C# 5.0 PROGRAMMER'S REFERENCE

Continues

C# 5.0

PROGRAMMER'S REFERENCE

C# 5.0

PROGRAMMER'S REFERENCE

Rod Stephens

A Wiley Brand

C# 5.0 Programmer's Reference

Published by
John Wiley & Sons, Inc.
10475 Crosspoint Boulevard
Indianapolis, IN 46256
www.wiley.com

Copyright © 2014 by John Wiley & Sons, Inc., Indianapolis, Indiana

Published simultaneously in Canada

ISBN: 978-1-118-84728-2
ISBN: 978-1-118-84697-1 (ebk)
ISBN: 978-1-118-84729-9 (ebk)

Manufactured in the United States of America

10 9 8 7 6 5 4 3 2 1

For general information on our other products and services please contact our Customer Care Department within the United States at (877) 762-2974, outside the United States at (317) 572-3993 or fax (317) 572-4002.

Wiley publishes in a variety of print and electronic formats and by print-on-demand. Some material included with standard print versions of this book may not be included in e-books or in print-on-demand. If this book refers to media such as a CD or DVD that is not included in the version you purchased, you may download this material at http://booksupport.wiley.com. For more information about Wiley products, visit www.wiley.com.

Library of Congress Control Number: 2014930410

ABOUT THE AUTHOR

 **ROD STEPHENS** started out as a mathematician, but while studying at MIT, he discovered how much fun programming is and has been programming professionally ever since. During his career, he has worked on an eclectic assortment of applications in such fields as telephone switching, billing, repair dispatching, tax processing, wastewater treatment, concert ticket sales, cartography, and training for professional football players.

Rod has been a Microsoft Visual Basic Most Valuable Professional (MVP) for more than 10 years and has taught introductory programming at ITT Technical Institute. He has written more than two dozen books that have been translated into languages from all over the world, and more than 250 magazine articles covering C#, Visual Basic, Visual Basic for Applications, Delphi, and Java.

Rod's popular *C# Helper* website (www.CSharpHelper.com) receives almost a million post visits per year and contains thousands of pages of tips, tricks, and example programs for C# programmers, as well as example code for this book. His *VB Helper* website (www.vb-helper.com) contains similar material for Visual Basic programmers.

You can contact Rod at RodStephens@CSharpHelper.com or RodStephens@vb-helper.com.

ABOUT THE TECHNICAL EDITOR

BRIAN HOCHGURTEL has been doing .NET development for more than 10 years, and actually started his .NET experience with Rod Stephens when they wrote the Wiley book *Visual Basic .NET and XML* in 2002. Currently Brian works with C#, SQL Server, and SharePoint at Riverside Technology in Fort Collins, CO.

CREDITS

ACKNOWLEDGMENTS

THANKS TO Bob Elliott, Adaobi Obi Tulton, John Mueller, San Dee Phillips, Daniel Scribner, and all the others who worked so hard to make this book possible.

Thanks also to technical editor Brian Hochgurtel for giving me the benefit of his valuable experience.

CONTENTS

PART II: C# LANGUAGE ELEMENTS

CHAPTER 4: DATA TYPES, VARIABLES, AND CONSTANTS   53

APPENDIX B: DATA TYPES   733

APPENDIX C: VARIABLE DECLARATIONS   737

INTRODUCTION

WHEN IT COMES TO PROGRAMMING, a little learning can indeed be a dangerous thing. If you read a book like *C# 5.0 All-in-One for Dummies* (Bill Sempf et al., 2013, For Dummies) or my book *Stephens' C# Programming with Visual Studio 2010 24-Hour Trainer* (Rod Stephens, 2010, Wrox), after only a few weeks you can easily think you know everything there is to know about programming.

I clearly remember when I finished my first programming class. The language we used was UCSD Pascal, and after only one class, I knew it quite well. I knew how to use the language, how to draw simple graphics, and how to read and write files. I was quite sure that with enough work I could write just about any program imaginable.

Since then I've had plenty of opportunities to realize just how wrong I was. I've worked on projects in about a dozen different programming languages, each with its own strengths and idiosyncrasies. I've worked on elegantly architected systems where adding new features was a breeze, and I've worked on badly designed 50,000 plus line monstrosities where you might need to study the code for a week before changing a single line for fear of breaking everything else. Since then I've also studied complexity theory and learned that there are literally thousands of provably hard (NP-complete) programs that you cannot solve in a reasonable amount of time. (I talk about some of them in my book *Essential Algorithms: A Practical Approach to Computer Algorithms*, Rod Stephens, 2013, Wiley.)

Even by itself, C# is a complex and powerful programming language. It includes all the language features that you would expect in any high-level language such as structures and classes, methods, complex error handling (`try`, `catch`, and `finally`), branching statements (`if-then` and `switch`), several kinds of loops (`for`, `foreach`, and `while`), and several ways to break out of loops (`break` and `return`).

In addition to the complexities of the language itself, C# provides many auxiliary features that make it even more powerful and more complicated. Features let you execute query-like operations on arrays, use parallel processing, serialize and deserialize objects, and let a program inspect pieces of code to learn about the objects that it is using.

Finally, the environment that contains C# brings its own complexity. The .NET Framework contains more than 10,000 classes that give you access to libraries for cryptography, expression matching, interacting with the operating system, networking, and much more.

This book describes as much of that complexity as possible. It explains the pieces of the C# language in detail. It explains the syntax, data types, and control statements that go into C# applications. This book also describes some of the pieces of the .NET Framework that are most useful for building complex applications.

This book does not cover every possible topic related to C#, but it does cover the majority of the technologies that developers need to build sophisticated applications.

WHO SHOULD READ THIS BOOK

This book is intended for intermediate and advanced programmers who have already programmed in C# or some other language. This book describes C# in detail but it does so quickly and assumes you already understand basic programming concepts. If you're a beginner, you can still use this book to learn to program in C#, but it will be a bit harder. If you get stuck, feel free to e-mail me at RodStephens@CSharpHelper.com and I'll try to put you back on the right track.

One of the main reasons this book assumes you know programming basics is it's hard to find a simple order in which to present topics in depth. For example, declaring and using variables is one of the most basic concepts in programming. (This book covers that early in Chapter 4, "Data Types, Variables, and Constants.") However, in C# variable declarations are different depending on whether they are inside a class's method. (In some languages methods are also called procedures, subprocedures, routines, subroutines, or functions.) If you already know what a method is, then the book can cover variables in depth. If you are unfamiliar with methods, a book can present only the basics of variable declarations, then cover classes, and finally return to the topic of variables. This book assumes you know basics such as what a variable is and what methods are, so it can quickly move through topics without a lot of repeating and backtracking.

If fundamentals such as variable declarations, data types, classes, and arrays are familiar to you, you should have no problem with this book. The index and reference appendices should be particularly useful in helping you remember the syntax for performing various C# tasks such as creating a class or making a generic method.

If you don't know what data types are, what a for loop is, and what an if statement does, you can probably pick those things up as you go along, but you may need to go back and reread a few chapters after you get the hang of things.

APPROACH

A program can interact with the user in many ways. It can read and write text in a console window. It can use Windows Forms and controls to provide a more graphical interface. A program can use Windows Presentation Foundation (WPF) controls to build an interface that is even more richly graphical and interactive than Windows Forms interfaces. Recently, a Windows Store program can use controls similar to those used in a WPF application to run in the Windows 8 operating system. Some programs provide no interface for the user and instead provide tools and services for other programs to use behind the scenes.

Building applications that use these different approaches takes a lot of work. The steps you take to build a WPF application are different from those you use to build a console application. However, no matter which kind of application you build, behind the user interface sits a bunch of good old C# code. You use the same syntax to create classes, loops, methods, and variables whether you're building Windows Forms applications or WPF applications. The same C# language enables you to build applications to run in a console window, on the Windows desktop, in Windows 8, in a browser, or even in Windows Phone.

This book focuses on the C# programming language rather than on user interface design and construction. Chapter 2, "Writing a First Program," explains how to start with different kinds of applications so that you can make applications to test the code, but the main focus is on the code behind the user interface.

> **NOTE** *The main exception to this is Chapter 16, "Printing," because printing works differently in the different kinds of applications.*

This book also describes methods a program can use to interact with its environment. For example, the techniques and classes a program uses to create printouts or manipulate files aren't actually part of the C# language, but they are essential for many applications.

Finally, this book describes some advanced subjects that are useful in many applications. These include such topics as using regular expressions to match patterns, parallel programming, serialization, XML, databases, and cryptography.

WHICH EDITION OF VISUAL STUDIO SHOULD YOU USE?

Visual Studio is the integrated development environment that is most often used to write C# programs. Because this book focuses on the C# language and not on user interface issues, you can use it with any edition of Visual Studio. You can use one of the free Express editions or one of the more complete Professional, Premium, or Ultimate editions.

> **NOTE** *To read about or download one of the Visual Studio Express Editions,* go to www.visualstudio.com/products/visual-studio-express-vs.
>
> *For a comparison of the different Visual Studio editions, go to* www.visualstudio.com/products/compare-visual-studio-products-vs.

The examples that go with this book, and that are available for download on this book's website, were written in Visual Studio Express 2012 for Windows Desktop and were tested in Windows 8. I picked the Windows Desktop version because writing desktop applications is generally easier than writing Windows Store or Windows Phone applications. I picked the 2012 edition because a lot of people already have that version installed. Programs written in the 2012 edition should also be compatible with Visual Studio 2013 so you should be able to open them in the 2013 edition. If you have trouble opening the project, please let me know.

You can use other editions of Visual Studio to study C# programming. For example, you could use Visual Studio Express 2013 for Windows, which can build Windows Store applications. If you do, the C# code you write behind the scenes will be the same as the code you would write for Windows Desktop but building the user interface will be very different.

The C# language and the .NET Framework change from time to time but the basics remain the same. That means much of this book's material applies to other versions of C# as well as different editions of Visual Studio. For example, there are some differences between C# 4.0 and C# 5.0, but the two versions are mostly the same. That means you can use this book even if you have an older version of Visual Studio installed, such as Visual Studio 2010, as long as you understand that a few things may not work. (The `async` and `await` keywords are the biggest differences.)

HOW THIS BOOK IS ORGANIZED

The chapters in this book are divided into five parts plus appendices.

Part I: The C# Ecosystem

Chapters 1 through 3 explain how C# programs fit into the Visual Studio environment. They explain how C# code is converted into code that the computer can execute and how that conversion happens. They also explain what files go into a C# application and what those files contain.

Chapter 2 briefly explains how you can write simple console, Windows Forms, and WPF applications that can invoke C# code. The rest of the book focuses on that code and mostly ignores user interface issues.

Part II: C# Language Elements

Chapters 4 through 10 explain the bulk of the C# language and the objects that support it. They explain data types (`string`, `float`, and arrays), operators (`+`, `*`, and `%`), program control statements (`if`, `while`, and `for`), and error handling. They also explain how to edit and debug C# code.

Although Language-Integrated Query (LINQ) it is not strictly part of the C# language, it is closely tied to the language, so Chapter 8, "LINQ," covers it. That chapter also covers Parallel LINQ (PLINQ), a parallel version of LINQ that can provide improved performance on multicore systems.

Part III: Object-Oriented Programming

Chapters 11 through 15 explain fundamental concepts in object-oriented programming (OOP) with C#. They explains how to define classes and inheritance hierarchies, use collection classes, and build generic classes and methods.

Part IV: Interacting with the Environment

Chapters 16 through 20 explain how an application can interact with its environment. They show how the program can create printouts, use configuration files, manipulate the filesystem, and download information from the Internet.

Part V: Advanced Topics

Chapters 21 through 27 cover more advanced topics that are useful in many advanced applications. They include such topics as recognizing patterns in text, parallel programming, using databases, serialization, reflection, and encrypting and decrypting data.

Part VI: Appendices

Appendix A, "Solutions to Exercises," provides outlines of solutions to the exercises described at the end of each chapter. Programs that implement many of the solutions are available for download on the book's website. This appendix shows the most interesting parts of many of the programs, but to save space I omitted some of the less interesting details. Download the examples from www.wrox.com/go/csharp5programmersref to see all the code.

The book's other appendices provide a categorized reference of the C# language. You can use them to quickly review the syntax of a particular command or refresh your memory of what a particular class can do. The chapters earlier in the book give more context, explaining how to perform specific tasks and why one approach might be better than another. The appendices provide a brief summary.

HOW TO USE THIS BOOK

If you are an advanced C# programmer, you may want to skim the language basics covered in the first parts of the book. You still may find a few new details, so you might not want to skip these chapters entirely, but most of the basic language features are the same as in previous versions of C#.

Each chapter ends with a set of exercises you can use to test your understanding of the material covered in the chapter. Sometimes exercises point to more in-depth topics that don't fit well in the chapter's text. Even if you're an advanced C# developer, you may want to read the exercises to make sure you didn't miss anything.

Intermediate programmers and those with less C# experience should take these chapters a bit more slowly. The chapters in Part III, "Object-Oriented Programming," cover particularly tricky topics. Learning all the variations on inheritance and interfaces can be rather confusing. If you are unfamiliar with these topics, plan to spend some extra time on those chapters.

Particularly if you have experience with some other programming language but not C#, you should spend some extra time on these first ten or so chapters because they set the stage for the material that follows. It will be a lot easier for you to follow a discussion of file management or regular expressions if you are not confused by the error-handling code that the examples take for granted.

Programming is a skill best learned by doing. You can pick up the book and read through it quickly if you like (well, as quickly as you can, given how long it is), but the information is more likely to stick if you open Visual Studio and experiment with some programs of your own.

Throughout your work, you can refer to the appendices to get information on specific classes, controls, and syntax. For example, you can turn to Appendix R, "Streams," to quickly find classes you can use to manipulate files and directories. If you need more information, you can go back to Chapter 19, "File System Objects," or check the online help. If you just need to refresh your memory of the basic classes and their methods, however, scanning Appendix R will be faster.

NECESSARY EQUIPMENT

To build C# programs, you need a copy of Visual Studio. To download different editions, go to `www.visualstudio.com/downloads/download-visual-studio-vs`.

To run Visual Studio, you need a reasonably modern, fast computer with a lot of memory. The exact requirements depend on the version and edition of Visual Studio you are using. To get the details, see the download page for the version you want to use. (I use a dual-core 64-bit 1.60 GHz Intel Core i5-4200U system with 8 GB of memory and 1 TB of hard disk space running Windows 8. It has a Windows Experience Index of 5.6 and handles Visual Studio with no problems.)

> **NOTE** *Technically, you can build C# programs without Visual Studio. It's uncommon, harder than using Visual Studio, and doesn't let you use Visual Studio's amazing programming and debugging features, so this book doesn't discuss it. For more information, search the Internet for* **C# without Visual Studio.**

Much of C# 5 is compatible with earlier versions of C#, so if you're using an older version of Visual Studio, you may be able to make most of this book's examples work with your system. You cannot load the example programs directly into your version of Visual Studio, however. You need to open the source code files in an editor such as WordPad and copy and paste the significant portions of the code into your program.

CONVENTIONS

To help you get the most from the text and keep track of what's happening, I used a number of conventions throughout the book.

For styles in the text:

- ➤ Important words are *italicized* when they are introduced.
- ➤ Keyboard strokes are shown like this: Ctrl+A.
- ➤ Filenames, URLs, and code within the text are shown like this: `persistence.properties`.
- ➤ Code is presented in the following two different ways:

```
I use a monofont type for code examples.
I use bolded type to emphasize code that's particularly important in the present
context.
```

SOURCE CODE

As you work through the examples in this book, you may choose either to type in all the code manually or to use the source code files that accompany the book. Many of the examples in the text show only the code that is relevant to the current topic and may be missing some of the extra details that you need to make the example work properly.

All the source code used in this book is available for download at

`www.wrox.com/go/csharp5programmersref`

You can also search for the book at `www.wrox.com` to find the code. When at the site, simply locate the book's title (either by using the Search box or by using one of the title lists) and click the Download Code link on the book's detail page to obtain all the source code for the book.

> **NOTE** *Because many books have similar titles, you may find it easiest to locate the book by its ISBN: 978-1-118-84728-2.*

After you download the code, just decompress it with your favorite compression tool. Alternatively, you can go to the main Wrox code download page at `www.wrox.com/dynamic/books/download.aspx` to see the code available for this book and all other Wrox books.

> **WARNING** *File Explorer can open compressed files and let you browse them as if they were normal files and that can sometimes lead to confusion. People often open a compressed file in this way and double-click on a .sln or .csproj file to open it in Visual Studio. This is probably the most common reason why people cannot run downloaded code.*
>
> Unfortunately Visual Studio doesn't really understand how to work inside a compressed directory. When you try to load the project, you will usually see an error similar to the following.
>
> *One or more projects in the solution were not loaded correctly.*
>
> Occasionally the project will seem to load but if you try to edit the code or run the program you'll get an error similar to the following. The name of the missing file may differ for different programs.
>
> *The item 'Program.cs' does not exist in the project directory. It may have been moved, renamed, or deleted.*
>
> Visual Studio is confused because it cannot find some file that was not extracted from the compressed files. To avoid these problems, always extract the files from the compressed download before you try to open a project.

ERRATA

We make every effort to ensure that there are no errors in the text or in the code. However, no one is perfect, and mistakes do occur. If you find an error in one of my books, like a spelling mistake or faulty piece of code, I would be grateful for your feedback. By sending in errata you may save another reader hours of frustration, and at the same time you will be helping me provide even higher quality information.

To find the errata page for this book, go to www.wrox.com and locate the title using the Search box or one of the title lists. Then, on the book details page, click the Book Errata link. On this page you can view all errata that have been submitted for this book and posted by Wrox editors. A complete book list including links to each book's errata is also available at www.wrox.com/misc-pages/booklist.shtml.

If you don't spot "your" error on the Book Errata page, go to www.wrox.com/contact/techsupport.shtml and complete the form there to send us the error you have found. We'll check the information and, if appropriate, post a message to the book's errata page and fix the problem in subsequent editions of the book.

P2P.WROX.COM

For author and peer discussion, join the P2P forums at p2p.wrox.com. The forums are a web-based system for you to post messages relating to Wrox books and related technologies and to interact with other readers and technology users. The forums offer a subscription feature to e-mail you topics of interest of your choosing when new posts are made to the forums. Wrox authors and editors, other industry experts, and your fellow readers are present on these forums.

At p2p.wrox.com you can find a number of different forums that can help you not only as you read this book but also as you develop your own applications. To join the forums, just follow these steps:

1. Go to p2p.wrox.com and click the Register link.

2. Read the terms of use and click Agree.

3. Complete the required information to join, as well as any optional information you want to provide, and click Submit.

4. You will receive an e-mail with information describing how to verify your account and complete the joining process.

> **JOIN THE FUN**
>
> You can read messages in the forums without joining P2P, but to post your own messages, you must join.

After you join, you can post new messages and respond to messages other users post. You can read messages at any time on the web. If you want to have new messages from a particular forum e-mailed to you, click the Subscribe to this Forum icon by the forum name in the forum listing.

For more information about how to use the Wrox P2P, be sure to read the P2P FAQs for answers to questions about how the forum software works, as well as many common questions specific to P2P and Wrox books. To read the FAQs, click the FAQ link on any P2P page.

Using the P2P forums allows other readers to benefit from your questions and any answers they generate. I monitor my book's forums and respond whenever I can help.

If you have other comments, suggestions, or questions that you don't want to post to the forums, you can e-mail me at RodStephens@CSharpHelper.com. I can't promise to solve all your problems but I'll try to help you if I can.

IMPORTANT URLS

Here's a summary of important URLs related to this book:

➤ www.CSharpHelper.com—My C# website. Contains thousands of tips, tricks, and examples for C# developers.

➤ p2p.wrox.com—Wrox P2P forums.

➤ www.wrox.com—The Wrox website. Contains code downloads, errata, and other information. Search for the book by title or ISBN.

➤ RodStephens@CSharpHelper.com—My e-mail address. I hope to hear from you!

PART I
The C# Ecosystem

The C# Environment

➤ IL and the CLR

➤ JIT compiling

➤ Programs and assemblies

➤ The .NET Framework

WROX.COM DOWNLOADS FOR THIS CHAPTER

Please note that all the code examples for this chapter are available as a part of this chapter's code download on the book's website at www.wrox.com/go/csharp5programmersref on the Download Code tab.

A C# program cannot exist in isolation. You can't write C# programs without using other tools. You can't even run a compiled C# program without libraries that provide runtime support.

This chapter describes the tools that you need in the Windows environment to write, compile, and execute C# programs. Most of the time those tools work smoothly behind the scenes, so you don't need to be aware of their presence. It's still worth knowing what they are, however, so you know how all the pieces of the C# environment fit together.

VISUAL STUDIO

You can write a C# program in a text editor and then use a command-line interface to compile the program. (For example, see "Working with the C# 2.0 Command Line Compiler" at http://msdn.microsoft.com/library/ms379563.aspx for more information.)

That approach is a lot of work, however, so most C# programmers use Visual Studio.

Visual Studio is a powerful *integrated development environment* (IDE) that includes code editors, form and window designers, and flexible debugging tools. Some versions also include testing, profiling, team programming, and other tools.

The Visual Studio code editors provide IntelliSense help, which displays prompts and descriptions of items you need to enter into the code. The code editor's features such as IntelliSense make writing correct C# programs much easier than it is with a simple text editor.

If you haven't already installed Visual Studio, you should probably do it now. It takes a while, so be sure you have a fast Internet connection.

To learn about and download one of the Visual Studio Express Editions, go to `www.visualstudio.com/products/visual-studio-express-vs`.

To learn about the other Visual Studio editions, go to `www.microsoft.com/visualstudio/eng/products/compare`.

While Visual Studio is downloading and installing, you can read further.

The most important tool integrated into Visual Studio is the compiler, which turns C# code into a compiled executable program—well, sort of.

THE C# COMPILER

The C# compiler doesn't actually compile code into a truly executable program. Instead it translates your C# code into an assembly-like language called *Intermediate Language* (IL).

> ### WHAT'S IN A NAME?
>
> While under development, the intermediate language was called Microsoft Intermediate Language (MSIL). When .NET was released, the name was changed to IL.
>
> The international standards organization Ecma created the Common Language Infrastructure (CLI) standard that defines a Common Intermediate Language (CIL).
>
> To summarize the alphabet soup, MSIL is the old name for Microsoft's intermediate language; IL is the current name; and CIL is the name for the non-Microsoft standard. There are some differences between IL and CIL but many .NET developers use MSIL, IL, and CIL interchangeably.

> ### PROGRAMS AND ASSEMBLIES
>
> The C# compiler doesn't compile only programs; it can also compile other kinds of assemblies. An *assembly* is the smallest possible piece of compiled code. Assemblies include programs, code libraries, control libraries, and anything else you can compile. An executable program consists of one or more assemblies.

Consider the following C# code.

```
static void Main(string[] args)
{
    foreach (string arg in args) Console.WriteLine(arg);
    Console.WriteLine("Press Enter to continue");
    Console.ReadLine();
}
```

The C# compiler translates this into the following IL code.

```
.method private hidebysig static void  Main(string[] args) cil managed
{
  .entrypoint
  // Code size       51 (0x33)
  .maxstack  2
  .locals init ([0] string arg,
           [1] string[] CS$6$0000,
           [2] int32 CS$7$0001,
           [3] bool CS$4$0002)
  IL_0000:  nop
  IL_0001:  nop
  IL_0002:  ldarg.0
  IL_0003:  stloc.1
  IL_0004:  ldc.i4.0
  IL_0005:  stloc.2
  IL_0006:  br.s        IL_0017
  IL_0008:  ldloc.1
  IL_0009:  ldloc.2
  IL_000a:  ldelem.ref
  IL_000b:  stloc.0
  IL_000c:  ldloc.0
  IL_000d:  call        void [mscorlib]System.Console::WriteLine(string)
  IL_0012:  nop
  IL_0013:  ldloc.2
  IL_0014:  ldc.i4.1
  IL_0015:  add
  IL_0016:  stloc.2
  IL_0017:  ldloc.2
  IL_0018:  ldloc.1
  IL_0019:  ldlen
  IL_001a:  conv.i4
  IL_001b:  clt
  IL_001d:  stloc.3
  IL_001e:  ldloc.3
  IL_001f:  brtrue.s    IL_0008
  IL_0021:  ldstr       "Press Enter to continue"
  IL_0026:  call        void [mscorlib]System.Console::WriteLine(string)
  IL_002b:  nop
  IL_002c:  call        string [mscorlib]System.Console::ReadLine()
  IL_0031:  pop
  IL_0032:  ret
} // end of method Program::Main
```

> **DISPLAYING IL**
>
> You can use the ildasm program to view a compiled program's IL code. (Ildasm is pronounced "eye-ell-dazm" so it rhymes with "chasm." The name stands for "IL disassembler.") For information about ildasm, see `http://msdn.microsoft.com/library/f7dy01k1.aspx`.

The IL code is fairly cryptic; although, if you look closely you can see the method's declaration and calls to `Console.WriteLine` and `Console.ReadLine`.

IL code looks a lot like assembly language but it's not. Assembly language is a (barely) human-readable version of machine code that can run on a specific kind of computer. If the program were translated into assembly or machine code, it could run only on one kind of computer. That would make sharing the program on different computers difficult.

To make sharing programs on multiple computers easier, IL provides another layer between C# code and machine code. It's like a virtual assembly language that still needs to be compiled into executable machine code. You can copy the IL code onto different computers and then use another compiler to convert it into machine code at run time. In .NET, the *Common Language Runtime* (*CLR*) performs that compilation.

THE CLR

CLR is a virtual machine component of the .NET Framework that translates IL into native machine code when you run a C# program. When you double-click a C# program's compiled executable program, the CLR translates the IL code into machine code that can be executed on the computer.

The CLR uses a *just-in-time compiler* (*JIT compiler*) to compile pieces of the IL code only when they are needed. When the program is loaded, the loader creates a stub for each method. Initially, that stub points to the method's IL code.

When the program invokes the method, the JIT compiler translates its IL code into machine code, makes the stub point to it, and then runs the machine code. If the program calls the method again later, its stub already points to the machine code, so the method doesn't need to be compiled again.

Figure 1-1 shows the process graphically.

Usually, the time needed to compile a method is small, so you don't notice the tiny bits of extra time used as each method is called for the first time. After a method is compiled, it runs a tiny bit faster when it is called later.

If a method is never called by the program, it is never compiled by the JIT compiler, so the compiler saves some time.

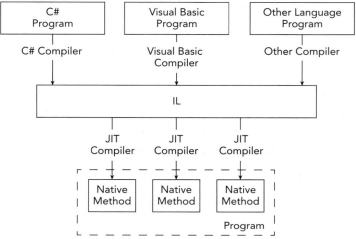

FIGURE 1-1: Compilers translate C# code (and code in other languages) into IL code. At run time, the JIT compiler translates methods from IL code into machine code as needed.

AHEAD-OF-TIME COMPILING

Normally .NET programs use the JIT compiler, but if you want to, you can use the NGen.exe program to precompile a program into native code. Then when you run the program, it is already compiled, so each method doesn't need to be compiled just in time.

This might not save you as much time as you would think. Hard drives are slow compared to operations performed in memory, so loading the compiled methods from disk may take much longer than the time saved precompiling the program.

You can speed things up if you give an assembly a strong name and install it in the system's Global Assembly Cache (GAC, pronounced "gack"). In that case, multiple programs that share the assembly may not need to load the compiled assembly from disk. The whole process is rather involved and only useful under specialized conditions, so it's not described in any greater detail here. For more information about NGen and the JIT compiler, see "Compiling MSIL to Native Code" at http://msdn.microsoft.com/library/ht8ecch6.aspx. For more information about using NGen and the GAC to improve performance, see "The Performance Benefits of NGen" at http://msdn.microsoft.com/magazine/cc163610.aspx.

In addition to providing JIT compilation, the CLR also provides some low-level services used by programs such as memory management, thread management, and exception handling. (Chapter 12, "Classes and Structures," describes the .NET memory management model. Chapter 6, "Methods," and Chapter 22, "Parallel Programming," discuss using multiple threads. Chapter 9, "Error Handling," describes exception handling in C#.)

THE .NET FRAMEWORK

The .NET Framework includes the CLR and a large library of powerful tools that make C# programming simpler. Those tools include just about everything you normally use in a C# program that isn't part of the C# language itself. Some of the tools included in the .NET Framework enable you to

➤ Add attributes to classes and their members to give extra information to runtime tools.

➤ Use collections such as lists, dictionaries, and hash tables.

➤ Work with databases.

➤ Find the computer's physical location using methods such as GPS, Wi-Fi triangulation, and cell tower triangulation.

➤ Interact with system processes, event logs, and performance data.

➤ Create sophisticated two-dimensional drawings.

➤ Interact with Active Directory.

➤ Provide globalization so that programs use appropriate text and images in different locales.

➤ Use LINQ (described in Chapter 8, "LINQ").

➤ Create and use message queues.

➤ Work with the filesystem.

➤ Play audio and video.

➤ Get information about and manage devices.

➤ Interact with networks and the Internet.

➤ Print documents.

➤ Examine the code entities defined by the program or another compiled assembly.

➤ Serialize and deserialize objects.

➤ Control program security.

➤ Support speech recognition.

➤ Run multiple threads of execution simultaneously.

➤ Process XML and JSON files.

➤ Encrypt and decrypt files.

➤ Much more.

By using all of these tools, you can build standalone programs to run on desktop systems, phone or tablet applications, websites, networked applications, and all sorts of other programs.

A compiled C# program needs the CLR to execute, and most programs also need the .NET Framework. That means to run a program, a computer must have the .NET Framework installed.

If Visual Studio is installed on the computer, the .NET Framework is also installed. That means you can usually copy a compiled C# application onto the computer and it will run. (Of course, you should never copy a compiled program from a source you don't trust! This method works if you want to share a program with your friends, but don't just grab any old compiled C# program off the Internet.)

Most installers also install the .NET Framework if needed, so if you use an installer, the .NET Framework will be installed if it's not already on the machine. For example, ClickOnce deployment installs the .NET Framework if necessary.

You can also install the .NET Framework manually by downloading an installer or by using a web installer. To find the latest installers, go to Microsoft's Download Center at `www.microsoft.com/download/default.aspx` and search for **.NET Framework**.

CLICKONCE

To use ClickOnce deployment, select Build ➪ Publish, and let the Publish Wizard guide you through the process. The wizard enables you to determine

➤ The location where the distribution package should be built

➤ Whether the user will install from a website, a file, or a CD or DVD

➤ Whether the application should check for updates when it runs

For more information on ClickOnce deployment, see `http://msdn.microsoft.com/library/142dbbz4.aspx`.

Most of the .NET Framework features are backward compatible, so usually you can install the most recent version, and programs built with older versions will still run. If you do need a particular version of the .NET Framework, search the Download Center for the version you need.

SUMMARY

A C# program cannot stand completely alone. To create, compile, and run a C# program, you need several tools. You can create a C# program in a text editor, but it's much easier to use Visual Studio to write and debug programs. After you write a program, the C# compiler translates the C# code into IL code. At run time, the CLR (which is part of the .NET Framework) uses JIT compilation to translate the IL code into native machine code for execution.

You can use NGen to precompile assemblies and install them in the GAC, so they don't need to be compiled at run time by the JIT compiler. In many cases, however, that won't save much time. If the program's methods are called when the user performs actions such as clicking buttons and invoking menu items, the small additional overhead probably won't be noticeable.

All that happens behind the scenes when you build and execute a C# program. The next chapter explains how you can start to build C# programs. It explains the most common types of C# projects and explains how you can use several of them to test C# code as you work through the rest of this book.

EXERCISES

1. Draw a diagram showing the major steps that Visual Studio performs when you write a C# program and press F5 to run it.

2. Suppose you have two applications. The first uses 50 methods to perform tasks as the user selects them. The second uses the same 50 methods to perform all the tasks when it starts. How will the performance of the two applications differ? How do NGen and the GAC apply to this situation?

3. For which of the following scenarios would NGen and the GAC be most useful?

    a. An interactive application that displays forms on the screen

    b. A code library that defines methods for performing tasks that your other programs use

    c. A control library that defines custom buttons, scroll bars, and other controls

    d. A console application that writes output to a console window

4. Suppose your program uses 100 methods as the user performs various actions. You add a parameter to each method, so you can tell it to return without doing anything. Then when the program starts (while the splash screen displays), the code calls every method telling it to return without doing anything. How would the CLR handle those methods?

Writing a First Program

WHAT'S IN THIS CHAPTER

➤ Solutions and projects

➤ Creating console, Windows Forms, WPF, and Windows Store applications

➤ Naming conventions

➤ How the CLR starts programs

WROX.COM DOWNLOADS FOR THIS CHAPTER

Please note that all the code examples for this chapter are available as a part of this chapter's code download on the book's website at www.wrox.com/go/csharp5programmersref on the Download Code tab.

Unless you plan to edit C# files in a text editor and then use the command-line interface to compile them, you will probably end up using Visual Studio to write and build C# programs. Because of that, this book does cover Visual Studio to some extent.

The book's goal, however, is to cover the C# language. This chapter explains the most common kinds of applications that you can build in C#. It shows how you can build programs that provide buttons or other methods for executing your C# code.

Visual Studio enables you to build many different kinds of applications. This chapter explains how to start with four of those types: console, Windows Forms, WPF, and Windows Store applications.

TYPES OF PROJECTS

A Visual Studio *solution* contains the files that you need to create some sort of result. Typically, the result is a single executable application; although, it could be a suite of related applications together with documentation and other related items.

The solution is defined by two files with .sln and .suo extensions. The .sln file stores information that defines the solutions and the projects it contains. The .suo file keeps track of customizations to the Visual Studio IDE.

A solution typically contains one or more *projects*. A project usually defines a compiled result such as a program, library, or custom control.

Simple applications often consist of a single solution that contains a single project that defines an executable program.

To create a new project in a new solution, select File ➪ New Project to display the New Project dialog. (To add a new project to an existing solution, select File ➪ Add ➪ New Project.)

The New Project dialog displays a hierarchical set of categories on the left and the associated project templates on the right. The appearance of the dialog and the templates that it contains depends on the version of Visual Studio that you run. Figure 2-1 shows the New Project dialog for Visual Studio Express 2012 for Windows Desktop. In Figure 2-1 the selected category is Installed ➪ Templates ➪ Visual C#, and only four templates are available for that category.

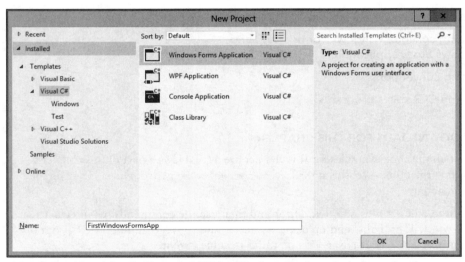

FIGURE 2-1: Visual Studio Express 2012 for Windows Desktop includes only a few C# project templates.

The following list summarizes the project types that are easiest to use with this book.

- ➤ **Windows Forms**—A program that uses Windows Forms controls and that runs on the Windows desktop
- ➤ **WPF (Windows Presentation Foundation)**—A program that uses WPF controls and that also runs on the Windows desktop
- ➤ **Console**—A program that reads text input and displays text output in a console window
- ➤ **Windows Store**—A Windows Store app

> **TIP** *For a more complete list of available project templates, see "Creating Projects from Templates" at* msdn.microsoft.com/library/0fyc0azh.aspx.

Both WPF and Windows Store applications use *extensible markup language* (*XAML*) code to define the WPF controls that make up their user interfaces. WPF controls are more flexible and graphically powerful than Windows Forms controls. For example, WPF controls can display gradient backgrounds, scale or rotate images, play video, and use animation to change their appearance over time, all things that are hard for Windows Forms controls.

However, WPF controls use more resources than Windows Forms controls, so the designers that let you edit WPF and Windows Store applications are slower. Taking full advantage of WPF capabilities also requires a lot of effort, so Windows Forms applications are usually easier to build.

Console applications have only a text interface, so they are even simpler, as long as you don't need graphical features such as a drawing surface or the mouse.

As you can see in Figure 2-1, Visual Studio Express 2012 for Windows Desktop enables you to make Windows Forms, WPF, and console applications.

Visual Studio Express 2012 for Windows 8 enables you to make Windows Store applications but not Windows Forms, WPF desktop, or console applications. (Both of these editions include a few other project types such as class libraries and control libraries.)

If you have a more full-featured version of Visual Studio than the Express edition, you can see other project templates. Figure 2-2 shows the New Project dialog for Visual Studio 2012 Ultimate. If you look closely you can see that the dialog includes all the templates provided by both of the Express editions plus many more.

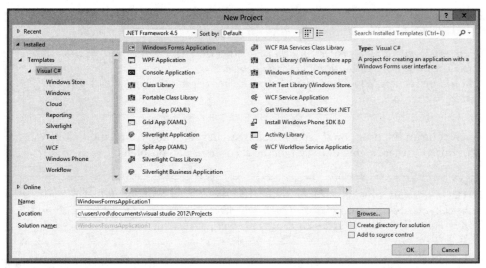

FIGURE 2-2: Visual Studio Ultimate 2012 includes many more project templates than the Express edition does.

This book focuses on the C# language and not on user interface design, so it doesn't say too much more about creating fully functional applications. However, it is worth knowing a bit more about how the different kinds of projects work. The following sections provide a bit more information on the four main application project types: console, Windows Forms, WPF, and Windows Store.

CONSOLE APPLICATIONS

When you make a console application, Visual Studio creates a file called Program.cs that defines a class named Program. The following code shows the initial Program class created by Visual Studio Express 2012 for Windows Desktop.

```
using System;
using System.Collections.Generic;
using System.Linq;
using System.Text;
using System.Threading.Tasks;

namespace MyConsoleApplication
{
    class Program
    {
        static void Main(string[] args)
        {
        }
    }
}
```

> **NOTE** *When you create a new project in Visual Studio Express 2012 for Windows Desktop, the New Project dialog makes you enter a project name. When you first save the project by using the File menu's Save All command, Visual Studio prompts you for the directory in which to save the project.*
>
> *When you create a new project in other versions of Visual Studio 2012, the New Project dialog makes you enter the project's name and the directory where it should be stored. When you click OK to create the new project, the project is created in that location.*

By default, when you run the program, Visual Studio searches for a static method named Main and executes it. Initially, there's only one such method, so there's no problem.

> **NOTE** *If you have previous programming experience, you probably know all about classes, objects, instances, and methods. If you don't, you can learn all about them in Part III, "Object-Oriented Programming," of this book.*

However, if you create another class and give it a static method named Main, Visual Studio cannot figure out which one to launch. You can resolve that problem in a couple ways. First, you can rename all but one of the Main methods, so Visual Studio can figure out which one to execute.

Another approach is to select Project ⇨ Properties to open the application properties window, as shown in Figure 2-3. Open the Startup Object drop-down, and select the class that contains the Main method that Visual Studio should execute.

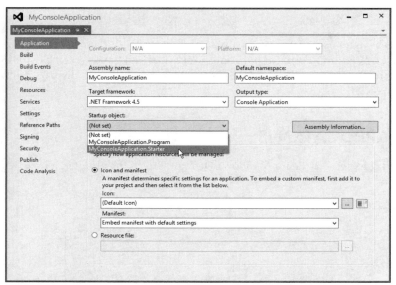

FIGURE 2-3: The application properties window enables you to specify the application's startup class.

Inside the Main method, you can add whatever code you need the program to execute. For example, the following code displays a message and then waits for the user to press the Enter key.

```
static void Main(string[] args)
{
    Console.WriteLine("Press Enter to continue");
    Console.ReadLine();
}
```

Figure 2-4 shows the running program. When you press the Enter key, the `Console.ReadLine` statement finishes and the Main method exits. When that method exits, the program ends and the console window disappears.

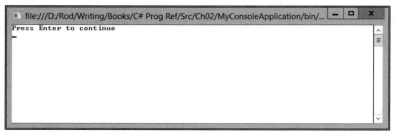

FIGURE 2-4: A console application runs in a text-only console window.

> **WARNING** *A console application ends as soon as the* Main *method exits. If the code doesn't include a* Console.ReadLine *statement or some other statement that pauses execution, the program may disappear before the user has a chance to read any output it produces.*

Because console applications have no user interfaces, many C# books write all their examples as console applications. However, Windows Forms applications look nicer and have greater flexibility. For example, a Windows Forms application can display images, draw graphics, and display results in controls such as combo boxes or lists.

WINDOWS FORMS APPLICATIONS

Figure 2-5 shows Visual Studio Express 2012 for Windows Desktop after it has created a new Windows Forms application.

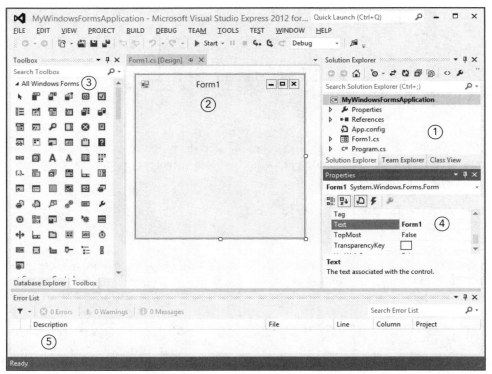

FIGURE 2-5: After creating a new Windows Forms application, Visual Studio displays the default form Form1.

The following list describes the numbered areas on Visual Studio, as shown in Figure 2-5.

1. **Solution Explorer**—This area lists the files associated with the project. Double-click a file to open it in the designer area.

2. **Designer**—This area contains designers that enable you to edit different kinds of files. For example, the Code Editor enables you to edit C# code, and the Form Designer enables you edit forms. Figure 2-5 shows the Form Designer editing the user interface for the form defined by the file Form1.cs.

3. **Toolbox**—While you are editing a form, you can click a control in the Toolbox to select it. Then you can click and drag to place an instance of that control on the form.

4. **Properties**—If you select a control in the Window Designer, this area displays that control's properties and enables you to edit them. In Figure 2-5 the form is selected, so this area is showing the form's properties. For example, you can see in the Properties Window that the form's Text property is set to Form1. In the Form Designer, you can see that the form displays its text at the top.

5. **Other windows**—This area typically holds other windows such as the Error List and Output Window. The program shown in Figure 2-5 does not currently have any errors, so the Error List is empty.

> **NOTE** *Visual Studio is extremely configurable. You can hide or show windows, drag windows into new positions, dock windows next to other windows, and make multiple windows share the same area as tabs. If you rearrange things, your Visual Studio installation may not look much like the figures in this book.*

The goal in this book is to let you build enough of a program to execute C# code behind the scenes. In a Windows Forms application, objects such as controls can execute code when events occur. For example, when the user clicks a button, the program can execute a Click event handler.

To create a button, click the Button tool in the Toolbox. Then click and drag in the Window Designer to place a button on the window. If you like, you can use the Properties window to set the button's properties. For example, you can set its caption by setting the Text property to something like Click Me.

Scroll to the top of the Properties Window to set the control's Name property. For example, if the button says Click Me, you might make its name **clickMeButton**.

To create a Click event handler for the button, double-click it in the Form Designer. When you do, Visual Studio creates the following empty Click event handler and opens it in the Code Editor.

```
private void clickMeButton_Click(object sender, EventArgs e)
{

}
```

C# NAMING CONVENTIONS

The naming convention used by many C# developers uses Pascal Case for class names and CamelCase for instance names.

In *Pascal Case*, words are run together with the first letter of each word capitalized. For example, a class that holds detail information for customer orders might be called `CustomerOrderDetail`.

CamelCase is similar to Pascal Case except the first letter is not capitalized. For example, an instance of the `CustomerOrderDetail` class representing a new item in an order might be called `newCustomerOrderDetail`.

Therefore, for the current example a button labeled Click Me has the name `clickMeButton`.

Now you can add whatever code you want the event handler to execute inside the braces. For example, the following code changes the button's caption to Clicked.

```
private void clickMeButton_Click(object sender, EventArgs e)
{
    clickMeButton.Text = "Clicked";
}
```

Recall from the previous section that a console application starts by executing the `Program` class's `Main` method. If you look closely at Figure 2-5, you can see that a Windows Forms program also includes a file named Program.cs. If you double-click that file, the Code Editor opens and displays the following code.

```
using System;
using System.Collections.Generic;
using System.Linq;
using System.Threading.Tasks;
using System.Windows.Forms;

namespace MyWindowsFormsApplication
{
    static class Program
    {
        /// <summary>
        /// The main entry point for the application.
        /// </summary>
        [STAThread]
        static void Main()
        {
            Application.EnableVisualStyles();
            Application.SetCompatibleTextRenderingDefault(false);
            Application.Run(new Form1());
        }
    }
}
```

If you skip down a bit to the first indented line of code, you can see that this file defines a `Program` class that is somewhat similar to the one created for console applications. Like the version used by the console application, this `Program` class defines a `static Main` method. As before, when you run the program, Visual Studio executes this method.

In a Windows Forms application, the `Main` method initializes some visual style text rendering attributes. It then executes the `Application.Run` method passing it a new instance of the `Form1` class. This is how the program displays its main form. The `Application.Run` method displays the form it is passed as a parameter and enters an event loop where it processes messages until the form closes.

When the form closes, the call to `Application.Run` finishes. That is the last statement in the `Main` method, so `Main` exits. As is the case with a console application, when the `Main` method exits, the application ends.

> **TIP** *Some C# developers build Windows Forms applications by creating a console application and then adding code similar to the previous code to display a form. That seems like a lot of unnecessary work. If you want to make a Windows Forms application, you may as well create one and let Visual Studio do some of the work for you.*

WPF APPLICATIONS

Creating a WPF application is similar to creating a Windows Forms application. Select File ➪ New Project, select the WPF Application template, and enter a project name. If you do not use Visual Studio Express 2012 for Windows Desktop, enter a project location. Then click OK to create the project.

Figure 2-6 shows a newly created WPF application. If you compare Figures 2-6 and 2-5, you can see many of the same windows. The center of Visual Studio contains a Window Designer similar to the Form Designer in Figure 2-5. The Solution Explorer and Properties Window are on the right. (Although, there are many differences between the two versions of the Properties Window.) The Error List appears at the bottom of both figures.

One notable difference between the two displays is the XAML code window at the bottom of the Window Designer. The window's controls and appearance are determined by the XAML code in this area. When you add controls to the window, the XAML code updates to reflect the new controls.

Conversely, if you modify the XAML code, the Window Designer updates to display your changes.

A second major difference between Figures 2-5 and 2-6 is the Document Outline to the left of the Window Designer in Figure 2-6. This window shows a hierarchical view of the structure of the window. In Figure 2-6, the main `Window` object contains a single `Grid` object. You would add new controls to the `Grid`.

If you look at the bottom of the Document Outline, you can see three tabs labeled Database... ("Explorer" is cut off), Toolbox, and Document... ("Outline" is cut off). You can click the Toolbox tab to get a toolbox similar to the one shown in Figure 2-5. Then you can add a button to the program much as you added one to the Windows Forms application. Click the button tool to select it. Then click and drag to create a button on the window.

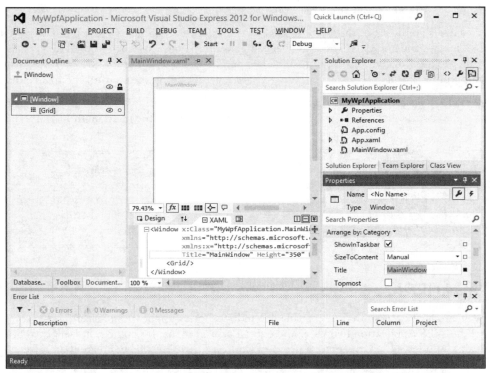

FIGURE 2-6: After creating a new WPF application, Visual Studio displays the default window `MainWindow`.

Use the Properties Window to set the button's properties. Note that in WPF applications the button's `Content` property determines its caption or other contents, not the `Text` property used by a Windows Forms button.

To associate an event handler with the button, double-click it as you would for a Windows Forms application. The following code shows the initial empty `Click` event handler.

```
private void clickMeButton_Click(object sender, RoutedEventArgs e)
{

}
```

This is similar to the previous Windows Forms `Click` event handler. The only difference is the second parameter has the type `RoutedEventArgs` instead of `EventArgs`.

Add whatever code you want to execute when the button is pressed. For example, the following code changes the button's caption to Clicked.

```
private void clickMeButton_Click(object sender, RoutedEventArgs e)
{
    clickMeButton.Content = "Clicked";
}
```

If you look at the Solution Explorer in Figure 2-6, you won't find the Program.cs class file created for a Windows Form application. Instead you find an App.xaml file.

If you double-click App.xaml, Visual Studio opens the file in the XAML editor. The following code shows an initial App.xaml file.

```
<Application x:Class="MyWpfApplication.App"
             xmlns="http://schemas.microsoft.com/winfx/2006/xaml/presentation"
             xmlns:x="http://schemas.microsoft.com/winfx/2006/xaml"
             StartupUri="MainWindow.xaml">
    <Application.Resources>

    </Application.Resources>
</Application>
```

The `Application` element's `StartupUri` attribute indicates that the program should initially display the window defined in the MainWindow.xaml file.

The App.xaml file is marked read-only, so you shouldn't change the startup window by editing it. Instead select Project ➪ Properties as you would for a Windows Forms application. This opens an application properties window similar to the one shown in Figure 2-3. Use the Startup Object drop-down to select the window that you want to display at startup.

WINDOWS STORE APPLICATIONS

Windows Store applications are programs designed to run in Windows 8. They support the look and feel of Windows 8 applications. For example, they can display tiles on the start screen and can update those tiles at runtime to tell the user what they are doing. (For more information about the Windows Store, go to www.windowsstore.com.)

To create a Windows Store application, select File ➪ New Project, select one of the Windows Store templates, enter a project name, and enter a project location. Then click OK to create the project.

Figure 2-7 shows a newly created Windows Store application in Visual Studio Express 2012 for Windows 8. Initially, the file App.xaml.cs displays in the code editor.

To add a button to the application, double-click MainPage.xaml in Solution Explorer to open the `MainPage` class in the designer. The `MainPage` class is similar to the `MainWindow` used by the WPF applications described in the previous section, and you can use the designer to edit them similarly. Use the Toolbox to place a button on the page. Use the Properties Window to set the button's properties. Double-click the button to create an event handler for the button, and add whatever code you like to it.

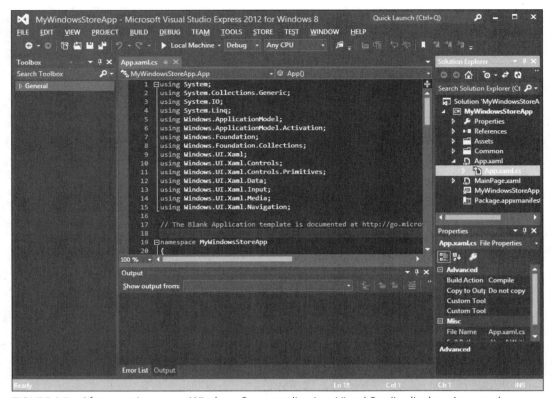

FIGURE 2-7: After creating a new Windows Store application, Visual Studio displays App.xaml.cs.

The way a Windows Store application starts is a bit more complicated than the way the previous kinds of applications start. The App.xaml.cs file defines a class named App. That class includes some startup code including the following OnLaunched method, which executes when the application starts normally:

```
protected override void OnLaunched(LaunchActivatedEventArgs args)
{
    Frame rootFrame = Window.Current.Content as Frame;

    // Do not repeat app initialization when the Window already has content,
    // just ensure that the window is active
    if (rootFrame == null)
    {
        // Create a Frame to act as the navigation context and navigate
        // to the first page
        rootFrame = new Frame();

        if (args.PreviousExecutionState == ApplicationExecutionState.Terminated)
        {
            //TODO: Load state from previously suspended application
        }
```

```
        // Place the frame in the current Window
        Window.Current.Content = rootFrame;
    }

    if (rootFrame.Content == null)
    {
        // When the navigation stack isn't restored navigate to the first page,
        // configuring the new page by passing required information as a
        // navigation parameter
        if (!rootFrame.Navigate(typeof(MainPage), args.Arguments))
        {
            throw new Exception("Failed to create initial page");
        }
    }
    // Ensure the current window is active
    Window.Current.Activate();
}
```

If the application's `Frame` is `null`, the code creates a new `Frame`.

Then if the `Frame`'s content was `null`, the bold line of code uses the `Frame`'s `Navigate` method to navigate to a new instance of the `MainPage` class. (If the `Frame`'s content is not `null`, it is a previously created instance of the `MainPage` class and it is reused.)

Finally, the code activates the current window, and at that point the `MainPage` appears.

SUMMARY

Unless you plan to edit C# files in a text editor and then use the command-line interface to compile them, you will end up using Visual Studio to write and build C# programs. Because of that, the book does cover Visual Studio to some extent.

The book's goal, however, is to cover the C# language. This chapter explains the most common kinds of applications that you can build in C#. It shows how you can build programs that provide buttons or other methods for executing your C# code.

Visual Studio enables you to build many different kinds of applications. This chapter explains how to start with four of those types: console, Windows Forms, WPF, and Windows Store applications. The remainder of this book assumes you can create one of those kinds of applications so that you can run C# code.

Although this book doesn't explain user interface programming or Windows Forms, WPF, and Windows Store applications in more detail, you should look into them when you have a chance. C# code alone enables you to produce some amazing results, but you need a great user interface to actually show them off.

When you create a new program, Visual Studio creates all sorts of files to represent forms, windows, code, resources, and other data associated with the project. Chapter 3, "Program and Code File Structure," describes the most common kinds of files associated with C# projects.

EXERCISES

1. Create a new console application named ConsoleShowArgs and enter the following code into its main method.

    ```
    foreach (string arg in args) Console.WriteLine(arg);
    Console.WriteLine("Press Enter to continue");
    Console.ReadLine();
    ```

    This code displays any command-line arguments passed to the program when it executes.

    a. Save the program in a directory and run it. What happens?

    b. Next, select Project ➪ Properties, open the Debug tab, and in the Command Line Arguments text box, enter **Red Green Blue**. Run the program again. What happens this time?

2. Use File Explorer to find the compiled executable program that was created for the program you built in Exercise 1. (It is probably in the project's bin\Debug directory and is named after the project with a .exe extension.) Double-click the program to run it. What happens?

3. Right-click File Explorer or the desktop, and select New ➪ Shortcut. Browse to set the shortcut's target to the location of the executable program you built. Add the text **Apple Banana Cherry** after the target's path. For example, on my system I used the following target (all on one line and the double quotes are included):

    ```
    "D:\Rod\Writing\Books\C# Prog Ref\Src\847282ch02src\
    ConsoleShowArgs\bin\Debug\ConsoleShowArgs.exe" Apple Banana Cherry
    ```

    Double-click the shortcut to run the program. What happens?

4. Open a command window, navigate to the executable program's directory, type the program's name, and press Enter to run the program. What happens?

    Now run the program with command-line arguments by typing in the following text at the command prompt.

    ```
    ConsoleShowArgs Ant Bear Cat
    ```

    What happens this time?

5. Repeat Exercise 1 with a Windows Forms application named WindowsFormsShowArgs. Place a ListBox named argsListBox on the form and set its Dock property to Fill. Double-click the form (not the ListBox) and add the bold code in the following snippet to the form's Load event handler.

    ```
    private void Form1_Load(object sender, EventArgs e)
    {
        foreach (string arg in Environment.GetCommandLineArgs())
            argsListBox.Items.Add(arg);
    }
    ```

    What do you think will happen when you run the program? Run the program to find out. Then define the command-line arguments as described in Exercise 1 and run the program again. What actually happens?

6. Repeat Exercise 2 for the program you built in Exercise 5. What do you think will happen when you run the program? What actually happens?

7. Repeat Exercise 3 for the program you built in Exercise 5. What do you think will happen when you run the program? What actually happens?

8. You've probably got the hang of this by now, but if you want to try WPF (or if you skipped the previous exercises because you care about only WPF), repeat Exercise 1 with a WPF application named WPFShowArgs. Place a ListBox named argsListBox on the form and set its Height and Width properties to Auto. Click the form (not the ListBox) to select it. In the Properties window, click the Event button (the lightning bolt) and double-click in the box to the right of the Loaded event. Add the bold code in the following snippet to the form's Load event handler.

```
private void Window_Loaded(object sender, RoutedEventArgs e)
{
    foreach (string arg in Environment.GetCommandLineArgs())
        argsListBox.Items.Add(arg);
}
```

What do you think will happen when you run the program? Run the program to find out. Then define the command-line arguments as described in Exercise 1 and run the program again. What actually happens?

9. Repeat Exercise 2 for the program you built in Exercise 8. What do you think will happen when you run the program? What actually happens?

10. Repeat Exercise 3 for the program you built in Exercise 8. What do you think will happen when you run the program? What actually happens?

3

Program and Code File Structure

WHAT'S IN THIS CHAPTER

- ➤ Project files, including hidden files
- ➤ Changing project properties, references, resources, and assembly information
- ➤ Preprocessor directives
- ➤ The `using` directive and `namespace` statements
- ➤ End-of-line, multiline, and XML comments

WROX.COM DOWNLOADS FOR THIS CHAPTER

Please note that all the code examples for this chapter are available as a part of this chapter's code download on the book's website at www.wrox.com/go/csharp5programmersref on the Download Code tab.

A C# *solution* contains one or more related projects. A *project* includes all the files related to whatever output it produces. That output might be an executable program, a custom control, or a code library that other programs can use. The files relating to the output might include files full of C# code, documentation, data files, and any other files you want to include in the project.

This chapter describes the structure of a typical C# project and explains the purposes of some of the most common types of files you can find in a C# project. This chapter also describes the basic structure of C# source code files. It explains how you can use regions and namespaces to group related pieces of code. It also describes some typographic features such as comments, XML comments, and line labels that you can use to make C# code easier to understand.

HIDDEN FILES

Figure 3-1 shows the Solution Explorer window for a solution named TurtleSolution that contains two projects named TurtleLib and TurtleTest.

Each project contains a Properties folder that represents the project's properties. Each project also contains a References item that represents references to libraries used by the project.

In addition to the Properties and References items, the projects contain files related to the project. In this example, the TurtleLib project includes the class definition file Turtle.cs, and the TurtleTest project contains the form definition file Form1.cs.

In the TurtleTest project the Show All Files button has been clicked (the button third from the right at the top of the figure) so that you can see all the project's files. The TurtleLib project has similar files, but they are hidden by default.

These files are generated by Visual Studio for various purposes. For example, the bin and obj directories contain files generated when the projects are compiled.

The following list describes the items contained in the TurtleTest project, as shown in Figure 3-1. The exact files you see for an application may be different from those shown here, but this list should give you an idea of what's involved in building a project. Note that most of these files are generated automatically by Visual Studio, and you shouldn't edit them manually. If you change them directly, you are likely to lose your changes when Visual Studio rebuilds them. You may even confuse Visual Studio so it can't load the project.

FIGURE 3-1: A solution contains one or more projects that contain files related to the project.

➤ **TurtleTest**—This item represents the entire project. You can expand or collapse it to show and hide the project's details.

➤ **Properties**—This item represents the project's properties. To change the properties, either right-click this item and select Open or select Project ➪ Properties. Figure 3-2 shows the TurtleTest project's properties pages.

➤ **AssemblyInfo.cs**—This file contains information about the project's assembly. Instead of editing this file directly, select Project ➪ Properties to open the project's properties page, and then on the Application tab, click the Assembly Information button. Figure 3-3 shows the TurtleTest project's assembly information.

➤ **Resources.Designer.cs**—This file contains definitions of project resources such as strings and images. Instead of editing this file directly, select Project ➪ Properties to open the project's properties page and then go to the Resources tab.

➤ **Settings.Designer.cs**—This file contains definitions of project settings. Instead of editing this file directly, select Project ➪ Properties to open the project's properties page and then go to the Settings tab.

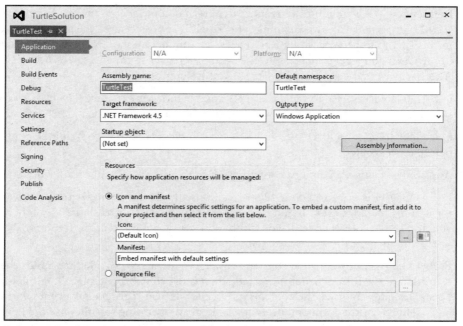

FIGURE 3-2: A project's properties pages lets you set project properties, resources, and settings.

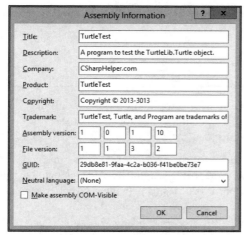

FIGURE 3-3: A project's assembly information lets you specify values such as the project's name, copyright information, and version.

➤ **References**—This item lists references to external components such as libraries and COM components. In this example, the TurtleTest project uses the `Turtle` class defined in the TurtleLib project, so its References section includes a reference to the TurtleLib library. (To add a reference, right-click the References item, and select Add Reference. Alternatively, you can select Project ⇨ Add Reference.)

➤ **bin**—This folder is used to build the application before it is executed. The Debug or Release subfolder contains the compiled .exe file (depending on whether this is a debug or release build).

➤ **obj**—This folder and its Debug and Release subfolders are used to build the application before it is executed.

➤ **App.config**—This file contains configuration settings that the application reads when it starts.

➤ **Form1.cs**—This is a form code file. It contains the C# code you write that goes into the form. This includes event handlers for the form and its controls, and any other methods you add to the form's code. If you double-click this file in Solution Explorer, Visual Studio opens the form in the Form Designer.

➤ **Form1.Desginer.cs**—This file contains designer-generated C# code that builds the form. It initializes the form when it is created, creates the controls you placed on the form in the Form Designer, and sets the controls' properties. It also registers any event handlers that you have defined for the form and its controls. Instead of editing this file, use the Form Designer to modify the form and its controls.

➤ **Form1**—This entry represents the code behind Form1. If you double-click this file in Solution Explorer, Visual Studio opens the form's code in the code editor.

➤ **Program.cs**—This file contains the automatically generated `Main` method that Visual Studio executes to start the program.

RESOURCES AND SETTINGS

Resources are chunks of data distributed with the application but that are not intended to be modified by the program. These might include prompt strings, error message strings, icons, pictures, and sound files.

Settings are values that control the execution of the application. These might include flags telling the program what options to display or how to perform certain tasks. For example, you could build different profiles to provide settings that make the program run in a restricted demo mode or in a fully licensed mode.

If you expand code items such as Form1 and Program, Solution Explorer lists the program elements contained inside. That includes variables, methods, event handlers, and other class-level items defined inside the class. You can double-click one of these items to open its definition in the Code Editor.

If you look closely at the bottom of Figure 3-1, you can see that the Solution Explorer window has three tabs. The first tab displays the Solution Explorer, which lists the files that make up the project. In Figure 3-1 that tab is selected so Solution Explorer is displayed.

The second tab opens Team Explorer, a tool that helps you manage your work in a team environment. For more information, see msdn.microsoft.com/library/hh500420.aspx.

The third tab opens the Class View. This tool enables you to view the classes defined by your projects. You can expand the classes to learn about their inheritance hierarchies. If you click a class, the bottom of the window shows you the class's properties, methods, and events. If you double-click one of these items, Visual Studio opens the code that defines it in the Code Editor.

Figure 3-4 shows the Class View displaying information about the Turtle class defined in the TurtleLib project.

Some projects may have other hidden files. For example, when you add controls to a form, the designer adds a resource file to the form to hold any resources needed by the controls.

Normally, you do not need to work directly with the hidden files, and doing so can mess up your application. At best, the changes you make will be lost. At worst, you may confuse Visual Studio, so it can no longer load your project.

Instead you should use other tools to modify the hidden files indirectly. For example, the files holding resources used by a form are automatically updated when you modify the form and its controls.

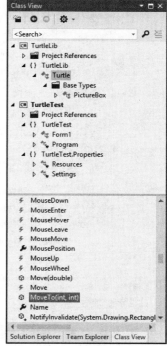

FIGURE 3-4: The Class View lets you examine the classes defined by a project.

PREPROCESSOR DIRECTIVES

Preprocessor directives are commands for the C# compiler. They tell the compiler such things as which pieces of code to include in compilation and how the Code Editor should group lines of code.

The following sections describe the most useful C# preprocessor directives.

#define and #undef

The #define directive defines a *preprocessor symbol* that you can then use with the #if, #else, #elif, and #endif directives described next. Preprocessor symbols are either defined or not defined. They do not have values like constants inside the code do.

> **NOTE** *A program can create variables and constants with the same names as defined preprocessor symbols.*

The #undef directive removes the definition of a defined symbol.

The #define and #undef directives must come before any programming statements including using directives. They apply for the entire file that contains them.

WHY #UNDEF?

If all #define and #undef directives must appear at the beginning of the file, you may wonder why you would ever use #undef. After all, if you're going to undefine something you just defined, why bother defining it in the first place?

The answer is in the program's property pages. If you select Project ⇨ Properties and then go to the Build tab, you see the property page, as shown in Figure 3-5.

By default, Visual Studio defines the DEBUG and TRACE symbols. Uncheck the appropriate boxes if you don't want them defined.

You can also add your own symbols by typing their names in the Conditional Compilation Symbols text box.

The #undef directive enables you to define symbols on the Build property page and then undefine them as needed in specific files.

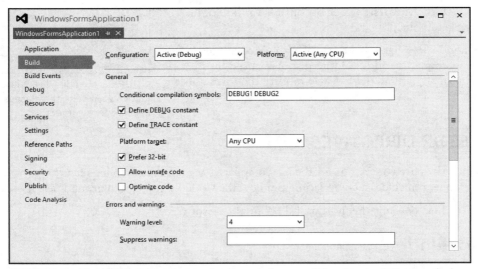

FIGURE 3-5: The Build property page lets you define conditional compilation symbols.

Visual Studio defines different sets of compilation symbols for different build configurations. The two standard configurations are Debug and Release. By default, Visual Studio defines the DEBUG and TRACE symbols for Debug builds and defines only the TRACE symbol for Release builds.

To change these values, use the Configuration Manager (found by selecting Build ⇨ Configuration Manager) to select the Debug or Release build. Then use the Build property page to determine which symbols are defined.

The DEBUG and TRACE symbols play a special role in program debugging. The Debug and Trace classes provide tools that make it easier to tell what a program is doing as it runs. The Debug class's methods execute only if the DEBUG symbol is defined. Similarly, the Trace class's methods execute only if the TRACE symbol is defined. By defining or not defining these symbols, you can easily turn the Debug and Trace methods on and off. Chapter 10, "Tracing and Debuging," says more about these classes.

#if, #else, #elif, and #endif

These statements enable you to use compilation symbols to decide which code is included in the program when it is compiled.

For example, the following code displays a different message box depending on which symbols are defined.

```
            private void Form1_Load(object sender, EventArgs e)
            {
#if DEBUG_LEVEL1
                MessageBox.Show("Debug level is 1");
#elif DEBUG_LEVEL2
                MessageBox.Show("Debug level is 2");
#else
                MessageBox.Show("Debug level is undefined");
#endif


            ...
            }
```

In this example, if the symbol DEBUG_LEVEL1 is defined, the first message box displays. If that symbol is not defined but DEBUG_LEVEL2 is defined, the second message box displays. If neither of those symbols is defined, the third message box displays.

Visual Studio evaluates compilation symbols while you write code and grays out code that won't be included in the compilation, so it's easy to see what code will be used.

In addition to the simple tests shown in the preceding code snippet, the #if and #elseif directives can include parentheses and the !, &&, and || boolean operators. For example, the following code displays a message if SKIP_DEBUG is defined, or DEBUG_LEVEL1 and DEBUG_LEVEL2 are both undefined.

```
#if SKIP_DEBUG || (!DEBUG_LEVEL1 && !DEBUG_LEVEL2)
            MessageBox.Show("Don't display debugging messages.");
#endif
```

You can also use the != and == operators to compare symbols to the values true and false. For example, the following code displays a message box if the symbol SHOW_GREETING is defined.

```
#if SHOW_GREETING == true
    MessageBox.Show("Hello!");
#endif
```

The syntax #if SHOW_GREETING is simpler and usually easier to read, so most developers use that approach.

DEBUGGING LEVELS

Sometimes, it's helpful to easily adjust the level of diagnostic output a program generates. You could define a set of conditional compilation symbols named DEBUG_ LEVEL1, DEBUG_LEVEL2, and so forth. The program would then send diagnostic messages to the Output Window or to a log file depending on the debug level.

For example, you might place level 1 Debug statements in major subroutines, level 2 statements in secondary routines, and level 3 statements throughout important routines to provide step-by-step information. Then you can define the debug level symbols to quickly give you the amount of information you want.

This is particularly useful when you test and debug a program. Instead of removing test code from the program, you can surround it with #if #endif directives, so you can reactivate it later if you find bugs in the code.

For more information on debugging C# applications, see Chapter 10.

Note that the code not included by the conditional compilation statements is completely omitted from the executable program. That means excluded code doesn't take up space in the executable program.

That also means Visual Studio doesn't check the correctness of code that isn't included. Visual Studio won't warn you if excluded code contains typographical errors and invalid C# code.

#warning and #error

The #warning directive generates a level 1 warning. It is listed in the Error List but won't stop the program from compiling. One reason to do this is to flag deprecated code so that developers know they are using old code, as in the following example.

```
#if OLD_VERSION
#warning You are using an old version of this library
#endif
```

The #error directive is similar to the #warning directive except it generates an error instead of a warning. An error prevents Visual Studio from compiling the program.

#line

The #line directive enables you to control the file's line number and name for reporting purposes. This directive can take one of the three forms described in the following list.

➤ #line *number* [*file*]—This sets the line number and optionally the filename for the following line. If a #warning or #error directive follows this directive, it reports the given line number and file. If it is included, the *file* must be enclosed in double quotes.

➤ #line hidden—This hides the lines that follow from the debugger until the next #line directive is reached.

➤ #line default—This restores the file's line number and name to their true values.

The following example demonstrates the #line directives.

```
#if OLD_VERSION

#line 10 "Tools Module"
#warning This code is deprecated.
#endif

#line hidden
    ... lots of code omitted ...
#line default
```

If the symbol OLD_VERSION is defined, this code's first #line directive sets the line number to 10 and the filename to "Tools Module". Then the #error directive displays a message in the Error List that says there's an error on line 10 in the file Tools Module.

The #line hidden directive hides the omitted code from the debugger. If you try to step through the code in the debugger, the Code Editor skips over those lines. They are still executed, but you can't step through them.

The final #line default directive restores the file to normal line numbering, name, and ends line hiding.

> **WARNING** *In some versions of Visual Studio, the Code Editor doesn't seem to completely end line hiding until it reaches a* #line default *directive.*

#region and #endregion

Some code constructs such as class and method definitions define regions that you can collapse in the Visual Studio Code Editor. If you look closely at a class statement, you can see a minus sign to the left in the Code Editor. If you click the minus sign, the editor collapses the class into a single line and changes the minus sign to a plus sign. Click the plus sign to expand the class again.

In Figure 3-6, the Person class and the PrintInvoice method in the Customer class are collapsed.

The #region directive enables you define other sections of code that you can collapse and expand in a similar manner. The section of code extends to a corresponding #endregion directive.

The #region and #endregion directives can be followed by a string that identifies them. You can use that string to identify the region, so you can make sure the directives match up. However, the Code Editor completely ignores that string, so if a #region directive's string doesn't match the string used in the corresponding #endregion directive, Visual Studio doesn't care.

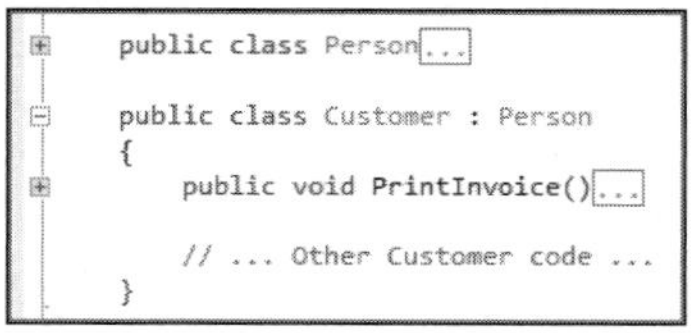

```
public class Person...

public class Customer : Person
{
    public void PrintInvoice()...

    // ... Other Customer code ...
}
```

FIGURE 3-6: The Code Editor lets you expand and collapse blocks of code such as classes and methods.

For example, suppose an Employee class contains a lot of code for calculating payroll. You could place the payroll-related properties, methods, and other code in a region. Then you could hide that region so that it doesn't get in the way while you work on other code in the class. The following code snippet shows how you could define this kind of region.

```
public class Employee : Person
{
    #region PayrollCode

    ... Payroll-related code here ...

    #endregion PayrollCode

    ... Other Employee code ...
}
```

Sometimes, it may be easier to move related pieces of code into separate files. For example, if a class becomes so large it's hard to find things in it, it may be easier to move sections of the class into separate files. The `partial` keyword described in the section "Class Definitions' later in this chapter enables you to place parts of a class in different files. For example, you could move the `Employee` class's payroll-related code into a partial piece of the `Employee` class in a separate file.

#pragma

The `#pragma` directive gives special information to the compiler. This directive comes in two basic forms: `#pragma warning` and `#pragma checksum`.

The `#pragma warning` directive comes in the two forms described in the following list.

➤ `#pragma warning disable [warning_list]`—This disables warnings for a comma-separated list of warning codes. If you omit the warning codes, this disables all warnings.

➤ `#pragma warning restore [warning_list]`—This re-enables warnings for a comma-separated list of warning codes. If you omit the warning codes, this re-enables all warnings.

For example, suppose you have XML documentation enabled. (This is described in the section "XML Comments" later in this chapter.) In that case, all public classes and all their public members should have XML comments describing them. If any of those comments are missing, Visual Studio displays an error message.

If you have XML documentation enabled, you should probably supply all those comments. If you want to omit a comment for a particular method, however, you can use `#pragma warning disable` to disable the warning on that method.

For example, consider the following `Employee` class.

```
    /// <summary>
    /// Represents an employee.
    /// </summary>
    public class Employee
    {
#pragma warning disable 1591
    public void PrintTimesheet()
```

```
        {
            ...
        }
#pragma warning restore 1591

        ...
    }
```

The class begins with an XML comment, so it doesn't cause a warning. The `PrintTimesheet` method does not have an XML comment, so it would cause a warning if the `#pragma warning disable` directive didn't disable the error.

After the `PrintTimesheet` method ends, the code restores the warning, so the compiler can report it for the class's later public members.

The `#pragma checksum` directive has the following format.

```
#pragma checksum "file" "{guid}" "bytes"
```

This directive is useful for debugging ASP.NET applications. It's outside the scope of this book, so it isn't described here. For more information, see `msdn.microsoft.com/library/ms173226.aspx`.

FINDING WARNING NUMBERS

Unfortunately, the Error List doesn't display the warning numbers you need to use with the `#pragma warning` directive. One way to find a warning number is to right-click the warning in the Error List and select Show Error Help. That opens a web page that describes the warning and gives the warning number.

You can find a summary of compiler errors and warnings at `msdn.microsoft .com/library/vstudio/ms228296.aspx`, although the warnings are listed by number and not name, so that won't help you find the number you want.

CODE FILE STRUCTURE

The following code shows the file Form1.cs from a newly created program named WindowsFormsApplication1. This is a Windows Forms program created in Visual Studio Express 2012 for Windows Desktop.

```
using System;
using System.Collections.Generic;
using System.ComponentModel;
using System.Data;
using System.Drawing;
using System.Linq;
using System.Text;
using System.Threading.Tasks;
```

```
using System.Windows.Forms;

namespace WindowsFormsApplication1
{
    public partial class Form1 : Form
    {
        public Form1()
        {
            InitializeComponent();
        }
    }
}
```

The following sections describe three key pieces of this program that are typical of C# programs: the using directive, the namespace statement, and class definitions.

The using Directive

In .NET, *namespaces* are used to identify related classes, structures, interfaces, and other programming items. Namespaces can be nested within other namespaces, so they form a hierarchical system that categorizes programming items.

For example, the Form class is defined in the Forms namespace, which is inside the Windows namespace, which in turn is inside the System namespace. You can specify the complete path through a series of namespaces by separating them with dots. For example, the fully qualified path to the Form class is System.Windows.Forms.Form.

A using directive enables you to use a class without including its full namespace path. The previous code begins with a series of using directives that let the code refer to classes within the indicated namespaces without using the namespaces.

> **WARNING** *Don't confuse the* using *directive with the* using *statement. The* using *directive provides a short way to refer to namespaces. The* using *statement makes it easier to call an object's* Dispose *method. You learn more about the* using *statement in Chapter 12, "Classes and Structures."*

For example, the following statement shows the final using directive in the previous code.

```
using System.Windows.Forms;
```

This statement enables the program to use classes defined in the System.Windows.Forms namespace without giving the namespace path. Later the code uses the following statement.

```
public partial class Form1 : Form
```

This statement refers to the Form class without providing its full namespace path.

The using directive can also create an alias for a namespace or type. For example, the following tatement makes the alias d2d represent the System.Drawing.Drawing2D namespace.

```
using d2d = System.Drawing.Drawing2D;
```

UNNECESSARY NAMESPACES

The initial program shown earlier includes nine `using` directives, but the only one that is actually used by the code is the one that includes the `System.Windows.Forms` namespace.

When you compile a program, Visual Studio includes only the libraries that it actually needs, so the extra `using` directives don't affect the compiled assembly.

However, when Visual Studio compiles a program, it may need to search several namespaces to resolve class names. For example, when Visual Studio sees the reference to the `Form` class in the previous code, it cannot find a definition for that class in the local code, so it searches the namespaces included by `using` directives. If the program includes lots of unnecessary `using` directives, Visual Studio may waste some time fruitlessly searching those namespaces before it finds the right one.

The end result is the same, but removing unnecessary `using` directives can make compiling faster.

Removing unneeded namespaces can also prevent namespace pollution, a situation in which two namespaces define classes or other items with the same names.

To easily remove unneeded `using` directives, open a file in the Code Editor, right-click the code, and select Organize Usings. That item's subitems include three self-explanatory commands: Remove Unused Usings, Sort Usings, and Remove and Sort.

The code could then use the following statement to declare a variable named `matrix` that has type `System.Drawing.Drawing2D.Matrix`.

```
d2d.Matrix matrix;
```

Usually `using` directives are placed at the beginning of a file, but you can also place them inside `namespace` statements. If you place a `using` directive in a namespace, it must come before all elements in the namespace and applies only to that instance of the namespace. If you have another piece of code that defines part of the same namespace, in the same file or in another one, then the `using` statement does not apply to the other piece of the namespace.

For example, the following code includes two `namespace` statements with some omitted code in between. Both declare statements that define classes that inherit from the Form class, so both include the `using System.Windows.Forms` directive.

```
namespace MyNamespace
{
    using System.Windows.Forms;

    class EmployeeForm : Form
    {
        ...
    }
}
```

```
... Omitted code ...

namespace MyNamespace
{
    using System.Windows.Forms;

    class CustomerForm : Form
    {
        ...
    }
}
```

The namespace Statement

You can use the namespace statement to create your own namespaces. You can use namespaces to group related classes and other program elements. By placing different classes in separate namespaces, you allow pieces of code to include only the namespaces they are actually using. That makes it easier to ignore classes that a piece of code isn't using. It also allows more than one namespace to define items that have the same names.

For example, you could define an Accounting namespace that contains the AccountsReceivable and AccountsPayable namespaces. Each of those might contain a class named Invoice. The program could select one version or the other by using either Accounting.AccountsReceivable.Invoice or Accounting.AccountsPayable.Invoice.

> **TIP** *Different namespaces can define classes with the same names, but if you give classes different names, you reduce the chance of confusion.*

The following example defines the Accounting namespace. That namespace defines the CustomerType enumeration and the two classes PayableItem and ReceivableItem. It also contains the nested namespace OrderEntry, which defines the OrderEntryClerk class. All the classes and namespaces could define other items.

```
namespace Accounting
{
    public enum CustomerType
    {
        CashOnly,
        Credit30,
        Credit90
    }

    public class PayableItem
    {
        ...
    }

    public class ReceivableItem
    {
        ...
```

```
        }

    namespace OrderEntry
    {
        public class OrderEntryClerk
        {
            ...
        }

        ...
    }
}
```

If a file includes a `using` directive to indicate that it is using a namespace, it does not need to explicitly identify the namespace to use the classes and other items it defines. You only need to explicitly use the namespace if multiple included namespaces define items with the same name.

All program elements in a C# program must be inside a namespace. By default, any code files you create include a namespace named after the project you initially created. For example, if you create an application named OrderEntrySystem, by default its code is contained in the `OrderEntrySystem` namespace.

You can view and modify the project's default namespace by selecting Project ⇨ Properties and looking on the Application tab. Figure 3-7 shows the Application tab for the WindowsFormsApplication1 project. The default namespace is WindowsFormsApplication1.

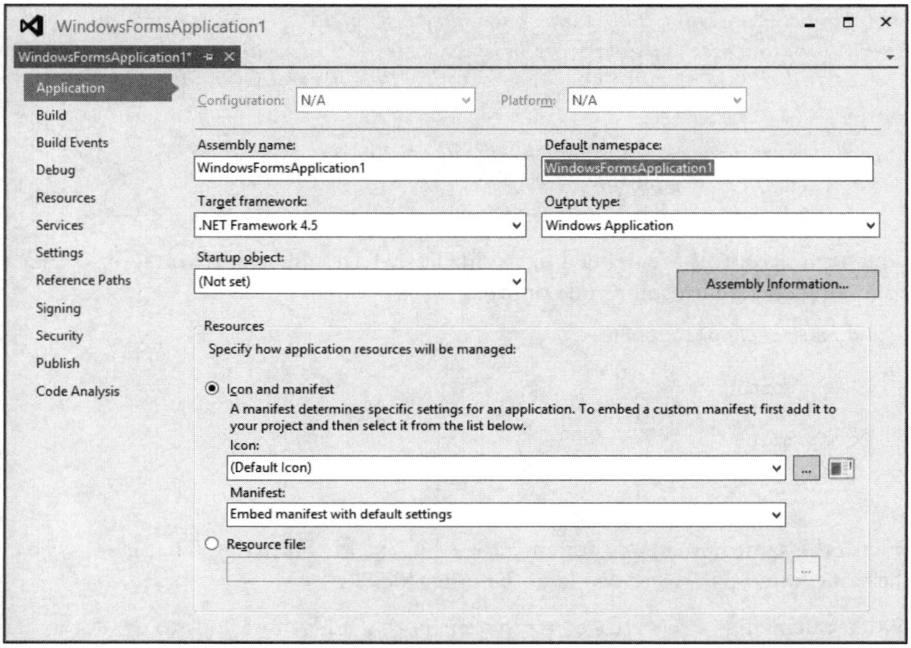

FIGURE 3-7: A project's property pages let you view and change the project's default namespace.

If you change the project's default namespace, any classes that you create in the future are placed in the new namespace.

Class Definitions

The WindowsFormsApplication1 example program shown earlier included the following class definition.

```
public partial class Form1 : Form
{
    public Form1()
    {
        InitializeComponent();
    }
}
```

Chapter 12 has a lot more to say about classes. For now you should know that all classes (and structures, enumerations, and other program elements) must be declared inside some namespace.

One last fact about classes is worth mentioning here during the discussion of program and code file structure. If you look at the previous class definition, you see that it includes the `partial` keyword. That keyword means that this is only part of the class's definition and that other class statements may contain more pieces of the class.

> **TIP** *Usually a code file includes a single namespace and that defines some or all of a single primary class. The namespace may also include helper structures, classes, and other elements used by the primary class. You can define as many namespaces and classes as you like in a single file, but then managing the file becomes harder.*
>
> *If you use the Project menu's Add Class and other commands to create new classes, you'll get one class per file.*

In this example, the form's controls are defined in the file Form1.Desginer.cs. If you look at that file, you can see the following code (with some code omitted).

```
namespace WindowsFormsApplication1
{
    partial class Form1
    {
        ... Code omitted ...
    }
}
```

This code begins with the same `namespace` statement used in the file Form1.cs. That means the code in this file is in the same namespace as the code in the other file.

Inside the `namespace` statement is a `partial class` statement that adds more code to the `Form1` class.

If a class is split into multiple pieces, then all the pieces must use the `partial` keyword. That means if you see a class declared with that keyword, you know there are other pieces somewhere.

COMMENTS

Comments can help other developers (or you at a later date) understand the program's purpose, structure, and method. Although comments aren't executed by the program, they can make the code easier to understand. That makes the code easier to debug and modify over time.

C# provides three kinds of comments: end-of-line comments, multiline comments, and XML comments.

End-of-line and Multiline Comments

An end-of-line comment begins with the two characters // that are not inside a quoted string. This kind of comment extends to the end of the current line of code.

A multiline comment begins with the characters /* and ends with the characters */. The compiler ignores everything between those sets of characters.

The following code demonstrates end-of-line and multiline comments.

```
/* This class defines a student. It includes contact information,
 * billing information, past and current courses, and past and
 * current intramural activities.
 */
public class Student
{
    // The student's name.
    public string FirstName { get; set; }
    public string LastName { get; set; }

    // The student's contact information.
    public string Street { get; set; }
    public string City { get; set; }
    public string State { get; set; }
    public string Zip { get; set; }          // ZIP+4.
}
```

This code begins with a multiline comment containing a short paragraph describing the class. Many developers begin each line of a multiline comment with an asterisk, so you can tell that the line is part of a comment even if the /* and */ characters are scrolled off the screen at the time. Actually, Visual Studio automatically adds the asterisk if you press Enter while the cursor is inside a multiline comment.

After the class's opening brace, the code includes an end-of-line comment that says, "The student's name." It then defines the FirstName and LastName properties.

Next, the code includes another end-of-line comment followed by the definition of the Street, City, State, and Zip properties. The line defining the Zip property also includes an end-of-line comment.

Although many developers begin each line in a multiline comment with an asterisk, that is not required, so you can use multiline comments to quickly comment out large sections of code. For example, the following code shows the previous example with all the code inside the `Student` class commented out with a multiline comment.

```
/* This class defines a student. It includes contact information,
 * billing information, past and current courses, and past and
 * current intramural activities.
 */
public class Student
{
    /*
    // The student's name.
    public string FirstName { get; set; }
    public string LastName { get; set; }

    // The student's contact information.
    public string Street { get; set; }
    public string City { get; set; }
    public string State { get; set; }
    public string Zip { get; set; }         // ZIP+4.
    */
}
```

> **TIP** *In addition to using a multiline comment to comment out large chunks of code, you could also use an `#if` directive. The following code shows the previous example with the* Student *class's body removed by this approach.*
>
> ```
>     /* This class defines a student. It includes contact
> information,
>      * billing information, past and current courses, and past and
>      * current intramural activities.
>      */
>     public class Student
>     {
> #if false
>         // The student's name.
>         public string FirstName { get; set; }
>         public string LastName { get; set; }
>
>         // The student's contact information.
>         public string Street { get; set; }
>         public string City { get; set; }
>         public string State { get; set; }
>         public string Zip { get; set; }         // ZIP+4.
> #endif
>     }
> ```

Visual Studio's Standard toolbar also includes command and uncomment tools. Click and drag to select lines of code. Then click the Comment tool to add the `//` characters at the beginning of each of the selected lines. Click the Uncomment tool to remove the initial `//` characters from each line. (You can also find those commands in the Edit ➪ Advanced menu.)

Use comments to make your code clear. Comments do not slow the executable program down (some superstitious developers think they must slow the code because they make the file bigger), so there's no good reason to avoid them.

XML Comments

A normal comment is just a piece of text that gives information to a developer trying to read your code. XML comments enable you to add some context to a piece of code. For example, you can preface a method with a brief description of the method, its parameters, and the meaning of its return result.

If you want it to, Visual Studio can automatically extract XML comments to build an XML file describing the project. This file displays the hierarchical shape of the project, showing comments for the project's namespaces, classes, and other elements. The result is not particularly easy to read, but you can use it to automatically generate more useful documentation such as reports or web pages. For example, third-party tools such as NDoc (ndoc.sourceforge.net) and Sandcastle (shfb.codeplex .com) can process the XML comments to produce documentation. You can also write your own programs to process XML comments, for example, by using XSLT as described in Chapter 24, "XML."

You can place a block of XML comments before code elements that are not contained in methods. These include such items as classes, structures, enumerations, properties, methods, and events.

To begin a comment block, place the cursor on the line before the element you want to describe and type ///. Visual Studio automatically inserts a template for an appropriate XML comment block. If the element that follows takes parameters, it includes sections describing the parameters, so it is in your best interest to completely define the parameters before you create the XML comment block. (Otherwise you need to add the appropriate comment sections by hand later.)

The following code shows the XML comment block created for the CreateStudent method. It includes a summary section where you can describe the method and two param sections where you can describe the method's parameters.

```
/// <summary>
///
/// </summary>
/// <param name="firstName"></param>
/// <param name="lastName"></param>
public void CreateStudent(string firstName, string lastName)
{
}
```

Note that XML elements can span multiple lines, as the summary element does in this example.

If you start a new line between XML comment entries, Visual Studio automatically adds /// to the beginning of the new line. If you then type <, IntelliSense presents a list of standard XML comment sections. You can select one or you can type a new section of your own. For example, the following code adds some content for the comments in the previous code and an extra WrittenBy element that contains a date attribute:

```
/// <summary>
/// Create a new student record in the database.
/// </summary>
/// <param name="firstName">The student's first name.</param>
/// <param name="lastName">The student's last name.</param>
/// <WrittenBy date="4/1/2020">Rod Stephens</WrittenBy>
public void CreateStudent(string firstName, string lastName)
{
}
```

COMMENT CONVENTIONS

I just made up the `WrittenBy` element and its `date` attribute—they're not part of some XML comment standard. You can put anything you want in there; although, the comments will be most useful if you use standard elements such as `param` and `remarks` whenever possible.

To allow Visual Studio to create XML documentation from the XML comments, select Project ⇨ Properties and go to the Build tab. If the whole tab isn't visible, scroll to the bottom and check the XML Documentation File box, as shown in Figure 3-8. If you don't want the documentation file to have its default name, you can change that, too.

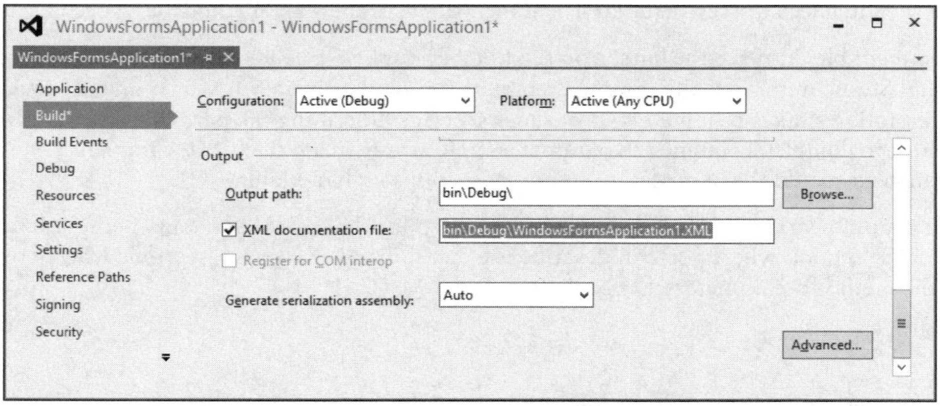

![Visual Studio Build properties dialog showing the XML documentation file checkbox checked with path bin\Debug\WindowsFormsApplication1.XML]

FIGURE 3-8: Check the XML Documentation File box to create XML documentation.

In addition to providing documentation for your use, XML comments let IntelliSense provide additional information about your code. Figure 3-9 shows IntelliSense displaying information about the `CreateStudent` method. At this point, I had typed the method call's open parenthesis, so IntelliSense displays information about the `firstName` parameter.

When you compile the application, Visual Studio extracts the XML comments and places them in an XML file with the name indicated on the Build property page. The result isn't readable, but you can use it to generate more palatable documentation.

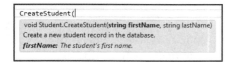

FIGURE 3-9: IntelliSense uses XML comments to display information about methods and their parameters.

The following text shows a sample result. (I've added a few line breaks in long lines.) The bold lines show the information defined by XML comments.

```xml
<?xml version="1.0"?>
<doc>
    <assembly>
```

```
        <name>WindowsFormsApplication1</name>
    </assembly>
    <members>
        <member name="F:WindowsFormsApplication1.Form1.components">
            <summary>
            Required designer variable.
            </summary>
        </member>
        <member name="M:WindowsFormsApplication1.Form1.Dispose(System.Boolean)">
            <summary>
            Clean up any resources being used.
            </summary>
            <param name="disposing">true if managed resources should be disposed;
                otherwise, false.</param>
        </member>
        <member name="M:WindowsFormsApplication1.Form1.InitializeComponent">
            <summary>
            Required method for Designer support - do not modify
            the contents of this method with the code editor.
            </summary>
        </member>
        <member name="M:WindowsFormsApplication1.Program.Main">
            <summary>
            The main entry point for the application.
            </summary>
        </member>
        <member name="T:WindowsFormsApplication1.Student">
            <summary>
            This class defines a student. It includes contact information,
            billing information, past and current courses, and past and
            current intramural activities.
            </summary>
        </member>
        <member name="M:WindowsFormsApplication1.Student.CreateStudent(
          System.String,System.String)">
            <summary>
            Create a new student record in the database.
            </summary>
            <param name="firstName">The student's first name.</param>
            <param name="lastName">The student's last name.</param>
            <WrittenBy date="4/1/2020">Rod Stephens</WrittenBy>
        </member>
        <member name="T:WindowsFormsApplication1.Properties.Resources">
            <summary>
              A strongly-typed resource class, for looking up localized
              strings, etc.
            </summary>
        </member>
        <member name="P:WindowsFormsApplication1.Properties.Resources.
          ResourceManager">
            <summary>
              Returns the cached ResourceManager instance used by this class.
            </summary>
        </member>
        <member name="P:WindowsFormsApplication1.Properties.Resources.Culture">
```

```
      <summary>
        Overrides the current thread's CurrentUICulture property for all
        resource lookups using this strongly typed resource class.
      </summary>
    </member>
  </members>
</doc>
```

SUMMARY

A Visual Studio solution contains a hierarchical arrangement of items. At the top level, it contains one or more projects. Each project contains files that define such items as forms, application settings, and resources. This chapter explained the purposes of the most common of these types of files.

This chapter also explained preprocessor directives such as #define, #if, and #region that you can include in a C# source file to control the way Visual Studio and the C# compiler manage the file. It also explained some basic elements of code file structure such as the using and namespace statements, class declarations, and different kinds of comments.

Now that you understand the basic elements that make up a C# project and code file, you can start learning about the language itself. The chapters in the next part of the book describe the basic elements of the C# programming language. Chapter 4, "Data Types, Variables, and Constants," begins by explaining data types, variables, and constants that hold information while a program manipulates it.

EXERCISES

The exercises for this chapter are actually things you should practice rather than questions to test your understanding. Take a few minutes to give them a try. These exercises and the rest of the book assume you use Visual Studio 2012 Express for Windows Desktop. If you prefer to use some other version of Visual Studio, you may need to adapt the exercises and their solutions somewhat.

For exercises 1 through 5, follow these steps to build a test application:

1. Create a new Windows Forms application.

2. Add a button and give it these property values:

   a. Name = setBackgroundProperty

   b. Text = Set Background

   c. Anchor = None

   d. Make the button big enough to display its text.

3. Use the Format ⇨ Center in Form menu to position the button in the middle of the form.

4. Open Project ⇨ Properties and select the Resources tab. Open the Add Resources drop-down (click to the right on its drop-down arrow) and add a picture to the project. Use any picture you like.

5. Create the button's `Click` event handler and insert the following line of code, replacing `dog` with the name of the resource you added as it appears on the Resources tab.

```
BackgroundImage = Properties.Resources.dog;
```

Use the program to answer the following questions.

1. Resize the form.

   a. What happens to the button's position?

   b. What happens if you change the button's `Anchor` property to `Top, Left`? (Experiment a bit with the graphical editor for setting this property.)

   c. What if `Anchor` is `Bottom, Right`?

   d. What if `Anchor` is `Top, Bottom, Left, Right`?

2. Set the button's `Anchor` property to `Top, Bottom, Left, Right`.

   a. What happens to the button if you make the form small?

   b. Can you still "click" the button by pressing Enter?

   c. Change the button's `MinimumSize` property to `50, 15`. Now what happens if you make the form small?

3. Click the button.

   a. What happens when you click the button?

   b. What happens if you change the form's `BackgroundImageLayout` property to `None`?

   c. What if `BackgroundImageLayout` is `Center`?

   d. What if `BackgroundImageLayout` is `Stretch`?

   e. What if `BackgroundImageLayout` is `Zoom`?

4. Add the following lines of code to the button's `Click` event handler. What happens when you click the button now?

```
setBackgroundButton.BackColor = Color.Yellow;
setBackgroundButton.ForeColor = Color.Red;
```

5. Use a multiline comment to comment out the code you entered for Exercise 4 and add the following code. What happens now when you click the button?

```
BackColor = Color.Red;
ForeColor = Color.Blue;
```

6. Suppose you have the following code that includes nested multiline comments.

```
/*
Comment.

/*
Inner comment.
*/

*/
```

How do you think Visual Studio will interpret this code?

7. Suppose you have the following code that defines two overlapping regions.

```
#region Region1
// Code Block 1 ...
#region Region2
// Code Block 2 ...
#endregion Region1
// Code Block 3 ...
#endregion Region2
```

    a. What happens if you collapse Region1? (Try to figure it out by using what you know about regions. Then try it to see if you're correct.)

    b. What happens if you collapse Region2?

PART II
C# Language Elements

Data Types, Variables, and Constants

WROX.COM DOWNLOADS FOR THIS CHAPTER

Please note that all the code examples for this chapter are available as a part of this chapter's code download on the book's website at www.wrox.com/go/csharp5programmersref on the Download Code tab.

A *variable* is a program element that stores a value. Some of the values that a variable might contain include a number, string, character, date, or object representing something complex such as a customer or business report.

A program uses variables to hold and manipulate values. For example, if some variables hold numbers, the program can apply arithmetic operations to them. If the variables hold strings, the program can use string operations on them such as concatenating them, searching them for particular substrings, and extracting substrings from them.

Four factors determine a variable's exact behavior:

➤ *Data type* determines the kind of the data the variable can hold (integer, character, string, and so forth).

➤ *Scope* defines the code that can access the variable. For example, if you declare a variable inside a `for` loop, only other code inside the loop can use the variable. If you declare a variable at the top of a method, only the code in the method can use the variable.

> **NOTE** *Methods are described in greater detail in Chapter 6, "Methods." For now you can think of a method (sometimes called a function, routine, subroutine, or procedure) as a piece of code wrapped in a package, so it's easy to invoke from multiple places in the program.*

➤ *Accessibility* determines what code in other modules can access the variable. If you declare a variable inside a class at the class level (outside of any method in the class) and you use the `private` keyword, only the code in the class (or derived classes) can use the variable. In contrast, if you declare the variable with the `public` keyword, code in other classes can use the variable, too.

➤ *Lifetime* determines how long the variable's value is valid. For example, a variable declared inside a method is created when the method begins and is destroyed when it exits. If the method runs again, it creates a new copy of the variable and its value is reset.

Visibility is a concept that combines scope, accessibility, and lifetime. It determines whether a certain piece of code can use a variable. If the variable is accessible to the code, the code is within the variable's scope, and the variable is within its lifetime (has been created and not yet destroyed), then the variable is visible to the code.

This chapter explains the syntax for declaring variables in C#. It explains how you can use different declarations to determine a variable's data type, scope, accessibility, and lifetime. It discusses some of the issues you should consider when selecting a type of declaration and describes some concepts, such as anonymous and nullable types, that can complicate variable declarations. This chapter also explains ways you can initialize objects, arrays, and collections quickly and easily.

Constants, parameters, and properties all have concepts of scope and data type that are similar to those of variables, so they are also described here.

DATA TYPES

The smallest piece of data a computer can handle is a *bit*, a single value that can be either 0 or 1. (Bit is a contraction of "binary digit.")

Eight bits are grouped into a *byte*. Computers typically measure disk space and memory space in kilobytes (1,024 bytes), megabytes (1,024 kilobytes), gigabytes (1,024 megabytes), and terabytes (1,024 gigabytes).

Multiple bytes are grouped into *words* that may contain 2, 4, or more bytes depending on the computer hardware. Most computers these days use 4-byte (32-bit) words, although 8-byte (64-bit) computers are becoming more common.

C# also groups bytes in different ways to form data types with a greater logical meaning. For example, it uses 4 bytes to make an integer, a numeric data type that can hold values between −2,147,483,648 to 2,147,483,647.

The following table summarizes C#'s elementary data types.

NAME	TYPE	SIZE	VALUES
Boolean	bool	2 bytes	True or False.
Byte	byte	1 byte	0 to 255.
Signed byte	sbyte	1 byte	−128 to 127.
Character	char	2 bytes	0 to 65,535.
Short integer	short	2 bytes	−32,768 to 32,767.
Unsigned short integer	ushort	2 bytes	0 through 65,535.
Integer	int	4 bytes	−2,147,483,648 to 2,147,483,647.
Unsigned integer	uint	4 bytes	0 through 4,294,967,295.
Long integer	long	8 bytes	−9,223,372,036,854,775,808 to 9,223,372,036,854,775,807.
Unsigned long integer	ulong	8 bytes	0 through 18,446,744,073,709,551,615.
Decimal	decimal	16 bytes	0 to +/−79,228,162,514,264,337,593,543,950,335 with no decimal point; 0 to +/−7.9228162514264337593543950335 with 28 places to the right of the decimal place.
Single-precision floating point number	float	4 bytes	−3.4028235E+38 to −1.401298E-45 (negative values); 1.401298E-45 to 3.4028235E+38 (positive values).
Double-precision floating point number	double	8 bytes	−1.79769313486231570E+308 to −4.94065645841246544E-324 (negative values); 4.94065645841246544E-324 to 1.79769313486231570E+308 (positive values).
String	string	varies	Depending on the platform, a string can hold approximately 0 to 2 billion Unicode characters.

continues

(continued)

NAME	TYPE	SIZE	VALUES
Date and time	`DateTime`	8 bytes	January 1, 0001 0:0:00 to December 31, 9999 11:59:59 pm.
Object	`object`	4 bytes	Points to any type of data.
Class	`class`	varies	Class members have their own ranges.
Structure	`struct`	varies	Structure members have their own ranges.

> **TIP** *Because the* `decimal` *data type has greater precision and a smaller range than the* `float` *and* `double` *data types, Microsoft recommends that you store currency values with the* `decimal` *data type.*

Many of these data types are actually C#-style shorthand for types defined in the System namespace. For example, `sbyte` is the same as `System.SByte` and `ulong` is the same as `System.UInt64`.

> **TIP** *Some of the types defined in the System namespace explicitly include their sizes. For example, the* `UInt64` *type occupies 64 bits. Whenever possible you should use the less specific type name* `ulong` *and let Visual Studio figure out how to map that to the more specific type* `UInt64`. *That way if later versions of C#, perhaps running on 128-bit computers, redefine* `ulong` *to be a 128-bit unsigned integer, you won't need to rewrite your code to work properly.*

Normally in a program you can think of the `char` data type as holding a single character. That could be a simple Roman letter or digit, but C# uses 2-byte Unicode characters, so the `char` type can also hold more complex characters from other alphabets such as Greek, Kanji, and Cyrillic.

The `int` data type usually provides the best performance of the integer types, so you should stick with `int` unless you need the extra range provided by `long` and `decimal`, or you need to save space with the smaller `char` and `byte` types. In many cases, the space savings you get using the `char` and `byte` data types isn't worth the extra time and effort, unless you work with a large array of values.

Note that you cannot safely assume that a variable's storage requirements are exactly the same as its size. In some cases, the program may move a variable so that it begins on a boundary that is natural for the hardware platform. For example, if you make a structure containing several `short` (2-byte) variables, the program may insert 2 extra bytes between them so that they can all start on 4-byte boundaries because that may be more efficient for the hardware. For more information on structures, see Chapter 12, "Classes and Structures."

Some data types also come with some additional overhead. For example, an array stores some extra information about each of its dimensions.

ALIGNMENT ATTRIBUTES

Actually, you can use the `StructLayout` attribute to change the way C# allocates the memory for a structure. In that case you may determine exactly how the structure is laid out. This is a fairly advanced topic and is not covered in this book. For more information, see `http://msdn.microsoft.com/system .runtime.interopservices.structlayoutattribute.aspx`.

Value Versus Reference Types

There are two kinds of variables in C#: value types and reference types.

A *value type* is a relatively simple data type such as an `int` or `float` that represents the data it contains directly. If you declare an `int` variable named `numItems` and assign it the value 27, the program allocates a chunk of memory and stores the value 27 in it.

In contrast, a *reference type* variable contains a reference to another piece of memory that actually contains the variable's data. For example, suppose you define an `OrderItem` class that has `PartNumber`, `PriceEach`, and `Quantity` properties. Now suppose your program creates an `OrderItem` object named `item1` that has `PartNumber` = 3618, `PriceEach` = 19.95, and `Quantity` = 3. The program allocates a chunk of memory to hold those property values. It also creates another piece of memory that is a reference to the first piece of memory. The variable named `item1` is actually this reference and not the memory containing the properties.

Figure 4-1 shows how the two variables `numItems` and `item1` are stored in memory. The dark box on the right shows the pieces of memory that are part of the object referred to by `item1`.

Most of the types described in the previous section that hold a single piece of data are value types. Those include the numeric types, `bool`, and `char`.

Class and structure data types hold multiple related values so, looking at Figure 4-1, you might assume they are reference types. Actually, classes are reference types but structures are value types. That's one of the biggest differences between the two. Chapter 12 has lots more to say about classes, structures, and their differences.

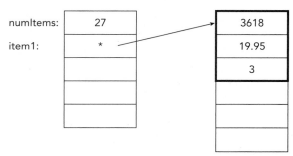

FIGURE 4-1: Value type variables hold their values directly. Reference type variables hold references to their data.

The `DateTime` data type is a structure that holds information about a date and time. Like other structures, it is a value type.

Perhaps the most unexpected fact about value and reference types is that the `string` class is a reference type. A `string` variable contains a reference to some information that describes the actual textual value.

The var Keyword

The var keyword is like a special data type that makes Visual Studio determine the data type that a variable should have based on the value that it is assigned. For example, the following code uses the var keyword to declare the variable numTypes.

```
var numTypes = 13;
```

This code assigns the value 13 to the variable numTypes. Because C# interprets the literal value 13 as an int, the program makes numTypes an int.

> ### STRING STRUCTURE
>
> In C# (and other .NET languages), strings are *immutable*. That means when a string has been assigned a value, it can never be changed. Of course, a program might like to create a string variable and change its value many times.
>
> To get around this seeming inconsistency, string is a reference type that refers to a location called the *intern pool* where the string's value is actually kept.
>
> Only one instance of a given piece of text exists and is stored in the intern pool. If two string variables represent the same piece of text, they both refer to the same location in the intern pool. This saves space if the program uses many variables that contain the same text; although, it does make things a bit more confusing.
>
> When you set a string variable to a new value, the program doesn't actually place the new value inside the string. Instead it looks for the new value in the intern pool. If the value isn't in the intern pool, the program adds it. It then makes the variable point to the entry in the intern pool.
>
> For most purposes, you can ignore the intern pool and pretend a string variable actually holds its text.

You can only use the var keyword inside methods, and you must assign a value to the variable when you declare it (so Visual Studio can figure out what type it should be).

The var keyword is powerful because it can handle all sorts of data types. For example, the following code uses var to declare an array of int and an object with an anonymous type.

```
var values = new[] { 1, 2, 3 };
var person = new { FirstName = "Rod", LastName = "Stephens" };
```

Some programmers use the var type extensively. Unfortunately, to correctly understand the code, you need to easily determine the data type that Visual Studio assigns to the variable. For example, see if you can quickly determine the data types assigned to each of the following variables.

```
var value1 = 100;
var value2 = 1000000000;
var value3 = 10000000000;
var value4 = 100000000000000000000;
```

```
var value5 = 1.23;
var value6 = new { Description= "Pencils", Quantity = 12, PriceEach = 0.25m };
```

EXPOSING THE ANONYMOUS

If you want to know the actual name of an anonymous type created by a var declaration, you can use a statement similar to the following.

```
Console.WriteLine(person.GetType().Name);
```

For the preceding definition of the person variable, this returns the unwieldy type
name <>f__AnonymousType0`2.

The first five data types are int, int, long (because int is too small), syntax error (because this value
is too big to fit in a long but Visual Studio won't automatically promote it to a float), and double.

It's not too hard to figure out that last value is an object with the three fields Description, Quantity,
and PriceEach. What's less obvious is that this object has a class type and not a structure type. Even
worse, suppose the program later uses the following code.

```
var value7 = new { Description= "Notepad", Quantity = "6", PriceEach = 1.15m };
```

This code is similar to the previous code, but here the Quantity value is a string, not an int. If you
don't notice that the two declarations have slightly different formats, you won't know that the two
variables have different data types.

To avoid possible confusion, I generally use explicit data types except where var is necessary. In
particular, the data types created by LINQ expressions can be weird and hard to discover, so for
LINQ using var makes sense. Chapter 8 says more about LINQ.

VARIABLE DECLARATION SYNTAX

Inside a method, the syntax for declaring a variable is simple.

```
«const» type«[]» name «= value»;
```

SYNTAX CONVENTIONS

In syntax definitions for this book, items enclosed in double brackets « » are optional.

Italicized items should be replaced by actual values. Depending on the item, the
actual values might come from a list of allowed choices or they might be names that
you invent.

The | symbol means you can use one of the choices on either side. For example, «A
| B» means you can optionally include either A or B (but not both).

The pieces of this declaration are

➤ const—If you include this, the variable is a constant and its value cannot be changed later. Use the *value* to assign the constant a value.

➤ *type*—The data type you want the variable to have.

➤ [] —Include empty square brackets [] to make an array.

➤ *name*—The name you want the variable to have.

➤ = *value*—The value you want the variable to initially have.

For example, the following snippet declares two variables, an int initialized to 13 and an array of bool.

```
int numPlayers = 13;
bool[] isActive;
```

To create multidimensional arrays, include commas to indicate the number of dimensions. For example, the following code declares a two-dimensional array.

```
int[,] values;
```

You would access a value in this array as in the following code.

```
values[1, 2] = 1001;
```

You can include as many commas as you like to create higher-dimensional arrays.

ARRAYS OF ARRAYS

In addition to creating multidimensional arrays, you can also create arrays of arrays. The following code declares an array of arrays of integers.

```
int[][] values;
```

You would access a value in this array as in the following code.

```
values[1][2] = 987;
```

Declaring a variable that is not inside a method is slightly more complicated because the declaration can include attributes, access specifiers, and other modifiers. The following text shows the syntax for declaring a variable inside a class but not inside any method.

```
«attributes» «accessibility»
    «const | readonly | static | volatile | static volatile»
    type«[]» name «= value»
```

FIELDS

A variable that is declared at the class level, outside of any method, is called a *field*. Most developers recommend that you use properties instead of fields. Properties are described in the section "Properties" later in this chapter.

The pieces of this declaration are

➤ *attributes*—One or more attributes that specify extra properties for the variable. The following section, "Attributes," describes attributes in more detail.

➤ *accessibility*—This determines which code can access the variable. The section "Accessibility" later in this chapter describes accessibility values in more detail.

➤ const—If you include this, the variable is a constant and its value cannot be changed later. Use the *value* to assign the constant a value.

➤ readonly—If you include this, the variable is similar to a constant except its value can be set either with a *value* clause or in the class's constructor.

➤ static—This keyword indicates the variable is shared by all instances of the class.

➤ volatile—This keyword indicates the variable might be modified by code running in multiple threads running at the same time.

➤ *type*—The data type you want the variable to have.

➤ []—Include empty square brackets [] to make an array.

➤ *name*—The name you want the variable to have.

➤ = *value*—The value you want the variable to initially have.

For example, the following code defines a publically visible constant int variable named NumSquares and initializes it to the value 8.

```
public const int NumSquares = 8;
```

The section "Static, Constant, and Volatile Variables" later in this chapter provides more detail on the static, const, readonly, and volatile keywords.

You can define and even initialize multiple variables of the same type in a single statement. The following statement declares and initializes two int variables.

```
public int value1 = 10, value2 = 20;
```

> **TIP** *Many developers prefer not to initialize multiple variables in the same statement to keep the code easier to read.*

Name

A variable's `name` must be a valid C# identifier. It should begin with a letter, underscore, or @ symbol. After that it can include letters, numbers, or underscores. If the name begins with @, it must include at least one other character.

Identifier names cannot contain special characters such as &, %, #, and $. They also cannot be the same as C# keywords such as `if`, `for`, and `public`. The following table lists some examples.

NAME	VALID?
numEmployees	Valid
NumEmployees	Valid
num_employees	Valid
_manager	Valid (but unusual)
_	Valid (but confusing)
1st_employee	Invalid (doesn't begin with a letter, underscore, or @ symbol)
#employees	Invalid (contains the special character #)
return	Invalid (keyword)

The @ character is mainly used to allow a program to have a variable with the same name as a keyword. For example, you could define a variable named `@for`. The @ symbol tells the compiler that this is not a keyword. However, the compiler ignores the @ symbol after it decides it isn't the beginning of a keyword. For example, if you declare a variable named `@test`, then the program considers `test` and `@test` to be the same name.

You can avoid a lot of potential confusion if variable names aren't keywords, don't use the @ symbol, and aren't weird combinations such as _, ____, and _1_2_. For a list of C# keywords, go to `http://msdn.microsoft.com/library/x53a06bb.aspx`.

Attributes

The optional attribute list is a series of attribute objects that provide extra information about the variable. An attribute further refines the definition of a variable to give more information to the compiler, the runtime system, and other tools that need to manipulate the variable.

> ### DELIGHTFUL DECORATIONS
>
> Applying an attribute to a class, variable, method, or other code entity is sometimes called *decorating* the entity.

Attributes are fairly specialized and address issues that arise when you perform specific programming tasks. For example, serialization is the process of converting objects into a textual representation. When you write code to serialize and deserialize data, you can use serialization attributes to gain more control over the process.

The following code defines the OrderItem class. This class declares three public variables: ItemName, Price, and Quantity. It uses attributes to indicate that ItemName should be stored as text, Price should be stored as an XML attribute named Cost, and Quantity should be stored as an XML attribute with its default name, Quantity.

```
[Serializable()]
public class OrderItem
{
    [XmlText()]
    public string ItemName;

    [XmlAttribute(AttributeName = "Cost")]
    public decimal Price;

    [XmlAttribute()]
    public int Quantity;
}
```

(These attributes are defined in the System.Xml.Serialization namespace, so the program uses the statement using System.Xml.Serialization, although that statement isn't shown in the code here.)

The following code shows the XML serialization of an OrderItem object.

```
<OrderItem Cost="1.25" Quantity="12">Cookie</OrderItem>
```

Chapter 25, "Serialization," says more about serialization. Because attributes are so specialized, they are not described in more detail here. For more information, see the sections in the online help related to the tasks you need to perform. For information on attributes in general, see these web pages:

➤ Attributes (C# and Visual Basic), http://msdn.microsoft.com/library/z0w1kczw.aspx.

➤ Attributes Tutorial, http://msdn.microsoft.com/library/aa288454.aspx.

➤ Attribute Hierarchy, http://msdn2.microsoft.com/2e39z096.aspx.

Accessibility

A variable declaration's accessibility clause can take one of the following values (in order of decreasing accessibility):

➤ public—Indicates the variable should be available to all code inside or outside of the variable's class. This allows the most access to the variable.

➤ internal—Indicates the variable should be available to all code inside or outside of the variable's class within the same assembly only. The difference between this and public is that public allows code in other assemblies to access the variable. The internal keyword is useful, for example, if you write a library for use by other assemblies and you want some of the variables inside the library to be visible only inside the library.

➤   `protected`—Indicates the variable should be accessible only to code within the same class or a derived class. The variable is available to code in the same class or a derived class, even if the instance of the class is different from the one containing the variable. For example, one `Employee` object can access a `protected` variable inside another `Employee` object.

➤   `internal protected`—This is the union of the `internal` and `protected` keywords. It indicates a variable is accessible only to code within the same class or a derived class and only within the same assembly.

➤   `private`—Indicates the variable should be accessible only to code in the same class or structure. The variable is available to other instances of the class or structure. For example, the code in one `Customer` object can access a `private` variable inside another `Customer` object.

If you omit the accessibility, a declaration is `private` by default. In the following code, the two variables `value1` and `value2` are both `private`.

```
private int value1;
int value2;
```

Static, Constant, and Volatile Variables

A variable declaration can include any of the following keywords:

➤   `const`

➤   `readonly`

➤   `static`

➤   `volatile`

➤   `static volatile`

The `const` keyword indicates the value cannot be changed after it is created. The variable's declaration must include an initialization statement to give the constant a value. If you don't include an initialization or if the code tries to change the constant's value, Visual Studio flags the statement as an error.

The `readonly` keyword makes the variable similar to a constant except its value can be set in its declaration or in a class constructor. The following code shows how you could create a `Car` class with a `readonly` `MilesPerGallon` variable.

```
class Car
{
    public readonly float MilesPerGallon = 40f;

    public Car()
    {
        MilesPerGallon = 20;
    }
}
```

```
        public Car(float milesPerGallon)
        {
            MilesPerGallon = milesPerGallon;
        }
    }
```

The class starts by declaring `MilesPerGallon`, initially setting it to the somewhat optimistic value 40.

Next, a parameterless constructor sets `MilesPerGallon` to 20. When the program uses this constructor to create a new `Car` instance, its `MilesPerGallon` value is set to 20.

A second constructor takes a `float` value as a parameter and sets the new instance's `MilesPerGallon` value to the parameter's value. Because all the class's constructors set `MilesPerGallon`, the declaration of the variable doesn't need to give it a value, too. (Chapter 12 covers classes and constructors in greater detail.)

No other code either inside the class or outside of it can modify the `readonly` variable's value.

> **NOTE** *You cannot use the* var *keyword with a* const *or* readonly *declaration.*
> *If you use* const *or* readonly, *you must include an explicit data type.*

The `static` keyword indicates the variable is shared by all instances of the class. If a variable is not declared `static`, each instance of the class has its own copy of the variable.

For example, suppose you build a `Car` class to represent a fleet of identical cars. Each `Car` object needs its own `Miles` property because each car may have driven a different number of miles. However, if all the cars get the same number of miles per gallon, they can share a `MilesPerGallon` property. The following code shows how you might create this class.

```
    class Car
    {
        public static float MilesPerGallon;
        public float Miles;
    }
```

Because all the instances of the `Car` class share the same `MilesPerGallon` variable, if the code in any instance of the class changes this value, all the instances see the new value.

The `volatile` keyword indicates the variable might be modified by code running in multiple threads running at the same time. This prevents the compiler from optimizing the variable in a way that would prevent code on a separate thread from modifying the value. For more information on this keyword, see `http://msdn.microsoft.com/library/x13ttww7.aspx`.

INITIALIZATION

The final (and optional) part of a variable declaration is initializing it.

If you do not initialize a variable, it takes a default value that depends on its data type. Numeric and `char` variables take the value 0, and `bool` variables take the value `false`.

Structures are also value types. When a structure is declared, each of its properties and fields takes its default value. For example, if a structure has a `int` field, it is set to `0`.

Reference values (including class variables and `string`s) get the special value `null`, which means "this reference doesn't point to anything."

If you don't want a variable to take its default value, you can include an initialization. Follow the variable's name with an equal sign and the value you want it to take. For simple types such as `int` and `bool`, this is straightforward. For example, the following code declares the `bool` variable `ready` and initializes it to the value `false`.

```
bool ready = false;
```

For more complex data types such as classes, structures, arrays, and lists, initialization is a bit more complicated. The following sections explain how to initialize variables of those types.

Classes and Structures

There are two main ways to initialize an object that has a class or structure type. (The steps are the same for classes and structures, so the following text assumes you are working with a class.)

First, you can use a `new` statement to create the new object and follow it with a list of property or field initializers. Each initializer consists of the property's or field's name, an equal sign, and the value that it should receive.

For example, suppose you define the following `Person` class.

```
class Person
{
    public string FirstName, LastName;
}
```

Now the program can use the following code to create and initialize an instance of the class.

```
Person rod = new Person() { FirstName = "Rod", LastName = "Stephens" };
```

The properties (or fields) do not need to be listed in the order in which they are defined in the class.

The second way to initialize an instance of a class is to give the class a constructor that takes parameters it can use to initialize the object. For example, consider the following `Person` class.

```
class Person
{
    public string FirstName, LastName;

    public Person(string firstName, string lastName)
    {
        FirstName = firstName;
        LastName = lastName;
    }
}
```

This code uses the `firstName` and `lastName` parameters to initialize the object's `FirstName` and `LastName` fields.

Now the program can use the following code to create and initialize an instance of the class.

```
Person rod = new Person("Rod", "Stephens");
```

With this approach, the new statement must provide the parameters in the order expected by the constructor.

> **INTELLISENSE INITIALIZATION**
>
> Visual Studio's IntelliSense provides useful feedback when you use either of these methods of initializing an object. If you type new Person(, IntelliSense lists the parameters that the class's constructors can accept. If you type new Person() { and a space, IntelliSense lists the class's properties and fields so you can pick one.

Arrays

When you declare an array, a C# program doesn't automatically create the array. After declaring the array, there are two ways you can initialize it.

First, you can follow the variable name with the equal sign, the new keyword, the array items' data type, and the number of items you want the array to hold surrounded by square brackets. The following code uses this method to create an array of 10 decimal values.

```
decimal[] salaries = new decimal[10];
```

All array indices start with 0, so this creates an array with values salaries[0] through salaries[9].

Initially array entries take on their default values. For example, the salaries array initialized in the preceding code would be filled with 10 copies of the value 0. The code can then loop through the array and initialize each entry.

Instead of initializing each array entry separately, you can use the second method for initializing an array. For this method, follow the variable's name with the equal sign and a comma-delimited list of values surrounded by braces. For example, the following code declares a decimal array and fills it with four values.

```
decimal[] salaries =
{
    32000m,
    51700m,
    17900m,
    87300m,
};
```

> **TIP** *The comma after the final item in the initialization list is optional.*

When you use this method for initializing an array, the program determines the number of items in the array by looking at the values you supply.

If you are initializing an array of objects, the items inside the braces would be values of the appropriate type. For example, the following code declares and initializes an array containing four `Person` references, the last of which is initialized to `null`.

```
Person[] customers =
{
    new Person() { FirstName="Ann", LastName="Archer"},
    new Person() { FirstName="Ben", LastName="Blather"},
    new Person() { FirstName="Cindy", LastName="Carver"},
    null,
};
```

To initialize a multidimensional array, include an array initializer for each entry. For example, the following code declares and initializes a two-dimensional array.

```
int[,] values =
{
    {1, 2, 3},
    {4, 5, 6},
};
```

Note that you must provide a consistent number of items for each of the array's dimensions. For example, the following declaration is invalid because the array's first row contains three elements, but the second row contains only two elements.

```
int[,] values =
{
    {1, 2, 3},
    {4, 5},
};
```

To initialize an array of arrays, make an array initializer where each item is a new array. The following code declares and initializes an array of arrays holding values similar to those in the preceding two-dimensional array.

```
int[][] values2 =
{
    new int[] {1, 2, 3},
    new int[] {4, 5, 6},
};
```

Collections

Collection classes that provide an `Add` method (such as `List`, `Dictionary`, and `SortedDictionary`) have their own initialization syntax that is similar to a combination of the two kinds of array initializers. After the variable's name, include the equal sign and a new object as you would for any other class. Follow that with a comma-delimited list of values that should be added to the collection surrounded by braces.

For example, the following code declares and initializes a `List<string>` (a list of strings).

```
List<string> pies = new List<string>
{
    "Apple", "Banana", "Cherry", "Coconut Cream"
};
```

> **NOTE** *The syntax* List<string> *creates a* List *object that manipulates* strings. List *is a generic class and in this example* string *is its generic parameter. Chapter 14, "Collection Classes," says more about generic collection classes.*

The items inside the braces must include all the values needed by the collection's Add method. For example, the Dictionary class's Add method takes two parameters giving a key/value pair that should be added. That means each entry in the initializer should include a key and value.

The following code initializes a Dictionary<string, string> (dictionary with keys that are strings and associated values that are strings). The parameters to the class's Add method are an item's key and value so, for example, the value 940-283-1298 has the key Alice Artz. Later you could look up Alice's phone number by searching the Dictionary for the item with the key "Alice Artz".

```
Dictionary<string, string> directory = new Dictionary<string, string>()
{
    {"Alice Artz", "940-283-1298"},
    {"Bill Bland", "940-237-3827"},
    {"Carla Careful", "940-237-1983"}
};
```

INITIALIZING WITHOUT ADD

Some collection classes such as Stack and Queue don't have an Add method, so this kind of initializer doesn't work for them. Fortunately, they have constructors that take a parameter that can be an enumerable type such as a list or array. That means you can pass the constructor an array of values to be added to the Stack or Queue as in the following code.

```
Stack<int> stack = new Stack<int>(new int[] { 1, 2, 3, 4 });
Queue<int> queue = new Queue<int>(new int[] { 4, 3, 2, 1 });
```

LITERAL TYPE CHARACTERS

If your code includes a literal value such as a number, C# uses a set of rules to interpret the value. For example, the value 2000000000 fits in the int data type, so when a C# program sees that value, it assumes it is an int.

In contrast, the value 3000000000 does not fit in the int data type, so the program assumes this value is a uint, which is big enough to hold the value. A uint cannot hold a negative value, however, so if the program contains the value –3000000000, C# makes it a long.

When a value looks like an integer, the program tries to interpret it as the smallest integer data type at least as large as int (so it doesn't consider byte, sbyte, short, or ushort).

When a value includes a decimal point, the program assumes it is a double.

For the smaller integer data types, the program automatically converts integer values if possible. For example, consider the following statement.

```
short count = 15000;
```

This statement declares a variable named count that has type short. The program considers the literal value 15000 to be an int. Because the value 15000 can fit in a short, the program converts the int into a short and stores the result in the variable.

Often this all works without any extra work on your part, but occasionally it can cause problems. The following code demonstrates one of the most common of those.

```
float distance = 1.23;
```

This statement declares a variable named distance that has type float. The program considers the literal value 1.23 to be a double. Because all double values cannot necessarily fit in a float, the program flags this as an error at design time and displays this error:

Literal of type double cannot be implicitly converted to type 'float'; use an 'F' suffix to create a literal of this type

One way to avoid this problem is to use a *literal type character* to tell C# what type the literal should have. The following code solves the preceding code's problem. The f at the end of the literal tells the program that the value 1.23 should be treated as a float instead of a double.

```
float distance = 1.23f;
```

The following table lists C#'s literal type characters.

CHARACTER	DATA TYPE
U	uint
L	long
UL, LU	ulong
F	float
D	double
M	decimal

You can use uppercase or lowercase for literal type characters. For example, 1.23f and 1.23F both give a float result. For the UL and LU characters, you can even mix case as in 10uL; although, that might make the code more confusing than necessary.

> **TIP** *Because the lowercase letter l looks a lot like the numeral 1, Visual Studio marks a line with warning if you use the lowercase l in a literal type character as in 10l or 10lu.*

C# also lets you precede an integer literal with 0x or 0X (in both cases, the first character is a zero not the letter O) to indicate that it is a hexadecimal (base 16) value. For example, the following two statements set the variable flags to the same value. The first statement uses the decimal value 100 and the second uses the hexadecimal value 0x64.

```
flags = 100;    // Decimal 100.
flags = 0x64;   // Hexadecimal 0x64 = 6 * 16 + 4 = 100.
```

BASE CONVERSIONS

You can use the Convert.ToInt32 method to convert between bases other than decimal and hexadecimal. See http://msdn.microsoft.com/library/sf1aw27b.aspx.

Surround string literals with double quotes and char literals with single quotes, as shown in the following code.

```
string name = "Rod";
char ch = 'a';
```

Within a string or char literal, a character that follows the \ character has a special meaning. For example, the combination \n represents a new line. These combinations are called *escape sequences*. The following table lists C#'s escape sequences.

ESCAPE SEQUENCE	CHARACTER
\'	Single quote
\"	Double quote
\\	Backslash
\0	Null
\a	Alert (bell)
\b	Backspace
\f	Form feed
\n	New line
\r	Carriage return
\t	Tab
\v	Vertical tab

For example, the following code defines a string that contains four column headers' values separated by tabs.

```
string header = "Item\tPrice Each\tQuantity\tTotal";
```

If a `string` contains backslashes but no escape sequences, it can be cumbersome to represent each backslash with \\. For example, Windows file paths such as C:\Temp\Projects\CurrentWork\ project.txt may include a lot of backslashes. The following code shows how you would assign this value to a `string` variable.

```
string filename = "C:\\Temp\\Projects\\CurrentWork\\project.txt";
```

In C# you can place an @ symbol in front of a string to make working with this kind of text easier. In that case the `string` ignores all escape sequences and includes the characters between its quotes as they appear.

```
string filename = @"C:\Temp\Projects\CurrentWork\project.txt";
```

This kind of string continues until it reaches its closing " and can even span multiple lines.

If you need the string to contain a " character, you can't simply type it in the text because the program would think it represented the end of the string. You also cannot use \" because this kind of string ignores escape sequences.

Instead of adding a " character to the string, double up the character. The following code initializes a `string` variable to hold a two-line string that contains double quotes and then displays it in the Console window.

```
            string greeting = @"Welcome to Project
""Do What I Meant""";
            Console.WriteLine(greeting);
```

The following text shows the result.

```
Welcome to Project
"Do What I Meant"
```

DATA TYPE CONVERSION

Normally, you assign a value to a variable that has the same data type as the value. For example, you assign a string value to a `string` variable, you assign an integer value to an `int` variable, and so forth. Often, however, a program must convert a value from one data type to another. For example, it might need to convert an `int` into a `float` or it might need to convert a `string` containing a numeric value into a `decimal`.

The following sections discuss several ways you can convert data from one to another. Those methods include

➤ Implicit conversion

➤ Casting

➤ Using the `as` operator

➤ Parsing

➤ Using `System.Convert`

➤ Using `System.BitConverter`

Implicit Conversion

Suppose a program needs to save a value in a variable. If the variable can hold any value that the program might want to use, then the program can safely store the value in the variable.

For example, suppose the program creates an `int` variable and puts some value in it. It then wants to save the value in a `long` variable. A `long` variable can hold any value that an `int` variable can hold, so this is guaranteed to succeed.

Storing a value in a variable of a different type that is guaranteed to hold the value is called a *widening conversion*. Storing an `int` value in a `long` is an example of a widening conversion. (If you think of the variables as envelopes or boxes, this makes sense. You can put a smaller value in a wider envelope without trouble.)

In contrast, a *narrowing conversion* is one in which the source value cannot necessarily fit in the destination variable. For example, suppose a program has an `int` variable and wants to copy its value into a `byte` variable. This may or may not succeed depending on the value. For example, if the value is 10, this succeeds because 10 will fit in a `byte` variable. However, if the value is 900, this fails because 900 cannot fit in a `byte`.

A C# program can make widening conversions implicitly. For example, the following code saves an `int` value in a `long` variable.

```
int theInt = 1337;
long theLong = theInt;
```

A C# program will not perform implicit narrowing conversions. For example, the following code is not allowed even though the value stored in `theLong` would fit in an `int` variable.

```
long theLong = 100;
int theInt = theLong;
```

In this case, Visual Studio displays the following error message:

Cannot implicitly convert type 'long' to 'int'. An explicit conversion exists (are you missing a cast?)

LOSS OF PRECISION

Some widening conversions can still result in a loss of precision. For example, a `decimal` variable can store more significant digits than a `float` can. A `float` can hold any value that a `decimal` can but not with the same precision. If you assign a `decimal` value to a `float` variable, you may lose some precision.

For example, consider the following code.

```
decimal dPrice = 1.2345678901234567890m;
Console.WriteLine(dPrice);

float fPrice = (float)dPrice;
Console.WriteLine(fPrice);
```

The following text shows the result in the Console window.

```
1.2345678901234567890
1.234568
```

Microsoft considers the `decimal` to `float` conversion widening because the `decimal` value will fit in a `float`, just possibly with some loss of precision. A C# program cannot perform that conversion implicitly, however.

If you need to perform a narrowing conversion, then you must use one of the explicit conversion methods described in the following sections. The most common of those methods, and the one suggested by the error message, is casting.

For a table listing C#'s implicit numeric conversions, see `http://msdn.microsoft.com/library/y5b434w4.aspx`.

For a table listing C#'s explicit numeric conversions, see `http://msdn.microsoft.com/library/aa288039.aspx`.

Casting

A *cast operator* explicitly tells a program to convert a value from one type to another type. To cast a value into a type, place the type surrounded by parentheses in front of the value. For example, the following code casts a `long` value into an `int` variable. The bold text shows the cast operator.

```
long theLong = 100;
int theInt = (int)theLong;
```

The following sections provide more detail about casting numbers and casting objects.

Casting Numbers

If the `long` value fits in the `int` variable, then this cast succeeds. If the value does not fit, then the cast fails. By default, C# does not warn you that the cast failed. Instead the converted value causes an overflow or underflow and leaves garbage in the `int` variable.

You can protect the code by enclosing it in a checked block. If an integer cast overflows or under-flows while inside a checked block, the program throws a System.OverflowException. (A program throws different kinds of exception objects to signal runtime errors. Chapter 9, "Error Handling," has more to say about exceptions and how to handle them.) The following code shows the preceding example rewritten to use a checked block.

```
checked
{
    theLong = 3000000000;
    theInt = (int)theLong;
}
```

Now the program can catch the exception as described in Chapter 9.

Unfortunately a checked block does not throw an exception if the program tries to convert a double value into a float and the value won't fit. For example, the following code tries to squeeze the value −1e200 into a variable of type float.

```
float theFloat;
double theDouble = -1e200;

theFloat = (float)theDouble;
```

The value −1e200 is too small to fit in a float so this cast fails. The program doesn't throw an exception, and a checked block will not detect this error.

If the value is too large or small, the program sets the variable's value to positive or negative infinity. The float class provides the methods IsPositiveInfinity, IsNegativeInfinity, and IsInfinity to determine whether a variable is holding one of these special values. The following code shows the preceding example rewritten to deal with values that are too big or too small to fit in a float.

```
float theFloat;
double theDouble = -1e200;

theFloat = (float)theDouble;
if (float.IsInfinity(theFloat)) ... Do something about it ...
```

CASTING A FLOAT TO AN INTEGER

If you cast a floating point value into an integer type, the value is truncated. For example, the expression (int)99.9 gives the value 99.

If you want to round the value to the nearest integer instead of truncating it, use the System.Convert class's ToInt32 method (which is described in the section "Using System.Convert" later in this chapter) or the Math.Round method instead.

Casting Objects

Converting an object to an ancestor class is a widening conversion. For example, suppose the Student class inherits from the Person class. In that case, all Students are Persons so converting a Student into a Person is a widening conversion. That means the following implicit conversion works.

```
Student student = new Student();
Person person;

person = student;
```

A variable of an ancestor class can hold objects of a derived class. For example, a Person variable can hold a Student object because a Student is a type of Person. However, not all Person objects are Students. That means casting a Person to a Student is a narrowing conversion and may or may not succeed depending on whether the Person actually is a Student or something else such as a Teacher or Janitor.

The following code demonstrates two narrowing object conversions.

```
Person personA = new Student();
Person personB = new Janitor();
Student student;

student = (Student)personA;
student = (Student)personB;
```

The first conversion casts personA into a Student. Variable personA happens to hold a Person object, so this works.

The second conversion casts personB into a Student. Variable personB happens to hold a Janitor. A Janitor is not a kind of Student so this fails at run time with a System.InvalidCastException.

One way to determine whether a cast from one object type to another is valid is to try it and catch the InvalidCastException if it occurs. Another method is to use the is operator. The is operator determines whether an object is compatible with a given type.

For example, suppose the variable person holds a reference to an object that might be a Student or a Janitor. The following code tests whether that object can be cast into a Student before performing the conversion.

```
if (personB is Student)
{
    student = (Student)personB;

    // Do something with the Student...
}
```

Using the as Operator

The as operator provides a shorthand for converting objects from one type to another. The following code converts the value in variable person into a Student and saves it in variable student.

```
student = person as Student;
```

This is similar to a cast if the variable person holds a value that can be converted into a Student. If the value cannot be converted into a Student (for example, if it is a Janitor), then the as operator returns the special value null. That leaves the variable student referring to no object.

Casting Arrays

Casting lets you convert values between primitive and object types. It also lets you cast arrays of objects.

For example, in some sense an array of Student objects is also an array of Person objects because a Student is a type of Person. That means a C# program can implicitly convert an array of Student into an array of Person, and it can explicitly convert an array of Person into an array of Student. The following code demonstrates those implicit and explicit conversions.

```
// Make an array of Students.
Student[] students = new Student[10];

// Implicit cast to an array of Persons.
// (A Student is a type of Person.)
Person[] persons = students;

// Explicit cast back to an array of Students.
students = (Student[])persons;
```

Parsing

Each of the fundamental data types (except for string) has a Parse method that tries to convert a string into that type. For example, the following code saves the value 112358 in a string variable. It then uses the int class's Parse method to convert that string into an int.

```
string text = "112358";
int value = int.Parse(text);
```

Some of these parsing methods can take additional parameters to control the conversion. For example, the numeric methods can take a parameter that gives the international number style the string should have.

If the string passed to the Parse method doesn't make sense, the method throws an exception. A program can catch the exception as described in Chapter 9. Alternatively, the code can use a corresponding TryParse method. Each class's TryParse method attempts to parse a string much as Parse does. Unlike Parse, TryParse returns the parsed value through an output parameter, and the method's return value is true if parsing was successful and false otherwise. The following code shows how a program might use TryParse.

```
string text = "112358";
int value;
if (int.TryParse(text, out value))
{
    // Do something with value ...
}
```

TIP *Many programs use the* Parse *and* TryParse *methods to convert values entered by the user into numbers. For example, if* priceTextBox *is a* TextBox *where the user enters a price, the following code reads the value, parses it, and saves the result in the variable* price.

```
decimal price;
if (!decimal.TryParse(priceTextBox.Text, out price))
{
    MessageBox.Show("Error parsing price value " +
        priceTextBox.Text);
    return;
}

// Do something with price...
```

This code declares the variable price. *It then uses* TryParse *to attempt to parse the text in the* TextBox's Text *property. If the parsing fails (*TryParse *returns* false*), the code displays an error message and returns from the method.*

If the parsing succeeds, the code continues to do whatever is appropriate with price.

Using System.Convert

The Convert class has a variety of methods that convert values from one data type to another. For example, the following code uses the ToInt64 method to convert the string "61" into a 64-bit integer.

```
long value = Convert.ToInt64("61");
```

These methods are easy to understand so they make the code simple to read. Unfortunately, they work with particular data type sizes such as 32- or 64-bit integers rather than with the system's default integer size, so they may require you to change your code in the future. If a later version of C# assumes that long means 128-bit integer, you may need to update your calls to Convert.ToInt64.

Using System.BitConverter

The System.BitConverter defines methods that convert values to and from arrays of bytes.

The GetBytes method returns an array of bytes representing a value. Methods such as ToInt32 and ToDouble convert values stored in byte arrays back into specific data types.

Often these methods are used to convert values returned by API functions into more usable types. For example, an API function might return two 16-bit integer values packed into the halves of a single 32-bit value. You could use these methods to convert the 32-bit value into an array of 4 bytes and then convert the two pairs of bytes into 16-bit values.

The BitConverter class's methods are quite specialized, so they are not described further here. For more information, see "BitConverter Class" at msdn.microsoft.com/library/system .bitconverter.aspx.

ToString

The ToString method is so useful it deserves special mention. Every object has a ToString method that returns a string representation of the object. For example, the following code converts the decimal value totalCost into a string and saves the result in the variable totalString.

```
string totalString = totalCost.ToString();
```

The value returned by ToString depends on the object. Simple objects such as the primitive data types (byte, int, long, decimal, string, and so on) return their values. More complicated objects often return their class names rather than their values. (You can override a class's ToString method to make it return something more useful if that makes sense. For example, you could make the Person class's ToString method return the person's first and last names.)

The ToString method can take as a parameter a format string to change the way the method formats its result. For example, the following code displays the value of the decimal variable cost with two digits after the decimal point.

```
MessageBox.Show(cost.ToString("0.00"));
```

Appendix P, "Date and Time Format Specifiers," and Appendix Q, "Other Format Specifiers," describe format specifiers in greater detail.

SCOPE

A variable's scope determines which other pieces of code can access it. For example, if you declare a variable inside a method, only code within that method can access the variable. The three possible levels of scope are (in increasing size of scope) block, method, and class.

Block Scope

A *block* is a series of statements enclosed in braces. If you declare a variable within a block of code, the variable has block scope, and only other code within that block can access the variable. Furthermore, only code that appears after the variable's declaration can see the variable.

Variables declared in the block's opening statement are also part of the block. Note that a variable is visible within any subblock contained within the variable's scope.

For example, consider the following code snippet.

```
for (int i = 1; i <= 5; i++)
{
    int j = 3;
    if (i == j)
    {
        int sum = i + j;
        Console.WriteLine("Sum: " + sum);
    }
    else
    {
```

```
            int product = i * j;
            Console.WriteLine("Product: " + product);
        }

        int k = 123;
        Console.WriteLine("k: " + k);
    }
```

This code uses a for loop with the looping variable i declared in the for statement. The scope of variable i is the block defined by the for loop. Code inside the loop can see variable i, but code outside of the loop cannot.

Inside the loop, the code declares variable j. This variable's scope is also the for loop's block.

If i equals j, the program declares variable sum and uses it. This variable's scope includes only the two lines between the if and else statements.

If i doesn't equal j, the code declares variable product. This variable's scope includes only the two lines between the else statement and the closing brace.

The program then declares variable k. This variable also has block scope, but it is available only after it is declared, so the code could not have accessed it earlier in the for loop.

Other code constructs that define blocks include the following:

➤ switch statements—All the case statements exist within the block defined by the switch statement.

➤ try catch finally statements—The try section, catch sections, and finally section all define separate blocks. Note also that the exception variable used by each catch statement is in the block defined by its catch statement. (That means they can all have the same name.)

➤ while loops—Variables declared inside the loop are local to the loop.

➤ using statements (not using directives)—Resources acquired by the block and variables declared inside the block are local to the block.

Because block scope is the most restrictive, you should use it whenever possible to reduce the chances for confusion. The section "Restricting Scope" later in this chapter talks more about restricting variable scope.

Method Scope

If you declare a variable inside a method but not within a block, the variable is visible to any code inside the procedure that follows the declaration. The variable is not visible outside of the method. In a sense, the variable has block scope where the block is the method.

A method's parameters also have method scope. For example, in the following code, the scope of the order and item parameters is the AddOrderItem method.

```
public void AddOrderItem(Order order, OrderItem item)
{
    order.OrderItems.Add(item);
}
```

Class Scope

A variable with class (or structure) scope is available to all code in its class (or structure) even if the code appears before the variable's declaration. For example, the following code works even though the `DisplayLoanAmount` method is declared before the `LoanAmount` variable that it displays.

```
public class Lender
{
    public void DisplayLoanAmount()
    {
        MessageBox.Show(LoanAmount.ToString());
    }

    private decimal LoanAmount;
    ...
}
```

Depending on its accessibility keyword, the variable may be visible outside of the class. For example, if you declare the variable with the `public` keyword, it is visible to all code outside of the class. See the section "Accessibility" earlier in this chapter for more information.

Restricting Scope

There are several reasons why you should give variables the most restrictive scope possible that still lets them do their jobs.

Limited scope keeps the variable localized, so programmers cannot use the variable incorrectly in far off code that is unrelated to the variable's main purpose.

Having fewer variables with wide scope (such as public) means programmers have less to remember when they work on the code. They can concentrate on their current work, rather than worry about what an object's p and q fields mean.

Limiting scope keeps variables closer to their declarations, so it's easier for programmers to check the declaration. One of the best examples of this situation is when a `for` loop declares its looping variable right in the `for` statement. A programmer can easily see that the looping variable is an integer (for example) without scrolling to the top of the method hunting for its declaration. It is also easy to see that the variable has block scope, so other variables with the same names can be used outside of the loop.

Finally, limited scope means a programmer doesn't need to worry about whether a variable's old value will interfere with the current code or whether the final value after the current code exits will later interfere with some other code This is particularly true for looping variables. If a program declares variable i at the top of a method and then uses it many times in various loops, you might need to do a little thinking to be sure the variable's past values won't interfere with new loops. If you declare i separately in each `for` statement, each loop has its own version of i, so there's no way they can interfere with each other.

PARAMETER DECLARATIONS

A parameter declaration for a method defines the names and types of the parameters passed into it. Parameters always have method scope. C# creates parameter variables when a method begins and destroys them when the method ends. The method's code can access the parameters, but code outside of the method cannot.

For example, the following method takes an integer named id as a parameter. Code within the method can access id, and code outside of the method cannot.

```
public void DisplayEmployee(int id)
{
    . . .
}
```

A parameter's basic scope is straightforward (method scope), but parameters have some special features that complicate the situation. Although this isn't exactly a scoping issue, it's related closely enough to scope that it's worth covering here.

There are three ways you can pass values into a method: by value, by reference, and for output.

By Value

By default a parameter's value is passed into the method *by value*. That means the method receives a *copy* of the parameter's value. If the method modifies the parameter, it modifies only the copy, so the value in the calling code remains unchanged.

For example, consider the following code.

```
private void DoubleTest()
{
    int value = 10;
    DoubleIt(value);
    Console.WriteLine("DoubleTest: " + value.ToString());
}

private void DoubleIt(int number)
{
    number *= 2;
    Console.WriteLine("DoubleIt: " + number.ToString());
}
```

The DoubleTest method creates variable value and initializes it to 10. It then calls the DoubleIt method, passing it value as an argument. (In the calling code, a value passed to a method is called an *argument*.)

The DoubleIt method receives the value as the parameter number. (When a method receives a value, it is called a *parameter*.) Notice that the parameter's name doesn't need to be the same as the argument. Actually, often the argument isn't a simple variable as it is in this case. The DoubleTest method could have used an arithmetic statement as an argument as in DoubleIt(value / 3).

The DoubleIt method doubles the value of its parameter and displays the result in the Console window. Control then returns to the DoubleTest method.

Because the parameter was passed to the `DoubleIt` method by value, the original variable value in the `DoubleTest` method is unchanged.

If you run this code, the following text appears in the Console window.

```
DoubleIt: 20
DoDouble: 10
```

By Reference

One alternative to passing a value into a method by value is to pass it *by reference*. In that case the method receives a reference to the argument's value, not a copy of the value. That means if the method changes the parameter, the argument in the calling code is also changed.

WHEN SHOULD YOU PASS BY REFERENCE?

You should pass a parameter by reference whenever you want a method to both use and update the parameter.

For example, suppose you wrote a method that takes as parameters the X and Y coordinates where it should print some text on a printout. When it is finished, the method should update those coordinates to indicate the position where the next piece of text should be printed so it doesn't overlap the current piece of text. This could be at a new position on the same line (a new X value but the same Y value), or it could be on a new line (new X and Y values).

In this case, you could pass the coordinates into the method by reference so the method can read their values and update them.

To pass a value by reference, add the keyword `ref` before the parameter declaration. If a parameter is declared with the `ref` keyword, the argument in the calling code must also include the `ref` keyword to make it obvious that you are passing the value by reference. That will hopefully prevent you from being surprised when the calling code modifies the argument's value. (Actually, you wouldn't declare a parameter with the `ref` keyword unless you intended the method to modify it.)

The following code shows the previous example with the method's parameter passed by reference. The `ref` keywords are shown in bold.

```
private void DoubleTest()
{
    int value = 10;
    DoubleIt(ref value);
    Console.WriteLine("DoubleTest: " + value.ToString());
}

private void DoubleIt(ref int number)
{
    number *= 2;
    Console.WriteLine("DoubleIt: " + number.ToString());
}
```

If you run the code now, the following text appears in the Console window.

```
DoubleIt: 20
DoDouble: 20
```

This time the `DoubleIt` method doubled its parameter, and the change was reflected in the `value` argument in the calling code.

For Output

The final way you can pass a value into a method uses the `out` keyword. This keyword means the parameter is intended to be an output parameter. The argument is passed into the method by reference so the method can set its value. The method does not assume the value has been initialized before it is passed into the method, and the method assigns a value to the parameter before it returns.

> ### WHEN SHOULD YOU PASS FOR OUTPUT?
>
> You should pass parameters for output whenever you want a method to initialize a parameter but the method doesn't need to use the parameter's initial value.
>
> For example, suppose a method fetches data about a particular model of car and uses output parameters to return information about the model such list price, miles per gallon, horsepower, and number of cup holders. In that case, the method initializes those values before it returns but doesn't use any values that those parameters might have on input, so the parameters should be declared for output.
>
> If you have the choice between declaring a parameter by reference or for output, declare it for output because that is more restrictive and may help you catch bugs. When you declare a parameter for output, Visual Studio does not require the calling code to initialize the parameter passed into the method. It also flags any code that uses the parameter's input value as an error because marking the parameter for output indicates that its input value is not needed.

As is the case for the `ref` keyword, if you add the `out` keyword to a parameter declaration, you must also include it with the argument. The following code shows the previous example modified to use the `out` keyword.

```
private void DoubleTest()
{
    int value;
    DoubleIt(out value);
    Console.WriteLine("DoubleTest: " + value.ToString());
}

private void DoubleIt(out int number)
{
    number = 50;
    Console.WriteLine("DoubleIt: " + number.ToString());
}
```

Because the `DoubleIt` method doesn't require that its parameter be initialized, the `DoubleTest` method does not initialize its `value` variable. The `DoubleIt` method sets the parameter's value and displays it. Because the parameter is declared `out`, the value returns to the calling code, so in the `DoubleTest` method `value` becomes 50.

The following text shows the result.

```
DoubleIt: 50
DoubleTest: 50
```

Unusual Circumstances and Exceptions

Even if you know how to pass arguments by value, by reference, and for output, there are situations that can be confusing. Recall that some variables are value types and others are reference types. When you pass a value type variable by value, the method receives a copy of the value and all is as you would expect.

If you pass a reference variable by value, the method receives a copy of the reference, not a copy of the reference's data. That means the method cannot change the reference (because it was passed by value) but it can change the data associated with the reference.

For example, consider the following method.

```
private void SetCity(Person person)
{
    person.City = "Bugsville";
    person.Zip = 12345;
}
```

This method takes a `Person` parameter passed by value, changes the object's `City` and `Zip` values, and ends.

If `Person` is a class, it is a reference type so the method receives a copy of the reference. That means the parameter refers to the same object as the argument in the calling code, so any changes to the object's properties are also changes to the original object.

In the calling code, the `Person` object hasn't changed but its `City` and `Zip` values have.

Now consider the following version of the `SetCity` method.

```
private void SetCity(Person person)
{
    person = new Person() { City = "Programmeria", Zip = 54321 };
}
```

This version sets the `person` parameter to a new `Person` object. Because the parameter was passed by reference, however, the calling code's `Person` object isn't changed. You can make the calling code receive the new value by declaring the parameter `ref` or `out`.

A similar phenomenon occurs when you pass arrays into a method. If the array is passed by value, the method can change its values, but if it sets the parameter equal to a new array, the change does not return to the calling code. If the array parameter is declared `ref` or `out`, the method can set the parameter equal to a new array, and the change returns to the calling code.

Chapter 6 has more to say about methods.

PROPERTIES

In C# a *property* is similar to a field in a class except it is implemented by *accessor methods* instead of as a simple variable. A property's get and set accessors allow the program to get and set the property's value.

The following code shows a simple Name property.

```
private string _Name;
public string Name
{
    get
    {
        return _Name;
    }
    set
    {
        _Name = value;
    }
}
```

The code begins by declaring a private string variable _Name. Sometimes this private variable is called the property's *backing field* because it holds the value for the property.

The next statement begins the definition of the public Name property. The get accessor simply returns the value in the _Name variable.

The set accessor sets the _Name variable equal to the special value parameter. The value parameter is implicitly declared for the set accessor. It acts like any other parameter except you don't need to define it.

A program could use these methods exactly as if there were a public field. For example, if this code is in the Employee class, the following code shows how a program could set and then get the Name property for an Employee object named emp.

```
emp.Name = "Rod Stephens";
Console.WriteLine(emp.Name);
```

You might want to use properties instead of public fields for several reasons. First, the accessors give you extra control over how the program stores and retrieves the property's value. For example, the set accessor could use code to validate the value before saving it in the backing field. The code could verify that a postal code or phone number has the proper format and throw an exception if the value is badly formatted.

You can also set breakpoints in property methods. Suppose your program is crashing because a piece of code is setting a value incorrectly. The crash doesn't occur right away, so the value may have been set long before the crash. If you implement the value with a property, you can set a breakpoint in the set accessor and stop whenever the program sets the value.

Properties also enable you to set and get values in formats other than those you want to actually use to store the value. For example, the following code defines a Name property that saves a full name in first and last name variables.

```
private string _FirstName, _LastName;
public string Name
{
    get
    {
        return _FirstName + " " + _LastName;
    }
    set
    {
        _FirstName = value.Split(' ')[0];
        _LastName = value.Split(' ')[1];
    }
}
```

Here the get accessor returns the concatenation of the _FirstName and _LastName fields. The set accessor uses the string class's Split method to split the new value into two pieces delimited by a space character. It saves the first part of the value in _FirstName and the second part in _LastName.

Finally, you can use properties to create read-only and write-only values. The following code shows how to make a read-only NumEmployees property method and a write-only NumCustomers property method. (Write-only property methods are unusual but legal.)

```
private int _NumEmployees;
public int NumEmployees
{
    get
    {
        return _NumEmployees;
    }
}

private int _NumCustomers;
public int NumCustomers
{
    set
    {
        _NumCustomers = value;
    }
}
```

To make a property read-only or write-only, the code simply omits the accessor that it doesn't need. The properties' backing fields are still visible to code inside the class so that code can get and set the values as needed.

> **NOTE** *A property must define at least one of the* get *and* set *accessors. Otherwise it's not much use.*

A backing field isn't the only way you can store a property's value. For example, you could store the value in a database, text file, or configuration setting. Still, backing fields are quite popular. They're so popular that C# provides auto-implemented properties that use backing fields behind the scenes.

To create an auto-implemented property, simply omit the body of the accessors as in the following example.

```
public string Name { get; set; }
```

> **NOTE** *Auto-implemented properties must include both* get *and* set *accessors.*

The advantage of auto-implemented properties is that you don't need to write as much code. The disadvantage is that you can't set breakpoints in the accessors.

ENUMERATIONS

An *enumeration* (also called an *enumerated type* or simply an *enum*) is a discrete list of specific values called *enumerators*. You define the enumeration and the values allowed. Later, you can declare a variable of the enumeration's type so it can take only those values.

For example, suppose that you build a large application where users can have one of three access levels: clerk, supervisor, and administrator. You could define an enumeration named AccessLevels that contains the enumerators Clerk, Supervisor, and Administrator. Now, if you declare a variable to be of type AccessLevels, C# allows the variable to take only those values.

The following code shows a simple example.

```
// Define the access level values.
public enum AccessLevels
{
    Clerk,
    Supervisor,
    Administrator,
}

// The user's access level.
private AccessLevels Level;

// Set supervisor access level.
public void MakeSupervisor()
{
    Level = AccessLevels.Supervisor;
}
```

This code defines the AccessLevels type and declares the variable Level of the type. Later the MakeSupervisor method sets Level to the value AccessLevels.Supervisor. (Note that the value is prefixed with the enumerated type's name.)

The syntax for declaring an enumerated type is as follows:

```
«attributes0» «accessibility» name
    «: type»
{
    «attributes1» name1 «= value1»,
    «attributes2» name2 «= value2»,
    ...
}
```

The pieces of this declaration are

➤ *attributes0*—Attributes that specify extra properties for the enumeration. See the section "Attributes" earlier in this chapter for more information.

➤ *accessibility*—This determines which code can access the variable. See the section "Accessibility" earlier in this chapter for more information.

➤ *name*—The name you want to give the enumeration.

➤ *: type*—All enumerations are stored internally as integer values. By default, an enumeration's type is int. You can use this part of the declaration to change the underlying type to byte, sbyte, short, ushort, int, uint, long, or ulong. (Any integer type except char.)

➤ *attributes1*, *attributes2*—Attributes that specify extra properties for the enumerators.

➤ *name1*, *name2*—The names of the enumerators.

➤ *value1*, *value2*—The integer value that should be used to store this enumerator. By default, the first enumerator is represented by 0 and the values of subsequent enumerators are increased by 1.

The following code provides a more complicated example.

```
public enum Meal : sbyte
{
    Breakfast = 1,
    Lunch = Breakfast * 10,
    Dinner = 100,
    Supper = Dinner,
}
```

This code defines an enumeration named Meal that stores its enumerators with the sbyte data type. The enumerator Breakfast is represented by the value 1, Lunch is represented by 10 times the value of Breakfast, and Dinner is represented by the value 100.

The enumerator Supper is defined to be the same as the enumerator Dinner. Both are stored as the value 100 internally, so the program cannot distinguish between the two values.

Usually, all that's important about an enumeration is that its values are distinct, so you don't need to change the underlying data type or initialize the values.

Normally, a program should set a variable's value to one of the allowed enumerators as in the statement Level = AccessLevels.Supervisor. If for some reason you need to set the value to a calculated result, you can cast the result into the enumeration's type. For example, the following code sets the `Meal` variable `food` to the value 1 cast into a `Meal`.

```
Meal food = (Meal)1;
```

INVALID ENUMERATORS

If you cast a value to an invalid enumerator value, the invalid value is stored. For example, using the previous `Meal` enumeration, the following sets the variable `meal` to the invalid value 3.

```
Meal meal = (Meal)3;
```

The program happily stores this value and may lead to problems later when you try to use the value. This kind of bug can be hard to track down because the code that causes it by saving the invalid value may be far from the code that tries to use the invalid value.

To avoid this kind of bug, don't cast values into an enumeration type unless you absolutely must.

You can declare an enumeration inside a class or namespace.

If you define an enumeration inside a namespace, code within the namespace can refer to it by its name. If the enumeration's accessibility level permits, code outside the namespace can refer to it by giving the namespace and the enumeration. For example, suppose the `Meal` enumeration is defined in the `FoodStuff` namespace. Then a piece of code in some other namespace could use the enumeration as in the following code.

```
FoodStuff.Meal meal = FoodStuff.Meal.Breakfast;
```

> **TIP** *If a* using *directive refers to the namespace containing the enumeration, you don't need to include the namespace when you refer to the enumeration.*

If you define an enumeration inside a class and its accessibility permits, code outside of the class can refer to the enumeration by including the class name. If the code is in another namespace, it should add that, too.

For example, suppose the `FoodStuff` namespace contains the `Oven` class, which defines the `Meal` enumeration. The following code shows how a method inside the `Oven` class could use the enumeration.

```
Meal meal = Meal.Breakfast;
```

The following code shows how a method outside of the `Oven` class but inside the `FoodStuff` namespace could use the enumeration.

```
Oven.Meal meal = Oven.Meal.Breakfast;
```

The following code shows how a method in another namespace could use the enumeration.

```
FoodStuff.Oven.Meal meal = FoodStuff.Oven.Meal.Breakfast;
```

Enumerations have several advantages. First, they encourage you to use meaningful values instead of "magic numbers" in your code. Instead of using the potentially confusing value 1, you can use the value Breakfast.

Second, enumerations allow Visual Studio to provide IntelliSense help. If you type Meal meal = IntelliSense provides the choice Meal. If you select it and type a period, IntelliSense displays the possible enumerators.

A final benefit of enumerations is that they provide a ToString method that returns the textual name of the value. For example, the following code displays the message "Breakfast."

```
Meal meal = Meal.Breakfast;
Console.WriteLine(meal.ToString());
```

(Actually the Console.WriteLine method calls the ToString method for any object that it is passed, so you could write the second statement as Console.WriteLine(meal).)

If you have a variable that can take only a fixed number of values, you should probably make it an enumerated type. Also, if you discover that you have defined a series of constants to represent related values, you should consider converting them into an enumerated type. Then you can gain the benefits of the improved type checking and IntelliSense.

FLAGS

If you decorate an enumeration with the Flags attribute, the enumeration represents a combination of values. The code can use the bitwise operators to combine values.

To make the enumeration work properly, you should explicitly give the enumerators values that are powers of 2 so that they can be combined in any arrangement.

For example, the following code defines a Direction enumeration to let the program specify any combination of Up, Down, Left, and Right. The code also creates a value None to represent no value and a value All to represent every value.

```
[Flags] enum Direction
{
    None = 0,
    Up = 1,
    Down = 2,
    Left = 4,
    Right = 8,
    All = Up | Down | Left | Right,
}
```

continues

continued

The following code creates a variable to represent moving in the upper-right direction.

`Direction direction = Direction.Up | Direction.Right;` Normally, you use | (bitwise "or") to combine values but you can also use & (bitwise "and") and ~ (bitwise "not"). The following code sets the variable `direction` to all the `Direction` values except `Right`.

```
Direction direction = Direction.All & ~Direction.Right
```

This expression on the right side of the equal sign sets `direction` to the value `All`. The expression `~Direction.Right` creates a value that has bits set where those in the value `Direction.Right` are clear and vice versa. The & operator makes `direction`'s final value have bits set where they are set in `Direction.All` and also in `~Direction.Right` (which are all the bits except the one representing `Right`). The result `direction` has bits set for `Up`, `Down`, and `Left`.

NULLABLE TYPES

Most relational databases have a concept of a null data value. A null value indicates that a field does not contain any data. It lets the database distinguish between valid zero or blank values and non-existing values. For example, a null bank balance would indicate that there is no known balance, whereas a 0 would indicate that the balance was 0.

You can create a nullable variable in C# by adding a question mark after the variable's data type. The following code declares a nullable `int` variable.

```
int? count;
```

BEHIND NULLABLE

Behind the scenes, a nullable type is implemented by the generic `Nullable` structure. For example, the type `int?` is actually implemented as `Nullable<int>`. You can even declare variables to have the type `Nullable<int>` if you like; although, the ? syntax is easier to write and read.

To make a nullable variable "null," set it equal to `null`. To give a variable a non-null value, simply set it equal to the value. The following code sets variable `count` to `null` and then 1337.

```
int? count;
count = null;
count = 1337;
```

To determine whether a nullable variable contains a value, either use its `HasValue` property or simply compare it to `null`. The following code determines whether the variable `count` holds a value in a couple different ways.

```
if (count.HasValue) Console.WriteLine("count = " + count);
else Console.WriteLine("count = null");
if (count != null) Console.WriteLine("count = " + count);
if (count == null) Console.WriteLine("count = null");
```

The first line of code uses the variable's `HasValue` property. If `count` has a value, the code displays it.

The `else` statement on the next line displays "count = null" if the variable has no value.

The next two lines use `!=` and `==` to compare the variable to the value `null`.

The syntax used by nullable variables makes them remarkably easy to use and understand. There's only one slightly complex issue: *null propagation*. When you perform a calculation with a nullable variable that holds no value, its "nullness" propagates into the result. For example, if a nullable integer contains no value, it probably doesn't make sense to add another number to it. (What is `null` + 11?)

If any of the operands in an expression contains a `null` value, the result is a `null` value. Any time you need to use a nullable value, you should first check to see whether it is `null` or a usable value.

DELEGATES

A *delegate* is a special data type that refers to a method. The method can be an instance method provided by an object or a static method defined by a class. Like other types such as classes and enumerations, delegates can be defined in namespaces and classes but not inside methods.

A delegate variable acts as a pointer to a method. Delegate variables are sometimes called *type-safe function pointers*.

The `delegate` keyword defines a delegate type and specifies the parameters and return type of the method to which the delegate refers.

After you have defined a delegate type, you can declare variables that are of that type. You can set those variables equal to methods that match the delegate's parameters and return value.

For example, the following code defines a delegate type named `ShowMessageType`. This delegate represents methods that take a single `string` as a parameter and that don't return any result.

```
private delegate void ShowMessageType(string msg);
```

The following defines a `ShowInConsoleWindow` method, which simply displays a message in the Console window.

```
// Display a message in the Console window.
private void ShowInConsoleWindow(string message)
{
    Console.WriteLine(message);
}
```

The `ShowInConsoleWindow` method takes a single `string` parameter and returns no result, so it matches the `ShowMessageType` delegate.

The following code creates a delegate variable and makes it refer to the `ShowInConsoleWindow` method.

```
// Create a delegate variable holding a
// reference to the ShowInConsoleWindow method.
ShowMessageType say = ShowInConsoleWindow;
```

Now that the delegate variable refers to a method, the code can invoke that method by using the variable. The following code shows how a program can invoke the method referred to by the `say` variable.

```
// Invoke the method.
say("Hello");
```

DELEGATES THE EASY WAY

The .NET Framework defines two families of delegates that you can use instead of writing your own delegate types in many cases. These two kinds of delegates are named `Action` and `Func`.

An `Action` delegate represents a method that takes between 0 and 16 parameters and returns no value. These are generic delegates, so you need to specify the data types of the method's parameters.

Generics are described in detail in Chapter 15. For now an example should make this clear. The following code creates a delegate variable that represents a method that takes a `string` as a parameter and returns no result.

```
Action<string> say = ShowInConsoleWindow;
```

The generic parameter `<string>` indicates the delegate takes a `string` as a parameter.

The predefined `Func` delegates represent methods that take 0 to 16 parameters and return a value. The delegate's initial generic types indicate the types of the method's parameters. The final generic type gives the method's return type.

The following code declares a delegate variable that takes as parameters two `floats` and returns a `double`.

```
Func<float, float, double> mapping;
```

Delegate variables are similar to any other kind of variable and the same rules apply to them. You can change their values, pass them as arguments into methods, and use them as members of classes and structures. (Chapter 12 says more about creating classes and structures.)

For a more interesting example, consider the following `ProcessApplicant` method.

```
// Process a job applicant.
private void ProcessApplicant(Person applicant, ShowMessageType status)
{
    status("Processing applicant " + applicant.Name);

    // Process the applicant ...

    status("Done processing applicant " + applicant.Name);
}
```

This method takes as parameters a `Person` object to process and a method of type `ShowMessageType`. It starts by calling the method to display status information saying it is starting to process the applicant. The method then does whatever it needs to do to process the applicant. It finishes by calling the status method again to say it is done processing the applicant.

Depending on what you want to do with the status information, you can pass different status methods to `ProcessApplicant`. For example, the following code passes `ProcessApplicant` the method `ShowInConsoleWindow` to make the status messages appear in the Console window.

```
ProcessApplicant(person, ShowInConsoleWindow);
```

The following code uses the `ShowInMessageBox` method to make the status messages appear in message boxes.

```
ProcessApplicant(person, ShowInMessageBox);
```

You could define other methods to write status messages into a log file, save messages in a database, e-mail messages to someone, or ignore the messages completely. The main program can pass any of these methods into the `ProcessApplicant` method to make it handle the messages differently.

SUMMARY

Two of the most important things you control with a variable declaration are its data type and its visibility. Visibility combines scope (the piece of code that contains the variable such as a `for` loop, method, or class), accessibility (the code that is allowed to access the variable determined by keywords such as `private`, `public`, and `protected`), and lifetime (when the variable has been created and not yet destroyed).

To avoid confusion, explicitly declare the data type whenever possible and use the most limited scope possible for the variable's purpose.

Code that uses LINQ (described in Chapter 8) complicates matters somewhat. The results of LINQ expressions often have weird data types, and it can be extremely difficult to use those exact types. In that case you can use the `var` data type to let the program determine the true data type at runtime.

Now that you know how to declare variables, you can learn how to combine them. Chapter 5, "Operators," explains the symbols (such as +, *, and %) that you can use to combine variables to produce new results.

EXERCISES

1. Suppose the variable `student` has type `Student`, the variable `person` has type `Person`, and the `Student` class inherits from the `Person` class. Use an `if` statement and the `is` operator to write code that is equivalent to the following statement but without the `as` operator.

```
student = person as Student;
```

2. Write a statement that declares an `int` array named `fibonacci` that holds values 1, 1, 2, 3, 5, 8, 13, 21, 34, 55, and 89.

3. Write a statement that declares an 8 × 8 array named `board` that holds instances of the `Person` class where each entry is initially `null`.

4. Repeat Exercise 2 using an array of arrays.

5. Create a `Person` class with text fields `FirstName`, `LastName`, `Street`, `City`, and `State`. Also give the class a numeric `Zip` field that is just big enough to hold five-digit ZIP codes. Define the fields so all code can see them.

6. Write a statement that declares a 2 × 2 array containing objects of the `Person` class you created for Exercise 5. Initialize them to hold the names Ann Archer, Ben Baker, Cindy Cant, and Dan Deevers.

7. Write a statement that declares and initializes a three-dimensional 2 × 2 × 3 array of `strings` where each entry gives its position in the array. For example, `values[0, 1, 1]` should hold the value "011."

8. Write a method that takes a `ref` parameter. What happens if you try to pass in an argument that has not been initialized in the calling code?

9. Modify the method you wrote for Exercise 8 so that it uses an `out` parameter instead of a `ref` parameter. What happens if the calling code does not initialize the argument before passing it into the method? What if it does initialize the argument?

10. What happens if you modify the method you wrote for Exercise 8 so that it doubles its parameter when it starts?

11. What happens if you modify the method you wrote for Exercise 8 so that it does nothing with its parameter?

12. What happens if you try to pass an expression such as 12 * 3 into a method that takes an `int` parameter by reference?

13. Make an `Oven` class that has `TempFahrenheit` and `TempCelsius` properties to get and set the temperature in degrees Fahrenheit and Celsius, respectively. Store the temperature in a single `private` variable. (You decide whether to store the temperature in Fahrenheit or Celsius.) Use the following equations to convert from one to the other.

$$F = C \times \tfrac{9}{5} + 32$$

$$C = (F - 32) \times \tfrac{5}{9}$$

14. Make two methods Combine1 and Combine2 that both take two ints as parameters and return a string. The first should return the values concatenated as in "(12, 34)." The second should return them concatenated as in "R12C34."

Next declare a delegate variable named combiner to hold a reference to these methods. Use combiner to test the methods as in the following code.

```
combiner = Combine1;
Console.WriteLine(combiner(1, 2));
combiner = Combine2;
Console.WriteLine(combiner(1, 2));
```

5

Operators

WROX.COM DOWNLOADS FOR THIS CHAPTER

Please note that all the code examples for this chapter are available as a part of this chapter's code download on the book's website at `www.wrox.com/go/csharp5programmersref` on the Download Code tab.

An *operator* is a basic code element that performs some operation on one or more values to create a result. The values the operator acts upon are *operands*. For example, in the following statement, the operator is + (addition), the operands are B and C, and the result is assigned to the variable A.

```
A = B + C
```

C# operators fall into five categories: arithmetic, concatenation, comparison, logical, and bitwise. This chapter first explains these categories and the operators they contain; it then discusses other operator issues such as precedence, assignment operators, and operator overloading.

ARITHMETIC OPERATORS

The following table lists the arithmetic operators provided by C#. Most of these should be familiar to you.

OPERATOR	PURPOSE	EXAMPLE	RESULT
++	Increment	x++ or ++x	Sets x = x + 1
--	Decrement	x-- or --x	Sets x = x - 1
-	Negation	-x	Sets x = -x
+	Unary plus	+x	Sets x = +x (leaves x unchanged)
*	Multiplication	2 * 3	6
/	Division	3.0 / 2	1.5
%	Modulus	17 mod 5	2
+	Addition	2 + 3	5
-	Subtraction	3 - 2	1
<<	Bit left shift	10110111 << 1	01101110
>>	Bit right shift	10110111 >> 1	01011011

The % operator returns the remainder after dividing its first operand by its second. For example, 17 % 5 = 2 because 17 = 3 × 5 with a remainder of 2.

Result Data Type

An operator's result data type depends on the operands' data types. If an expression combines values with different data types, those with narrower types (smaller ranges) are automatically promoted to the type with the wider type (greater range). For example, consider the following expression.

```
var x = 1.2 + 3;
```

The operands 1.2 and 3 are a double and an int, respectively. Because the result may not fit in an int, the value 3 is promoted to a double. The calculation is then performed and the final result is a double.

The / operator performs both integer and floating point division. If the operands are both integers, the / operator performs integer division and discards any remainder. If either of the operands has a floating point type, the / operator performs floating point division. The following code shows examples.

```
float x = 9 / 10;   // Result 0.0.
float y = 9f / 10;  // Result 0.9.
float z = 9 / 10f;  // Result 0.9.
```

The + symbol represents both numeric addition and string concatenation. The following code shows an example of string concatenation.

```
string firstname = "Rod";
string lastname = "Stephens";
string name = firstname + ' ' + lastname;   // Result "Rod Stephens"
```

The third line of code in this example uses the + operator to combine the string `firstname`, a space character, and the string `lastname`.

If one of the + operator's operands is a `string`, then the result is a `string` and the other operand is converted into a string if necessary. For example, the following code concatenates a `string`, `double`, `string`, and `bool`.

```
string message = "Data point " + 37.2 + " is " + false;
```

The result in this example is the `string` "Data point 37.2 is False."

Shift Operators

The `<<` operator shifts the bits of an integer value to the left, padding the empty bits on the right with zeros. For example, the `byte` value with bits 10110111 shifted 1 bit to the left gives 01101110. The leftmost bit doesn't fit in the `byte` so it is dropped.

The `>>` operator shifts the bits of a value to the right, padding the empty bits on the left with zeros. For example, the byte value with bits 10110111 shifted 1 bit to the right gives 01011011.

Unfortunately, you can't put binary literals such as 10110111 in your code. Instead, you must write this value as 0xB7 in hexadecimal or 183 in decimal.

> **CALCULATOR CLEVERNESS**
>
> The Calculator application that comes with Windows enables you to easily convert between binary, octal, hexadecimal, and decimal. In newer versions of the calculator, open the View menu and select Programmer. If your version doesn't have Programmer mode, open the View menu and select Scientific. Now you can click the Bin, Oct, Dec, or Hex radio buttons to select a base, enter a value in that base, and then select another base to convert the value into the new base.

Increment and Decrement Operators

The statements ++x and x++ both increment the value of the variable x but they have slightly different side effects. These two forms of the increment operator are sometimes called *pre-increment* and *post-increment* operations, respectively. (This discussion also applies to the pre-decrement and post-decrement operators --x and x--.)

The pre-increment operator ++x increments x and then returns its new value. The post-increment operator x++ returns x's original value and then increments x. The difference is small and in simple calculations isn't important. For example, many programs use one or the other of these operators to increment a variable and nothing more. The following code simply increments the variable numProcessed.

```
numProcessed++;
```

These operators are also often used in for loops as in the following code. The post-increment operator is highlighted in bold.

```
for (int i = 0; i < 5; i++) Console.WriteLine("i: " + i);
```

In both these examples, the increment operation takes place on its own, so it doesn't matter whether you use the pre-increment or post-increment version. In more complicated calculations, however, the difference can be important.

For example, suppose a bill-of-sale application has variables priceEach and numItems. The user clicks a button to add a new item to the sale, and the program uses the following code to update the total cost.

```
decimal totalCost = numItems++ * priceEach;
```

Because this code uses the post-increment operator, the calculation uses the current value numItems and then increments it afterward. This gives an incorrect result because the calculation uses the old value for numItems. For example, suppose priceEach is 10 and numItems is 1 when this statement executes. The code calculates totalCost = 10 * 1 = 10 and then increments numItems to 2.

The following version uses the pre-increment operator.

```
decimal totalCost = ++numItems * priceEach;
```

This version increments numItems and then performs the calculation so it gets the correct result. If priceEach is 10 and numItems is 1 when this statement executes, the code first increments numItems to 2 and then calculates totalCost = 10 * 2 = 20, which is the correct result.

> **TIP** *Often the pre- and post-increment operators are easy enough to understand. If they make the program confusing, you can rewrite the code to make things easier to understand. The following code does what the preceding example does, but it separates the increment operator from the calculation to reduce confusion.*
>
> ```
> ++numItems;
> decimal totalCost = numItems * priceEach;
> ```

COMPARISON OPERATORS

Comparison operators compare one value to another and return a boolean value (true or false), depending on the result. The following table lists the comparison operators provided by C#. The first six (==, !=, <, <=, >, and >=) are relatively straightforward. Note that the logical negation operator ! is not a comparison operator, so it is not listed here. It is described in the next section, "Logical Operators."

OPERATOR	PURPOSE	EXAMPLE	RESULT
==	Equals	A == B	true if A equals B
!=	Not equals	A != B	true if A does not equal B
<	Less than	A < B	true if A is less than B
<=	Less than or equal to	A <= B	true if A is less than or equal to B
>	Greater than	A > B	true if A is greater than B
>=	Greater than or equal to	A >= B	true if A is greater than or equal to B
is	Object is or inherits from a certain type	obj is Manager	true if obj is an object that inherits from Manager

When its operands are reference types, the == and != operators compare the operands, not the values to which they refer. For example, the following code defines two Person objects and sets them equal to the same value.

```
Person person1 = new Person();
Person person2 = person1;
```

After this code executes, person1 and person2 refer to the same Person object so the == operator reports them as equal.

The following code creates two different Person objects.

```
Person person1 = new Person() { FirstName = "Zaphod", LastName = "Beeblebrox" };
Person person2 = new Person() { FirstName = "Zaphod", LastName = "Beeblebrox" };
```

These are two separate objects even though they happen to have the same FirstName and LastName values. Even if all the objects' properties and fields have the same values, these are still two separate objects so the == operator reports them as different.

LOGICAL OPERATORS

Logical operators combine two boolean values and return true or false, depending on the result. The following table summarizes C#'s logical operators.

OPERATOR	PURPOSE	EXAMPLE	RESULT
!	Negation	!A	true if A is false
&	And	A & B	true if A and B are both true
|	Or	A | B	true if A or B or both are true
^	Xor (Exclusive Or)	A ^ B	true if A is true or B is true but both are not true
&&	And with short-circuit evaluation	A && B	true if A and B are both true (see the following notes)
||	Or with short-circuit evaluation	A || B	true if A or B or both are true (see notes)

The operators !, &, and | are relatively straightforward.

"Xor" stands for "exclusive or," and the Xor operator returns true if one but not both of its operands is true. The expression A ^ B is true if A is true or B is true but both are not true.

Xor is useful for situations in which exactly one of two things should be true. For example, suppose you run a small software conference with two tracks, so two talks are going on at any given time. Each attendee should sign up for one talk in each time slot but cannot sign up for both because they're at the same time. You might use code similar to the following to check whether an attendee has signed up for either talk 1a or talk 1b but not both:

```
if (talk1a ^ talk1b)
{
    // This is okay
    ...
}
```

The && and || operators are similar to the & and | operators, except that they provide short-circuit evaluation. In *short-circuit evaluation*, C# is allowed to stop evaluating operands if it can deduce the final result without them. For example, consider the expression A && B. If C# evaluates the value A and discovers that it is false, the program knows that the expression A && B is also false no matter what value B has, so it doesn't need to evaluate B.

Similarly for the expression A || B, if A is true, then the entire expression is true no matter what value B has, so the program doesn't need to evaluate B.

Whether the program evaluates both operands doesn't matter much if A and B are simple boolean variables. However, assume that they are time-consuming methods. For example, the TimeConsumingFunction routine might need to look up values in a database or download data from a website. In that case, not evaluating the second operand might save a lot of time.

```
if (TimeConsumingFunction("A") && TimeConsumingFunction("B"))
{
    ...
}
```

Because && and || do the same thing as & and | but are sometimes faster, you might wonder why you would ever use & and |. The main reason is that the operands may have side effects. A *side effect* is some action a method performs that is not obviously part of the method. For example, suppose that the NumEmployees method opens an employee database and returns the number of employee records, leaving the database open. The fact that this method leaves the database open is a side effect.

Now, suppose that the NumCustomers function similarly opens the customer database, and then consider the following statement.

```
if ((NumEmployees() > 0) && (NumCustomers() > 0))
{
    ...
}
```

After this code executes, you cannot be certain which databases are open. If NumEmployees returns 0, the && operator's first operand is false, so it doesn't evaluate the NumCustomers method, and that method doesn't open the customer database.

The && and || operators can improve application performance under some circumstances. However, to avoid possible confusion and long debugging sessions, do not use && or || with operands that have side effects.

AVOID SIDE EFFECTS

Side effects in general make the code harder to understand, so you should avoid them whenever possible. In the preceding example, you could pull the database opening features of the NumEmployees and NumCustomers methods and put them in separate methods. The following code is slightly longer than the previous version but avoids confusing side effects.

```
OpenEmployeeDatabase();
OpenCustomerDatabase();
if ((NumEmployees() > 0) && (NumCustomers() > 0))
{
    ...
}
```

BITWISE OPERATORS

Bitwise operators work much like logical operators do, except they compare integer values one bit at a time.

Many programs use bitwise operators for a variety of purposes. Some of the most common include:

➤ Reading and setting bit fields—Here the bits in a single number have specific meanings. For example, suppose you want to store a value indicating whether an object should be attached to the left, right, top, and bottom edges of its container. You could store that information with four separate boolean values, or you could store it as four bits in a single value.

➤ Working with devices—Many devices such as communications ports use bits to get and set information about the device.

➤ Encryption and compression—These operations often need to work with bits.

➤ Graphics—Many graphics algorithms use bits to represent colors and other important values. For example, different bits in a single number may represent a pixel's red, green, and blue color components.

The bitwise negation operator ~ flips the bits in its operand from 1 to 0 and vice versa. The following shows an example:

```
  ~10110111
= 01001000
```

The bitwise And operator & places a 1 in a result bit if both of its operands have a 1 in that position. The following shows an example:

```
  10101010
& 00110110
= 00100010
```

The bitwise Or operator | places a 1 in the result if either of its operands has a 1 in the corresponding position. The following shows an example:

```
  10101010
| 00110110
= 10111110
```

The bitwise Xor operator ^ places a 1 bit in the result if exactly one of its operands, but not both, has a 1 in the corresponding position. The following shows an example:

```
  10101010
^ 00110110
= 10011100
```

There are no bitwise equivalents for the && and || operators.

CONDITIONAL AND NULL-COALESCING OPERATORS

The *conditional operator* ?:, which is sometimes called the *ternary operator*, takes three operands. The first operand is a boolean value. If that value is true, the operator returns its second operand. If the first operand is false, the operator returns its third operand.

For example, suppose the variable amount holds a dollar value and you want to display it in the Label control named amountLabel. If amount is negative, you want to display its value in red. If amount is not negative, you want to display its value in blue. The following code sets the amountLabel control's text and color appropriately.

```
amountLabel.Text = amount.ToString("c");
amountLabel.ForeColor = (amount < 0) ? Color.Red : Color.Blue;
```

FORMATTING CURRENCY

If you pass the ToString method the parameter "C" or "c", it uses a currency format that is appropriate for the computer's locale. In the United States, it formats positive values as in $123.45 and negative values as in ($123.45).

One way you might use the conditional operator is to set one variable equal to another variable's value or some default value if the second variable's value is null.

For example, suppose a sales program is trying to place an order. If the order is for an existing customer, the variable customer is a Customer object representing the customer. If this is a new customer, then customer is null. The following code uses the conditional operator to set variable orderedBy to either the existing customer or a new Customer object.

```
Customer orderedBy = (customer != null) ? customer : new Customer();
```

This code essentially sets orderedBy equal to customer or a default value (a new Customer object) if customer is null. This is a common enough procedure that C# provides a special operator to do just this.

The *null-coalescing operator* ?? takes two operands. It returns its left operand if its value is not null. If the left operand is null, it returns its right operand. The ?? operator's left operand can be any value that might be null including a reference variable or a nullable type such as int?.

The following code shows the preceding example rewritten to use the ?? instead of ?:.

```
Customer orderedBy = customer ?? new Customer();
```

ASSIGNMENT OPERATORS

A fairly common operation in C# programs is to set a variable equal to its value after performing some operation on it. For example, the following code adds 10 to the value x.

```
x = x + 10;
```

To make this sort of operation easier, C# provides a set of assignment operators. These consist of a normal operator followed by =. For example, the following statement shows the preceding code rewritten to use the += assignment operator.

```
x += 10;
```

This operator basically means, "Set x equal to its current value plus 10."

The complete list of assignment operators is: =, +=, -=, *=, /=, %=, &=, |=, ^=, <<=, and >>=.

OPERATOR PRECEDENCE

When C# evaluates a complex expression, it must decide the order in which to evaluate the operators. For example, consider the expression `1 + 2 * 3 / 4 + 2`. The following text shows three orders in which you might evaluate this expression to get three different results.

```
1 + (2 * 3) / (4 + 2) = 1 + 6 / 6 = 2
1 + ((2 * 3) / 4) + 2 = 4
((1 + 2) * 3) / (4 + 2) = 1
```

Precedence determines which operator C# executes first. For example, the C# precedence rules say the program should evaluate multiplication and division before addition, so the second equation above is the correct interpretation.

The following table lists the operators in order of precedence. When evaluating an expression, the program evaluates an operator before it evaluates those lower than it in the list.

OPERATOR	DESCRIPTION
( )	Grouping (parentheses)
x++	Post-increment
x--	Post-decrement
+	Unary plus
-	Numeric negation
!	Logical negation
~	Bitwise negation
++x	Pre-increment
--x	Pre-decrement
(T)	Casting
*	Multiplication
/	Division
%	Modulus
+	Concatenation
+	Addition
-	Subtraction
<<	Left shift
>>	Right shift

OPERATOR	DESCRIPTION
<	Less than
>	Greater than
<=	Less than or equal to
>=	Greater than or equal to
is	Inherits from
==	Equals
!=	Does not equal
&	Logical And
^	Logical Xor
|	Logical Or
&&	Conditional And
||	Conditional Or
??	Null-coalescing
?:	Conditional
=	Assignment operators
+=	
-=	
...	

When operators are in the same section in the table, or if an expression contains more than one instance of the same operator, the program evaluates them in left-to-right order.

For example, % and * are in the same section in the table, so the expression 17 % 5 * 5 is evaluated as (17 % 5) * 5 = 10 not as 17 % (5 * 5) = 17.

Parentheses are not actually operators, but they do have a higher precedence than the true operators, so they're listed to make the table complete. You can always use parentheses to explicitly dictate the order in which C# performs an evaluation.

PLENTIFUL PARENTHESES

If there's the slightest doubt about how C# will evaluate an expression, add parentheses to make it obvious. Even if you can figure out what an expression means, parentheses often make the code even easier to read and understand. There's no extra charge for using parentheses, and they may avoid some unnecessary confusion.

THE STRINGBUILDER CLASS

The + operator is useful for concatenating a few strings together, but if you must combine a large number of strings, you may get better performance by using the StringBuilder class. This class is optimized for performing long sequences of concatenations to build big strings.

The following code compares the performance of string concatenation and the StringBuilder class.

```
const int numTrials = 10000;
System.Diagnostics.Stopwatch watch =
    new System.Diagnostics.Stopwatch();

// Test +=.
watch.Start();
for (int i = 0; i < numTrials; i++)
{
    string test = "";
    for (int j = 0; j < 1000; j++) test += "A";
}
watch.Stop();
Console.WriteLine("Using += took " +
    watch.Elapsed.TotalSeconds.ToString("0.00") + " seconds");

// Test StringBuilder.
watch.Reset();
watch.Start();
for (int i = 0; i < numTrials; i++)
{
    StringBuilder builder = new StringBuilder();
    for (int j = 0; j < 1000; j++) builder.Append("A");
    string test = builder.ToString();
}
watch.Stop();
Console.WriteLine("Using StringBuilder took " +
    watch.Elapsed.TotalSeconds.ToString("0.00") + " seconds");
```

This code performs 10,000 trials using string concatenation and the StringBuilder class. For each trial, it builds a string containing the character A 1,000 times.

To test string concatenation, the program enters a loop that uses the += operator 1,000 times. To test the StringBuilder class, the program creates a StringBuilder object and calls its Append method 1,000 times.

After each test, the program displays the elapsed time in the Console window. The following text shows a sample output.

```
Using += took 6.10 seconds
Using StringBuilder took 0.19 seconds
```

For small pieces of code, the difference between concatenation and using StringBuilder is negligible. If you need to concatenate a dozen or so strings once, using a StringBuilder won't make much difference in run time, will make the code more confusing, and may even slow performance slightly.

However, if you make huge strings built up in pieces, or if you build simpler strings but many times in a loop, StringBuilder may make your program run faster.

DATETIME AND TIMESPAN OPERATIONS

The `DateTime` data type is fundamentally different from other data types. When you perform an operation on most data types, you get a result that has the same type or that is at least of some compatible type. For example, if you subtract two `int`s, the result is an `int`.

In contrast, if you subtract two `DateTime` variables, the result is not a `DateTime`. For example, what's August 7 minus July 20? It doesn't make sense to think of the result as a date.

Instead, C# defines the difference between two `DateTime`s as a `TimeSpan`, a data type that represents an elapsed time. In this example, August 7 minus July 20 is 18 days. (And yes, `TimeSpan`s know all about leap years.)

The following equations define `DateTime` and `TimeSpan` arithmetic.

```
DateTime - DateTime = TimeSpan
DateTime + TimeSpan = DateTime
TimeSpan + TimeSpan = TimeSpan
TimeSpan - TimeSpan = TimeSpan
```

The `TimeSpan` class also defines unary negation (`timespan2 = -timespan1`), but other operations (such as multiplying a `TimeSpan` by a number) are not defined. In some cases you can still perform the calculation if you must.

For example, the following code makes variable `timespan2` twice as long as `timespan1`.

```
TimeSpan timespan2 = new TimeSpan(timespan1.Ticks * 2);
```

This code takes the number of ticks in `timespan1`, multiplies that value by 2, and passes the result into a `TimeSpan` class constructor to make the new `TimeSpan` value. (A tick is 100 nanoseconds or 100 billionths of a second.)

Sometimes using operators to combine `DateTime` and `TimeSpan` values can be a bit cumbersome. For example, the following statement adds 7 days to the current date. (As you can probably guess, `DateTime.Now` returns a `DateTime` that represents the current date and time.)

```
DateTime nextWeek = DateTime.Now + new TimeSpan(7, 0, 0, 0, 0);
```

To make these sorts of calculations easier to read, `DateTime` provides methods for performing common operations.

The `Add` method returns a new `DateTime` representing a `DateTime`'s value plus the duration represented by a `TimeSpan`. (`DateTime` also provides a `Subtract` method that subtracts a `TimeSpan`.) For example, the following code returns the current date and time plus 7 days.

```
DateTime.Now.Add(new TimeSpan(7, 0, 0, 0, 0));
```

This isn't a great improvement in readability over the previous version, but the other `DateTime` methods are easier to read. Each adds a given number of a specific time unit to a `DateTime`. For example, the following code uses the `AddDays` method to add 7 days to the current date and time.

```
DateTime.Now.AddDays(7);
```

This code does the same thing as the previous two examples but is easier to read.

The DateTime methods that add durations are AddYears, AddMonths, AddDays, AddHours, AddMinutes, AddSeconds, AddMilliseconds, and AddTicks.

DateTime does not provide methods for subtracting specific kinds of durations such as SubtractDays. Fortunately, you can pass a negative value into the other methods. For example, the following statement returns the date and time 7 days before the current date and time.

```
DateTime.Now.AddDays(-7);
```

OPERATOR OVERLOADING

C# defines operators for expressions that use standard data types such as int and bool. It defines a few operators such as is for object references, but operators such as * and % don't make sense for objects in general.

However, you can define those operators for your structures and classes by using the operator statement. This is a more advanced topic, so if you're relatively new to C#, you may want to skip this section and come back to it later, perhaps after you have read Chapter 12, "Classes and Structures."

To overload an operator in a class, create a static method that returns the appropriate data type. Instead of giving the method a name, use the keyword operator followed by the operator symbol you want to overload. Next, define the parameters that the operator takes. Finally, write the code that the operator should return.

For example, suppose you want to define a Complex class to represent complex numbers. The following code shows the beginning of the class. Here Re holds the number's real part and Im holds the number's imaginary part. (If you don't remember how complex numbers work, see http://en.wikipedia.org/wiki/Complex_number.)

```
public class Complex
{
    public double Re = 0, Im = 0;
}
```

You could define methods such as Add and Multiply to add and multiply Complex objects, but the + and * operators would be much more intuitive and easy to read.

The following code overrides the + operator for this class.

```
public static Complex operator +(Complex operand1, Complex operand2)
{
    return new Complex()
    {
        Re = operand1.Re + operand2.Re,
        Im = operand1.Im + operand2.Im
    };
}
```

The operator's declaration indicates that the + operator takes two Complexes as parameters and returns a Complex. The code creates a new Complex object and uses object initialization syntax to set its Re and Im fields equal to the sums of the operands' Re and Im values. It then returns the new object.

The following code shows a `*` operator for this class.

```
public static Complex operator *(Complex operand1, Complex operand2)
{
    return new Complex()
        {
            Re = operand1.Re * operand2.Re - operand1.Im * operand2.Im,
            Im = operand1.Re * operand2.Im + operand1.Im * operand2.Re
        };
}
```

Some operators such as unary negation (`-x`) and unary plus (`+x`) take only one operand. To overload an operator that has only one operand, give the operand only one parameter.

The following code shows a unary negation operator for the `Complex` class.

```
public static Complex operator -(Complex operand1)
{
    return new Complex()
        {
            Re = -operand1.Re,
            Im = -operand1.Im
        };
}
```

Unary operators that you can overload include: `+`, `-`, `!`, `~`, `++`, `--`, `true`, and `false`. Binary operators that you can overload include: `+`, `-`, `*`, `/`, `%`, `&`, `|`, `^`, `<<`, and `>>`. Note that the second operand for the shift operators `<<` and `>>` must be an `int`.

The assignment operators are automatically overloaded if you overload the corresponding operator. For example, if you overload `*`, then C# overloads `*=` for you.

The following sections provide some extra detail about different kinds of overloaded operators.

Comparison Operators

Comparison operators that you can overload include `==`, `!=`, `<`, `>`, `<=`, and `>=`. These operators must be overloaded in pairs. For example, if you overload `<`, you must also overload `>`. The pairs are `<` and `>`, and `<=` and `>=`, and `==` and `!=`. Similarly the `true` and `false` operators come as a pair.

There are two notions of equality for objects. *Reference equality* means two references point to the same object. *Value equality* means two objects contain the same values.

For example, if two `Person` objects refer to the same object, they have reference equality. If they refer to different objects that happen to have the same properties and fields, they have value equality.

Normally the `==` and `!=` operators test reference equality, so if that's the kind of test you want, you don't need to overload these operators.

For the `Complex` class, two instances of the class that represent the same number should be treated as equal, so the class should implement value equality and therefore the `==` and `!=` operators.

If you overload those operators, Visual Studio also expects you to override the `Equals` and `GetHashCode` methods (which all classes inherit from the ultimate base class, `Object`).

To summarize, if you want a class to provide value equality, you must overload == and !=, and you must override Equals and GetHashCode. This is some work but it's not quite as bad as it sounds.

The following code shows the overridden Equals method.

```
public override bool Equals(object obj)
{
    if (obj == null) return false;
    if (!(obj is Complex)) return false;

    Complex complex = obj as Complex;
    return ((this.Re == complex.Re) && (this.Im == complex.Im));
}
```

This is an instance method so there is some instance of the Complex class for which the code is running. The this keyword provides a reference to that object. (Again if this is too confusing, come back to it after you read Chapter 12.)

The method starts by checking the input parameter. If that parameter is null, it cannot equal the object referred to by this so the method returns false. (The object this cannot be null. Otherwise for what object is the code running?)

Next if the parameter is not a Complex, for example, if it's a Person or Frog, the method returns null.

If the method has not already returned by this point, you know the parameter is a Complex and is not null. In that case the method returns true if the real and imaginary parts of the parameter are the same as those for the this object.

The following code shows the GetHashCode method.

```
public override int GetHashCode()
{
    return (Re.GetHashCode() + Im).GetHashCode();
}
```

This method must return a hash code for use by algorithms and data structures such as the one provided by the HashTable class. This method invokes the real part's GetHashCode method. It adds the imaginary part to the result and invokes the sum's GetHashCode method.

The following code shows the == operator.

```
public static bool operator ==(Complex operand1, Complex operand2)
{
    // If both refer to the same object (reference equality), return true.
    if ((object)operand1 == (object)operand2) return true;

    // If one is null but not the other, return false.
    if (((object)operand1 == null) || ((object)operand2 == null)) return false;

    // Compare the field values.
    return (operand1.Re == operand2.Re) && (operand1.Im == operand2.Im);
}
```

The code first compares the two operands to see if they refer to the same object. It first casts both operands to the generic object type, so the program doesn't try to use the == operator that we are currently defining to compare them. Without these casts, this statement recursively calls this same == operator, which calls the same == operator, and so on until the recursive calls fill the stack and the program crashes.

If the operands don't have reference equality, the code checks whether one of them is null. If they were both null, they would have reference equality, so the method would already have returned true. If that didn't happen and either of the operands is null, one is null and the other is not, so the method returns false.

If the method has not yet returned, both operands are not null. In that case the method returns true if their real and imaginary parts match.

The following code shows the != operator.

```
public static bool operator !=(Complex operand1, Complex operand2)
{
    return !(operand1 == operand2);
}
```

This operator simply uses the == operator to compare the operands and negates the result.

Logical Operators

The true and false operators are a bit confusing. The true operator should return the boolean value true if its operand should be regarded as true. Similarly, the false operator should return the boolean value true if its operand should be regarded as false.

Note that an operand might be neither true nor false depending on what it represents. For example, an object reference might be null, in which case you might not want to consider it true or false.

If you define the true and false operators, objects of the class can control tests such as those used by the if statement and while loops.

For example, suppose you consider a Complex object to be true if either its real or imaginary part is non-zero. Then if the variable complex is a Complex, the following code would work.

```
if (complex) Console.WriteLine("complex is true");
```

You cannot overload the && and || operators, but if you overload true, false, &, and |, these are defined for you and they use short-circuit evaluation.

Type Conversion Operators

Type conversion operators enable the program to convert values from one type to another. For example, you can regard any complex number as a real number with imaginary part 0. That means you can convert a float, double, or other numeric value into a Complex.

The reverse is not always true. Not all complex numbers are also real numbers. To use terminology defined in Chapter 4, "Data Types, Variables, and Constants," converting from a double to a Complex is a widening conversion and converting from a Complex to a double is a narrowing conversion.

To define a widening conversion, create an operator overload where the operator's name is the new data type. Use the keyword `implicit` to indicate that this is a widening conversion, so the code doesn't need to explicitly cast to make the conversion.

The following code shows an implicit conversion operator that converts a `double` to a `Complex`.

```
public static implicit operator Complex(double real)
{
    return new Complex() { Re = real, Im = 0 };
}
```

This operator returns a new `Complex` with the real part equal to the `double` parameter and imaginary part 0.

After you define this operator, you can implicitly convert a `double` into a `Complex` as in the following code.

```
Complex complex = 12.3;
```

Note that C# already knows how to implicitly convert from `int`, `long`, `float`, and other numeric types to `double` so it can convert those types into a `Complex`. For example, the following statement converts the character value `'A'` into the `double` 65.0. (65 is the Unicode value for A.) It then uses the conversion operator to convert that into a `Complex`.

```
Complex complex = 'A';
```

To define a narrowing conversion, create an operator overload as before, but replace the `implicit` keyword with the keyword `explicit`. The following code shows an explicit conversion operator that converts from `Complex` to `double`.

```
public static explicit operator double(Complex complex)
{
    return complex.Re;
}
```

After you define this operator, you can explicitly convert a `Complex` into a `double` as in the following code.

```
Complex complex = new Complex() { Re = 13, Im = 37 };
double real = (double)complex;
```

Although you normally cannot make two versions of a method that differ only in their return types, you can do that for conversion operators. When the program tries to make a conversion, it can tell by the type of the result which conversion operator to use. For example, the following code defines a conversion from `Complex` to `int`.

```
public static explicit operator int(Complex complex)
{
    return (int)complex.Re;
}
```

In this case it may be better to just have one conversion to `double` and let the program convert the `double` to `int`.

It is easy to get carried away with operator overloading. Just because you can define an operator for a class doesn't mean you should. For example, you might concoct some meaning for + with the `Employee` class, but it would probably be a counterintuitive operation. It would probably be better to write a method with a meaningful name instead of an ambiguous operator such as + or >>.

SUMMARY

A program uses operators to manipulate variables, constants, and literal values to produce new results. In most cases, using operators is straightforward and intuitive.

Operator precedence determines the order in which C# applies operators when evaluating an expression. In cases in which an expression's operator precedence is unclear, add parentheses to make the order obvious. Even if you don't change the way that C# handles the statement, you can make the code more understandable and avoid possibly time-consuming bugs.

Because the `string` type is a reference type that usually acts like a value type, performing long sequences of concatenations can be inefficient. The `StringBuilder` class makes that kind of `string` processing faster. If your program works only with a few short strings, using the `string` data type will probably be fast enough and will make your code easier to read. However, if your application builds enormous strings or concatenates a huge number of strings, you may save a noticeable amount of time by using `StringBuilder`.

The `DateTime` data type also behaves differently from other types. Normal operators such as + and – have different meanings for this class. For example, subtracting two `DateTime`s gives a `TimeSpan` as a result, not another `DateTime`. These operations generally make sense if you think carefully about what dates and time spans are.

Addition, subtraction, and other operations have special meaning for `DateTime` and `TimeSpan` values. Similarly, you can override operators to perform special operations on your classes. Defining / or >> may not make much sense for the `Employee`, `Customer`, or `Order` classes but in some cases custom operators can make your code more readable.

A program uses operators to combine variables to create new results. A typical program may perform the same set of calculations many times under different circumstances. For example, a point-of-sales program might need to add up the prices of the items in a customer order in many different parts of the program. Instead of performing that calculation every time it needed, you can move the calculation into a method and then call the method to perform the calculation. Chapter 6, "Methods," explains how you can use methods to break a program into manageable pieces that you can then reuse to make performing the calculations simpler, more consistent, and easier to debug and maintain.

EXERCISES

1. Can you use both the pre- and post-increment operators on the same variable as in ++x++? If you can't figure it out, try it and try to understand what Visual Studio tells you about it.

2. Sometimes the conditional and null-coalescing operators can make the code confusing, particularly if their operands are complicated expressions. Rewrite the following code to use `if` statements instead of `?:` and `??`.

```
amountLabel.ForeColor = (amount < 0) ? Color.Red : Color.Blue;
Customer orderedBy = customer ?? new Customer();
```

3. In the section "Comparison Operators" the code for the overloaded `==` operator does not check whether both operands are `null`. Why does it not need to do that?

4. Create a subtraction operator for the `Complex` class described in this chapter.

5. Create a `Fraction` class and define the `*` and `/` operators for it.

6. Create a conversion operator to convert `Fraction` to `double`. Is this a widening or narrowing conversion?

7. Create a `>` operator for the `Fraction` class.

8. Create an `==` operator for the `Fraction` class.

9. Calculate the result of each of the following statements.

   a. `1 + 2 * 3 - 4 / 5`

   b. `9 * 5 / 10`

   c. `2 * 5 / 10`

   d. `2 / 10 * 5`

   e. `12 / 6 * 4 / 8`

10. Add parentheses to the following expressions to make them true.

    a. `4 * 4 - 4 / 4 + 4 = 19`

    b. `4 * 4 - 4 / 4 + 4 = 16`

    c. `4 * 4 - 4 / 4 + 4 = 11`

    d. `4 * 4 - 4 / 4 + 4 = 4`

    e. `4 * 4 - 4 / 4 + 4 = 0`

11. Before each of the following statements, `int` variable x holds the value `11`. What are the values of x and y after each of the following statements?

    a. `int y = x / 4;`

    b. `int y = x++ / 4;`

    c. `int y = ++x / 4;`

    d. `float y = x / 4;`

    e. `double y = x / 4f;`

12. If x is an `int` variable holding the value `7`, then the statement `float y = x / 2` sets y equal to `3.0`. Give three ways to modify this statement to make y equal `3.5`.

13. If x is an `int` variable holding the value `7`, why does the statement `float y = x / 2.0` raise an error? How could you fix it?

14. C# provides `|=` and `&=` operators but does not provide `||=` or `&&=` operators. If those operators existed, what would they do? Would they provide any additional benefit?

Methods

WHAT'S IN THIS CHAPTER

➤ Method declarations

➤ Optional and named parameters

➤ Method overloading

➤ Extension methods

➤ Lambda expressions

➤ Covariance and contravariance

➤ Asynchronous method execution

WROX.COM DOWNLOADS FOR THIS CHAPTER

Please note that all the code examples for this chapter are available as a part of this chapter's code download on the book's website at www.wrox.com/go/csharp5programmersref on the Download Code tab.

Methods enable you to break an otherwise unwieldy chunk of code into manageable pieces. They enable you to extract code that you may need to use under more than one circumstance and place it in a single location where you can call it as needed.

This enables you to maintain and update the code in a single location. If you later need to modify the code, you need to do it only in one place, so you don't need to keep multiple copies of the code synchronized.

> ### METHOD TERMINOLOGY
>
> Methods that don't return a value (have a void return type) are sometimes called *subroutines*, *routines*, *procedures*, or *subprocedures*. Methods that return a value are sometimes called *functions*.

This chapter describes methods and explains the syntax for declaring them. It also provides some tips for making methods more maintainable.

METHOD DECLARATIONS

In C# all methods must be inside a class. The syntax for creating a method follows:

```
«attributes» «accessibility» «modifiers» return_type name(«parameters»)
{
    code...
}
```

Many of these pieces of the declaration are similar to those described for declaring variables. For example, variable declarations can also include attributes and accessibility keywords. See the corresponding sections in Chapter 4, "Data Types, Variables, and Constants," for basic information about those features.

The following sections provide extra information about the pieces of a method declaration.

Attributes

The optional attribute list is a series of attribute objects that provide extra information about the method. An attribute further refines the definition of a method to give more information to the compiler, the runtime system, and other tools that need to manipulate the method.

Attributes are specialized and address issues that arise when you perform specific programming tasks. For example, the `System.Diagnostics.Conditional` attribute means a (method) is conditional upon the definition of some preprocessor symbol. If the symbol is not defined, then the method is silently ignored.

For example, consider the following code snippet.

```
#define INTERACTIVE
...
[Conditional("INTERACTIVE")]
private void DisplayGreeting()
{
    MessageBox.Show("Hello");
}
...
private void Form1_Load(object sender, EventArgs e)
{
    DisplayGreeting();
}
```

The code first defines the preprocessor symbol INTERACTIVE. Later it uses the `Conditional` attribute in the definition of the `DisplayGreeting` method. That method displays a message box.

The form's `Load` event handler calls the `DisplayGreeting` method. If the INTERACTIVE constant is defined, the method executes and displays its message box. If INTERACTIVE is not defined, the method call is ignored and the program continues.

See the section "Attributes" in Chapter 4 for more detail on attributes in general, including some links you can follow to get more information.

The following list describes some of the most useful method attributes. Many of these apply to property methods (see the section "Properties" in Chapter 4) and fields. Most of them are in the System.ComponentModel namespace. Check the online help for more detail.

➤ AttributeUsage—If you build your own custom attribute, this attribute tells how your attribute can be used. For example, it determines whether an item can have multiple instances of your attribute, whether your attribute can be inherited by a derived class, and the kinds of things that can have your attribute (assembly, class, method, and so forth).

➤ Browsable—This indicates whether a property or event should be displayed in an editor such as the Properties window or a PropertyGrid control.

➤ Category—This indicates the grouping that should hold the property or event in a visual designer such as the Properties window or a PropertyGrid control.

➤ DefaultEvent—This gives a class's default event name. If the class is a control or component and you double-click it in the Form Designer, the code editor opens to this event's handler.

➤ DefaultProperty—This gives a class's default property name.

➤ DefaultValue—This gives a property a default value. If you right-click the property in the Properties window and select Reset, the property is reset to this value.

➤ Description—This gives a description of the item. If a property has a Description and you select the property in the Properties window, the window displays the description text at the bottom.

➤ Localizable—This determines whether a property should be localizable, so you can easily store different versions of the property for different languages and locales.

➤ MergableProperty—This indicates whether the property can be merged with the same property provided by other components in the Properties window. If this is true and you select multiple controls with the same value for this property, the Properties window displays the value. If you enter a new value, all the controls are updated.

➤ ParenthesizePropertyName—This indicates whether editors such as the Properties window should display parentheses around the property's name.

➤ ReadOnly—This indicates whether designers should treat this property as read-only.

➤ RecommendedAsConfigurable—This indicates that a property should be tied to the configuration file. When you select the object at design time and expand the (Dynamic Properties) item, the property is listed. If you click the ellipsis to the right, a dialog box appears that enables you to map the property to a key in the configuration file.

➤ RefreshProperties—This indicates how an editor should refresh the object's *other* properties if *this* property is changed. The value can be Default (do not refresh the other properties), Repaint (refresh all other properties), or All (requery and refresh all properties).

➤ Conditional—This indicates that the method is ignored if a preprocessor symbol is undefined.

➤ `DebuggerHidden`—This tells debuggers whether a method should be debuggable. If `DebuggerHidden` is `true`, the debugger skips over the method and does not stop at breakpoints inside it.

➤ `DebuggerStepThrough`—This tells debuggers whether to let the developer step into a method in the debugger. If the `DebuggerStepThrough` attribute is present, the IDE does not step into the method.

➤ `ToolboxBitmap`——This tells the IDE where to find a control or component's Toolbox bitmap. This can be a file, or it can be a type in an assembly that contains the bitmap and the bitmap's name in the assembly. It's awkward but essential if you're developing controls or components.

➤ `Obsolete`—This indicates that the item (class, method, property, or whatever) is obsolete. Optionally, you can specify the message that the code editor should display to the developer if code uses the item (for example, "Use the NewMethod instead"). You can also indicate whether the IDE should treat using this item as a warning or an error.

Accessibility

The method's accessibility value can be one of `public`, `internal`, `protected`, `internal protected`, and `private`. These have the same meanings as the same keywords when used to declare variables. See the section "Accessibility" in Chapter 4 for more information.

Modifiers

The method's modifiers give more information about the method. The following sections describe the allowed keywords.

new

A derived class can define a method with the same name as a method it inherits from the parent class. In that case, the new version of the method *hides* the parent's version. This is allowed but Visual Studio flags it with a warning. The `new` keyword tells Visual Studio that this is not an accident and suppresses the warning.

For example, suppose the `Person` class includes `FirstName`, `LastName`, `Street`, `City`, `State`, and `Zip` fields. It also provides the following `Address` method that returns those values formatted as an address string.

```
public string Address()
{
    return FirstName + " " + LastName + '\n' +
        Street + '\n' +
        City + " " + State + " " + Zip;
}
```

Now suppose the `Employee` class is derived from `Person`. The `Employee` class adds a new `Office` field and provides the following new `Address` method that includes the `Office` value.

```
public new string Address()
{
    return FirstName + " " + LastName + ", " + Office + '\n' +
        Street + '\n' +
        City + " " + State + " " + Zip;
}
```

Without the `new` keyword, this would raise the warning.

static

As Chapter 4 explained, a variable declared with the `static` keyword is shared by all instances of the class. Similarly, a `static` method applies to all instances of the class. In that case, the method applies to the class itself rather than to a particular instance of the class.

For example, suppose the `Person` class has a `LookupPerson` method that looks up a person's name in a database and returns a `Person` object representing that person. It wouldn't make sense to require you to create a `Person` object just to invoke its `LookupPerson` method. Instead you can make this a `static` method.

To invoke a static method, use the class name as in `Person.LookupPerson("Eddie Russett")`.

virtual and override

The `virtual` keyword and `override` keywords go together.

Suppose the `Person` and `Employee` classes have `Address` methods as described in the previous sections. The `Employee` class's version of `Address` hides the `Person` class's version. Now consider the following code.

```
Employee employee = new Employee { FirstName = "Rod", ... };
Console.WriteLine("Employee:\n" + employee.Address());
Console.WriteLine();

Person person = employee;
Console.WriteLine("Person:\n" + person.Address());
```

The code creates an `Employee` object and displays the result of its `Address` method in the Console window. This includes the object's `FirstName`, `LastName`, `Office`, `Street`, `City`, `State`, and `Zip` values.

Next the code sets a `Person` variable equal to the same `Employee`. This is allowed because an `Employee` is a kind of `Person`. The code then displays the result of the `Person` object's `Address` method. Because this is a `Person` object, its `Address` method doesn't include the object's `Office` value. Even though this object is actually an `Employee`, the `Person` class's version of the `Address` method doesn't include the `Office` value. The following text shows the result.

```
Employee:
Rod Stephens, B-24
1337 Leet St
Bugsville HI 98765
```

```
Person:
Rod Stephens
1337 Leet St
Bugsville HI 98765
```

However, there is a way to let the object use its "native" `Address` method instead of the one given by the type of the variable holding it. In this case, the `Employee` object would use its `Address` method even if it were represented by a `Person` variable.

To do this, add the `virtual` keyword to the `Person` class's version of the method as in the following code.

```
public virtual string Address()
{
    return FirstName + " " + LastName + '\n' +
        Street + '\n' +
        City + " " + State + " " + Zip;
}
```

The `virtual` keyword tells C# that a derived class may replace this method with a version of its own.

Next add the `override` keyword to the `Employee` class's `Address` method as in the following code.

```
public override string Address()
{
    return FirstName + " " + LastName + ", " + Office + '\n' +
        Street + '\n' +
        City + " " + State + " " + Zip;
}
```

This tells the program to replace the `Address` method for `Employee` objects with this version, even if they are referred to by a `Person` variable.

The following text shows the new result.

```
Employee:
Rod Stephens, B-24
1337 Leet St
Bugsville HI 98765

Person:
Rod Stephens, B-24
1337 Leet St
Bugsville HI 98765
```

sealed

If you override a method, you can also add the keyword `sealed` to indicate that no further derived class can override the method. For example, suppose the `Person` class defines the `virtual` method `Address` and the `Employee` class defines the following overridden version of the method.

```
public override sealed string Address()
{
    return FirstName + " " + LastName + ", " + Office + '\n' +
```

```
                Street + '\n' +
                City + " " + State + " " + Zip;
    }
```

Now if the `Manager` class inherits from the `Employee` class, it cannot override this method because it is sealed.

> **TIP** *The* `Manager` *class cannot override the* `Address` *method, but it can hide it with a new version that is declared with the* new *keyword.*

abstract

The `abstract` keyword prevents a program from making instances of the class. Instead the program must make instances of other classes derived from it. If a class contains an `abstract` member, then the class must also be marked `abstract`.

For example, a class might include an abstract method. In that case derived classes must provide a body for the `abstract` method. This lets a class determine what its derived classes should do but not how they work.

A class with an `abstract` method is incomplete. If you were to create an instance of the class, you could not invoke the method because the class has not provided an implementation for it. To avoid this conundrum, C# does not let you create an instance of a class that has an abstract method.

The following code shows an abstract `Person` class.

```
abstract class Person
{
    public string FirstName = "", LastName = "",
        Street = "", City = "", State = "", Zip = "";

    public abstract string Address();
}
```

The following code shows a `Student` class that inherits from `Person` and implements the `Address` method.

```
class Student : Person
{
    public override string Address()
    {
        return FirstName + " " + LastName + ", " +
            Street + '\n' +
            City + " " + State + " " + Zip;
    }
}
```

extern

The `extern` keyword indicates that the method is defined outside of the assembly. This keyword is often used to declare methods defined in libraries. For example, the following code declares the external `SendMessage` function. The `DllImport` attribute tells the program to look for the method in the user32.dll library.

```
[System.Runtime.InteropServices.DllImport("user32.dll")]
public static extern int SendMessage(
    IntPtr hWnd, uint Msg, int wParam, int lParam);
```

The following code shows how a program could use `SendMessage` to make the button `dangerButton` display the User Access Control (UAC) shield.

```
private void Form1_Load(object sender, EventArgs e)
{
    const Int32 BCM_SETSHIELD = 0x160C;

    // Give the button the flat style and make it display the UAC shield.
    dangerButton.FlatStyle = System.Windows.Forms.FlatStyle.System;
    SendMessage(dangerButton.Handle, BCM_SETSHIELD, 0, 1);
}
```

This code defines the constant `BCM_SETSHIELD`. The value 0x160C is a message code that means a control should display the UAC shield.

The code then sets the button's `FlatStyle` property to `System`. Finally, it calls `SendMessage` to send the button the `BCM_SETSHIELD` message, which makes it display the shield. Figure 6-1 shows the result.

FIGURE 6-1: The external `SendMessage` function can make a button display the UAC shield.

Name

The method's name must be a valid C# identifier. It should begin with a letter, underscore, or @ symbol. After that it can include letters, numbers, or underscores. If the name begins with @, it must include at least one other character. The name cannot include special characters such as &, %, #, and $. It also cannot be the same as C# keywords such as `if`, `for`, and `public`.

Most developers use *CamelCase* when naming a method so a method's name consists of several descriptive words with their first letters capitalized. A good method for generating method names is to use a short phrase beginning with a verb and describing what the method does. Some examples include `LoadData`, `SaveNetworkConfiguration`, and `PrintExpenseReport`.

Return Type

A method's *return_type* is the type of the value the method returns. To return a value, use the `return` keyword followed by the value the method should return. For example, the following method multiplies two values and returns the result.

```
private float Multiply(float value1, float value2)
{
    return value1 * value2;
}
```

If the method doesn't return any value, set the return type to void. If you want the method to return before its last line of code, you can use the return statement with no following value. For example, the following method asks the user whether it should delete a file. If the user clicks No, the method returns. Otherwise the method deletes the file.

```
private void DeleteFile(string filename)
{
    // Make the user confirm.
    if (MessageBox.Show("Are you sure you want to delete "
        + filename + "?",
        "Delete File?",
        MessageBoxButtons.YesNo,
        MessageBoxIcon.Question)
            == DialogResult.No)
                return;

    // Delete the file.
    //...
}
```

Parameters

A method's parameter declaration defines the names and types of the parameters passed into it. Parameter lists are somewhat similar to variable declarations, so they are described in the section "Parameter Declarations" in Chapter 4. See that section for more information.

Two new features that don't apply to variables and are therefore not described in Chapter 4 are *optional arguments* and *named arguments*.

Optional parameters must come at the end of the parameter list, after any required parameters. To make a parameter optional, follow its declaration with an equal sign and a default value. The calling code can omit any of the optional arguments at the end of the parameter list, and those parameters take their default values. The code cannot include arguments that follow missing arguments, at least without using argument names.

Named arguments allow calling code to explicitly indicate the argument values by name. That makes the code more readable, particularly if the method has a long argument list and if some arguments are optional. It also lets the calling code give the arguments in any order and omit any optional arguments without omitting those that follow in the parameter list. To use an optional parameter, the calling code includes the parameter's name, a colon, and the parameter's value.

The following code defines a FindOverdueAccounts method that looks for overdue customer accounts and takes appropriate action.

```
private void ListOverdueAccounts(
    int daysPastDue, decimal amount = 50.00m,
    bool disconnect = false, bool printInvoices = false)
{
    ...
}
```

The method takes four parameters. The `daysPastDue` parameter is required but the others are optional.

The following code shows several ways the program might call this method.

```
// daysPastDue = 90, other parameters take defaults.
ListOverdueAccounts(90);

// daysPastDue = 90, amount = $100.00, other parameters take defaults.
ListOverdueAccounts(90, 100.00m);

// daysPastDue = 90, disconnect = true, other parameters take defaults.
// This version is not allowed because you cannot include an argument
// after a missing argument.
ListOverdueAccounts(90, , true);

// daysPastDue = 90, disconnect = true, other parameters take defaults.
// This version is allowed because it uses named arguments.
ListOverdueAccounts(90, disconnect: true);

// daysPastDue = 30, amount = $100.00. Other parameters take defaults.
ListOverdueAccounts(30, amount: 100);

// All arguments specified in new order.
ListOverdueAccounts(disconnect: true, amount: 100,
    printInvoices: false, daysPastDue: 60);
```

The third call to `ListOverdueAccounts` is not allowed because it provides an argument after an omitted argument. The fourth call provides the same arguments. That version works because it uses named arguments.

Optional Versus Overloading

A C# program can define multiple methods with the same name but that differ in their parameter lists. This is called *method overloading*. For example, the following code defines two versions of the `FireEmployee` method.

```
private void FireEmployee(string name)
{
    ...
}

private void FireEmployee(string name, string reason)
{
    ...
}
```

At compile time, the compiler uses the arguments passed into a method call to decide which version of the method to use.

Overloaded methods cannot differ only in optional parameters. Otherwise if a call to the method omitted the optional parameters, the program would be unable to tell which version of the method to use.

The following code shows a single version of the `FireEmployee` method that uses optional parameters instead of overloading.

```
private void FireEmployee(string name, string reason = "Unknown reason")
{
    ...
}
```

Different developers have varying opinions on whether it is better to use optional parameters or overloaded methods under different circumstances.

One argument in favor of optional parameters is that overloaded methods might duplicate a lot of code. However, it is easy to make each version of the method call another version that allows more parameters, passing in default values. For example, in the following code the first version of the `FireEmployee` method simply invokes the second version:

```
private void FireEmployee(string name)
{
    FireEmployee(name, "Unknown reason");
}

private void FireEmployee(string name, string reason)
{
    ...
}
```

Overloading is generally better when the different versions of the method need to do something different or when they take completely different parameters. For example, the following code shows two versions of the `FireEmployee` method, one that takes the employee's name as a parameter and one that takes an `Employee` object as a parameter.

```
private void FireEmployee(string name)
{
    ...
}

private void FireEmployee(Employee employee)
{
    ...
}
```

In this case, it would probably be confusing to make a single method with optional `name` and `employee` parameters and require the calling code to pass in only one of those values. (These two methods would probably also do a lot of the same work, so they should probably both invoke a third method to do that common work.)

Parameter Arrays

Sometimes it's useful to have methods that can take any number of parameters. For example, a method might take as parameters a message and a series of e-mail addresses. It would send the message as an e-mail to each of the addresses.

One approach would be to give the method a long list of optional `string` parameters with the default value `null`. The method would examine each of the parameters and send the message to those that were not `null`.

Unfortunately, the method would need to use separate code to process each address separately. The number of parameters would place an upper limit on the number of e-mail addresses that could be included.

A better solution is to use the `params` keyword to make the method's final argument a parameter array. A *parameter array* contains an arbitrary number of parameter values. At run time, the method can loop through the array to process the parameter values. The following code shows an example.

```
private void SendEmails(string message, params string[] addresses)
{
    if (addresses != null)
    {
        foreach (string address in addresses)
            Console.WriteLine("Send " + message + " to " + address);
    }
}
```

The `SendEmails` method takes two parameters, a `string` called `message` and a parameter array of `strings` holding e-mail addresses. The code first checks whether the parameter array is `null`. If the array is not `null`, the code loops through it and displays each e-mail address and the message in the Console window. (A real application would send the message to each e-mail address.)

The following code shows how the program could use this method to send a message to two e-mail addresses.

```
SendEmails("I need C# help!",
    "RodStephens@CSharpHelper.com",
    "RodStephens@vb-helper.com"
);
```

Parameter arrays are subject to the following restrictions:

➤ A method can have only one parameter array, and it must come last in the parameter list.

➤ Parameter lists cannot be declared with the `ref` or `out` keywords.

➤ The calling code may pass the value `null` in the place of the parameter array. (That's why the code in the previous example checked whether the array was `null` before using it.)

➤ The calling code can provide any number of values for the parameter array including zero.

➤ All the items in the parameter array must have the same data type. However, you can use an array that contains the generic `object` data type and then it can hold just about anything.

The program can also pass an array of the appropriate data type in place of a series of values. The following code passes an array of `strings` into the `SendEmails` method.

```
string[] addresses =
{
    "RodStephens@CSharpHelper.com",
```

```
        "RodStephens@vb-helper.com",
};
SendEmails("I need C# help!", addresses);
```

Implementing Interfaces

An *interface* defines a set of properties, methods, and events that a class implementing the interface must provide. An interface is a lot like a class with all its properties, methods, and events declared with the `abstract` keyword. Any class that inherits from the base class must provide implementations of those properties, methods, and events. Similarly, a class that implements an interface must provide the properties, methods, and events defined by the interface.

> **NAMING CONVENTION**
>
> Developers often begin the name of interfaces with a capital *I* so that it's obvious that it's an interface. Actually, it's such a common practice and has no disadvantages that it should practically be a requirement. Start interface names with "I" so that other developers know they are interfaces.

The following code defines the `IDrawable` interface.

```
public interface IDrawable
{
    void Draw(Graphics gr);
    Rectangle GetBounds();
    bool IsVisible { get; set; }
}
```

The `IDrawable` interface defines a `Draw` method, a `GetBounds` function, and a `bool` property named `IsVisible`.

To indicate that a class implements an interface, add a colon followed by the interface's name after the class's name. The following code shows the declaration for a `DrawableRectangle` class that implements the `IDrawable` interface.

```
public class DrawableRectangle : IDrawable
{

}
```

If you build an empty class such as this one that includes the `:  IDrawable` clause, you can right-click the interface name and select the Implement Interface submenu. The submenu has two choices: Implement Interface and Implement Interface Explicitly. When you select one of those commands, Visual Studio adds empty properties, methods, and events to the class to implement the interface. How the class uses those items depends on whether you implement the interface implicitly or explicitly.

Implicit Implementation

The following code shows the `DrawableRectangle` class with code added by Visual Studio for implicit implementation.

```
public class DrawableRectangle : IDrawable
{
    public void Draw(Graphics gr)
    {
        throw new NotImplementedException();
    }

    public Rectangle Bounds()
    {
        throw new NotImplementedException();
    }

    public bool IsVisible
    {
        get
        {
            throw new NotImplementedException();
        }
        set
        {
            throw new NotImplementedException();
        }
    }
}
```

You should edit this code to replace the `throw` statements with whatever code is necessary.

If a class implements an interface implicitly, you can use its members just as you would for any other class's members. For example, consider the following code.

```
DrawableRectangle rect = new DrawableRectangle();
Console.WriteLine(rect.GetBounds());

IDrawable drawable = rect;
Console.WriteLine(drawable.GetBounds());
```

This code creates a `DrawableRectangle`. It then invokes its `GetBounds` method and displays the result in the Console window.

Next, the code creates an `IDrawable` variable and makes it refer to the same `DrawableRectangle`. This works because a `DrawableRectangle` is a kind of `IDrawable`.

The code then displays the result of the `IDrawable`'s `GetBounds` method.

Explicit Implementation

If you select Implement Interface Explicitly, Visual Studio also creates the necessary code, but it adds the interface's name to each item. The following code shows this form of the Draw method with the interface name highlighted.

```
void IDrawable.Draw(Graphics gr)
{
    throw new NotImplementedException();
}
```

If a class implements an interface explicitly, the program cannot access the interface's members from a variable of that class's type. Instead it must use a variable of the interface's type.

Consider again the following code, which was shown earlier for the implicit interface implementation.

```
DrawableRectangle rect = new DrawableRectangle();
Console.WriteLine(rect.GetBounds()); // Doesn't work.

IDrawable drawable = rect;
Console.WriteLine(drawable.GetBounds());
```

With the explicit implementation, the first call to GetBounds doesn't work. Because the class implements the interface explicitly, the code must use the IDrawable variable to use the interface's members.

EXTENSION METHODS

Extension methods enable you to add new methods to an existing class without rewriting it or deriving a new class from it. To make an extension method, place a static method in a static class. Add the keyword this before the method's first parameter and give that parameter the type that you want to extend.

For example, the following code defines a RemoveNonLetters extension method for the string class.

```
public static class StringExtensions
{
    public static string RemoveNonLetters(this string text)
    {
        string result = "";
        foreach (char ch in text)
            if (((ch >= 'a') && (ch <= 'z')) ||
                ((ch >= 'A') && (ch <= 'Z')))
                result += ch;
            else
                result += "?";

        return result;
    }
}
```

The code is defined in the static StringExtensions class.

> **TIP** *If you name static extension classes as in* StringExtensions, *it's easy to tell which class you are extending and that this is an extension class.*

The static RemoveNonLetters method's first parameter uses the this keyword, so you know this is an extension method. The parameter following this has type string so this extension method extends the string class.

The method's code loops through a string's characters and replaces any that are not letters with question marks. It then returns the result.

The following code shows how a program might use this method.

```
string text = "When in worry or in doubt, run in circles scream and shout";
Console.WriteLine(text.RemoveNonLetters());
```

This code creates a string variable. It then invokes the RemoveNonLetters method just as if that were a normal method defined by the string class.

LAMBDA EXPRESSIONS

Lambda expressions are methods defined within the flow of the program's code instead of as separate methods. Often they are defined, used, and forgotten in a single statement without ever being given a name.

You can use normal methods instead of lambda expressions, but sometimes lambda expressions make the code simpler and easier to read. Many LINQ queries (described in Chapter 8, "LINQ") use functions to select values that meet certain criteria. You can write those functions as separate methods but they may only be used once inside the LINQ query so making them separate methods clutters the code unnecessarily.

The following sections group lambda expressions into three categories: expression lambdas, statement lambdas, and async lambdas.

Expression Lambdas

An *expression lambda* consists of a list of zero or more parameters, the => operator, and a single expression that evaluates to some result. The lambda expression returns the result of the expression.

The following code uses a simple expression lambda (in bold).

```
Action note = () => MessageBox.Show("Hi");
note();
```

Recall from the section "Delegates" in Chapter 4 that Action is a type that represents a method that takes no parameters and returns void. The code creates a variable note with that type. It sets that variable equal to the expression lambda defined by () => MessageBox.Show("Hi"). This lambda takes no parameters and executes the expression `MessageBox.Show("Hi")`. (The empty parentheses are required as a placeholder if the lambda expression takes no parameters.)

The following code modifies the previous expression lambda so that it takes a parameter.

```
Action<string> note = message => MessageBox.Show(message);
note("Hello");
```

This expression lambda takes a string parameter and passes it to `MessageBox.Show`.

The two examples shown so far call `MessageBox.Show`, which returns `void`. The following example shows how an expression lambda can return a value.

```
Func<float, double> root = value => Math.Sqrt(value);
Console.WriteLine(root(13));
```

The variable `root` has type `Func<float, double>` so it represents a method that takes a `float` parameter and returns a `double` result. The code sets `root` equal to an expression lambda that uses `Math.Sqrt` to take the square root of its input parameter. The lambda's return result is the result of that expression.

Statement Lambdas

An expression lambda executes a single statement and returns its result. A *statement lambda* is similar except it can execute multiple statements. To group the statements, this kind of lambda uses braces. It also uses the `return` statement to return its result.

The following code demonstrates a statement lambda.

```
Func<int, int, int, int> middle = (v1, v2, v3) =>
    {
        // Sort the items.
        int[] values = { v1, v2, v3 };
        Array.Sort(values);

        // Return the middle item.
        return values[1];
    };
Console.WriteLine(middle(2, 3, 1));
```

This code sets `middle` to a lambda that picks the middle of three integers. The lambda copies its three parameters into an array, sorts the array, and returns the middle item.

The code then calls the lambda to pick the middle of the values 2, 3, and 1.

NOT SO LITTLE LAMBDAS

A statement lambda can be quite long but at some point it just makes the code more confusing. If the lambda is too long, consider making it a separate named method instead.

Async Lambdas

The section "Using Async and Await" later in this chapter discusses one method for running methods asynchronously. At this point it's worth briefly explaining how that technique works with lambda expressions.

In brief, you can use the `async` keyword to indicate that a method can run asynchronously. The program can then use the `await` keyword to wait for an `async` method to complete. Usually, you use `async` with named methods but you can also use it to make lambda expressions asynchronous, too.

ASYNCHRONICITY

When a method runs asynchronously, it runs on a separate *thread of execution* while the main program continues running on the main thread. If the computer has multiple processors, the two threads may be able to run on different processors so they truly run at the same time.

Even if the computer has only a single processor, the result may be faster if one thread is blocked waiting for some resource. For example, the method's thread might need to fetch data from a database on a hard drive, which can take a lot longer than performing calculations in memory. While the method's thread is waiting, the main program can continue.

The following `Form Load` event handler uses an asynchronous statement lambda.

```
private void Form1_Load(object sender, EventArgs e)
{
    countButton.Click += async (button, args) =>
    {
        for (int i = 0; i < 5; i++)
        {
            Console.WriteLine(i);
            await System.Threading.Tasks.Task.Delay(1000);
        }
    };
}
```

This code adds an event handler to the `countButton`'s control's `Click` event. The event handler is defined by the lambda expression. The expression's declaration includes the `async` keyword so it can run asynchronously.

The statement lambda makes variable `i` loop from 1 to 5. For each value of `i`, the lambda displays the value of `i` in the Console window and then waits for 1 second.

If you add this code to a Windows Forms program with a button named `countButton` and click the button, the statement lambda executes and displays its count in the Console window. Because the lambda is asynchronous, you can click the button several times to see several counts running at the same time.

VARIANCE

Suppose the `Student` class is derived from the `Person` class. In that case you can save a `Student` value in a `Person` variable as in the following code because a `Student` is a kind of `Person`.

```
Person person = new Student();
```

It should come as no surprise that you can do something similar with method parameters and return types. For example, suppose the `EnrollStudent` method takes a `Person` as a parameter, creates necessary database records to enroll that `Person` in school, and returns a new `Student` object representing the new student. The following code shows the method's signature.

```
private Student EnrollStudent(Person person)
{
    ...
}
```

The calling code might save the result in some variable. The code could save the result in a `Student` variable. Because a `Student` is a kind of `Person`, the code could also save the result in a `Person` variable.

The method's parameter has type `Person`. Because a `Student` is a type of `Person`, the calling code could pass a `Student` into the method. (Although you might want the method to prevent that so that you don't enroll the same student twice.)

The following code shows how the program could call this method without matching the method's parameter and return types.

```
Student student = new Student();
...
Person person = EnrollStudent(student);
```

None of this should come as a big surprise.

Similarly, you can store a reference to a method in a delegate variable with parameters and return type that don't exactly match those used by the method.

For example, the following code defines a delegate representing methods that take a `Student` parameter and return a `Person`.

```
private delegate Person ReturnsPersonDelegate(Student student);
```

A program could use the delegate as in the following code.

```
ReturnsPersonDelegate del = EnrollStudent;
```

The `EnrollStudent` method doesn't return a `Person` as the delegate type requires, but it returns a `Student`, which is a type of `Person`. The fact that you can assign a method to a delegate when the method returns a more derived type than the delegate is called *covariance*.

The `EnrollStudent` method also doesn't take a `Student` parameter as the delegate type requires. Instead it takes a `Person` parameter. A `Student` is a kind of `Person` so the program could call the method with a `Student` as an argument. The fact that you can assign a method to a delegate when the method has parameters of a less derived type than the delegate is called *contravariance*.

ASYNCHRONOUS METHODS

Normally a program calls a routine and control passes to that routine. When the routine finishes executing, control returns to the calling code, which resumes executing its own code. All this happens synchronously, so the calling code waits until the called routine finishes all its work before it continues.

C# provides several methods that you can use to execute code asynchronously. In those cases a calling piece of code can launch a routine in a separate thread and continue executing before the routine finishes. If your computer has multiple cores or CPUs, the calling code and the asynchronous routine may both be able to execute simultaneously on separate processors, potentially saving a lot of time.

The following sections describe three of the more manageable approaches to executing methods asynchronously.

Calling EndInvoke Directly

This method uses a delegate's `BeginInvoke` method to start a routine executing asynchronously. Later the code calls `EndInvoke` to wait for the routine to finish and to process the result.

To use this method, first define a delegate that represents the routine that you want to run asynchronously. Call the delegate's `BeginInvoke` method, passing it whatever parameters the method needs plus two additional parameters: a callback method and a parameter to pass to the callback method. For this technique, set the extra parameters to `null` so the routine does not invoke a callback when it completes. (The following section explains how to use the callback.)

The call to `BeginInvoke` launches the asynchronous code on its own thread and then returns immediately so the calling code can perform other tasks.

After the calling code has done as much as it can before the asynchronous thread finishes, it should invoke the delegate's `EndInvoke` method. That method waits until the asynchronous thread finishes (if it isn't already finished) and returns the result of the original method.

> ### ALWAYS CALL ENDINVOKE
>
> It is important that the code calls `EndInvoke` even if the thread executes a `void` method, and the calling code doesn't care about any returned result. The call to `EndInvoke` lets the program free resources used by the asynchronous thread.

The BeginInvoke example program, which is available for download on the book's website, uses the following simple `Count` method.

```
private void Count(int max)
{
    for (int i = 1; i <= max; i++)
    {
        System.Threading.Thread.Sleep(1000);
        Console.WriteLine("Count: " + i);
    }
}
```

This method counts to an indicated value displaying numbers in the Console window and sleeping 1 second between each number.

The following code runs the Count method asynchronously.

```
// Start the Count method on a new thread.
Action<int> countDelegate = Count;
IAsyncResult result = countDelegate.BeginInvoke(5, null, null);

// Count to 3.
for (int i = 1; i <= 3; i++)
{
    System.Threading.Thread.Sleep(1000);
    Console.WriteLine("Main: " + i);
}

// Wait for the other thread to complete.
countDelegate.EndInvoke(result);
Console.WriteLine("Main: done");
```

This code creates a delegate of type Action<int> to represent a method that takes an int parameter and has void return type. It sets the variable equal to the Count method.

The code then calls the delegate variable's BeginInvoke method, passing it the parameter 5 (to send to the Count method) and two null parameters. It saves the result returned by BeginInvoke, which is an IAsynchResult object.

Next, the code counts to 3, pausing 1 second between values.

The code then calls the delegate's EndInvoke method passing it the IAsyncResult value it got from BeginInvoke. That call makes the main program wait until the delegate finishes running.

Finally when the delegate's other thread finishes and EndInvoke returns, the code displays a completion message.

The following text shows the result of one trial.

```
Main: 1
Count: 1
Main: 2
Count: 2
Main: 3
Count: 3
Count: 4
Count: 5
Main: done
```

In a real application, the main program and the asynchronous thread would perform time-consuming tasks instead of just sleeping.

Handling a Callback

The technique described in the previous section directly calls EndInvoke to make the main user interface thread wait until its asynchronous threads have finished before the main program continues.

Another approach is to let the main program continue without waiting for the threads to complete and then have the threads invoke a callback method when they finish.

This approach lets the main program ignore the asynchronous threads for most purposes, but it does make the flow of execution less predictable. While the threads are running, the user can do other things, perhaps even starting new threads that duplicate those that are already running. When a thread finishes, the callback routine executes, possibly interrupting whatever the user is doing at the time.

There's one important catch to working with callbacks: Only the thread that created the user interface (called the *UI thread*) can directly interact with the controls in the user interface. That means the asynchronous threads cannot directly assign images to `PictureBoxes`, display text in `Labels` or `TextBoxes`, move controls around, or otherwise manipulate the controls. Because the threads invoke the callback methods, those methods cannot directly interact with the controls, either.

You can get around this restriction by using the form's `Invoke` method. `Invoke` executes one of the form's methods on the UI thread.

The HandleCallback example program, which is available for download on the book's website, uses a callback instead of calling `EndInvoke` in the program's main flow of execution. This program, which is shown in Figure 6-2, uses a callback to let the main program know when the asynchronous thread has finished.

The main program displays a count in the `Label` while the thread displays its count in the Console window. (You could use `Invoke` to make it display its count in the `Label` but this is complicated enough without that.)

FIGURE 6-2: The HandleCallback example program uses a callback instead of `EndInvoke`.

The program uses the following code to start the thread and display its count.

```
// Start the countDelegate method on a new thread.
Func<int, int> countDelegate = Count;
IAsyncResult result = countDelegate.BeginInvoke(5,
    new AsyncCallback(CountCallback), "Thread: ");

// Count to 3.
for (int i = 1; i <= 3; i++)
{
    System.Threading.Thread.Sleep(1000);
    countLabel.Text = i.ToString();
    countLabel.Refresh();
}

// Display a finished message.
countLabel.Text = "Main: done";
```

First, the code creates a delegate variable to hold a reference to the `Count` method described shortly. This version of `Count` takes an `int` parameter and returns an `int` result.

Next, the code calls the delegate's `BeginInvoke` method. This time it passes the method the value that should be passed to the `Count` method (5), a new `AsyncCallback` object initialized to represent the `CountCallback` method, and a value to be passed to the callback (the string `Thread:`). At this point, a new thread starts running the `Count` method.

The code then enters its own loop where it displays the numbers 1 through 3 in the form's `Label` control, pausing for 1 second between numbers. Notice that the code refreshes the `Label` each time it displays a new value. If the code didn't do this, the `Label` would not refresh until the code finished so the user would not see the count. After it finishes its count, the code displays the message `Main: done` in the `Label`.

Meanwhile the other thread has been running the following `Count` method.

```
// Count pausing 1 second between numbers.
// Return the final value displayed.
private int Count(int max)
{
    for (int i = 1; i <= max; i++)
    {
        System.Threading.Thread.Sleep(1000);
        Console.WriteLine("Count: " + i);
    }
    return max;
}
```

This method displays a count in the Console window and then returns the largest number it displayed. Notice that this method doesn't know anything about the callback.

When the method finishes, the following callback (which was registered in the call to `BeginInvoke`) executes.

```
// The asynchronous thread finished.
private void CountCallback(IAsyncResult iresult)
{
    // Get an AsyncResult.
    AsyncResult result = (AsyncResult)iresult;

    // Get the delegate that ran.
    Func<int, int> caller = (Func<int, int>)result.AsyncDelegate;

    // Get the parameter we passed to BeginInvoke.
    string parameter = (string)result.AsyncState;

    // Get the method's return value.
    int value = (int)caller.EndInvoke(result);

    // Use Invoke to display the result.
    Action<string> updater = SetLabel;
    string message = parameter + value;
    this.Invoke(updater, message);
}
```

The callback method receives as a parameter an `IAsyncResult` object that gives information about the method that finished running.

The method first casts the IAsyncResult parameter into an AsyncResult object. (AsyncResult is defined in the System.Runtime.Remoting namespace. The program includes a using directive to simplify the code.)

Next, the code casts the result's AsyncDelegate property into a delegate that represents the method that ran asynchronously.

The result's AsyncState property contains the parameter that was given to the BeginInvoke method to pass on to the callback. In this example, that was the string Thread:. This example simply passes a fixed string in this value, but more generally you can use this value to identify different asynchronous calls to the same method. The code gets this value and casts it into a string to recover the original value.

Next, the code calls the delegate's EndInvoke method passing it the result object. This frees the resources used by the thread and lets the program retrieve the method's returned result. In this example, the Count method returns an int so the code casts the value returned by EndInvoke into an int.

At this point the callback would like to display a success message in the form's Label. Unfortunately, the callback is executing in the asynchronous thread rather than the UI thread, so it cannot directly set the Label's Text property.

To work around this problem, the callback creates a delegate to represent the SetLabel method described next. It composes a message and calls the form's Invoke method passing it the delegate and the message. This makes the form run the SetLabel method on its UI thread.

The following code shows the SetLabel method.

```
// Set the Label's text.
private void SetLabel(string text)
{
    countLabel.Text = text;
}
```

The SetLabel method simply sets the Label's Text property. (This is the only simple part of the whole process.)

Using Async and Await

Calling EndInvoke directly in the UI thread makes the code relatively simple, but it means the program is blocked until the asynchronous thread finishes running. Using a callback allows the main UI thread to finish before the threads do so the user interface can interact with the user, but the code is more complex, particularly if the callback must manipulate controls, so it needs to use the form's Invoke method.

C# provides two keywords that make it easier to use the callback approach without actually writing callbacks and calling Invoke yourself.

The async keyword indicates that a routine may have parts that should run asynchronously. You should apply this keyword to event handlers and other methods that will start tasks asynchronously and then wait for them.

The await keyword makes the program wait until a particular task has finished running asynchronously. When it sees the await keyword, C# essentially converts the rest of the method into a callback that it automatically invokes when the task has finished. One really nice feature of this "virtual callback" is that it executes on the UI thread so it can manipulate controls directly without using the form's Invoke method.

The AsyncAwait example program, which is available for download on this book's website, is similar to the HandleCallback example program, but it uses the async and await keywords instead of a callback.

The following code shows the event handler that executes when you click the program's Count button. The async and await keywords are highlighted in bold.

```csharp
// Count on a separate thread.
private async void countButton_Click(object sender, EventArgs e)
{
    // Disable the button.
    countButton.Enabled = false;
    countLabel.Text = "";
    countButton.Refresh();
    countLabel.Refresh();

    // Start the Count method on a new thread.
    Func<object, int> countDelegate = Count;
    Task<int> task = new Task<int>(countDelegate, 5);
    task.Start();

    // Count to 3.
    for (int i = 1; i <= 3; i++)
    {
        System.Threading.Thread.Sleep(1000);
        countLabel.Text = i.ToString();
        countLabel.Refresh();
    }

    // Display a finished message.
    countLabel.Text = "Main: done";

    // Enable the button.
    countButton.Enabled = true;

    // Wait for the task to complete.
    int result = await task;

    // Display the result message.
    countLabel.Text = "Thread: " + result;
}
```

Because this event handler has parts that run asynchronously, its declaration includes the async keyword.

After some preliminaries, the code creates a delegate that refers to the Count method. The Task class used next can pass a state value to the method, but Task expects that value to be of the generic object class, so the countDelegate variable is declared to represent methods that take an object parameter and return an int.

Next, the code creates a `Task` object for the method represented by the `countDelegate` variable. The `Task` constructor takes as parameters the delegate and the value 5 that it should pass to the delegate's method.

The code then calls the `Task`'s `Start` method to start the task running on a new thread.

The program then performs its own count on the UI thread. When it finishes it displays a message in the `Label` and re-enables the program's `Button`.

Having finished its work, the code uses the `await` keyword to wait for the `Task` to finish and saves the result returned in the variable `result`.

The code finishes by displaying the result it received from the asynchronous thread.

The following code shows the new version of the `Count` method.

```
// Count pausing 1 second between numbers.
// Return the final value displayed.
private int Count(object maxObj)
{
    int max = (int)maxObj;
    for (int i = 1; i <= max; i++)
    {
        System.Threading.Thread.Sleep(1000);
        Console.WriteLine("Count: " + i);
    }
    return max;
}
```

This is similar to the earlier versions except its parameter is declared as an `object` instead of an `int`. It must then convert the `object` into an `int` before it starts its loop.

At first this example may seem similar to the BeginInvoke example described earlier. Both start an asynchronous thread, do some counting on the UI thread, and then wait for the asynchronous thread to finish before continuing.

The difference is that the BeginInvoke example is blocked while it waits for the asynchronous thread to finish. In contrast, the AsyncAwait example returns as soon as the code uses the `await` keyword. Later when the asynchronous thread finishes, it invokes a hidden callback and execution returns to the main program right after the `await` keyword. This lets the UI thread remain responsive while it's waiting for the other thread to finish.

SUMMARY

Methods let you break an application into manageable, reusable pieces. This chapter explained how to declare methods that define how objects behave. It also explained techniques related to methods, such as how to create extension methods and use covariance and contravariance.

This chapter also explained some of the ways you can execute pieces of code simultaneously on different threads of execution. If your computer has multiple cores or CPUs, that may allow you to greatly improve performance.

The chapters so far have not explained how to write anything other than straight-line code that executes one statement after another with no deviation. Some examples have used loops and other constructs, but up until now this book hasn't explained the details of how to use those statements.

Most programs need to follow more complex paths of execution than simply executing a series of statements. They may need to perform some statements only under certain conditions and repeat other statements many times. Chapter 7, "Program Control Statements," describes the statements that a C# program uses to control the flow of code execution. These include decision statements (if-else and switch) and looping statements (for, foreach, while, and do-while).

EXERCISES

1. Create an IContactable interface that specifies a method Contact that takes a string parameter and returns a bool. (In a real application, this method would try to contact someone via e-mail, text message, or some other method and return true to indicate success or false to indicate failure.)

2. Create an Emailable class that implicitly implements the interface you built for Exercise 1. First, do it by hand. Then use Visual Studio's Implement context menu command to do it again. (You don't need to give the method a real body. Just make it return true.)

3. Create a Textable class that explicitly implements the IContactable interface you built for Exercise 1. First, do it by hand. Then use Visual Studio's Implement context menu command to do it again.

4. Create a Contactable class that you could use instead of the IContactable interface you built for Exercise 1.

5. Create a non-abstract Mailable class that inherits from the Contactable class you built for Exercise 4.

6. Create a double extension method named Root that uses Math.Sqrt to return the square root of a number.

7. The Math class's Sqrt method returns a number's square root, but the class has no method that returns other roots such as the third root. However, the Math class's Pow method returns a number raised to a power, and you can use that method to calculate roots. For example, the third root of a number would be Math.Pow(number, 1.0 / 3.0). Write an overloaded version of the Root extension method you built for Exercise 6 that takes the root's base as a parameter and uses Math.Pow to calculate the result.

8. Suppose you're building a checkers program and you want a Piece class to represent a piece. The King class inherits from Piece and represents a piece that has been crowned. The Piece class defines a CanMoveTo method that takes a row and column number as inputs and returns true or false to indicate whether the piece can move to that position. The King class must replace this method with a new version. Finally, you want to represent all pieces whether crowned or not by Piece objects. For example, to keep track of the pieces' positions, the program will use an array defined by the following code.

```
Piece[] Board = new Piece[8, 8];
```

Create simple `Piece` and `King` classes. For testing purposes, make the `Piece` class's `CanMoveTo` method always return `false` and make the `King` class's version always return `true`.

9. Suppose a program has the inheritance hierarchy `Person` ⇨ `Employee` ⇨ `Manager` ⇨ `Executive`. Define a delegate type named `ManagersFromEmployeesDelegate` to represent methods that take an array of `Employees` as an input and that return an array of `Managers`. Create a `Promote` method that has the same signature and make a variable to hold that method.

10. Use covariance and contravariance to make a new `Promote2` method that is as different as possible from the `Promote` method you built for Exercise 9. Create a new `ManagersFromEmployeesDelegate` variable and make it hold a reference to the new method.

11. (Hard) Make an application similar to the one shown in Figure 6-3. (You can't tell from the picture in this book, but the upper-left image uses shades of red, the upper-right image uses shades of green, the lower-left image uses shades of blue, and the lower-right image uses shades of gray.)

FIGURE 6-3: The ColorizeBitmap example program creates red, green, blue, and gray versions of an image synchronously and asynchronously.

The File menu has two commands: Open (opens an image file) and Exit (closes the program). The Process menu also has two commands: Synchronously (processes images synchronously) and Asynchronously (processes images asynchronously).

You can use the following enumeration and `ProcessBitmap` method.

```
// The colorization types.
private enum ColorizationType
{
    Red,
    Green,
    Blue,
    Gray,
}

// Process a Bitmap.
private void ProcessBitmap(Bitmap bm, ColorizationType colorType)
{
    for (int y = 0; y < bm.Height; y++)
    {
        for (int x = 0; x < bm.Width; x++)
        {
            Color color = bm.GetPixel(x, y);
            int average = (color.R + color.G + color.B) / 3;
            if (colorType == ColorizationType.Red)
                bm.SetPixel(x, y, Color.FromArgb(average, 0, 0));
            else if (colorType == ColorizationType.Green)
                bm.SetPixel(x, y, Color.FromArgb(0, average, 0));
            else if (colorType == ColorizationType.Blue)
                bm.SetPixel(x, y, Color.FromArgb(0, 0, average));
            else
                bm.SetPixel(x, y, Color.FromArgb(average, average, average));
        }
    }
}
```

When the user selects the Synchronously command, use the `ProcessBitmap` method to process four copies of the loaded image and display the results.

When the user selects the Asynchronously command, use `BeginInvoke` and `EndInvoke` to perform the same tasks asynchronously.

Use the `System.Diagnostics.Stopwatch` class to time the two techniques.

12. Would there be any advantage to modifying the program you wrote for Exercise 11 so it uses a callback or `async` and `await`?

7

Program Control Statements

Program control statements tell an application which other statements to execute under different circumstances. They control the path that execution takes through the code. They include commands that tell the program to execute some statements but not others and to execute certain statements repeatedly.

The two main categories of control statements are decision statements (or conditional statements) and looping statements. The following sections describe in detail the decision and looping statements provided by C#.

DECISION STATEMENTS

A *decisions statement* or *conditional statement* represents a branch in the program. It marks a place where the program can execute one set of statements or another, or possibly no statements at all, depending on some condition. These include several kinds of `if` statements and `switch` statements.

if-else Statements

The `if-else` statement has the following syntax:

```
if (condition1) statement1;
else if (condition2) statement2;
else if (condition3) statement3;
...
else statementElse;
```

The conditions are logical expressions that evaluate to either `true` or `false`. The statements are the statements that should be executed if the corresponding condition is `true`.

The program evaluates each of the conditions until it finds one that is `true`. It then evaluates the corresponding statement and skips all the rest of the series of `else` and `if` statements.

SHORT CIRCUITING IFS

Because the program skips any remaining `else` and `if` statements, a series of `if-else` statements provides short-circuit evaluation similar to the behavior given by the `||` operator. In particular, the program doesn't evaluate the conditions used by those statements. Normally, that's okay and saves the program some time, but it can be a problem if those conditions invoke methods with side effects.

For example, suppose a condition calls the `EmployeeExists` method. If that method opens an employee database and leaves it open, that is a side effect. If you don't know whether that condition will be checked, after the series of `if-else` statements finishes, you won't know whether the database has been opened.

The best way to avoid this issue is to not write methods that have unexpected side effects. For more on side effects, see the discussion of the `&&` and `||` operators in the section "Logical Operators" in Chapter 5.

If none of the conditions are `true`, the program executes `statementElse`.

For example, consider the following code snippet.

```
string greeting = "";

if (DateTime.Now.DayOfWeek == DayOfWeek.Monday)
    greeting = "Sorry, it's Monday.";
else if (DateTime.Now.DayOfWeek == DayOfWeek.Friday)
    greeting = "Finally, it's Friday!";
else
    greeting = "Welcome to " + DateTime.Now.DayOfWeek.ToString();

MessageBox.Show(greeting);
```

The code starts by creating the `string` variable `greeting` and initializing it to a blank string. It then begins a series of `if-else` statements.

If it's Monday, the program sets `greeting` to `"Sorry, it's Monday."`

If it's not Monday and it is Friday, the program sets `greeting` to `"Finally, it's Friday!"`

If it's neither Monday nor Friday, the program sets `greeting` to `"Welcome to"` followed by the current day of the week.

After the series of `if-else` statements, the program displays the greeting in a message box.

The final `else` section is optional. If you don't include it and none of the conditions are `true`, the program doesn't execute any of the corresponding statements.

All the `else if` statements are also optional. If the code includes only an `if` statement, either the program executes the statement that follows or it doesn't, depending on the value of the condition.

For example, the following code uses a single `if` statement to display a message box only if it's Monday. If it's any other day of the week, the program does nothing.

```
if (DateTime.Now.DayOfWeek == DayOfWeek.Monday)
    MessageBox.Show("Sorry, it's Monday.");
```

The "statement" that the program executes when a condition is `true` can actually be a block of statements surrounded by braces. The following shows the syntax.

```
if (condition1)
{
    statement1;
}
else if (condition2)
{
    statement2;
}
else if (condition3)
{
    statement3;
}
...
else
{
    statementElse;
}
```

You can place as many statements as you like between the braces.

switch Statements

The `switch` statement lets a program execute one of several pieces of code depending on a single value. The result is similar to a series of `if-else` statements that compare a single value to a series of other values.

The basic syntax is as follows:

```
switch (value)
{
    case expression1:
        statements1;
        break;
    case expression2:
```

```
        statements2;
        break;
    ...
  «default:
        statementsDefault
        break;»
}
```

Here the program compares `value` to the expressions until it finds one that matches or it runs out of expressions to test. The expressions must be constant statements and cannot duplicate each other.

If the program finds a match, it executes the corresponding code. If the program runs out of expressions, it executes the statements in the `default` section (if it is present).

EASY-TO-READ DEFAULTS

The `default` section of a `switch` statement does not need to be at the end of the list, but it's usually easier to read there than buried in the middle.

You can place multiple `case` statements in a group to make them all execute the same code. However, you cannot allow the code from one case section to fall through to the next. If the first section contains lines of code, it must end with a `break` statement before the next case begins.

THE NEED FOR SPEED

If a `switch` statement includes a long sequence of `case` sections, the C# compiler converts it into a lookup table. Finding items in a lookup table is very fast, so the `switch` statement is often faster than a corresponding sequence of `if-then-else` statements.

However, the `switch` statement is less flexible. A `switch` statement only compares a single value to a collection of other values, but a sequence of `if-else` statements can perform all sorts of tests. Unless the code is executed many times inside a loop, the difference in time will probably be small anyway. For that reason, you should generally use the approach that makes the code easiest to read and understand.

The following code is similar to the previous code that checks the day of the week except this version adds extra code for Saturday and Sunday.

```
string greeting = "";

switch (DateTime.Now.DayOfWeek)
{
    case DayOfWeek.Monday:
        greeting = "Sorry, it's Monday.";
        break;
    case DayOfWeek.Friday:
        greeting = "Finally, it's Friday!";
```

```
        break;
    case DayOfWeek.Saturday:
    case DayOfWeek.Sunday:
        greeting = "Yay! The weekend!";
        break;
    default:
        greeting = "Welcome to " + DateTime.Now.DayOfWeek.ToString();
        break;
}

MessageBox.Show(greeting);
```

GIVE BREAK A BREAK

Actually each `case` section in a `switch` statement does not need to end with a `break` statement. Rather it must end in a statement that cannot allow control to pass by to the next `case` section. The `break` statement satisfies that condition, but a few other statements do, too.

For example, consider the following code.

```
switch (choice)
{
    case 1:
        // Do something...
        throw new ArgumentException();

    case 2:
        for (; ; )
        {
            // Do something...
        }

    case 3:
        int i = 1;
        while (i > 0)
        {
            // Do something (that doesn't modify i) ...
        }
}
```

The first `case` section ends by throwing an exception. Because control cannot get past that statement, this is okay.

The second `case` section contains an infinite loop. The C# compiler is smart enough to know that the loop never ends, so control cannot get past, which is also okay.

The third `case` section ends in a loop that will be infinite as long as the code inside the loop doesn't modify variable `i`. The compiler isn't smart enough to realize that this loop never ends, so it doesn't allow this.

This code initializes the greeting variable and then executes a switch statement. Depending on the values of DateTime.Now.DayOfWeek, the program executes the code in the appropriate case section.

The values DayOfWeek.Monday and DayOfWeek.Friday have their own sections. The two values DayOfWeek.Saturday and DayOfWeek.Sunday both execute code that sets greeting to "Yay! The weekend!"

If DateTime.Now.DayOfWeek is not any of those values, the default section sets greeting equal to "Welcome to" followed by the day of the week.

Enumerated Values

The switch statement works naturally with lists of discrete values because each case statement can handle one value.

Enumerated types also work with discrete values, so they work well with switch statements. The enumerated type defines the values and the switch statement uses them, as shown in the following code fragment.

```
private enum JobStates
{
    Pending,
    Assigned,
    InProgress,
    ReadyToTest,
    Tested,
    Released,
}
private JobStates JobState;
...
switch (JobState)
{
    case JobStates.Pending:
        ...
        break;
    case JobStates.Assigned:
        ...
        break;
    case JobStates.InProgress:
        ...
        break;
    case JobStates.ReadyToTest:
        ...
        break;
    case JobStates.Tested:
        ...
        break;
    case JobStates.Released:
        ...
        break;
}
```

To catch bugs when changing an enumerated type, many developers include a default section that throws an exception. If you later add a new value to the enumerated type but forget to add corresponding code to the switch statement, the default section throws an exception, so you can fix the code.

For more information on enumerated types, see the section "Enumerations" in Chapter 4.

Conditional and Null-coalescing Operators

The conditional or ternary operator ?: evaluates a boolean expression and returns one of two values, depending on whether the expression is true or false. For example, the following code examines an Employee object's IsManager property. If IsManager is true, the code sets the employee's Salary to 90,000. If IsManager is false, the code sets the employee's Salary to 10,000.

```
emp.Salary = emp.IsManager ? 90000 : 10000;
```

This is equivalent to the following if-else statement.

```
if (emp.IsManager) emp.Salary = 90000;
else emp.Salary = 10000;
```

The null-coalescing operator ?? examines a reference value. It returns that value if it is not null. It returns its second argument if the first value is null. For example, the following code sets variable orderedBy equal to customer if customer is not null. If customer is null, the code sets orderedBy equal to a new Customer object.

```
Customer orderedBy = customer ?? new Customer();
```

This is equivalent to the following if-else statement.

```
Customer orderedBy;
if (customer != null) orderedBy = customer;
else orderedBy = new Customer();
```

For more information on the conditional and null-coalescing operators, see the section "Conditional and Null-coalescing Operators" in Chapter 5.

LOOPING STATEMENTS

Looping statements make the program execute a series of statements repeatedly. C# provides four kinds of loops: for loops, while loops, do loops, and foreach loops.

for Loops

A for loop has the following syntax.

```
for («initialization»; «test»; «increment») statement;
```

The parts of the loop are as follows:

➤   *initialization*—This piece of code can initialize the loop. Usually it declares and initializes the looping variable; although, you can place other code here as well.

➤   *test*—Each time the program is about to execute the code inside the loop, it evaluates this as a boolean expression. If the result is true, the loop continues. If the result is false, the loop ends. (Note that this means the loop might not execute even once if the condition is false when the loop starts.)

➤   *increment*—After the program has executed the code inside the loop but before it checks *test* again, it executes this code. Usually this code increments the looping variable.

➤   *statement*—This is the piece of code that is executed repeatedly as long as *test* is true. You can make the loop include multiple statements by enclosing them in braces.

LOOP SCOPE

Variables declared inside a loop, including those created in the loop's *initialization* section, have scope equal to the loop. That means code outside of the loop cannot see them. If you need the code after the loop to see a variable, declare it before the loop, not inside the loop.

It's a good practice to declare the looping variable inside the for statement. That limits the variable's scope, so you don't need to remember what the variable means in other pieces of code. It keeps the variable's declaration and initialization close to the code where it is used, so it's easier to remember the variable's data type and value. It also lets you more easily reuse counter variables in other loops without confusion.

The following code shows a simple for loop.

```
for (int i = 1; i <= 10; i++)
{
    Console.WriteLine(i);
}
```

The *initialization* part of the for statement declares integer variable i and sets it equal to 1. The *test* part of the loop determines whether i is less than or equal to 10. The *increment* part of the loop increases i by 1. Taken together, these pieces of the for statement make the loop run for values i = 1, i = 2, i = 3, ..., i = 10. For each value of i, the program executes the Console.WriteLine statement to display the value of i.

Usually the loop's *initialization* piece declares and initializes a single value as in the previous code. If the looping variable has already been declared, you can leave this section blank or only initialize the variable. For example, the following code declares the looping variable i outside of the loop.

```
int i;
for (i = 1; i < 10; i++)
{
    Console.WriteLine(i);
}
```

OUT OF CONTROL

Your code can change the value of looping variables inside the loop, but that's generally not a good idea. A `for` loop's intent is usually to make one variable (or at most a few variables) loop over specific values. If you change the value inside the loop, the result can be confusing. If you must modify looping variables in complicated ways, consider using the `while` or `do` loop instead. Then programmers reading the code won't expect a simple incrementing loop.

The *initialization* section can also declare and initialize multiple variables of the same type, and the *increment* section can execute multiple commands separated by commas. For example, the following code shows a `for` loop that uses three looping variables: a, b, and c.

```
for (int a = 0, b = 1, c = 1; a < 1000; a = b, b = c, c = a + b)
{
    Console.WriteLine("a: " + a);
}
```

In this example, the *initialization* code declares and initializes the three looping variables, the `test` section makes the loop run as long as a < 1000, and the `increment` section updates all three variables.

If you omit the *test* entirely, the loop runs indefinitely. In that case the loop's code usually contains a `return` or other statement to break out of the loop. For example, the following code enters an infinite loop. Each time through the loop, it does something and then asks the user whether it should continue. If the user clicks No, the loop's `return` statement makes the program exit the method that contains the loop.

```
for (; ; )
{
    // Do something ...

    if (MessageBox.Show("Continue?", "Continue?", MessageBoxButtons.YesNo)
        == DialogResult.No) return;
}
```

Noninteger for Loops

Usually a `for` loop's control variable has an integral data type such as a `int` or `long`. Because you can do all sorts of strange things inside a `for` loop's initialization and increment sections, you aren't restricted to integer looping variables. For example, the following code uses a `float` variable to display the values 1.0, 1.5, 2.0, 2.5, and 3.0.

```
for (float x = 1f; x <= 3f; x += 0.5f)
    Console.WriteLine(x.ToString("0.0"));
```

Because floating-point numbers cannot exactly represent every possible value, these data types are subject to rounding errors that can lead to unexpected results in `for` loops. The preceding code works as you would expect, at least on my computer. The following code, however, has problems. Ideally, this code would display values between 1 and 2, incrementing them by 1/7. Because of rounding errors, however, the value of x after seven trips through the loop is approximately 1.85714316. The program adds 1/7 to this and gets 2.00000024. This is greater than the stopping value 2, so the program exits the loop and the `Console.WriteLine` statement does not execute for x = 2.

```
for (float x = 1; x <= 2; x += 1f / 7f)
{
    Console.WriteLine(x);
}
```

One solution to this type of problem is to convert the loop into one that uses an integer control variable. Integer variables don't have the same problems with rounding errors that floating-point numbers have, so you get more precise control over the values used in the loop.

The following code does roughly the same thing as the previous code. However, this version uses an integer control variable, so this loop executes exactly eight times as desired. The final value printed into the Console window by the program is 2.

```
float x = 1;
for (int i = 1; i <= 8; i++, x += 1f / 7f)
{
    Console.WriteLine(x);
}
```

while Loops

A `while` loop has the following syntax.

```
while (test)
    statement;
```

As long as the `test` evaluates to `true`, the loop executes its statement. Note that this means the loop might not execute even once if the test is `false` when the loop starts.

You cannot omit the `test` but you can set it to `true` to make the `while` loop repeat indefinitely. If you want to execute more than one statement inside the loop, enclose them in braces. Usually the code inside the loop makes something change so the `test` eventually evaluates to `false` and stops the loop.

For a simple example of a `while` loop, suppose values is an array of integers. The following code uses a `while` loop to search the array for the value 37.

```
int index = 0;
while ((index < values.Length) && (values[index] != 37))
    index++;
```

The code initializes the variable `index` to 0. Then as long as `index` is a valid index in the array and the `values[index]` entry isn't 37, the loop increments `index`. (After the loop finishes, if `index` is equal to the length of the array, the value wasn't found.)

do Loops

A do loop has the following syntax.

```
do
    statement;
while (test);
```

A do loop is similar to a while loop except it performs its test after the loop has executed instead of before it executes. That means a do loop always executes at least once.

The following code shows a do loop version of the previous example that searches an array for the value 37.

```
int index = -1;
do
    index++;
while ((index < values.Length) && (values[index] != 37));
```

As is the case for a while loop, if you want to execute multiple statements in a do loop, you should enclose them in braces.

foreach Loops

A foreach loop iterates over the items in a collection, array, or other container class that supports foreach loops. A foreach loop has the following syntax.

```
foreach (variable in group)
    statement;
```

Here, group is a collection, array, or other object that supports foreach. As in for loops, the looping variable must be declared either in or before the foreach statement.

> **ENABLING ENUMERATORS**
>
> To support foreach, the group object must implement the System.Collections.IEnumerable interface. This interface defines a GetEnumerator method that returns an enumerator. For more information, see the next section, "Enumerators."

The following code shows a simple foreach loop.

```
foreach (Employee employee in employees)
{
    Console.WriteLine(employee.Name);
}
```

Each time through the loop, the program sets the variable employee equal to the next item in the employees array. The code inside the loop displays the employee object's Name in the Console window.

The looping variable must be of a data type compatible with the objects contained in the group. If the group contains `Employee` objects, the variable could be an `Employee` object. It could also be a generic `object` or any other class that readily converts into an `Employee` object. For example, if `Employee` inherits from the `Person` class, the variable could be of type `Person`.

C# doesn't automatically understand what kinds of objects are stored in a collection or array until it tries to use them. If the looping variable's type is not compatible with a value in the collection, the program throws an `InvalidCastException` when it tries to assign the looping variable to that value.

That means if a collection or array contains more than one type of object, the looping variable must be of a type that can be converted into all the objects' types. If the objects in a collection do not inherit from a common ancestor class, the code must use a control variable of type `object`.

LIMITING SCOPE

As is the case with `for` loops, declaring the looping variable in the `foreach` statement is a good practice. That limits the variable's scope, so you don't need to remember what the variable means in other pieces of code. It keeps the variable's declaration and initialization close to the code where it is used, so it's easier to remember the variable's data type and value. It also lets you easily reuse counter variables in other loops without confusion.

Your code can change the value of the looping variable inside the loop, but that has no effect on the loop's progress through the collection or array. The loop resets the variable to the next object and continues as if you had never changed the variable's value. To avoid confusion, don't bother.

The program cannot modify the collection itself while the loop is executing. For example, if the code is looping over a list of `Employee` objects, the code inside the loop cannot add or remove objects from the list. (That could be confusing, so this probably wouldn't be a good idea even if it were allowed.)

CREATIVE COLLECTIONS

If you must modify a collection while looping through it, create a new collection and modify that one instead. For example, suppose you want to loop through the original collection and remove some items. Make the new collection and then loop through the original, copying the items that you want to keep into the new collection.

In complicated situations, you may need to use a `while` loop and some careful indexing instead of a `foreach` loop.

One common scenario when dealing with collections is examining every item in the collection and removing some of them. A `foreach` loop won't let you remove items while you're looping over them so that's not an option.

One approach that seems like it might work (but doesn't) is to use a `for` loop, as shown in the following code.

```
for (int i = 0; i < employees.Count; i++)
{
    if (employees[i].ShouldBeRemoved) employees.RemoveAt(i);
}
```

Unfortunately, if the code removes an object from the collection, the loop skips the next item because its index has been reduced by one and the loop has already passed that position in the collection.

One solution to this problem is to use a `for` loop to examine the collection's objects in reverse order, as shown in the following example.

```
for (int i = employees.Count - 1; i >= 0; i--)
{
    if (employees[i].ShouldBeRemoved) employees.RemoveAt(i);
}
```

In this version, the code never needs to use an index after it has been removed because the code is counting backward. The index of an object in the collection also doesn't change unless that object has already been examined by the loop. The loop examines every item exactly once, no matter which objects are removed.

Enumerators

An *enumerator* is an object that lets you move through the objects contained by some sort of container class. For example, collections, arrays, and hash tables provide enumerators. This section discusses enumerators for collections, but the same ideas apply for these other classes.

You can use an enumerator to view the objects in a collection but not to modify the collection itself. You can use the enumerator to alter the objects in the collection (for example, to change their properties), but you can generally not use it to add, remove, or rearrange the objects in the collection.

Initially, an enumerator is positioned before the first item in the collection. Your code should use the enumerator's `MoveNext` method to step to the next object in the collection. `MoveNext` returns `true` if it successfully moves to a new object or `false` if there are no more objects in the collection.

The `Reset` method restores the enumerator to its original position before the first object, so you can step through the collection again.

The `Current` method returns the object that the enumerator is currently reading. Invoking `Current` throws an exception if the enumerator is not currently reading any object. That happens if the enumerator is before the first object or after the last object.

The following example uses an enumerator to loop through the items in a list named `employees`.

```
IEnumerator<Employee> enumerator = employees.GetEnumerator();
while (enumerator.MoveNext())
{
    Console.WriteLine(enumerator.Current.Name);
}
```

This code creates an enumerator to enumerate over Employee objects. It then enters a while loop. If enumerator.MoveNext returns true, the enumerator has successfully moved to the next object in the collection. As long as it has read an object, the program uses enumerator.Current to get the current object and displays that object's Name property in the Console window.

When it reaches the end of the employees list, the enumerator's MoveNext method returns false and the loop ends.

A foreach loop provides roughly the same access to the items in a container class as an enumerator. Under some circumstances, however, an enumerator may provide a more natural way to loop through a container class than a foreach loop. For example, an enumerator can skip several items without examining them closely. You can also use an enumerator's Reset method to restart the enumeration. To restart a foreach loop, you would need to start the loop over.

The IEnumerable interface defines the features needed for enumerators, so any class that implements the IEnumerable interface provides enumerators. Any class that supports foreach must also implement the IEnumerable interface, so any class that supports foreach also supports enumerators. A few of the classes that implement IEnumerable include the following:

Array	HybridDictionary	SqlDataReader
ArrayList	ListDictionary	Stack
Collection	MessageQueue	String
CollectionBase	OdbcDataReader	StringCollection
ControlCollection	OleDbDataReader	StringDictionary
DataView	OracleDataReader	TableCellCollection
DictionaryBase	Queue	TableRowCollection
DictionaryEntries	ReadOnlyCollectionBase	XmlNode
Hashtable	SortedList	XmlNodeList

Iterators

An *iterator* is similar in concept to an enumerator. It also provides methods that enable you to step through the items in some sort of container object. Iterators are more specialized than enumerators and work with particular classes.

For example, a GraphicsPath object represents a series of connected lines and curves. A GraphicsPathIterator object can step through the line and curve data contained in a GraphicsPath object.

Iterators are much more specialized than enumerators. How you use them depends on what you need to do and on the kind of iterator, so they are not described in detail here.

break Statements

Each type of loop has a normal termination condition. For example, a while loop continues to execute as long as the test in the while statement is true. When the test becomes false, the loop ends.

In addition to a loop's standard method for ending, there are a few other ways a program can leave a loop.

One way to break out of a loop early is to execute a return statement. When the program encounters a return statement, the method immediately exits, even if that means breaking out of one or more loops.

The break statement immediately stops the innermost loop containing the statement and passes control to the end of the loop. For example, suppose the Machine class represents the machines in a workshop. The following code searches the array machines for a machine that isn't busy.

```
Machine idleMachine = null;
foreach (Machine machine in machines)
{
    if (machine.IsIdle)
    {
        idleMachine = machine;
        break;
    }
}

if (idleMachine != null)
{
    // Assign work to the machine.
}
```

First, the program declares the variable idleMachine and initializes it to null. It then loops through the Machines array. If it finds an object in the array with IsIdle property true, it saves that machine in the variable idleMachine and uses the break statement to end the loop.

After the loop finishes, the code checks idleMachine to see if it found an idle machine.

A loop can also end early if it encounters an exception and doesn't include code to handle it. In that case, the loop ends and control passes to an enclosing try catch finally block if there is one. If the loop isn't enclosed in a try catch finally block, control leaves the executing method and passes up the call stack to the method that called it. If there is an active try catch finally block at that level, it handles the exception. If there is still no try catch finally block, control continues to pass up the call stack until the exception is handled or control pops off the stack, in which case the program crashes. (For more information about try catch finally blocks, see Chapter 9, "Error Handling.")

continue Statements

The continue statement lets a program skip the rest of its current pass through a loop and start the next pass early.

For example, suppose you need to process a collection of `Employee` objects. If an employee is not exempt, you need to perform some overtime calculations for that employee. The following code shows how a program could use the `continue` statement to do this.

```
foreach (Employee employee in employees)
{
    if (employee.IsExempt) continue;

    // Process the employee.
    ...
}
```

Inside the loop, the code checks the `Employee` object's `IsExempt` property. If `IsExempt` is `true`, the program uses the `continue` statement to skip the rest of the loop and process the next `Employee`.

SUMMARY

Control statements form the heart of any program. Decision statements determine what commands are executed, and looping statements determine how many times they are executed.

The `if` and `switch` statements are the most commonly used decision statements in C#. The `?:` and `??` are less common operators that act as decision statements.

C# provides the `for`, `while`, `do`, and `foreach` looping statements. Some container classes also support enumerators that let you step through the items in the container. An enumerator provides more flexibility and can sometimes be more natural than a `foreach` loop.

Using the looping statements described in this chapter, you can perform complex searches over collections of objects. For example, you can loop through an array of numbers to find their maximum, minimum, and average values. The next chapter explains how you can use database-like query syntax to perform similar operations more easily. It tells how you can use LINQ to select, filter, and arrange data taken from lists, collections, arrays, and other data structures.

EXERCISES

1. Suppose `person` is a variable of type `Person`. The `Person` class has a `Type` property of the enumeration type `PersonType`. The enumeration includes the values `Customer`, `Employee`, and `Manager`. How are the following two blocks of code different?

```
// Block 1.
if (person.Type == PersonType.Customer)
{
    ...
}
else if (person.Type == PersonType.Employee)
{
    ...
}
```

```
    else if (person.Type == PersonType.Manager)
    {
        . . .
    }

    // Block 2.
    if (person.Type == PersonType.Customer)
    {
        . . .
    }
    if (person.Type == PersonType.Employee)
    {
        . . .
    }
    if (person.Type == PersonType.Manager)
    {
        . . .
    }
```

2. Rewrite the previous code in Block 1 to use a `switch` statement instead of `if` statements.

3. Suppose the `Person` class has a `GetBirthMonth` method that looks a person up in a database and returns the person's birth month as a number between 1 and 12. Your program should use that method to determine the person's birthstone. Should you use a series of `if` statements or a `switch` statement? Why?

4. Write a series of `if` statements and a `switch` statement with roughly the same performance to find birthstones as described in Exercise 3.

5. Suppose you want to assign a letter grade depending on a student's test score: 90–100 = A, 80–89 = B, 70–79 = C, 60–69 = D, 0–59 = F. Should you use a `switch` statement or a series of `if` statements? Why? Write the code using your chosen approach.

6. The section "for Loops" in this chapter used the following code as an example.

```
for (int a = 0, b = 1, c = 1; a < 1000; a = b, b = c, c = a + b)
{
    Console.WriteLine("a: " + a);
}
```

This code works but it's rather confusing because its initialization and increment sections contain so many statements. Rewrite this loop to move the initialization out of the loop and the increment statements inside the loop.

7. Write a `for` loop that adds up the numbers in the array `values`.

8. Write a `while` loop that adds up the numbers in the array `values`.

9. Write a `do` loop that adds up the numbers in the array `values`.

10. Write a `for` loop that uses a `char` looping variable to display the letters A through Z.

11. The following code sets an overdue `Bill` object's `Penalty` property to $5 or 10 percent of the outstanding balance, whichever is greater.

```
bill.Penalty = bill.Status == BillStatus.Overdue ?
    bill.Balance < 50m ? 5m : bill.Balance * 0.1m : 0m;
```

Rewrite this code so that it doesn't use the `?:` operator.

12. Rewrite the following code so that it doesn't use the `??` operator.

```
Student student = GetStudent("Steward Dent") ?? new Student("Steward Dent");
```

13. Write a `for` loop that displays the multiples of 3 between 0 and 100 in largest-to-smallest order.

14. What values does the following loop display?

```
for (int i = 1; i < 100; i += i) Console.WriteLine(i);
```

15. Write a program that displays the dates that are Friday the 13ths starting at the beginning of the current year. Display dates one year at a time as long as the user clicks Yes in a dialog asking if the program should continue for the next year.

16. Rewrite the following `foreach` loop so that it doesn't use the `continue` statement.

```
foreach (Employee employee in employees)
{
    if (employee.IsExempt) continue;

    // Process the employee.
    ...
}
```

What advantage does the `continue` statement have over your solution? When would it be even more useful?

LINQ

WROX.COM DOWNLOADS FOR THIS CHAPTER

Please note that all the code examples for this chapter are available as a part of this chapter's code download on the book's website at www.wrox.com/go/csharp5programmersref on the Download Code tab.

Language Integrated Query or *LINQ* (pronounced "link") is a data retrieval mechanism that enables programs to filter, select, and group data in much the same way a program can gather data from a database. The difference is that LINQ enables the program to select data from all kinds of data sources, not just databases. LINQ enables a program to select data from arrays, lists, collections, XML data, relational databases, and a wide variety of other data sources.

LINQ enables a program to use a (sort of) natural query language to make complex data selections with little code. For example, suppose you want to search a collection of customer records, find those with balances greater than $50 that are overdue by at least 30 days, and display the list sorted by balance. You could easily write code to loop through the collection to find the appropriate customers and copy them into a new collection. You could then write code to sort that collection. This isn't terribly hard, but it does take a moderate amount of code that would give you several opportunities to make mistakes.

> **LOTS OF LINQ**
>
> This chapter describes the standard LINQ providers that a C# program can use to select data from such sources as arrays, lists, XML data, and relational databases. However, you can build providers to let LINQ interact with just about any data source. There are providers that select data from Amazon.com, Active Directory, Excel, Flickr, Google, JSON, JavaScript, MySQL, Oracle, SharePoint, and many other sources. For a list of some of the many providers available, see Charlie Calvert's blog post "Link to Everything: A List of LINQ Providers" at `blogs .msdn.com/b/charlie/archive/2008/02/28/link-to-everything-a-list-of-linq-providers.aspx`.

In contrast, a LINQ query can define this search and sort operation concisely. The program can then execute the query to get the results with little code and little chance to make mistakes. The result may not be as fast as optimized C# code, but LINQ is often much simpler and easier to implement.

LINQ provides dozens of extension methods that apply to all sorts of objects that can hold data such as arrays, dictionaries, and lists. (For more information on extension methods, see the section "Extension Methods" in Chapter 6, "Methods.") For example, an array of integers by itself is basically just a chunk of memory that holds a bunch of numbers. LINQ adds extension methods to integer arrays that let you perform such tasks as the following:

- ➤ Finding the minimum, maximum, and average value
- ➤ Converting the array into an enumerable list of `float` or some other data type
- ➤ Concatenating the array with another array
- ➤ Determining whether the array contains a particular value
- ➤ Counting the number of values that meet some condition
- ➤ Returning the first value that meets some condition
- ➤ Returning the distinct values (the values without duplicates)
- ➤ Grouping the values by some criterion
- ➤ Finding the items that are in the array that are also in another array
- ➤ Sorting the items in the array
- ➤ Reversing the order of the items in the array
- ➤ Returning the sum of the items in the array

C# provides a syntax that converts queries into LINQ extension method calls to select, order, and otherwise manipulate the data and return a result.

The standard LINQ tools are divided into the following three broad categories:

- ➤ *LINQ to Objects*—LINQ methods that interact with C# objects such as arrays, dictionaries, and lists.

➤ *LINQ to XML*—LINQ features that read and write XML data. LINQ lets you easily move data between XML hierarchies and other C# objects.

➤ *LINQ to ADO.NET*—LINQ features that let you write LINQ-style queries to extract data from relational databases.

The following section provides an intuitive introduction to LINQ. Many of LINQ's details are so complex and technical that they can be quite confusing if they're stated precisely. However, the basic ideas are mostly straightforward and easy to understand with a few examples. To make things as easy to understand as possible, this chapter relies heavily on examples.

The next section, "Basic LINQ Query Syntax," describes the most useful LINQ query commands. These enable you to perform queries that select, filter, and arrange data. The section after that, "Advanced LINQ Query Syntax," describes additional LINQ query commands that you are likely to use less frequently.

The section "Other LINQ Methods" describes methods provided by LINQ but not supported by C#'s LINQ query syntax. To use these methods, you must invoke them as methods for the arrays, dictionaries, lists, and other objects that they extend.

After describing the tools provided by LINQ, most of the rest of the chapter describes the three main categories of LINQ: LINQ to Objects, LINQ to XML, and LINQ to ADO.NET. The chapter finishes by describing Parallel LINQ (PLINQ).

LINQ to Objects is a bit easier to understand than LINQ to XML and LINQ to ADO.NET because it doesn't require special knowledge beyond C#. To understand LINQ to XML properly, you need to understand XML, which is a complex topic in its own right. Similarly, to get the most out of LINQ to ADO.NET, you need to understand relational databases such as SQL Server, a huge topic about which many books have been written.

Because LINQ to Objects is easiest to cover, this chapter focuses on it, and most of the examples in this chapter use LINQ to Objects. Similar concepts apply to the other forms of LINQ as well. The final sections of the chapter provide some information about LINQ to XML and LINQ to ADO. NET, however, to give you an idea of what is possible in those areas.

INTRODUCTION TO LINQ

The LINQ extension methods add new features to data stored in various data structures such as arrays and lists. C# provides a higher-level query syntax that makes it easier to use the lower-level extension methods. These higher-level *query expressions* define the data that should be selected from the data source and the way it should be arranged. LINQ query syntax is somewhat similar to the standard database Structured Query Language (SQL) so it should seem familiar if you have worked with relational databases.

For example, suppose a program defines a `Customer` class with properties such as `Name`, `Phone`, `Street`, `City`, `State`, `Zip`, `Balance`, and so forth. Suppose also that the `customers` array holds all of the application's `Customer` objects. Then the following expression defines a query that selects customers with negative account balances. It orders the results by balance in ascending order, so customers with the most negative balances (who owe the most) are listed first.

```
var overdue =
    from customer in customers
    where customer.Balance < 0
    orderby customer.Balance ascending
    select new { customer.Name, customer.Balance };
```

Behind the scenes, C# transforms the query expression into calls to the LINQ API and fetches the selected data. The program can then loop through the results as shown in the following code:

```
foreach (var customer in overdue)
    Console.WriteLine(customer.Name + ": " + customer.Balance);
```

There are a couple of interesting things to note about this code. First, the previous code fragments do not declare an explicit data type for the `overdue` query expression or the looping variable `customer` in the `foreach` loop. C# automatically infers the data type for both of these variables. If you use a statement such as `Console.WriteLine(overdue.GetType().Name)` for the `overdue` and `customer` variables, you'll discover that they have the following ungainly type names:

```
WhereSelectEnumerableIterator`2
<>f__AnonymousType0`2
```

Because these data types have such awkward names, you don't want to try to guess them. It's much easier to use the `var` data type and let C# figure out the data types for you.

A second interesting fact about this code is that the program doesn't actually fetch any data when the query expression is defined. It accesses the data source (in this case the `customers` array) when the code tries to access the result in the `foreach` loop.

Many programs don't need to distinguish between when the expression is declared and when it is executed. In this example, if the code iterated through the results right after defining the query, there wouldn't be much difference. However, if it may be a long time between defining the query and using it or if the query takes a long time to execute, the difference may matter.

Third, if you have any experience with relational databases, you'll notice that the `select` clause is in a different position from where it would be in a SQL statement. In SQL the SELECT clause comes first but in LINQ it comes at the end. (This placement is due to issues Microsoft encountered while implementing IntelliSense for LINQ.)

> **INTELLISENSE DEFERRED**
>
> Basically IntelliSense doesn't know what "fields" you can select until it knows what fields are available. In the preceding example, the `from` clause indicates that the data will be selected from the `customers`, an array of `Customer` objects. It isn't until after the `from` clause that IntelliSense knows that the `select` statement can pick from the `Customer` class's properties.

The following sections explain the most useful LINQ keywords supported by C#.

BASIC LINQ QUERY SYNTAX

The following text shows the typical syntax for a LINQ query:

```
from ... where ... orderby ... select ...
```

The following sections describe these four standard clauses. The sections after those describe some of the other most useful LINQ clauses.

from

The `from` clause tells where the query should get the data and defines the name by which it is known within the LINQ query. Its basic form is

```
from queryVariable in dataSource
```

Here `queryVariable` is a variable that you are declaring to manipulate the items selected from `dataSource`. This is similar to declaring a looping variable in a `for` or `foreach` statement.

You can supply a data type for `queryVariable` if you know its type; although, because of the anonymous types used by LINQ, it's often easiest to let LINQ infer the data type automatically. For example, the following query explicitly indicates that the query variable `customer` is from the `Customer` class:

```
var query = from Customer customer in customers select customer.Name;
```

A query can include multiple `from` clauses to select values from multiple data sources. For example, the following query selects data from the `customers` and `orders` arrays.

```
var customerOrders =
    from customer in customers
    from order in orders
    select new { customer.Name, order.OrderId };
```

In database terms, this query returns the *cross-product* of the two arrays. In other words, it returns every possible {`Customer`, `Order`} pair from the two arrays. For every `Customer` in the `customers` array, it returns that `Customer` plus every `Order` in the orders array.

If the `customers` array contains Art, Betty, and Carl, and the `orders` array contains orders numbered 1, 2, and 3, then this query selects the following nine results:

```
Art      1
Art      2
Art      3
Betty    1
Betty    2
Betty    3
Carl     1
Carl     2
Carl     3
```

Usually, you include a `where` clause to connect the objects selected from the two lists. For example, if customers and orders are related by a common `CustomerId` property, you might use the following query to select customers together with their corresponding orders rather than all orders:

```
var customerOrders =
    from customer in customers
    from order in orders
    where order.CustomerId == customer.CustomerId
    select new { customer.Name, order.OrderId };
```

If Art, Betty, and Carl have `CustomerId` values 1, 2, 3, and the three orders have the corresponding `CustomerId` values, the preceding query would return the following results:

```
Art       1
Betty     2
Carl      3
```

where

The `where` clause filters the records selected by the `from` clause. It can include tests involving the objects selected and properties of those objects. The last example in the preceding section shows a particularly useful kind of query that *joins* objects from two data sources that are related by common property values. The `where` clause often performs simple tests and comparisons, but it can also execute methods on the selected objects and properties to decide if they should be included in the results.

For example, suppose the `Customer` class has `Balance` and `PaymentIsLate` properties, and suppose the `PreferredCustomer` class inherits from `Customer`. Also suppose the `customers` array contains both `Customer` and `PreferredCustomer` objects.

The `OwesALot` method defined in the following code returns `true` if a `Customer` owes at least $50. The query that follows selects objects from `customers` where the object is not a `PreferredCustomer`, has a `PaymentIsLate` value of `true`, and for which function `OwesALot` returns `true`.

```
private bool OwesALot(Customer customer)
{
    return customer.Balance <= -50m;
}
...
var query =
    from customer in customers
    where !(customer is PreferredCustomer) &&
        customer.PaymentIsLate &&
        OwesALot(customer)
    select customer;
```

The `where` clause can include just about any boolean expression, usually involving the selected objects and their properties. As the preceding example shows, it can include `!`, `is`, `&&`, and method calls.

Expressions can use any of the arithmetic, date, string, or other comparison operators. The following query selects `Order` objects from the `orders` array where the `OrderDate` property is after April 1, 2015:

```
var query =
    from order in orders
```

```
where order.OrderDate > new DateTime(2015, 4, 1)
select order;
```

orderby

The `orderby` clause sorts a query's results. Usually the values used to sort the results are properties of the objects selected. For example, the following query selects `Customer` objects from the `customers` array and sorts them by their `Balance` properties:

```
var query =
    from customer in customers
    orderby customer.Balance
    select customer;
```

This query sorts the customers by their `Balance` properties in ascending order.

If an `orderby` clause includes more than one field, the results are sorted by the first value and any ties are broken by the remaining fields. For example, the following query selects customers ordered by `Balance`. If two customers have the same `Balance`, they are ordered by `LastName`. If two customers have the same `Balance` and `LastName`, they are ordered by `FirstName`.

```
var query =
    from customer in customers
    orderby customer.Balance, customer.LastName, customer.FirstName
    select customer;
```

To arrange items in descending order, simply add the keyword `descending` after an ordering expression. Each expression can have its own `descending` keyword, so you can arrange them independently. For example, you could order customers by `Balance` ascending, `FirstName` descending, and `LastName` descending.

An `orderby` clause can include calculated values. For example, suppose the `Order` class has `Subtotal`, `Tax`, and `Shipping` properties. The following query orders its results by the sum of those values.

```
var query =
    from order in orders
    orderby order.Subtotal + order.Tax + order.Shipping
    select order;
```

Note that the values used for ordering results are not necessarily the values selected by the query. For example, the preceding query selects all the `Order` objects in the `orders` array, not those objects' total costs. The next section explains the `select` clause.

select

The `select` clause lists the fields that the query should select into its result. This can be an entire object taken from a data source or it can be one or more fields taken from multiple data sources. It can include the results of methods or calculations performed on the object's fields. It can even include more complicated things such as the results of nested queries.

The following query selects the concatenated first and last names of the `Customer` objects in the `customers` array.

```
var query =
    from customer in customers
    orderby customer.FirstName + " " + customer.LastName
    select customer.FirstName + " " + customer.LastName;
```

If you want to select more than one field from the query's objects, use the `new` keyword followed by the values enclosed in braces. For example, the following query selects `Customer` objects' concatenated first and last names plus their `Balance` values.

```
var query =
    from customer in customers
    orderby customer.FirstName + " " + customer.LastName
    select new
    {
        Name = customer.FirstName + " " + customer.LastName,
        customer.Balance
    };
```

This technique creates objects of an *anonymous type* that has properties holding the selected values.

If you select a simple property from a query object, the anonymous type's property has the same name. In this example, the value `customer.Balance` is stored in the anonymous object's `Balance` property.

If you select a calculated value, you must specify a name for the anonymous type's property. In this example, the calculated value `customer.FirstName + " " + customer.LastName` is stored in a property called `Name`.

> **DUPLICATE NAMES**
>
> If you select values with the same name from multiple objects, you must give a new name to at least one of them so that the anonymous type doesn't have two properties with the same name.

Later you can use the anonymous type's property names when you process the results. The following code shows how a program might display the results from the preceding query.

```
foreach (var obj in query)
    Console.WriteLine(obj.Name + ": " + obj.Balance);
```

The queries shown so far return objects of an anonymous type. If you like, you can define a type to hold the results and then create new objects of that type in the `select` clause. For example, suppose the `BalanceInfo` class has `Name` and `Balance` properties. The following query selects the same data as the preceding query but this time saves the results in new `BalanceInfo` objects:

```
var query =
    from customer in customers
    orderby customer.FirstName + " " + customer.LastName
```

```
select new BalanceInfo
{
    Name = customer.FirstName + " " + customer.LastName,
    Balance = customer.Balance
};
```

THE NAME GAME

If you like, you can give new names to noncalculated values selected from the query objects. For example, the following query selects the concatenated name and balance from Customer objects. It calls the concatenated name Name and it calls the balance OutstandingBalance.

```
var query =
    from customer in customers
    orderby customer.FirstName + " " + customer.LastName
    select new
    {
        Name = customer.FirstName + " " + customer.LastName,
        OutstandingBalance = customer.Balance
    };
```

The result contains BalanceInfo objects instead of objects with an anonymous type. That means the program can use an explicitly typed BalanceInfo object to loop through the result as shown in the following code.

```
foreach (BalanceInfo info in query)
    Console.WriteLine(info.Name + ": " + info.Balance);
```

You can also use a class's constructors to select a new instance of the class. For example, suppose the BalanceInfo class has a constructor that takes a name and account balance as parameters. The following code shows how you could modify the previous query to use that constructor.

```
var query =
    from customer in customers
    orderby customer.FirstName + " " + customer.LastName
    select new BalanceInfo(
        customer.FirstName + " " + customer.LastName,
        customer.Balance);
```

Using LINQ Results

A LINQ query expression returns an IEnumerable containing the query's results. A program can iterate through this result and process the items that it contains.

To determine what objects are contained in the IEnumerable result, you need to look carefully at the select clause. If this clause picks a simple value such as a string or int, the result contains those simple values.

For example, the following query selects customer first and last names concatenated into a single string. The result is a `string`, so the query's `IEnumerable` result contains `strings` and the `foreach` loop can treat them as `strings`.

```
var query =
    from customer in customers
    select customer.FirstName + " " + customer.LastName;

foreach (string name in query)
    Console.WriteLine(name);
```

Often the `select` clause picks some sort of object. The following query selects the `Customer` objects contained in the `customers` array. The result contains `Customer` objects, so the code can use an explicitly typed `Customer` for its looping variable.

```
var query =
    from customer in customers
    select customer;

foreach (Customer customer in query)
    Console.WriteLine(customer.FirstName + " " + customer.LastName);
```

ADVANCED LINQ QUERY SYNTAX

So far this chapter has described basic LINQ commands that you might expect to use regularly, but there's much more to LINQ than these simple queries. The following sections describe some of the more advanced LINQ commands that are less intuitive and that you probably won't need to use as often.

join

The `join` keyword selects data from multiple data sources matching up corresponding fields. The following pseudocode shows the `join` clause's syntax:

```
from variable1 in dataSource1
join variable2 in dataSource2
  on variable1.field1 equals variable2.field2
```

For example, the following query selects `Customer` objects from the `customers` array. For each `Customer` object, it selects `Order` objects from the `orders` array where the two records have the same `CustomerId` value.

```
var query =
    from customer in customers
    join order in orders on customer.CustomerId equals order.CustomerId
    select new { customer, order };
```

> **FINICKY JOINS**
>
> The syntax for the `join` clause is fairly finicky. The on portion must list the "`from`" variable first and the "`join`" variable second. It must also include the `equals` keyword and you cannot include other operators such as `==`, `<=`, or `!=`.
>
> If you need to use an operator such as `!=`, try using a `where` clause instead of a `join`.

join into

You can add an `into` clause to the `join` clause to group the joined values into a list with a specified new name. For example, consider the following query. (The new elements are shown in bold.)

```
var query =
    from customer in customers
    join order in orders on customer.CustomerId equals order.CustomerId
        into CustomerOrders
    select new { customer, CustomerOrders };
```

This query selects `Customer` and `Order` data much as the previous query did. This time, however, the `Order` items selected by the `join` clause are placed in a list named `CustomerOrders`. The `select` clause then selects each `Customer` object plus its `CustomerOrders` list.

The following code shows how a program could loop through the results.

```
foreach (var group in query)
{
    Console.WriteLine(group.customer.FirstName + " " + group.customer.LastName);
    foreach (Order order in group.CustomerOrders)
        Console.WriteLine("    Order: " + order.OrderId);
}
```

For each group object in the results, the program displays that group's customer name. It then loops through the group's `CustomerOrders` list, displaying each `Order` object's `OrderId`. The following text shows some sample output.

```
Art Anderson
    Order: 1
    Order: 2
Betty Baker
    Order: 3
Carl Carter
```

In this example, customer Art Anderson had two orders with `OrderId` values 1 and 2, Betty Baker had one order with `OrderId` 3, and Carl Carter had no orders.

group by

Like `join into`, `group by` enables a program to gather related values together into groups. It also returns an `IEnumerable` that holds objects, each containing another `IEnumerable`.

The following code shows an example.

```
var query =
    from order in orders
    group order by order.CustomerId;
```

This query selects `Order` objects from the `orders` array. The `group order` part of the query means you want to select the `order` objects and you want to group them. The `by order.CustomerId` part of the query means the objects should be grouped by their `CustomerId` properties.

The result is a list of objects representing the groups. Each of those objects has a `Key` property that gives the value that was used to build that group. In this example, the `Key` is the value of the objects' `CustomerId` values.

Each of the objects is also enumerable so the program can loop through the objects that are in its group.

The following code shows how a program could display the results of this query.

```
foreach (var group in query)
{
    Console.WriteLine("Customer " + group.Key + ":");
    foreach (Order order in group)
        Console.WriteLine("    Order: " + order.OrderId);
}
```

This code loops over the groups in the query's results. For each group object, the program displays the group's `Key`. It then loops through the group displaying its `Order` objects.

If you add an `into` clause after the `group by` section, you can give the group data a name that you can use later in a `select` clause. For example, consider the following query.

```
var query =
    from order in orders
    group order by order.CustomerId into CustomerOrders
    select new { ID = CustomerOrders.Key, Orders = CustomerOrders };
```

Like the previous example, this query selects `Order` objects grouped by `CustomerId`. It gives the grouped data the name `CustomerOrders`. The `select` clause then uses that name to select the grouped data's `Key` and the grouped data itself.

The following code shows how a program could display the results.

```
foreach (var group in query)
{
    Console.WriteLine("Customer " + group.ID + ":");
    foreach (Order order in group.Orders)
        Console.WriteLine("    Order: " + order.OrderId);
}
```

This code is similar to the previous version except it uses the names `ID` and `Orders` that the `select` clause used to name the selected pieces of data.

Aggregate Values

When you group data, you can use *aggregate methods* to select combined values. For example, suppose you select Order objects grouped by CustomerId so each group in the result contains the orders placed by a single customer. Then you could use the Sum method to calculate the sum of the prices of the orders in each group. The following query shows an example with the Sum method highlighted in bold.

```
var query =
    from order in orders
    group order by order.CustomerId into Orders
    select new
    {
        ID = Orders.Key,
        Orders,
        TotalPrice = Orders.Sum(order => order.Price)
    };
```

This query selects Order objects from the orders array, groups them by CustomerId, and gives the name Orders to the groups.

The select clause selects each group's Key (which is the CustomerId value used to create the group) and the group itself.

For a final selection, the query takes the Orders group and calls its Sum extension method. The Sum method takes as a parameter a method that it should use to select a numeric value from the objects over which it is taking the sum, in this case the Order objects in the group. This example uses a lambda expression that simply returns an Order object's Price property. (For information on lambda expressions, see the section "Lambda Expressions" in Chapter 6.)

The following code shows how a program can display the results.

```
foreach (var group in query)
{
    Console.WriteLine("Customer " + group.ID + ": " +
        group.TotalPrice.ToString("C"));
    foreach (Order order in group.Orders)
    {
        Console.WriteLine("    Order " + order.OrderId + ": " +
            order.Price.ToString("C"));
    }
}
```

This code loops over the groups returned by the query. For each group, it displays the group's ID (which holds the CustomerId used to build the group) and the group's TotalPrice (which was calculated by the Sum method). The code then loops through the Order objects that make up the group and displays the objects' OrderId and Price properties.

The following text shows some sample output.

```
Customer 1: $41.50
    Order 1: $16.00
    Order 3: $25.50
Customer 2: $13.20
    Order 2: $13.20
```

The following list summarizes LINQ's aggregate methods.

➤ `Aggregate`—Uses a method that you specify to perform some calculation on the values

➤ `Average`—Returns the average of the values

➤ `Count`—Returns the number of items that satisfy a condition

➤ `Sum`—Returns the sum of the values

➤ `LongCount`—Returns the number of items that satisfy a condition as a `long`

➤ `Max`—Returns the maximum value

➤ `Min`—Returns the minimum value

Set Methods

Set methods modify a set of items. For example, the `Union` method creates the union of two sets. C# does not provide a special syntax for including these methods in a LINQ query, so you must invoke the methods directly. Fortunately these methods are easy to use.

For example, suppose the `ordersPaid` and `ordersDue` arrays contain `Order` objects representing customer orders that have been paid and that are due, respectively. The following statement uses the `Union` method to create a new array containing all the orders in both arrays.

```
Order[] allOrders = ordersPaid.Union(ordersDue).ToArray();
```

The result of the `Union` method is an iterator that you could loop over with a `foreach` statement. This example calls the result's `ToArray` method to convert it into an array.

You can apply these methods to the results of a query. For example, the following query examines the `orders` array and selects the `Order` objects' `CustomerId` values. The code then uses the `Distinct` method to restrict the result to only distinct values. The following `foreach` statement displays the distinct values.

```
var query =
    (from order in orders select order.CustomerId).Distinct();
foreach (int id in query)
    Console.WriteLine(id);
```

The following list summarizes LINQ's set methods.

`Concat`—Returns two result sets concatenated

`Distinct`—Returns a set without duplicates

`Except`—Returns the items in one set except those that are also in a second set

`Intersect`—Returns the items that are in both of two set

`Union`—Returns the items that are in either of two set

Limiting Results

The following list summarizes methods that LINQ provides for limiting the results returned by a query.

➤ `First`—Returns the first result and discards the rest. If the result includes no values, this throws an exception.

➤ `FirstOrDefault`—Returns the first result and discards the rest. If the query contains no results, it returns a default value.

➤ `Last`—Returns the last result and discards the rest. If the result includes no values, this throws an exception.

➤ `LastOrDefault`—Returns the last result and discards the rest. If the query contains no results, it returns a default value.

➤ `Single`—Returns the single item selected by the query. If the query does not contain exactly one result, this throws an exception.

➤ `SingleOrDefault`—Returns the single item selected by the query. If the query contains no results, this returns a default value. If the query contains more than one item, this throws an exception.

➤ `Skip`—Discards a specified number of results and keeps the rest.

➤ `SkipWhile`—Discards results as long as some condition is `true` and then keeps the rest. (The condition is given by a method, often a lambda expression.)

➤ `Take`—Keeps a specified number of results and discards the rest.

➤ `TakeWhile`—Keeps results as long as some condition is `true` and then discards the rest.

For example, the following query selects `Customer` objects in order of increasing `Balance` property. The expression `Take(10)` selects the first 10 values and discards the rest. (If the result holds fewer than 10 values, the statement takes them all.) The result is a list of the 10 customers with the smallest balances.

```
var query =
    (from customer in customers
     orderby customer.Balance
     select customer).Take(10);
```

The following query uses the `TakeWhile` method to select all Customer objects with Balance properties less than −50.

```
var query =
    (from customer in customers
     orderby customer.Balance
     select customer).TakeWhile(customer => customer.Balance < -50m);
```

OTHER LINQ METHODS

LINQ provides several other extension methods that are not supported by C#'s query syntax. You cannot use them in queries, but you can apply them to the results of queries.

The following list describes some of the more useful remaining LINQ extensions that aren't supported by C#'s query syntax.

➤ `Contains`—Returns `true` if the result contains a specific value.

➤ `DefaultIfEmpty`—If the query's result is not empty, returns the result. If the result is empty, returns an `IEnumerable` containing a default value.

➤ `ElementAt`—Returns the element at a specific position in the query's result. If there is no element at that position, this throws an exception.

➤ `ElementAtOrDefault`—Returns the element at a specific position in the query's result. If there is no element at that position, this returns a default value.

➤ `Empty`—Creates an empty `IEnumerable`.

➤ `Range`—Creates an `IEnumerable` containing a range of integer values. For example, `Enumerable.Range(100, 5)` returns five numbers starting at 100: 100, 101, 102, 103, and 104.

➤ `Repeat`—Creates an `IEnumerable` containing a value repeated a specified number of times.

➤ `SequenceEqual`—Returns `true` if two sequences are identical.

LINQ also provides methods that convert results into new data types. The following list summarizes these methods.

➤ `AsEnumerable`—Converts the result into a typed `IEnumerable<T>`

➤ `AsQueryable`—Converts an `IEnumerable` into an `IQueryable`

➤ `OfType`—Removes items that cannot be cast into a specified type

➤ `ToArray`—Returns an array containing the results

➤ `ToDictionary`—Places the results in a `Dictionary` using a selector function to set each item's key

➤ `ToList`—Returns a `List<T>` containing the results

➤ `ToLookup`—Places the results in a `System.Linq.Lookup` (one-to-many dictionary) using a selector function to set each item's key

Note that the `ToArray`, `ToDictionary`, `ToList`, and `ToLookup` functions force the query to execute immediately instead of waiting until the program accesses the results.

INTRODUCTION TO GENERICS

Chapter 15, "Generics," explains generics, but they play a big role in LINQ, so you should at least have some idea of what they are before continuing. A generic class or method takes a data type as a *generic parameter*. Its code can then create variables of that type and manipulate them.

For example, the `AsEnumerable` method described in the preceding list converts a result into a typed `IEnumerable<T>`. This is an object that implements the `IEnumerable<T>` interface, an interface that takes a generic parameter. The actual result could be `IEnumerable<int>`, `IEnumerable<decimal>`, or `IEnumerable<Person>` depending on what kind of data you pass into the `AsEnumerable` method.

In this chapter, you can mostly ignore these generic parameters, and LINQ will use the type that's appropriate for your data. See Chapter 15 for more on generics.

LINQ EXTENSION METHODS

As was mentioned earlier in this chapter, C# doesn't actually execute LINQ queries. Instead it converts them into a series of method calls (provided by extension methods) that perform the query. Though C#'s LINQ query syntax is generally easier to use, it is sometimes helpful to understand what those method calls look like.

The following sections explain the general form of these method calls. They explain how the method calls are built, how you can use these methods directly in your code, and how you can extend LINQ to add your own query methods.

Method-Based Queries

Suppose a program defines an array of `Customer` objects named `customers` and then defines the following query.

```
var query =
    from customer in customers
    where customer.Balance < 0
    orderby customer.Balance
    select new
    {
        CustName = customer.FirstName + " " + customer.LastName,
        CustBalance = customer.Balance
    };
```

This query finds customers that have `Balance` less than zero, orders them by `Balance`, and returns a result that can enumerate their names and balances.

To perform this selection, C# converts the query into a series of function calls to form a *method-based query* that performs the same tasks as the original query. For example, the following method-based query returns roughly the same results as the original LINQ query:

```
var query =
    customers.Where(OwesMoney).
    OrderBy(OrderByAmount).
    Select(MakeObject);
```

This code calls the customers list's Where method. It passes that method the OwesMoney method, which returns true if a Customer object has a negative account balance.

The code then calls the OrderBy method of the result returned by Where. It passes OrderBy the OrderByAmount method, which returns a decimal value that OrderBy can use to order the results of Where.

Finally, the code calls the Select method of the result returned by OrderBy. It passes Select the MakeObject method. That method creates a CustInfo object that has CustName and CustBalance properties.

The exact series of method calls generated by C# to evaluate the LINQ query is somewhat different from the one shown here. The version shown here uses the OwesMoney, OrderByAmount, and MakeObject methods defined in the program to help filter, order, and select data. The method-based query generated by C# uses automatically generated anonymous types and lambda expressions, so it is much uglier.

The following code shows the OwesMoney, OrderByAmount, and MakeObject methods.

```
// Return true if this Customer has Balance < 0.
private bool OwesMoney(Customer customer)
{
    return customer.Balance < 0;
}

// Return the Customer's balance. This is used to order results.
private decimal OrderByAmount(Customer customer)
{
    return customer.Balance;
}

// A class to hold selected Customer information.
class CustInfo
{
    public string CustName { get; set; }
    public decimal CustBalance{ get; set; }
}

// Create a new CustInfo object.
private CustInfo MakeObject(Customer customer, int index)
{
    return new CustInfo()
    {
        CustName = customer.FirstName + customer.LastName,
```

```
            CustBalance = customer.Balance
    };
}
```

This code defines the methods that are passed as parameters to the query's `Where`, `OrderBy`, and `Select` calls, but where are `Where`, `OrderBy`, and `Select` defined? They are called as if they are methods provided by `customers`, but `customers` is simply an array of `Customer` objects and it doesn't define those methods.

It turns out that `Where`, `OrderBy`, and `Select` are extension methods added to the `IEnumerable` interface by the LINQ library. Arrays implement that interface so they gain these extension methods.

Similarly, LINQ adds other extension methods to the `IEnumerable` interface such as `Any`, `All`, `Average`, `Count`, `Distinct`, `First`, `GroupBy`, `OfType`, `Repeat`, `Sum`, `Union`, and many more.

Method-Based Queries with Lambda Functions

Lambda expressions make building method-based queries somewhat easier. When you use lambda expressions, you don't need to define separate methods to pass as parameters to LINQ methods such as `Where`, `OrderBy`, and `Select`. Instead, you can pass a lambda expression directly into the method.

The following code shows a revised version of the previous method-based query. Here the method bodies have been included as lambda expressions.

```
var query =
    customers.Where(customer => customer.Balance < 0).
    OrderBy(customer => customer.Balance).
    Select(customer => new CustInfo()
        {
            CustName = customer.FirstName + " " + customer.LastName,
            CustBalance = customer.Balance
        }
    );
```

This is more concise because it doesn't require you to build separate methods, but it can be a lot harder to read and understand. Passing a simple lambda expression to the `Where` or `OrderBy` method may not be too confusing, but if you need to perform complex tests, you may be better off making separate methods.

Whether you use methods or lambda expressions, the standard LINQ query syntax is usually easier to understand, so you may prefer to use that version whenever possible. Unfortunately, many references describe the LINQ extension methods as if you are going to use them in method-based queries rather than in LINQ queries. For example, the description of the OrderBy method at msdn.microsoft.com/library/bb534966.aspx includes the following definition:

```
public static IOrderedEnumerable<TSource> OrderBy<TSource, TKey>(
        this IEnumerable<TSource> source,
        Func<TSource, TKey> keySelector
)
```

This declaration is quite confusing, but you can figure it out of you must. In this case the declaration means the following:

➤ The method is named `OrderBy`.

➤ It takes two generic type parameters: `TSource` and `TKey`.

➤ The method's return value has type `IOrderedEnumerable<TSource>`.

➤ The method extends `IEnumerable<TSource>`.

➤ The method takes as a parameter a `Func<TSource, TKey>`.

For more information on extension methods, see the section "Extension Methods" in Chapter 6. For more information on generics, see Chapter 15.

As previously mentioned, C#'s LINQ query syntax is usually easier to understand. One time when you need to use the more confusing method-style syntax is when you want to add your own LINQ extensions. The following section explains how you can write extension methods to add new features to LINQ.

Extending LINQ

LINQ queries return some sort of `IEnumerable` object. (Actually, they return some sort of `SelectIterator` creature but the result implements `IEnumerable`.) The items in the result may be simple types such as `int`, `string`, or `Customer` objects, or they may be of some bizarre anonymous type that groups several selected fields together. Whatever the items are, the result is some sort of `IEnumerable`.

Because the result is an `IEnumerable`, you can add new methods to the result by creating extension methods for `IEnumerable`.

For example, the following code defines a standard deviation function. It extends the `IEnumerable<decimal>` interface so it applies to the results of a LINQ query that fetches `decimal` values.

```
public static class MyLinqExtensions
{
    // Return the standard deviation of
    // the values in an IEnumerable<decimal>.
    public static decimal StdDev(this IEnumerable<decimal> source)
    {
        // Get the total.
        decimal total = source.Sum();

        // Calculate the mean.
        decimal mean = total / source.Count();

        // Calculate the sums of the deviations squared.
        var deviationsSquared =
            from decimal value in source
            select (value - mean) * (value - mean);
        decimal totalDeviationsSquared = deviationsSquared.Sum();
```

```
        // Return the standard deviation.
        return (decimal)Math.Sqrt((double)
            (totalDeviationsSquared / (source.Count() - 1)));
    }
}
```

> **NONSTANDARD STANDARDS**
>
> There are a couple different definitions for standard deviation. This topic is outside the scope of this book so it isn't explored here. For more information, see `mathworld.wolfram.com/StandardDeviation.html`.

Now the program can apply this method to the result of a LINQ query that selects decimal values. The following code uses a LINQ query to select Balance values from the customers array where the Balance is less than zero. It then calls the StdDev extension method and displays the result.

```
var query =
    from customer in customers
    where customer.Balance < 0
    select customer.Balance;
Console.WriteLine(query.StdDev());
```

The following code performs the same operations without storing the query in an intermediate variable:

```
Console.WriteLine(
    (from customer in customers
     where customer.Balance < 0
     select customer.Balance).StdDev());
```

LINQ TO OBJECTS

LINQ to Objects refers to methods that let a program extract data from objects that are extended by LINQ extension methods. These methods extend IEnumerable so that they apply to any class that implements IEnumerable including arrays, Dictionary, HashSet, LinkedList, Queue, SortedDictionary, SortedList, Stack, and others.

All the examples shown previously in this chapter use LINQ to Objects, so this section says no more about them. See the previous sections for more information and examples.

LINQ TO XML

LINQ to XML refers to methods that let a program move data between XML objects and other data-containing objects. For example, using LINQ to XML you can select customer data from arrays and use it to build an XML document. Chapter 24 explains general ways a C# program can manipulate XML data. The sections that follow describe LINQ to XML methods.

LINQ comes with its own assortment of XML elements. These classes, which are contained in the `System.Xml.Linq` namespace, correspond to similar classes in the `System.Xml` namespace; although their names begin with X instead of Xml. For example, the `System.Xml.Linq.XElement` class corresponds to `System.Xml.XmlElement`.

The LINQ versions of the XML classes provide many of the same features as the `System.Xml` versions, but they also provide support for LINQ features.

The following section explains how you can easily include XML data in your program. The two sections after that describe methods for using LINQ to move data into and out of XML objects.

XML Literals

C# does not support XML literals so you cannot type XML data directly into your program. You can, however, pass an XML object's `Parse` method a string containing XML data. If you prefix the string with the @ character, the string can even span multiple lines.

For example, the following code creates an `XElement` object containing an `<Employees>` element that holds three `<Employee>` elements.

```
// Read the XElement.
XElement xelement = XElement.Parse(
@"<Employees>
    <Employee FirstName=""Ann"" LastName=""Archer""/>
    <Employee FirstName='Ben' LastName='Baker'/>
    <Employee>
      <FirstName>Cindy</FirstName>
      <LastName>Cant</LastName>
    </Employee>
  </Employees>
");
```

The three `<Employee>` elements demonstrate three ways to give the elements `FirstName` and `LastName` values. The first uses two sets of double quotes to represent quotes in the data. When the C# compiler sees two pairs of double quotes inside a quoted string, it places a single double quote in the string's data.

The second `<Employee>` delimits its name values with single quotes. XML data can use single or double quotes to delimit values. Using single quotes makes the C# code a lot easier to read than using pairs of double quotes.

The first two `<Employee>` elements hold their `FirstName` and `LastName` values in attributes. The third `<Employee>` holds its values in sub-elements.

Building the same XML hierarchy by using `System.Xml` objects would take a lot more work. You would need to write code to create the `<Employees>` element. Then you would need to write code to create each of the `<Employee>` elements. You would need to add code to set the first two `<Employees>` elements' `FirstName` and `LastName` properties, and you would need to add code to create the final `<Employee>` element's `FirstName` and `LastName` child elements.

This is all reasonably straightforward but it is cumbersome. Parsing a string is much easier. Because the string shows the XML data's structure, parsing is also more intuitive.

LINQ into XML

LINQ's XML classes provide constructors that let you build XML documents relatively easily. Each constructor's parameter list ends with a parameter array so you can pass any number of items into it.

The constructors also know what to do with parameters of different types. For example, if you pass an XElement into another XElement's constructor, then the first element becomes a child of the second. If you pass an XAttribute object into an XElement's constructor, then the XAttribute object becomes an attribute of the XElement.

This lets you build XML structures in a fairly intuitive manner. The following code shows how you could use constructors to build the previous XML fragment.

```
XElement employees = new XElement("Employees",
    new XElement("Employee",
        new XAttribute("FirstName", "Ann"),
        new XAttribute("LastName", "Archer")
    ),
    new XElement("Employee",
        new XAttribute("FirstName", "Ben"),
        new XAttribute("LastName", "Baker")
    ),
    new XElement("Employee",
        new XElement("FirstName", "Cindy"),
        new XElement("LastName", "Cant")
    )
);
```

The code starts by creating the <Employees> element. It passes that object's constructor three <Employee> XElement objects so they become its children in the XML document.

The code passes the constructors for the first and second <Employee> elements two XAttribute objects so those objects become attributes of the elements.

The third <Employee> element's constructor takes as parameters two additional XElement objects so that element stores its FirstName and LastName values as separate elements.

This technique of building an XML document by using constructors is called *functional construction*.

The result is the same as the result given by parsing XML text in the previous section. Figure 8-1 shows a message box displaying the results of the employees object's ToString method.

Functional construction is reasonably straightforward, but it's still not quite as easy as parsing XML text, as demonstrated in the previous section. Functional construction does offer one advantage, however. If you pass an XML class's constructor an object that implements IEnumerable, the constructor enumerates it and adds all the items it contains to the XML hierarchy in an appropriate manner. That means you can use a LINQ query to create pieces of the XML structure.

FIGURE 8-1: Functional construction enables you to build XML documents relatively easily and intuitively.

For example, suppose a program has an array named `employees` that contains `Employee` objects. The following code uses LINQ and functional construction to build an XML fragment containing elements for each of the `Employee` objects.

```
// Use LINQ to create a list of <Employee> elements.
var makeEmployees =
    from employee in employees
    select new XElement("Employee",
        new XAttribute("FirstName", employee.FirstName),
        new XAttribute("LastName", employee.LastName));

// Create the XML document.
XElement document = new XElement("Employees", makeEmployees);
```

The code starts with a LINQ query that selects information from the `employees` array. For each `Employee` in the array, the query creates an `XElement`. It uses the `Employee` object's `FirstName` and `LastName` properties to create `XAttribute` objects for the `XElement`.

You can even include the LINQ query directly inside the top-level constructor, as shown in the following code.

```
XElement document2 = new XElement("Employees",
    from employee in employees
    select new XElement("Employee",
        new XAttribute("FirstName", employee.FirstName),
        new XAttribute("LastName", employee.LastName)));
```

LINQ out of XML

The LINQ XML objects provide a standard assortment of LINQ methods that make moving data from those objects into `IEnumerable` objects simple. Using these functions, it's about as easy to select data from the XML objects as it is from `IEnumerable` objects such as arrays and lists.

XML objects represent hierarchical data. To make using that data easier, the XML classes also provide methods to help you search those data hierarchies. For example, the `XElement` object provides a `Descendants` method that searches the object's descendants for elements of a certain type.

For example, the following code searches the `XElement` named `document` for descendants named "Employee" and displays their `FirstName` and `LastName` attributes.

```
var selectEmployee =
    from employee in document.Descendants("Employee")
    select new
    {
        FirstName = employee.Attribute("FirstName").Value,
        LastName = employee.Attribute("LastName").Value
    };
foreach (var obj in selectEmployee)
    Console.WriteLine(obj.FirstName + " " + obj.LastName);
```

The LINQ query selects objects from `document.Descendants("Employee")`. Each of the objects returned by the `Descendants` method is an `XElement`. The query uses that object's `Attribute` method to get the object's `FirstName` and `LastName` attributes. Those attributes are `XAttribute` objects, so the code uses their `Value` properties to get the attribute values. Finally, the query creates a new object of an anonymous type holding the `FirstName` and `LastName` attribute values.

The following table describes other methods supported by `XElement` that a program can use to navigate through an XML hierarchy. Most of these methods return `IEnumerable` objects that you can use in LINQ queries.

FUNCTION	RETURNS
Ancestors	IEnumerable containing all ancestors of the element.
AncestorsAndSelf	IEnumerable containing this element followed by all of its ancestors.
Attribute	The element's attribute with a specific name.
Attributes	IEnumerable containing the element's attributes.
Descendants	IEnumerable containing all descendants of the element.
DescendantsAndSelf	IEnumerable containing this element followed by all of its descendants.
DescendantNodes	IEnumerable containing all descendant nodes of the element. These include all nodes such as XElement and XText.
DescendantNodesAndSelf	IEnumerable containing this element followed by all its descendant nodes.
Element	The first child element with a specific name.
Elements	IEnumerable containing the immediate children of the element.
ElementsAfterSelf	IEnumerable containing the siblings of the element that come after this element.
ElementsBeforeSelf	IEnumerable containing the siblings of the element that come before this element.
Nodes	IEnumerable containing the nodes that are immediate children of the element. These include all nodes such as XElement and XText.
NodesAfterSelf	IEnumerable containing the sibling nodes of the element that come after this element.
NodesBeforeSelf	IEnumerable containing the sibling nodes of the element that come before this element.

Most of the methods that return an `IEnumerable` take an optional parameter that indicates the names of the elements to select. For example, if you pass the `Descendants` function the parameter "Customer," the function returns only the descendants of the element that are named "Customer."

LINQ TO ADO.NET

LINQ to ADO.NET provides tools that let you apply LINQ-style queries to objects used by ADO.NET to store and interact with relational data. LINQ to ADO.NET includes three components: LINQ to SQL, LINQ to Entities, and LINQ to DataSet. The following sections briefly give additional details about these three pieces.

LINQ to SQL and LINQ to Entities

LINQ to SQL and LINQ to Entities are object-relational mapping (O/RM) tools that build strongly typed classes for modeling databases. They generate classes to represent the database and the tables that it contains. LINQ features provided by these classes allow a program to query the data model objects.

For example, to build a database model for use by LINQ to SQL, select Project ➪ Add New Item command and add a new LINQ to SQL Classes item. This opens a designer where you can define the database's structure.

If you have SQL Server installed and running, you can drag SQL Server database objects from the Server Explorer to build the database model. If you drag all the database's tables onto the designer, you should see all the tables and their fields, primary keys, relationships, and other structural information. (Alternatively, you can use the designer's tools to build the data model yourself instead of building a model from the database's structure.)

As you create the data model, LINQ to SQL creates corresponding classes to represent the database and its tables. For example, it defines a class that inherits from DataContext to represent the database. If you named the data model SalesInfo, LINQ to SQL defines the class SalesInfoDataContext to represent the database.

Now suppose the program creates an instance of that class named db. Then the following code selects all the records from the database's Customers table ordered by name:

```
var query =
    from customer in db.Customers
    orderby customer.FirstName, customer.LastName
    select new { customer.FirstName, customer.LastName };
```

Microsoft intends LINQ to SQL to be a tool for quickly building LINQ-enabled classes for use with SQL Server databases. The designer can take a SQL Server database, build a model for it, and then create the necessary classes.

LINQ to Entities provides support for writing queries against Entity Framework data models. The Entity Framework is intended for use in more complicated enterprise scenarios than LINQ to SQL. It allows extra abstraction that decouples a data object model from the underlying database. For example, the Entity Framework allows you to store pieces of a single conceptual object in more than one database table.

Building and managing SQL Server databases and the Entity Framework are topics too large to cover in this book so LINQ to SQL and LINQ to Entities are not described in more detail here. For more information, consult the online help or Microsoft's website. Some of Microsoft's relevant web pages include:

➤ LINQ to SQL (msdn.microsoft.com/bb386976.aspx)

➤ LINQ to Entities (msdn.microsoft.com/library/bb386964.aspx)

➤ LINQ to SQL: .NET Language-Integrated Query for Relational Data (msdn.microsoft.com/bb425822.aspx)

➤ Data Developer Center ➪ Learn ➪ Entity Framework (msdn.microsoft.com/en-US/data/ef)

LINQ to DataSet

LINQ to DataSet lets a program use LINQ-style queries to select data from `DataSet` objects. A `DataSet` contains an in-memory representation of data contained in relational tables.

A `DataSet` can hold data and provide query capabilities whether the data was loaded from SQL Server, from some other relational database, or by the program's code.

The `DataSet` object itself doesn't provide many LINQ features. It is mostly useful because it holds `DataTable` objects that represent groupings of items, much as `IEnumerable` objects do.

The `DataTable` class does not directly support LINQ either, but it has an `AsEnumerable` method that converts the `DataTable` into an `IEnumerable`, which you already know supports LINQ.

> ### WHERE'S IENUMERABLE?
>
> Actually, the `AsEnumerable` method converts the `DataTable` into an `EnumerableRowCollection` object but that object implements `IEnumerable`.

The LinqToDataSetScores example program, which is available for download on the book's website, demonstrates several LINQ to `DataSet` techniques. This program builds a `DataSet` that holds two tables. The `Students` table has fields `StudentId`, `FirstName`, and `LastName`. The `TestScores` table has fields `StudentId`, `TestNumber`, and `Score`. The tables' `StudentId` fields provide the link between the two tables.

The program uses the following code to get references to the `DataTable` objects that represent the tables.

```
// Get references to the tables.
DataTable studentsTable = testScoresDataSet.Tables["Students"];
DataTable scoresTable = testScoresDataSet.Tables["TestScores"];
```

The program then uses the following code to select the names of students with `LastName` before "F" alphabetically:

```
var namesBeforeFQuery =
    from student in studentsTable.AsEnumerable()
    where (student.Field<string>("LastName").CompareTo("F") < 0)
```

```
            orderby student.Field<string>("LastName")
            select new
            {
                FirstName = student.Field<string>("FirstName"),
                LastName = student.Field<string>("LastName")
            };
    namesBeforeDDataGrid.DataSource = namesBeforeFQuery.ToList();
```

There are only a few differences between this query and previous LINQ queries. First, the `from` clause calls the `DataTable` object's `AsEnumerable` method to convert the table into something that supports LINQ.

Second, the syntax `student.Field<string>("FirstName")` lets the query access the `LastName` field in the `student` object. (The `student` object is a `DataRow` within the `DataTable`.)

Finally, the last line of code in this example sets a `DataGrid` control's `DataSource` property equal to the result returned by the query to make the control display the results. The `DataGrid` control cannot display the `IEnumerable` result. so the code calls the `ToList` method to convert the result into a list, which the `DataGrid` can use.

The following list summarizes the key differences between a LINQ to DataSet query and a normal LINQ to Objects query:

➤ The LINQ to DataSet query must use the `DataTable` object's `AsEnumerable` method to make the object queryable.

➤ The code can access the fields in a `DataRow`, as in `student.Field<string>("LastName")`.

➤ If you want to display the results in a bound control such as a `DataGrid` or `ListBox`, use the query's `ToList` method.

If you understand these key differences, the rest of the query is similar to those used by LINQ to Objects. The following code shows a second query demonstrated by the program:

```
    // Select all students and their scores.
    var allScoresQuery =
        from student in studentsTable.AsEnumerable()
        join score in scoresTable.AsEnumerable()
            on student.Field<int>("StudentId") equals score.Field<int>("StudentId")
        orderby student.Field<int>("StudentId"), score.Field<int>("TestNumber")
        select new
        {
            ID = student.Field<int>("StudentId"),
            Name = student.Field<string>("FirstName") + " " +
                student.Field<string>("LastName"),
            Test = score.Field<int>("TestNumber"),
            Score = score.Field<int>("Score")
        };
    allScoresDataGrid.DataSource = allScoresQuery.ToList();
```

This query selects records from the `Students` table, joins them with the corresponding records in the `TestScores` table, and orders the results by student ID and test number. It selects student

ID, first and last names, test number, and score. It then displays the result of the query in the `allScoresDataGrid` control.

The following code shows a more complicated example.

```
// Make a function to convert a numeric grade to a letter grade.
Func<double, string> letterGrade = score =>
{
    if (score >= 90) return "A";
    if (score >= 80) return "B";
    if (score >= 70) return "C";
    if (score >= 60) return "D";
    return "F";
};

// Display names, averages, and grades for A students.
var aStudents =
    from student in studentsTable.AsEnumerable()
    join score in scoresTable.AsEnumerable()
        on student.Field<int>("StudentId") equals score.Field<int>("StudentId")
    group score by student into studentGroup
    where studentGroup.Average(s => s.Field<int>("Score")) >= 90
    orderby studentGroup.Average(s => s.Field<int>("Score")) descending
    select new
    {
        Name = studentGroup.Key.Field<string>("FirstName") + " " +
            studentGroup.Key.Field<string>("LastName"),
        Average = studentGroup.Average(s => s.Field<int>("Score")),
        Grade = letterGrade(studentGroup.Average(s => s.Field<int>("Score")))
    };
aStudentsDataGrid.DataSource = aStudents.ToList();
```

This code starts by defining a `Func<double, string>` delegate and setting it equal to a statement lambda that converts a numeric grade into a letter grade.

Next, the code defines a query that selects corresponding records from the `Students` and `TestScores` tables. It groups the records by `student`, so the records for a particular `student` are gathered in a group called `studentGroup`.

The `where` clause uses the `studentGroup`'s `Average` method to calculate the average of the `Score` values in the group. (The items in `studentGroup` are the `TestScore` records for a `student`. This statement takes the average of the `Score` fields in those `TestScore` objects.) The `where` clause then picks the records where the average of the student's test scores is at least 90.

The `orderby` clause orders the results by the students' average scores.

Finally, the `select` clause selects the students' first and last names, average test score, and average test score converted into a letter grade.

The snippet finishes by displaying the results in the `aStudentsDataGrid` control. Figure 8-2 shows the program displaying this information.

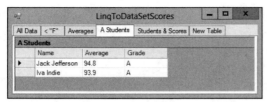

FIGURE 8-2: Example program LinqToDataSetScores displays (among other things) name, test score average, and letter grade for A students.

LINQ to DataSet not only allows you to pull data out of a `DataSet` but also provides a way to put data into a `DataSet`. If the query selects `DataRow` objects, then the query's `CopyToDataTable` method converts the query results into a new `DataTable` object that you can then add to a `DataSet`. The following code demonstrates this technique.

```
// Make a new table.
var newTableQuery =
    from student in studentsTable.AsEnumerable()
    where student.Field<string>("LastName").CompareTo("D") < 0
    select student;
DataTable newDataTable = newTableQuery.CopyToDataTable();
newDataTable.TableName = "NewTable";
testScoresDataSet.Tables.Add(newDataTable);
newTableDataGrid.DataSource = newDataTable;
```

This code selects records from the `Students` table for students with last name that come before "D" alphabetically. It then uses `CopyToDataTable` to convert the result into a `DataTable`. It gives the table a name and adds it to the `DataSet`. It finishes by displaying the results in the `newTableDataGrid` control.

PLINQ

Parallel LINQ (PLINQ pronounced "plink") allows a program to execute LINQ queries across multiple processors or cores in a multicore system. If you have multiple cores or CPU's and a nicely parallelizable query, PLINQ may improve your performance considerably.

So what kinds of queries are "nicely parallelizable?" The short, glib answer is, "It doesn't really matter." Microsoft has gone to great lengths to minimize the overhead of PLINQ, so using PLINQ may help for some queries and shouldn't hurt you too much for queries that don't parallelize nicely.

Simple queries that select items from a data source often parallelize well. If the items in the source can be examined, selected, and otherwise processed independently, then the query is parallelizable.

Queries that must use multiple items at the same time do not parallelize as efficiently. For example, adding an `orderby` clause to the query forces the program to gather all the results and sort them so that part of the query at least will not benefit from PLINQ.

Adding parallelism to LINQ is remarkably simple. Simply add a call to `AsParallel` to the enumerable object that you're searching. The FindPrimes example program, which is available for download on the book's website, uses PLINQ to find prime numbers. The program uses the following `IsPrime` method.

```
private static bool IsPrime(int number)
{
    if (number % 2 == 0) return false;
    for (int i = 3; i * i <= number; i += 2)
        if (number % i == 0) return false;
    return true;
}
```

THE NEED FOR SPEED

Some feel that adding parallelism to LINQ is kind of like giving caffeine to a snail. A snail is slow. Giving it caffeine might speed it up a bit (or perhaps kill it), but you'd get a much bigger performance gain if you got rid of the snail and got a cheetah instead.

Similarly, LINQ isn't all that fast. Adding parallelism will speed it up, but you'll probably get a larger speed improvement by moving the data into a database or using special-purpose algorithms designed to manage your particular data.

This argument is true, but you don't use LINQ because it's fast; you use it because it's convenient, easy to use, and flexible. Adding parallelism makes it a bit faster and is so easy that it doesn't cost you much effort.

If you really need significant performance improvements, you should consider moving the data into a database or more sophisticated data structure, but if you're using LINQ anyway, you may as well take advantage of PLINQ when you can.

The program uses the `IsPrime` method in the following PLINQ query. The call to `AsParallel` is highlighted in bold.

```
var primes =
    from number in Enumerable.Range(2, maxNumber).AsParallel()
    where IsPrime(number)
    select number;
```

The program times this query with and without the call to `AsParallel`. On my dual-core system, this query without `AsParallel` takes approximately 12.38 seconds to find all the primes between 2 and 10 million. Using PLINQ the program takes only 7.34 seconds. This is more than one-half the time for the nonparallel version because there's some overhead in managing the parallel threads. It's still a nice speed improvement for little extra typing.

PUZZLING PARALLELISM

For small enumerable objects (lists containing only a few items) and on computers that have only a single CPU, the overhead of using `AsParallel` may actually slow down execution slightly.

SUMMARY

LINQ lets you perform SQL-like queries in C# code. Depending on which form of LINQ you use, the development environment may provide strong type checking and IntelliSense support.

LINQ to Objects lets you query arrays, lists, and other objects that implement the IEnumerable interface.

LINQ to XML and the LINQ XML classes let you use LINQ to extract data from XML hierarchies. You can generate XML documents by parsing text or by using functional construction.

LINQ to ADO.NET (which includes LINQ to SQL, LINQ to Entities, and LINQ to DataSet) allows a program to perform queries on objects representing data in a relational database. Together these LINQ tools allow a program to select data in powerful new ways.

If you have a multicode system, PLINQ can sometimes speed up your LINQ queries with little effort on your part.

For much more information on the various LINQ technologies, see the online help and the web. The following list includes several useful Microsoft web pages that you can visit to learn more about LINQ. Some are a bit old but they still provide valuable information.

➤ **Getting Started with LINQ in C#**—msdn.microsoft.com/library/bb397933.aspx.

➤ **Hooked on LINQ (a wiki with some useful "5 Minute Overviews")**—www.hookedonlinq .com/LINQtoSQL5MinuteOverview.ashx.

➤ **LINQ to Objects**—msdn.microsoft.com/library/bb397919.aspx.

➤ **LINQ to XML**—msdn.microsoft.com/library/bb387098.aspx.

➤ **LINQ to SQL**—msdn.microsoft.com/bb386976.aspx.

➤ **101 C# LINQ Samples**—code.msdn.microsoft.com/101-LINQ-Samples-3fb9811b.

➤ **LINQ jump page**—msdn.microsoft.com/bb397926.aspx.

➤ **Querying DataSets—Introduction to LINQ to DataSet (by Erick Thompson, ADO. NET Program Manager, in the ADO.NET team blog)** — blogs.msdn.com/adonet/ archive/2007/01/26/querying-datasets-introduction-to-linq-to-dataset.aspx.

➤ **LINQ to SQL: .NET Language-Integrated Query for Relational Data**—msdn.microsoft .com/bb425822.aspx.

➤ **Entity Framework Overview**—msdn.microsoft.com/library/bb399567.aspx.

➤ **Parallel LINQ (PLINQ)**—msdn.microsoft.com/dd460688.aspx.

The LINQPad tool available at www.linqpad.net helps you interactively write LINQ queries and can execute them against a database without compiling a program. It comes in free, pro, and premium editions.

Using the C# statements and techniques described in Chapters 4 through 8, you can build applications that are extremely powerful and complex. Actually, you can build applications that are so complex it's hard to ensure that they work correctly. Even a relatively simple application can run into problems and large applications are practically guaranteed to contain bugs. Chapter 9, "Error Handling," explains how you can protect an application from unexpected errors and let it take action to correct problems, or at least to avoid crashing.

EXERCISES

1. Write a program that uses functional construction to build an `XElement` representing the following XML volleyball league data.

```
<League Night='Wednesday'>
    <Teams>
        <Team Name='Bling'>
            <Players>
                <Player FirstName='Anthony' LastName='Bell' />
                <Player FirstName='Jacqueline' LastName='Walker' />
            </Players>
        </Team>
        <Team Name='Flying Dolphins'>
            <Players>
                <Player FirstName='Steve' LastName='Foster' />
                <Player FirstName='Phyllis' LastName='Henderson' />
            </Players>
        </Team>
    </Teams>
    <Matches>
        <Match>
            <Team Name='Bling' Score='25'/>
            <Team Name='Flying Dolphins' Score='19'/>
        </Match>
    </Matches>
</League>
```

If `root` is the name of the root `XElement`, display the data by using the statement `Console.WriteLine(root.ToString())`.

2. The VolleyballTeams example program has an `XmlString` method that returns a string containing XML data similar to the data shown in Exercise 1 but with more teams, players, and match data. Download that program and modify it so it parses the data to build an XML hierarchy and displays the result.

3. Copy the program you build for Exercise 2 and modify it to use LINQ to XML to display the teams and their players. The result should look like the following:

```
Bling
    Anthony Bell
    Jacqueline Walker
    ...
Flying Dolphins
    Steve Foster
    Phyllis Henderson
    ...
...
```

4. Copy the program you build for Exercise 2 and modify it to use LINQ to XML to display the teams and the numbers of points they won in each of their matches. The result should look like the following:

```
Team                   Points
====                   ======
Bling                      25
Bling                      25
Bling                      14
Bling                      19
Bling                      25
Flying Dolphins            19
Flying Dolphins            25
Flying Dolphins            22
Flying Dolphins            14
Flying Dolphins            19
. . .
```

5. Copy the program you build for Exercise 4 and modify it to display each team's total number of wins (assume a team wins if it got 25 points in a match) and total number of points. Order the results by total wins followed by total points, both descending so the best teams come first. The result should look like the following:

```
Name                 Wins    Points
====                 ====    ======
Sand Crabs              4       119
Golden Spikers          4       117
Bling                   3       108
The Wee Free People     2        95
Flying Dolphins         1        99
Hurricanes              1        95
```

6. Copy the program you build for Exercise 2 and modify it to use LINQ to DataSet to create a volleyball league `DataSet`. The `DataSet` should hold three `DataTables` with the following structure:

```
Teams
    TeamName         string
Players
    FirstName        string
    LastName         string
    TeamName         string
Matches
    TeamName         string
    VersusTeamName   string
    Score            int
```

7. Copy the program you build for Exercise 6. Modify it to repeat Exercise 3 but using LINQ to DataSet instead of LINQ to XML.

8. Copy the program you build for Exercise 6. Modify it to repeat Exercise 4 but using LINQ to DataSet instead of LINQ to XML.

9. Copy the program you build for Exercise 6. Modify it to repeat Exercise 5 but using LINQ to DataSet instead of LINQ to XML.

10. In actual volleyball leagues, teams are ranked by their win percentage (in case teams don't all play the same number of games). If two teams have the same win percentage, their point differentials (total points "for" minus total points "against") break any ties, not simply the teams' total points.

    Copy the program you build for Exercise 9 and modify it so it displays each team's name, wins, losses, win percentage, points "for," points "against," and point differential. Order the results by team rankings.

    The result should look like the following:

    ```
    Name                Won   Lost   Win %   Pts+   Pts-   Diff
    ====                ===   ====   =====   ====   =====  ====
    Golden Spikers       4     1     80.00    117    88      29
    Sand Crabs           4     1     80.00    119    97      22
    Bling                3     2     60.00    108    108      0
    The Wee Free People  2     3     40.00     95    108    -13
    Hurricanes           1     4     20.00     95    110    -15
    Flying Dolphins      1     4     20.00     99    122    -23
    ```

11. Copy the program you build for Exercise 10. Modify it to insert a Standings element inside the League XML element. Use LINQ to XML to insert Team elements in the Standings element to record the standings. If root is the root of the XML hierarchy, use Console .WriteLine(root.ToString()) to verify that the result looks like the following:

```
<League>
    <Teams>
        . . .
    </Teams>
    <Matches>
        . . .
    </Matches>
    <Standings>
        <Team Name="Golden Spikers" Wins="4" Losses="1" WinPercent="80"
            PointsFor="117" PointsAgainst="88" PointDifferential="29" />
        <Team Name="Sand Crabs" Wins="4" Losses="1" WinPercent="80"
            PointsFor="119" PointsAgainst="97" PointDifferential="22" />
        <Team Name="Bling" Wins="3" Losses="2" WinPercent="60"
            PointsFor="108" PointsAgainst="108" PointDifferential="0" />
        <Team Name="The Wee Free People" Wins="2" Losses="3" WinPercent="40"
            PointsFor="95" PointsAgainst="108" PointDifferential="-13" />
        <Team Name="Hurricanes" Wins="1" Losses="4" WinPercent="20"
            PointsFor="95" PointsAgainst="110" PointDifferential="-15" />
        <Team Name="Flying Dolphins" Wins="1" Losses="4" WinPercent="20"
            PointsFor="99" PointsAgainst="122" PointDifferential="-23" />
    </Standings>
</League>
```

Error Handling

Although it is theoretically possible to write a program that perfectly predicts every conceivable situation that it might encounter, in practice that's difficult for nontrivial programs. For large applications, it's practically impossible to plan for every eventuality. Errors in the program's design and implementation can introduce bugs that give unexpected results. Even if you correctly anticipate every normal condition, users, corrupted databases, and unreliable network communications may give the application values that it doesn't expect.

Similarly, changing requirements over time may introduce data that the application was never intended to handle. The Y2K bug is a good example. When engineers wrote accounting, auto registration, financial, inventory, and other systems in the 1960s and 1970s, they never dreamed their programs would still be running in the year 2000. At the time, disk storage and memory were relatively expensive, so they stored years as 2-byte values (for example, 89 meant 1989). When the year 2000 rolled around, the applications couldn't tell whether the value 01 meant the year 1901 or 2001. In one humorous case, an auto registration system started issuing horseless carriage license plates to new cars because it thought cars built in 00 must be antiques. The Y2K problem wasn't actually a bug. It was a case of software used with data that wasn't part of its original design.

This chapter explains different kinds of exceptional conditions that can arise in an application. These range from unplanned data (as in the Y2K problem), to unexpected inputs (as when the user types "ten" into a numeric field), to bugs where the code is just plain wrong. With some advance planning, you can build a robust application that can keep running gracefully, even when the unexpected happens.

BUGS VERSUS UNDESIRABLE CONDITIONS

Several different types of unplanned conditions can derail an otherwise high-quality application. How you should handle these conditions depends on their nature.

For this discussion, a *bug* is a mistake in the application code. Some bugs become apparent right away and are easy to fix. These usually include simple typographic errors in the code and cases in which you misuse an object (for example, by using the wrong property). Other bugs are subtler and may be detected only long after they occur. For example, a data-entry routine might place invalid characters into a rarely used field in a `Customer` object. Only later when the program tries to access that field will you discover the problem. This kind of bug is difficult to track down and fix, but you can take some proactive steps to make these sorts of bugs easier to find.

> **BUGS THROUGHOUT HISTORY**
>
> On a historical note, the term "bug" has been used since at least the time of the telegraph to mean some sort of defect. Probably the origin of the term in computer science was an actual moth that was caught between two relays in an early computer in 1947. For a bit more information, including a picture of this first computer bug, see `www.jamesshuggins.com/h/tek1/first_computer_bug.htm`.

An *undesirable condition* is some predictable condition that you don't want to happen, but that you know could happen despite your best efforts. For example, there are many ways that a simple printing operation can fail. The printer might be unplugged, disconnected from its computer, disconnected from the network, out of toner, out of paper, experiencing a memory fault, clogged by a paper jam, or just plain broken. These are not bugs because the application software is not at fault. There is some condition outside of the program's control that must be fixed.

Another common undesirable condition occurs when the user enters invalid data. You may want the user to enter a value between 1 and 10 in a text box, but the user might enter 0, 9999, or "lunch" instead.

You can't fix undesirable conditions but you can try to make your program handle them gracefully and produce some meaningful result instead of crashing.

Catching Bugs

By definition, bugs are unplanned. No reasonable programmer sits down and thinks, "Perhaps I'll put a bug in this variable declaration."

Because bugs are unpredictable, you cannot know ahead of time where a bug will lie. However, you can watch for behavior in the program that indicates that a bug may be present. For example, suppose that you have a method that sorts a purchase order's items by cost. If the method receives an order with 100,000 items, something is probably wrong. If one of the items in the order is a computer keyboard with a price of $73 trillion, something is probably wrong. If the customer who placed the order doesn't exist, something is probably wrong.

This method could go ahead and sort the 100,000 items with prices ranging from a few cents to $73 trillion. Later, the program would try to print a 5,000-page invoice with no shipping or billing address. Only then would the developers realize that there was a problem.

Rather than trying to work around the weird data and continue running, it would be better if the program immediately told developers that something was wrong so that they could start looking for the problem. Bugs are easier to find the sooner they are detected. This bug will be easier to find if the sorting method notices it, rather than waiting until the application tries to print an invalid invoice. Your methods can protect themselves and the program as a whole by proactively validating inputs and outputs, and reporting anything suspicious to developers.

Some developers object to making methods spend a lot of time validating data that they "know" is correct. After all, one method generated this data and passed it to another, so you *know* that it is correct because the first method did its job properly. That's only true if every method that touches the data works perfectly. Because bugs are by definition unexpected, you cannot safely assume that all the methods are perfect and that the data remains uncorrupted.

AUTOMATED BUG CATCHERS

Many companies use automated testing tools to try to flush out problems early. Regression testing tools can execute code to verify that its outcome isn't changed when you make modifications to other parts of the application. If you build a suite of testing routines to validate data and method results, you may work them into an automated testing system, too.

To prevent validation code from slowing down the application, you can use the `System.Diagnostics` `.Debug` class's `Assert` method to check for strange conditions. The idea is that the method asserts that some statement is true.

The `Debug.Assert` method comes in several overloaded versions. The simplest form takes two parameters, a boolean expression and a string. If the boolean expression evaluates to `false`, the assertion fails and the method displays an error message.

The `Debug` class's `Fail` method is similar to the `Assert` method except it always displays an error message. Normally, you would use C# code to determine when to call this method. For example, if a `switch` statement has `case` sections to handle all the possible values of an enumerated type, you could add a `default` section that calls `Debug.Fail`. Then if an unexpected value appears, the program tells you.

When you debug the program, `Debug.Assert` and `Debug.Fail` statements immediately notify you if an assertion fails. When you make a release build to send to customers, the `Debug.Assert` and

`Debug.Fail` code is automatically removed from the application. That makes the application faster and doesn't inflict cryptic error messages on the user.

You can also use the DEBUG and TRACE preprocessor symbols to add other input and output validation code. By default, both of these symbols are defined in debug builds. Only TRACE is defined in release builds.

Example program UseDebug, which is available for download from the book's website, uses the following code to validate a method's inputs. (This program doesn't actually do anything; it just demonstrates input and output validation code.)

```
            // Sort an order's items.
            // Use the Debug class to validate inputs and outputs.
            private void SortOrderItems(Order order)
            {
                // Validate inputs.
                Debug.Assert(order.Customer != null, "No customer");
                Debug.Assert(order.Items != null, "No Items list");
                Debug.Assert(order.Items.Count > 0, "Empty Items list");
                Debug.Assert(order.Items.Count < 100, "Too many order items");

                // Sort the items.
                //...
                Console.WriteLine(order.ToString());

                // Validate outputs.
#if DEBUG
                // Verify that the items are sorted.
                for (int i = 1; i < order.Items.Count; i++)
                {
                    OrderItem order_item1 = order.Items[i - 1];
                    OrderItem order_item2 = order.Items[i];
                    Debug.Assert(order_item1.Price <= order_item2.Price,
                        "Order items not properly sorted");
                }
#endif
            }
```

DEBUG AND TRACE

The Trace class provides methods similar to those provided by the Debug class. For example, it includes Trace.Assert and Trace.Fail methods.

The Debug class's methods do nothing if the DEBUG preprocessor symbol is not defined, which is the default case for release builds. Similarly, the Trace class's methods do nothing if the TRACE preprocessor symbol is not defined.

If you want to use these methods only in debug builds, use Debug.Assert and Debug.Fail. If you want to use these methods in both debug and release builds, use Trace.Assert and Trace.Fail.

The method starts by validating its inputs. It verifies that the `Order` object's `Customer` property and `Items` collection are not `null`. It also verifies that the order contains at least 1 and fewer than 100 items. If a larger order comes along during testing, developers can increase this number to 200 or whatever value makes sense, but there's no need to start with an unreasonably large default.

After the method sorts the order's items (that code isn't shown), it uses the directive `#if DEBUG` to make its output validation code disappear from release builds. If this is a debug build, the code loops through the sorted items and verifies that each item's `Price` is at least as large as the `Price` of the preceding item in the list.

After you have tested the application long enough, you should have discovered most of the errors that are caused by incorrect program logic. When you make the release build, the compiler automatically removes the validation code, making the finished executable smaller and faster.

Code Contracts

The .NET Framework version 4.0 added the `Contract` class to formalize the idea of using assertions to validate method inputs and outputs.

INSTALLING CONTRACTS

Code contracts don't work for the Visual Studio Express editions. If you use an Express edition, you may want to skip or skim this section. You can still use `Debug` and `Trace` methods as described in the preceding section.

If you use some other edition of Visual Studio, you still need to install code contracts to make them work. Even though the .NET Framework includes the `Contract` class, the class won't do anything until you install the library.

To use code contracts, go to the DevLabs site at `msdn.microsoft.com/devlabs` and search for "**Code Contracts for .NET**. Download" and install the latest version of the library.

Microsoft has also released extensions for the code editor to help when writing contracts. For example, the extension adds information to tooltips and IntelliSense. To install the extension, go to the DevLabs site and search for "**Code Contracts Editor Extensions.**"

The idea is for a method to begin with a contract stating preconditions, things that must be true when the method is called, and postconditions, things that the method guarantees are true when it finishes. The program can also define invariant conditions that should remain true while the program is running.

Preconditions and Postconditions

The `Contract` class's `Requires` method represents a precondition that the method requires to be true when it starts. The `Ensures` method represents a postcondition that the method guarantees to be true when it finishes.

Example program UseCodeContracts, which is available for download from the book's website, uses the following code to validate a method's inputs and outputs.

```
// Sort an order's items.
// Use the Debug class to validate inputs and outputs.
private void SortOrderItems(Order order)
{
    // Preconditions.
    Contract.Requires(order.Customer != null, "No customer");
    Contract.Requires(order.Items != null, "No Items list");
    Contract.Requires(order.Items.Count > 0, "Empty Items list");
    Contract.Requires(order.Items.Count < 100, "Too many order items");

    // Postconditions.
    Contract.Ensures(OrderItemsAreSorted(order),
        "Order items not properly sorted");

    // Sort the items.
    //...
    Console.WriteLine(order.ToString());
}

// Return true if the items in this list are sorted.
[Pure()]
private bool OrderItemsAreSorted(Order order)
{
    for (int i = 2; i < order.Items.Count; i++)
    {
        OrderItem order_item1 = order.Items[i - 1];
        OrderItem order_item2 = order.Items[i];
        if (order_item1.Price > order_item2.Price) return false;
    }
    return true;
}
```

This program is similar to the UseDebug program described in the preceding section except it uses code contracts instead of the `Debug.Assert` method to validate preconditions and postconditions.

Notice that the code places all the contract's preconditions and postconditions at the beginning of the method. This makes it easier to find all the required conditions. For example, if you use `Debug.Assert` statements to validate outputs, they must go at the end of the method and any other place where the method might exit. When you use code contracts, all the conditions are at the beginning.

Placing the conditions at the beginning of the method also encourages test-driven development. Here developers write tests to verify a method's correctness before they write its code. That makes it more likely that the tests will be effective and thorough. When developers write the method before the tests, they often skip some tests because they "know" that the method handles those cases properly.

Also notice that this version handles its postcondition slightly differently from the previous version. The UseDebug program described in the preceding section looped through the order's items and used `Debug.Assert` to verify that their prices were in order. The `Contract.Ensures` method examines a single boolean value so that it cannot perform a loop.

To work around this problem, the new version of the program makes `Contract.Ensures` call the `OrderItemsAreSorted` method. That method performs the loop and returns a boolean result that the `Contract.Ensures` method can use.

If the `Contract.Ensures` method invokes another method, in this case `OrderItemsAreSorted`, Visual Studio issues a warning unless that method is marked with the `Pure` attribute. That attribute indicates that the method does not modify any objects while it is examining them. You need to write your code so that the method has this property. (This makes some sense. It would be confusing if the method verifying a postcondition is modifying the object it is verifying.) In this example, the `OrderItemsAreSorted` method examines an object's order items but it doesn't modify the order or its items.

Making Contracts Work

Unfortunately, even if you put all this code in your program, contracts don't work automatically.

Just as the `Debug` and `Trace` classes don't do anything unless the `DEBUG` and `TRACE` preprocessor symbols are defined, most of the `Contract` class's methods don't do anything unless the `CONTRACTS_FULL` preprocessor symbol is defined.

If you use a `#define` directive to define that symbol, the `Contract` class's methods will work but they won't work properly. If you think about how postconditions work, you'll understand part of the problem. A postcondition should be verified before the method exits, but the contract in the previous example places the `Contract.Ensures` call before the main body of the method's code. The method must verify the postcondition before it exits, not just when it starts.

To move the postcondition checks to their correct location and otherwise prepare the contract for use, you need to invoke the rewriter tool ccrewrite.exe. That tool rearranges the IL code generated by the C# compiler so that contracts work properly. If you try to run the program without using the rewriter, the first call to a `Contract` method fails.

Fortunately there's an easier way to make contracts work. Don't bother with the `CONTRACTS_FULL` preprocessor symbol in your code. Instead select Project ➪ Properties to open the project's property pages. Select the Code Contracts tab to see the page shown in Figure 9-1. Click the Perform Runtime Contract Checking box to enable contracts. This defines the `CONTRACTS_FULL` preprocessor symbol for you and makes Visual Studio automatically invoke the rewriter after it compiles your program.

You can explore the Code Contracts property page to change the way contracts are verified. For example, you can use the drop-down to the right of the Perform Runtime Contract Checking box to check only preconditions and postconditions, or to check only preconditions.

Now if you step through the program's code in the debugger, you can see it execute the `Contract` class's method calls. The code first steps through the preconditions, then the method's body, and finally the postcondition defined by the `Contract.Ensures` method.

Invariants

An invariant is some condition that should remain true throughout an object's lifetime. To create a code contract invariant for a class, give the class a method that checks whatever the variant conditions are and decorate that method with the `ContractInvariantMethod` attribute.

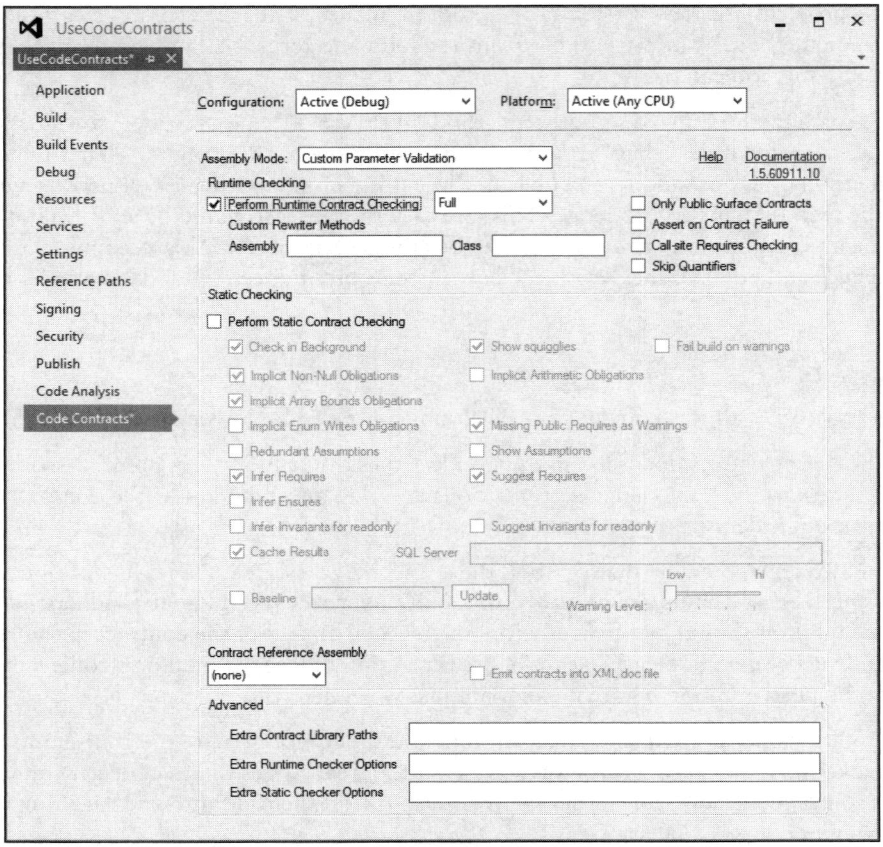

FIGURE 9-1: Use the Code Contracts property page to turn on code contracts.

Now whenever the program executes a public method from outside of the class's code, it checks the invariant after that method call returns to make sure the invariant property is still true.

For example, suppose the `Order` class has a `Customer` property and that property should never be `null` throughout the lifetime of the `Order` object. The following code shows how you might use a contract to enforce that condition in the `Order` class.

```
class Order
{
    public List<OrderItem> Items = new List<OrderItem>();

    public Customer Customer { get; set; }

    public Order(Customer customer)
    {
        Customer = customer;
    }
```

```
[ContractInvariantMethod]
private void CustomerIsNotNull()
{
    Contract.Invariant(this.Customer != null);
}
}
```

Here the `CustomerIsNotNull` method returns `true` if the `Customer` property is not `null`. Now any time the main program calls one of the `Order` class's public methods, the code contract invokes `CustomerIsNotNull` to see if this invariant has been violated.

The basic process for using an invariant is straightforward, but there are a couple important details.

First, code contracts check invariants only when code outside of the class invokes one of the class's methods. In this example, the `Order` class could have methods that set the `Customer` property to `null` and the invariant wouldn't notice.

Actually, if one of the class's public methods calls a second of the class's methods, the invariant is not verified after the call to the second method. The idea is that the second method may need to temporarily violate the invariant property and the original method call will fix things up before it returns. In other words, if code outside of the class calls one of the class's public methods, the variant property is verified only after the outermost call finishes.

The second important detail about invariants is that they apply only to public methods. In this example, the `Order` class's `Customer` value is implemented as a property with `get` and `set` accessors. Because the accessors are methods, the code contract system can verify the invariant after they execute.

If the `Customer` value were implemented as a public field, the code contract system could not verify the invariant after its value was changed.

For more information about code contracts, see the Code Contracts User Manual at `research.microsoft.com/projects/contracts/userdoc.pdf`.

Catching Undesirable Conditions

Although you don't want undesirable conditions to happen, with some careful thought, you can often predict where one might occur. Typically, these situations arise when the program must work with something outside of its own code. For example, when the program needs to access a file, printer, web page, floppy disk, or CD-ROM, that item may be unavailable. Similarly, whenever the program takes input from the user, the user may enter invalid data.

Notice how this differs from the bugs described in the previous section. After sufficient testing, you should have found and fixed most of the bugs. No amount of testing can remove the possibility of this kind of undesirable condition. No matter what code you use, the user may still remove a flash drive from the computer before the program is ready or unplug the printer while your program is using it.

Whenever you know that an undesirable condition might occur, you should write code to protect the program. It is generally better to test for these conditions ahead of time before you perform an action that might fail rather than simply attempt to perform the action and then catch the error when the program fails.

Testing for problem conditions generally gives you more complete information about what's wrong because you know what the program is trying to do at that point. It's also usually faster than catching an error because `try catch` blocks (described in the section "try catch Blocks" later in this chapter) come with considerable overhead.

For example, the following statement sets an integer variable to the value entered in a text box:

```
int numItems = int.Parse(numItemsTextBox.Text);
```

The user might enter a valid value in the text box. Unfortunately, the user may also enter something that is not a number, a value that is too big to fit in an integer, or a negative number when you are expecting a positive one. The user may even leave the field blank.

Often you can make error handling easier and more uniform by writing a validation method. The following method validates an integer value. It takes as parameters an output variable to hold the result, the `TextBox` holding the text, the value's name, and the minimum and maximum allowed values.

```
private bool IsValidInteger(out int result, TextBox txt, string name,
    int min = int.MinValue, int max = int.MaxValue)
{
    // Give result an initial value.
    result = int.MinValue;

    // Get the text.
    string text = txt.Text;

    // If there is something wrong, build an error message.
    string message = "";
    if (text.Length == 0) message = "Please enter " + name + ".";
    else if (!int.TryParse(text, out result))
        message = "Error parsing " + name + " '" + text + "'";
    else if ((result < min) || (result > max))
        message = name + " must be between " +
            min.ToString() + " and " + max.ToString() + ".";

    // See if we have an error message.
    if (message.Length > 0)
    {
        // Display the message, select the TextBox's text,
        // give it focus, and return false.
        MessageBox.Show(message, name + " Error",
            MessageBoxButtons.OK, MessageBoxIcon.Error);
        txt.Select(0, text.Length);
        txt.Focus();
        return false;
    }

    // The value is okay.
    return true;
}
```

This method initializes the output value to the minimum possible `int` value. It then gets the text in the `TextBox`.

Next, the code tests the text to see if it is valid. If the text is blank, cannot be parsed by `int.TryParse`, or is outside the allowed range, the method composes an appropriate error message.

After it finishes its test, the method checks to see if it has a nonblank error message. If the message is nonblank, the method displays the error message, selects the text in the `TextBox`, sets focus to the `TextBox`, and returns `false` to tell the calling code that the value was invalid.

If the error message is blank, the method returns `true` to tell the calling code that the value was valid.

Example program ValidateInteger, as shown in Figure 9-2, and available for download on the book's website, uses the `IsValidInteger` method to validate the values in three `TextBox`es.

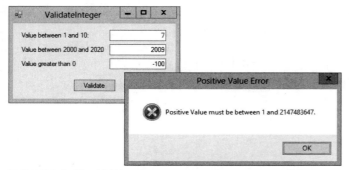

FIGURE 9-2: The ValidateInteger example program validates the values in three TextBoxes.

The following code shows how the ValidateInteger program uses the `IsValidInteger` method.

```
// Validate the values.
private void validateButton_Click(object sender, EventArgs e)
{
    int oneToTen, year, positive;

    // Validates the entries.
    if (!IsValidInteger(out oneToTen, oneToTenTextBox, "Value", 1, 10)) return;
    if (!IsValidInteger(out year, yearTextBox, "Year", 2000, 2020)) return;
    if (!IsValidInteger(out positive, positiveTextBox, "Positive Value", 1))
        return;

    // In a "real" application, you would perform other processing here.
    // ...

    MessageBox.Show("OK");
}
```

This code calls `IsValidInteger` three times and returns if any of those calls returns `false`. If all the calls to `IsValidInteger` return true, all the values are valid, so the program continues processing them.

You can write similar methods to validate other types of data fields such as phone numbers, e-mail addresses, street addresses, and so forth.

Global Exception Handling

Normally, you should try to catch an error as close as possible to the place where it occurs. An error is easiest to fix if you catch it right away in the method where it happens.

However, bugs often arise in unexpected places. Unless you protect every method with error-handling code (a fairly common strategy), a bug may arise in code that you have not protected.

ERRORS, ERRORS, EVERYWHERE

Some sources of errors are completely beyond your control. For example, power surges, static electricity, intermittent short circuits, or even stray radiation striking exactly the right part of a chip can make the computer's hardware misbehave, so code that should work correctly fails. There's little you can do to anticipate these kinds of errors but you can use global error handling to try to recover from them.

Of course, that doesn't excuse you from rigorously checking your code for errors. The vast majority of bugs are due to real mistakes in the code or data rather than to magical cosmic rays flipping a single bit on a memory chip.

When you write a global exception handler, you probably won't know where the exception will occur, so it's hard to figure out how to keep the program running effectively. You can log the error, save data if necessary, and possibly display a message for the user before closing the program. You can make the program attempt to ignore the error and continue running, but it may be difficult to actually fix the problem.

LET THE USER ESCAPE

If you decide to make the program ignore the error and keep running, display a message first and give the user a chance to close the program. Otherwise, the program might get stuck in an infinite loop where it ignores the error and then retries whatever operation caused the error in the first place.

How you install a global error handler depends on the type of program you run. The following sections explain how to install global exception handlers for Windows Forms, WPF, and console applications.

Note that global exception handlers don't work inside Visual Studio. In all three kinds of programs, if the program throws an unhandled exception, Visual Studio springs into action and catches the error. To test the programs, you need to run a compiled executable program outside of Visual Studio.

Windows Forms Applications

To catch unhandled exceptions in a Windows Forms application, add an event handler to the `Application` object's `ThreadException` event. The WindowsFormsGlobalException example program, which is available for download on this book's website, uses the following code to install its event handler.

```
// Install the global exception handler.
private void Form1_Load(object sender, EventArgs e)
{
    Application.ThreadException += ThreadException;
}
```

The following code shows the example program's `ThreadException` event handler.

```
// Handle global exceptions.
private static void ThreadException(object sender, ThreadExceptionEventArgs e)
{
    try
    {
        string message = e.Exception.Message + '\n' +
            "Do you want to try to continue?";
        if (MessageBox.Show(message, "Unhandled Exception",
            MessageBoxButtons.YesNo, MessageBoxIcon.Stop) == DialogResult.No)
        {
            Application.Exit();
        }
    }
    catch
    {
        Application.Exit();
    }
}
```

The event handler does all its work inside a `try catch` block. If anything goes wrong, the code simply closes the application.

The code builds and displays a message that describes the exception and asks the user if the program should try to continue. (You might also want to log the error, including a stack trace, into a log file or a system log.) If the user clicks No, the method calls `Application.Exit` to end the program.

If the user clicks Yes, the program continues running.

When you click the program's Throw Exception button, the following code executes.

```
// Throw an exception.
private void throwExceptionButton_Click(object sender, EventArgs e)
{
    throw new ArgumentException();
}
```

This code simply throws an `ArgumentException`. Because this code doesn't use a `try catch` block, the global exception handler catches it.

WPF Applications

To catch unhandled exceptions in a WPF application, add an event handler to the `Application` `.Current` object's `DispatcherUnhandledException` event. The WpfGlobalException example program, which is available for download on the book's website, uses the following code to install its event handler.

```
// Install the global exception handler.
private void Window_Loaded(object sender, RoutedEventArgs e)
{
    Application.Current.DispatcherUnhandledException += UnhandledException;
}
```

The following code shows the example program's `UnhandledException` event handler.

```
// Handle global exceptions.
private void UnhandledException(object sender,
    DispatcherUnhandledExceptionEventArgs e)
{
    try
    {
        string message = e.Exception.Message + '\n' +
            "Do you want to try to continue?";
        if (MessageBox.Show(message, "Unhandled Exception",
            MessageBoxButton.YesNo, MessageBoxImage.Stop) == MessageBoxResult.No)
        {
            Application.Current.Shutdown();
        }
        e.Handled = true;
    }
    catch
    {
        Application.Current.Shutdown();
    }
}
```

This event handler is similar to the one used by the previous example. Most of the differences are in the constants and method calls this version uses to perform the same tasks as the previous version.

One important difference is the following statement.

```
e.Handled = true;
```

This statement tells the program that the event has been handled and the program doesn't need to close. In a Windows Forms application, continuing is the default action. In a WPF application, closing is the default action.

When you click the program's Throw Exception button, the following code executes.

```
// Throw an exception.
private void throwExceptionButton_Click(object sender, RoutedEventArgs e)
{
    throw new ArgumentException();
}
```

This is similar to the code in the Windows Forms example. The only difference is that this version takes as its second parameter a `RoutedEventArgs` object instead of an `EventArgs` object.

Console Applications

To catch unhandled exceptions in a console application, add an event handler to the `AppDomain.CurrentDomain` object's `UnhandledException` event. The `Main` method used by the ConsoleGlobalException example program, which is available for download on the book's website, installs its event handler and enters a loop that runs until the program ends.

```
static void Main(string[] args)
{
    // Install the event handler.
    AppDomain.CurrentDomain.UnhandledException += UnhandledException;

    // Loop forever.
    for (; ; )
    {
        Console.WriteLine("1 - Continue, 2 - Throw exception, 3 - Exit");
        Console.Write("> ");
        string text = Console.ReadLine();
        int choice = int.Parse(text);

        switch (choice)
        {
            case 1:
                // Continue.
                Console.WriteLine("Continuing...\n");
                break;

            case 2:
                // Throw an exception.
                Console.WriteLine("Throwing exception...\n");
                throw new ArgumentException();

            case 3:
                // Exit.
                return;
        }
    }
}
```

The method installs the program's event handler and then enters an infinite loop. Each time through the loop, the method displays a prompt and then waits for the user's input. It parses the input and uses a `switch` statement to decide what to do next.

If the user enters 1, the program displays a message and continues its loop. If the user enters 2, the program throws an exception. If the user enters 3, the program exits the `Main` method and ends.

The following code shows the example program's `UnhandledException` event handler.

```
// Handle an exception.
private static void UnhandledException(object sender,
    UnhandledExceptionEventArgs e)
{
    Console.WriteLine("Caught exception:");
    Exception exception = (Exception)e.ExceptionObject;
```

```
        Console.WriteLine(exception.Message);
        Console.WriteLine("\n\n\nPress Enter to close the application");
        Console.ReadLine();
    }
```

This event handler is different from the previous two in two main ways. First, this is a console application so, instead of displaying messages boxes, it communicates to the user through the console window.

Second, this event handler cannot prevent the application from ending. (Although you could use a try catch block in the Main method to catch exceptions and try to keep the program running there.)

Figure 9-3 shows the ConsoleGlobalException example program after it has caught an exception. Initially, the event handler displayed the information starting at Throwing Exception and ending with Press Enter to Close the Application. When you press Enter, the system automatically displays the following text and the ConsoleGlobalException Has Stopped Working dialog.

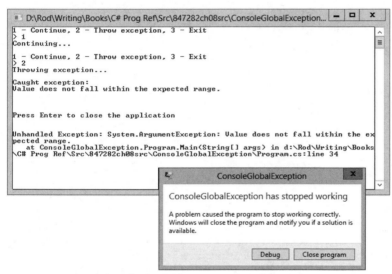

FIGURE 9-3: An UnhandledException event handler cannot prevent a console application from closing.

TRY CATCH BLOCKS

The try catch block provides structured error handling for C# programs. The syntax is as follows.

```
try
{
    tryStatements...
}
catch (exceptionType1 variable1)
{
    exceptionStatements1...
}
```

```
catch (exceptionType2 variable2)
{
    exceptionStatements2...
}
...
catch
{
    finalExceptionStatements...
}
finally
{
    finallyStatements...
}
```

The program executes the code in the *tryStatements* block. If any of that code throws an exception, the program jumps to the first catch block.

If the exception matches *exceptionType1*, the program executes the code in *exceptionStatements1*. The exception type might match the catch statement's exception class exactly, or it might be a sub-class of the listed class.

For example, suppose the *tryStatements* block performs an integer calculation that divides by zero. That raises a DivideByZeroException. That class inherits from the ArithmeticException class, which inherits from SystemException, which inherits from Exception. That means the code would stop at the first catch statement it finds that looks for DivideByZeroException, ArithmeticException, SystemException, or Exception.

CATCH CONTROL

Arrange catch statements so the most specific comes first. Otherwise, a more general statement catches errors before a more specific statement has a chance. For example, the generic Exception class matches all other exceptions, so if the first catch statement catches Exception, no other catch statement ever executes.

If two catch statements are unrelated, neither catches the other's exceptions, so put the exception more likely to occur first. That makes the code more efficient because it looks for the most common problems first. It also keeps the code most likely to execute near the top where it is easier to read.

If the raised exception does not match the first exception type, the program checks the next catch statement. The program keeps comparing the exception to catch statements until it finds one that applies, or it runs out of catch statements.

If no catch statement matches the exception, the exception "bubbles up" to the next level in the call stack, and C# moves to the method that called the current one. If that method has appropriate error-handling code, it deals with the error. If that method can't catch the error, the exception bubbles up again until C# eventually either finds error-handling code that can catch the exception or runs off the top of the call stack. If it runs off the call stack, C# calls the global UnhandledException event handler described in the previous sections, if one exists. If there is no `UnhandledException` event handler, the program crashes.

If you include a `catch` statement with no exception type, that block matches any exception. If the raised exception doesn't match any of the previous exception types, the program executes the `finalExceptionStatements` block of code. Note that the statement `catch (Exception ex)` also matches all exceptions, so it's just as good as `catch` by itself. It also gives you easy access to the exception object's properties and methods.

You can figure out what exception classes to use in `catch` statements in several ways. First, you can spend a lot of time digging through the online help. An easier method is to let the program crash and then look at the error message it produces.

Figure 9-4 shows the error message a program throws when it tries to use the `Integer.Parse` method to convert the non-numeric string `Hello` into an integer. The first line in the dialog makes it obvious that the program should catch `FormatException`.

FIGURE 9-4: When a program crashes, the message it generates tells you the type of exception it threw.

Another way to decide what types of exceptions to catch is to place a final generic `catch (Exception ex)` statement at the end of the `catch` list. Place code inside that `catch` block to display the exception's type name, as shown in the following code.

```
try
{
    . . .
}

... Catch blocks ...

catch (Exception ex)
{
    MessageBox.Show("Unexpected exception " + ex.GetType().Name);
}
```

When the final `catch` block reports a new exception type, you can create a new `catch` block to handle it.

CATCH CATASTROPHES

It may not be possible to take meaningful action when you catch certain exceptions. For example, if a program uses up all the available memory, C# throws an `OutOfMemoryException`. If there is no memory available, you may have trouble doing anything useful. Similarly, if there's a problem with the filesystem, you may be unable to write error descriptions into a log file.

After it finishes running the code in *tryStatements* and it executes any necessary exception code in a `catch` block, the program executes the code in *finallyStatements*. The statements in the `finally` section execute whether the code in *tryStatements* succeeds or fails.

A `try catch` block must include at least one `catch` section or a `finally` section; although, those sections do not need to contain any code. For example, the following `try catch` block calls method `DoSomething` and uses an empty `catch` section to ignore any errors that occur.

```
try
{
    DoSomething();
}
catch
{
}
```

Exception Objects

When a `catch` statement catches an exception, its exception variable contains information about the error that raised the exception.

REPEATED VARIABLES

The `try`, `catch`, and `finally` sections define their own scopes, so they can use variables with the same names without interfering with each other. Many programmers always give exception variables the name `ex`.

Different exception classes may provide different features, but they all provide the basic features defined by the `Exception` class from which they are all derived. The following table lists the most commonly used `Exception` class properties and methods.

ITEM	PURPOSE
InnerException	The exception that caused the current exception. For example, suppose that you write a tool library that catches an exception and then throws a new custom exception describing the problem in terms of your library. You should set InnerException to the exception that you caught before you throw the new exception.
Message	Returns a brief message that describes the exception.
Source	Returns the name of the application or object that threw the exception.
StackTrace	Returns a string containing a stack trace giving the program's location when the error occurred.
TargetSite	Returns the name of the method that threw the exception.
ToString	Returns a string describing the exception and including the stack trace.

Example program ShowExceptionInfo, which is available for download on this book's website, displays an exception's Message, StackTrace, and ToString values.

At a minimum, the program should log or display the Message value for any unexpected exceptions so that you know what exception occurred. The program might also log the StackTrace or the result of ToString so that you can see where the exception occurred.

The StackTrace and ToString values can help developers find a bug, but these values can be intimidating to end users. Even the abbreviated format used by the exception's Message property is usually not useful to a user. When the user clicks the Find Outstanding Invoices button, the message "Attempted to Divide by Zero" doesn't actually tell the user what the problem is or what to do about it.

When a program catches an exception, a good strategy is to record the full ToString message in a log file or e-mail it to a developer. Then display a message that restates the error message in terms the user can understand. For example, the program might say the following.

Unable to total outstanding invoices. A bug report has been sent to the development team.

The program should then try to continue as gracefully as possible. It may not be able to finish this calculation, but it should not crash, and it should allow the user to continue working on other tasks if possible.

Throwing Exceptions

In addition to catching exceptions, your program may need to generate its own exceptions. Because handling an exception is called *catching* it, raising an exception is called *throwing* it. (This is just a silly pun. People also catch lions and colds, but I don't think many people throw them. It's as good a term as any, however.)

To throw an exception, the program creates an instance of the type of exception it wants to generate, passing the constructor additional information describing the problem. The program can then set other exception fields if wanted. For example, it might set the exception's Source property to tell the code that catches the error where it originated. The program then uses the throw statement to throw the exception. If an error handler is active somewhere in the call stack, C# jumps to that point and the error handler processes the exception.

Example program DrawableRect, which is available for download on this book's website, uses the following code to show how the DrawableRectangle class protects itself against invalid input.

```
class DrawableRectangle
{
    public DrawableRectangle(int x, int y, int width, int height)
    {
        // Verify that new_width > 0.
        if (width <= 0)
        {
            throw new ArgumentException(
                "DrawableRectangle width must be greater than zero",
                    "width");
        }

        // Verify that new_height > 0.
        if (height <= 0)
        {
            throw new ArgumentException(
                "DrawableRectangle height must be greater than zero",
                    "height");
        }

        // Save the parameter values.
        //...
    }

    // Other code for this class omitted.
    //...
}
```

The class's constructor takes four arguments: an X and Y position, and a width and height. If the new object's width is less than or equal to zero, the program creates a new ArgumentException object. It passes the exception's constructor a description of the error and the name of the argument that is invalid. After creating the exception object, the program uses the throw statement to raise the exception. The code checks the new object's height similarly.

The following code shows how a program might use a try catch block to protect itself while creating a new DrawableRectangle object.

```
try
{
    DrawableRectangle rect = new DrawableRectangle(10, 20, 0, -100);
}
catch (Exception ex)
{
    MessageBox.Show(ex.Message);
}
```

When your application needs to throw an exception, it's easiest to use an existing exception class. There are a few ways to get lists of exception classes so that you can find one that makes sense for your application. Appendix O, "Useful Exception Classes," lists some of the more useful exception classes. The online help topic "Introduction to Exception Handling in Visual Basic" at msdn.microsoft.com/aa289505.aspx also has a good list of exception classes at the end. Microsoft's web page msdn.microsoft.com/system.exception_derivedtypelist.aspx provides a long list of exception classes derived from the System.Exception class.

Another method for finding exception classes is to open the Object Browser (select View ➪ Object Browser) and search for **Exception**.

When you throw exceptions, you must use your judgment about selecting these classes. For example, C# uses the System.Reflection.AmbiguousMatchException class when it tries to bind a method call to an object's method and it cannot determine which overloaded method to use. This happens at a lower level than your program will act, so you won't use that class for exactly the same purpose, but it still may be useful to throw that exception. For example, if your program parses a string and, based on the string, cannot decide what action to take, you might use this class to represent the error, even though you're not using it exactly as it was originally intended.

Be sure to use the most specific exception class possible. Using more generic classes such as Exception makes it much harder for developers to understand and locate an error. If you cannot find a good, specific fit, create your own exception class, as described in the section "Custom Exceptions" later in this chapter.

Rethrowing Exceptions

Sometimes when you catch an exception, you cannot completely handle the problem. In that case, it may make sense to rethrow the exception so that a method higher up in the call stack can take a crack at it.

To rethrow an error exactly as you caught it, just use the throw keyword, as in the following example.

```
try
{
    // Do something hard here.
    ...
}
catch (ArithmeticException ex)
{
    // We can handle this exception. Fix it.
    ...
}
catch
{
    // We don't know what to do with this one. Re-throw it.
    throw;
}
```

If your code can figure out more or less why an error is happening but it cannot fix it, it's sometimes a good idea to rethrow the error as a different exception type. For example, suppose a piece of code causes an ArithmeticException but the underlying cause of the exception is an invalid argument.

In that case it is better to throw an `ArgumentException` instead of an `ArithmeticException` because that can provide more specific information higher up in the call stack.

At the same time, however, you don't want to lose the information contained in the original `ArithmeticException`. The solution is to throw a new `ArgumentException` but to place the original `ArithmeticException` in its `InnerException` property so that the code that catches the new exception has access to the original information.

The following code demonstrates this technique.

```
try
{
    // Do something hard here.
    ...
}
catch (ArithmeticException ex)
{
    // This was caused by an invalid argument.
    // Re-throw it as an ArgumentException.
    throw new ArgumentException("Invalid argument X in function Whatever. ", ex);
}
catch
{
    // We don't know what to do with this one. Re-throw it.
    throw;
}
```

Custom Exceptions

When your application needs to throw an exception, it's easiest to use an existing exception class. Reusing existing exception classes makes it easier for developers to understand what the exception means. It also prevents exception proliferation, where the developer needs to watch for dozens or hundreds of bizarre types of exceptions.

Sometimes, however, the predefined exceptions don't fit your needs. For example, suppose that you build a class that contains data that may exist for a long time. If the program tries to use an object that has not refreshed its data for a while, you want to raise some sort of "data expired" exception. You could squeeze this into the `System.TimeoutException` class, but that exception doesn't quite fit this use. In that case, you can build a custom exception class.

Building a custom exception class is easy. Make a new class that inherits from the `System.Exception` class. Then, provide constructor methods to let the program create instances of the class. That's all there is to it.

By convention, an exception class's name should end with the word `Exception`. Also by convention, you should provide at least three overloaded constructors for developers to use when creating new instances of the class. (For more information on what constructors are and how to define them, see the section "Constructors" in Chapter 12, "Classes and Structures.")

The first constructor takes no parameters and initializes the exception with a default message describing the general type of error.

The other two versions take as parameters an error message, and an error message plus an inner exception object. These constructors pass their parameters to the base class's constructors to initialize the object appropriately.

For completeness, you can also make a constructor that takes as parameters a `SerializationInfo` object and a `StreamingContext` object. This version can also pass its parameters to a base class constructor to initialize the exception object, so you don't need to do anything special with the parameters. (This constructor is useful if the exception will be serialized and deserialized. If you're not sure whether you need this constructor, you probably don't. If you do include it, however, you need to import the `System.Runtime.Serialization` namespace in the exception class's file to define the `SerializationInfo` and `StreamingContext` classes.)

Example program `CustomException`, which is available for download on the book's website, uses the following code to define the `ObjectExpiredException` class.

```
class ObjectExpiredException : Exception
{
    // No parameters. Use a default message.
    public ObjectExpiredException()
        : base("This object has expired")
    {
    }

    // Set the message.
    public ObjectExpiredException(string message)
        : base(message)
    {
    }

    // Set the message and inner exception.
    public ObjectExpiredException(string message, Exception innerException)
        : base(message, innerException)
    {
    }

    // Include SerializationInfo object and StreamingContext objects.
    public ObjectExpiredException(SerializationInfo info,
      StreamingContext context)
        : base(info, context)
    {
    }
}
```

After you have defined the exception class, you can throw and catch it just as you can throw and catch any exception class defined by C#. For example, the following code throws an `ObjectExpiredException`.

```
throw new ObjectExpiredException("This Customer object has expired.");
```

The parent class `System.Exception` automatically handles the object's `Message`, `StackTrace`, and `ToString` properties, so you don't need to implement them yourself.

SUMMARY

In practice, it's extremely difficult to anticipate every condition that might occur within a large application. You should try to predict as many incorrect situations as possible, but you should also plan for unforeseen errors. You should write error-checking code that makes bugs obvious when they occur and recovers from them if possible. You may not anticipate every possible bug, but with a little thought you can make the program detect and report obviously incorrect values.

You should also look for unplanned conditions (such as the user entering a phone number in a Social Security number field) and make the program react gracefully. Your program cannot control everything in its environment (such as the user's actions, printer status, and network connectivity), but it should be prepared to work when things aren't exactly the way they should be.

You may never remove every last bug from a 100,000-line program, but you can make any remaining bugs relatively harmless and appear so rarely that the users can do their jobs in relative safety.

Visual Studio provides a rich set of tools for debugging an application. Using the development environment, you can stop the program at different lines of code and examine variables, change variable values, look at the call stack, and call methods to exercise different pieces of the application. You can step through the program, executing the code one statement at a time to see what it is doing. You can even make some modifications to the source code and let the program continue running. Chapter 10, "Tracing and Debugging," describes tools and techniques you can use to debug applications.

EXERCISES

1. Consider the following `Student` class.

```
public class Student
{
    public string Name;
    public List<Course> Courses = new List<Course>();

    // Constructor.
    public Student(string name)
    {
        Name = name;
    }
}
```

Add `Debug.Assert` statements to the class to require the following conditions.

   ➤ The `Name` property must always be at least 1 character long.

   ➤ The `Courses` value can never be `null`. (Although the list can be empty.)

2. Repeat Exercise 1 using code contract preconditions and postconditions instead of `Debug` `.Assert` statements. (Put in postconditions even though you "know" they're unnecessary.)

3. Repeat Exercise 1 using code contract invariants instead of preconditions, postconditions, or `Debug.Assert` statements.

4. Suppose you anticipate occasions when the main program might try to violate the conditions listed for Exercise 1. Instead of using Debug.Assert or code contracts to catch these occasions during testing, you want to raise exceptions and let the main program catch them. Repeat Exercise 1 so it does that.

5. The section "Console Applications" earlier in this chapter showed a console application that throws an exception if you enter the value 2 in the console window. Can you think of any other ways to make the program throw an exception?

6. Rewrite the program described in Exercise 5 so that it can handle any input without throwing an exception (except the input 2, which is supposed to throw an exception).

7. The program described in the section "Console Applications" earlier in this chapter uses an UnhandledException event handler to catch unhandled exceptions. However, all the code in a console application runs directly or indirectly from the Main method. That means you could put a try catch block in that method to catch all exceptions that aren't handled anywhere else.

Rewrite the example shown in that section to use this technique. What are the advantages and disadvantages of this method compared to using an UnhandledException event handler?

8. Suppose the Factorial program uses the following code.

```
// Calculate the entered number's factorial.
private void calculateButton_Click(object sender, EventArgs e)
{
    long number = long.Parse(numberTextBox.Text);
    resultLabel.Text = Factorial(number).ToString();
}

// Return number!
private long Factorial(long number)
{
    long result = 1;
    for (long i = 2; i <= number; i++) result *= i;
    return result;
}
```

What kinds of error-handling statements would be appropriate in this example? Would it make sense to use Debug.Assert? Code contracts? Add the appropriate error-handling statements to this code.

10

Tracing and Debugging

WHAT'S IN THIS CHAPTER

- ➤ Breakpoints
- ➤ The Watches and Autos windows
- ➤ Breakpoint conditions, hit counts, and filters
- ➤ Enabling and disabling breakpoints
- ➤ Debug and trace listeners

WROX.COM DOWNLOADS FOR THIS CHAPTER

Please note that all the code examples for this chapter are available as a part of this chapter's code download on the book's website at www.wrox.com/go/csharp5programmersref on the Download Code tab.

Visual Studio's code editor includes tools that help you avoid bugs. Some of the things the editor does to help you include

- ➤ Providing IntelliSense to help you use methods and parameters correctly
- ➤ Identifying variables that are used before initialization or that are declared but never used
- ➤ Detecting unreachable code
- ➤ Flagging methods with a non-void return type that don't return a value on all code paths
- ➤ Providing a renaming tool so that you can easily rename objects without missing references

Despite those tools, however, bugs are as certain in programming as death and taxes. Although it is theoretically possible for a program to be bug-free, chances are good that any nontrivial program contains bugs. Actually, in some testing strategies it's an axiom that the program contains bugs. The goal is not to fix every bug but to fix so many of the bugs that those that remain occur extremely rarely.

Although this book is about the C# language and not Visual Studio, any reasonably complete C# book should provide some coverage of debugging tools and techniques. This chapter briefly describes some of the tools Visual Studio provides to help you track down and eliminate bugs. It also explains tracing methods that you can use to figure out what a program is doing and hopefully what it is doing wrong.

THE DEBUG MENU

The Debug menu contains commands that are generally useful when you debug a program. They include commands to set and clear breakpoints, one of Visual Studio's most useful features.

A *breakpoint* is a spot in the code that is marked to suspend execution. When the program reaches a line marked with a breakpoint, execution pauses so that you can examine the program's status. While execution is paused, you can hover over variables to see their values, enter expressions in the Immediate window to evaluate them, and change values by setting variables equal to new values in the Immediate window. You can even edit the code to some extent and then continue running.

To set a breakpoint, place the cursor in the code editor on the line where you want to pause execution. Then press F9 or click in the margin to the left of the line of code to create the breakpoint. To remove a breakpoint, place the cursor on the line, and press F9 or click in the margin again.

The commands that are visible in the Debug window change depending on several conditions, such as the type of file you have open, whether the program is running, the line of code that contains the cursor, and whether that line contains a breakpoint. The following list briefly summarizes the most important items available in the Debug menu while execution is stopped at a breakpoint.

➤ **Windows**—This submenu's commands display other debugging-related windows. The following section describes this menu's most useful commands.

➤ **Continue** (F5)—This command makes the program continue execution until it finishes or it reaches another breakpoint.

➤ **Break All** (Ctrl+Break)—This command pauses the program's execution. You can then examine the program's state, examine and change variables' values, and modify the code before you resume execution.

➤ **Stop Debugging** (Ctrl+Alt+Break)—This command stops the program and ends its debugging session. Note that this stops the program immediately, so it doesn't get a chance to run form closing event handlers and any other cleanup code that it would run if it halted normally.

➤ **Step Into** (F8 or F11)—This command makes the debugger execute the current line of code. If that code calls a method, the debugger steps into that method.

➤ **Step Over** (Shift+F8 or F10)—This command makes the debugger execute the current line of code. If that code calls a method, the debugger steps over that method. (If the method contains a breakpoint, execution pauses there.)

➤ **Step Out** (Ctrl+Shift+F8)—This command makes the debugger run until it leaves the method it is currently executing (or until it reaches a breakpoint). Execution pauses when the program reaches the line of code that called this method.

➤ **QuickWatch** (Shift+F9)—This command displays a dialog box that gives information about the selected code object. If the object is a variable, the dialog enables you to reevaluate it or change its value. Click the Add Watch button to add the value to a watch window. (See the entry "Watch" in the next section for more information on watch windows.)

➤ **Exceptions** (Ctrl+Alt+E)—This command displays the dialog box shown in Figure 10-1. Use the dialog to make the debugger stop the program when a particular kind of exception is thrown or unhandled.

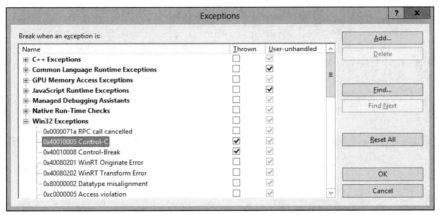

FIGURE 10-1: The Exceptions dialog box enables you to determine how the debugger handles exceptions.

➤ **Toggle Breakpoint** (F9)—This command toggles whether the current code line contains a breakpoint.

➤ **New Breakpoint**—This submenu's single command Break At Function (Ctrl+B) displays a dialog box that enables you to specify a function and a line within that function where the program should break.

➤ **Delete All Breakpoints (Ctrl+Shift+F9)**—This command removes all breakpoints from the entire solution.

➤ **Enable All Breakpoints**—This command enables all disabled breakpoints.

➤ **Disable All Breakpoints**—This command disables all breakpoints but leaves them in the solution so that you can re-enable them later. (You can disable individual breakpoints by right-clicking the breakpoint's margin and selecting Disable Breakpoint.)

THE DEBUG ⇨ WINDOWS SUBMENU

The Debug menu's Windows submenu contains commands that display debugging-related windows. The following list briefly describes the most useful of these windows. The sections that follow this one provide more detail about the Breakpoints, Command, and Immediate windows.

➤ **Immediate** (Ctrl+G)—This window enables you to examine variable and execute C# statements. The section "The Immediate Window" later in this chapter describes this window in more detail.

➤ **Locals** (Ctrl+Alt+V, L)—This window displays the values of variables defined in the local context. To change a value, click it and enter the new value. Click the plus and minus signs to the left of a complex value such as an object to expand or collapse it.

➤ **Breakpoints** (Ctrl+Alt+B)—This window, which is shown in Figure 10-2, displays the solution's breakpoints, their locations, and their conditions. Use the toolbar to create a new function breakpoint, delete a breakpoint, delete all breakpoints, enable or disable all breakpoints, go to a breakpoint's source code, and change the columns displayed by the dialog box. Select or clear the check boxes on the left to enable or disable breakpoints. Right-click a breakpoint to change its properties. See the section "The Breakpoints Window" later in this chapter for more detail.

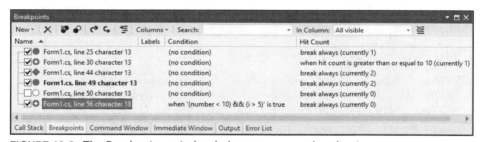

FIGURE 10-2: The Breakpoints window helps you manage breakpoints.

➤ **Output**—This window displays output produced by `Console` statements.

➤ **Autos** (Ctrl+Alt+V, A)—This window displays the values of local and global variables used in the current and previous lines of code.

➤ **Call Stack** (Ctrl+L)—This window lists the methods that have called other methods to reach the program's current point of execution. Double-click a line to jump to the corresponding code in the program's call stack.

➤ **Watch**—The Watch submenu contains the commands Watch 1, Watch 2, Watch 3, and Watch 4. These commands display four different watch windows that display the values of variables and expressions when the program is paused. When you create a watch using the QuickWatch command described in the preceding section, the new watch is placed in the Watch 1 window. You can click and drag a watch from one watch window to another to make a copy of the watch in the second window.

➤ **Modules**—This window displays information about the DLL and EXE files used by the program. It shows each module's filename and path; whether it is optimized; whether it is your code (rather than an installed library); and whether debugging symbols are loaded. It also shows each module's load order (lower-numbered modules are loaded first), version, and timestamp.

Often it is useful to make the visible debug windows occupy separate tabs in the same area at the bottom of the IDE. That enables you to switch between them quickly and easily without them taking up too much space.

THE BREAKPOINTS WINDOW

The Breakpoints window lists all the breakpoints. If you double-click a breakpoint in the list, you can easily jump to the code that holds it.

The icons to the left of the breakpoints shown in Figure 10-2 give information about their properties. The following list describes the icons.

➤ Solid red circle—This indicates an ordinary breakpoint.

➤ White plus sign—This indicates the breakpoint is modified by a condition, hit count, or filter. The following text describes these.

➤ Diamond—This indicates the breakpoint performs some special action when it is reached. Normally, the action prints a message in the Immediate window showing values that you specify.

➤ Hollow circle or diamond—This indicates the breakpoint has been disabled.

Right-click a breakpoint and select Condition to display the dialog box shown in Figure 10-3. By default, a breakpoint pauses execution whenever it is reached. You can use this dialog box to add an additional condition that determines whether the breakpoint pauses the program when it is reached. In Figure 10-3, the breakpoint pauses execution if the expression `(number < 10) && (i > 5)` is `true` when the code reaches the breakpoint.

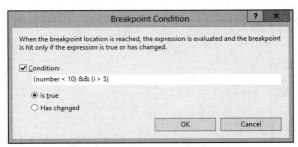

FIGURE 10-3: The Breakpoint Condition dialog box enables you to specify a condition that determines whether execution pauses at the breakpoint.

> **NOTE** *Specifying a breakpoint condition can slow execution considerably because the debugger must evaluate the condition frequently.*

Right-click a breakpoint and select Hit Count to display the Breakpoint Hit Count dialog box, as shown in Figure 10-4. Each time the code reaches a breakpoint, it increments the breakpoint's hit count. You can use this dialog box to make the breakpoint interrupt execution when it has been reached a specific number of times, a multiple of some number of times, or at least a certain number of times.

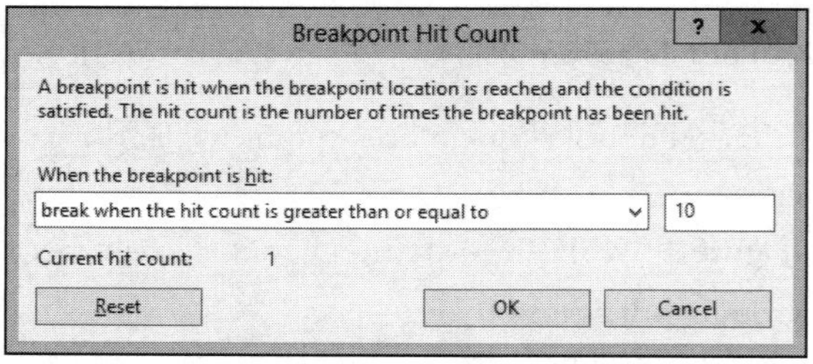

FIGURE 10-4: The Breakpoint Hit Count dialog box enables you to make a breakpoint's activation depend on the number of times the code has reached it.

Right-click a breakpoint and select Filter to display the Breakpoint Filter dialog box, shown in Figure 10-5. You can enter a filter expression to make the breakpoint pause execution only for certain machines, processes, or threads.

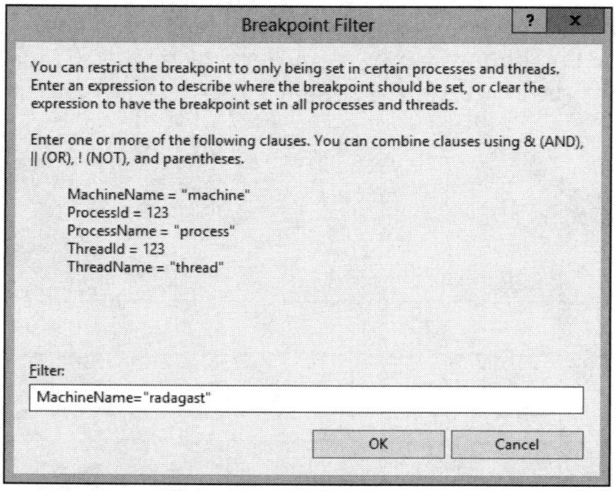

FIGURE 10-5: The Breakpoint Filter dialog box enables you to make a breakpoint's activation depend on the machine, process, or thread.

Right-click a breakpoint and select When Hit to display the When Breakpoint Is Hit dialog box, as shown in Figure 10-6. Here you can specify the actions the debugger takes when the breakpoint is activated. Select the Print a Message check box to make the program display a message in the Immediate window. Select the Continue Execution check box to make the program continue running without stopping after it displays its message.

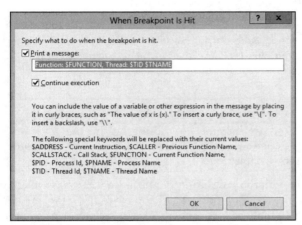

FIGURE 10-6: The When Breakpoint Is Hit dialog box enables you to make a breakpoint display a message when it is hit.

THE IMMEDIATE WINDOW

The Immediate window enables you to evaluate expressions and execute commands while the program is stopped in the debugger. One of the more useful commands displays a variable's or expression's value. Simply type the variable or expression and press Enter to see its value.

You can also set a variable's value in the Immediate window. Simply type the variable's name, the equal sign, and its new value. For example, the statement Width = 300 sets Width equal to 300. If the code is running in a Windows Form, and no other variable named Width is defined, this would set the form's width to 300.

In addition to viewing and modifying variable values, the Immediate window enables you to execute methods so that you can easily test them. For example, suppose you have written a CheckPrinter method. Then you could type the statement CheckPrinter() in the Immediate window to execute that method.

Executing methods in the Immediate window enables you to test them quickly and easily without writing user interface code to handle all possible situations. You can call a method passing it different parameters to see what happens. If you set breakpoints within the method, the debugger pauses execution there.

The Debug and Trace classes provide several methods such as Write and WriteLine for displaying output. They let your program display information about what it is doing.

When you initially configure Visual Studio for C#, that information is written into the Immediate window. You can change that behavior in two ways. First, you can select Tools ➪ Options, go to Debugging, and select General. If you uncheck the "Redirect All Output Window text to the Immediate Window" option, the `Debug` and `Trace` writing methods send output to the Output window instead of the Immediate window. (Even though that option says it redirects *all* output, it actually redirects only `Debug` and `Trace` output, not output generated by `Console` writing methods such as `Console.WriteLine`.)

The second method for changing where `Debug` and `Trace` output goes is to implement trace listeners. This is a useful and complicated enough technique that it is described in the following section.

TRACE LISTENERS

The breakpoints described in the previous sections are extremely useful for figuring out what a program is doing. They let you step through the code as it executes to see what steps the program executes and to see what values are contained in variables.

However, sometimes a breakpoint can interfere with the program's operation, so it prevents you from observing its normal behavior. For example, if the program uses event handlers to track the mouse's position, a breakpoint stops the event handlers so that the program can't track the mouse anymore.

Sometimes it's hard to predict when an error will occur. For example, if a program encounters a bug only after running for several hours, it may be impractical to step through the code until a mistake occurs.

In those cases, it may be better to record events as they occur in a log or text file and then look at the record later. By default the `Trace` and `Debug` classes send their output to the Immediate or Console window. However, those classes share a `Listeners` collection that keeps track of listener objects that should receive that output.

Initially, that collection holds the `DefaultTraceListener` object, but you can remove that object or add new listeners if you like. Other listeners can send output to other locations such as log files, system event logs, or text files.

The .NET Framework provides the following three kinds of trace listener classes.

➤ `ConsoleTraceListener`—Sends output to the Console window

➤ `EventLogTraceListener`—Sends output to an event log

➤ `TextWriterTraceListener`—Sends output to a stream such as a `FileStream`

The TraceIntoTextFile example program, which is available for download on the book's website, uses the following code to demonstrate a trace listener.

```
private void Form1_Load(object sender, EventArgs e)
{
    // Create the trace output file.
    Stream stream = File.Create("DebugLog.txt");

    // Create a TextWriterTraceListener for the trace output file.
```

```
        Debug.Listeners.Add(new TextWriterTraceListener(stream));

        // Write a startup note into the trace file.
        Debug.WriteLine(DateTime.Now.ToString() + ": Debugging session started");
    }

    // Create and process a Student.
    private void processButton_Click(object sender, EventArgs e)
    {
        Student student = new Student()
        {
            FirstName = firstNameTextBox.Text,
            LastName = lastNameTextBox.Text,
            Street = streetTextBox.Text,
            City = cityTextBox.Text,
            State = stateTextBox.Text,
            Zip = zipTextBox.Text
        };
        ProcessStudent(student);
    }


    // Process a student.
    private void ProcessStudent(Student student)
    {
        Debug.WriteLine("ProcessStudent");
        Debug.Indent();
        Debug.WriteLine("Name:    " + student.FirstName + " " + student.LastName);
        Debug.WriteLine("Address: " + student.Street);
        Debug.WriteLine("         " + student.City + " " + student.State + " " +
            student.Zip);
        Debug.Unindent();

        ///... Process the student here...
    }

    // Close the Debug trace file.
    private void Form1_FormClosing(object sender, FormClosingEventArgs e)
    {
        Debug.WriteLine(DateTime.Now.ToString() + ": Debugging session ended");
        Debug.Close();
    }
```

When the form loads, the program creates a file named DebugLog.txt. It uses that file's stream to create a new TextWriterTraceListener and adds it to the Debug object's Listeners collection.

The program then uses Debug.WriteLine to write a start message. Because the Debug object's Listeners collection contains the default listener in addition to the new TextWriterTraceListener, the message is displayed in the Immediate window and written into the file.

If you enter information about a student in the form's TextBoxes and then click the Process button, the processButton_Click event handler executes. It creates a new Student object and passes it to the ProcessStudent method.

The `ProcessStudent` method uses `Debug` statements to display the `Student`'s information in the Immediate window and to write it into the listener file. The method uses `Debug.Indent` and `Debug.Unindent` to indent the `Student`'s information.

When you later close the form, the `Form1_FormClosing` event handler uses `Debug.WriteLine` to display an ending message. It then calls `Debug.Close` to flush any output that hasn't been written into the listener file and to close the file. If you skip this step, some of the output is likely to be lost.

> ### AUTOFLUSH
>
> If you set the `Debug` or `Trace` class's `AutoFlush` property to `true`, then the class automatically flushes its output every write time you use the object's write methods.

The following text shows sample output written into the listener file.

```
4/1/2014 3:06:25 PM: Debugging session started
ProcessStudent
    Name:    Rod Stephens
    Address: 1337 Leet St
             Bugsville AZ 87654
4/1/2014 3:06:27 PM: Debugging session ended
```

You can make a couple of useful changes to the previous program. First, you can open the listener file for appending instead of writing over previous output. Second, you can allow sharing when you open the file, so other programs such as Microsoft Word and Notepad can view the file while the program is still running. (If you allow sharing, you need to flush output every time you write or set `AutoFlush` to `true`. Otherwise the other program won't see the latest items written into the file.)

The following code shows how you can open the listener file and allow sharing.

```
// Open the trace output file. Allow sharing and use AutoFlush.
Stream stream = File.Open("DebugLog.txt",
    FileMode.Append, FileAccess.Write, FileShare.Read);
Debug.AutoFlush = true;
```

SUMMARY

C# and Visual Studio cannot debug your programs for you, but they do provide the tools you need to do it yourself. Breakpoints are particularly useful. They enable you to pause execution at selected lines of code, so you can examine the program's variables and step through execution line by line to see what the program is doing, and hopefully what it is doing wrong. You can place conditions on breakpoints, so they stop the program only under certain conditions, such as when a breakpoint has been reached a certain number of times or when a variable contains a particular value.

The `Debug` and `Trace` classes provide methods that the program can use to display diagnostic information in the Immediate window. By adding trace listeners to those classes, you can save information in other places such as event logs or text files without interrupting the program. Later you can analyze that information to see what the program did.

The chapters in Part II, "C# Language Elements," of this book focus on small-scale programming issues. They explain how to create variables, perform calculations, and overload operators; how to control program flow with statements such as `if`, `switch`, `for`, and `while`; how to select and arrange data with LINQ; and how to use debugging and tracing tools to understand what a program is doing and find bugs.

The chapters in Part III, "Object-Oriented Programming," move to a higher level and describe object-oriented concepts. They explain key object-oriented concepts, how to build structures and classes, how to use collection classes, and how to use generics to make one class work with many data types.

EXERCISES

1. The following code shows a recursive implementation of a Factorial function. (Recursive means it calls itself.)

    ```
    private long Factorial(long number)
    {
        if (number <= 1) return 1;
        return number * Factorial(number - 1);
    }
    ```

    Use the `Debug` class's methods to trace this method's execution. Each call to the `Factorial` method should indicate when it is called and with what parameter. Before returning, each call should display its result. Use indentation to make it easier to match calls and results. For example, the following text shows the output while calculating `Factorial(4)`.

    ```
    Factorial(4)
        Factorial(3)
            Factorial(2)
                Factorial(1)
                Result: 1
            Result: 2
        Result: 6
    Result: 24
    ```

2. Modify the program you wrote for Exercise 1 so that each call to the `Factorial` method displays its parameter and result as in the following text.

    ```
    Factorial(1) = 1
    Factorial(2) = 2
    Factorial(3) = 6
    Factorial(4) = 24
    ```

3. Can you modify the program you wrote for Exercise 2 to efficiently use `Debug` statements to display each call and its result in the order in which they are called? For example, can you make the program display the following trace when calling `Factorial(4)`?

    ```
    Factorial(4) = 24
    Factorial(3) = 6
    Factorial(2) = 2
    Factorial(1) = 1
    ```

4. Suppose your customer *insists* that you produce an output similar to the one described in Exercise 3. Modify the `Factorial` method to produce this kind of display. (Hint: You may want to make larger changes to the method, for example, changing its parameter list or return value.)

5. The `Debug` and `Trace` classes let a program provide different levels of output depending on whether the `DEBUG` and `TRACE` preprocessor symbols are defined. Create a `PrintMessage` method that takes two parameters: a debugging level and a message. If the debugging level is less than or equal to a corresponding preprocessor symbol, display the message in the Console window. (For example, if the symbol `DEBUG2` is defined and the method's debugging level is less than or equal to 2, display the message.)

Compare this method to the `Debug` and `Trace` classes. How could you improve this method?

6. Build a program that writes `Debug` and `Trace` messages into the file Messages.txt instead of displaying them in the Console or Immediate window. Open the file for append, allow read-only sharing, automatically flush the log files, and include the time with each message. Write a few messages using `Debug`, `Trace`, and `Console`. Before the program closes the file, open the file with Microsoft Word and Notepad to verify that you can do it.

7. One limitation to the `Debug` and `Trace` classes is that they share the same `Listeners` collection, so you can't send `Debug` output to one location and `Trace` output to another. Write a method called `LogMessage` that takes two parameters: a filename and a message. The method should append the current time plus the message to the indicated file. (Chapter 19, "File System Objects," has a lot to say about reading and writing files. For now just use `System.IO.File.AppendAllText` to add text to the file.) Then rewrite the program you wrote for Exercise 6 to use that method to write messages into the files DebugLog.txt and TraceLog.txt.

PART III
Object-Oriented Programming

11

OOP Concepts

WHAT'S IN THIS CHAPTER

➤   Properties, methods, and events

➤   Inheritance, refinement, and abstraction

➤   Hiding and overriding

➤   Encapsulation, information hiding, and polymorphism

WROX.COM DOWNLOADS FOR THIS CHAPTER

Please note that all the code examples for this chapter are available as a part of this chapter's code download on the book's website at www.wrox.com/go/csharp5programmersref on the Download Code tab.

This chapter describes the basic concepts behind *object-oriented programming (OOP)*. It explains how to define classes and how to derive one class from another. It also describes the three fundamental features of OOP programming languages: encapsulation, inheritance, and polymorphism. It explains how C# provides those features and what benefits you can gain from using them properly.

CLASSES

A *class* is a programming entity that packages the data and behavior of some sort of programming abstraction. It encapsulates the idea that it represents in a package that has a well-defined interface to code that lies outside of the package. The interface determines how other pieces of code can interact with objects defined by the class. The interface determines which pieces of data are visible outside of the class and which pieces of data are hidden inside the class.

The three main sets of characteristics of a class are the properties, methods, and events that it defines. The public (externally visible) properties, methods, and events let the program work with the class:

➤ A *property* is some sort of data value. It may be a simple value (such as a string or int), or it may be a more complex item (such as an array, list, or object containing its own properties, methods, and events). Properties determine some feature of an object such as its name, color, or behavior.

➤ A *method* is a routine that performs some action. A method makes an object defined by the class do something.

➤ An *event* provides notification that something happened to an object defined by the class. An event can invoke other pieces of code to tell other parts of the program that something has happened to the object.

For a concrete example, imagine a Job class that represents a piece of work to be done by an employee. This class might have the properties shown in the following table.

PROPERTY	PURPOSE
JobDescription	A string describing the job.
EstimatedHours	The number of hours initially estimated for the job.
ActualHours	The actual number of hours spent on the job.
Status	An enumeration giving the job's status (New, Assigned, InProgress, or Complete).
ActionTaken	A string describing the work performed, parts installed, and so forth.
Customer	An object of the Customer class that describes the customer for whom the job is performed. (That class has properties such as Name, Address, PhoneNumber, and ContractNumber.)
AssignedEmployee	An object of the Employee class that describes the employee assigned to the job. (That class has properties such as Name, PhoneNumber, EmployeeId, and SocialSecurityNumber.)

The JobDescription, EstimatedHours, ActualHours, Status, and ActionTaken properties are relatively simple string and numeric values. The Customer and AssignedEmployee properties are objects themselves with their own properties, methods, and events.

This Job class might provide the methods shown in the following table.

METHOD	PURPOSE
AssignJob	Assigns the `Job` to an `Employee`
PrintInvoice	Prints an invoice for the `Customer` after the job is completed
EstimatedCost	Calculates and returns an estimated cost based on the customer's service contract type and `EstimatedHours`

The class could provide the events shown in the following table to keep the main program informed about the job's progress.

EVENT	PURPOSE
Created	Occurs when the `Job` is first created
Assigned	Occurs when the `Job` is assigned to an `Employee`
Rejected	Occurs if an `Employee` refuses to do the job, perhaps because the `Employee` doesn't have the right skills or equipment to do the work
Canceled	Occurs if the `Customer` cancels the job before it is started
Finished	Occurs when the job is completed

The class packages the data and behavior of some programming abstraction such as a `Job`, `Employee`, `Customer`, `Menu`, `SquashMatch`, `SoftwareProject`, or anything else you might want to manipulate as a single entity.

After you have defined a class, you can create as many instances of the class as you like. An *instance* of the class is an object of the class type. For example, the `Job` class represents jobs in general. After you have defined the `Job` class, you can make instances of the class to represent specific jobs. You could create instances to represent building a brick wall, planting a tree, or repairing a telephone switch. The process of creating an instance of a class is called *instantiation*.

There are a couple common analogies to describe instantiation. One compares the class to a blueprint. After you define the class, you can use it to create any number of instances of the class, much as you can use the blueprint to make any number of similar houses (instances).

The different houses have much in common. For example, the blueprint defines the number, size, and relative placement of the houses' rooms. These are analogous to features defined by the class that apply to all the instances. (In the `Job` class example, all instances have a `PrintInvoice` method that prints an invoice. Although exactly what is printed depends on the instance's properties.)

The houses can also have differences such as different colors, front doors, and appliances. Those correspond to the class's property values. For example, a `House` class could define `ExteriorColor` and `ExteriorTrim` properties that determine the color of each instance of the class.

A second analogy compares a class definition to a cookie cutter. After you create the cookie cutter, you can use it to make any number of cookies (instances). The cookie cutter (class) defines the cookies' size and shape. Specific instances might have different properties such as thickness, dough type (chocolate chip, sugar, gingerbread, and so on), and frosting type (none, single color, and patterned).

CLASSES, CLASSES EVERYWHERE

The .NET Framework is full of classes. Every type of control and component (`Form`, `TextBox`, `Label`, `Timer`, `Window`, and so forth) is a class. Their parent classes `Control` and `Component` are classes. The Framework also includes classes that represent containers, queues, messages, random number generators, web pages, XML documents, XPS documents, cryptographic functions, printers, operating system features, and all sorts of other things.

Even `Object`, from which all other classes derive, is a class. Whenever you work with any of these (getting or setting properties, calling methods, and responding to events), you are working with instances of classes. In total, the .NET Framework contains somewhere on the order of 10,000 public classes.

Actually, every piece of code you write in C# must be contained in a class. There's no escaping classes!

Because all classes ultimately derive from the `Object` class, every instance of every class is in some sense an `Object`, so they are often simply called *objects*. If you don't know or don't care about an item's class, you can simply refer to it as an object.

OUTSTANDING OBJECTS

When you read the section "Polymorphism" later in this chapter, you'll see that this makes technical, as well as intuitive, sense. Because all classes eventually derive from the `Object` class, all instances of all classes are actually `Object`s.

The following sections provide more details about the more important features provided by OOP languages in general and C# in particular.

ENCAPSULATION

A class's *public interface* is the set of properties, methods, and events that are visible to code outside of the class. The class may also have private properties, methods, and events that it uses to do its job. For example, the `Job` class described in the previous section provides an `AssignJob` method. That method might call a private `FindQualifiedEmployee` method that looks through an employee database to find someone who has the skills and equipment necessary to do the job. That routine is not used outside of the class, so it can be declared private.

PRIVATE PROPERTY

Many developers underestimate the value of private properties and simply use private variables (fields) instead. Just because a value is private, doesn't mean you won't get any benefit from making it a property. Property accessors let you validate new values, perhaps with code contracts or the `Debug.Assert` method. If a value is being set incorrectly, you can also set a breakpoint in a property accessor to see when the value is changing. (See Chapter 9, "Error Handling," for information about code contracts and `Debug.Assert`.)

The `FindQualifiedEmployee` method *should* be declared private to hide it from code outside of the class. That makes the interface easier to understand and use. Making `FindQualifiedEmployee` public would clutter the interface (and IntelliSense) with unnecessary information.

The class may also include private properties and events. These hidden properties, methods, and events are not part of the class's public interface.

The class *encapsulates* the programming abstraction that it represents (a `Job` in this ongoing example). Its public interface determines what is visible to the application outside of the class. It hides the ugly details of the class's implementation from the rest of the world. Because the class hides its internals in this way, encapsulation is also sometimes called *information hiding*.

By hiding its internals from the outside world, a class prevents exterior code from messing around with those internals. It reduces the dependencies between different parts of the application, allowing only those dependencies that are explicitly permitted by its public interface.

Removing dependencies between different pieces of code makes the code easier to modify and maintain. If you must change the way the `Job` class assigns a job to an employee, you can modify the `AssignJob` method appropriately. The code that calls the `AssignJob` routine doesn't need to know that the details have changed. It simply continues to call the method and leaves the details up to the `Job` class.

Removing dependencies also helps break the application into smaller, more manageable pieces. A developer who calls the `AssignJob` method can concentrate on the job at hand, rather than on how the method works. This makes developers more productive and less likely to make mistakes while modifying the encapsulated code.

To make using a class as easy and safe as possible, you should hide as much information as possible about the class's internals while still allowing outside code to do its job. If the external code doesn't need to know something about how the class works, it shouldn't.

To make public properties, methods, and events easy to use, you should make them simple (at least as seen from outside of the class) and tightly focused. A set of small methods that do a single simple task each is easier to use than a single method that can do a huge number of different things depending on its parameters.

For example, the `Graphics` class provides methods to draw and fill various shapes. The `DrawEllipse`, `DrawRectangle`, `DrawLine`, and `DrawPolygon` methods outline different kinds of shapes. Similarly, the `FillEllipse`, `FillRectangle`, `FillRegion`, and `FillPolygon` methods fill different kinds of shapes.

You could probably replace all those methods with a single DrawShape method that draws and outlines or fills various kinds of shapes depending on the parameters that it received. That would make the code harder to understand because you would have to carefully study the parameters in a specific call to figure out what it was doing. By using separate methods, the class makes the code obvious. If the program calls DrawRectangle, it is drawing a rectangle.

DON'T OVERGENERALIZE

Creating methods that try to do too much is sometimes called the "kitchen sink" approach because the method contains everything "including the kitchen sink." Sometimes it's easy to slip into this approach by trying to generalize a method unnecessarily.

For example, suppose you need a method to print an invoice. Some other part of the program needs to print an employee timesheet. Because they both involve printing, you might try to make a single method to do both. That's probably a mistake. The two tasks both involve printing and may require common printer setup code, but they don't have much in common logically. (The fact that you might want to name the method something confusing like PrintInvoiceOrTimeSheet is a hint that the method is being asked to do too much.)

A better approach would be to make separate PrintInvoice and PrintTimeSheet methods. If they share a lot of common code, then you can move that code into a PrintMethods class that handles printing details. For example, that class might provide SelectPrinter, InitializePrinter, and FinishPrinting methods.

When you are working on the PrintInvoice method, you will be focused on printing, so calling SelectPrinter, InitializePrinter, and FinishPrinting makes sense.

When other pieces of code need to print an invoice, they simply call PrintInvoice and the details of setting up the printer are hidden.

Making methods perform a single, tightly focused task can be a difficult concept for beginning programmers. Adding more features seems like it would give developers more power, so you might think it would make their jobs easier. However, it often makes development more confusing and difficult. Instead of thinking in terms of giving the developer more power, you should think about the fact that this approach gives the developer more things to worry about and more ways to make mistakes. Ideally, you should not expose any more features than the developer actually needs.

INHERITANCE

Inheritance lets you derive a *child class* from a *parent class*. The child class inherits all the properties, methods, and events defined by the parent class. It can then modify, add to, or subtract from the parent class. Making a child class inherit from a parent class is also called *deriving* the child class from the parent, and *subclassing* the parent class to form the child class.

For example, suppose you define a `Person` class that includes properties named `FirstName`, `LastName`, `Street`, `City`, `State`, `Zip`, `Phone`, and `Email`. It might also include a `PrintEnvelope` method that prints an envelope addressed to the person represented by the `Person` object.

Now you could derive the `Employee` class from `Person`. The `Employee` class inherits the `FirstName`, `LastName`, `Street`, `City`, `State`, `Zip`, `Phone`, and `Email` properties. It then adds new `EmployeeId`, `SocialSecurityNumber`, `OfficeNumber`, `Extension`, and `Salary` properties.

The `Employee` class might *override* the `Person` class's `PrintEnvelope` method, so it addresses the envelope to the employee's office instead of the home address.

Now you can derive other classes from those classes to create a whole hierarchy of classes. You could derive the `Manager` class from the `Employee` class and add fields such as `Secretary` that would refer to another `Employee` object that represents the manager's secretary. Similarly, you could derive a `Secretary` class from `Employee` that includes a reference to a `Manager` object. You could derive `ProjectManager`, `DepartmentManager`, and `DivisionManager` from the `Manager` class; `Customer` from the `Person` class; and so on for other types of people that the application needs to use. Figure 11-1 shows an inheritance hierarchy containing these classes.

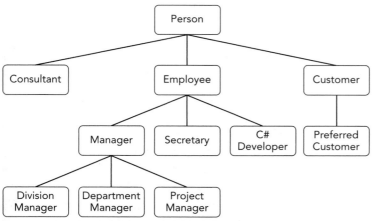

FIGURE 11-1: You can derive classes from other classes to form complex inheritance relationships.

Inheritance Hierarchies

One of the key benefits of inheritance is *code reuse*. When you derive a class from a parent class, the child class gets to reuse the code you wrote for the parent class. For example, all the classes referred to in Figure 11-1 inherit their `FirstName`, `LastName`, `Street`, `City`, `State`, `Zip`, `Phone`, and `Email` properties from the `Person` class, so they don't need to implement those properties separately.

The `Consultant`, `Employee`, `Customer`, and `PreferredCustomer` classes also inherit the `PrintEnvelope` method defined by the `Person` class. The `Employee` class overrides that method, so it doesn't get to reuse the `Person` class's version. However, the new version does something different from the original version, so you have no choice but to write new code. In addition, the six classes that inherit from `Employee` get to reuse the new version.

Code reuse not only saves you the effort needed to write the same code multiple times but also saves you time for debugging and maintenance. For example, if you find a bug in the PrintEnvelope method, you need to fix it only in one place instead of in each of the classes that inherits it. That saves time and prevents you from fixing the bug in one class but forgetting to fix it in another.

Code reuse also helps you make modifications. Suppose you decide to change the Zip property to store ZIP codes with the ZIP+4 format instead of the original 5-digit format. In that case you need to change only the representation in the Person class, and all the other classes inherit the change.

Of course, then you'll probably want to change the PrintEnvelope method to use the new Zip format. Again, you have to make the change only in the Person class and the other classes inherit the change.

Similarly, if you need to add, modify, or delete a property or method, you need to make the change only in the class where it is defined, not in all the classes that inherit it. If you want to add a SendEmail method, you need to add it only to the Person class.

Refinement and Abstraction

You can think about the relationship between a parent class and its child classes in a top-down or bottom-up way. Those two points of view lead to the ideas of refinement and abstraction.

Refinement

Using a top-down view of inheritance, you can think of the child classes as *refining* the parent class. They provide extra detail that differentiates among different types of the parent class.

For example, suppose that you start with a class that covers a broad category such as Person. The Person class would need general fields that apply to all people such as FirstName, LastName, Address, and PhoneNumber.

Some kinds of people might need additional fields that don't apply to every kind of person. For example, a school's instructors might also need Title, CoursesAssigned, Advisees, Office, and OfficeHours properties. Students might need StudentId, Year, CoursesTaken, and GPA fields.

You could add all these fields to the Person class, but that would force the class to play two different roles. That would be complicated and confusing. It would also be somewhat wasteful because a Person acting as an instructor wouldn't use any of the student properties, and a Person acting as a student wouldn't use any of the instructor properties.

A better solution is to derive new Instructor and Student classes that refine the Person class's definition and add their new properties. Now each class represents a specific kind of person.

Abstraction

Using a bottom-up view of inheritance, you can think of the parent as *abstracting* the features of its children. The parent class gathers together the common features of the child classes. Because the parent class is more general than the child classes (it includes a larger group of objects), abstraction is sometimes called *generalization*.

For example, suppose you're making a drawing application and you define various classes to represent shapes such as Circle, Rectangle, Ellipse, and Polygon. When you build the program, you may discover that these classes have a lot in common. For example, at times the program may need to find bounding rectangles for each of the objects. You may find that the objects have common ForegroundColor and BackgroundColor properties. You may want each class to provide a PointIsOver method that returns true if the given point is over the shape. You might also want to make each class raise a Clicked event when the user clicks on its shape.

MULTIPLE INHERITANCE

Some languages allow *multiple inheritance*, where a class can have multiple parent classes. For example, suppose that you create a Boat class that defines properties of boats (NumberOfPassengers, Draft, MaximumSpeed, HasGps, and so forth) and a House class that defines properties of living spaces (SquareFeet, NumberOfBedrooms, NumberOfBathrooms, and so forth). Using multiple inheritance, you could derive a HouseBoat class that inherits from both the Boat and House classes. This class would have the properties, methods, and events of both of the classes. (You would also need a tie-breaking scheme to figure out what to do if, for example, the Boat and House classes both had a Price property.)

C# does not allow multiple inheritance. A class can have as many child classes as you like, but it can have at most one parent class. That means relationships such as those shown in Figure 11-1 form a treelike inheritance hierarchy.

An alternative to multiple inheritance is *interface inheritance*. Instead inheriting from multiple parent classes, the child inherits from one class and implements other features defined by an interface. For example, the HouseBoat class might inherit from Boat and implement an IHouse interface. Although a class can have only one parent, it can implement as many interfaces as you like.

Unfortunately, you need to write the code to implement the interface because you can't inherit it. You lose the benefit of code reuse, but at least you keep the benefits of polymorphism (described in the section "Polymorphism" later in this chapter).

You can also use delegation to provide a form of code reuse. Suppose you create an IHouse interface and a House class that implements the interface. Now you can place an instance of the House class inside the HouseBoat class, perhaps as a private variable. Now when you implement the IHouse interface, you can delegate all the work to the House instance. This isn't as easy as multiple inheritance, but it does give you most of the same code reuse.

(For more information on interfaces, see the section "Implementing Interfaces" in Chapter 6, "Methods.")

After you realize that these classes have so much in common, you might decide to extract those common features and move them into a common parent class named Drawable. That class would define the common features that the other classes need to implement. For example, the Drawable class could implement the ForegroundColor and BackgroundColor properties for the other classes to inherit.

Some of the child classes might override the default implementations in the Drawable class. It might even be impossible for the Drawable class to provide some of the features it defines. For example, each type of shape would need a different PointIsOver method because you need to use different techniques to determine whether a point is over a rectangle, circle, or polygon. You could give the Drawable class a default implementation, perhaps making it treat its shape as a rectangle, but you wouldn't gain much by doing that. You would still need to override that method in every class except Rectangle. Providing the default implementation would also incorrectly imply that the method is useful for something other than a single child class.

In this case you're probably better off marking the method as abstract and not providing a method body so that the child classes are required to override it. (For more information on the abstract keyword, see the section "abstract" in Chapter 6.)

A FAMILY NAME

To make the relationship among child classes more obvious, you can give them similar names. For the drawing example, you could call the child classes DrawableRectangle, DrawableCircle, DrawablePolygon, and so forth. This makes it easier to remember that the classes are all types of Drawables. It also helps differentiate them from .NET Framework classes such as Rectangle, Ellipse, and Polygon.

Making a Drawable parent class also allows the program to treat all drawing objects uniformly as Drawables. For example, it can create a collection named AllDrawables to hold the current picture's drawing objects. Then when the user moves the mouse, the program could loop through the collection calling each object's PointIsOver method to determine whether the mouse was over an object. The section "Polymorphism" later in this chapter provides more details.

Using Refinement and Abstraction

Often a program's classes are defined by using refinement. You know the general categories of things the program needs such as Person, Report, and Job. As you go through the project requirements, you can refine those to create the specific kinds of objects the program will need. Person becomes Employee, Manager, Secretary, Programmer, Customer, and Contractor. Report becomes TimeSheet, JobRequirements, ProgressReport, and Invoice.

During the project's design phase, the classes tend to map naturally to the requirements, so it's relatively easy to imagine their relationships.

Abstraction often arises during development. As you define and work with the classes, you may discover they have unexpected things in common. For example, suppose you're working with the Person class and the descendant classes described earlier. After a while you realize that Manager and Programmer are salaried positions but Secretary is hourly. You could add a Salary property to Manager and Programmer, and add HourlyRate to Secretary. Unfortunately, that would require a duplicate Salary property. It would also mean you couldn't treat Manager and Programmer objects uniformly.

The solution is to create a new `SalariedEmployee` class to act as a new parent for the `Manager` and `Programmer` classes. Figure 11-2 shows the new class hierarchy.

Refinement is an important technique for building inheritance hierarchies, but it can sometimes lead to *unnecessary refinement* or *over-refinement*. For example, suppose that you define a `Vehicle` class. You then refine this class by creating `Auto`, `Truck`, and `Boat` classes. You refine the `Auto` class into `Wagon` and `Sedan` classes and further refine those for different drive types (four-wheel drive, automatic transmission, and so forth). If you really go crazy, you could define classes for specific manufacturers, body styles, and colors.

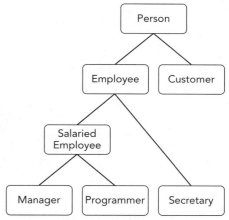

FIGURE 11-2: You can derive classes from other classes to form complex inheritance relationships.

The problem with this hierarchy is that it captures a lot more detail than you need. If you're building a program to manage a fleet of delivery vehicles, then you probably need to know the vehicle's capacity, but you probably don't need to keep track of its manufacturer, transmission type, and color. You may want to track some of that information so that you can identify each vehicle properly, but you don't need to make these separate classes.

As far as a delivery scheduling application is concerned, the color is irrelevant. Creating lots of unnecessary classes makes the object model harder to understand and can lead to confusion and mistakes.

Avoid unnecessary refinement by refining a class only when doing so lets you capture new information that the application actually needs to know.

Just as you can take refinement to ridiculous extremes, you can also overdo abstraction. Because abstraction is driven by code rather than intuition, it sometimes leads to unintuitive inheritance hierarchies.

For example, suppose that your application needs to mail purchase orders to vendors and invoices to customers. If the `PurchaseOrder` and `Invoice` classes have enough in common, you might decide to create a more abstract `MailableItem` class that contains the code needed to create and mail a document to someone.

At some point you may discover that you also need to e-mail items to vendors or customers, so you create the idea of an `EmailableItem` class. The `MailableItem` and `EmailableItem` classes probably share some common features because they both represent sending something to someone, so you may then be tempted to create an even more abstract `SendableItem` class.

Although all this makes a sort of weird sense from a coding point of view, it doesn't make much intuitive sense. That means programmers need to spend extra time figuring out what the classes are for and how to use them. It also means programmers are more likely to make mistakes that can slow development and create annoying bugs.

CONTEXT IS KING

The classes mentioned here probably don't make sense for most programs, but some may make perfect sense in the proper context. If you're building a program to manage a mailroom, you may want classes to represent things that you can mail.

If a class makes intuitive sense, it's probably a reasonable class. If the program doesn't need to treat the instances of a class differently than it treats instances of child or parent classes, it's probably unnecessary. And you should take a long look at a class if its name makes developers scratch their heads, make funny faces, and ask, "What on Earth is *that* for?"

You can sometimes avoid over-abstraction by moving common features into libraries instead of creating separate classes to represent them. For example, you could make a library containing methods to send items via e-mail or postal mail. Then the program can call those methods as needed. Unless the program is some sort of a message tracking system, it probably doesn't need an object to represent e-mails and letters.

Over-refinement and over-abstraction sometimes lead to inflated inheritance hierarchies. Sometimes the hierarchy grows tall and thin. Other times the design might include many separate but small inheritance hierarchies, a parent class with a single child, or a class that is never used.

If your inheritance hierarchy starts to take on one of these odd forms, you should spend some time to reevaluate your classes. Make sure each adds something meaningful to the application and that the relationships are reasonably intuitive. Too many classes with confusing relationships can drag a project to a halt as developers spend more time trying to understand the hierarchy than they spend writing code.

HORRIBLE HIERARCHIES

I've worked on a few projects that failed because of overly complicated object models. Their class hierarchies were so confusing that developers couldn't understand how to use the classes to get anything done.

In one case the hierarchy was designed with all sorts of useful abstraction and refinement, but the classes were so non-intuitive that only the person who made the design could figure out how they all fit together.

In another case, the hierarchy grew up over time as pieces were added to the system. Eventually, the hierarchies grew so deep and confusing that no one but the person who had created the hierarchy could figure out how anything worked.

If you are unsure whether you should add a new class, leave it out. You can add it later if you discover that it is necessary after all. Usually it's easier to add a new class than it is to remove an unnecessary class after developers have started using it.

Has-a and Is-a Relationships

In refinement you create child classes to differentiate among different kinds of objects. In abstraction you create a parent class to represent features that are common between two or more child classes. Both of these techniques create parent/child relationships between classes.

Another concept that sometimes masquerades as a parent/child relationship is *containment*. In containment, one object contains another object as an attribute.

The ideas of inheritance and containment are sometimes referred to as *is-a* and *has-a* relationships.

For example, a Student is-a specific type of Person object. The is-a relation maps naturally into inheritance hierarchies. Because a Student is-a Person, it makes sense to derive the Student class from the Person class.

In contrast a Person object has-a street address, city, state, and ZIP code. The has-a relation maps most naturally to embedded items. For example, you could give the Person class the Street, City, State, and Zip properties.

To see why the difference between the is-a and has-a relationships is important, suppose your program works with the Person and Student classes. Suppose it also works with FinancialAidPayment, RegistrationFee, and other classes that have street, city, state, and ZIP code information. Using abstraction, you might make a HasPostalAddress class that contains those values. Then you could derive the Person, FinancialAidPayment, and RegistrationFee classes as children of HasPostalAddress. Unfortunately, that makes a rather unintuitive inheritance hierarchy. Deriving all those classes from the same parent class also makes them seem closely related when they are actually related only coincidentally.

A better solution is to encapsulate the postal address data in its own Address class and then include an instance of that class in the Person, FinancialAidPayment, and RegistrationFee classes.

You make a parent class through abstraction in part to avoid duplication of code. The parent class contains a single copy of the common variables and code, so the child classes don't need to have their own separate versions for you to debug and maintain. Placing an instance of the Address class in each of the other classes provides the same benefit without complicating the inheritance hierarchy.

Sometimes you can use either is-a or has-a to describe a relationship. For example, a Person has-an address, but at the same time a Person is-a thing that has an address. In cases like this, you need to use your common sense and intuition to decide which makes more sense. One hint is that it is easy to describe something that "has an address" but the phrase "is a thing that has an address" is more awkward and ill-defined.

You can also think about how a relationship might affect other classes. Are the Person, FinancialAidPayment, and RegistrationFee classes truly closely related? Or do they just share some common information?

Adding and Modifying Class Features

Adding new properties, methods, and events to a child class is easy. You simply declare them as you would in any other class. The parent class knows nothing about them, so the new items are added only to the child class.

The following code shows how you could implement the `Person` and `Employee` classes in C#.

```
// A general person.
public class Person
{
    public string FirstName, LastName, Street, City, State, Zip, Phone, Email;

    // Dial the phone.
    public void DialPhone()
    {
        // Dial the number Phone...
    }
}

// An employee.
public class Employee : Person
{
    public string EmployeeId, SocialSecurityNumber, OfficeNumber, Extension;
    public decimal Salary;

    // Print a timesheet for the employee.
    public void PrintTimesheet()
    {
        // Print the timesheet...
    }
}
```

The `Person` class defines name and address values. For simplicity, they are implemented as fields, but in practice you might want to make them properties. This class also defines a `DialPhone` method that dials the person's phone number.

The `Employee` class is derived from the `Person` class. (That's what ": `Person`" means at the end of the class declaration.) This class adds some new values and then defines a new `PrintTimesheet` method.

There are two ways a child class can modify the behavior of a method defined in its parent class (or any ancestor class): hiding and overriding.

Hiding and Overriding

First, the child class can *hide* the parent class's version of a method. To do that, add the keyword new to indicate that you want to use a new version of the method. The following code shows how the `Employee` class could hide the `DialPhone` method to create a new version that includes the `Employee`'s `Extension`. The new keyword is highlighted in bold.

```
// Dial the phone + extension.
public new void DialPhone()
{
    // Dial the number Phone + Extension...
}
```

The second way a child class can modify a parent method is to *override* it.

This method requires some cooperation from the parent class. The parent class must mark the method with the `virtual` or `abstract` keyword. (The parent class can also have overridden the method. In that case, some ancestor class declared the original method with the `virtual` or `abstract` keyword.)

The following code shows the new version of the `Person` class's `DialPhone` method with the `virtual` keyword highlighted in bold.

```
// Dial the phone.
public virtual void DialPhone()
{
    // Dial the number Phone...
}
```

The `virtual` keyword indicates that this method can be overridden by descendant classes. The following code shows how the `Employee` class could override the `DialPhone` method.

```
// Dial the phone + extension.
public override void DialPhone()
{
    // Dial the number Phone + Extension...
}
```

Overriding a method in this way is a powerful technique. When you invoke an overridden method for an object, you get the version defined by the object's true class, even if you are referring to the object with a variable of an ancestor class.

In contrast, when you hide a method, you get only that version if you use a variable of the class that defined the new version.

These are confusing concepts, so here's a detailed example. Consider the following stripped-down `Person` and `Employee` classes.

```
public class Person
{
    public string Name;

    public virtual void IsVirtual()
    {
        Console.WriteLine(Name + ": Person.IsVirtual");
    }

    public void HideMe()
    {
        Console.WriteLine(Name + ": Person.HideMe");
    }
}

public class Employee : Person
{
    public override void IsVirtual()
    {
        Console.WriteLine(Name + ": Employee.IsVirtual");
    }
```

```
        public new void HideMe()
        {
            Console.WriteLine(Name + ": Employee.HideMe");
        }
    }
```

The `Person` class defines two methods. The `IsVirtual` method is defined with the `virtual` keyword. The `HideMe` method is defined without the `virtual` keyword.

The `Employee` class overrides `IsVirtual` and hides `HideMe`.

All four of these methods simply display their object's name, the method's class, and the method's name in the Console window.

Now consider the following code that uses these methods.

```
Person ann = new Person() { Name = "Ann" };
Employee bob = new Employee() { Name = "Bob" };
Person person = bob;

ann.IsVirtual();
bob.IsVirtual();
person.IsVirtual();
Console.WriteLine();
ann.HideMe();
bob.HideMe();
person.HideMe();
```

The code creates a `Person` object and an `Employee` object. It then creates a `Person` variable and makes it refer to the `Employee` object it just created. (You can do that because an `Employee` is a kind of `Person`.)

Next, the code calls each of the objects' `IsVirtual` methods. The object `ann` is a `Person`, so it calls the `Person` version of `IsVirtual`. The object `bob` is an `Employee`, so it calls the `Employee` version of `IsVirtual`.

The `person` object has type `Person`, but it actually refers to the `Employee` object `bob`. Because the `Employee` class overrode the definition of this method, the `person` object uses the version defined by the object's true class, in this case `Employee`. Even though it looks like the code is invoking `Person.IsVirtual`, it actually invokes `Employee.IsVirtual`.

The case with the `HideMe` method is somewhat simpler. As before, the `ann` and `bob` objects call their respective class's versions of the method.

The `person` object has type `Person`. Because this method is hidden in the `Employee` class, the `Person` class doesn't know anything about that version. When the code calls the `Person` object's `HideMe` method, it gets the `Person` class's version.

The following text shows the code's output.

```
Ann: Person.IsVirtual
Bob: Employee.IsVirtual
Bob: Employee.IsVirtual
```

```
Ann: Person.HideMe
Bob: Employee.HideMe
Bob: Person.HideMe
```

The object `person` invokes the `Employee` class's version of `IsVirtual` (the third line of output) but it invokes the `Person` class's version of `HideMe` (the last line of output).

> **TIP** *Hiding and overriding are important but confusing concepts. If the difference isn't clear, you should reread this section.*

There are two other keywords that affect overriding: `abstract` and `sealed`.

abstract

An abstract method is one that doesn't have a method body. It defines the name, parameters, and return type of the method but doesn't provide an implementation. (This is similar to the way interfaces define method signatures but don't provide an implementation.)

If you give a class an abstract method, there's a sort of placeholder in the class for the method. Because the placeholder is empty, you cannot create an instance of the class because it is incomplete. For that reason, if a class contains an abstract method, you must also mark the class as abstract.

Note that the class could define other non-abstract properties, methods, and events. (Some people call a non-abstract method, class, or other item *concrete*.) If it contains even one abstract method, then the class must be abstract.

ABSOLUTELY ABSTRACT

You can also mark a class `abstract` to prevent someone from creating an instance of it even if it doesn't contain any abstract methods.

An abstract method is also considered virtual, so a child class can override it to give it a method body. Then the child class can be concrete and you can create instances of it.

For an example, consider the following code.

```
public abstract class Report
{
    public abstract void GenerateReport();
    public abstract void DistributeReport();
}
public abstract class PersonnelReport : Report
{
    public override void DistributeReport()
    {
        // Code to distribute the report to the personnel department...
    }
}
```

```
public class Timesheet : PersonnelReport
{
    public override void GenerateReport()
    {
        // Code to generate a timesheet.
    }
}
```

The idea here is that the Report class defines broad features that should be provided by any report. The class defines two abstract methods: GenerateReport and DistributeReport. Because the class contains an abstract method, it must also be abstract. (In this case that's okay. The Report class doesn't represent a specific kind of report, so it doesn't make sense to create an instance of one anyway.)

The PersonnelReport class derived from Report represents a report that should be sent to everyone in the personnel department. It overrides the DistributeReport method to send the report to everyone in the department. The class still contains an abstract method (GenerateReport) so it must be marked abstract.

The Timesheet class derived from PersonnelReport overrides the GenerateReport method to actually create a report. This class has no abstract methods so this can be a concrete class.

sealed

The final keyword that affects overriding is sealed. If you mark an overridden method as sealed in a child class, then further descendant classes cannot override that method.

Sealed methods have a couple of odd quirks. First, you cannot seal a method in the class where it is originally defined, only in a class that overrides it. Second, you cannot override a sealed method in a descendant class but you can hide it, so sealing a method doesn't completely protect it from later tampering.

For example, consider the following code.

```
public abstract class Animal
{
    public abstract string FoodType();
}

public class Herbivore : Animal
{
    public override sealed string FoodType()
    {
        return "Vegetation";
    }
}

public class Koala : Herbivore
{
    public new string FoodType()
    {
```

```
        return "Eucalyptus";
    }
}
```

The `Animal` class defines an abstract `FoodType` method.

The `Herbivore` class derived from `Animal` overrides `FoodType` to return the string `"Vegetation"`.

The `Herbivore` class marks the method `sealed` so the `Koala` class, which is derived from `Herbivore`, cannot override `FoodType`. It can, however, use the `new` keyword to hide the `Herbivore` implementation of the method with a new version.

> ### RESPECT THE SEAL
>
> If a method is marked `sealed`, it's probably for a good reason, so you shouldn't hide that method. Don't hide a sealed method unless you really must.
>
> By the same token, it's hard to predict what future developers will need to do with a method, so it's hard to know they will never need to override it. Don't seal a method unless you're certain no one will ever need to override it.

POLYMORPHISM

Loosely speaking, *polymorphism* is the ability to treat one object as if it were an object of a different type. In OOP terms, it means that you can treat an object of one class as if it were from an ancestor class.

For example, suppose `Employee` and `Customer` are both derived from the `Person` class. Then you can treat `Employee` and `Customer` objects as if they were `Person` objects because, in a sense, they are. They are specific types of `Person` objects. They inherited all the properties, methods, and events of a `Person` object, so they should act as `Person` objects.

C# enables you to make a variable of one class refer to an object of a derived class. In this example, you can use a `Person` variable to hold a reference to an `Employee` or `Customer` object, as shown in the following code.

```
Employee employee = new Employee();      // Make an Employee
Customer customer = new Customer();       // Make a Customer
Person person = new Person();             // Make a Person.

person = employee;    // Okay because an Employee is a type of Person.
person = customer;    // Okay because a Customer is a type of Person.
employee = person;    // Not okay because a Person is not necessarily an Employee.
```

One common reason to use polymorphism is to treat a collection of objects in a uniform way that makes sense in the context of the parent class. For example, suppose that the `Person` class defines the `FirstName` and `LastName` properties. The program could define a collection named `AllPeople` and add references to `Customer` and `Employee` objects to represent all the people that the program needs to manage. The code could then loop through the collection, treating each object as a `Person`, as shown in the following code.

```
foreach (Person person in AllPeople)
{
    Console.WriteLine(person.FirstName + " " + person.LastName);
}
```

When you use an object polymorphically, you can access only the features defined by the type of variable you actually use to refer to an object. For example, if you use a `Person` variable to refer to an `Employee` object, you can use only the features defined by the `Person` class, not those added by the `Employee` class.

If you know an object has a specific type, you can convert the object into that type before you work with it. For example, the following code loops through the `AllPeople` list and takes special action for objects that are `Employees`.

```
foreach (Person person in AllPeople)
{
    if (person is Employee)
    {
        // Do something Employee-specific with the person.
        Employee employee = person as Employee;
        ...
    }
}
```

The code uses the statement `if (person is Employee)` to determine whether the variable `person` can be treated as an `Employee` object. It is important to realize that this doesn't mean `person` actually is an `Employee`. It means `person` is an `Employee` or a class derived from `Employee`, so it can be treated as an `Employee`. For example, if the `Manager` class is derived from `Employee`, then `person is Employee` returns `true` for `Manager` objects.

The code uses the following statement to convert the `Person` looping variable into an `Employee` variable.

```
Employee employee = person as Employee;
```

The `as` keyword converts the variable `person` into an `Employee` if possible. If `person` cannot be converted into an `Employee`, then `as` returns `null`. (In this example, you know `person` can be converted into an `Employee` because the code just checked.) The `as` statement is roughly equivalent to the following code.

```
Employee employee = null;
if (person is Employee) employee = (Employee)person;
```

Sometimes you might want to invoke the base class's version of an overridden method. For example, suppose you override the `Person` class's `ToString` method but you also want to be able to call the version defined in the `Object` class from which `Person` is derived. In that case you could add the following `BaseToString` method to the `Person` class.

```
public string BaseToString()
{
    return base.ToString();
}
```

OVERRIDING TOSTRING

A particularly useful combination of overriding and polymorphism involves the `ToString` method. This method is declared `virtual` by the `Object` class. Because `Object` is the ultimate granddaddy of all classes, all classes inherit it. The default implementation returns the object's class name.

Because this method is declared `virtual`, you can override it. For example, the following code shows how you might override `ToString` in the `Person` class.

```
public class Person
{
    public string Name, FirstName, LastName;

    public override string ToString()
    {
        return FirstName + " " + LastName;
    }
}
```

Now when you call a `Person` object's `ToString` method, you get the new version. Polymorphism means you get the new version even if the variable referring to the `Person` object is of some other class such as `Object`. The following code demonstrates this type of override.

```
Object alice = new Person()
    { FirstName = "Alice", LastName = "Almer" };
Console.WriteLine(alice.ToString());
```

The code makes an `Object` variable refer to a `Person` object. It then calls the object's `ToString` method and displays the result. Even though the variable is of type `Object`, polymorphism lets it use the `Person` class's version of `ToString`.

Here the keyword `base` tells the program to use the version of `ToString` defined in the parent class. Now the program can use the `Object` class's version of `ToString` by calling the `BaseToString` method.

The code inside the `Person` class can invoke the parent class's version of `ToString` as shown here, but there is no way for the program to invoke an object's overridden base class methods directly. If you don't define a method similar to `BaseToString`, the program cannot call the `Object` class's version of the method.

Also note that there is no way to call further up the inheritance chain.

SUMMARY

Classes are programming abstractions that group data and related behavior in tightly encapsulated packages. After you define a class, you can create instances of that class.

Inheritance lets you derive a child class from a parent class, possibly adding, hiding, or overriding the parent's behavior. The `new`, `virtual`, `abstract`, `override`, and `sealed` keywords give you a fair amount of control over how methods are inherited and modified.

Interfaces give you another method for defining behavior that doesn't follow an inheritance hierarchy. Like an abstract class, an interface lets you determine a class's behavior without providing an implementation. Because interfaces don't need to follow a derivation hierarchy, you can use them to implement nonhierarchical relationships such as multiple inheritance (interface inheritance).

Polymorphism enables you to treat an object as if it were of an ancestor's type. For example, the following text shows the inheritance hierarchy for the Windows Forms `PictureBox` control.

```
System.Object
    System.MarshalByRefObject
        System.ComponentModel.Component
            System.Windows.Forms.Control
                System.Windows.Forms.PictureBox
```

This means you can treat a `PictureBox` as if it is a `PictureBox`, `Control`, `Component`, `MarshalByRefObject`, or `Object`.

This chapter described these features and briefly mentioned how you can implement many of them in C#. The next chapter explains the syntax for creating classes and structures in greater detail. It also explains the differences between the two and how to decide when to use classes and when to use structures.

EXERCISES

For the exercises that require you to build an inheritance hierarchy, draw abstract classes with dashed outlines and concrete classes with solid outliines.

1. Consider the inheritance hierarchy shown Figure 11-2. Suppose you decide you also need a `PartTimeProgrammer` class to represent programmers who are paid hourly. How would you update the hierarchy?

2. Consider the following code.

```
foreach (Person person in AllPeople)
{
    if (person is Employee)
    {
        // Do something Employee-specific with the person.
        Employee employee = person as Employee;
        ...
    }
}
```

Rewrite the code so that it doesn't use is. (Hint: Place the as statement before the new if statement.) Which version is better?

3. Draw an inheritance hierarchy for a pet store application that includes the classes shown in the following table. Add parent classes as needed. (Hint: If you include the properties defined by each class, there shouldn't be a lot of duplication.)

CLASS	PROPERTIES
Janitor	Name, Address, EmployeeId, Hours, HourlyPay
ShiftManager	Name, Address, EmployeeId, Hours, Salary
Customer	Name, Address, CustomerId, Pets
Groomer	Name, Address, Hours, HourlyRate
Supplier	Name, Address, SupplierId, Products
StoreManager	Name, Address, EmployeeId, Hours, Salary
SalesClerk	Name, Address, EmployeeId, Hours, HourlyPay
Trainer	Name, Address, Classes, Hours, HourlyRate

Are there some classes that should be abstract? Why? How would you make them abstract?

4. Build a program that implements the hierarchy you designed for Exercise 3. For properties with non-obvious data types such as Pets and Classes, use string as a placeholder. (If you're not sure how to build the classes, read the next chapter and then come back to this exercise.)

5. Suppose you're building a fantasy role-playing game. Each player has one of three races: Human, Elf, or Dwarf. Each player also has a weapon. Right now you have defined Sword, Bow, and Wand, but you plan to add other weapons later such as other bladed weapons (Spear, Dagger, and Axe), missile weapons (Sling, Atlatl, and Dart), and magic weapons (Potion, Pendant, and VoodooDoll).

    How would you design the Player class to handle all this? Draw an inheritance hierarchy to show the relationships among the classes.

6. Suppose you decide to modify the game described in Exercise 5 so that players have a profession. The basic professions are Fighter and MagicUser. A player can be one of the basic professions or can be a specialist. The initial Fighter specialties are Knight, Ranger, and Archer. The initial MagicUser specialties are Illusionist, Witch, and Chemist. How would you modify the definition of the Player class? Draw the class inheritance hierarchy.

7. Suppose software developers are assigned to departments. They may also be assigned to a primary development project and up to two secondary projects. How would you design the Developer class to handle this?

8. Suppose you're building a program for a college and you need the classes and properties shown in the following table.

CLASS	PROPERTIES
Student	Name, Address, StudentId, CurrentClasses, PastClasses
Instructor	Name, Address, EmployeeId, CurrentClasses, PastClasses
TeachingAssistant	Name, Address, StudentId, EmployeeId, CurrentClasses, PastClasses, CurrentClassesTaught, PastClassesTaught
ResearchAssistant	Name, Address, StudentId, EmployeeId, Sponsor

(The Sponsor property is the Instructor for whom a ResearchAssistant works.)

How would you implement these classes? Draw the inheritance hierarchy. (Hint: Change the names of some properties if that helps.)

9. Build a program that implements the hierarchy you designed for Exercise 8. For properties with non-obvious data types such as CurrentClasses, use string as a placeholder. (If you're not sure how to build the classes, read the next chapter and then come back to this exercise.) Make classes that implement an interface do so directly without delegation.

10. Modify the classes you built for Exercise 9 so that they use delegation to implement the IStudent interface. What are the advantages and disadvantages of the approaches used in Exercises 9 and 10?

11. In Exercise 10, why shouldn't you make the Student class implement the IStudent interface directly and then make the TeachingAssistant and ResearchAssistant classes delegate the interface to a Student object?

12. In the model you built for Exercises 10 and 11, suppose you want to derive the LabAssistant class from ResearchAssistant. How would the new class handle the IStudent interface?

12

Classes and Structures

WHAT'S IN THIS CHAPTER

- ➤ Defining classes and structures
- ➤ Value and reference types
- ➤ Memory requirements, and heap and stack performance
- ➤ Boxing and unboxing
- ➤ Constructors and destructors
- ➤ Garbage collection and `Dispose`

WROX.COM DOWNLOADS FOR THIS CHAPTER

Please note that all the code examples for this chapter are available as a part of this chapter's code download on the book's website at www.wrox.com/go/csharp5programmersref on the Download Code tab.

A variable holds a single value. It may be a simple value, such as an `int` or `string`, or a reference to a more complex entity such as a class or structure.

Classes and structures are both *container types*. They group related data values and methods into a convenient package that you can manipulate as a group.

For example, a `Recipe` class would contain fields or properties holding information about a recipe such as ingredients, temperature, instructions, and number of servings. It could also include methods to convert measurements between English and metric, to scale the recipe for different numbers of servings, and to print the recipe.

If you make an instance of the `Recipe` class and fill it with the data for a particular recipe, you can move the object around as a single unit instead of passing around separate variables holding the ingredients, temperature, instructions, and number of servings. The object also contains methods for manipulating the recipe, so you don't need to write a separate module containing methods to convert measurements, scale the recipe, and print. The class keeps all these things together, so they're easy to find.

This chapter explains how to define and instantiate classes and structures. It explains the key differences between classes and structures and provides some recommendations about which to use under different circumstances.

Classes and structures provide almost exactly the same features. For example, both can have properties, methods, and events. The following sections start by describing classes. As you read about classes, be aware that most of those features also apply to structures. Sections later in the chapter explain where the two differ.

CLASSES

A class packages data and related behavior. The `Recipe` class described earlier is an example. It contains information about a recipe and methods for manipulating its data.

Here's the syntax for declaring a class.

```
«attributes» «accessibility» «abstract|sealed|static» «partial»
    class name «inheritance»
{
    statements
}
```

The only thing all class declarations require is the `class` clause (including the class's name). Everything else is optional. The following code describes a valid (albeit not very interesting) class.

```
class Person
{
}
```

The following sections describe the pieces of the general declaration in detail.

attributes

The optional *attributes* section is a list of attributes that apply to the class. An attribute further refines the definition of a class to give more information to the compiler and the runtime system.

Attributes are rather specialized and address issues that arise when you perform specific programming tasks. For example, if you need to copy instances of the class from one application to another, you can mark the class with the `Serializable` attribute. This isn't something you need to do for every class. Actually, some attributes are so specialized that you may never use them.

Because attributes are so specialized, they are not described in detail here. (Although Chapter 25, "Serialization," says more about serialization.) For more information, consult the Internet and the online help.

For more information on attributes, go to these web pages:

➤ Attributes (C# and C#) (msdn.microsoft.com/library/z0w1kczw.aspx)

➤ Attributes Tutorial (msdn.microsoft.com/library/aa288454.aspx)

For a list of 578 attributes that you can use, go to Microsoft's "Attribute Class" web page at msdn.microsoft.com/system.attribute.aspx and look at the "Inheritance Hierarchy" section at the bottom.

accessibility

If a class is declared directly within a namespace, its *accessibility* clause must be either public or internal. You can also omit accessibility, in which case the default is internal.

If a class is declared inside a structure, its *accessibility* clause can be public, private, or internal. If the class is declared within a class, the clause can also take the values protected and protected internal.

The following table summarizes the meanings of these values and when they are allowed.

KEYWORD	ALLOWED IN	MEANING
public	namespace structure class	The class is visible to all code inside or outside of the class's assembly.
internal	namespace structure class	The class is visible only to code inside the class's assembly.
private	structure class	The class is visible only to code inside the containing namespace, structure, or class.
protected	structure class	The class is visible only to code inside the containing structure or class, or in a class derived from the containing class.
protected internal	structure class	Combines protected and internal.

For example, the following code defines a Person class.

```
namespace OrderProcessor
{
    public class Person
    {
```

```
    internal struct Address
    {
        public string Street, City, State, Zip;
    }

    public string FirstName, LastName;
    internal Address PostalAddress;
    }
}
```

The Person class is defined at the namespace level. It is declared public, so all code can see its definition.

The Person class defines the Address structure. It is declared internal, so this structure is visible only to code within the assembly. If you use the Person class from code in another assembly, that code won't see the definition of the Address structure.

After defining the Address class, the Person class defines FirstName, LastName, and PostalAddress fields. The PostalAddress field is declared internal, so it's not visible to code outside the assembly. If you use the Person class from code in another assembly, that code won't see the PostalAddress field.

abstract | sealed | static

If a class's declaration includes the abstract keyword, you cannot make instances of the class. To make use of the class's features, you must derive another class from it. You can then make instances of the derived class.

If a class's declaration includes the sealed keyword, you cannot derive other classes from it.

If a class's declaration includes the static keyword, you cannot derive other classes from it or create instances of it. You invoke the members of a static class by using the class's name instead of an instance. Note that all members of a static class must also be declared static.

For example, consider the following LogTools class.

```
public static class LogTools
{
    public static void RecordMessage(string message)
    {
        Console.WriteLine(message);
    }
}
```

This static class defines a static RecordMessage method. In this example, the method writes a message to the Console window, although, you could modify it to write the message into a log file.

The following code shows how a program can invoke the RecordMessage method.

```
LogTools.RecordMessage("Started " + DateTime.Now.ToString());
```

Notice how the code invokes the method by using the class's name (highlighted in bold).

> ### EXTENSION TENSION
>
> You can add an extension method to a class even if it is declared `sealed`. If you add features that don't match the class's original purpose, you can make the class more confusing and harder to use correctly. Adding new features to a sealed class also violates the idea that the class is in some sense "finished." To avoid confusion, don't add extension methods to a sealed class unless you must.
>
> For more information on extension methods, see the section "Extension Methods" in Chapter 6, "Methods."

partial

The `partial` keyword tells C# that the current declaration defines only part of the class. The following code shows the `Person` class broken into two pieces.

```
partial class Person
{
    public string FirstName, LastName;
}

partial class Person
{
    public string Street, City, State, Zip;
}
```

You can break a class into any number of pieces. (If you do break a class into pieces, all of them must include the `partial` keyword.) At compile time, C# finds the pieces and combines them to define the class.

Normally, you wouldn't break a class into pieces within a single module. In fact, it's not a good idea to break a class into pieces unless you must. Keeping all the class's code in one piece makes it easier to find.

> ### PICKING UP THE PIECES
>
> The reason partial classes were introduced was to hide automatically generated code from developers.
>
> For example, when you create a form in a Windows Forms application, the project contains a lot of code to create and initialize the form's controls. That code is confusing, and if you modify it, you can break the form so that it won't work anymore.
>
> To help protect that code from accidental breakage, Visual Studio places it in a separate module with a name similar to Form1.Designer.cs. Any code you add to the form goes into the similarly named file Form1.cs. The `partial` keyword lets both of these pieces of code help define the `Form1` class.

Keeping all the pieces together makes it easier to find the pieces, but there are a few circumstances in which splitting a class may make sense. Some of those times include

➤ To separate automatically generated code from code written by developers

➤ To split a large class so that multiple developers can work on it simultaneously

➤ To break the class into pieces that each focus on some aspect of the class's behavior

➤ To place the implementations of different interfaces in different files

All the pieces of a class must have the same accessibility and parent class. You only need to declare those in one of the pieces, but if you declare them multiple times, they must agree. For example, you cannot make one piece of the HonorStudent class inherit from Student while another piece inherits from Person.

You can make different pieces of the class implement different interfaces. For example, the following code is legal.

```
public partial class Student : Person, Interface1
{
    . . .
}

partial class Student : Interface2
{
    . . .
}
```

> ### CONSISTENCY IS KING
>
> Using different accessibility and inheritance clauses can be confusing. Remember, at any given moment, you may be working with only one piece of the class. To make the code as obvious as possible, make the declarations for every piece of a class look exactly the same.

inheritance

If it is included, the class's *inheritance* clause can include a parent, one or more interfaces, or both a parent class and interfaces. If the declaration includes a parent class and interfaces, the parent class must come first.

For example, the following code defines a Student class that inherits from the Person class and that implements the IComparable and IFormattable interfaces.

```
class Student : Person, IComparable, IFormattable
{
    . . .
}
```

The class automatically inherits its parent's properties, methods, and events but is responsible for providing implementations for its interfaces. (For more information on implementing interfaces, see the section "Implementing Interfaces" in Chapter 6.)

Recall from Chapter 11, "OOP Concepts," that C# allows a class to inherit from at most one parent class and to implement any number of interfaces. See the sidebar "Multiple Inheritance" in Chapter 11 for more information.

STRUCTURES

In many respects, structures are similar to classes. They let you group properties, methods, events, fields, and other members in a package that you can manipulate as a group.

One of the most obvious differences between structures and classes is that structures do not support inheritance. You cannot derive one structure from another. (You also cannot derive a structure from a class or vice versa.)

Structures can implement interfaces much as classes can.

The fact that structures don't support inheritance is reflected in the following declaration syntax.

```
«attributes» «accessibility» «partial» struct name «interfaces»
{
    statements
}
```

The structure's *attributes* and *accessibility* clauses and the `partial` keyword work the same way they do for classes. The *interfaces* section is similar to a class's *inheritance* section except it supports only interfaces not inheritance. See the earlier sections discussing these pieces of the class declaration for details.

There is one other huge difference between structures and classes: structures are value types but classes are reference types. This is an important but confusing issue, so the following sections spend quite a bit of time explaining what that difference means.

Value Versus Reference Types

The biggest difference between a structure and a class is in how each allocates memory for its data. Classes are *reference types*. That means an instance of a class is actually a reference to the object's storage in some other part of memory.

In contrast, structures are *value types*. An instance of a structure contains the data inside the structure rather than simply points to it. Figure 12-1 illustrates the difference.

The following sections describe some of the more important consequences of the way value and reference types allocate memory.

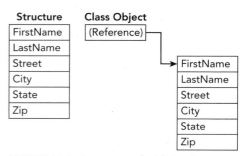

FIGURE 12-1: A structure holds its data, but a class holds a reference to its data.

Memory Requirements

The difference in the amount of memory required by classes and structures is small when you consider only a single object. In Figure 12-1, the class needs to allocate only one additional memory location to hold the reference. (The reference takes 4 bytes on 32-bit systems or 8 bytes on 64-bit systems.)

However, the difference can add up in an array. An array of structures contains only the data in the structures. An array of objects requires references in addition to the memory used by the objects. If the array contains 1,000 items, then it uses 4,000 more bytes of memory (assuming a 32-bit system).

When an array is first allocated, however, its entries are initially set to null, so they don't refer to any objects. At that point the array uses only the memory required by its references. Figure 12-2 compares an array of structures to an empty array of objects.

For example, suppose a structure or object requires 1 KB of memory. An array containing 1,000 structures occupies 1 MB. When an array of objects is first created, it occupies 4 KB for its null references. When the array is full, it occupies 1 MB for its data plus 4 KB for its (no longer null) references.

Suppose a program needs to use a large array of items. If relatively few of the items will be allocated at any given moment, an array of objects will use relatively little memory. If the program needs many of the items to be allocated at the same time, an array of structures will use slightly less memory because it doesn't need to allocate references.

Structure Array	Object Array
FirstName	<null>
LastName	<null>
Street	<null>
City	
State	
Zip	
FirstName	
LastName	
Street	
City	
State	
Zip	
FirstName	
LastName	
Street	
City	
State	
Zip	

FIGURE 12-2: An array of structures uses lots of memory even before it is initialized. An array of objects uses little memory until its entries refer to objects.

PERFORMANCE ANXIETY

In theory, an array of structures might also be slightly faster than an array of objects, particularly if you want items initialized to their default values. The structure array will be allocated in a single step. Its memory will be contiguous, which may reduce paging in some applications. It will also be allocated and freed in a single step instead of in a series of allocations, one for each object in an object array.

The garbage collector can also mark an array of structures as in use in a single step. In contrast, it must follow the references in an array of objects to mark them all individually. (Garbage collection is described in detail in the section "Garbage Collection" later in this chapter.)

In practice, however, the difference in performance between using an array of structures and using an array of objects is small enough that you probably shouldn't use performance as the deciding factor. Usually, you should pick the technique that makes the most logical sense and not worry about a slight difference in performance.

Heap and Stack Performance

C# programs allocate variables from two pools of memory called the *stack* and the *heap*. Memory for value types (such as `int` and `double`) comes from the stack. Memory for reference types comes from the heap.

Any number of references can point to the same piece of memory in the heap. That complicates garbage collection and other heap-management issues, so working with reference types can be slightly slower than working with value types.

Note that arrays are themselves reference types derived from the `Array` class. That means all arrays are allocated from the heap even if the values they contain are allocated from the stack.

Object Assignment

One of the most important functional differences between structures and objects lies in object assignment.

When you set a value variable equal to another value variable, the program copies the data in one variable into the other. If you change the data in one variable, the other variable is unchanged because it is a copy residing in its own memory.

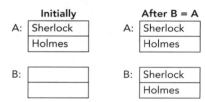

FIGURE 12-3: When you set one value type variable equal to another, the program copies the data.

Figure 12-3 shows this situation. Initially, variable A holds the values `Sherlock` and `Holmes`. Variable B holds blank values. When you execute the statement B = A, the program copies the values stored in variable A into variable B.

In contrast, when you set a reference variable equal to another reference variable, the program makes both variables point to the same memory. If you change the data in one reference, the change is reflected in the other because they both point to the same object.

Figure 12-4 shows this situation. Initially variable A holds the values `Sherlock` and `Holmes`. Variable B is null. When you execute the statement B = A, the program makes variable B point to the same object pointed to by variable A.

Parameter Passing

The difference between value and reference type variables can be particularly confusing when you consider parameter passing methods. For example, assume `Employee` is a class and consider the following method declaration.

```
public void SelectEmployee(Employee employee)
{
    . . .
}
```

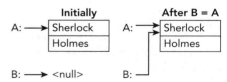

FIGURE 12-4: When you set one reference type variable equal to another, the program makes them both refer to the same object.

The parameter `employee` is passed by value, so it is a *copy* of the argument used in the calling code. (Here *parameter* refers to the value inside the method and *argument* refers to the value passed into the method in the calling code.) The parameter has type `Employee`, so the argument and parameter are reference types. That means the parameter `employee` contains a copy of the reference to the actual `Employee` object. Figure 12-5 shows conceptually how the argument and parameter are arranged in memory.

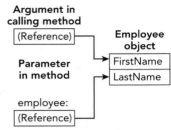

FIGURE 12-5: When you pass a reference type by value, the parameter contains a copy of the reference.

In this example, the parameter refers to the same object as the argument. If you use the parameter to change the `Employee` object's properties (for example, if you execute the statement `employee .FirstName = "Linda"`), the calling code sees that change because the argument points to the same object.

If you change the parameter to make it point to a new `Employee` object, the parameter and the argument will refer to two separate objects. The calling code will not see that change.

Now consider the following modified version of the `SelectEmployee` method.

```
public void SelectEmployee(ref Employee employee)
{
    . . .
}
```

Here the `ref` keyword means the argument is passed into the method by reference. (The `out` keyword would also pass the argument by reference.) Now the `employee` parameter is a reference to the argument, which is a reference to an `Employee` object. Figure 12-6 shows this situation conceptually.

Now the parameter is a reference to the argument not to the `Employee` object. If you use the parameter to change the `Employee` object's properties (for example, if you execute the statement `employee .FirstName = "Linda"`), the calling code sees that change as before.

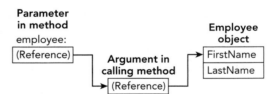

FIGURE 12-6: When you pass a reference type by reference, the parameter is a reference to a reference to the object.

If you change the parameter to make it point to a new `Employee` object, you are actually changing the argument. That means the calling code sees the change.

Because structures are value types, they behave differently than objects when you pass them into a method by reference or by value. For example, suppose `Address` is a structure and consider the following code.

```
public void PrintAddress(Address address)
{
    . . .
}
```

The parameter `address` is passed by value, so it is a *copy* of the argument used in the calling code. Because structures are value types, all the data in the structure is copied into the parameter. Figure 12-7 shows conceptually how the argument and parameter are arranged in memory.

The parameter holds a completely separate copy of all the argument's data. If you change the parameter's data (for example, if you execute the statement `address.Street = "1337 Leet St"`), the argument is unaffected, so the calling code doesn't see the change. If you set the parameter equal to a new `Address` structure, the argument is still unaffected, so the calling code doesn't see that change either.

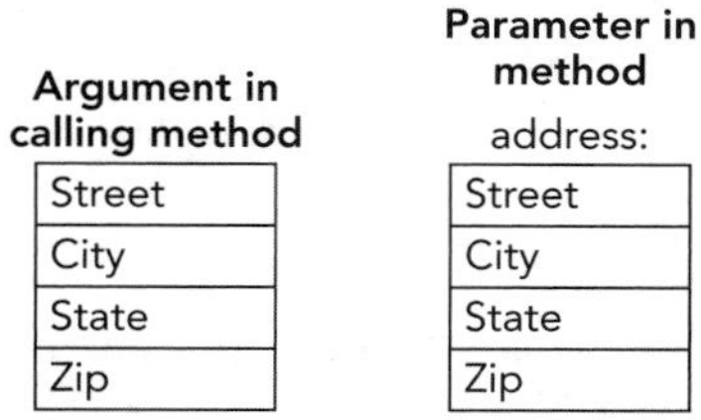

Basically, nothing you do to the parameter will affect the calling code. This is different from the behavior you get when you pass an object into the method. In that case changes to the object's properties are visible to the calling code.

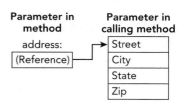

FIGURE 12-7: When you pass a structure by value, the parameter contains a copy of the structure and all its data.

Now consider the following modified version of the `PrintAddress` method.

```
public void PrintAddress(ref Address address)
{
    . . .
}
```

Here the `ref` keyword means the argument is passed into the method by reference. Now the `address` parameter is a reference to the argument. Figure 12-8 shows this situation conceptually.

The parameter is a reference to the argument. If you use the parameter to change the `Address` structure's properties (for example, if you execute the statement `address.Street = "1337 Leet St"`), the calling code sees that change.

If you change the parameter itself to make it point to a new `Address` structure, you are actually changing the argument. That means the calling code sees the change.

FIGURE 12-8: When you pass a structure by reference, the parameter is a reference to the structure.

Remember that arrays are reference types. An array variable is a reference to the block of memory that contains the items in the array. If those items are also reference types, for example, in an array of `Employee` objects, then you have a reference to a block of memory containing references. If you then pass the array by references, you get a reference to a reference to a block of memory containing references. Figure 12-9 shows conceptually how the memory is arranged when you pass an array of `Employee` objects named `employees` into a method by reference.

Fortunately, you usually don't need to worry about the mess shown in Figure 12-9. The only thing you need to remember is that any changes to the `employees` parameter are reflected in the argument.

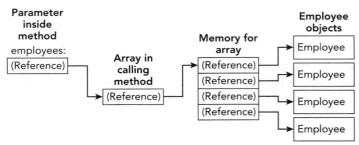

FIGURE 12-9: An array passed by reference is actually a reference to a reference to a block of memory containing references.

The following table summarizes how changes to a parameter affect the argument in the calling code for reference and value types passed by value or by reference.

ARGUMENT TYPE	PASSED BY	EFFECTS
Value type (`int`)	Value	Changing the parameter does not change the argument.
Value type (`int`)	Reference	Changing the parameter changes the argument.
Structure (`Address`)	Value	Changes to the structure's properties are not seen in the calling code. Setting the parameter to a new value does not change the argument in the calling code.
Structure (`Address`)	Reference	Changes to the structure's properties are seen in the calling code. Setting the parameter to a new object changes the argument in the calling code.
Reference type (`Employee`)	Value	Changes to the object's properties are seen in the calling code. Setting the parameter to a new value does not change the argument in the calling code.
Reference type (`Employee`)	Reference	Changes to the object's properties are seen in the calling code. Setting the parameter to a new object changes the argument in the calling code.

ARGUMENT TYPE	PASSED BY	EFFECTS
Array (`Employee[]`)	Value	Changes to an array entry's properties are seen in the calling code.
		Setting an entry in the array to a new value affects the values in the array in the calling code.
		Setting the parameter to point to a new array or `null` does not affect the array in the calling code.
Array (`Employee[]`)	Reference	Changes to an array entry's properties are seen in the calling code.
		Setting an entry in the array to a new value affects the values in the array in the calling code.
		Setting the parameter to point to a new array or `null` changes the array in the calling code.

Passing objects and structures by value or reference can also affect performance. When you pass an object by value, the program passes only a copy of a reference to the method. When you pass a structure by value, the program must copy all the structure's data. If the structure is large, that will take a bit longer.

Boxing and Unboxing

C# allows a program to treat any variable as if it were an object. For example, consider the following method.

```
public void ShowStringValue(object obj)
{
    Console.WriteLine(obj.ToString());
}
```

This method can take any kind of object as a parameter.

Now suppose you call this method with the statement `ShowStringValue(13)`. The number `13` is an `int`, not an object. To allow the method to work, the program wraps the value `13` in an object and passes the object to the method.

The process of wrapping a value type such as an `int` in an object is called *boxing*. Later, if the program needs to use the `int` as a value type again, the program *unboxes* it.

Because structures are value types, the program must box and unbox them whenever it treats them as objects.

Some operations that require boxing and possibly unboxing include assigning a structure to an object variable, passing a structure to a routine that takes an object as a parameter, or adding a structure to a collection class that holds objects. Note that this last operation includes adding a structure to a collection used by a control or other object. For example, adding a structure to a `ListBox` control's `Items` collection requires boxing.

Because arrays are reference types, treating an array as an object doesn't require boxing.

Boxing and unboxing add some overhead to a program. If the program needs to box and unbox only a few items, the difference is small. If the program must box and unbox a huge number of items, the extra time can add up.

CHOOSING BETWEEN CLASSES AND STRUCTURES

Microsoft provides some recommendations at `msdn.microsoft.com/library/ms229017.aspx`. It recommends that you consider using a structure if instances are short-lived or commonly embedded in other objects. It also says to use a structure only if the type has all of the following characteristics:

➤ It logically represents a single value.

➤ It occupies fewer than 16 bytes.

➤ It is immutable.

➤ It will not have to be boxed and unboxed frequently.

All of these rules are designed to prevent you from shuffling large amounts of data around accidentally. For example, if you pass a 100 KB structure to a method by value, the program makes a 100 KB copy to pass to the method.

Many developers use classes exclusively. That has the advantage that you don't need to remember how a variable was defined to understand how it is passed to methods. Using only classes means you lose the memory allocation features of structures but it may be worth it to avoid possible confusion.

CONSTRUCTORS

Chapter 4, "Data Types, Variables, and Constants," briefly mentioned constructors. A *constructor* is special method that has no name and that returns the type of the class or structure that contains it. (Alternatively, you can think of a constructor as having the same name as its class and returning no type, not even `void`.)

You can overload constructors by giving different versions different signatures, just as you can overload any other method. For example, the following code shows a simple `Person` class with two constructors highlighted in bold.

```
public class Person
{
    string FirstName { get; set; }
    string LastName { get; set; }

    public Person()
    {
        FirstName = "unknown";
        LastName = "unknown";
    }

    public Person(string firstName, string lastName)
    {
        FirstName = firstName;
        LastName = lastName;
    }
}
```

A CONSTRUCTOR BY ANY OTHER NAME

A constructor with no parameters is called a *parameterless constructor* or sometimes an *empty constructor*.

Whenever the program creates a new instance of a class or structure, the program invokes a constructor. The program uses the parameters in the `new` statement to determine which constructor to use. For example, the following code creates a new `Person` object. Because the `new` statement uses two string parameters, the program uses the previous code's second constructor.

```
Person person = new Person("Rufus", "Firefly");
```

If you do not provide any constructors for a class or structure, C# automatically provides a default parameterless constructor. If you create any constructors of your own, C# does not create a default constructor.

You can use that fact to ensure that the program initializes new objects or structures with required values. For example, if the previous version of the `Person` class did not include a parameterless constructor, then the program would be forced to use the other constructor, which takes first and last names as parameters. The program could not create a `Person` object without giving it first and last name values. (Although it could still mess things up by setting those values to blank strings or `null`. You could modify the constructor to check for that.)

You can define your own parameterless constructors for classes. Structures cannot have explicitly defined parameterless constructors.

As is the case with other methods, you can give constructors optional parameters. For example, the following constructor can take zero, one, or two parameters.

```
public Person(string firstName = "unknown", string lastName = "unknown")
{
    FirstName = firstName;
    LastName = lastName;
}
```

Constructors have two additional options that are not available to methods in general. First, a constructor can use the `this` keyword to automatically invoke another constructor. For example, consider the following code.

```
public Person(string firstName, string lastName)
{
    FirstName = firstName;
    LastName = lastName;
}

public Person()
    : this("(Unknown)", "(Unknown)")
{
}
```

This code defines a constructor that takes first and last names as parameters. That constructor saves its input parameters in the object's `FirstName` and `LastName` properties.

The code then defines another constructor. The `this` clause highlighted in bold invokes the first constructor, passing it the values (Unknown) and (Unknown) as parameters.

In the second option that is unavailable to other methods, a constructor uses the `base` keyword to invoke a constructor in the parent class. For example, consider the following `Employee` class derived from the `Person` class.

```
public class Employee : Person
{
    public int EmployeeId { get; set; }

    public Employee(string firstName, string lastName, int employeeId)
        : base(firstName, lastName)
    {
        EmployeeId = employeeId;
    }

    public Employee(string firstName, string lastName)
        : this(firstName, lastName, 0)
    {
    }
}
```

The first constructor takes a first name, last name, and employee ID as parameters. The `base` clause highlighted in bold invokes a `Person` class constructor, passing it the first and last names as parameters. The constructor then saves the employee ID.

The `Employee` class's second constructor uses `this` to invoke the first constructor, passing it the first and last names, and the employee ID 0.

> **STRUCTURAL DIFFERENCES**
>
> There are a few differences between constructors for classes and structures.
>
> As mentioned earlier, structures cannot have explicitly declared parameterless constructors.
>
> Because structures do not support inheritance, their constructors cannot use the `this` or `base` clauses.

STRUCTURE INSTANTIATION DETAILS

Structures handle instantiation somewhat differently from classes. When you declare a reference variable, C# does not automatically allocate the object to which the variable points. In contrast, when you declare a value type such as a structure, C# automatically allocates space for the variable's data. That means you don't need to use the `new` keyword to instantiate a structure.

For example, the following code creates an `Address` structure and initializes its `Street` property.

```
Address address;
address.Street = "711 Maple Street";
```

Although you don't need to use the `new` keyword to instantiate a structure, you can if you want. That's a useful way to reinitialize a structure and set its data to default values. For example, consider the following code.

```
// Create an Address.
Address address;
address.Street = "711 Maple Street";
...
// Reinitialize the Address.
address = new Address();
address.Street = "742 Evergreen Terrace";
...
```

This code creates an `Address` structure and sets its `Street` property. It works with the structure for a while and then uses `new` to reinitialize the structure. It then sets the `Street` property to a new value and continues using the structure.

You can also use the `new` keyword if you want to use initialization syntax to initialize the structure. For example, the following code uses `new` to create an `Address` structure and set its `Street` property.

```
Address address = new Address() { Street = "1313 Mockingbird Lane" };
```

GARBAGE COLLECTION

When a program starts, the system allocates a chunk of memory for the program called the *managed heap*. When it allocates data for reference types (class objects), C# uses memory from this heap.

Suppose your program creates a `Person` object and then later sets the only reference to that object equal to `null`. The program can no longer access the object, so its heap memory is "lost."

The *garbage collector* (*GC*) is in charge of recycling that lost memory. At some later point, the garbage collector's optimizing engine may decide that there is too much lost memory in the heap, so it decides to clean house.

Exactly how garbage collection works is fairly complicated and not terribly important for most applications, so this section provides only an overview. For more precise details, see the web page "Garbage Collection" at `msdn.microsoft.com/library/0xy59wtx.aspx`.

Basically when it runs, the garbage collector marks all the heap memory as not in use. It then examines all the program's reference variables, parameters that are object references, CPU registers, and other items that might point to heap objects. For each of those references, the garbage collector marks the object to which the reference points as in use.

Next, the garbage collector compacts heap memory that is still in use and updates program references so that they can find any items that it moved. The garbage collector then updates the heap itself so that the program can allocate memory from the unused portion.

> ### THE FINAL WORD IN FINALIZATION
>
> Because you can't tell when garbage collection will occur, this process is called *nondeterministic finalization*.

When it destroys an object, the garbage collector frees the object's memory and any managed resources it contains. It may not free unmanaged resources, however. You can determine when and how an object frees its managed and unmanaged resources by using destructors and the `Dispose` method.

Destructors

When it destroys an object, the garbage collector automatically frees any managed resources used by that object. For example, suppose an unused object contains a reference to an open file stream. When the garbage collector runs, it notices that the file stream is inaccessible to the program, so it destroys the file stream, as well as the object that refers to it.

However, suppose that the object uses an unmanaged resource that is outside of the scope of objects that C# understands. For example, suppose the object holds an integer representing a file handle, network connection, or channel to a hardware device that C# doesn't understand. In that case, the garbage collector doesn't know how to free that resource.

In that case, you can give the class a *destructor*, a method that runs when objects are destroyed. Before it permanently destroys an object, the garbage collector calls that object's destructor so the destructor can clean up unmanaged resources.

Note that there are no guarantees about exactly when the garbage collector calls this method, or the order in which different objects' destructors are called. Two objects' destructors may be called in either order even if one contains a reference to the other or if one was freed long before the other. That means a destructor cannot use any references to objects created outside of the destructor because those objects may no longer exist.

To create a destructor, create a method named after the class with a ~ character in front of it. For example, the following code shows a destructor for the `Person` class.

```
~Person()
{
    // Free unmanaged resources here.
    ...
}
```

FINALIZATION AND DESTRUCTION

Technically, the program doesn't really call the destructor. Instead Visual Studio translates the destructor into a method named `Finalize` that overrides the parent class's `Finalize` method. The `Finalize` method performs whatever actions you put in the destructor and then calls its parent class's `Finalize` method.

For example, consider the following destructor.

```
~Person()
{
    // Free unmanaged resources here.
    ...
}
```

This code is converted into the following `Finalize` method.

```
protected override void Finalize()
{
    try
    {
        // Free unmanaged resources here.
        ...
    }
    finally
    {
        base.Finalize();
    }
}
```

Because the program actually calls the `Finalize` method, not the destructor, the destruction of a .NET object is called *finalization*.

When a program ends normally, it calls the destructors for all the objects that were created. If the program crashes or you halt it abnormally, for example, by using the Debug menu's Stop Debugging command, the program doesn't run the destructors. Sometimes that may leave unmanaged resources locked or otherwise unavailable to the operating system. For example, a file editing program may leave open files locked if it crashes.

Dispose

Because C# doesn't keep track of whether an object is reachable at any given moment, it doesn't know when it can permanently destroy the object until the program ends or the garbage collector reclaims it. That means the object's memory and resources may remain unavailable for quite a while.

Unavailable memory itself isn't a big issue. If the program's heap runs out of space, the garbage collector runs to reclaim the unused memory. However, if an object contains a reference to a resource (managed or unmanaged), that resource isn't freed until the object is destroyed, and that can sometimes have dire consequences. You generally don't want control of a file, network connection, scanner, or other scarce system resource left to the whims of the garbage collector.

By convention, the `Dispose` method frees an object's resources. Before a program frees an object that contains important resources, it can call that object's `Dispose` method to free the resources explicitly.

To handle the case in which the program doesn't call `Dispose`, the class should also free any unmanaged resources that it holds in its destructor. Because the destructor is executed regardless of whether the program calls `Dispose`, the class must be able to execute both the `Dispose` method and the destructor without harm. For example, if the program shuts down some piece of unusual hardware, it probably should not shut down the hardware twice.

To make `Dispose` methods a little more consistent, C# defines the `IDisposable` interface, which declares the `Dispose` method. If a class implements this interface, then the `using` statement will automatically call an object's `Dispose` method, so you don't need to do it explicitly.

Finally, if the `Dispose` method has freed all the object's resources, there's no need to invoke the destructor when the object is eventually destroyed. You can make destruction a bit more efficient by having the `Dispose` method call `GC.SuppressFinalize` to tell the garbage collector to skip the object's destructor.

The following list summarizes the key destruction issues.

➤ The destructor is called automatically when an object is destroyed.

➤ The destructor cannot refer to managed objects because they may have already been destroyed. In particular, the destructor cannot free managed resources because they may have already been destroyed.

➤ The destructor must free unmanaged resources. This is the last chance the object has for freeing those resources.

➤ Instead of making the program wait an unknowable amount of time for the destructor to execute, you can provide a `Dispose` method that disposes of all resources when the object is done with them.

➤ If you implement the IDisposable interface, the using statement calls Dispose automatically.

➤ Either it must be safe for the Dispose method and the destructor to both run, or you can ensure that they both can't run by making the Dispose method call GC.SuppressFinalize.

The following code defines a UseResources class that uses both managed and unmanaged resources.

```
// A class with managed and unmanaged resources.
public class UseResources : IDisposable
{
    // Code to initialize and use resources.
    ...

    // Destructor.
    // Cannot free managed resources.
    // Must free unmanaged resources.
    ~UseResources()
    {
        // Free unmanaged resources here.
        ...
    }

    // Dispose.
    // Frees managed and unmanaged resources.
    // Suppresses the destructor.
    public void Dispose()
    {
        // Free managed resources here.
        ...

        // Free unmanaged resources here.
        ...

        // Suppress the destructor.
        GC.SuppressFinalize(this);
    }
}
```

The class implements IDisposable so the using statement will automatically call the Dispose method.

The bulk of the class's code, which initializes and uses the resources, isn't shown here.

The class's destructor frees the unmanaged resources.

The Dispose method frees both managed and unmanaged resources. It then calls GC.SuppressFinalize to prevent the destructor from running and freeing the unmanaged resources again.

The parameter to GC.SuppressFinalize is the object for which the destructor should not be called. The code passes this to that method so the current object's destructor isn't called.

In this class, either the Dispose method or the destructor is called but not both.

> ### DISPOSE ONCE
>
> If you study the `UseResources` class, you'll see that it contains code to dispose of unmanaged resources in two places: in the destructor and in the `Dispose` method. Both of those pieces of code won't execute for a given object, but the class still contains duplicated code.
>
> You can avoid that duplication by moving the code that frees unmanaged resources into a new method. Then you can make the destructor and the `Dispose` method call the new method.
>
> Many developers use a more complicated approach in which the new method frees both managed and unmanaged resources. In that case, the new method needs to know whether it is being called by the destructor or the `Dispose` method so it knows whether to free managed resources. That approach can be a bit more confusing, but it achieves the same goals as the version shown here.

EVENTS

Chapter 4 explained how to create properties, and Chapter 6 explained how to make methods. In some sense properties and methods let program code outside of a class communicate with an object. Properties let the program view and modify the object's data. Methods let the program make the object do something.

Events do the reverse: They let the object send information back to the program when something interesting occurs. The object raises an event to tell the main program about a situation so the main program can decide what to do about it.

For example, some of the most common events are button and menu `Click` events. When the user selects a menu item or clicks a button, the menu item or button raises a `Click` event. The main program catches that event and takes appropriate action.

The following sections describe events. They explain how a class declares events and how other parts of the program can catch them.

Declaring Events

An object can raise events whenever it needs to notify the program of changing circumstances. The class declares the event using the `event` keyword. The following text shows the `event` statement's syntax.

```
«attributes» «accessibility» «new|virtual|override|abstract|sealed» «static»
    event delegate name;
```

The following list describes the declaration's pieces.

➤ *attributes*—Attributes provide extra information about the event for use by the compiler, the runtime system, and other tools.

➤ *accessibility*—This can be `public`, `private`, `protected`, `internal`, or `protected internal` and is similar to the accessibility for other items such as classes, properties, and methods. The keywords have the following meanings:

> ➤ `public`—The event can be caught by any code.

> ➤ `private`—The event can be caught only by code inside the class.

> ➤ `protected`—The event can be caught only by code inside the class or a derived class.

> ➤ `internal`—The event can be caught only by code inside the class's assembly.

> ➤ `protected internal`—The event can be caught only by code inside the class or a derived class within the class's assembly.

➤ `new|virtual|override|abstract|sealed`—These are similar to the keywords used by methods described in Chapter 6. They have the following meanings:

> ➤ `new`—Hides an event with the same name defined in an ancestor class.

> ➤ `virtual`—If you mark an event as virtual, you can later replace it in a derived class by overriding it.

> ➤ `override`—If an ancestor class defines a virtual event, you can use the `override` keyword to override it.

> ➤ `abstract`—This keyword indicates the event is abstract, so derived classes must override the event to give it an implementation. As is the case with `abstract` methods, a class that contains an `abstract` event must be `abstract` and cannot be instantiated.

> ➤ `sealed`—This keyword indicates the event is no longer `virtual` so it cannot be overridden in derived classes.

➤ `static`—This indicates the class itself raises the event rather than instances of the class.

➤ *delegate*—This is a delegate type that defines the parameters that will be passed to event handlers for the event.

➤ *name*—This is the name you want to give the event.

Much of this should seem familiar to you from similar keywords used with methods. In fact, events seem a lot like methods. The class that defines the event "invokes" it much as you invoke a method, and the event handler that catches the event is just a method.

However, there are some major differences between events and methods. The following sections provide some more detail about events and explain the reasons why events are more than simply methods in disguise. Those sections also include some examples that show how to declare, raise, and catch events.

Raising Events

To raise an event, the code must first determine whether any other pieces of code have registered to catch the event. It does that by comparing the event to `null`. (This is a fairly odd syntax but that's the way C# does it.)

If the event handler isn't `null`, the code "invokes" it, passing it any required parameters. The program then invokes each of the registered event handlers in turn, passing them those parameters.

For example, suppose the `Student` class defined a `GradeChanged` event. Then the following snippet inside the `Student` class raises the event, passing it the current `Student` object as a parameter.

```
if (GradeChanged != null) GradeChanged(this);
```

Catching Events

To subscribe to an event, a program uses the `+=` operator to "add" the event handler to the event.

For example, suppose the `Person` class defines a `NameChanged` event. Suppose the main program creates an instance of the `Person` class named `MyPerson`. Finally, suppose the main program defines an event handler named `MyPerson_NameChanged` to handle that event. Then the main program could use the following code to subscribe to the event.

```
MyPerson.NameChanged += MyPerson_NameChanged;
```

If the program executes this code multiple times, then when the event is raised, the event handler will be called multiple times.

To unsubscribe from an event, use the `-=` operator. The following code shows how a program might unsubscribe from the `Person` class's `NameChanged` event.

```
MyPerson.NameChanged -= MyPerson_NameChanged;
```

(This example is described further in the next section.)

---

1 − 2 = 0

A program can unsubscribe from an event more times than it subscribed to it without causing any harm. For example, if the program uses `+=` to subscribe to the event three times and then uses `-=` to unsubscribe from it four times, nothing bad happens. The program just doesn't catch the event.

Using Event Delegate Types

The *delegate* part of the event declaration is a delegate type that defines the parameters that the event handler takes when it catches the event. You can create your own delegate type, use a predefined `Action` delegate type, or use the special `EventHandler` delegate type.

The EventHandler type defines an event that gives the handler two parameters. The first is an object that represents the object that raised the event. The second parameter is another item that gives information about the event. Microsoft recommends that you make the second parameter an object with a name that starts with the name of the event and ends in EventArgs.

For example, the PersonEvent example program, which is available for download on this book's website, defines a Person class with a Name property. When the Name property changes, the Person object raises a NameChanged event. That event handler's second parameter is a NameChangedEventArgs object.

Figure 12-10 shows the PersonEvent program in action. Enter a new name in the text box and click Set Name. This displays a message box asking you to confirm the name change. If you click Yes, the program updates the name and displays the new name in the bottom text box.

FIGURE 12-10: The PersonEvent example program demonstrates event handling.

The following code shows the example's NameChangedEventArgs class.

```
public class NameChangedEventArgs
{
    public string OldName, NewName;
    public bool Cancel;

    public NameChangedEventArgs(string oldName, string newName)
    {
        OldName = oldName;
        NewName = newName;
        Cancel = false;
    }
}
```

This class has three fields. The OldName and NewName fields tell the main program what the Person object's name is being changed from and to. The Cancel property lets the main program cancel the name change.

The NameChangedEventArgs class also defines a constructor that the Person class can use to initialize the old and new name values.

The following code shows the Person class.

```
class Person
{
    // Raised when the person's name changes.
    public event EventHandler<NameChangedEventArgs> NameChanged;
```

```
            // The Name property.
            private string _Name = "";
            public string Name
            {
                get { return _Name; }
                set
                {
                    // Prepare the argument object.
                    NameChangedEventArgs args =
                        new NameChangedEventArgs(_Name, value);

                    // If any code is registered to receive the event, raise the event.
                    if (NameChanged != null) NameChanged(this, args);

                    // If the code didn't cancel the change, make the change.
                    if (!args.Cancel) _Name = value;
                }
            }
        }
```

The class starts by declaring its NameChanged event. The EventHandler<NameChangedEventArgs> part of the declaration indicates that this event will pass its event handlers the object that is raising the event and a NameChangedEventArgs object.

Next, the class defines a Name property. The set accessor starts by creating a NameChangedEventArgs object and initializing its name values.

To raise an event, the code must first determine whether any other pieces of code have registered to catch the event. It does that by comparing the event to null.

If the event handler isn't null, the code "invokes" it, passing it a reference to the object raising the event (this) and the NameChangedEventArgs object. That makes the program raise the event for each of the program elements that are registered to catch it. The same NameChangedEventArgs object is passed to each of the registered event handlers in turn.

Next, the accessor checks the NameChangedEventArgs object's Cancel field to see if the event handlers set that value to true. If Cancel is false, the accessor sets the property's backing field _Name to the new name value.

The program's main form uses the following code to declare and initialize a Person object.

```
// A Person.
private Person MyPerson = new Person();
```

The following code shows the program's NameChanged event handler.

```
// The event handler.
private void MyPerson_NameChanged(object sender, NameChangedEventArgs e)
{
    e.Cancel =
        MessageBox.Show(
            "Change the name from " + e.OldName + " to " + e.NewName + "?",
            "Change Name?",
```

```
        MessageBoxButtons.YesNo)
            == System.Windows.Forms.DialogResult.No;
}
```

The event handler takes two parameters. The first is an object named `sender` that refers to the `Person` object that is raising the event. The second parameter is the `NameChangedEventArgs` object created by the `Person` object when it raises the event.

The event handler displays a message box telling the user the `NameChangedEventArgs` object's old and new names, and asking if the change should be allowed. It sets the `NameChangedEventArgs` object's `Cancel` value to indicate whether the user clicks Yes or No.

The following code shows the program's `Load` event handler.

```
private void Form1_Load(object sender, EventArgs e)
{
    // Set and display an initial name.
    MyPerson.Name = "Ann";
    nameTextBox.Text = MyPerson.Name;

    // Register the event handler.
    MyPerson.NameChanged += MyPerson_NameChanged;
}
```

This code initializes the `Person` object's `Name` property and displays the name in the `nameTextBox`. At that point, no event handler is registered with the object so the event isn't raised.

The code then registers the `MyPerson_NameChanged` method to catch the `NameChanged` event.

The final piece to the program is the following `Click` event handler, which executes when the user clicks the Set Name button.

```
// Change the person's name.
private void setNameButton_Click(object sender, EventArgs e)
{
    MyPerson.Name = newNameTextBox.Text;
    nameTextBox.Text = MyPerson.Name;
}
```

When the user clicks the button, this code sets the `Person` object's `Name` property to the value entered in the `nameTextBox`.

The following list shows the complete sequence of events that occur when you click the button.

➤ The main program sets the `Person` object's `Name` property to a new value.

➤ The `Person` object's `set` accessor raises the `NameChanged` event.

➤ The main program's `MyPerson_NameChanged` event handler catches the event and displays a message box asking you to confirm the change.

➤ The `Person` object's `set` accessor checks the `NameChangedEventArgs` object's `Cancel` value to see whether it should cancel the name change. If `Cancel` is `false`, the accessor saves the new name value.

Using Static Events

Static events are mostly like nonstatic events except the event is provided by the class itself rather than an instance of the class.

The StaticEvent example program, which is available for download on this book's website, defines a `ReportManager` class that provides a static `ReportError` event.

The main program uses the following code to subscribe to the event. Notice how it uses the class instead of an instance to identify the event.

```
ReportManager.ReportError += MyReportManager_ReportError;
```

One important difference between static and nonstatic events has to do with the way objects are destroyed and recycled by the garbage collector. When one object registers for a second object's event, the second object keeps a reference to the first object. For example, suppose the `Form1` class's code registers to catch a `Person` object's `NameChanged` event. In that case, the `Person` object holds a reference to the `Form1` object.

Now if the program removes all references to those `Form1` and `Person` objects, the garbage collector can reclaim them as usual.

However, suppose `NameChanged` is a static event provided by the `Person` class. In that case, when the `Form1` object registers to receive the event, the `Person` class receives a reference to the `Form1` object. Later if the program doesn't need the `Form1` object any more, the garbage collector cannot reclaim it because the `Person` class still holds a reference to it. The `Form1` object's memory is lost forever.

You can avoid this situation by using the `-=` operator to unregister the event handler before releasing the `Form1` object. (You can also avoid this problem if you don't use static events.)

Hiding and Overriding Events

Events are a bit unusual because they are not inherited the same way properties and methods are. A derived class cannot raise the events declared by its ancestors.

For example, suppose the `BankAccount` class defines the `Overdrawn` event, and suppose the `OverdraftAccount` class is derived from the `BankAccount` class. Then the code in the `OverdraftAccount` class cannot raise the `Overdrawn` event.

The `OverdraftAccount` class can use the `new` keyword to hide the `Overdrawn` event with a new version.

If the `BankAccount` class declares the event with the `virtual` keyword, then the `OverdraftAccount` class can use the `override` keyword to override the event with a new version.

The `new`, `virtual`, and `override` keywords work much as they do for methods. See the sections "new" and "virtual and override" in Chapter 6 for more information.

Raising Parent Class Events

As the previous section mentioned, a derived class cannot raise an event declared by one of its ancestors. However, sometimes you might like to do just that. The derived class cannot invoke the ancestor class's event, but it can invoke code in the ancestor class and that code can invoke the event.

The solution is to give the ancestor a method that raises the event. The derived class can then call that method. By convention that method is usually named after the event with On added at the beginning.

To continue the previous example, you might like the OverdraftAccount class to raise the Overdrawn method defined by the BankAccount class instead of create a new event of its own that hides or overrides the BankAccount version. It cannot raise that event directly, but you can add an OnOverdrawn method to raise the event.

For example, you could create the following OnOverdrawn method.

```
protected void OnOverdrawn(decimal value)
{
    if (Overdrawn != null) Overdrawn(this, value);
}
```

Now when it needs to raise the Overdrawn event, the OverdraftAccount class invokes the OnOverdrawn method.

Implementing Custom Events

You can use code similar to the following to create an auto-implemented property.

```
public string Name { get; set; }
```

Behind the scenes, Visual Studio creates get and set accessors to support the property.

Similarly, the following statement declares a simple event.

```
public event EventHandler<NameChangedEventArgs> NameChanged;
```

This time Visual Studio creates *event accessors* that add and remove event handlers from a list of event handlers. These are similar to the get and set accessors provided for auto-implemented properties except they are named add and remove.

You can explicitly implement a property if you want to add extra features beyond those provided by auto-implemented properties. Similarly, you can explicitly implement add and remove event accessors if you want. If you take that approach, you must also write code to invoke any registered event handlers.

For example, consider the following code.

```
// A private event to represent the public event.
private EventHandler<VoteEventArgs> VoteEvent;

// The event.
public event EventHandler<VoteEventArgs> Vote
{
    add
    {
        VoteEvent += value;
    }
    remove
    {
        VoteEvent -= value;
    }
}
```

This code declares a private event named VoteEvent. It then defines a Vote event. That event's add and remove accessors delegate their jobs to the private event.

Later, the class can use code similar to the following to raise the event.

```
// Make the event args object.
VoteEventArgs args = new VoteEventArgs(this.Description);

// Call the event handlers.
if (VoteEvent != null) VoteEvent(this, args);
```

This code creates a VoteEventArgs object to provide information about the event. (Don't worry about the details. What's important is that it creates the object.) It then raises the private event named VoteEvent. Because the add and remove accessors simply passed add and remove requests to the private event, that event invokes any registered event handlers.

This example simply passes event requests to a private event so it actually doesn't add anything. It does basically the same thing as an auto-implemented public Vote event.

However, you could modify the program to do other things. For example, the custom event could delegate to an object contained in this class. Suppose the Car class has a Crashed event and suppose the Driver class has a Car property that represents the driver's car. Then the Driver class could make its own Crashed event that delegates to the Car object's event.

STATIC METHODS

Static methods are a bit less intuitive than static variables. Like static variables, you access static methods by using the class itself rather than an instance of the class. For example, consider the following Student class.

```
public class Student
{
    public int StudentId { get; set; }
    public string FirstName { get; set; }
    public string LastName { get; set; }
    ...

    // Make a Student.
    public static Student LookupStudent(int id)
    {
        // Look up the student ID in the database and create object theStudent.
        ...

        return theStudent;
    }
}
```

The class starts with some property declarations. It then defines the static LookupStudent method. This method takes a student's ID as a parameter, looks the student up in a database (that code isn't shown), and returns a Student object representing the student.

This kind of method that creates a new instance of a class is called a *factory method* because it acts as a factory that creates objects on demand.

> ## WORK AT THE FACTORY
>
> Factory methods enable a program to work with multiple classes that have a common ancestor without needing to know the details about which subclass it is using. It enables you to move the details of creating the particular subclass into the method and remove it from the main program.
>
> For example, suppose a program needs to work with a database. The DbConnection class represents a connection to a database at a high level. Child classes, such as OdbcConnection, OleDbConnection, OracleConnection, and SqlConnection, represent connections to specific kinds of databases.
>
> In this scenario, you could write a factory method that creates a database connection and returns a DbConnection object that the program can use. Later, if you decide to change the kind of database you're using, you can modify the factory method so it creates the new kind of connection object. The main program would still work with the parent class DbConnection so its code wouldn't need to change.
>
> By convention, the names of factory methods usually end in Factory as in DbConnectionFactory.

The following code shows how a program might use the LookupStudent method.

```
// Get the ID.
int id = int.Parse(lookupIdTextBox.Text);

// Get the student.
Student student = Student.LookupStudent(id);
if (student == null)
{
    firstNameTextBox.Clear();
    lastNameTextBox.Clear();
    idTextBox.Clear();
}
else
{
    firstNameTextBox.Text = student.FirstName;
    lastNameTextBox.Text = student.LastName;
    idTextBox.Text = student.StudentId.ToString();
}
```

This code gets an ID from a text box. It calls the LookupStudent method to find the student in the database and then either clears its result text boxes or displays the student's ID and name properties.

You could use a constructor instead of a factory method. In this example, the constructor would take the student's ID as a parameter, look up the student's record in the database, and initialize the Student object's properties.

Unfortunately, if the student didn't appear in the database, the constructor could throw an exception, but it couldn't return a null value. A factory method can return null if appropriate.

Even if you define a factory method, the main program could still create a Student object that didn't represent a student in the database. You can prevent that by giving the class a private constructor. Then code outside of the class cannot create an instance of the class, so it must use the factory method. (Because the factory method is inside the class, it can use the constructor if that helps.)

One restriction on static methods is that they cannot use instance properties or methods. That makes sense because a static method doesn't depend on a particular instance, so what instance's properties or methods would it use?

For example, the static LookupStudent method couldn't access the FirstName property because that property is defined only for instances of the class and not for the class itself. (Of course, the method could make an instance of the class and then use that instance's FirstName property. That's how the factory method creates a new Student object.)

SUMMARY

Classes and structures are similar. Both are container types that group related variables, methods, and events in a single entity.

Many developers use only classes, mostly because they are more familiar with classes, but there are some important reasons why you might pick one over the other. For example, structures don't support inheritance.

Structures are also value types and classes are reference types. This makes them behave differently when you define, initialize, and pass values into methods. The concepts described in this chapter should help you decide which of the two types is better in different situations.

Whether you use structures or classes, if you build large enough programs or collections of programs, you may run into naming conflicts. Names such as Person, Customer, and Order are so intuitive that developers working on different parts of the application may want to use the same names. Having two Customer classes around can cause confusion and lead to programs that don't work well together.

Namespaces help solve this problem by letting you categorize code and differentiate classes with the same names. For example, if you define separate billing, personnel, and order processing namespaces, all those namespaces can define their own Person, Employee, and Customer classes without conflict.

The next chapter describes namespaces in detail. It explains how to create namespaces and how to use them to refer to classes created in different assemblies.

EXERCISES

1. Draw a diagram similar to Figure 12-9 showing the memory layout used by the following `Customer` class, assuming `Address` and `Order` are structures.

```
public class Customer
{
    public Address MailingAddress, BillingAddress;
    public Order[] Orders;
}
```

(You don't need to show how it would be passed into a method. Just show how an object is laid out.)

2. Repeat Exercise 1 assuming `Address` and `Order` are classes instead of structures.

3. Consider the `Customer` classes used in Exercises 1 and 2. How large is the difference between the two structures if you pass a `Customer` object into a method by value? By reference? Would the differences be larger or smaller if `Customer` were a structure instead of a class?

4. Download the PersonEvent example program. What happens if the `Person` class's `Name` property's set accessor doesn't check whether `NameChanged` is `null` and simply "invokes" the event handler?

5. Create a `BankAccount` class that has a `Balance` property. If `Balance` is set to a negative amount, the set accessor should raise an `Overdrawn` event and not save the new value. Write a program to test the class. If the program tries to reduce the balance to less than $0.00, display a message box.

6. Create an `OverdraftAccount` class that is derived from the `BankAccount` class you built for Exercise 5. Override the `Overdrawn` event. Also override the `Balance` property so that the set accessor only raises the event if the balance is set to a value less than –$100.00.

7. Modify the program you wrote for Exercise 6 so that the `OverdraftAccount` class raises the `BankAccount` class's `Overdrawn` event instead of overrides that event.

8. Modify the program you wrote for Exercise 6 so that the `OverdraftAccount` class hides the `Overdrawn` event. Make the main program use code similar to the following to create its `OverdraftAccount` object.

```
private BankAccount Account = new OverdraftAccount();
```

What happens when you run the program? Why does it do that?

9. Write a program that uses the custom event handler described in the section "Implementing Custom Events." Make a `BallotIssue` class that provides the `Vote` event. That event passes the event handlers a `VoteEventArgs` object that has a boolean field named `IsVetoed`.

Also give the `BallotIssue` class a boolean `IsVetoed` method. When the program calls that method, the class should raise its `Vote` event. The idea is that any of the registered event handlers could veto the `BallotIssue`.

Give the main program three different event handlers that use a message box to ask if you want to veto the issue.

Unfortunately, the way the `BallotIssue` class delegates the event requires it to invoke every event handler even if one vetoes the issue. That means a later event handler could reset `e.Cancel` to `false` even if an earlier event handler set it to `true`.

To prevent that, make each event handler check `e.Cancel`. If the value is `true`, the event handler should return without doing anything.

10. The problem with the program you wrote for Exercise 9 is that a later event handler can override the veto choice of an earlier event handler, essentially vetoing the veto.

Write a program that avoids this problem by making the `BallotIssue` class store its event handlers in a private `List<EventHandler<VoteEventArgs>>` instead of delegating to a private event.

To raise the event, the new version should loop through the list of event handlers. After it calls each, the code can check `e.Cancel`. If `e.Cancel` is `true`, it can break out of the loop so later event handlers cannot reset `e.Cancel`.

11. Make a program that defines a `Student` class that has a `LookupStudent` factory method similar to the one described in the section "Static Methods." Instead of using a database, place arrays containing first and last names in the method and use the student's ID as an index into the arrays. If the user enters an ID that is outside of the arrays' bounds, return `null`. Finally, give the class a private constructor and make the factory method use it.

13

Namespaces

WROX.COM DOWNLOADS FOR THIS CHAPTER

Please note that all the code examples for this chapter are available as a part of this chapter's code download on the book's website at `www.wrox.com/go/csharp5programmersref` on the Download Code tab.

In large applications, name collisions are fairly common. A developer working on a billing system might create a `Customer` class. Meanwhile another developer working on a customer complaint tracking system might define a different `Customer` class. Each class will have different properties, methods, and events that are useful for its application.

Having two classes with the same name like this won't cause any problems until you try to integrate the two programs. At that point, the program won't be able to tell which kind of `Customer` class to use under different circumstances.

This situation in which multiple items have the same name is called a *namespace collision* or *namespace pollution*.

Namespaces enable you to group code so that you can tell the program where to find a particular class. For example, the developer working on the billing system might use the `Billing` namespace and the developer working on the complaint tracking system might use the `CustomerSatisfaction` namespace.

Now when you glue code from the two programs together in one mega-program, you can refer to the two classes as `Billing.Customer` and `CustomerSatisfaction.Customer` and the two classes can peacefully coexist.

Namespaces can contain other namespaces, so you can build a hierarchical structure that groups different entities. You can divide the `Billing` namespace into pieces such as `OverdueAccounts` and `PaidAccounts` to give developers working on that project some isolation from each other.

Namespaces can be confusing at first, but they are fairly simple. They just group the code in manageable pieces so that you can tell different chunks of code apart from each other.

This chapter describes namespaces. It explains how to use namespaces to categorize programming items and how to use them to select the right versions of items with the same name.

COLLISIONS IN .NET

Name collisions are uncommon in the .NET Framework because the designers were careful to give classes with similar purposes different names. If no two classes have the same name, then there's no problem.

For example, the `System.Data` namespace includes several subnamespaces such as `Odbc` and `OleDb` to work with different kinds of databases (in this case, ODBC and OLE DB databases). Those namespaces contain similar classes, but their names are prefixed with the namespace name so that they don't conflict. For example, those namespaces contain the `OdbcConnection` and `OleDbConnection` classes.

However, there are a few cases in which classes have exactly the same names. For example, the `System.Windows.Forms`, `System.Windows.Controls`, and `System.Web.UI.WebControls` namespaces all define `Label`, `TextBox`, and `Button` classes.

Those namespaces represent different ways of building user interfaces (Windows Forms, WPF/XAML, and web page) so it is quite unusual for a program to include more than one of those kinds of controls. If you ever do, however, you'll need to use namespaces to indicate which you are using in different parts of the code.

THE USING DIRECTIVE

Visual Studio defines thousands of classes, constants, and other entities to provide tools for your applications. It categorizes them in namespaces to prevent name collisions and to make it easier for you to find the items you need.

The .NET Framework root namespaces are named `Microsoft` and `System`.

The `Microsoft` namespace includes namespaces that support different programming languages and tools. For example, typical namespaces include `CSharp`, `JScript`, and `VisualBasic`, which contain types and tools that support the C#, JScript, and Visual Basic languages. The `Microsoft` namespace also includes the `Win32` namespace, which includes classes that handle operating system events and that manipulate the registry.

The System namespace contains a huge number of useful programming items, including many nested namespaces. For example, the System.Drawing namespace contains classes related to drawing; System.Data contains classes related to databases; System.Threading holds classes dealing with multithreading; and System.Security includes classes for working with security and cryptography.

Note that these namespaces are not necessarily available to your program at all times. For example, by default, the Microsoft.JScript namespace is not available to C# programs. To use it, you must first add a reference to the Microsoft.JScript.dll library.

Visual Studio includes so many programming tools that the namespace hierarchy is truly enormous. Namespaces are refined into subnamespaces, which may be further broken into more namespaces until they reach a manageable size. Although this makes it easier to differentiate among all the different programming entities, it makes the fully qualified names of some classes rather cumbersome.

For example, the following code draws a rectangle with a dashed border. Notice the long series of namespaces used by the Dash enumeration value (highlighted in bold).

```
private void Form1_Paint(object sender, PaintEventArgs e)
{
    using (Pen pen = new Pen(Color.Blue))
    {
        pen.DashStyle = System.Drawing.Drawing2D.DashStyle.Dash;
        e.Graphics.DrawRectangle(pen, 10, 10, 100, 50);
    }
}
```

You can use a using directive at the top of the file to make using namespaces easier. For example, suppose the program begins with the following statement.

```
using System.Drawing.Drawing2D;
```

Now the program can use the following simpler code to draw the dashed rectangle.

```
private void Form1_Paint(object sender, PaintEventArgs e)
{
    using (Pen pen = new Pen(Color.Blue))
    {
        pen.DashStyle = DashStyle.Dash;
        e.Graphics.DrawRectangle(pen, 10, 10, 100, 50);
    }
}
```

The using directive tells the compiler where to look for classes, structures, enumerations, and other items that are not defined locally. When it sees the value DashStyle.Dash, the compiler tries to locate DashStyle in the current file. When it doesn't find it, the compiler searches the namespaces listed in using directives. In this example, it eventually finds DashStyle in the System.Drawing.Drawing2D namespace.

If a program contains two using directives for namespaces that define classes with the same names, C# may become confused and give you an Ambiguous Reference error. To fix the problem, the code must use fully qualified names to select the right versions.

OVERUSING USING

A code file can include any number of `using` directives without affecting the size of the compiled executable program. The compiler includes only items in namespaces that it actually uses, so extra `using` directives don't make any difference to the end result.

However, when the compiler needs to figure out where some symbol is defined, it searches the namespaces listed in `using` statements. If the file includes lots of unused namespaces, the compiler may waste a lot of time searching them.

For example, a typical Windows Forms application might include the following `using` directives by default in a new application.

```
using System;
using System.Collections.Generic;
using System.ComponentModel;
using System.Data;
using System.Drawing;
using System.Linq;
using System.Text;
using System.Threading.Tasks;
using System.Windows.Forms;
```

A program that draws a dashed rectangle needs only the following three `using` directives.

```
using System.Drawing;
using System.Windows.Forms;
using System.Drawing.Drawing2D;
```

You can help the compiler find symbols more efficiently by removing unnecessary `using` directives. An easy way to do that is to right-click the code editor and open the Organize Usings context menu item. That menu contains the following three commands.

Remove Unused Usings—This command removes `using` directives for namespaces that are not needed by the code.

Sort—This command sorts `using` directives alphabetically.

Remove and Sort—This command removes unnecessary `using` directives and then sorts them.

For example, the following code creates two `Customer` objects, one using the class defined in the `Billing` namespace and one using the class defined in the `CustomerSatisfaction` namespace.

```
Billing.Customer customer1 = new Billing.Customer();
CustomerSatisfaction.Customer customer2 = new CustomerSatisfaction.Customer();
```

Sometimes, including a fully qualified namespace can make the code unwieldy and hard to read. In this example, the CustomerSatisfaction namespace makes the second statement so long it barely fits on a single line. In other cases, such as with the System.Drawing.Drawing2D.DashStyle.Dash value used earlier, deeply nested namespaces makes the code awkward.

In addition to including a namespace for the compiler to use, the using directive can define an alias to make using long namespaces easier. For example, the following using directives define aliases for the System.Drawing.Drawing2D and CustomerSatisfaction namespaces.

```
using D2D = System.Drawing.Drawing2D;
using CS = CustomerSatisfaction;
```

The following code shows how you could use those aliases.

```
pen.DashStyle = D2D.DashStyle.Dash;
CS.Customer customer2 = new CS.Customer();
```

ABSTRUSE ABBREVIATIONS

Be sure your abbreviations aren't more confusing than the original namespace names. In the previous example, D2D and CS are too short to be descriptive, so they may cause confusion unless you use them often enough to get used to them. Abbreviations such as Draw2D and Satisfaction would be longer but more intuitive.

Project Templates

When you create a new project, Visual Studio includes whatever using directives are defined by the project's template. The included directives were chosen by the Microsoft development team because it thought those directives would be useful under many common situations, but the results may not suit your needs.

If the template doesn't do exactly what you need, it's easy to add a few using directives manually. It's even easier to remove unwanted directives by using the Remove Unused Usings context menu command. (See the tip "Overusing Using" earlier in this chapter.)

However, if you build a large number of projects or add a lot of modules that need the same directives, you can make the process a bit easier by defining your own templates.

To create a project template, start a new project. Add any forms, windows, or other modules that you want the template to have, and edit them so they contain the wanted using directives. When you have the project the way you want it, use the File menu's Export Template command to open the Export Template Wizard, as shown in Figure 13-1.

To create a project template, select the Project Template option, and click Next to display the page shown in Figure 13-2. Enter a name and description for the template. If you want, you can also define an icon for Visual Studio to display and a preview image. When you finish, click Finish to create the template.

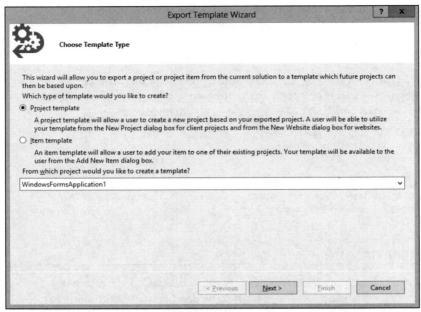

FIGURE 13-1: The Export Template Wizard enables you to build project or item templates.

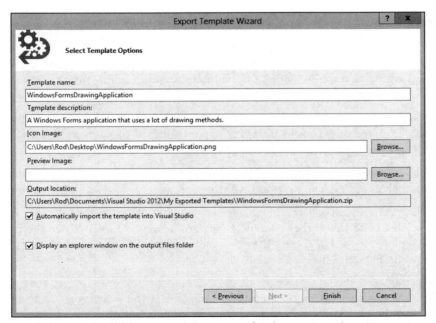

FIGURE 13-2: Specify a name and description for the new template. You can also define an icon and preview image if you like.

Now when you start a new project, the New Project dialog includes your template, as shown in Figure 13-3.

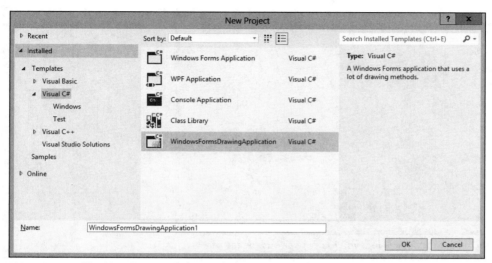

FIGURE 13-3: The New Project dialog includes your templates.

When you create a new project based on your template, the new project includes whatever files you included in the template, and those files contain the using directives that you included.

> **MORE POWERFUL TEMPLATES**
>
> Templates can not only define the modules and using directives that are initially included in a project but also define other code. For example, you could make templates that include standard splash screen code or that contain standard menu items.

Item Templates

When you add a new form or other modules to a project, Visual Studio uses an item template to determine what code and what using directives are added. Just as you can define new project templates, you can define new item templates.

For example, create a form that includes the using directives you want. Then select the File menu's Export Template command to display the Export Template Wizard as before. On the wizard's first page, select Item Template and click Next to display the page shown in Figure 13-4.

Check the parts of the program that you want to include in the template and click Next to display the page shown in Figure 13-5.

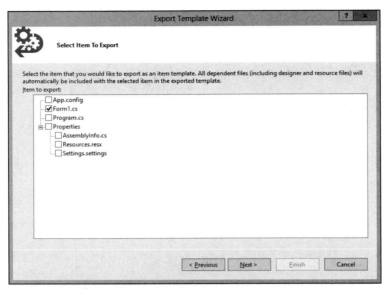

FIGURE 13-4: An item template lets you export various pieces of a program such as forms or settings.

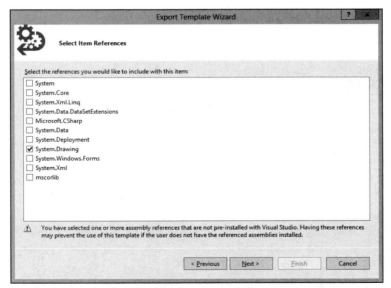

FIGURE 13-5: An item template lets you include references to system libraries.

Check the references that you want to include, and click Next to display the page shown in Figure 13-2. Enter the template name and description as before, and click Finish to create the template.

Now when you select the Project menu's Add New Item command, you can select the item you defined.

THE DEFAULT NAMESPACE

Every project has a default namespace, and every item in the project is contained directly or indirectly within that namespace.

Initially, the default namespace has the same name as the project. For example, if you create a project named OrderExplorer, then every module's code is initially contained in the `OrderExplorer` namespace.

To view or change the project's default namespace, use Project ➪ Properties to open the project's property pages, and select the Application page, as shown in Figure 13-6. You can view and change the default namespace in the Default Namespace text box.

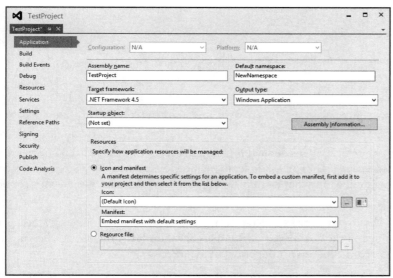

FIGURE 13-6: Use the Application property page to change an application's default namespace.

If you change the default namespace, any modules you add to the project in the future use that namespace.

MAKING NAMESPACES

You can create new namespaces nested within the default namespace to further categorize your code. Simply add a namespace statement to the code.

You can create a namespace outside of any other namespace. You can also place a namespace inside another namespace at the top level (not inside any class, structure, or other code item). For example, consider the following code.

```
namespace OrderExplorer
{
    public class Person
```

```
    {
        public CustomerData.Customer customer;
    }

    namespace CustomerData
    {
        public class Customer : Person
        {
            public Person person;
        }
    }
}

namespace DrawingTools
{
    public class Shape
    {
        public OrderExplorer.CustomerData.Customer customer;
    }
}
```

This code defines two top-level namespaces: OrderExplorer and DrawingTools. The OrderExplorer namespace contains the CustomerData namespace.

The code inside a namespace can refer to items defined in that namespace or any enclosing namespace without explicitly giving a namespace path. For example, in the previous code, the Customer class can refer to the Person class without indicating that its fully qualified namespace path is OrderExplorer .CustomerData.

In contrast, the Person class must refer to the Customer class as CustomerData.Customer because the Person class is not contained in the CustomerData namespace. Similarly, the Shape class must refer to the Customer class as OrderExplorer.CustomerData.Customer.

A using directive can change this behavior. For example, if the module contains the following using directive, then all the classes in this example could refer to the Customer class without any namespace information.

```
using OrderExplorer.CustomerData;
```

A program can place code in a namespace in multiple places by using multiple namespace statements. For example, two modules could use the statement namespace DrawingTools to add code to the DrawingTools namespace.

NAMESPACES GONE WILD

Scattering pieces of a namespace throughout your code will probably confuse other developers. One case in which it might make sense to break a namespace into pieces would be if you want to put different classes in different code files, either to prevent any one file from becoming too big or to allow different programmers to work on the files at the same time. In that case, it might make sense to place related pieces of the application in the same namespace but in different files.

RESOLVING NAMESPACES

Normally, C# does a good job of resolving namespaces, so you don't need to worry too much about the process. You can insert a `using` directive and then omit the namespace in the declarations that you use. If you don't include a `using` directive, you can still use fully qualified declarations. You can even create a namespace alias so that you can specify the namespace without typing it out in full.

However, there are some in-between cases that can be confusing. To understand them, it helps to know a bit more about how C# resolves namespaces.

When the compiler sees a reference that uses a fully qualified namespace, it looks in that namespace for the item it needs and that's that. It either succeeds or fails. For example, the following code declares a variable of type `System.Collections.Hashtable`. The compiler looks in the `System.Collections` namespace and tries to find the `Hashtable` class. If the class is not there, the declaration fails.

```
System.Collections.Hashtable hashtable = new System.Collections.Hashtable();
```

When the compiler finds a reference to a qualified namespace, it initially assumes the namespace is fully qualified. If it cannot resolve the reference as described in the preceding paragraph, it assumes the reference is partially qualified, and it looks in the current namespace for a resolution. For example, suppose you declare a variable as shown in the following code.

```
CustomerData.Customer customer;
```

In this case, the compiler searches the current namespace for a nested namespace called `CustomerData`. If it finds such a namespace, it looks for the `Customer` class in that namespace.

If the compiler cannot resolve a namespace using these methods, it moves up the namespace hierarchy and tries again. Movement up the namespace hierarchy can sometimes be confusing. It may lead the compiler to resolve references in an ancestor of the current namespace, in some sort of uncle/aunt namespace, or in a cousin namespace.

For example, consider the namespace hierarchy shown in Figure 13-7. The clouds represent namespaces and the boxes represent classes.

Suppose the `Customer` class includes the following declaration.

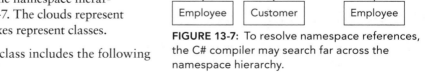

FIGURE 13-7: To resolve namespace references, the C# compiler may search far across the namespace hierarchy.

```
public Employee SalesRep { get; set; }
```

The `Customer` class is in the `BusinessClasses` namespace. That namespace defines an `Employee` class so that's the class the compiler uses for the `SalesRep` property.

Now suppose the `Customer` class uses the following declaration instead of the preceding one.

```
public AssignmentTools.Employee SalesRep { get; set; }
```

In this case, the compiler first assumes `AssignmentTools.Employee` is a fully qualified name. It looks at the root of the namespace hierarchy for the `AssignmentTools` namespace, but it doesn't find one.

Next, the compiler looks in the current namespace `BusinessClasses` to see if it contains a namespace `AssignmentTools`. The compiler doesn't find such a namespace, so it moves up the hierarchy to the `ContractBuilder` namespace.

The compiler looks again for an `AssignmentTools` namespace and this time finds it. The compiler looks in the new namespace for the `Employee` class and finds it, so its search is over.

If you understand how the compiler resolves namespaces, you can eventually figure out that the property in this example has type `ContractBuilder.AssignmentTools.Employee`. If you add `using` directives to the code, things can get more confusing.

Suppose the program includes the following directives.

```
using BusinessClasses;
using AssignmentTools;
```

Now if a piece of code in the `ContractBuilder` namespace declares a variable of type `Employee`, the compiler won't know which version to use. At that point it gives up and reports an Ambiguous Reference error.

You can come up with combinations of `using` directives, namespace aliases, and fully or partially qualified namespace paths to make the code do exactly what you want, but the result can be confusing. In this example, you would probably be better off rearranging the namespaces and possibly renaming one of the `Employee` classes to make things more obvious.

> ### WHICH NAMESPACE?
>
> If you aren't sure which namespace the compiler has decided to use in a particular situation, right-click the type (for example, `Employee`) and select Go to Definition. If the type is defined in your code, the code editor jumps to that definition. If the type is defined in a library, Visual Studio opens the Object Browser to the type's definition.

THE GLOBAL NAMESPACE

Different namespaces can contain program items that have the same names. One namespace might define a class named `Shutdown`; another might create an enumeration named `Shutdown`; and a third might define a structure named `Shutdown`. As long as you use the right namespaces, you can use any of the versions.

One situation in which this can cause problems is if a namespace defines a symbol that hides a symbol in the global namespace. For example, suppose you define the following `Player` class for a game program.

```
public class Player
{
    public string Name { get; set; }
```

```
    private ConsoleTyes Console { get; set; }

    // Display the Person's name.
    public void ShowName()
    {
        Console.WriteLine(Name);
    }
}
```

The intent is for the `Console` property to store the player's console type. Unfortunately, when the compiler sees `Console` in the `ShowName` method, it finds the property, not the class, that displays messages in the Console window.

If you place `global::` in front of a namespace, the compiler begins searching for the symbol in the global namespace instead of looking for it locally. That means you can use the following statement to correctly find the `Console.WriteLine` method.

```
    global::System.Console.WriteLine(Name);
```

Usually it is better to avoid names that conflict with the system namespaces. For example, if you change the property's name to `ConsoleType`, there's no confusion.

SUMMARY

Namespaces are everywhere in C#. Every piece of code you write is contained in some namespace, even if it is only the application's root namespace. Despite the pervasiveness of namespaces, many developers never need to use them explicitly, so they find them somewhat mystifying.

Namespaces are quite simple. They merely divide programming items into a hierarchy to prevent name collisions, and they enable you to group related items.

The `using` directive lets a program refer to items in a namespace without using fully qualified names. The `using` directive can also define an alias for a namespace, so you can refer to it by using a short abbreviation. This is particularly useful for resolving names that appear in more than one of the namespaces that your program uses.

The .NET Framework contains hundreds of namespaces, some of which are more useful than others. The next chapter describes classes that are in two of the most useful namespaces: `System.Collections` and `System.Collections.Generic`. The classes in those namespaces let you arrange and manage objects in particularly useful ways such as in stacks, queues, lists, and dictionaries.

EXERCISES

1. Suppose you are writing a program that uses the `System.Security.Cryptography.SHA512Managed` class but you (understandably) don't want to type all that out. Give two methods for shortening this in your code. What are the advantages and disadvantages of each?

2. Suppose your program needs to use the `System.Windows.Controls.Calendar` control and the `System.Globalization.Calendar` class. Give three methods for differentiating between the two classes in your code. What are the advantages and disadvantages of each?

For Exercises 3 through 8 use the namespace hierarchy shown in Figure 13-8. (No, I don't recommend this kind of design.)

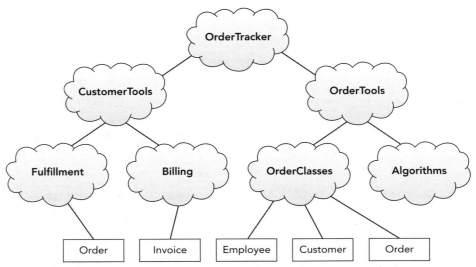

FIGURE 13-8: Clouds represent namespaces and rectangles represent classes.

3. Without any `using` directives, what is the shortest way code in the `Algorithms` namespace can refer to the `Order` classes in both the `OrderClasses` and `Fulfillment` namespaces?

4. Without any `using` directives, what is the shortest way code in the `OrderTools` namespace can refer to the `Order` classes in both the `Fulfillment` and `OrderClasses` namespaces?

5. What `using` directives would you create to allow code in the `Algorithms` namespace to refer to either of the `Order` classes with an alias? Show code that uses those aliases to define objects of the two classes.

6. What is the most concise way for the `Customer` class to include both kinds of `Order` objects? Show code that defines objects of both classes.

7. What is the easiest way to allow code throughout the namespace hierarchy to use the `Invoice` class?

8. How could you improve the design shown in Figure 13-8?

14

Collection Classes

WHAT'S IN THIS CHAPTER

- ➤ Arrays and array objects
- ➤ Collection classes
- ➤ Generic collections
- ➤ Collection initialization
- ➤ Iterators

WROX.COM DOWNLOADS FOR THIS CHAPTER

Please note that all the code examples for this chapter are available as a part of this chapter's code download on the book's website at www.wrox.com/go/csharp5programmersref on the Download Code tab.

Many applications must store and manipulate groups of objects. For example, an application might need to manage a group of Customers, Orders, Students, or Invoices.

An array lets you store a group of objects. Unfortunately, arrays don't let you easily rearrange the objects. For example, to add an object at the end of an array in C#, you need to create a new array that's one position bigger than the old array, copy the existing items into the new array, add the new item, and then set the reference to the old array equal to the new one. Adding or removing an item from the beginning or middle of an array is even more time-consuming.

Because these sorts of operations are common, many algorithms have been devised over the years to make them easier. The .NET Framework includes an assortment of collection classes that implement those algorithms, so you don't have to do it yourself.

This chapter describes collection classes provided by the Framework. It explains how you can use them to store and manipulate groups of objects and provides tips for selecting the right collection for different purposes. The following section starts by describing the simplest kind of collection: the array.

ARRAYS

C# provides two basic kinds of arrays. First, it provides the normal arrays that you get when you use the new keyword and brackets surrounding the number of items the array should hold. For example, the following code declares an array of int named squares and initializes it to contain 10 entries.

```
int[] squares = new int[10];
```

The C# Array class provides another kind of array. This kind is actually an object that provides methods for managing the items stored in the array.

The following code shows the previous version of the code rewritten to use an Array object:

```
Array squares = Array.CreateInstance(typeof(int), 10);
```

This version creates the array by passing to the static Array.CreateInstance method the data type the array should contain and the number of items that it should hold.

One of the nice features of the Array class is that it provides methods that also work on normal arrays. For example, if values is an ordinary array of strings, then the statement Array.Sort(values) sorts the strings in the array.

The following sections provide more details about arrays and the Array class.

Dimensions

Both normal arrays and Array objects can support multiple dimensions. The following statement declares a three-dimensional array with 10 items in the first dimension, 5 in the second, and 20 in the third. It then sets the value for the item in position (1, 2, 3).

```
int[, ,] values = new int[10, 5, 20];
values[1, 2, 3] = 123;
```

The following code does the same thing with an Array object.

```
Array values = Array.CreateInstance(typeof(int), 10, 5, 20);
values.SetValue(123, 1, 2, 3);
```

Lower Bounds

A normal array always has lower bound 0 in every dimension. For example, the previous array had dimensions 0 through 9, 0 through 4, and 0 through 19.

You can pretend an array has nonzero lower bounds, but it requires extra work on your part. You must add or subtract an appropriate amount from each index to map the indexes you want to use to the underlying zero-based indexes.

`Array` objects can handle nonzero lower bounds for you. Pass the `CreateInstance` method the array's data type, an array giving the lengths of each dimension, and an array giving each dimension's lower bounds.

For example, suppose you want to store quarterly sales data for the years 2001 through 2010. The following code creates a two-dimensional array with indexes ranging from 2001 to 2010 in the first dimension and 1 to 4 in the second dimension.

```
int[] lengths = {10, 4};
int[] lowerBounds = {2001, 1};
Array sales = Array.CreateInstance(typeof(decimal), lengths, lowerBounds);
sales.SetValue(10000m, 2005, 3);
```

The code first defines an array containing the number of elements for each dimension (10 in the first dimension and 4 in the second). Next, it creates an array containing the lower bounds for each dimension. (The first dimension starts with index 2001 and the second starts with index 1.)

The code then calls `Array.CreateInstance`, passing it the `int` data type, the array of lengths, and the array of lower bounds. The code finishes by setting the value for the third quarter in the year 2005 to 10,000.

Resizing

To resize an array, you need to allocate a new array, copy any items that you want to preserve into it, and then set the reference to the original array equal to the new one. For example, the following code adds the value 5 to the end of an array.

```
// Create the initial array.
int[] values = { 0, 1, 2, 3, 4 };

// Add the value 5 at the end.
int[] newValues = new int[6];
for (int i = 0; i < values.Length; i++)
    newValues[i] = values[i];
newValues[5] = 5;
values = newValues;
```

Like a normal array, an `Array` object cannot resize. However, the `Array` class's `CopyTo` method makes it relatively easy to copy items from one `Array` to another. For example, the following code is similar to the preceding code except it uses `Array` objects instead of ordinary arrays.

```
// Create the initial array.
Array values = Array.CreateInstance(typeof(int), 5);
for (int i = 0; i < values.Length; i++) values.SetValue(i, i);

// Add the value 5 at the end.
Array newValues = Array.CreateInstance(typeof(int), 6);
values.CopyTo(newValues, 0);
newValues.SetValue(5, 5);
values = newValues;
```

The `Array` class's static `Copy` method allows you even greater control. It lets you specify the index in the source array where the copy should start, the index in the destination array where the items should be copied, and the number of items to be copied.

One of the nice things about the `Array` class's methods is that many of them also work with normal arrays. For example, the following code shows the earlier code for extending a normal array, but this version uses the `Array.Copy` method (highlighted in bold) instead of copying items with a `for` loop.

```
// Create the initial array.
int[] values = { 0, 1, 2, 3, 4 };

// Add the value 5 at the end.
int[] newValues = new int[6];
Array.Copy(values, newValues, 5);
newValues[5] = 5;
values = newValues;
```

This code is still rather long, but the `Array.Copy` method is quite fast, so the code is fairly efficient.

Speed

There's no doubt that arrays of variables are much faster than `Array` objects. In one test, setting and getting values in an `Array` object took more than 20 times as long as performing the same operations in a variable array.

Microsoft has also optimized one-dimensional arrays, so they are faster than multidimensional arrays. The difference is much less dramatic than the difference between arrays and the `Array` class, however.

If your application performs only a few hundred array operations, the difference is unimportant. If your application must access array values many millions of times, you may need to consider using an array of variables even if the `Array` class would be more convenient for other reasons (such as nonzero lower bounds).

Example program ArraySpeeds, which is available for download on this book's website, compares the speeds of variable arrays and `Array` objects. Enter the number of items that you want to use in the arrays, and click Go. The program builds one- and two-dimensional arrays and `Array` objects holding the same number of integers. It then fills the arrays for a large number of trials and displays the elapsed time.

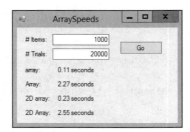

FIGURE 14-1: Variable arrays are faster than `Array` objects.

Figure 14-1 shows the results. Variable arrays are much faster than `Array` objects, and one-dimensional variable arrays generally seem to be slightly faster than two-dimensional arrays.

Other Array Class Features

The `Array` class provides several other useful static methods that work with both arrays and `Arrays`. For example, the `IndexOf` and `LastIndexOf` methods return the position of a particular item in an `Array`.

The following table summarizes some of the most useful `Array` class methods.

PROPERTY/METHOD	PURPOSE
BinarySearch	Returns the index of an item in the previously sorted array. The items must implement the IComparable interface, or you must provide an IComparer object.
Clear	Removes all the items from the array.
ConvertAll	Converts an array of one type into an array of another type.
Copy	Copies some or all the items from a position in one array to a position in another.
Exists	Determines whether the array contains a particular item.
IndexOf	Returns the index of the first item with a given value.
LastIndexOf	Returns the index of the last item with a given value.
Resize	Resizes the array.
Reverse	Reverses the order of the items in the array.
Sort	Sorts the items in the array. The items must implement the IComparable interface, or you must provide an IComparer object.

SYSTEM.COLLECTIONS

The collection classes in the System.Collections namespace basically hold items and don't provide a lot of extra functionality. Other classes described later in this chapter are more powerful, so you should generally use them.

The following sections describe the ArrayList, StringCollection, and NameValueCollection classes.

ArrayList

The System.Collections.ArrayList class represents a resizable array implemented internally as a list. You can add and remove items from any position in the list and it resizes itself accordingly. The following table describes some of the class's more useful properties and methods.

PROPERTY/METHOD	PURPOSE
Add	Adds an item at the end of the list.
AddRange	Adds the items in an object that implements the ICollection interface to the end of the list.

continues

(continued)

PROPERTY/METHOD	PURPOSE
BinarySearch	Returns the index of an item in the previously sorted list. The items must implement the `IComparable` interface, or you must provide the method with an `IComparer` object.
Capacity	Gets or sets the number of items that the list can hold.
Clear	Removes all the items from the list.
Contains	Returns `true` if a specified item is in the list.
CopyTo	Copies some of the list or the entire list into a one-dimensional `Array` object.
Count	Returns the number of items currently in the list. This is always less than or equal to `Capacity`.
GetRange	Returns an `ArrayList` containing the items in part of the list.
IndexOf	Returns the zero-based index of the first occurrence of a specified item in the list.
Insert	Adds an item at a particular position in the list.
InsertRange	Adds the items in an object that implements the `ICollection` interface to a particular position in the list.
Item	Returns the item at a particular position in the list.
LastIndexOf	Returns the zero-based index of the last occurrence of a specified item in the list.
Remove	Removes the first occurrence of a specified item from the list.
RemoveAt	Removes the item at the specified position in the list.
RemoveRange	Removes the items in the specified positions from the list.
Reverse	Reverses the order of the items in the list.
SetRange	Replaces the items in part of the list with new items taken from an `ICollection` object.
Sort	Sorts the items in the list. The items must implement the `IComparable` interface, or you must provide the method with an `IComparer` object.
ToArray	Copies the list's items into a one-dimensional array. The array can be an array of objects, an array of a specific type, or an `Array` object (holding `objects`).
TrimToSize	Reduces the list's allocated space so that it is just big enough to hold its items. This sets `Capacity = Count`.

WHY BOTHER?

If the classes described later are generally better, why would you bother with these simpler classes? Sometimes, you need to use the simpler classes because some other object or method returns them to your code. For example, suppose you want to add an array of strings to an application's settings. You can use Project ➪ Properties to open the project's property pages and open the Settings page, as shown in Figure 14-2.

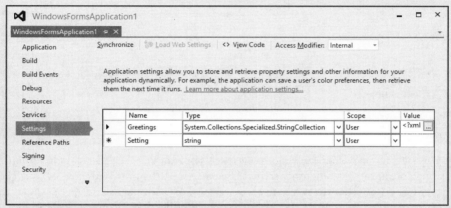

FIGURE 14-2: The Settings property page doesn't support arrays of strings but it does support the `StringCollection` type.

The Settings page doesn't support the `string[]` type, but it does support the `StringCollection` type. If you click the ellipsis in the Value column, the String Collection Editor opens and lets you edit the strings. After you close the editor, you can select the text in the Value field and copy it to the clipboard. If you then paste it into a text editor, you'll see XML code similar to the following.

```xml
<?xml version="1.0" encoding="utf-16"?>
<ArrayOfString xmlns:xsi="http://www.w3.org/2001/XMLSchema-instance"
xmlns:xsd="http://www.w3.org/2001/XMLSchema">
  <string>Hello</string>
  <string>Good morning</string>
  <string>Greetings</string>
</ArrayOfString>
```

At run time, the program can use code similar to the following to display one of the values in the `StringCollection` named `greetings`.

```csharp
StringCollection greetings = Properties.Settings.Default.Greetings;
MessageBox.Show(greetings[0]);
```

A single `ArrayList` object can hold objects of many different kinds. For example, the following code creates an `ArrayList`, adds several items of different types to it, and then loops through the list displaying the values.

```
ArrayList list = new ArrayList();
list.Add("What?");
list.Add(this);
list.Add(7331);
list.Add(new Bitmap(32, 32));
foreach (object obj in list)
    Console.WriteLine(obj.ToString());
```

The following text shows the result.

```
What?
WindowsFormsApplication1.Form1, Text: Form1
7331
System.Drawing.Bitmap
```

StringCollection

The `System.Collections.Specialized` namespace's `StringCollection` class is similar to `ArrayList`, except that it can hold only strings. Because it works only with strings, this class provides some extra type checking that the `ArrayList` does not. For example, if your program tries to add an `Employee` object or `Bitmap` to a `StringCollection`, the collection throws an exception.

A `StringCollection` can hold duplicate values and `null` values.

The following code shows how the UseStringCollection example program, which is available for download on the book's website, demonstrates a `StringCollection`.

```
// The values.
private StringCollection Values = new StringCollection();

// Add a value to the collection.
private void addButton_Click(object sender, EventArgs e)
{
    Values.Add(valueTextBox.Text);
    valueTextBox.Clear();
    valueTextBox.Focus();
    ListValues();
}

// Display the name/values groups.
private void ListValues()
{
    valueListBox.Items.Clear();
    foreach (string value in Values)
    {
        valueListBox.Items.Add(value);
    }
}
```

The code starts by creating a new StringCollection. When you enter a string in the TextBox and click Add, the button's Click event handler adds the value to the StringCollection and calls the ListValues method to display the collection's values. The ListValues method loops through the collection's values and displays them in the program's ListBox.

To take advantage of this extra error checking, you should always use a StringCollection instead of an ArrayList if you are working with strings. Of course, if you need other features (such as the fast lookups provided by a Dictionary), you should use one of the classes described in the following sections.

NameValueCollection

The System.Collections.Specialized namespace's NameValueCollection class is a collection that can hold more than one string value for a particular key (the value's "name"). For example, you might use people's names as keys. The strings associated with a particular key could include the postal address, phone number, e-mail address, and so forth.

Of course, you could also store the same information by putting the postal address, phone number, e-mail address, and other fields in an object or structure, and then storing the objects or structures in some sort of collection class such as an ArrayList. A NameValueCollection, however, is useful if you don't know ahead of time how many strings will be associated with each key.

The following code shows how the UseNameValueCollection example program, which is available for download on the book's website, demonstrates a NameValueCollection.

```
// The NameValueCollection.
private NameValueCollection Values = new NameValueCollection();

// Add a new name/value.
private void addButton_Click(object sender, EventArgs e)
{
    Values.Add(nameTextBox.Text, valueTextBox.Text);
    valueTextBox.Clear();
    valueTextBox.Focus();
    ListValues();
}

// Display the name/values groups.
private void ListValues()
{
    valueListBox.Items.Clear();
    foreach (string key in Values.AllKeys)
    {
        valueListBox.Items.Add(key + ": " + Values[key]);
    }
}
```

The code starts by declaring a NameValueCollection. If you enter name and value in the program's TextBoxes and click Add, the program's Click event handler adds the name/value pair to the collection. It then calls the ListValues method to display the current list of names and values.

The ListValues method loops through the keys in the collection and displays them together with their values. The values are shown separated by commas. For example, if you add the values Eggs, Toast, and Juice to the name Breakfast, then the ListBox displays the text "Breakfast: Eggs,Toast,Juice."

The following table describes some of the NameValueCollection class's most useful properties and methods.

PROPERTY/METHOD	DESCRIPTION
Add	Adds a new name/value pair to the collection. If the collection already holds an entry for the name, it adds the new value to that name's values.
AllKeys	Returns a string array holding all the key values.
Clear	Removes all names and values from the collection.
CopyTo	Copies items starting at a particular index into a one-dimensional Array object. This copies only the items, not the keys.
Count	Returns the number of keys in the collection.
Get	Gets the items for a particular index or name as a comma-separated list of values.
GetKey	Returns the key for a specific index.
GetValues	Returns a string array containing the values for a specific name or index.
HasKeys	Returns true if the collection contains any non-null keys.
Keys	Returns a collection containing the keys.
Remove	Removes a particular name and all its values.
Set	Sets the item for a particular name.

Note that there is no easy way to remove a particular value from a name. For example, if a person's name is associated with a postal address, phone number, and e-mail address, it is not easy to remove only the phone number. Instead you must remove the name and add it again omitting the value you want to remove.

DICTIONARIES

A *dictionary* is a collection that associates keys with values. You look up a key, and the dictionary provides you with the corresponding value. This is similar to the way a NameValueCollection works, except a dictionary's keys and values need not be strings, and a dictionary associates each key with a single value.

The `System.Collections.Specialized` namespace contains several different kinds of dictionary classes that are optimized for different uses. Their differences come largely from the ways in which they store data internally. Although you don't need to understand the details of how the dictionaries work internally, you do need to know how they behave so that you can pick the best one for a particular purpose.

Because all the dictionary classes provide the same service (associating keys with values), they have roughly the same properties and methods. The following table describes the most useful.

PROPERTY/METHOD	DESCRIPTION
Add	Adds a key/value pair to the dictionary.
Clear	Removes all key/value pairs from the dictionary.
Contains	Returns true if the dictionary contains a specific key.
CopyTo	Copies the dictionary's data starting at a particular position into a one-dimensional array of DictionaryEntry objects. The DictionaryEntry class has Key and Value properties.
Count	Returns the number of key/value pairs in the dictionary.
Item	Gets or sets the value associated with a key.
Keys	Returns a collection containing all the dictionary's keys.
Remove	Removes the key/value pair with a specific key.
Values	Returns a collection containing all the dictionary's values.

You can index a dictionary much as you can index an array. For example, the following code creates a `ListDictionary`, adds the value `Apple pie` with the key `dessert`, and then displays that value in a message box.

```
ListDictionary dict = new ListDictionary();
dict["dessert"] = "Apple pie";
MessageBox.Show((string)dict["dessert"]);
```

Notice how the code uses `["dessert"]` as the index for the dictionary.

The dictionary treats all its keys and values as plain `objects`, so the code must convert the result into a `string` before displaying it in the message box.

The following sections describe different dictionary classes in more detail.

ListDictionary

A `ListDictionary` is a dictionary that stores its data in a linked list. In a linked list, each item is held in an object that contains its data plus a reference (or *link*) to the next item in the list.

Figure 14-3 illustrates a linked list. This list contains the key/value pairs Appetizer/Salad, Entrée/Sandwich, Drink/Water, and Dessert/Cupcake. The link out of the Dessert/Cupcake item is set to null, so the program can tell when it has reached the end of the list. A reference variable inside the ListDictionary class, labeled Top in Figure 14-3, points to the first item in the list.

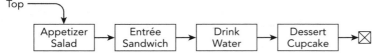

FIGURE 14-3: Each item in a linked list holds a reference to the next item in the list.

The links in a linked list make adding and removing items relatively easy. The ListDictionary simply rearranges the links to add or remove objects. For example, to add a new item at the top of the list, you create the new item, set its link to point to the item that is currently at the top, and then make the list's Top variable point to the new item. Other rearrangements are almost as easy. (For more information on how linked lists work, see a book on algorithms and data structures such as my book *Essential Algorithms: A Practical Approach to Computer Algorithms*, Wiley, 2013.)

Unfortunately, if the list grows long, finding items in it can take a long time. To find an item in the list, the program starts at the top and works its way down, following the links between items, until it finds the one it wants. If the list is short, that doesn't take long. If the list holds 100,000 items, this means potentially a 100,000-item crawl from top to bottom. That means a ListDictionary object's performance degrades if it contains too many items.

If you need to store only a few hundred items in the dictionary and you don't need to access them frequently, a ListDictionary is fine. If you need to store a huge number of entries, or if you need to access the dictionary's entries an enormous number of times, you may get better performance using a fancier class such as a Hashtable. A Hashtable has more overhead than a ListDictionary but is faster at accessing its entries.

Hashtable

A Hashtable looks a lot like a ListDictionary on the outside, but internally it stores its data in a different way. Rather than using a linked list, this class uses a hash table to hold data.

A hash table is a data structure that allows extremely fast access to items using their keys. Exactly how hash tables work is interesting but outside the scope of this book. (For more information, see a book on algorithms and data structures such as my book *Essential Algorithms*.)

You don't need to know how to create your own hash table to use one, but to use hash tables effectively, you do need to know a little bit about how they work. Hash tables provide extremely fast lookup but they require a fair amount of extra space. If a hash table becomes too full, it starts to slow down, taking longer than normal to store and retrieve values. To improve performance, the hash table must resize itself and rearrange the items it contains. Resizing a hash table can take some time, so the Hashtable class provides some extra tools to help you avoid resizing.

One overloaded version of the Hashtable's constructor takes a parameter that tells how many items the table should initially be able to hold. If you know you are going to load 1,000 items into the Hashtable, you might initially give it enough room to hold 1,500 items. Then the program could add all 1,000 items without filling the table too much, so it would still give good performance. If you don't set an initial size, the hash table might start out too small and need to resize itself many times before it could hold 1,000 items, and that will slow it down.

Another version of the constructor lets you specify the hash table's load factor. The *load factor* is a number between 0.1 and 1.0 that gives the largest fraction of the table that can be used before the Hashtable enlarges itself. For example, if the load factor is 0.8, then the Hashtable will resize itself if it is more than 80 percent full.

The following code creates a Hashtable, adds the value Apple pie with the key dessert, and then displays that value in a message box.

```
Hashtable dict = new Hashtable();
dict["dessert"] = "Apple pie";
MessageBox.Show((string)dict["dessert"]);
```

This code is the same as the code shown earlier that demonstrates a ListDictionary except it uses a Hashtable.

For high-performance lookups, the Hashtable class is a great solution as long as it doesn't resize too often and doesn't become too full.

HybridDictionary

A HybridDictionary is a cross between a ListDictionary and a Hashtable. If the dictionary is small, the HybridDictionary stores its data in a ListDictionary. If the dictionary grows too large, the HybridDictionary switches to a Hashtable.

If you know that you will need only a few items, use a ListDictionary. If you know you will need to use lots of items, use a Hashtable. If you are unsure whether you will have few or many items, you can hedge your bet with a HybridDictionary. It'll take a bit of extra time to switch from a list to a Hashtable if you add a lot of items, but you'll save time in the long run if the list does turn out to be enormous.

StringDictionary

The StringDictionary class uses a hash table to manage keys and values that are strings. Its methods are strongly typed to require strings, so they provide extra type checking that can make finding potential bugs a lot easier. For that reason, you should use a StringDictionary instead of a generic ListDictionary or Hashtable if you are working with strings.

SortedList

The SortedList class acts as a combination of a Hashtable and an Array. When you access a value by a key, it acts as a hash table. When you access a value by an index, it acts as an array containing items sorted by key value.

STRONG TYPING

A strongly typed method is one that uses specific data types such as `string`, `DateTime`, or `Student`. In contrast, a weakly typed method uses ambiguous data types such as interfaces, parent classes, or the `object` type.

Strongly typed methods are generally safer because Visual Studio and the .NET Framework can ensure that your program calls them only with the correct data types. For example, the `Hashtable` class is weakly typed, so it will allow you to add anything to its table. Even if you intend a `Hashtable` named `Employees` to hold `Employee` objects, the program could add `Employees`, `Customers`, `strings`, and even other `Hashtables` to it. You can even add a `Hashtable` to itself as its own key. (Although I'm hard pressed to think why.)

Strongly typed methods are also usually more efficient than weakly typed ones because you don't need to convert items to and from the weak type. For instance, the example earlier in the section "Dictionaries" used the following code to display the dessert value stored in the `ListDictionary` dict.

```
MessageBox.Show((string)dict["dessert"]);
```

Because the `ListDictionary` stores `objects`, the code must convert the result from an `object` into a `string`, and that conversion slows the program.

The moral of the story is that you should use strongly typed collections when you can. The section "Generic Collections" later in this chapter describes several collections that provide strong typing.

For example, suppose you add a number of `Job` objects to a `SortedList` named `jobs` using their priorities as keys. Then `jobs.GetByIndex(0)` always returns the job with the smallest priority value.

The following code shows how the SortedJobs example program, which is available for download on the book's website, demonstrates a `SortedList`.

```
// The list of jobs.
private SortedList Jobs = new SortedList();

// Add a job.
private void addButton_Click(object sender, EventArgs e)
{
    Jobs.Add(priorityNumericUpDown.Value, jobTextBox.Text);
    ListJobs();
}

// List the jobs in priority order.
private void ListJobs()
{
    jobsListBox.Items.Clear();
    for (int i = 0; i < Jobs.Count; i++)
    {
```

```
            jobsListBox.Items.Add(Jobs.GetKey(i) + ": " + Jobs.GetByIndex(i));
        }
    }
```

Enter a job name, select a priority, and click Add. The program adds the new job to the `SortedList` and calls the `ListJobs` method to list the jobs in their sorted order.

The `ListJobs` method loops through the indices of the items in the list and displays their keys and values.

A `SortedList` is more complicated (and hence slower) than a `Hashtable` or an array, so you should use it only if you need its special properties.

COLLECTIONSUTIL

Normally, `Hashtables` and `SortedLists` are case-sensitive. The `CollectionsUtil` class provides two shared methods, `CreateCaseInsensitiveHashtable` and `CreateCaseInsensitiveSortedList`, which create `Hashtables` and `SortedLists` that are case-insensitive.

If you can use case-insensitive `Hashtables` and `SortedLists`, you may be better off using them because they will prevent the program from accidentally adding the same item twice with different capitalization.

STACKS AND QUEUES

Stacks and queues are specialized data structures that are useful in many programming applications that need to add and remove items in a particular order. The .NET Framework `Stack` and `Queue` classes implement stacks and queues.

The difference between a stack and a queue is the order in which they return the items stored in them. The following two sections describe stacks and queues and explain the ways in which they return items.

Stack

A *stack* returns items in last-in-first-out (LIFO, pronounced *life-o*) order. Because of its LIFO behavior, a stack is sometimes called a *LIFO list* or simply a *LIFO*.

Adding an item to the stack is called *pushing the item onto the stack* and removing an item is called *popping the item off the stack*. These operations have the names push and pop because a stack is like a spring-loaded stack of plates in a cafeteria or buffet. You push new plates down onto the top of the stack and the plates sink into the counter. You pop the top plate off and the stack rises to give you the next plate. Figure 14-4 illustrates this kind of stack.

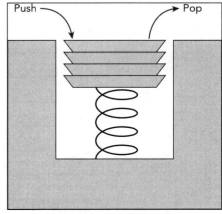

FIGURE 14-4: A `Stack` lets you remove items in last-in-first-out (LIFO) order.

You can also think of a stack as a stack of papers on a desk. You can add things on the top and take them off of the top, but you can't pull papers out of the middle or the bottom of the stack without the whole thing toppling over.

Normally, you use the Stack class's Push and Pop methods to add and remove items from a stack, but the class also provides a few methods that let you cheat by peeking at the top item without removing it or by converting the Stack into an array.

The following table describes the Stack class's most useful properties and methods.

PROPERTY/METHOD	PURPOSE
Clear	Removes all the items.
Contains	Returns true if the Stack contains a particular object.
CopyTo	Copies some or all of the Stack's objects into a one-dimensional array.
Count	Returns the number of items in the Stack.
Peek	Returns a reference to the Stack class's top item without removing it from the Stack.
Pop	Returns the Stack class's top item and removes it from the Stack.
Push	Adds an item to the top of the Stack.
ToArray	Returns a one-dimensional array containing references to the objects in the Stack. The Stack class's top item is placed first in the array.

A Stack allocates memory to store its items. If you Push an object onto a Stack that is completely full, the Stack must resize itself to make more room and that slows things down.

Like the Hashtable class, the Stack class provides overloaded constructors that let you determine how much memory should initially be allocated. The first constructor takes no parameters and allocates a default amount of memory.

The second constructor takes as a parameter the number of items the Stack should initially hold. If you know that you will add 10,000 items to the Stack, you can avoid a lot of resizing by initially allocating room for 10,000 items.

The third version of the constructor takes as a parameter an object that implements the ICollection interface. The constructor allocates enough room to hold the items in the ICollection and copies them into the Stack.

The following short example demonstrates a Stack.

```
Stack stack = new Stack();
stack.Push("Apple");
stack.Push("Banana");
stack.Push("Cherry");
Console.WriteLine(stack.Pop());
```

```
Console.WriteLine(stack.Pop());
Console.WriteLine(stack.Pop());
```

This code creates a `Stack` and pushes three strings onto it. It then pops the three values back off the `Stack`, displaying the results in the Console window. The following text shows the results.

```
Cherry
Banana
Apple
```

Notice that the items are popped off the `Stack` in last-in-first-out order.

The UseStack example program enables you push and pop items interactively. Download the example to see how it works.

Queue

A *queue* returns items in the opposite of the order used by a stack. A queue returns its items in first-in-first-out (FIFO, pronounced *fife-o*) order. Because of its FIFO behavior, a queue is sometimes called a *FIFO list* or simply a *FIFO*.

A queue is similar to a line at a customer service desk. The first person in line is the first person to leave it when the service desk is free. Figure 14-5 shows the idea graphically.

FIGURE 14-5: Customers leave a queue in first-in-first-out (FIFO) order.

Queues are particularly useful for processing items in the order in which they were created. For example, an order-processing application might keep orders in a queue so that orders placed first are fulfilled first.

Historically, the routines that add and remove items from a queue are called *enqueue* and *dequeue*. The following table describes the most useful properties and methods provided by the `Queue` class.

PROPERTY/METHOD	PURPOSE
Clear	Removes all the items.
Contains	Returns `true` if the `Queue` contains a particular object.
CopyTo	Copies some or all of the `Queue`'s objects into a one-dimensional array.

continues

(continued)

PROPERTY/METHOD	PURPOSE
Count	Returns the number of items in the Queue.
Dequeue	Returns and removes the item at the front of the Queue.
Enqueue	Adds an item to the back of the Queue.
Peek	Returns a reference to the item at the front of the Queue without removing it.
ToArray	Returns a one-dimensional array containing references to the objects in the Queue. The item at the front of the Queue is placed first in the array.
TrimToSize	Frees any empty space in the Queue.

Like Stacks, Queues must resize themselves if they become full and that slows things down. Also like Stacks, Queues provide overloaded constructors that let you determine how big the Queue is initially.

The first constructor takes no parameters and allocates a default initial capacity. If the Queue is full, it enlarges itself by a default growth factor.

The second constructor takes as a parameter the Queue's initial capacity. If you know that you will add 1,000 items to the Queue, you can save some time by initially allocating room for 1,000 items. With this constructor, the Queue also uses a default growth factor.

The third constructor takes as a parameter an object that implements the ICollection interface. The constructor allocates enough room to hold the items in the ICollection and copies them into the Queue. This version also uses a default growth factor.

The final version of the constructor takes as parameters an initial capacity and a growth factor between 1.0 and 10.0. A larger growth factor means the Queue resizes itself less often, but also means it may contain a lot of unused space.

The following short example demonstrates a Queue.

```
Queue queue = new Queue();
queue.Enqueue("Apple");
queue.Enqueue("Banana");
queue.Enqueue("Cherry");
Console.WriteLine(queue.Dequeue());
Console.WriteLine(queue.Dequeue());
Console.WriteLine(queue.Dequeue());
```

This code creates a Queue and adds three strings to it. It then dequeues the three values, displaying the results in the Console window. The following text shows the results.

```
Apple
Banana
Cherry
```

Notice that the items are removed from the Queue in first-in-first-out order.

The UseQueue example program enables you enqueue and dequeue items interactively. Download the example to see how it works.

GENERIC COLLECTIONS

A generic class or method is one that takes a data type as a parameter. The class or method can then use that type as if it were any other type.

For example, the Dictionary class is a generic collection class. It takes two type parameters giving the types of the dictionary's keys and values.

In C# you specify a class's generic parameters after the class name and enclosed in pointy brackets. The following code declares and instantiates a Dictionary that uses keys that are strings and values that are ints. It then sets the value for the key "Mark" equal to 23. It finishes by getting the value for the key "Mark" from the Dictionary and storing it in an int variable.

```
Dictionary<string, int> ages = new Dictionary<string, int>();
ages["Mark"] = 23;
int age = ages["Mark"];
```

The System.Collections.Generic namespace includes several generic collection classes that you can use to build strongly typed collections. These collections work with one or more specific data types that you supply in a variable's declaration (as shown in the preceding code).

You cannot directly modify a generic collection class, but you can add extension methods to it. For example, suppose you have defined a Person class. Then the following code creates an AddPerson extension method for the generic List<Person> class. This method takes as parameters a first and last name, uses those values to make a Person object, adds it to the list, and returns the new Person.

```
static class GenericExtensions
{
    public static Person AddPerson(this List<Person> list,
        string firstName, string lastName)
    {
        Person person = new Person()
            { FirstName = firstName, LastName = lastName };
        list.Add(person);
        return person;
    }
}
```

The following code shows how a program could use this extension method.

```
List<Person> people = new List<Person>();
people.AddPerson("Rod", "Stephens");
```

(For more information on extension methods, see the section "Extension Methods" in Chapter 6, "Methods.")

You can also derive a class from a generic class. For example, the following code defines an EmployeeList class that inherits from the generic List<Employee> class. The code adds an overloaded version of the Add method that takes first and last names as parameters.

```
public class EmployeeList : List<Employee>
{
    public Employee Add(string firstName, string lastName)
    {
        Employee employee = new Employee()
            { FirstName = firstName, LastName = lastName};
        base.Add(employee);
        return employee;
    }
}
```

NO OVERLOADS ALLOWED

Extension methods cannot overload a class's methods. If you want multiple versions of the Add method, as in this example, you need to use a derived class.

The following table lists some of the most useful collection classes defined by the System.Collections.Generic namespace.

COLLECTION	PURPOSE
Comparer	Compares two objects of a specific type and returns –1, 0, or 1 to indicate whether the first is less than, equal to, or greater than the second
Dictionary	A strongly typed dictionary
LinkedList	A strongly typed linked list
LinkedListNode	A strongly typed node in a linked list
List	A strongly typed list
Queue	A strongly typed queue
SortedDictionary	A strongly typed sorted dictionary
SortedList	A strongly typed sorted list
Stack	A strongly typed stack

STAY TUNED FOR MORE GENERICS

Chapter 15, "Generics," explains how you can build and use generic classes of your own to perform similar actions for objects of various types. For example, you could build a Tree class that makes a tree holding any kind of object. Then, for example, you could build a tree containing Employee objects to represent an organizational hierarchy.

COLLECTION INITIALIZERS

Initializers allow you to easily add items to collection classes that have an Add method. To initialize a collection, follow the variable's instantiation with the items you want to add to it surrounded by braces.

For example, suppose you have defined an Author class that has a constructor that takes first and last names as parameters. Then the following code creates and initializes a List<Author>.

```
List<Author> authors = new List<Author>()
{
    new Author("Terry", "Pratchett"),
    new Author("Jasper", "Fforde"),
    new Author("Tom", "Holt"),
};
```

If a collection's Add method takes more than one parameter, simply include the appropriate values for each item inside its own sets of braces. For example, each of the Dictionary class's entries includes a key and a value. The following code initializes a Dictionary that matches names with phone numbers.

```
Dictionary<string, string> phoneNumbers = new Dictionary<string, string>()
{
    {"Arthur", "808-567-1543"},
    {"Betty", "808-291-9838"},
    {"Charles", "808-521-0129"},
    {"Debbie", "808-317-3918"},
};
```

The same technique works for other collections that need two values such as ListDictionary, Hashtable, HybridDictionary, StringDictionary, and SortedList.

Unfortunately, you cannot use this method to initialize the Stack and Queue classes because this kind of initialization requires the class to have an Add method. For historical reasons, the methods in those classes that add new items are called Push and Enqueue instead of Add.

Fortunately, those classes have constructors that can take IEnumerable objects as parameters. That means, for example, that you can pass the constructors an array holding the objects that should be added to the collection. The following code uses that technique to initialize a `Stack` and `Queue` of `Author` objects.

```
Stack<Author> authorStack = new Stack<Author>(
    new Author[]
    {
        new Author("Terry", "Pratchett"),
        new Author("Jasper", "Fforde"),
        new Author("Tom", "Holt"),
    }
);

Queue<Author> authorQueue = new Queue<Author>(
    new Author[]
    {
        new Author("Terry", "Pratchett"),
        new Author("Jasper", "Fforde"),
        new Author("Tom", "Holt"),
    }
);
```

ITERATORS

One advantage of collection classes is that you can use a `foreach` loop to enumerate over their items.

C# also allows you to write iterators. An *iterator* is a method that yields a sequence of results. The program can use a `foreach` loop to enumerate the values the iterator yields. In that sense iterators resemble collections; although they don't need to store items in some sort of data structure.

The easiest way to make an iterator is to create a method that returns `IEnumerable` or a generic type such as `IEnumerable<String>`. The method should generate its values and use a `yield return` statement to return them to the code that is looping over the enumeration.

For example, the following iterator yields a list of prime numbers between `startNumber` and `stopNumber`.

```
// Enumerate prime numbers between startNumber and stopNumber.
public IEnumerable Primes(int startNumber, int stopNumber)
{
    // Define a lambda expression that tests primality.
    Func<int, bool> isPrime = x =>
    {
        if (x == 1) return false;      // 1 is not prime.
        if (x == 2) return true;       // 2 is prime.
        if (x % 2 == 0) return false;  // Even numbers are not prime.
        for (int i = 3; i * i <= x; i += 2)
            if (x % i == 0) return false;
        return true;
    };

    for (int i = startNumber; i <= stopNumber; i++)
    {
```

```
            // If this number is prime, enumerate it.
            if (isPrime(i)) yield return i;
        }
    }
```

This code makes a delegate variable named `isPrime` to hold a lambda expression that returns `true` if a number is prime. The iterator then loops through the numbers between `startNumber` and `stopNumber`, calls the `isPrime` for each, and uses `yield return` to return the values that are prime.

The following code shows how a program could use the iterator to display prime numbers.

```
foreach (int i in Primes(1, 100)) primesListBox.Items.Add(i);
```

This code iterates over the sequence generated by calling `Primes(1, 100)`. That call invokes the iterator and makes it produce the sequence of prime numbers between 1 and 100. The program adds each value in the sequence to the `primesListBox` control's items.

HOW DOES YIELD WORK?

When the iterator reaches the `yield return` statement, the program saves its state and returns the new value to the `foreach` loop. The loop processes the value, and then the program resumes running the iterator right after the `yield return` statement.

An iterator can use the `yield break` statement to end an enumeration.

For more information on iterators, see "Iterators (C# and Visual Basic)" at msdn.microsoft.com/library/dscyy5s0.aspx.

SUMMARY

This chapter explained several types of collection classes. Even the simplest of these, an array of variables, can be extremely useful. An array itself doesn't provide many features, but the `Array` class has a lot of useful methods, such as `Reverse` and `Sort`, that can manipulate arrays.

The `Array` class also lets you build multidimensional arrays with nonzero lower bounds. The performance isn't as good as that of arrays of values, but in some applications the convenience may be worth reduced performance.

Other collection classes store data in different ways. A `StringCollection` is a simple collection of strings. A `NameValueCollection` associates string keys with multiple string values. A `Dictionary` associates keys (of any type) with a single value each (also of any type).

A `Stack` provides access to items in last-in-first-out (LIFO) order. A `Queue` gives access to items in first-in-first-out (FIFO) order.

Although these classes have different features for adding, removing, finding, and ordering objects, they share some common traits. For example, those that provide an `Add` method support collection initialization and all of them support enumeration by `foreach` statements. They also support the methods used by LINQ to make queries possible.

This chapter explained how you can use the generic collection classes provided by the `System.Collections.Generic` namespace. The next chapter explains how you can build generic classes of your own. Generics let you build strongly typed classes that manipulate objects of any data type.

EXERCISES

1. A *palindrome* is a string that is the same forward as backward, ignoring capitalization and punctuation: "Taco cat" and "nurses run." Write a program that indicates whether a string entered by the user is a palindrome. (Hint: Don't use loops. Instead use the following facts.)

   ➤ You can treat a string as an `IEnumerable<char>`.

   ➤ `IEnumerable` provides a `Reverse` method.

   ➤ `IEnumerable` provides a `ToArray` method.

   ➤ The `string` class's constructor has a version that takes a `char[]` as a parameter.

   ➤ Convert to lowercase and remove spaces, but assume the user won't type any other punctuation characters.

2. Write a program that uses a dictionary of lists to store book titles grouped by author. (The dictionary's keys should be author names. Its values should be lists of book titles.) Use initialization code to create data for at least three authors with two books each. When the user enters or selects an author, display that author's books. (Hint: Use LINQ to get the values you need. In a Windows Forms application, you can set a `ListBox`'s `DataSource` property to an array.)

3. Modify the program you wrote for Exercise 2 so that it uses a `NameValueCollection` instead of a dictionary of lists. (Hint: You may find the string class's `Split` method useful.)

4. Write a program similar to the one shown in Figure 14-6 that lists information about cars.

   a. First, create a `Car` class with the properties `Name`, `Price`, `Horsepower`, and `SixtyTime` (the time in seconds to go from 0 to 60 mph). Create and initialize an array of `Car` objects. (Look up data on the Internet or just make some up if you prefer.) Override the class's `ToString` method so that it returns an object's concatenated values.

   b. Display the car data in a `ListBox`.

   c. Place four `RadioButtons` on the form labeled Name, Price, Horsepower, and 0–60 Time. When the user clicks one of the buttons, the program should sort the car data based on the selected criterion and redisplay the list.

   d. To sort the data, create a `CarComparer` class that implements `IComparer<Car>`. Give the class a `ComparisonTypes` enumeration that defines the possible comparison types. Give the class a `ComparisonType` property of the type `ComparisonTypes` to tell which type a comparer object should use. Make the `Compare` method required by the `IComparer` interface use the `ComparisonType` property to decide how to compare two `Car` objects.

e. Finally, to put it all together, when the user clicks one of the RadioButtons, make the program create a CarComparer, set its ComparisonType property, and use the comparer to sort the car data. Then make the ListBox display the sorted data.

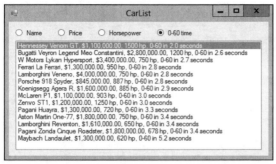

FIGURE 14-6: The CarList example program sorts car data by name, price, horsepower, or 0–60 time.

SORTING IN A LISTVIEW

The ListView control provides a nicer display than the ListBox because it can display data in rows and columns. It can also sort the data for you if you set its ListViewItemSorter property to an IComparer object.

This doesn't have much to do with generic collections, so I'm not including it as an exercise, but if you're up for a challenge, try repeating Exercise 4 with a ListView instead of a ListBox. Instead of using RadioButtons, let the user click the ListView's column headers to indicate which column should be used for sorting. For bonus points, if the user clicks a column twice, switch the sort from ascending to descending or vice versa. The CarListView example program, which is available for download on this book's website, shows one solution.

5. Write a program that initializes a List<char> to hold the characters A, B, C, D, and E. Reverse the items to create a new List<char> by using these methods:

   a. Use LINQ. (Hint: Convert the result into an array and pass it to the string constructor to make a string holding the list's characters.)

   b. Copy the list and use the copy's Reverse method. (Hint: Pass the original list into a constructor to make the list copy.)

   c. Use a stack.

6. How is an iterator different from a method that returns a collection such as an array or List? In other words, couldn't you make a method that returns the items in a List and use a foreach loop to enumerate them instead of using an iterator?

7. Make the `Primes` iterator shown in the section "Iterators" more efficient by making it handle the value 2 and other even numbers outside of its loop. Make a program similar to the one shown in Figure 14-7 to test the iterator.

FIGURE 14-7: The ListPrimes example program uses an iterator to enumerate prime numbers.

8. Make an `AllPrimes` iterator that yields prime numbers starting at 2 and continuing indefinitely. Modify the program you wrote for Exercise 1 so that it uses this new iterator. It also won't need the start number because the iterator starts at 2. (Hint: Make the `foreach` loop end when it has enumerated the required values. Don't make it run forever!)

15

Generics

WHAT'S IN THIS CHAPTER

➤ Defining generic classes and methods

➤ Constraining generic types

➤ Instantiating generic classes

➤ Using generic collection classes

➤ Defining generic extension methods

WROX.COM DOWNLOADS FOR THIS CHAPTER

Please note that all the code examples for this chapter are available as a part of this chapter's code download on the book's website at www.wrox.com/go/csharp5programmersref on the Download Code tab.

Chapter 11, "OOP Concepts," describes a class as like a blueprint or cookie cutter for creating objects. After you define a class, you can use it to create any number of objects with similar general characteristics but different details.

Similarly, a *generic* is like a cookie cutter for creating classes. After you define a generic, you can use it to create any number of classes that have similar features.

For example, the `System.Collections.Generic` namespace described in the preceding chapter defines a generic `List` class. That class lets you create lists of strings, lists of integers, lists of `Employee` objects, or lists of just about anything else.

This chapter explains how you can define and use your own generic classes.

ADVANTAGES OF GENERICS

A generic class takes one or more data types as parameters. When you create an instance of a generic class, those parameters are filled in with specific data types such as `string`, `int`, or `Employee`. Tying the class to specific data types gives it several advantages over nongeneric classes:

➤ **Strong typing**—Methods can take parameters and return values that have the class's instance type instead of a nonspecific `object` type. For example, a `List<string>` can hold only `string` values; its `Add` method can add only `strings` to the list; and its `Item` method returns `string` values. This makes it more difficult to accidentally add `ints`, `Employees`, or other incorrect types of objects to the list.

➤ **IntelliSense**—By providing strong typing, a class built from a generic lets Visual Studio provide IntelliSense. If you make a `List<Employee>`, Visual Studio knows that the items in the collection are `Employee` objects, so it can give you appropriate IntelliSense.

➤ **No boxing**—Because the class manipulates objects with a specific data type, your program doesn't need to convert items to and from the nonspecific `object` data type. For example, if a program stores `TextBox` controls in a nongeneric collection, the program must convert the `TextBox` controls to and from the `object` class when it adds and uses items in the collection. Avoiding these steps makes the code more efficient.

➤ **Code reuse**—You can use a generic class with more than one data type. For example, if you have built a generic `PriorityQueue` class, you can make `PriorityQueues` holding `Student`, `Applicant`, `MotorVehicle`, or `Donor` objects. Without generics, you would need to build four separate classes to build strongly typed priority queues for each of these types of objects. Reusing this code makes it easier to write, test, debug, and maintain the code.

The main disadvantage to generics is that they are slightly more complicated and confusing than nongeneric classes. If you know that you will only ever need to provide a class that works with a single type, you can simplify things slightly by not using a generic class. If you think you might want to reuse the code later for another data type, it's easier to just build the class generically from the start.

DEFINING GENERICS

C# allows you to define generic classes, structures, interfaces, methods, and delegates. The basic syntax for all those is similar, so when you know how to make generic classes, making generic structures, interfaces, and the others is fairly easy.

To define a generic class, make a class declaration as usual. After the class name, add one or more type names for data types surrounded by brackets. The type names are similar to the parameters names you would define for a method except they are types, not simple values. The class's code can use the names to refer to the types associated with the instance of the generic class. This may sound confusing, but an example should make it fairly easy to understand.

Suppose you want to build a binary tree that can hold any kind of data in its nodes. The following code shows how you could define a `BinaryNode` class to hold the tree's data. The type name `T` is highlighted in bold where it appears.

```
public class BinaryNode<T>
{
    public T Value;
    public BinaryNode<T> LeftChild, RightChild;
}
```

The class's declaration takes a type parameter named `T`. (Many developers use the name `T` for the type parameter. If the class takes more than one type parameter separated by commas, they start each name with `T` as in `TKey` and `TData`.)

The class defines a public field named `Value` that has type `T`. This is the data that is stored in the node.

The class also defines two fields that refer to the node's left and right children in the binary tree. Those fields are references to objects from this same class: `BinaryNode<T>`.

The following code shows how a program could use this class to build a small binary tree of `Employee` objects.

```
// Define the tree's root node.
BinaryNode<Employee> root = new BinaryNode<Employee>();
root.Value = new Employee("Ben", "Baker");

// Create the root's left child.
root.LeftChild = new BinaryNode<Employee>();
root.LeftChild.Value = new Employee("Ann", "Archer");

// Create the root's right child.
root.RightChild = new BinaryNode<Employee>();
root.RightChild.Value = new Employee("Cindy", "Carter");
```

This code first creates a new `BinaryNode<Employee>` to represent the tree's root. It sets that node's `Value` property to a new `Employee` object representing Ben Baker.

Next, the code sets the root's `LeftChild` equal to a new `BinaryNode<Employee>`. It sets that node's `Value` to a new `Employee` object representing Ann Archer.

Finally, the code uses similar steps to give the root a right child holding an `Employee` object representing Cindy Carter.

Generic Constructors

Like any other class, generic classes can have constructors. For example, the following constructor initializes a `BinaryNode` object's `LeftChild` and `RightChild` references.

```
// Set this node's value and children.
public BinaryNode(T value,
    BinaryNode<T> leftChild = null,
    BinaryNode<T> rightChild = null)
```

```
    {
        Value = value;
        LeftChild = leftChild;
        RightChild = rightChild;
    }
```

Notice how this code can use the type T without defining it. That type variable was defined in the class declaration, so it can be used throughout the class's code.

To use the constructor, the main program adds normal parameters after the type parameters in the object declaration. The following code uses the new constructor to create a binary tree similar to the previous one.

```
    // Define the child nodes.
    BinaryNode<Employee> leftChild =
        new BinaryNode<Employee>(new Employee("Ann", "Archer"));
    BinaryNode<Employee> rightChild =
        new BinaryNode<Employee>(new Employee("Cindy", "Carter"));

    // Define the tree's root node.
    BinaryNode<Employee> root = new BinaryNode<Employee>
    (
        new Employee("Ben", "Baker"),
        leftChild,
        rightChild
    );
```

This code uses the constructor to create the left and right child nodes. It doesn't pass children into those constructor calls, so the child nodes' left and right children are set to null.

The code then creates the root node, this time passing the constructor the root's left and right children.

> **NOTE** *The BinaryTree example program, which is available for download on this book's website, demonstrates this code.*

Multiple Types

If you want the class to work with more than one type, you can add other types to the declaration separated by commas. For example, suppose that you want to create a dictionary that associates keys with pairs of data items. Example program GenericPairDictionary uses the following code to define the generic PairDictionary class. This class acts as a dictionary that associates a key value with a pair of data values. The class declaration includes three data types named TKey, TValue1, and TValue2.

```
    // A Dictionary that associates a pair of data values with each key.
    public class PairDictionary<TKey, TValue1, TValue2>
    {
        // A structure to hold paired data.
        public struct ValuePair
        {
            public TValue1 Value1;
            public TValue2 Value2;
```

```csharp
        public ValuePair(TValue1 value1, TValue2 value2)
        {
            Value1 = value1;
            Value2 = value2;
        }
    }

    // A Dictionary to hold the paired data.
    private Dictionary<TKey, ValuePair> ValueDictionary =
        new Dictionary<TKey, ValuePair>();

    // Return the number of data pairs.
    public int Count
    {
        get { return ValueDictionary.Count; }
    }

    // Add a key and value pair.
    public void Add(TKey key, TValue1 value1, TValue2 value2)
    {
        ValueDictionary.Add(key, new ValuePair(value1, value2));
    }

    // Remove all data.
    public void Clear()
    {
        ValueDictionary.Clear();
    }

    // Return True if PairDictionary contains this key.
    public bool ContainsKey(TKey key)
    {
        return ValueDictionary.ContainsKey(key);
    }

    // Return a data pair.
    public void GetValues(TKey key, out TValue1 value1, out TValue2 value2)
    {
        ValuePair pair = ValueDictionary[key];
        value1 = pair.Value1;
        value2 = pair.Value2;
    }

    // Set a data pair.
    public void SetValues(TKey key, TValue1 value1, TValue2 value2)
    {
        ValueDictionary[key] = new ValuePair(value1, value2);
    }

    // Return a collection containing the keys.
    public Dictionary<TKey, ValuePair>.KeyCollection Keys
    {
        get { return ValueDictionary.Keys; }
    }
```

```
        // Remove a particular entry.
        public void Remove(TKey key)
        {
            ValueDictionary.Remove(key);
        }
    }
```

The `PairDictionary` class defines a `ValuePair` class to hold pairs of data values. The `ValuePair` class has two public fields of types `TValue1` and `TValue2`. Its only method is a constructor that makes initializing the values easier.

Notice that the `ValuePair` class is not generic. It uses the `TValue1` and `TValue2` types defined by the `PairDictionary` class's declaration, but it doesn't define any generic types of its own.

Next, the `PairDictionary` class declares a generic `Dictionary<TKey, ValuePair>` object named `ValueDictionary`. The class delegates its `Count`, `Add`, `Clear`, `ContainsKey`, `GetValues`, `SetValues`, `Keys`, and `Remove` methods to `ValueDictionary`.

The following code creates an instance of the generic `PairDictionary` class that uses integers as keys and strings for both data values. It adds three entries to the `PairDictionary` and then retrieves and displays the entry with key value 82.

```
// Create the PairDictionary and add some data.
PairDictionary<int, string, string> dictionary =
    new PairDictionary<int, string, string>();
dictionary.Add(21, "Arthur", "Ash");
dictionary.Add(82, "Betty", "Barter");
dictionary.Add(13, "Charlie", "Carruthers");

// Display the values for key value 82.
string value1, value2;
dictionary.GetValues(82, out value1, out value2);
Console.WriteLine(value1 + " " + value2);
```

> **NOTE** *The GenericPairDictionary example program, which is available for download on this book's website, demonstrates this code.*

Constrained Types

To get the most out of your generic classes, you should make them as general as possible. Depending on what the class is for, however, you may need to constrain the class's generic types.

For example, suppose you want to make a generic `SortedBinaryNode` class similar to the `BinaryNode` class described earlier but that keeps its values sorted. The node's `Add` method should insert a new value in the proper position in the tree.

When you call a node's `Add` method, the method compares the node's value to the new value. It then passes the new value to its left or right child depending on whether the new value is greater than or less than the node's value.

For example, suppose node A contains the value 20 and you pass its `Add` method the new value 15. The value 15 is less than 20, so node A sends the new value into its left subtree.

If node A has a left child, it calls that child's `Add` method to add the child somewhere in that subtree.

If node A has no left child, it creates a new node to hold the value 15 and takes that node as its new left child.

Determining whether a new value belongs in a node's left or right subtree is straightforward if the node holds `ints` or `strings`, but there's no obvious way to determine whether one `Employee` object should be placed before another. The `SortedBinaryNode` class works only if the data type of its objects allows comparison.

One way to ensure you can compare objects is to require that the type of the items implements the `IComparable` interface. Then the program can use the `CompareTo` method to see whether one item is greater than or less than another item.

To require that a generic type implements an interface, add a `where` clause after the class's declaration, as shown in the following code.

```
public class SortedBinaryNode<T> where T : IComparable<T>
{
    ...
}
```

This code requires that type `T` implements `IComparable<T>`.

The SortedBinaryTree example program, which is available for download on this book's website, uses the following complete `SortedBinaryNode` class.

```
public class SortedBinaryNode<T> where T : IComparable<T>
{
    public T Value;
    public SortedBinaryNode<T> LeftChild, RightChild;

    // Set this node's value and children.
    public SortedBinaryNode(T value,
        SortedBinaryNode<T> leftChild = null,
        SortedBinaryNode<T> rightChild = null)
    {
        Value = value;
        LeftChild = leftChild;
        RightChild = rightChild;
    }

    // Add a new value to this node's subtree.
    public void Add(T newValue)
    {
        // See if it belongs in the left or right child's subtree.
        if (newValue.CompareTo(Value) < 0)
        {
            // Left subtree.
            if (LeftChild == null)
                // Add it in a new left child.
```

```
                    LeftChild = new SortedBinaryNode<T>(newValue);
                else
                    // Add it in the existing left subtree.
                    LeftChild.Add(newValue);
        }
        else
        {
            // Right subtree.
            if (RightChild == null)
                // Add it in a new right child.
                RightChild = new SortedBinaryNode<T>(newValue);
            else
                // Add it in the existing right subtree.
                RightChild.Add(newValue);
        }
    }
}
```

The program uses an Employee class that implements IComparable<Employee>. Its CompareTo method, which is required by the interface, compares two Employee objects' full names and returns a value indicating which one comes first alphabetically.

The SortedBinaryTree example's main program uses the following code to build a small sorted tree of Employee objects.

```
// Create some Employees.
Employee jody = new Employee("Jody", "Adams");
Employee wanda = new Employee("Wanda", "Cortez");
Employee george = new Employee("George", "McGee");
Employee dom = new Employee("Dom", "Hall");
Employee linda = new Employee("Linda", "Brock");

// Create the root node.
SortedBinaryNode<Employee> root = new SortedBinaryNode<Employee>(jody);

// Add some other Employees to the tree.
root.Add(wanda);
root.Add(george);
root.Add(dom);
root.Add(linda);
```

The code first creates some Employee objects. It then makes a root node holding the Employee representing Jody Adams.

The program then calls the root node's Add method, passing it various Employee objects. You can follow each Employee as it is added to the tree. For example, Wanda Cortez comes alphabetically after Jody Adams, so the wanda Employee is added to the root node's right subtree. If you follow each of the Employee objects, you'll get the tree shown in Figure 15-1.

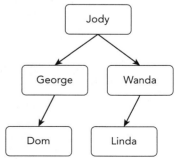

FIGURE 15-1: Example program SortedBinaryTree builds this tree of Employee objects.

A generic type's where clause can include one or more of the following elements.

ELEMENT	MEANING
struct	The type must be a value type.
class	The type must be a reference type.
new()	The type must have a parameterless constructor.
«baseclass»	The type must inherit from baseclass.
«interface»	The type must implement interface.
«typeparameter»	The type must inherit from typeparameter.

For example, the following code defines the StrangeGeneric class. This class takes three type parameters. Type T1 must implement the IComparable<T1> interface and must provide a parameterless constructor. Type T3 must inherit from the Control class. Type T2 must inherit from type T3.

```
public class StrangeGeneric<T1, T2, T3>
    where T1 : IComparable<T1>, new()
    where T3 : Control
    where T2 : T3
{

}
```

The following code creates an instance of the StrangeGeneric class.

```
StrangeGeneric<int, Panel, ScrollableControl> strange =
    new StrangeGeneric<int, Panel, ScrollableControl>();
```

The int class implements IComparable<int> and has a parameterless constructor. The ScrollableControl inherits from Control and Panel inherits from ScrollableControl. The full inheritance hierarchy for the Panel class is

```
System.Object
  System.MarshalByRefObject
    System.ComponentModel.Component
      System.Windows.Forms.Control
        System.Windows.Forms.ScrollableControl
          System.Windows.Forms.Panel
```

Constraining a type gives C# more information about that type, so it lets you use any known properties and methods. In the previous code, for example, the StrangeGeneric class knows that type T3 inherits from the Control class so you can safely use Control properties and methods such as Anchor, BackColor, and Font.

Default Values

The `new()` constraint requires a generic type to provide a parameterless constructor so the class's code can create a new instance of the type. For example, if the type's name is `T`, the class could execute the following statement.

```
T newValue = new T();
```

In addition to making a new instance of the type `T`, it may also be useful to set a variable of type `T` to a default value. Unfortunately, you can't know what a type's default value is until you know the type. For example, the default value for `int` is 0, the default value for a `struct` is an uninitialized structure, and the default value for a `string` or other reference type is `null`.

Fortunately, C# provides the default keyword, to let generic classes assign default values. The following statement creates a new variable of type `T` and sets it equal to whatever is the default value for that type.

```
T newValue = default(T);
```

INSTANTIATING GENERIC CLASSES

The previous sections have already shown a few examples of how to instantiate a generic class. The program declares the class and includes whatever data types are required inside brackets. The following code shows how a program might create a generic list of strings.

```
List<string> names = new List<string>();
```

To pass normal parameters to a generic class's constructor, simply add them inside the parentheses after the brackets.

GENERIC COLLECTION CLASSES

The `System.Collections.Generic` namespace defines several generic classes. These are basically collection classes that use generics to work with specific data types. See the section "Generic Collections" in Chapter 14, "Collection Classes," for more information and a list of the more useful predefined generic collection classes.

GENERIC METHODS

Generics are usually used to build classes that are not data type-specific such as the generic collection classes. You can also give a class (generic or otherwise) a generic method. Just as a generic class is not tied to a particular data type, the parameters of a generic method are not tied to a specific data type.

To make a generic method, include type parameters similar to those you would use for a generic class.

Example program Switcher uses the following code to define a generic `Switch` method.

```
public static class Switcher
{
    // Switch two values.
    public static void Switch<T>(ref T value1, ref T value2)
    {
        T temp = value1;
        value1 = value2;
        value2 = temp;
    }
}
```

The `Switch` method takes a generic type `T`. It also takes two parameters of type `T`. It creates a temporary variable of type `T` and uses it to swap the two values.

The following code shows how the main program uses the `Switch` method.

```
string value1 = value1TextBox.Text;
string value2 = value2TextBox.Text;
Switcher.Switch<string>(ref value1, ref value2);
value1TextBox.Text = value1;
value2TextBox.Text = value2;
```

This code gets two `string` values from `TextBox`es. It uses the `Switch` method to swap their values and displays the results.

TYPE NOT REQUIRED

In this example, Visual Studio is smart enough to infer the type parameter because the program is passing two `string` values into the method. In cases such as this, the code can omit the type parameter as in the following code.

```
Switcher.Switch(ref value1, ref value2);
```

You may want to include the type parameter anyway to make the code more self-documenting.

Note that the `Switcher` class is not generic but it contains a generic method. You can also create generic classes that contain both generic and nongeneric methods.

GENERICS AND EXTENSION METHODS

Extension methods let you add new features to existing classes, whether they're generic or nongeneric. For example, suppose you have an application that uses a `List<Student>`. This class is a generic collection class defined in the `System.Collections.Generic` namespace. It's not defined in your code so you can't modify it. However, you can add extension methods to it.

The following code adds an `AddStudent` method to `List<Student>` that takes as parameters a first and last name, uses those values to make a `Student` object, and adds it to the list.

```
public static class ListExtensions
{
    public static void AddStudent(this List<Student> students,
        string firstName,string lastName)
    {
        students.Add(new Student()
            { FirstName = firstName, LastName = lastName });
    }
}
```

This example works specifically with the `Student` type. It relies on the fact that this is the `List<Student>` class when it uses the `Student` class's constructor.

Sometimes, you can make a generic extension method that works with more general classes. For example, the following code adds a generic `NumDistinct` method to the generic `List<T>` class.

```
public static int NumDistinct<T>(this List<T> list)
{
    return list.Distinct().Count();
}
```

This method doesn't need to know what kind of objects the list contains. It just invokes the list's `Distinct` method, calls the `Count` method on the result, and returns the value given by `Count`.

For more information on extension methods, see the section "Extension Methods" in Chapter 6.

SUMMARY

A class is an abstraction that defines the properties, methods, and events that should be provided by instances of the class. After you define a class, you can make any number of instances of it, and they will all have the features defined by the class.

Generics take abstraction one level farther. A generic class abstracts the features of a set of classes. After you have defined a generic class, you can make any number of objects that have similar behaviors but that may work with different data types. Similarly, you can make generic structures, interfaces, methods, and delegates that can work with multiple data types.

Generics let you reuse the same code while working with different data types. They provide strong type checking, which lets you avoid boxing and unboxing. They also let Visual Studio provide IntelliSense support, which makes writing code easier and faster.

For more information on generics including some of their more esoteric syntax, see "An Introduction to C# Generics" at `msdn.microsoft.com/library/ms379564.aspx`.

The chapters so far have focused on programs that are relatively self-contained. They generate their own data or take input from the user, perform some calculations, and display the results on the program's user interface or in the Console window.

The chapters in the next part of the book describe techniques a program can use to interact with the outside system. They explain how to print documents, save settings that persist when the program isn't running, work with files and directories, and interact with networks. The next chapter starts the new focus by explaining how to generate output on a printer.

EXERCISES

1. Make a generic `PriorityQueue` class that associates keys with objects. Its `Dequeue` method should return the key/object pair with the lowest key value and remove that value from the queue. Make a program that uses a `PriorityQueue<int, string>`. (Hint: Use a `List<KeyValuePair>` to hold the items. Make the `Dequeue` method loop through the list to find the lowest key value.)

2. Make a generic `IncreasingQueue` class that stores objects in a queue and requires each object to be larger than the one before it in the queue. Make the class's constructor take as a parameter a lower bound for all entries. (In other words, all entries must be larger than the lower bound and added in increasing order.) Make a test program that demonstrates an `IncreasingQueue<float>`.

3. Write a generic `BoundValues` method that takes an array as a parameter and ensures that all its values are between a lower and upper bound. For example, if `prices` is an array of `decimal`, then `BoundValues(prices, 0, 1000)` would set any values in the array that are smaller than 0 to 0 and any values in the array that are larger than 1000 to 1000.

4. Repeat Exercise 3 but this time make the `BoundValues` method process an `IEnumerable` instead of an array and return a `List`.

5. Write a generic `MiddleValue` method that takes three values as parameters and returns the one in the middle.

6. Create a `CircularQueue` class. The `Enqueue` method adds an item to the end of the queue. The `NextItem` method returns the next item in the queue. If the object reaches the end of its queue, it starts over at the beginning. For example, if the queue contains the values A, B, and C, then repeatedly calling `NextItem` will return the values A, B, C, A, B, C, A, B, C, and so forth. (Hint: Use a `List` to hold the queue's values.)

7. Create a `Bundle` class that uses a `List` to hold items. Create an `Add` method so that the program can add items to a `Bundle`. Override its `ToString` method to return a string holding the items in the bundle separated by semicolons. For example, if the bundle contains the values "hello" and 13, the `ToString` method should return `hello;13`.

8. The `Bundle` class you built for Exercise 7 can delegate methods to the `List` object that it contains. At a minimum you need to give it an `Add` method so the program can put items in the `Bundle`. Unfortunately, the `List<T>` class supports more than 80 properties and methods that you could delegate. Delegating them all would be a huge amount of work.

Fortunately, there's an easier solution: Make `Bundle<T>` inherit from `List<T>`. Repeat Exercise 7 using this technique.

PART IV
Interacting with the Environment

16

Printing

WHAT'S IN THIS CHAPTER

- ➤ Windows Forms printing
- ➤ Print previews
- ➤ GDI+ drawing basics
- ➤ Printing a booklet
- ➤ WPF printing with paginators, `FlowDocument`s, and `FixedDocument`s

WROX.COM DOWNLOADS FOR THIS CHAPTER

Please note that all the code examples for this chapter are available as a part of this chapter's code download on the book's website at `www.wrox.com/go/csharp5programmersref` on the Download Code tab.

Windows Forms and WPF applications take two different approaches to printing. In a Windows Forms application, the program starts the printing process, and then a document object raises events to ask the program what it should draw on each printed page. A WPF application builds a document object that contains other objects representing printed items, such as text, images, and shapes.

The first part of this chapter describes printing in Windows Forms applications. The second part explains how to generate and print documents in WPF applications.

WINDOWS FORMS PRINTING

Although Windows Forms applications have some good printing tools, the basic process seems somewhat backward for many programmers. Instead of executing commands to tell a printer object what to print, the program must respond to events when a document object asks what it should print.

When you master the basic concepts, printing is mostly a matter of learning how to draw graphics. Drawing graphics in a Windows Forms application is practically the same whether you're drawing on a form, `PictureBox`, or printed page.

The following section describes the basic process. The sections after that explain how to print specific items, such as text, images, and shapes. The final Windows Forms example shows how to display page numbers, change margins for odd and even pages, and split paragraphs across multiple pages.

Basic Printing

The heart of the printing process in Windows Forms applications is the `PrintDocument` object. As its name implies, it represents a document to be printed.

You might expect the `PrintDocument` class to provide methods that you call to draw text, images, lines, and other items on the document. The process actually works in reverse. The program creates a `PrintDocument` object. It then directly or indirectly tells the object that it wants to generate a print preview or an actual printout. The `PrintDocument` then raises events asking the program what it should draw on each page of the printout. The program responds with drawing commands that determine the results.

> **PERCEPTIVE PRINTING**
>
> This process of the `PrintDocument` object raising event seems backward but it's actually fairly clever. The `PrintPage` event, which is described in detail shortly, passes the program a `Graphics` object on which to draw. This is the same kind of `Graphics` object that a program uses to draw on a `Form`, `PictureBox`, `Bitmap`, or anything else in .NET. By giving you a `Graphics` object, the `PrintPage` event enables you to use the same kind of code you use to draw anywhere else.
>
> In fact, if you design the program properly, you can use the same code to draw on a `Form`, `PictureBox`, and printout. If you place all your drawing commands in a method that takes a `Graphics` object as a parameter, you can use that method to generate results for the screen or the printer.

When a `PrintDocument` object must perform printing-related tasks, it raises four key events:

➤ `BeginPrint`—The `PrintDocument` raises its `BeginPrint` event when it is about to start printing. The program can initialize data structures, load data, connect to databases, and otherwise get ready to print.

➤ `QueryPageSettings`—Before it prints a page, the `PrintDocument` object raises this event. The program can catch this event and make changes that are specific to the page it is about to print. For example, if you are printing a booklet, the program can adjust the margins to leave extra space on the side of the page where the staples will be.

➤ `PrintPage`—The `PrintDocument` object raises the `PrintPage` event to generate a page. The program catches this event and uses the `e.Graphics` parameter to generate output. After it finishes printing the page, the program should set the value `e.HasMorePages` to `true` or `false` to tell the `PrintDocument` whether there are more pages to print after this one.

➤ **EndPrint**—When it finishes printing, the PrintDocument object raises its EndPrint event. The program can catch this event to clean up any resources it used while printing. It can free data structures, close data files and database connections, and perform any other necessary cleanup chores.

A SAFE DEFAULT

The PrintPage event handler's e.HasMorePages value is initially false, so you need to set only its value if you want to print more pages. That way if you forget to set its value, the program won't just keep spitting out an endless stream of blank pages.

After you create a PrintDocument and attach the event handlers that you want to use, you can do three things with it. First, you can call the object's Print method to immediately start the printing process. The PrintDocument object raises its events as necessary and sends the result to the currently selected printer.

Second, you can set a PrintPreviewDialog control's Document property to the PrintDocument object and then call the dialog box's ShowDialog method. The PrintPreviewDialog makes the PrintDocument generate a printout and displays it in a print preview dialog similar to the one shown in Figure 16-1.

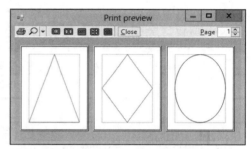

FIGURE 16-1: The PrintPreviewDialog lets the user zoom in and out, view the printout's various pages, and send the printout to a printer.

PREVIEW DON'T PRINT

Displaying print preview dialogs is easy in C#, so you may want to display previews instead of send output directly to the printer. Particularly when you debug programs or work through exercises, there's no reason to waste trees printing results you don't need to keep.

The print preview dialog's printer button on the left sends the printout to the currently selected printer. The magnifying glass button displays a drop-down that lets you select different scales. The next five buttons let the user display one, two, three, four, or six of the printout's pages at the same time. The Close button closes the dialog box and the Page up/down arrows let you move through the printout's pages.

The PrintPreviewControl displays a print preview much as the PrintPreviewDialog control does, except that it sits on your form. It does not provide all the buttons that the dialog box does, but it does provide methods that let you implement similar features. For example, your program can set the zoom level and the number of columns in the display.

PRINTOUT REGENERATION

When you click the `PrintPreviewDialog`'s print button, the PrintDocument regenerates the printout using its events and sends the result to the printer instead of to the print preview dialog box. It doesn't reuse the previously created preview document.

The third thing you can do with a `PrintDocument` is assign it to a `PrintDialog` object's `Document` property and then call the dialog's `ShowDialog` method. This displays a dialog box that lets you select the printer and set its properties. For example, you can set the printer's landscape or portrait orientation. When you click the dialog's Print button, the dialog uses the `PrintDocument` object to send the printout to the printer.

PREVIEW POSSIBILITIES

Your results could look different from those shown here. The print preview adjusts its appearance based on such factors as the type of printer you use, its settings, the size of the paper you use, and the paper's orientation.

The PrintShapes example program, which is available for download on this book's website, displays a preview in a `PrintPreviewControl`, sends a printout directly to a printer, and displays the print preview dialog shown in Figure 16-1. At design time, I added a `PrintPreviewControl`, `PrintDocument`, and `PrintPreviewDialog` to the form. I set the `Document` properties for the preview control and the preview dialog to the `PrintDocument` object.

When the program starts, the `PrintPreviewControl` automatically generates and displays its preview.

The following code shows how the program sends a printout to the printer.

```
// Send the printout to the currently selected printer.
private void printButton_Click(object sender, EventArgs e)
{
    samplePrintDocument.Print();
}
```

The following code shows how the program displays the preview dialog.

```
// Display a print preview.
private void previewButton_Click(object sender, EventArgs e)
{
    samplePrintPreviewDialog.ShowDialog();
}
```

Finally, the following code shows the most interesting part of the program in which the `PrintDocument` generates the printout.

```
// The next page number to print.
private int NextPage = 0;
```

```
// Start with page number 0.
private void samplePrintDocument_BeginPrint(object sender,
    System.Drawing.Printing.PrintEventArgs e)
{
    NextPage = 0;
}

// Print a page.
private void samplePrintDocument_PrintPage(object sender,
    System.Drawing.Printing.PrintPageEventArgs e)
{
    e.Graphics.SmoothingMode = SmoothingMode.AntiAlias;

    // Draw the margin bounds.
    e.Graphics.DrawRectangle(Pens.Orange, e.MarginBounds);

    // Draw a shape.
    int xmid = (e.MarginBounds.Left + e.MarginBounds.Right) / 2;
    int ymid = (e.MarginBounds.Top + e.MarginBounds.Bottom) / 2;
    switch (NextPage)
    {
        case 0:     // Triangle.
            Point[] trianglePoints =
            {
                new Point(xmid, e.MarginBounds.Top),
                new Point(e.MarginBounds.Right, e.MarginBounds.Bottom),
                new Point(e.MarginBounds.Left, e.MarginBounds.Bottom),
            };
            e.Graphics.DrawPolygon(Pens.Red, trianglePoints);
            break;
        case 1:     // Diamond.
            Point[] diamondPoints =
            {
                new Point(xmid, e.MarginBounds.Top),
                new Point(e.MarginBounds.Right, ymid),
                new Point(xmid, e.MarginBounds.Bottom),
                new Point(e.MarginBounds.Left, ymid),
            };
            e.Graphics.DrawPolygon(Pens.Green, diamondPoints);
            break;
        case 2:     // Ellipse.
            e.Graphics.DrawEllipse(Pens.Blue, e.MarginBounds);
            break;
    }

    // Page 2 is the last page.
    e.HasMorePages = (++NextPage <= 2);
}
```

The code first defines the NextPage variable that it uses to keep track of which page it is printing.

The BeginPrint event handler executes before the PrintDocument starts to generate the printout. In this example, this event handler sets NextPage to 0 so that the program knows it is about to print the first page.

The `PrintPage` event handler does all the drawing. It starts by setting the `Graphics` object's `SmoothingMode` property to make drawn shapes smoother. (Download the example, and comment this out to see what the difference is.)

DRAWING DETAILS

The `SmoothingMode` values and many other useful values for specifying graphics characteristics such as dash style and join style are defined in the `System.Drawing` `.Drawing2D` namespace. In a program in which you do a lot of drawing, you will probably want to include the following directive.

```
using System.Drawing.Drawing2D;
```

Next, the program draws an orange rectangle showing the page's margin bounds. Normally, anything you draw should be inside the margin bounds. (Don't worry too much yet about how to draw shapes. The following sections explain drawing basics.)

Depending on the page number, the code then draws a triangle, diamond, or ellipse. The event handler finishes by incrementing `NextPage` and setting `e.HasMorePages` to `true` if the next page has a number less than or equal to 2.

OUT OF BOUNDS

The `e.MarginBounds` value tells you where you should print to leave a reasonable margin around the edges of the page, but most printers can print outside of those bounds.

The `e.PageBounds` value gives the size of the paper, but most printers cannot print all the way up to the edges of the paper.

The `e.PageSettings.PrintableArea` value gives the area on which the printer should print, at least in theory.

All three of these areas are measured in hundredths of inches.

The following table shows the values for my printer.

VALUE	X	Y	WIDTH	HEIGHT
e.MarginBounds	100	100	650	900
e.PageBounds	0	0	850	1100
e.PageSettings .PrintableArea	25	6.833333	800	1042.667

The following sections provide a bit more information about how the `Graphics` object's drawing methods work.

Drawing Basics

The previous section explains how the `PrintShapes` example program draws some simple shapes. It focuses mostly on the `PrintPage` event and glosses over exactly how the graphics are drawn.

A program uses three things to draw shapes: a `Graphics` object, pens, and brushes. It uses those things whether it is drawing on a `Form`, `PictureBox`, `Bitmap`, or print document.

> **NOTE** *The classes that you use to draw in Windows Forms applications are contained in GDI+, the .NET version of the Graphics Device Interface (GDI) library.*

The following sections describe `Graphics` objects, pens, and brushes.

Graphics Objects

A `Graphics` object represents a drawing surface. You can think of it as the canvas or paper on which the program will draw.

The `Graphics` class provides many methods for drawing lines, rectangles, curves, and other shapes. The following table summarizes these methods.

METHOD	DESCRIPTION
DrawArc	Draws an arc of an ellipse.
DrawBezier	Draws a Bézier curve.
DrawBeziers	Draws a series of Bézier curves.
DrawClosedCurve	Draws a smooth closed curve that joins a series of points, connecting the final point to the first point.
DrawCurve	Draws a smooth curve that joins a series of points but doesn't connect the final point to the first point.
DrawEllipse	Draws an ellipse. (To draw a circle, draw an ellipse with equal width and height.)
DrawIcon	Draws an icon.
DrawIconUnstretched	Draws an icon without scaling. If you know that you will not resize the icon, this is faster than `DrawIcon`.
DrawImage	Draws an image. `Bitmap` is a subclass of `Image`, so you can use this method to draw a `Bitmap`.

continues

(continued)

METHOD	DESCRIPTION
DrawImageUnscaled	Draws an image without scaling. If you know that you will not resize the image, this is faster than DrawImage.
DrawLine	Draws a line.
DrawLines	Draws a series of connected lines. This is much faster than using DrawLine repeatedly.
DrawPath	Draws a GraphicsPath object.
DrawPie	Draws a pie slice taken from an ellipse.
DrawPolygon	Draws a polygon. This is similar to DrawLines except it connects the last point to the first point.
DrawRectangle	Draws a rectangle with horizontal and vertical sides. (In other words, it can't draw rotated rectangles.)
DrawRectangles	Draws a series of rectangles. This is much faster than using DrawRectangle repeatedly.
DrawString	Draws text.

The methods listed in the preceding table draw the outline of something such as a line, rectangle, or ellipse. The Graphics class provides corresponding methods that fill many of these shapes. For example, the DrawRectangle method outlines a rectangle, and the corresponding FillRectangle method fills a rectangle. The filling methods include FillClosedCurve, FillEllipse, FillPath, FillPie, FillPolygon, FillRectangle, and FillRectangles.

The Draw methods take a pen as a parameter and use that pen to determine how the outline is drawn. In contrast, the Fill methods take a brush as a parameter and use the brush to determine how to fill the area.

The one exception is the DrawString method, which uses a brush to fill text even though its name begins with Draw.

The sections "Pens" and "Brushes" later in this chapter describe pens and brushes in greater detail.

See the online help for specific information about the Graphics class's drawing and filling methods. You can find links to the pages describing these methods at the Graphics class's web page msdn.microsoft.com/library/system.drawing.graphics.

Obtaining Graphics Objects

There are several ways a program can obtain a Graphics object on which to draw. You've already seen that the PrintDocument's PrintPage event handler provides an e.Graphics parameter.

Similarly, a `Form`, `PictureBox`, or other control can provide a `Paint` event that includes an `e.Graphics` parameter on which a program can draw. The `Paint` event is raised when a control needs to redraw some or all of itself.

Note that the `Graphics` object included in a `Paint` event handler may clip its drawing methods, so it redraws only the parts of the control that actually need to be redrawn. That means any graphics drawn outside of those areas are ignored. You don't need to do anything special to make this work. Just be aware that some of your graphics may not actually be drawn.

For example, if you want to redraw an entire `PictureBox` to cover it with random circles, you need to refresh the entire `PictureBox` to ensure that everything you draw appears. (You can refresh a control by calling its `Refresh` method.)

The last common way to obtain a `Graphics` object is to create one that is associated with a `Bitmap`. The program can then use the `Graphics` object to draw on the `Bitmap`. The following code demonstrates this technique.

```
private void Form1_Load(object sender, EventArgs e)
{
    // Make a Bitmap.
    Bitmap bitmap = new Bitmap(100, 100);
    using (Graphics graphics = Graphics.FromImage(bitmap))
    {
        // Draw an ellipse on it.
        graphics.DrawEllipse(Pens.Brown, 0, 0, 99, 99);
    }

    // Display it on the form.
    this.BackgroundImage = bitmap;
}
```

This code creates a 100×100 pixel `Bitmap`. (Coordinates for all graphics in .NET are in pixels.) It then uses the `Graphics.FromImage` method to create a `Graphics` object associated with the `Bitmap`. The `Graphics` class provides a `Dispose` method, so the program includes a `using` statement to ensure that the method is called when the program is done with the object.

Next, the code uses the `Graphics` object's `DrawEllipse` method to draw a brown ellipse on the `Bitmap`. The code finishes by displaying the `Bitmap` in the form's `BackgroundImage` property.

Pens

The `Pen` object determines how lines are drawn. It determines a line's color, thickness, dash style, join style, and end cap style.

A program can explicitly create `Pen` objects, but often it can simply use one of the more than 280 stock pens that are predefined by the `Pens` class. For example, the following code draws a rectangle using a hot pink line that's one pixel wide.

```
gr.DrawRectangle(Pens.HotPink, 10, 10, 50, 50)
```

The following table summarizes the `Pen` class's constructors.

CONSTRUCTORS	DESCRIPTION
Pen(*brush*)	Creates a pen of thickness 1 using the indicated `Brush`
Pen(*color*)	Creates a pen of thickness 1 using the indicated color
Pen(*brush, thickness*)	Creates a pen with the indicated thickness (a `float`) using a `Brush`
Pen(*color, thickness*)	Creates a pen with the indicated thickness (a `float`) using the indicated color

The following table describes some of the `Pen` class's most useful properties and methods.

PROPERTY OR METHOD	PURPOSE
Brush	Determines the `Brush` used to fill a line.
Color	Determines the line's color.
CompoundArray	Lets you draw lines that are striped lengthwise.
CustomEndCap	Determines a line's end cap.
CustomStartCap	Determines a line's start cap.
DashCap	Determines the cap drawn at the ends of dashes. This can be `Flat`, `Round`, or `Triangle`.
DashOffset	Determines the distance from the start of a line to the start of its first dash.
DashPattern	An array of `float`s that specifies a custom dash pattern. The array entries tell how many pixels to draw, skip, draw, skip, and so forth. These values are scaled if the pen is not one pixel wide.
DashStyle	Determines the line's dash style. This value can be `Dash`, `DashDot`, `DashDotDot`, `Dot`, `Solid`, or `Custom`. If you set the `DashPattern` property, this value is automatically set to `Custom`. The dashes and gaps between them are scaled if the pen is not one pixel wide.
EndCap	Determines the cap used at the end of the line. This can be `ArrowAnchor`, `DiamondAnchor`, `Flat`, `NoAnchor`, `Round`, `RoundAnchor`, `Square`, `SquareAnchor`, `Triangle`, and `Custom`. If `LineCap` is `Custom`, you should use a `CustomLineCap` object to define the cap.
LineJoin	Determines how lines are joined by methods that draw connected lines such as `DrawLines` and `DrawPolygon`. This value can be `Bevel`, `Miter`, and `Round`.

PROPERTY OR METHOD	PURPOSE
SetLineCap	Specifies the pen's StartCap, EndCap, and LineJoin properties at the same time.
StartCap	Determines the cap used at the start of the line.
Width	The pen's width.

The PaintForm example program, which is available for download on this book's website, uses the following code to demonstrate some of these properties as it draws two shapes on the program's form.

```
private void Form1_Paint(object sender, PaintEventArgs e)
{
    e.Graphics.SmoothingMode = SmoothingMode.AntiAlias;

    // Draw a dashed ellipse.
    using (Pen ellipsePen = new Pen(Color.Black, 5))
    {
        ellipsePen.DashStyle = DashStyle.DashDotDot;
        e.Graphics.DrawEllipse(ellipsePen, 50, 50, 150, 100);
    }

    // Draw a polygon.
    using (Pen polygonPen = new Pen(Color.Gray, 10))
    {
        polygonPen.LineJoin = LineJoin.Bevel;
        Point[] points =
        {
            new Point(20, 20),
            new Point(200, 20),
            new Point(100, 50),
            new Point(260, 250),
            new Point(20, 170),
        };
        e.Graphics.DrawPolygon(polygonPen, points);
    }
}
```

The code creates a black pen of thickness 5. It sets the pen's DashStyle property to DashDotDot and draws an ellipse with it.

Next, the code creates a gray pen of thickness 10. It sets the pen's LineJoin property to Bevel and draws a polygon with it. Figure 16-2 shows the result.

You can learn more about the pen class at msdn .microsoft.com/library/system.drawing.pen.

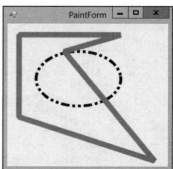

FIGURE 16-2: The PaintForm example program demonstrates dashed lines and beveled line joins.

Brushes

The `Brush` object determines how shapes are filled when you draw them using `Graphics` methods such as `FillClosedCurve`, `FillEllipse`, and `FillRectangle`. Different types of `Brushes` fill areas with solid colors, hatch patterns, color gradients, and images.

The `Brush` class is an abstract class, so you cannot make instances of the `Brush` class itself. Instead, you must create instances of one of the derived classes `SolidBrush`, `TextureBrush`, `HatchBrush`, `LinearGradientBrush`, and `PathGradientBrush`. The following table briefly describes these classes.

CLASS	PURPOSE
SolidBrush	Fills areas with a solid color
TextureBrush	Fills areas with a repeating image
HatchBrush	Fills areas with a repeating hatch pattern
LinearGradientBrush	Fills areas with a linear gradient of two or more colors
PathGradientBrush	Fills areas with a color gradient that follows a path

The BrushSamples example program, which is available for download on this book's website, uses the following code to demonstrate four kinds of brushes.

```
private void Form1_Paint(object sender, PaintEventArgs e)
{
    Rectangle rect = new Rectangle(10, 10, 120, 120);
    using (Brush solidBrush = new SolidBrush(Color.LightGray))
    {
        e.Graphics.FillRectangle(solidBrush, rect);
    }

    rect.Y += 130;
    using (Brush gradientBrush = new LinearGradientBrush(
        rect, Color.Black, Color.White, 45.0f))
    {
        e.Graphics.FillRectangle(gradientBrush, rect);
    }

    rect = new Rectangle(140, 10, 120, 120);
    using (Brush textureBrush = new TextureBrush(Properties.Resources.Smiley))
    {
        e.Graphics.FillRectangle(textureBrush, rect);
    }

    rect.Y += 130;
    using (Brush hatchBrush = new HatchBrush(
        HatchStyle.DiagonalBrick, Color.Black, Color.White))
    {
```

```
                e.Graphics.FillRectangle(hatchBrush, rect);
        }
    }
```

The code first creates a light gray solid brush and fills a rectangle.

Next, it moves the rectangle down 130 pixels and creates a linear gradient brush. The brush fills the rectangle starting with the color black and shading smoothly to the color white. The gradient's direction is 45° so the colors shade from black in the upper-left corner to white in the lower-right corner. After creating the brush, the program fills the rectangle with it.

The program then creates a new rectangle. It makes a texture brush, passing the brush's constructor the image stored in the program's `Properties.Resources.Smiley` resource. (Use the Project ⇨ Properties menu, and select the Resources page to add image resources.) When the program uses the texture brush, the rectangle is filled with repeating copies of the image.

FIGURE 16-3: The BrushSamples example program fills four rectangles with different kinds of brushes.

Finally, the program creates a `HatchBrush` that uses a diagonal brick pattern with a black foreground and white background. It finishes by filling a rectangle with the hatch brush. Figure 16-3 shows the result.

You can learn more about the brush classes at `msdn.microsoft.com/library/system .drawing.brush`.

Drawing Text

Many printing applications draw text more than anything else, so the `DrawString` method is particularly important. This method has six overloaded versions. All take a string to draw, the font to draw it with, and a brush to determine the text's appearance as their first three parameters.

Different versions let you specify the location for the text as X and Y `float` coordinates, a `PointF` (which has X and Y coordinates), or a `RectangleF` (which has top, left, width, and height values, again as `float`s).

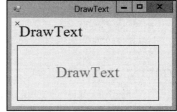

The final variation in the overloaded versions is that some let you include a `StringFormat` object to determine the way the text is laid out. For example, the `Alignment` and `LineAlignment` properties determine the text's horizontal and vertical alignment, respectively.

FIGURE 16-4: The DrawText example program draws text at a point and centered in a rectangle.

The DrawText example program, which is shown in Figure 16-4 and available for download on this book's website, uses the following code to demonstrate two of the overloaded versions of `DrawString`.

```
private void Form1_Paint(object sender, PaintEventArgs e)
{
```

```
        e.Graphics.SmoothingMode = SmoothingMode.AntiAlias;

    // Make a font.
    using (Font font = new Font("Times New Roman", 20))
    {
        // Draw text in the upper left corner.
        e.Graphics.DrawString("DrawText", font, Brushes.Black, 10, 10);
        e.Graphics.DrawLine(Pens.Black, 7, 7, 13, 13);
        e.Graphics.DrawLine(Pens.Black, 7, 13, 13, 7);

        // Draw text centered on the form.
        using (StringFormat sf = new StringFormat())
        {
            // Center vertically and horizontally.
            sf.Alignment = StringAlignment.Center;
            sf.LineAlignment = StringAlignment.Center;

            // Draw the text.
            Rectangle rect = new Rectangle(10, 50, 250, 100);
            e.Graphics.DrawRectangle(Pens.Black, rect);
            e.Graphics.DrawString("DrawText", font,
                Brushes.Gray, rect, sf);
        }
    }
}
```

After setting the `SmoothingMode`, the program creates a large font. It then draws the string "DrawText" using the font and a black brush at the point (10, 10). The `DrawString` method draws the text so its upper-left corner is just below that point.

The code then draws two lines to make an X over the point (10, 10) so you can see how the text is arranged with respect to this point.

Next, the program makes a `StringFormat` object. The object's `Alignment` and `LineAlignment` properties can take the values `Near` (left or top alignment), `Center` (centered), or `Far` (right or bottom alignment). This program sets both properties to center the text.

The code then creates a `Rectangle`, draws the `Rectangle`, and then draws the text using the `StringFormat` object to center the text in the `Rectangle`.

Printing Images

The `Graphics` class's `DrawImage` method draws an image. This method has 30 different overloaded versions. Some take the coordinates of a point where the image should be drawn. Others take rectangles or arrays of points to indicate which part of the image should be drawn at which location on the `Graphics` object. A few interesting versions let you map a rectangle to a parallelogram, possible flipping or skewing the image.

One of the more explicit versions takes a source rectangle that indicates the part of the image to print, and a destination rectangle that indicates where to print it.

The PrintImage example program, which is available for download on this book's website, uses the following `PrintPage` event handler to print an image centered on a page.

```
private void imagePrintDocument_PrintPage(object sender,
    System.Drawing.Printing.PrintPageEventArgs e)
{
    Bitmap bm = Properties.Resources.GrandCanyon;

    // The source rectangle includes the whole picture.
    Rectangle sourceRect = new Rectangle(0, 0, bm.Width, bm.Height);

    // Center the destination rectangle.
    int x = e.MarginBounds.Left + (e.MarginBounds.Width - bm.Width) / 2;
    int y = e.MarginBounds.Top + (e.MarginBounds.Height - bm.Height) / 2;
    Rectangle destRect = new Rectangle(x, y, bm.Width, bm.Height);

    // Draw the image.
    e.Graphics.DrawImage(Properties.Resources.GrandCanyon,
        destRect, sourceRect, GraphicsUnit.Pixel);

    // There are no more pages.
    e.HasMorePages = false;
}
```

The code starts by setting the variable bm equal to the image resource named `GrandCanyon`. (Use the Project ⇨ Properties menu, and select the Resources page to add image resources.) The code could work directly with the image. The variable bm is just used to make the code easier to read.

Next, the program defines a source rectangle that includes the entire image. It then defines a destination rectangle that is the same size as the image and centered within the page's margins.

The code then uses the `DrawImage` method to draw the entire image in the destination rectangle. It finishes by setting e.`HasMorePages` to false. Figure 16-5 shows the program's print preview.

A Booklet Example

The examples in this chapter so far have drawn simple shapes or text samples. This section describes a more complete and potentially useful example that prints a long series of paragraphs that may each use a different font size.

FIGURE 16-5: The PrintImage example program draws an image centered within the page's margins.

The PrintBooklet example program, which is available for download on this book's website, breaks text into pages. It assumes you will print the pages double-sided and then staple the pages into a booklet. To allow extra room for the staples, the program adds a *gutter* to the margin of each page on the side where the staples will be. The program assumes the first page goes on the outside of the booklet, so it adds the gutter to the left margin on odd-numbered pages and to the right margin on even-numbered pages. Finally, the program displays a page number in the upper corner opposite the gutter.

In addition to demonstrating event handlers for the `PrintDocument` class's events, this example shows how to use `StringFormat` objects to align text and break lines at word boundaries, wrap text within a target rectangle, and measure text to see how much will fit in a target rectangle.

Figure 16-6 shows the PrintBooklet program's print preview dialog, so you can understand the goals. The figure isn't big enough for you to read the text. The text (other than the headings) is gibberish anyway. It's just there so that you can see the shape of the document.

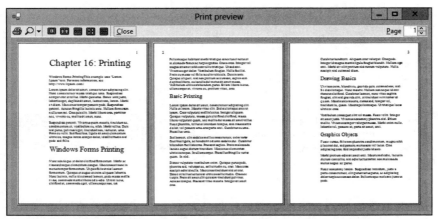

FIGURE 16-6: The PrintBooklet example program breaks text across pages, places a gutter on alternate sides, and draws page numbers on the side opposite the gutter.

If you look closely, you can see that the gutters are placed on alternate sides in odd and even pages. You can also see that the page numbers are in the upper corner on the side that doesn't have the gutter.

The program uses the following `ParagraphInfo` structure to store information about the text it will print.

```
// Information about the paragraphs to print.
private struct ParagraphInfo
{
    public int FontSize;
    public string Text;
    public ParagraphInfo(int fontSize, string text)
    {
        FontSize = fontSize;
        Text = text;
    }
}
```

The following code shows how the program prepares the text it will print.

```
// The paragraphs.
private List<ParagraphInfo> AllParagraphs, ParagraphsToPrint;
private int PagesPrinted;

// Load the paragraph info.
private void Form1_Load(object sender, EventArgs e)
{
    // Make the text to print.
    AllParagraphs = new List<ParagraphInfo>();
    AllParagraphs.Add(new ParagraphInfo(45, "Chapter 16: Printing"));
    AllParagraphs.Add(new ParagraphInfo(16,
        "This example uses \"Lorem Ipsum\" text. For more information," +
        "see http://www.lipsum.com/."));
    ... Code to initialize other ParagraphInfo structures omitted ...
}
```

This code declares two `List<ParagraphInfo>` objects. The `AllParagraphs` list holds all the text to be printed. The `ParagraphsToPrint` list holds the text that hasn't yet been printed while the program prints.

The `Form1_Load` event handler creates the `AllParagraphs` list and fills it with `ParagraphInfo` structures to print.

At design time I added a `PrintDocument` and `PrintPreviewDialog` to the program's form as usual. When you click the program's button Print Preview button, the program calls the dialog's `ShowDialog` method to start the printing process. When printing starts, the following `BeginPrint` event handler executes.

```
// Prepare to print.
private void bookletPrintDocument_BeginPrint(object sender, PrintEventArgs e)
{
    // We have not yet printed any pages.
    PagesPrinted = 0;

    // Make a copy of the text to print.
    ParagraphsToPrint = AllParagraphs.ToList();
}
```

> ## DODGING DESIGN TIME
>
> The examples in this chapter use `PrintDocument`, `PrintPreviewDialog`, and other objects created at design time and place them on a form. However, you can create those objects with code at run time instead if you prefer. Actually, some developers prefer to do just that because objects added to a form take up memory and resources even if they are never used. In contrast your code can create objects only as needed and can destroy them when it's done with them.

This code sets `PagesPrinted` to 0 because no pages have been printed yet during this round of printing. It then copies the `ParagraphInfo` structures from the `AllParagraphs` list (which holds all the data) into the `ParagraphsToPrint` list (which holds those paragraphs that have not yet been printed).

Before it prints each page, the `PrintDocument` object raises its `QueryPageSettings` event. The program uses the following code to catch this event and prepare the next page for printing.

```
// Set the margins for the next page.
private void bookletPrintDocument_QueryPageSettings(object sender,
    QueryPageSettingsEventArgs e)
{
    // Use a 1 inch gutter. (Printer units are 1/100th inch).
    const int gutter = 100;

    // See if the next page will be the first, odd, or even.
    if (PagesPrinted == 0)
    {
        // The first page. Increase the left margin.
        e.PageSettings.Margins.Left += gutter;
    }
    else if ((PagesPrinted % 2) == 0)
    {
        // It's an odd page. Shift the margins right.
        e.PageSettings.Margins.Left += gutter;
        e.PageSettings.Margins.Right -= gutter;
    }
    else
    {
        // It's an even page. Shift the margins left.
        e.PageSettings.Margins.Left -= gutter;
        e.PageSettings.Margins.Right += gutter;
    }
}
```

This code positions the new page's gutter. If this is the first page, then the page's margins have their default values and do not include a gutter. In that case, the code increases the left margin to add a 1-inch gutter.

If this isn't the first page, the code determines whether it is an odd or even page. If this is an even page, then the previous page was odd, so the gutter is currently on the left. To move the gutter to the right side of the page, the code adds 1 inch to the left margin and subtracts 1 inch from the right margin.

Similarly, if this is an even page, the code subtracts 1 inch from the left margin and adds 1 inch to the right margin.

After the `QueryPageSettings` event finishes, the `PrintDocument` object raises its `PrintPage` event to generate the next printed page. The program's `PrintPage` event handler is fairly long, so the following paragraphs describe it in pieces. (Download the example to see it all in one chunk.)

The following code shows how the event handler starts.

```
private void bookletPrintDocument_PrintPage(object sender, PrintPageEventArgs e)
{
    // Increment the page number.
```

```
        PagesPrinted++;

        // Draw the margins (for debugging).
        //e.Graphics.DrawRectangle(Pens.Red, e.MarginBounds);

        // Print the page number right justified
        // in the upper corner opposite the gutter
        // and outside of the margin.
        int x;
        using (StringFormat sf = new StringFormat())
        {
            // See if (this is an odd or even page.
            if ((PagesPrinted % 2) == 0)
            {
                // This is an even page.
                // The gutter is on the right and
                // the page number is on the left.
                x = (e.MarginBounds.Left + e.PageBounds.Left) / 2;
                sf.Alignment = StringAlignment.Near;
            }
            else
            {
                // This is an odd page.
                // The gutter is on the left and
                // the page number is on the right.
                x = (e.MarginBounds.Right + e.PageBounds.Right) / 2;
                sf.Alignment = StringAlignment.Far;
            }

            // Print the page number.
            using (Font font = new Font("Times New Roman", 20,
                FontStyle.Regular, GraphicsUnit.Point))
            {
                e.Graphics.DrawString(PagesPrinted.ToString(),
                    font, Brushes.Black, x,
                    (e.MarginBounds.Top + e.PageBounds.Top) / 2,
                    sf);
            }
```

The event handler starts by incrementing the number of pages printed so far. It then includes commented code to draw a rectangle around the page's margins. Drawing this rectangle often makes debugging printing routines easier because it lets you see how your printing relates to the page's margins.

Next, the code prepares to print the page number. It starts by creating a `StringFormat` object to align the page number. It sets the object's `Alignment` property to left-justify page numbers in the left margin and to right-justify page numbers in the right margin. The code also calculates an X coordinate to place the page number halfway between the margin and the page's bounds.

The code then creates the page number font and prints the page number at the point with the calculated X coordinate and halfway between the page's upper margin and page bounds. Depending on the alignment, the text is arranged so that it is to the left or right of that point.

The following code shows how the program prepares to print text.

```
// Draw the rest of the text left justified,
// wrap at words, and don't draw partial lines.
sf.Alignment = StringAlignment.Near;
sf.FormatFlags = StringFormatFlags.LineLimit;
sf.Trimming = StringTrimming.Word;

// Draw some text.
ParagraphInfo paragraphInfo;
int ymin = e.MarginBounds.Top;
RectangleF layoutRect;
SizeF textSize;
int charsFitted, linesFilled;
while (ParagraphsToPrint.Count > 0)
{
    // Print the next paragraph.
    paragraphInfo = ParagraphsToPrint[0];
    ParagraphsToPrint.RemoveAt(0);

    // Get the area available for this paragraph.
    layoutRect = new RectangleF(
        e.MarginBounds.Left, ymin,
        e.MarginBounds.Width,
        e.MarginBounds.Bottom - ymin);
    // Work around bug where MeasureString
    // thinks characters fit if (height <= 0.
    if (layoutRect.Height < 1) layoutRect.Height = 1;

    // See how big the text will be and
    // how many characters will fit.
    // Get the font.
    using (Font font = new Font("Times New Roman",
        paragraphInfo.FontSize, FontStyle.Regular, GraphicsUnit.Point))
    {
        textSize = e.Graphics.MeasureString(
            paragraphInfo.Text, font,
            new SizeF(layoutRect.Width, layoutRect.Height),
            sf, out charsFitted, out linesFilled);
```

This code resets the StringFormat object's properties to draw the text left-justified. Setting FormatFlags to LineLimit makes the program stop drawing when a complete line of text won't fit in the formatting rectangle. By default, a line would be drawn even if its bottom edge would stick out of the rectangle.

Setting Trimming to Word makes drawing stop when a complete word won't fit on a line. (Other settings let you stop at the nearest character and add an ellipsis after the final word or character if there's more text that wouldn't fit.)

The program sets ymin to the page's top Y coordinate and then enters a loop that runs as long as there are more paragraphs to print.

Inside the loop, the program gets the next paragraph to print and removes it from the ParagraphsToPrint list. It then creates a layout rectangle that contains the remaining space that is available for printing. Vertically this rectangle starts at the current Y coordinate `ymin` and extends to the bottom of the page. Horizontally the rectangle covers the width of the page.

Next, the code creates a font of the appropriate size for the paragraph. It then calls the `e.Graphics` `.MeasureString` method. The overloaded version of the method used by the program takes the paragraph's text and font, a size, and the `StringFormat` object as input parameters. It returns through output parameters the number of characters and lines that will fit in the indicated size. The program uses that information to determine how much of the paragraph will fit in the formatting rectangle.

Having determined how much text will fit in the available space, the program uses the following code to print it.

```
        // See if any characters will fit.
        if (charsFitted > 0)
        {
            // Draw the text.
            e.Graphics.DrawString(paragraphInfo.Text,
                font, Brushes.Black,
                layoutRect, sf);

            // Debugging: Draw a rectangle around the text.
            //e.Graphics.DrawRectangle(Pens.Green,
            //    layoutRect.Left,
            //    layoutRect.Top,
            //    textSize.Width,
            //    textSize.Height);

            // Increase the Y coordinate where the next
            // piece of text can start.
            // Add a little interparagraph spacing.
            ymin += (int)(textSize.Height +
                e.Graphics.MeasureString("M", font).Height / 2);
        }
    } // font
```

If any text fits in the layout rectangle, the program uses the `DrawString` method to print it. Commented out code lets you draw a rectangle around the text, again for debugging purposes.

The code then increases the available Y coordinate `ymin` by the height of the printed text plus half of an M character's height (for paragraph spacing).

At this point, the program has printed as much of the current paragraph as will fit in the available space. When the page first starts printing, that is probably the entire paragraph. It's only near the bottom of the page that a partial paragraph may be printed.

The following code shows how the program finishes printing the page.

```
        // See if (some of the paragraph didn't fit on the page.
        if (charsFitted < paragraphInfo.Text.Length)
        {
            // Some of the paragraph didn't fit.
            // Prepare to print the rest on the next page.
            paragraphInfo.Text = paragraphInfo.Text.
                Substring(charsFitted);
```

```
                ParagraphsToPrint.Insert(0, paragraphInfo);

                // That's all that will fit on this page.
                break;
            }
        } // while
    } // sf

    // If we have more paragraphs, we have more pages.
    e.HasMorePages = (ParagraphsToPrint.Count > 0);
}
```

If some of the paragraph's characters did not fit, the program resets the `ParagraphInfo` structure's text so that it holds whatever text did not fit. It then inserts the `ParagraphInfo` at the beginning of the `ParagraphsToPrint` list so that it is printed first on the next page. It then breaks out of the `while` loop so that it stops printing paragraphs on this page.

If all the paragraph's text did fit, the `while` loop continues printing the next paragraph. After the `while` loop ends, either because a paragraph didn't fit completely or because all the paragraphs have been printed, this page is done. The code sets `e.HasMorePages` to `true` if there are more paragraphs in the `ParagraphsToPrint` list.

When the last page has been printed, the `PrintDocument` object raises its `EndPrint` event. The following code shows the `EndPrint` event handler.

```
private void bookletPrintDocument_EndPrint(object sender, PrintEventArgs e)
{
    ParagraphsToPrint = null;
}
```

In this program, the `EndPrint` event handler simply sets the `ParagraphsToPrint` list to `null` so that the garbage collector can later recycle its memory. In this program, the list doesn't occupy much space, so freeing it is a small matter. In a program that allocated more elaborate data structures, cleaning up in this event handler might be more important.

WPF PRINTING

WPF programs have some big advantages over Windows Forms applications. For example, WPF controls are infinitely scalable. That means no matter how far you zoom in on a WPF control, the result is smooth and not pixelated.

WPF's approach to printing makes particularly good use of this infinite scalability. To create a printout, a WPF application creates objects that represent whatever needs to be printed. The program can scale those objects as necessary to fit the printout and the result takes advantage of the printer's capabilities.

There are several ways a WPF application can produce printouts. The following sections describe two of the more useful: using a paginator and creating documents.

Using a Paginator

A *paginator* is an object that generates a printout's pages. To create a printout by using a paginator, you derive a new class from the `DocumentPaginator` class and override its `GetPage` method to create the document's pages. You also need to override a few other methods to let the paginator know how many pages it will produce.

PAPERLESS PREVIEWS

WPF does not provide a print preview control. To view a printout without printing it and wasting paper, print to the Microsoft XPS Document Writer. The writer lets you pick the file where it will save the printout in XPS (XML Paper Specification) or OXPS (Open XPS) format.

Later, you can use Microsoft Reader to view the file. If you save the printout in the XPS format, you can also view the file by opening it in Internet Explorer.

The WpfPrintShapes example program, which is available for download on this book's website, uses a paginator to create a printout. Figure 16-7 shows the program's three pages displayed in Microsoft Reader.

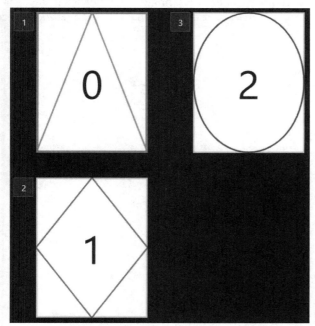

FIGURE 16-7: The WpfPrintShapes example program prints three pages.

When the WpfPrintShapes example program executes, it displays a Print button. When you click the button, the following code executes.

```
private void printButton_Click(object sender, RoutedEventArgs e)
{
    PrintDialog pd = new PrintDialog();
    if (pd.ShowDialog() == true)
    {
        // Print.
        pd.PrintDocument(
            new ShapesPaginator(
                new Size(pd.PrintableAreaWidth, pd.PrintableAreaHeight)),
            "Shapes");
    }
}
```

This code creates a PrintDialog object and calls its ShowDialog method to display it. If the user selects a printer and clicks Print, the ShowDialog method returns true. In that case, the program calls the dialog's PrintDocument method, passing it a new ShapesPaginator object and a description of the document being printed.

When the program creates the ShapesPaginator object, it passes the constructor a Size structure representing the page's printable area.

The ShapesPaginator object does all the interesting work of generating the document's printed pages. The following code shows the ShapesPaginator class, except for the GetPage method, which is described shortly.

```
public class ShapesPaginator : DocumentPaginator
{
    // The area in which to print.
    private Size MyPageSize;

    // Save the page size.
    public ShapesPaginator(Size pageSize)
    {
        MyPageSize = pageSize;
    }

    // Create and return the requested page.
    public override DocumentPage GetPage(int pageNumber)
    {
        ...
    }

    // If pagination is in progress and PageCount is not final, return false.
    // If pagination is complete and PageCount is final, return true.
    // In this example, there is no pagination to do.
    public override bool IsPageCountValid
    {
        get { return true; }
    }

    // The number of pages paginated so far.
```

```
// This example has exactly 3 pages.
public override int PageCount
{
    get { return 3; }
}

// The suggested page size.
public override Size PageSize
{
    get { return MyPageSize; }
    set { MyPageSize = value; }
}

// The element currently being paginated.
public override IDocumentPaginatorSource Source
{
    get { return null; }
}
}
```

The ShapesPaginator class inherits from DocumentPaginator. The class starts by declaring a private MyPageSize variable to hold the available printing area. The class's constructor takes a Size parameter and saves it in MyPageSize.

To produce a printout, the class overrides the following four properties.

➤ IsPageCountValid—Some programs may need to paginate all the printout's pages before the final PageCount value is correct. In that case, this property should return false while pagination is occurring and true after PageCount is set to its final correct value.

➤ PageCount—Returns the number of pages that have been formatted.

➤ PageSize—Gets or sets the suggested size of the printed page.

➤ Source—Returns the element being paginated.

The WpfPrintShapes example just prints three pages, so these overridden properties are relatively simple. The program doesn't need to format all the pages to determine how many pages there will be, so IsPageCountValid always returns true, PageCount always returns 3, PageSize returns the size saved by the class's constructor, and Source returns null.

In a Windows Forms application, a PrintDocument raises a PrintPage event to generate a printed page. Similarly, when a WPF application uses a paginator, it calls the paginator's GetPage method to get objects representing a printed page. The following code shows the GetPage method used by the ShapesPaginator class.

```
// Create and return the requested page.
public override DocumentPage GetPage(int pageNumber)
{
    // Create a grid.
    Grid grid = new Grid();
    grid.Width = MyPageSize.Width;
    grid.Height = MyPageSize.Height;
```

```
// Outline the drawing area.
Rectangle rectangle = new Rectangle();
rectangle.Width = MyPageSize.Width;
rectangle.Height = MyPageSize.Height;
rectangle.Stroke = Brushes.Orange;
rectangle.StrokeThickness = 10.0;
grid.Children.Add(rectangle);

// Display the page number.
TextBlock textBlock = new TextBlock();
textBlock.Text = pageNumber.ToString();
textBlock.FontSize = 300;
textBlock.HorizontalAlignment = HorizontalAlignment.Center;
textBlock.VerticalAlignment = VerticalAlignment.Center;
grid.Children.Add(textBlock);

// Generate the appropriate page.
switch (pageNumber)
{
    case 0:     // Triangle.
        Polygon triangle = new Polygon();
        triangle.Stroke = Brushes.Red;
        triangle.StrokeThickness = 10.0;

        PointCollection triangle_pts = new PointCollection();
        triangle_pts.Add(new Point(MyPageSize.Width / 2, 0));
        triangle_pts.Add(new Point(MyPageSize.Width, MyPageSize.Height));
        triangle_pts.Add(new Point(0, MyPageSize.Height));
        triangle.Points = triangle_pts;
        grid.Children.Add(triangle);
        break;

    case 1:     // Diamond.
        Polygon diamond = new Polygon();
        diamond.Stroke = Brushes.Green;
        diamond.StrokeThickness = 10.0;

        PointCollection diamond_pts = new PointCollection();
        diamond_pts.Add(new Point(MyPageSize.Width / 2, 0));
        diamond_pts.Add(new Point(MyPageSize.Width, MyPageSize.Height / 2));
        diamond_pts.Add(new Point(MyPageSize.Width / 2, MyPageSize.Height));
        diamond_pts.Add(new Point(0, MyPageSize.Height / 2));
        diamond.Points = diamond_pts;
        grid.Children.Add(diamond);
        break;

    case 2:     // Ellipse
        Ellipse ellipse = new Ellipse();
        ellipse.Stroke = Brushes.Blue;
        ellipse.StrokeThickness = 10.0;
        ellipse.Width = MyPageSize.Width;
        ellipse.Height = MyPageSize.Height;
```

```
                grid.Children.Add(ellipse);
                break;
    }

    // Make the grid arrange itself and its controls.
    Rect rect = new Rect(new Point(0, 0), MyPageSize);
    grid.Arrange(rect);

    // Wrap the grid in a DocumentPage and return it.
    return new DocumentPage(grid);
}
```

The code starts by creating a Grid control and making it fit the available print area.

Next, the program creates a Rectangle and makes it fit the available area. It sets the Rectangle's Stroke properties to draw an orange outline 10 pixels wide and adds the Rectangle to the Grid's children.

The code then creates a TextBlock to display the page number. It sets the object's text, font size, and alignment. It then adds the TextBlock to the Grid's children.

By now you can probably see the pattern. The code creates a new object to represent some output, sets its properties, and adds the object to the Grid's children.

Now, depending on the page number, the code creates a polygon representing a triangle, a polygon representing a diamond, or an ellipse.

After creating the content controls, the method calls the Grid's Arrange method to make it arrange its controls. It finishes by returning a new DocumentPage object. It passes the DocumentPage constructor the root visual object that it should contain (the Grid in this example).

Creating Documents

By using paginator objects as described in the preceding section, you can produce just about any document you like, at least in theory. In practice creating a layout for a complicated multipage printout with paragraphs flowing around pictures, tables, and charts would be a huge amount of work. The FlowDocument and FixedDocument classes make this sort of complex layout task much easier.

FlowDocuments

A FlowDocument object holds other objects that represent graphical output such as text, images, and shapes. It arranges its objects to take best advantage of whatever space is available, much as a web browser rearranges its contents when it is resized.

There isn't room here to completely cover XAML, and all the objects that can be contained in a FlowDocument, but the WpfFlowDocument program, which is shown in Figure 16-8 and available for download on this book's website, can serve as a small example.

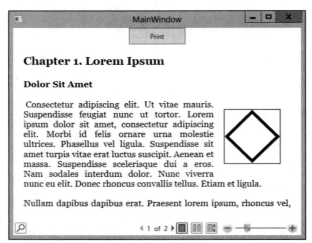

FIGURE 16-8: A `FlowDocument` rearranges its contents much as a web browser does when it is resized.

The following code shows the XAML used by the WpfFlowDocument program.

```
<Window x:Class="WpfFlowDocument.MainWindow"
        xmlns="http://schemas.microsoft.com/winfx/2006/xaml/presentation"
        xmlns:x="http://schemas.microsoft.com/winfx/2006/xaml"
        Title="WpfFlowDocument" Height="350" Width="525">
    <Grid>
        <Grid.RowDefinitions>
            <RowDefinition Height="30"/>
            <RowDefinition Height="*"/>
        </Grid.RowDefinitions>
        <Button Grid.Row="0"
            Content="Print" Click="printButton_Click"
            Width="100" Height="30" VerticalAlignment="Top"/>
        <FlowDocumentReader Grid.Row="1" VerticalAlignment="Top">
            <FlowDocument Name="sampleFlowDocument">
                <Paragraph FontSize="20" FontWeight="Bold">
                    Chapter 1. Lorem Ipsum
                </Paragraph>

                <Paragraph FontSize="16" FontWeight="Bold">
                    Dolor Sit Amet
                </Paragraph>

                <Paragraph>
                    <Floater HorizontalAlignment="Right">
                        <Paragraph>
                            <Grid Width="100" Height="100">
                                <Border BorderBrush="Black" BorderThickness="1"/>
                                <Polygon
                                    Points="50,5 95,50 50,95 5,50"
                                    Stroke="Black" StrokeThickness="5" />
```

```
                        </Grid>
                    </Paragraph>
                </Floater>
                Consectetur adipiscing elit ...
            </Paragraph>

            <Paragraph>
                Nullam dapibus dapibus ...
            </Paragraph>

            <Paragraph>
                Etiam lacus eros ...
            </Paragraph>

        </FlowDocument>
      </FlowDocumentReader>
    </Grid>
</Window>
```

The XAML code begins with a `Window` element that represents the program's window. That element contains a `Grid` with two rows: one that is 30 pixels tall and one that occupies the `Grid`'s remaining vertical space.

Next, the code defines a Print `Button` in the `Grid`'s first row. The code then defines a `FlowDocumentReader` to display the `FlowDocument`.

The `FlowDocument` element contains a sequence of `Paragraph` elements. The first two `Paragraphs` define headings. The third includes a `Floater` element. A `Floater` represents content that can be moved if necessary and around which other text can flow. In Figure 16-8 you can see how the text flows around the `Floater` on the right.

In this example, the `Floater` contains a `Paragraph` that holds a `Grid`. The `Grid` contains a `Border` and a `Polygon`.

The `Floater` is followed by more text in the same `Paragraph`.

Finally, the `FlowDocument` contains two other `Paragraphs`.

Printing a `FlowDocument` involves the following short but confusing sequence of steps.

1. Display a `PrintDialog` as usual.

2. Make an `XpsDocumentWriter` associated with the `PrintDialog`'s selected printer's queue.

3. Cast the `FlowDocument` into an `IDocumentPaginatorSource`.

4. Use the `XpsDocumentWriter`'s `Write` method to write into the print queue. Pass the method a paginator obtained by calling the `FlowDocument`'s `DocumentPaginator` property.

The following code shows how the WpfFlowDocument example prints.

```
private void printButton_Click(object sender, RoutedEventArgs e)
{
    PrintDialog pd = new PrintDialog();
    if (pd.ShowDialog() == true)
```

```
    {
        // Make an XPS document writer for the print queue.
        XpsDocumentWriter xpsWriter =
            PrintQueue.CreateXpsDocumentWriter(pd.PrintQueue);

        // Turn the FlowDocument into an IDocumentPaginatorSource.
        IDocumentPaginatorSource paginatorSource =
            (IDocumentPaginatorSource)sampleFlowDocument;

        // Write into the writer using the document's paginator.
        xpsWriter.Write(paginatorSource.DocumentPaginator);
    }
}
```

FixedDocuments

Like a `FlowDocument`, a `FixedDocument` holds graphical objects. Instead of rearranging its objects as space permits, a `FixedDocument` always places its objects in the same positions. This is similar to the way a PostScript document displays items at fixed positions.

The WpfFixedDocument example program, which is shown in Figure 16-9, and available for download on this book's website, displays and prints a `FixedDocument`.

FIGURE 16-9: A `FixedDocument` positions its contents in set positions on a fixed page.

The code to print a `FixedDocument` is similar to the code shown in the preceding section for printing a `FlowDocument`.

To display a `FixedDocument` in XAML code, include a `DocumentViewer` to hold the `FixedDocument`. Give the `FixedDocument` one or more `PageContent` elements to represent the printed pages. Each of those should hold a `FixedPage` element to generate content for the pager.

The following code shows the piece of XAML code used by the WpfFixedDocument example program to display its contents.

```
<DocumentViewer Grid.Row="1">
    <FixedDocument Name="sampleFixedDocument">
        <PageContent Width="850" Height="1100">
            <FixedPage Width="850" Height="1100" Margin="100">
                ... Page 1 content elements ...
            </FixedPage>
        </PageContent>
        <PageContent Width="850" Height="1100">
            <FixedPage Width="850" Height="1100" Margin="100">
                ... Page 1 content elements ...
            </FixedPage>
        </PageContent>
    </FixedDocument>
</DocumentViewer>
```

The details about how the program generates its content are long and not very interesting, so they aren't included here. They just use a long sequence of `StackPanel`, `TextBlock`, `Grid`, and other controls to create the output. Download the example and look at the code to see how it works.

FIXEDDOCUMENTS NEED FIXING

There is a well-known bug in Visual Studio's XAML designer that prevents it from correctly displaying XAML code that contains a `FixedDocument`. If you load XAML code into the designer, Visual Studio reports errors such as the following.

Property 'Pages' does not support values of type 'PageContent.'

The property 'Pages' is set more than once.

The specified value cannot be assigned. The following type was expected: "PageContentCollection."

If the XAML code is properly formed, however, the program compiles and runs without problems.

This has been a bug since the first version of WPF, so Microsoft doesn't seem to be rushing to fix this. I suspect it intends for programmers to use code to generate these objects at run time instead of using XAML code at design time. That certainly works but is more work and is outside the scope of this book.

SUMMARY

Windows Forms and WPF take different approaches to printing. In a Windows Forms application, a `PrintDocument` object represents a printout. It raises events such as `BeginPrint` and `PrintPage` to let the program determine what is printed. In the `PrintPage` event handler, you use `Graphics`, `Pen`, and `Brush` objects to produce output.

WPF applications use objects more directly to represent items to be printed. When you use a paginator, you derive a class from `DocumentPaginator` and you override the class's `GetPage` method to produce output. That output takes the form of a `DocumentPage` object containing other objects such as `TextBlock`, `Rectangle`, and `Polygon` objects that generate printed results.

If you prefer to use a `FlowDocument` or `FixedDocument` to produce output, you also use objects such as `TextBlock`, `Rectangle`, and `Polygon` to generate printed results. If you place the `FlowDocument` or `FixedDocument` inside a `FlowDocumentReader` or `DocumentViewer`, you can even use them as previews for the printout they will produce.

The programs described before this chapter interact only with the user. Printing is one way a program can interact with some other part of the system. The next chapter describes some other ways that a C# program can interact with the system by storing configuration and resource values for later use. These techniques let a program store and recover information between runs.

EXERCISES

To save paper, you may want to make all printing programs display print previews instead of printing.

1. Write a Windows Forms program that uses 20-pixel-wide blue lines to draw five-, seven-, and nine-pointed stars centered on three pages, as shown in Figure 16-10.

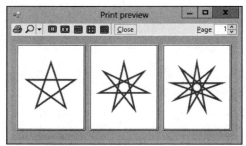

FIGURE 16-10: For Exercise 1, make a program that prints five-, seven-, and nine-pointed stars.

Hint: You can use the following code to generate points for the stars.

```
private List<PointF> StarPoints(float centerX, float centerY,
    float radius, int numPoints)
{
```

```
        // Calculate the difference in angles between points.
        double dtheta = (2 * Math.PI / numPoints) * (int)(numPoints / 2);

        // Generate the points.
        List<PointF> points = new List<PointF>();
        double theta = -Math.PI / 2;
        for (int i = 0; i < numPoints; i++)
        {
            double x = centerX + radius * Math.Cos(theta);
            double y = centerY + radius * Math.Sin(theta);
            points.Add(new PointF((float)x, (float)y));
            theta += dtheta;
        }

        return points;
}
```

2. Make a Windows Forms program that draws your name as large as possible centered inside the page's margins. (Hint: Use the `Graphics` object's `MeasureString` method to see how big the string will be when drawn with a particular font. Try fonts of different sizes until you find the largest that works. You only need to try integral font sizes.)

3. Make a Windows Forms program that generates prime numbers and prints them one per line in a 12-point font until it reaches the bottom of the page. Draw the margin bounds to verify that your text doesn't go beyond them. (Hints: Use 1.2 times the height of an M for the spacing between lines. To generate primes, use the `AllPrimes` iterator you built for Exercise 8 in Chapter 14, "Collection Classes.")

4. Repeat Exercise 1 with a WPF program that uses a paginator.

5. Repeat Exercise 1 with a WPF program that uses a `FixedDocument`. Hint: You don't need to create the stars at design time in XAML code. When the window loads, use code to add pages containing the stars to the `FixedDocument`. (This book doesn't explain how to build WPF interfaces in code, but you should be able to figure it out with a little experimentation. Create new `PageContent`, `FixedPage`, `Grid`, and `Polygon` objects. Add them to the appropriate objects' `Pages` or `Children` collections. If you get stuck, look at the solution in Appendix A "Solutions to Exercises," and download the program described there.)

17

Configuration and Resources

WHAT'S IN THIS CHAPTER

➤ Environment variables

➤ The registry

➤ Configuration files

➤ Resource files

➤ Localization

WROX.COM DOWNLOADS FOR THIS CHAPTER

Please note that all the code examples for this chapter are available as a part of this chapter's code download on the book's website at www.wrox.com/go/csharp5programmersref on the Download Code tab.

Most applications can take different actions depending on circumstances. Some applications decide how to act based on input provided by the user. Other applications use configuration information to determine how to behave.

For example, an application might display different kinds of data for different kinds of users. Data entry clerks, supervisors, managers, and billing specialists would all see different views of the same database. Similarly, you might configure an application for different levels of support. You might have different configurations for trial, basic, professional, and enterprise versions.

An application may also need to save state information between sessions. It might remember the types of forms that were last running, their positions, and their contents. The next time the program runs, it can restore those forms so that the user can get back to work as quickly as possible.

The .NET Framework provides many tools for storing and using application configuration and resource information. This chapter describes some of the most useful of those tools. It explains how an application can use environment variables, the registry, configuration files, resource files, and the Application object to save and restore configuration information.

FILE NOT FOUND

Configuration and resource files store information in files with specific formats. This chapter doesn't discuss more general uses of files. Reading and writing files, manipulating the filesystem, working with databases (which may be stored in files), and working with XML files are all topics covered by later chapters.

ENVIRONMENT VARIABLES

Environment variables give information about the operating system environment in which the program runs. They hold information such as the computer's name, the user's login name, the location of the system's temporary directory, the number of processors the system has, and the program's current working directory. You can also store configuration information in environment variables for your programs to use.

There are three types of environment variables that apply at the system, user, and process levels. System-level variables apply to all processes started on the system; user-level variables apply to processes started by a particular user; and process-level variables apply to a particular process and any other processes that it starts.

Environment variables are loaded when a process starts, and they are inherited by any process launched by the initial process. During program development, variables are loaded when you start Visual Studio. Their values are inherited by the program you are working on when you start it. If you make changes to the system's environment variables, you need to close and reopen Visual Studio before your program can see the changes.

A program can also create temporary process-level variables that are inherited by any processes you launch. Those values disappear when the original process ends.

A C# program can use the `System.Environment` class to read and write environment values. Before you learn how to use that class, however, you should learn how the operating system sets environment variables' values.

Setting Environment Variables

Environment variables are normally set on a systemwide basis before the program begins. In older operating systems, batch files such as autoexec.bat set these values. More recent systems provide Control Panel tools to set environment variables.

Newer systems also use an autoexec.nt file to set environment variables that apply only to command-line (console) applications, so they don't affect GUI applications. Sometimes, you can use this fact to your advantage by giving different kinds of applications different environment settings.

To set environment variables in newer versions of Windows, open the Control Panel, and search for the keyword "**environment**." In Windows 8, open the search tool, and search the Settings category for "**environment**." This search should produce two matches.

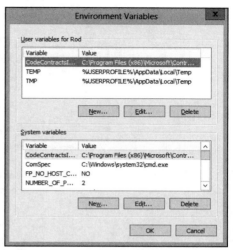

If you click the Edit the System Environment Variables choice, you should see the System Properties tool's Advanced tab. Now click the Environment Variables button to see the dialog, as shown in Figure 17-1.

If you click the Edit Environment Variables for Your Account choice, you should see a dialog similar to the one shown in Figure 17-1 except the bottom controls that modify the system's environment variables are disabled.

Use system variables when a value should apply to all processes started by all users. User user-level variables when a value should apply to all processes started by a particular user.

FIGURE 17-1: You can use system tools to set environment variables.

> **REFRESH REMINDER**
>
> Remember that Visual Studio won't see environment variable changes that you make after it is running. You need to close and reopen Visual Studio before your program will see the changes.

Using System.Environment

The `System.Environment` class provides methods for getting and setting process-level environment variables. It also provides properties and methods for working with many other items in the application's environment. The following table describes the `Environment` object's most useful properties.

PROPERTY	PURPOSE
CommandLine	Returns the process's command line.
CurrentDirectory	Gets or sets the fully qualified path to the current directory.
ExitCode	Gets or sets the processes' exit code.
HasShutdownStarted	Returns true if the Common Language Runtime is shutting down.
Is64BitOperatingSystem	Returns true if this is a 64-bit operating system.
Is64BitProcess	Returns true if the current process is a 64-bit process.

continues

(continued)

PROPERTY	PURPOSE
MachineName	Returns the computer's NetBIOS name.
NewLine	Returns the environment's defined new line string. For example, this might be a carriage return followed by a line feed.
OSVersion	Returns an `OperatingSystem` object containing information about the operating system. This object provides the properties `ServicePack` (name of the most recent service pack installed), `Version` (includes `Major`, `Minor`, `Build`, and `Revision`; `ToString` combines them all), `VersionString` (combines the operating system name, version, and most recent service pack), and `Platform`, which can be UNIX, Win32NT (Windows NT or later), Win32S (runs on 16-bit Windows to provide access to 32-bit applications), Win32Windows (Windows 95 or later), or WinCE.
ProcessorCount	Returns the number of processors on the computer.
StackTrace	Returns a string describing the current stack trace.
SystemDirectory	Returns the system directory's fully qualified path.
TickCount	Returns the number of milliseconds that have elapsed since the system started.
UserDomainName	Returns the current user's network domain name.
UserInteractive	Returns `true` if the process is interactive. This only returns `false` if the application is a service process or web service.
UserName	Returns the name of the user who started the process.
Version	Returns a `Version` object describing the Common Language Runtime. This object provides the properties `Major`, `Minor`, `Build`, and `Revision`. Its `ToString` method combines them all.
WorkingSet	Returns the amount of physical memory mapped to this process in bytes.

The following table describes the `System.Environment` object's most useful methods.

METHOD	PURPOSE
Exit	Ends the process immediately. `FormClosing` and `FormClosed` event handlers do not execute.

METHOD	PURPOSE

`ExpandEnvironmentVariables`	Replaces environment variable names in a string with their values. For example, the following code displays the name of the user and the computer:
	
	`MessageBox.Show(Environment`
	`.ExpandEnvironmentVariables("I am`
	`%username% on %computername%."))`

`GetCommandLineArgs`	Returns an array of strings containing the application's command-line arguments. The first entry (with index 0) is the name of the program's executable file.
`GetEnvironmentVariable`	Returns an environment variable's value.
`GetEnvironmentVariables`	Returns an `IDictionary` object containing the names and values of all environment variables. An optional parameter lets you determine whether you want to list variables defined for the machine, user, or process.
`GetFolderPath`	Returns the path to a system folder. This method's parameter is a `SpecialFolder` enumeration value such as `Cookies`, `Desktop`, `SendTo`, or `Recent`. See the online help for a complete list of available folders.
`GetLogicalDrives`	Returns an array of strings containing the names of the logical drives on the current computer.
`SetEnvironmentVariable`	Creates, modifies, or deletes an environment variable.

The `SetEnvironmentVariable` method lets you set environment variables at the system, user, and process levels. If you set a variable's value to `null`, this method deletes the variable. For system and user values, it updates the registry appropriately to set the values. For more information on the `SetEnvironmentVariable` method, see `msdn.microsoft.com/library/96xafkes.aspx`.

> **NOTE** *A program needs privilege to write to the registry to set a system-level environment variable.*

REGISTRY

The system registry is a hierarchical database that stores values for applications on the system. The hierarchy's root is named Computer and is divided into the several subtrees called *hives*. Which hives are available depends on your operating system. The following table summarizes the most commonly available hives. (The "HKEY" part of each name stands for "hive key.")

REGISTRY BRANCH	CONTAINS
HKEY_CLASSES_ROOT	Definitions of types of documents and properties associated with those types.
HKEY_CURRENT_CONFIG	Information about the system's current hardware configuration.
HKEY_CURRENT_USER	The current user's preferences (such as environment variable settings, program group information, desktop settings, colors, printers, network connections, and preferences specific to applications). Each user has a separate HKEY_CURRENT_USER hive.
HKEY_DYN_DATA	Performance data for Windows 95, 98, and Me. (Yes, this is a bit outdated but this hive is still there.)
HKEY_LOCAL_MACHINE	Information about the computer's physical state including bus type, system memory, installed hardware and software, and network logon and security information.
HKEY_USERS	Default configuration information for new users and the current user's configuration.

Depending on your operating system, the registry may also contain the unsupported keys HKEY_PERFORMANCE_DATA, HKEY_PERFORMANCE_NLSTEXT, and HKEY_PERFORMANCE_TEXT.

Many applications store information in the registry. The HKEY_CURRENT_USER subtree is particularly useful for storing individual users' preferences and other configuration information.

Lately, the registry has gone out of style for saving configuration information. Microsoft now recommends that you store this kind of data locally within a user's data storage area. This makes sense because it makes it easier to copy the settings (they're just files), helps reduce clutter in the registry, and reduces the chances that mistakes will corrupt the registry. (If the registry is corrupted badly enough, the system may become unbootable.) Instead of using the registry, you can store this information in configuration files (see the section "Configuration Files" later in this chapter) or XML files (see Chapter 24, "XML").

The keys to manipulating the registry are the `Registry` and `RegistryKey` classes in the `Microsoft.Win32` namespace.

The `Registry` class provides static fields that return `RegistryKey` objects representing the registry's hives. The following list describes the `Registry` class's hive fields.

FIELD	HKEY EQUIVALENT
ClassesRoot	HKEY_CLASSES_ROOT
CurrentConfig	HKEY_CURRENT_CONFIG
CurrentUser	HKEY_CURRENT_USER
DynData	HKEY_DYN_DATA

FIELD	HKEY EQUIVALENT
LocalMachine	HKEY_LOCAL_MACHINE
PerformanceData	HKEY_PERFORMANCE_DATA
Users	HKEY_USERS

Each registry key can contain values, subkeys, both, or neither. The `RegistryKey` class provides properties and methods that you can use to manipulate the key's values and subkeys. The following table summarizes the most useful `RegistryKey` properties and methods.

PROPERTY OR METHOD	PURPOSE
Close	Closes the key and flushes its data to the disk if it was modified
CreateSubKey	Creates a new subkey or opens an existing subkey for writing
DeleteSubKey	Deletes a subkey
DeleteSubKeyTree	Deletes a subkey and its subtree
DeleteValue	Deletes a value from the key
Dispose	Frees the object's resources
Flush	Writes the key's data to the disk
GetAccessControl	Returns access control security information for the key
GetSubKeyNames	Returns an array holding the key's subkey names
GetValue	Returns a value
GetValueKind	Returns a `RegistryValueKind` enumeration that indicates a value's type such as binary, multistring, or string
GetValueNames	Returns an array holding the key's value names
OpenSubKey	Opens a subkey
Name	Returns the key's name
SetAccessControl	Changes the key's access control security settings
SetValue	Sets a value for the key
SubKeyCount	Returns the key's number of subkeys
ValueCount	Returns the key's number of values

Using the `Registry` and `RegistryKey` classes is reasonably easy. Use a `Registry` field to get the hive you want to use. Use the `OpenSubKey` and `CreateSubKey` methods to create or open existing keys. Use `GetValue` and `SetValue` to get and set values. When you finish modifying a key, use its `Close` method to close it and ensure that the changes are written to disk.

POWERFUL PRIVILEGES

Windows protects the registry so that you cannot inadvertently damage critical values. If you mess up some values, you can wreak havoc on the operating system, and even make the system unbootable. To prevent possible chaos, newer versions of Windows don't let you edit some parts of the registry without elevated privileges.

Although the process is easy, it's also fairly awkward. You can make the process easier if you write `GetRegistryValue` and `SetRegistryValue` methods as shown in the following code.

```
public static class RegistryTools
{
    // Get a registry value.
    public static T GetRegistryValue<T>(RegistryKey hive,
        string subkeyName, string valueName, T defaultValue)
    {
        using (RegistryKey subkey = hive.OpenSubKey(subkeyName, false))
        {
            if (subkey == null) return defaultValue;
            T result = (T)subkey.GetValue(valueName, defaultValue);
            subkey.Close();
            return result;
        }
    }

    // Set a registry value.
    public static void SetRegistryValue<T>(RegistryKey hive,
        string subkeyName, string valueName, T value)
    {
        RegistryKey subkey = hive.OpenSubKey(subkeyName, true);
        if (subkey == null) subkey = hive.CreateSubKey(subkeyName);

        subkey.SetValue(valueName, value);
        subkey.Close();
        subkey.Dispose();
    }
}
```

A GENERIC TIP

These methods use a generic type parameter to make using them a bit more flexible. For example, when you invoke the `GetRegistryValue` method, the program can infer the data type `T` by the type of the final parameter. The method can then return the appropriate data type, so the program doesn't need to cast the result into the correct data type.

The following code uses the `GetRegistryValue` method to retrieve the value `Left` from the `Software\C# Projects\SaveRegistrySettings\Settings` key in the HKEY_CURRENT_USER hive.

```
int left = RegistryTools.GetRegistryValue(Registry.CurrentUser,
    @"Software\C# Projects\SaveRegistrySettings\Settings",
    "Left", 0);
```

Notice that the code specifies the complete path to the key. The code doesn't need to slowly move down through the registry hierarchy one key at a time.

Here I picked the location `Software\C# Projects\SaveRegistrySettings\Settings` somewhat arbitrarily. The HKEY_CURRENT_USER hive already contains a `Software` key. I added the subkey `C# Projects` to hold values saved by my C# projects. Inside that the subkey `SaveRegistrySettings` holds values saved by the SaveRegistrySettings example program, which is available for download on this book's website. The final subkey, `Settings`, holds setting values for the program.

Even the preceding code is somewhat more verbose than really needed by the example program because every call to get or set a registry value will use the same hive and key. To make things even easier, the program defines the following two helper methods.

```
// Get a registry value.
private T GetValue<T>(string name, T defaultValue)
{
    return RegistryTools.GetRegistryValue(Registry.CurrentUser,
        @"Software\C# Projects\SaveRegistrySettings\Settings",
        name, defaultValue);
}

// Save a registry value.
private void SetValue<T>(string name, T value)
{
    RegistryTools.SetRegistryValue(Registry.CurrentUser,
        @"Software\C# Projects\SaveRegistrySettings\Settings",
        name, value);
}
```

These methods simply call the methods defined in the `RegistryTools` class, passing them the correct hive and subkey path.

The program provides two buttons that let you set the form's foreground and background colors. Then when the program starts and stops, it gets and sets the saved colors plus the form's size and position. The following code shows how the program saves these values when the form is about to close.

```
// Save the current settings.
private void Form1_FormClosing(object sender,
    System.Windows.Forms.FormClosingEventArgs e)
{
    SetValue("Width", this.Width);
    SetValue("Height", this.Height);
    SetValue("Left", this.Left);
    SetValue("Top", this.Top);
    SetValue("BackColor", this.BackColor.ToArgb());
    SetValue("ForeColor", this.ForeColor.ToArgb());
}
```

The following code shows how the program restores those values when it next starts.

```
// Restore saved settings.
private void Form1_Load(object sender, EventArgs e)
{
    // Allow the form to position itself.
    this.StartPosition = FormStartPosition.Manual;

    this.Width = GetValue("Width", this.Width);
    this.Height = GetValue("Height", this.Height);
    this.Left = GetValue("Left", this.Left);
    this.Top = GetValue("Top", this.Top);
    this.BackColor = Color.FromArgb(
        GetValue("BackColor", this.BackColor.ToArgb()));
    this.ForeColor = Color.FromArgb(
        GetValue("ForeColor", this.ForeColor.ToArgb()));
}
```

NEATNESS COUNTS

As part of its uninstallation procedure, a program should remove any registry entries it has made. All too often, programs leave the registry cluttered with garbage. This not only makes it harder to figure out what real values the registry contains but can also slow the system down.

In an attempt to combat this problem, Microsoft is promoting Xcopy compatibility, where applications store values in configuration files instead of the registry. Then you can easily copy and remove these files rather than modify the registry.

CONFIGURATION FILES

A configuration file stores information for a program to use at run time. You can change the values in the configuration file and restart the program to make it use the new values. That lets you modify the application's behavior without needing to recompile the executable program.

The easiest way to use configuration files is through dynamic properties. Your program automatically loads dynamic properties at run time from the configuration file.

To define the settings you need to bind to the dynamic properties, use Project ➪ Properties, and click the Settings tab to see the property page shown in Figure 17-2. Use this page to define the configuration settings to load at run time.

If you give a setting the Application scope, its value is shared by all users. Settings with User scope are stored separately for each user, so different users can use and modify their own values.

After you define the settings, add a control to a form and select it. In the Properties window, expand the ApplicationSettings entry at the top, click the PropertyBinding subitem, and click the ellipsis to the right to display a list of the control's properties.

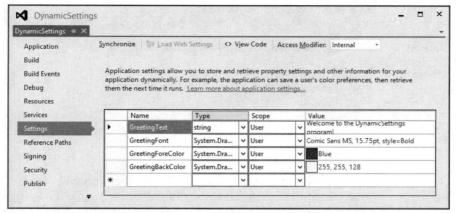

FIGURE 17-2: Use the Settings page to define values that are stored in a configuration file.

Select a property that you want to load dynamically, and click the drop-down arrow on the right to see a list of defined settings that you might assign to the property. Figure 17-3 shows the Application Settings dialog box with this drop-down list displayed for a control's `ForeColor` property. From the list, select the setting that you want to assign to the property.

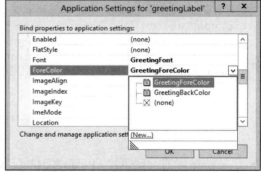

FIGURE 17-3: Use the drop-down list to assign a setting to a dynamic property.

Visual Studio adds the setting to the program's configuration file. If you open Solution Explorer and double-click the app.config entry, you see the dynamic properties.

The following text shows the configuration setting sections of an `App.config` file. The `userSettings` section defines the settings shown in Figure 17-2.

```xml
<?xml version="1.0" encoding="utf-8" ?>
<configuration>
    <configSections>
        ...
    </configSections>
    <startup>
        <supportedRuntime version="v4.0" sku=".NETFramework,Version=v4.5" />
    </startup>
    <userSettings>
        <DynamicSettings.Properties.Settings>
            <setting name="GreetingText" serializeAs="String">
                <value>Welcome to the DynamicSettings program!</value>
            </setting>
```

```
            <setting name="GreetingFont" serializeAs="String">
                <value>Comic Sans MS, 15.75pt, style=Bold</value>
            </setting>
            <setting name="GreetingForeColor" serializeAs="String">
                <value>Blue</value>
            </setting>
            <setting name="GreetingBackColor" serializeAs="String">
                <value>255, 255, 128</value>
            </setting>
        </DynamicSettings.Properties.Settings>
    </userSettings>
</configuration>
```

When you build the program, Visual Studio copies the App.config file into the executable directory and gives it the same name as the program with .config added at the end. For example, the config file for the DynamicSettings example program, which is available for download on this book's website, is called DynamicSettings.config. When the program starts, it loads the config file if it is present, reads the settings, and assigns their values to any properties bound to them.

So far, this is just a roundabout way to set the control's property values. The real benefit of this method comes later when you want to change a setting. Simply edit the config file in the program's executable directory and make any changes you want. Now when you run the program, it uses the new settings. Instead of recompiling the whole application, you only need to change the config file. If you have distributed the application to a large number of users, you only need to give them the revised configuration file and not a whole new executable.

Your program can also access the program's settings as shown in the following code.

```
MessageBox.Show(Properties.Settings.Default.GreetingText);
```

MULTIPLE CONFIGURATION FILES

You could define multiple config files and load them separately. For example, you might use one config file to hold properties used in one part of a program and use a second file to hold properties used by another part of the program.

However, loading config files manually takes some extra work and you don't gain much. Configuration files are just specially formatted XML files. Instead of using config files, you could store settings in some other XML file or in a serialization file. Chapter 24 explains how you can read XML files. Chapter 25, "Serialization," explains how to serialize and deserialize objects in files.

All the settings you defined are available in `Properties.Settings.Default`, and all are strongly typed, so you don't need to convert them from strings or objects into their correct types.

The `Properties.Settings.Default` object provides two other methods that can be useful for working with settings. First, the `Reload` method reloads the settings from the config file. This is useful if the program has modified the settings and you want to reload their original values.

Second, the `Save` method saves any changes the program has made into the config file. This method can save only settings that have User scope. Settings with Application scope are read-only.

When a program closes, it automatically saves any changes to User scope settings. However, if the program crashes, it does not have a chance to save any changes. If you want to be sure changes are saved, call `Properties.Settings.Default.Save` after the settings have been changed.

RESOURCE FILES

Like config files, resource files contain values that the application loads at run time. Config files are intended to let you tweak one or two settings. The intent of resource files is to let you easily replace a whole set of resources with another without recompiling.

One of the most common uses of resource files is to provide different resources for different languages. To create installation packages for different languages, you simply ship the executable and a resource file that uses the right language. Alternatively, you can ship resource files for all the languages you support and then let the application pick the appropriate file at run time based on the user's computer settings.

Resource files are not intended to store application configuration information and settings. They are intended to hold values that you might want to change, but only infrequently. You should store frequently changing data in configuration files or the system registry rather than in resource files.

The distinction is small and frankly somewhat arbitrary. Both configuration files and resource files store data that you can swap without recompiling the application. Rebuilding resource files can be a little more complex, however, so perhaps the distinction that configuration and setting data changes more frequently makes some sense.

Resource files can also be embedded within a compiled application. In that case, you cannot swap the resource file without recompiling the application. Although this makes embedded resource files less useful for storing frequently changing information, they still give you a convenient place to group resource data within the application. This is particularly useful if several parts of the application must use the same pieces of data. For example, if every form should display the same background image, it makes sense to store the image in a common resource file that they can all use.

The following sections describe the three most common types of resources: application, embedded, and localization.

Application Resources

To create application resources in C#, select Project ➪ Properties, and click the Resources tab. Use the drop-down on the left to select one of the resource categories: Strings, Images, Icons, Audio, Files, or Other. Figure 17-4 shows the application's Resources tab displaying the application's images.

To add an existing file to the program's resources, click the Add Resource drop-down list, and select Add Existing File. Use the drop-down's Add New String, Add New Icon, or Add New Text File commands to add new items from scratch. The drop-down's New Image item opens a cascading submenu that lets you create new PNG, BMP, GIF, JPEG, and TIFF images.

FIGURE 17-4: Use the Resources tab to define images and other resources used by the application.

When you create application resources, Visual Studio automatically generates code that adds strongly typed resource properties to the `Properties.Resources` class. Your program can use those resources as needed. For example, the ApplicationResources example program, which is available for download on this book's website, uses the following code to make its form display the image resource named HalfJack2.

```
private void Form1_Load(object sender, EventArgs e)
{
    this.BackgroundImage = Properties.Resources.HalfJack2;
}
```

Embedded Resources

Normally, when you add a resource to a program, Visual Studio stores it in the file Resources.resx. (You can see that file in Project Explorer if you expand the Properties entry. Double-clicking that file opens the Resources property page.)

You can also add other resource files to the application. Select Project ⇨ Add New Item. Pick the Resources File template, give the file a meaningful name, and click OK.

After you add a resource file to the project, you can double-click it in Solution Explorer to open it in the resource editor. Then you can add resources to the file exactly as you do for the application's resource file.

Just as it generates strongly typed properties for application resources, Visual Studio generates similar code for other embedded resource files. You can access these properties by adding the resource file's name after the resource file's name. For example, to use the image resource named `Logo` from the Images resource file, the program would use `Images.Logo`.

Localization Resources

One of the most important reasons for inventing resource files was to allow localization: supporting different text, images, and other items for different languages and cultures. Resources make localization in Visual Studio .NET easy.

First, create a form using whatever language you typically use from day to day. For me, that's English as spoken in the United States. Open the form in the form designer and give it whatever controls you need. Set the form's and controls' properties as usual.

Next, set the form's `Localizable` property to `true` and set the form's `Language` property to the first language you want to support other than the default language that you have been working with so far. Modify the controls' properties for the new language.

As you modify a form, Visual Studio saves the changes you make to a new resource file attached to the form. If you open Solution Explorer and expand the form's entry, you can see these resource files below the form's file.

Example program Localized uses default settings for United States English. It also includes localizations for generic German (as opposed to German as spoken in Switzerland, Germany, Liechtenstein, or some other country). If you expand the form's entry in Solution Explorer, you'll find the files `Form1.resx` holding the default settings and `Form1.de.resx` holding the German settings.

When you build the program, Visual Studio compiles the resources and saves them in a DLL file named Localized.resources.dll in a directory named after the locale. (The "Localized" part of the file's name comes from the program's name.) At run time, the application automatically checks the computer's regional settings and selects the resource file that matches most closely.

For example, suppose your computer is configured for the German/Switzerland (de-CH) locale. The program first looks for Localized.resources.dll in a subdirectory named de-CH. If it doesn't find the DLL, it looks for the generic German resources DLL in the subdirectory de (the code for generic German). If the program still can't find a resource DLL, it uses the default implementation that is included in the form itself.

Later, if you need to modify the resources for a locale, you can rebuild the application and then copy the new Localized.resources.dll into the appropriate subdirectory.

Normally, you should let the application pick the appropriate resource file automatically, but you can explicitly select a resource file for testing purposes. To do that, open the form's code file and add the following using directives.

```
using System.Threading;
using System.Globalization;
```

Next, find the form's constructor and add the bold lines shown in the following code.

```
public Form1()
{
    // Set the culture and UI culture to German.
    Thread.CurrentThread.CurrentCulture = new CultureInfo("de-DE");
    Thread.CurrentThread.CurrentUICulture = new CultureInfo("de-DE");

    InitializeComponent();
}
```

Now when the form is created, it loads the resources for the German de-DE localization. (The Localized example program includes these lines commented out. Uncomment them to make the program load the German localization.)

CULTURE COMES FIRST

The program must set the culture and user interface culture before it calls `InitializeComponent` because `InitializeComponent` is where the program sets the form and control properties.

For a list of culture codes, see `msdn.microsoft.com/library/ee825488.aspx`.

SUMMARY

Visual Studio provides many ways to store application configuration and resource information. Some of the most useful of these methods include environment variables, the registry, configuration files, and resource files.

The registry and configuration files generally hold user-specific information that changes relatively often. You can use them to store information such as user preferences and form layout.

You can store less volatile resources that determine the application's appearance in resource files. You can use embedded resource files to hold images, strings, audio, and other resources.

If you will distribute the application in multiple languages, localized resource files make displaying locale-appropriate resources easier. If necessary, you can change the data stored in configuration and resource files and redistribute them to your users without rebuilding the entire application.

Using all these techniques, you can make your application easily configurable. You can satisfy the needs of different kinds of users and customize the application without recompiling it.

This chapter explained ways that a program can save configuration and resource information using tools such as the registry, environment variables, and resource files. Generally, these kinds of data are of relatively limited size. If an application needs to store larger amounts of data, it should probably use a database or file.

The next chapter explains classes that a C# application can use to work with stream data in general and files in particular. Using streams attached to files, a program can read and write large amounts of data without cluttering up the registry, environment variables, or resource files.

EXERCISES

1. Write a program that lists all the environment variables at the machine, user, and process levels.

2. Write a program that displays the version of Visual Studio that it is running. (Hint: Look through the environment variables until you find the one you need.) What happens if you run the program by double-clicking the compiled executable? Why does that happen?

3. If you type the name of a program at a command prompt, the operating system checks the locations defined by the PATH environment variable to try to find the program. Write a program that displays the paths listed in the PATH variable.

4. Write a program that has TextBoxes for first name, last name, street, city, and ZIP code. Also give it a ComboBox for selecting a state. Make the program load and save the controls' values when it starts and stops. (Hint: You don't need to save and restore each value separately. Instead loop through the form's Controls collection and save and restore the value for TextBoxes and ComboBoxes.)

5. Write a program that displays a label with the font loaded from a configuration file. Initially, use 20-point Times New Roman and run the program. Then manually edit the config file to use 30-point Comic Sans MS and run the compiled executable. What happens if you then run the program from Visual Studio? What happens if you delete the config file and run the compiled executable? What happens if you then run the program from Visual Studio?

6. Localization lets you localize control properties, but you can use a similar technique to localize resources that are not stored in control properties. Create a program, add a new resource file named MyStrings.resx, and give it a string resource named Greeting with value "Hello." Now create a second resource file named MyStrings.fr.resx, and give it a string resource named Greeting with value Salut. In the form's Load event handler, display the value in a message box. What happens when your program loads the French locale (fr-FR)? What localization directories and files does Visual Studio create?

7. Setting the current thread's culture does more than make the program load the right localized resources. It also makes locale-aware methods such as those that use standard number, currency, and date formats display results that are appropriate for the locale.

Write a program that displays the locale, current date, and the currency amount 12,345.67 in each of the following locales: fr-FR, de-DE, de-CH, es-MX, es-ES, en-US, and en-GB. (Hint: Set the CurrentCulture as shown in the section "Localization Resources." Use the ToShortDateString method to format the date. Use ToString("C") to format the currency value.)

18

Streams

WROX.COM DOWNLOADS FOR THIS CHAPTER

Please note that all the code examples for this chapter are available as a part of this chapter's code download on the book's website at `www.wrox.com/go/csharp5programmersref` on the Download Code tab.

At a basic level, all pieces of data are just collections of bytes. The computer doesn't actually store invoices, employee records, and recipes. At its most basic level, the computer stores bytes of information. (Or even bits, but the computer naturally groups them in bytes.) It is only when a program interprets those bytes that they acquire a higher-level meaning that is valuable to the user.

Usually it's not helpful to treat high-level data as undifferentiated bytes, but there are times when it's useful to ignore the higher-level structure of the data and treat it as just a bunch of bytes.

One important way of thinking about data is the *stream*, an ordered series of bytes. Files, data flowing across a network, messages moving through a queue, and even the memory in an array can all fit this description.

Defining the abstract idea of a stream lets applications handle these different types of objects uniformly. For example, a cryptographic algorithm can process the bytes in a stream without knowing whether they represent employees, prescription information, or an image.

Visual Studio provides several classes for manipulating different kinds of streams. It also provides higher-level classes for working with streams that represent specific kinds of data. For example, it includes classes for working with streams that represent text files.

This chapter describes some of the classes you can use to manipulate streams. It explains lower-level classes that you may use only rarely and higher-level classes that let you read and write strings and files relatively easily.

The following table summarizes the most useful stream classes.

CLASS	USE
Stream	The parent class of other stream classes. Tools that manipulate streams in the most general way work with Stream objects.
FileStream	Read and write bytes in a file.
MemoryStream	Read and write bytes in memory.
BinaryReader, BinaryWriter	Read and write specific data types in a stream.
StringReader, StringWriter	Read and write text with or without new lines in a string.
StreamReader, StreamWriter	Read and write text with or without new lines in a stream (usually a file stream).

> **TIP** *All these classes are in the* System.IO *namespace, so if you use them, you may want to include the following* using *directive in your code.*
>
> ```
> using System.IO;
> ```

The following sections describe some of these classes in greater detail.

STREAM

The Stream class defines properties and methods that derived stream classes must provide. These let the program perform relatively generic tasks with streams such as determining whether the stream allows writing and deciding when the stream has reached its end.

The following table describes the Stream class's most useful properties.

PROPERTY	PURPOSE
CanRead	True if the stream supports reading.
CanSeek	True if the stream supports seeking to a particular position in the stream.
CanTimeout	True if the stream supports timing out of read and write operations.
CanWrite	True if the stream supports writing.

PROPERTY	PURPOSE
Length	The number of bytes in the stream.
Position	The stream's current position. For a stream that supports seeking, the program can set this value to move to a particular position.
ReadTimeout	The number of milliseconds that a read operation waits before timing out.
WriteTimeout	The number of milliseconds that a write operation waits before timing out.

The following table describes the Stream class's most useful methods.

METHOD	PURPOSE
BeginRead	Starts an asynchronous read.
BeginWrite	Starts an asynchronous write.
Close	Closes the stream and releases its resources.
Dispose	Releases the stream's resources.
EndRead	Waits for an asynchronous read to finish.
EndWrite	Ends an asynchronous write.
Flush	Flushes data from the stream's buffers into the underlying storage such as a file or piece of memory.
Read	Reads bytes from the stream and advances its position by that number of bytes.
ReadByte	Reads a byte from the stream and advances its position by one byte.
Seek	If the stream supports seeking, sets the stream's position.
SetLength	Sets the stream's length. If the stream is currently longer than the new length, it is truncated. If the stream is shorter than the new length, it is enlarged. The stream must support both writing and seeking for this method to work.
Write	Writes bytes into the stream and advances the current position by this number of bytes.
WriteByte	Writes 1 byte into the stream and advances the current position by 1 byte.

PROPER CLEANUP

Because the `Stream` class has a `Dispose` method, you should use it when you are done with the object. You can use the `using` statement to make disposing of the object automatic.

To clean up properly, the `Dispose` method flushes any buffered output and closes the stream. That means if you call `Dispose`, you don't need to call `Flush` or `Close`.

For more information about the `Stream` class, see `msdn.microsoft.com/system.io.stream.aspx`.

FILESTREAM

The `FileStream` class represents a stream associated with a file. Its parent class `Stream` defines most of its properties and methods. See the preceding section for descriptions of those properties and methods.

`FileStream` adds two useful new properties to those it inherits from `Stream`. First, `IsAsync` returns `true` if the `FileStream` was opened asynchronously. Second, the `Name` property returns the name of the file passed into the object's constructor.

The class also adds two new, useful methods to those it inherits from `Stream`. The `Lock` method locks the file, so other processes can read it but not modify it. `Unlock` removes a previous lock.

Overloaded versions of the `FileStream` class's constructor let you specify the following.

➤ A filename or file handle

➤ File mode (`Append`, `Create`, `CreateNew`, `Open`, `OpenOrCreate`, or `Truncate`)

➤ Access mode (`Read`, `Write`, or `ReadWrite`)

➤ File sharing (`Inheritable`, which allows child processes to inherit the file handle; `None`; `Read`; `Write`; or `ReadWrite`)

➤ Buffer size

➤ File options (`Asynchronous`, `DeleteOnClose`, `Encrypted`, `None`, `RandomAccess`, `SequentialScan`, or `WriteThrough`)

Example program WriteIntoFileStream, which is available for download on this book's website, uses the following code to create and write into a text file.

```
string filename = filenameTextBox.Text;
using (FileStream filestream = new FileStream(filename, FileMode.Create))
{
    byte[] bytes = new UTF8Encoding().GetBytes(textTextBox.Text);
    filestream.Write(bytes, 0, bytes.Length);
}
```

This code gets the file's name from the `filenameTextBox`. It passes the name and the file access parameter `Create` to the `FileStream` constructor.

The `UTF8Encoding` object represents UTF-8 encoded characters. The code creates such an object and uses its `GetBytes` method to create a byte array representing the text in `textTextBox`.

The code then writes the bytes into the file stream. The `using` statement ensures that the stream is disposed, and that flushes and closes the stream.

> **NOTE** *The 8-bit UTF encoding is the most popular type on the web; although, there are other encoding formats such as UTF-7 and UTF-16. For additional information, see* `unicode.org/faq/utf_bom.html` *and* `en.wikipedia.org/wiki/Unicode`.

As this example demonstrates, the `FileStream` class provides only low-level methods for reading and writing files. These methods let you read and write bytes, but not integers, strings, or the other types of data that you are more likely to want to use.

The `BinaryReader` and `BinaryWriter` classes make it easier to work with binary data. Similarly, the `StringReader` and `StringWriter` classes make it easier to work with strings. See the sections "`BinaryReader` and `BinaryWriter`" and "`StringReader` and `StringWriter`" later in this chapter for more information on those classes.

MEMORYSTREAM

The `MemoryStream` class represents a stream with data stored in memory. Like the `FileStream` class, it provides relatively primitive methods for reading and writing data. Usually, you'll want to attach a higher-level object to the `MemoryStream` to make it easier to use.

Example program WriteIntoMemoryStream, which is available for download on this book's website, uses the following code to write and read from a `MemoryStream` object.

```
// Create the stream.
MemoryStream stream = new MemoryStream();

// Write into the stream.
BinaryWriter writer = new BinaryWriter(stream);
writer.Write(textTextBox.Text);

// Read from the stream.
stream.Seek(0, SeekOrigin.Begin);
BinaryReader reader = new BinaryReader(stream);
MessageBox.Show(reader.ReadString());

// Clean up.
writer.Dispose();
reader.Dispose();
stream.Dispose();
```

The code first creates a MemoryStream. It then creates a BinaryWriter associated with the stream and uses its Write method to write a string into it.

Next, the code uses the Seek method to rewind the stream to the beginning of the data. It then creates a BinaryReader associated with the stream, uses its ReadString method to read a string from the stream, and displays the string in a message box.

The code finishes by disposing of the objects it used. This is a bit more confusing than usual because the reader and writer are associated with the stream. When the program disposes of the reader or writer, those objects automatically close their underlying stream. That means you cannot dispose of the writer before you finish with the reader. If you are careful, you can use a properly ordered sequence of using statements, but this example seems simpler if you just dispose of the objects all at once at the end.

BINARYREADER AND BINARYWRITER

The BinaryReader and BinaryWriter classes are helper classes that work with stream classes. They provide an interface that makes it easier to read and write data in a stream. For example, the BinaryReader class's ReadInt32 method reads a 4-byte (32-bit) signed integer from the stream. Similarly, the ReadUInt16 method reads a 2-byte (16-bit) unsigned integer.

These classes still work at a relatively low level, and you should generally use higher-level classes to read and write data if possible. For example, you shouldn't tie yourself to a particular representation of an integer (32- or 16-bit) unless you must.

Both the BinaryReader and BinaryWriter classes have a BaseStream property that returns a reference to the underlying stream. Note that their Close and Dispose methods automatically close their underlying streams.

The following table describes the BinaryReader class's most useful methods.

METHOD	PURPOSE
Close	Closes the BinaryReader and its underlying stream.
PeekChar	Reads the stream's next character but does not advance the reader's position.
Read	Reads characters from the stream and advances the reader's position.
ReadBoolean	Reads a bool from the stream and advances the reader's position by 1 byte.
ReadByte	Reads a byte from the stream and advances the reader's position by 1 byte.

METHOD	PURPOSE
ReadBytes	Reads a specified number of `bytes` from the stream into a `byte` array and advances the reader's position by that number of bytes.
ReadChar	Reads a `char` from the stream and advances the reader's position appropriately for the stream's encoding.
ReadChars	Reads a specified number of `chars` from the stream, returns the results in a `char` array, and advances the reader's position appropriately for the stream's encoding.
ReadDecimal	Reads a `decimal` value from the stream and advances the reader's position by 16 bytes.
ReadDouble	Reads an 8-byte `double` from the stream and advances the reader's position by 8 bytes.
ReadInt16	Reads a 2-byte `short` from the stream and advances the reader's position by 2 bytes.
ReadInt32	Reads a 4-byte `int` from the stream and advances the reader's position by 4 bytes.
ReadInt64	Reads an 8-byte `long` from the stream and advances the reader's position by 8 bytes.
ReadSByte	Reads a signed `sbyte` from the stream and advances the reader's position by 1 byte.
ReadSingle	Reads a 4-byte `float` from the stream and advances the reader's position by 4 bytes.
ReadString	Reads a `string` from the current stream and advances the reader's position past it.
ReadUInt16	Reads a 2-byte unsigned `ushort` from the stream and advances the reader's position by 2 bytes.
ReadUInt32	Reads a 4-byte unsigned `uint` from the stream and advances the reader's position by 4 bytes.
ReadUInt64	Reads an 8-byte unsigned `ulong` from the stream and advances the reader's position by 8 bytes.

The following table describes the `BinaryWriter` class's most useful methods.

METHOD	PURPOSE
Close	Closes the `BinaryWriter` and its underlying stream.
Flush	Writes any buffered data into the underlying stream.
Seek	Sets the position within the stream.
Write	Writes a value into the stream. This method has many overloaded versions to write `char`, `char[]`, `int`, `string`, `ulong`, and other data types into the stream.

For more information about these classes, see `msdn.microsoft.com/system.io.binarywriter .aspx` and `msdn.microsoft.com/system.io.binaryreader.aspx`.

TEXTREADER AND TEXTWRITER

Like the `BinaryReader` and `BinaryWriter` classes, the `TextReader` and `TextWriter` classes provide an interface for an underlying stream. As you can probably guess from their names, these classes provide methods for working with text.

`TextReader` and `TextWriter` are abstract classes, so you cannot create instances of them. They define behaviors for the derived classes that you can instantiate.

For example, the `StringWriter` and `StreamWriter` classes derived from `TextWriter` let a program write characters into a string or stream, respectively.

Normally, you would use these derived classes to read and write text, but you might want to use the `TextReader` or `TextWriter` classes to manipulate the underlying classes more generically. You may also find .NET Framework methods that require a `TextReader` or `TextWriter` object as a parameter. In that case, you could pass the method either a `StringReader`/`StringWriter` or a `StreamReader`/`StreamWriter`. (For more information on these classes, see the sections "StringReader and StringWriter" and "StreamReader and StreamWriter" later in this chapter.)

The following table describes the `TextReader` class's most useful methods.

METHOD	PURPOSE
Close	Closes the reader and releases its resources.
Peek	Reads the next character from the input without changing the reader's state, so other methods can read the character later.

METHOD	PURPOSE
Read	Reads data from the input. Overloaded versions of this method read a single char or an array of char up to a specified length.
ReadBlock	Reads data from the input into an array of char.
ReadLine	Reads a line of characters from the input and returns the data in a string.
ReadToEnd	Reads any remaining characters in the input and returns them in a string.

The TextWriter class has three useful properties. Encoding specifies the text's encoding (ASCII, UTF-8, Unicode, and so forth).

The FormatProvider property returns an object that controls formatting. For example, you can build a FormatProvider object that knows how to display numbers in different bases (such as hexadecimal or octal).

The NewLine property gets or sets the string used by the writer to end lines. Usually, this value is something similar to a carriage return or a carriage return plus a line feed.

The following table describes the TextWriter class's most useful methods.

METHOD	PURPOSE
Close	Closes the writer and releases its resources.
Flush	Writes any buffered data into the underlying stream.
Write	Writes a value into the stream. This method has many overloaded versions that write char, char[], int, string, ulong, and other data types.
WriteLine	Writes data into the output followed by the new-line sequence.

For more information about the TextWriter and TextReader classes, see msdn.microsoft.com/system.io.textwriter.aspx and msdn.microsoft.com/system.io.textreader.aspx.

STRINGREADER AND STRINGWRITER

The StringReader and StringWriter classes let a program read and write text in a string.

These classes are derived from TextReader and TextWriter, so they inherit most of their properties and methods from those classes. See the preceding section for details.

The StringReader class provides methods for reading lines, characters, or blocks of characters from a string. The StringReader class's constructor takes as a parameter the string that it should process. Its ReadToEnd method returns the part of the string that has not already been read.

The StringWriter class lets an application build a string. It provides methods to write text into the string with or without a new-line sequence afterward. Its ToString method returns the string represented by the object.

The StringWriter stores its string in an underlying StringBuilder object. The StringBuilder class is designed to make incrementally building a string more efficient than building a string by concatenating a series of values onto a string variable. For example, if an application needs to build a large string by concatenating a series of long substrings, it may be more efficient to use a StringBuilder rather than add the strings to a normal string variable by using the + operator. StringWriter provides a simple interface to the StringBuilder class.

The most useful method provided by StringWriter that is not defined by the TextWriter parent class is GetStringBuilder. This method returns a reference to the underlying StringBuilder object that holds the object's data.

Example program StringWriterAndReader, which is available for download on this book's website, uses the following code to demonstrate the StringWriter and StringReader classes.

```
// Use a StringWriter to write into a string.
using (StringWriter writer = new StringWriter())
{
    // Write the strings entered by the user.
    writer.WriteLine(textBox1.Text);
    writer.WriteLine(textBox2.Text);
    writer.WriteLine(textBox3.Text);

    // Display the result.
    string result = writer.ToString();
    MessageBox.Show(result);

    // Read the result with a StringReader.
    using (StringReader reader = new StringReader(result))
    {
        // Read one line.
        MessageBox.Show(reader.ReadLine());
        // Read the rest.
        MessageBox.Show(reader.ReadToEnd());
    }
}
```

The code starts by creating a StringWriter and using its WriteLine method three times to add the text entered by the user in TextBoxes to the string.

The code then saves the StringWriter's underlying string into the variable result and displays it in a message box.

Next, the code creates a StringReader associated with the result string. It uses the reader's ReadLine method to read one line from the string and displays it. The program finishes by using the ReadToEnd method to read and display the rest of the string.

STREAMREADER AND STREAMWRITER

The `StreamReader` and `StreamWriter` classes let a program read and write data in a stream, usually a `FileStream`. You can pass a `FileStream` into these classes' constructors, or you can pass a filename and the object creates a `FileStream` automatically.

The `StreamReader` class provides methods for reading lines, characters, or blocks of characters from the stream. Its `ReadToEnd` method returns any parts of the stream that have not already been read. The `EndOfStream` property is `true` when the `StreamReader` has reached the end of its stream.

Example program ReadLines, which is available for download on this book's website, uses the following code fragment to read the lines from a file and add them to a `ListBox` control.

```
using (StreamReader reader = new StreamReader("Animals.txt"))
{
    // Read until we reach the end of the file.
    do
    {
        animalListBox.Items.Add(reader.ReadLine());
    }
    while (!reader.EndOfStream);
}
```

The `StreamWriter` class provides methods to write text into the stream with or without a new-line character.

`StreamReader` and `StreamWriter` are derived from the `TextReader` and `TextWriter` classes and inherit most of their properties and methods from those classes. See the section "`TextReader` and `TextWriter`" earlier in this chapter for a description of those properties and methods.

The `StreamWriter` class adds a new `AutoFlush` property that determines whether the writer flushes its buffer after every write. This is useful if the program periodically writes to the same file and you want to make sure the contents are flushed. For example, a program could write into a log file every few minutes. If you set `AutoFlush` to `true`, then the output is always written into the file, so you can use Notepad or some other program to look at the file and see the latest entries.

Example program WriteLog, which is available for download on this book's website, uses the following code to demonstrate the `StreamWriter` class's `AutoFlush` property.

```
// The log file stream.
private StreamWriter Writer;

// Open the log file.
private void Form1_Load(object sender, EventArgs e)
{
    Writer = new StreamWriter("Log.txt", true);
    Writer.AutoFlush = true;
}

// Write an entry into the log.
private void writeButton_Click(object sender, EventArgs e)
{
    Writer.WriteLine(DateTime.Now.ToString() + ": " + entryTextBox.Text);
```

```
        entryTextBox.Clear();
        entryTextBox.Focus();
    }

    // Close the log file.
    private void Form1_FormClosing(object sender, FormClosingEventArgs e)
    {
        Writer.Dispose();
    }
```

The program's `Form_Load` event handler opens the log file and sets the `StreamWriter`'s `AutoFlush` property to `true`.

When you click its Write button, the program adds the current time and the text you entered in the `TextBox` to the log file.

The program's `FormClosing` event handler disposes of the `StreamWriter`.

While the program is running, use Notepad to view the log file and see the most recent entries. Comment out the code that sets `AutoFlush` to `true` and run the program again to see what happens.

EXISTS, OPENTEXT, CREATETEXT, AND APPENDTEXT

The `System.IO.File` class provides four shared methods that are particularly useful for working with `StreamReader` and `StreamWriter` objects associated with text files. The following table summarizes these four methods.

METHOD	PURPOSE
Exists	Returns `true` if a file with a given path exists
OpenText	Returns a `StreamReader` that reads from an existing text file
CreateText	Creates a new text file, overwriting the file if it exists, and returns a `StreamWriter` that lets you write into the new file
AppendText	Opens or creates the file and returns a `StreamWriter` that lets you append text at the end of the file

MAKE SURE IT EXISTS

Before you try to open a file, use `File.Exists` to see if it's there. Testing to see whether the file exists is faster and more proactive than using a `try catch` block.

Of course, you should still probably use a `try catch` block in case you cannot open the file, for example, if it is locked by another program.

CUSTOM STREAM CLASSES

The .NET Framework also provides a few other stream classes with more specialized uses.

The CryptoStream class applies a cryptographic transformation to the data passing through it. For example, if you attach a CryptoStream to a file, the CryptoStream can automatically encrypt or decrypt the data as it reads or writes to the file. (Chapter 27, "Cryptography," has more to say about cryptography.)

The NetworkStream class represents a socket-based stream over a network connection. You can use this class to make different applications communicate over a network. For more information about this class, see msdn.microsoft.com/library/system.net.sockets.networkstream.aspx.

Three special streams represent a program's standard input, standard output, and standard error. Console applications define these streams for reading and writing information to and from the console. Applications can also interact directly with these streams by accessing the Console class's In, Out, and Error properties. A program can change those streams to new stream objects such as StreamReaders and StreamWriters by calling the Console class's SetIn, SetOut, and SetError methods. For example, a program could redirect the error stream into a file. For more information on these streams, see msdn.microsoft.com/library/system.console.aspx.

> **STANDARD NAMES**
>
> Sometimes programmers refer to the standard output, input, and error streams by their traditional names: stdin, stdout, and stderr.

SUMMARY

Streams let a program treat a wide variety of data sources in a uniform way. That's useful for generalizable methods such as cryptographic algorithms or data compression routines, but in practice you often want to use specialized classes that make working with particular kinds of data easier.

For example, the StringReader and StringWriter classes read and write text in strings, and the StreamReader and StreamWriter classes read and write text in streams (usually files). The File class's Exists, OpenText, CreateText, and AppendText methods are particularly useful for working with StreamReader and StreamWriter objects associated with text files.

Stream classes let a program interact with files. The next chapter explains other classes that you can use to interact with the filesystem. These classes let a program examine, rename, move, and delete files and directories.

EXERCISES

1. The WriteIntoMemoryStream example program uses `Dispose` statements to free its `MemoryStream`, `BinaryWriter`, and `BinaryReader` objects. Rewrite the code with `using` statements instead. Which version is easier to read?

2. What happens if you don't dispose of a stream attached to a file? A memory stream? Which case is worse?

3. Write a program that reads and uses `File` class methods and streams to save and restore some text when it starts and stops. When it starts, the program should open a text file (if it exists) and display its contents in a multiline `TextBox`. When it is closing, the program should save the `TextBox`'s contents into the file, overwriting its previous contents.

4. One way a solution to Exercise 3 can save text is by using a `StreamWriter`'s `Write` or `WriteLine` method. Which of those methods should you use and why?

5. Modify the program you wrote for Exercise 3 to prompt the user to ask if it should overwrite the file. Take appropriate action when the user clicks Yes, No, or Cancel.

6. Write a program that indicates whether the lines in a file are in alphabetical order. Assume the file is huge, so the program must read the file one line at a time and compare each line to the previous one. (That way it needs to store only two lines of text at any given time. It can also stop if it ever finds two lines out of order.)

7. Modify the program you wrote for Exercise 14-8 so that it writes the primes into the file Primes.txt in addition to displaying them in a `ListBox`.

8. Modify the program you wrote for Exercise 7 so that it saves the primes in a binary file named Primes.dat. When the program starts, it should read that file (if it exists) and display the saved values in the `ListBox`. (Hint: The `BinaryReader` class doesn't have an `EndOfStream` property. To let it know how many values to read, save the number of primes at the beginning of the file.)

19

File System Objects

WHAT'S IN THIS CHAPTER

- ➤ `Directory` and `File` classes
- ➤ `DriveInfo`, `DirectoryInfo`, and `FileInfo` classes
- ➤ `FileSystemWatcher` and `Path` classes
- ➤ Managing the recycle bin

WROX.COM DOWNLOADS FOR THIS CHAPTER

Please note that all the code examples for this chapter are available as a part of this chapter's code download on the book's website at `www.wrox.com/go/csharp5programmersref` on the Download Code tab.

The preceding chapter described stream classes that you can use to read and write files. (It also described the `File` class, which isn't a stream class but is just too useful to ignore when you use streams.) Those classes are handy but even those like `StreamWriter` that work at the highest levels still represent only the contents of files. They don't give you any tools for working with the filesystem. Some of their methods can create a file, but they cannot rename or delete a file, or create or delete a directory.

This chapter describes classes that represent the filesystem. They allow you to create, rename, and delete files and directories. The final section in this chapter explains another important file-managing topic: how to use the recycle bin (wastebasket).

USING SYSTEM.IO

All these classes are in the System.IO namespace, so if you use them, you may want to include the following `using` directive in your code.

```
using System.IO;
```

FILESYSTEM PERMISSIONS

A program cannot perform a task unless the user has the appropriate permissions. Although this is true of every application, it's a particular issue for those that work with files. Users need the appropriate permissions to read, write, create, and delete files and directories.

A common mistake is for developers to build and test an application from an account that has a lot of privileges. The program runs fine from the developer's account, but normal users can't use it because they don't have the necessary privileges.

To ensure that users can use a program, you should always test it from an account that has typical user privileges.

.NET FRAMEWORK CLASSES

The System.IO namespace provides several classes for working with the filesystem. The DirectoryInfo and FileInfo classes let you work with specific filesystem objects. For example, a FileInfo object represents a particular file and provides methods to create, rename, delete, and get information about that file.

The Directory and File classes provide static methods that you can use to manipulate the filesystem without creating instances of helper objects. For example, the Directory class's Delete method lets you delete a directory without creating a DirectoryInfo object associated with the directory.

The following sections describe these and the other classes that the .NET Framework provides to help you work with the filesystem.

Directory

The Directory class provides static methods for working with directories. These methods let you create, rename, move, and delete directories. They also let you enumerate the files and subdirectories within a directory, and get and set directory information such as the directory's creation and last access times.

The following table describes the Directory class's static methods.

METHOD	PURPOSE
CreateDirectory	Creates a directory. This method creates ancestor directories if necessary.
Delete	Deletes a directory and its contents. This method can remove the entire directory tree.
Exists	Returns true if a path points to an existing directory.
GetCreationTime	Returns a directory's creation date and time.

METHOD	PURPOSE
`GetCreationTimeUtc`	Returns a directory's creation date and time in Coordinated Universal Time (UTC).
`GetCurrentDirectory`	Returns the application's current working directory.
`GetDirectories`	Returns an array of strings holding the fully qualified names of a directory's subdirectories.
`GetDirectoryRoot`	Returns the directory root for a path, for example, `C:\`.
`GetFiles`	Returns an array of strings holding the fully qualified names of a directory's files. Optionally, you can search for files that match a pattern and you can search subdirectories.
`GetFileSystemEntries`	Returns an array of strings holding the fully qualified names of a directory's files and subdirectories. Optionally, you can search for files and directories that match a pattern and you can search subdirectories.
`GetLastAccessTime`	Returns a directory's last access date and time.
`GetLastAccessTimeUtc`	Returns a directory's last access date and time in UTC.
`GetLastWriteTime`	Returns the date and time when a directory was last modified.
`GetLastWriteTimeUtc`	Returns the date and time in UTC when a directory was last modified.
`GetLogicalDrives`	Returns an array of strings listing the system's logical drives as in `A:\`. The list includes only drives that are attached. For example, it lists an empty floppy drive and a connected flash drive but doesn't list a flash drive after you disconnect it.
`GetParent`	Returns a `DirectoryInfo` object representing a directory's parent.
`Move`	Moves a directory and its contents to a new location on the same disk volume.
`SetCreationTime`	Sets a directory's creation date and time.
`SetCreationTimeUtc`	Sets a directory's creation date and time in UTC.
`SetCurrentDirectory`	Sets the application's current working directory.
`SetLastAccessTime`	Sets a directory's last access date and time.
`SetLastAccessTimeUtc`	Sets a directory's last access date and time in UTC.
`SetLastWriteTime`	Sets a directory's last write date and time.
`SetLastWriteTimeUtc`	Sets a directory's last write date and time in UTC.

SPECIAL DIRECTORIES

The `System.Environment.SpecialFolder` enumeration defines `SpecialFolder` objects representing folders such as `MyDocuments`, `History`, and `CommonProgramFiles`. Use a `SpecialFolder` object's `ToString` method to get the folder's name. Use `Environment.GetFolderPath` to get the directory's path.

The ListSpecialFolders example program, which is available for download on this book's website, uses the following code to list the special directories.

```
private void Form1_Load(object sender, EventArgs e)
{
    foreach (Environment.SpecialFolder folderType
        in Enum.GetValues(typeof(Environment.SpecialFolder)))
    {
        txtFolders.AppendText(
            String.Format("{0,-25}{1}\r\n",
                folderType.ToString(),
                Environment.GetFolderPath(folderType)
            )
        );
    }
    txtFolders.Select(0, 0);
}
```

The only special trick here is the way the program uses the `Enum.GetValues` method to enumerate the values defined by the `Environment.SpecialFolder` enumeration.

File

The preceding chapter mentioned the `File` class and specifically its `Exists` method. This class provides many other static methods for working with files. These methods let you create, rename, move, and delete files. They also make working with file streams a bit easier.

The following table describes the `File` class's most useful static methods.

METHOD	PURPOSE
AppendAllLines	Adds text to the end of a file, creating it if it doesn't exist.
AppendText	Opens a file for appending UTF-8 encoded text and returns a `StreamWriter` object attached to it.
Copy	Copies a file.
Create	Creates a new file and returns a `FileStream` attached to it.
CreateText	Creates or opens a file for writing UTF-8 encoded text and returns a `StreamWriter` object attached to it.

METHOD	PURPOSE
Delete	Permanently deletes a file.
Exists	Returns `true` if the specified file exists.
GetAttributes	Gets a file's attributes. This is a combination of `FileAttributes` flags that can include `Archive`, `Compressed`, `Device`, `Directory`, `Encrypted`, `IntegrityStream`, `Hidden`, `Normal`, `NoScrubData`, `NotContextIndexed`, `Offline`, `ReadOnly`, `ReparsePoint`, `SparseFile`, `System`, and `Temporary`.
GetCreationTime	Returns a file's creation date and time.
GetCreationTimeUtc	Returns a file's creation date and time in UTC.
GetLastAccessTime	Returns a file's last access date and time.
GetLastAccessTimeUtc	Returns a file's last access date and time in UTC.
GetLastWriteTime	Returns a file's last write date and time.
GetLastWriteTimeUtc	Returns a file's last write date and time in UTC.
Move	Moves a file to a new location.
Open	Opens a file and returns a `FileStream` attached to it. Parameters let you specify the mode (`Append`, `Create`, `CreateNew`, `Open`, `OpenOrCreate`, or `Truncate`), access (`Read`, `Write`, or `ReadWrite`), and sharing (`Read`, `Write`, `ReadWrite`, or `None`) settings.
OpenRead	Opens a file for reading and returns a `FileStream` attached to it.
OpenText	Opens a UTF-8-encoded text file for reading and returns a `StreamReader` attached to it.
OpenWrite	Opens a file for writing and returns a `FileStream` attached to it.
ReadAllBytes	Returns a file's contents in an array of bytes.
ReadAllLines	Returns a file's lines in an array of strings.
ReadAllText	Returns a file's contents in a string.
Replace	Takes three file paths as parameters, representing a source file, a destination file, and a backup file. If the backup file exists, this method permanently deletes it. It then moves the destination file to the backup file, and moves the source file to the destination file.
SetAttributes	Sets a file's attributes. This is a combination of flags defined by the `FileAttributes` enumeration. (See the `GetAttributes` method's entry for the possible values.)

continues

(continued)

METHOD	PURPOSE
SetCreationTime	Sets a file's creation date and time.
SetCreationTimeUtc	Sets a file's creation date and time in UTC.
SetLastAccessTime	Sets a file's last access date and time.
SetLastAccessTimeUtc	Sets a file's last access date and time in UTC.
SetLastWriteTime	Sets a file's last write date and time.
SetLastWriteTimeUtc	Sets a file's last write date and time in UTC.
WriteAllBytes	Creates or replaces a file, writes an array of bytes into it, and closes the file.
WriteAllLines	Creates or replaces a file, writes an array of strings into it, and closes the file.
WriteAllText	Creates or replaces a file, writes a string into it, and closes the file.

DriveInfo

A `DriveInfo` object represents one of the computer's drives. The following table describes the properties provided by this class. Note that some of these properties are available only when the drive is ready, as indicated in the following table's Must Be Ready column. If you try to access them when the drive is not ready, C# throws an exception.

PROPERTY	PURPOSE	MUST BE READY
AvailableFreeSpace	Returns the amount of free space available on the drive in bytes.	Yes
DriveFormat	Returns the name of the filesystem type such as NTFS (NT File System) or FAT32 (32-bit File Allocation Table). (For a comparison of these, see www.ntfs.com/ntfs_vs_fat.htm.)	Yes
DriveType	Returns a `DriveType` enumeration value indicating the drive type. This value can be `CDRom`, `Fixed`, `Network`, `NoRootDirectory`, `Ram`, `Removable`, or `Unknown`.	No
IsReady	Returns `true` if the drive is ready.	No
Name	Returns the drive's name. This is the drive's root name (as in `A:\` or `C:\`).	No

PROPERTY	PURPOSE	MUST BE READY
RootDirectory	Returns a DirectoryInfo object representing the drive's root directory. (See the following section "DirectoryInfo" for more information on this class.)	No
TotalFreeSpace	Returns the total amount of free space on the drive in bytes.	Yes
VolumeLabel	Gets or sets the drive's volume label.	Yes

The DriveInfo class also has a public static GetDrives method that returns an array of DriveInfo objects describing the system's drives.

DirectoryInfo

A DirectoryInfo object represents a directory. You can use its properties and methods to create and delete directories and to move through a directory hierarchy. The following table describes the most useful public properties and methods provided by the DirectoryInfo class.

PROPERTY OR METHOD	PURPOSE
Attributes	Gets or sets the directory's attributes. This is a combination of FileAttributes flags that can include Archive, Compressed, Device, Directory, Encrypted, IntegrityStream, Hidden, Normal, NoScrubData, NotContextIndexed, Offline, ReadOnly, ReparsePoint, SparseFile, System, and Temporary.
Create	Creates the directory. (Create a DirectoryInfo object, passing its constructor the fully qualified name of a directory that doesn't exist, and then use the Create method to create the directory.)
CreateSubdirectory	Creates a subdirectory within the directory and returns a DirectoryInfo object representing it. The subdirectory's path is relative to the DirectoryInfo object's directory, but can contain intermediate subdirectories.
CreationTime	Gets or sets the directory's creation time.
CreationTimeUtc	Gets or sets the directory's creation time in UTC.
Delete	Deletes the directory if it is empty. A parameter lets you tell the object to delete its contents, too, if it isn't empty.
Exists	Returns true if the directory exists.

continues

(continued)

PROPERTY OR METHOD	PURPOSE
Extension	Returns the extension part of the directory's name. Normally, this is an empty string for directories.
FullName	Returns the directory's fully qualified path.
GetDirectories	Returns an array of DirectoryInfo objects representing the directory's subdirectories. An optional parameter gives a pattern to match. This method does not recursively search the subdirectories.
GetFiles	Returns an array of FileInfo objects representing files inside the directory. An optional parameter gives a pattern to match. This method does not recursively search subdirectories.
GetFileSystemInfos	Returns a strongly typed array of FileSystemInfo objects, representing subdirectories and files inside the directory. The items in the array are DirectoryInfo and FileInfo objects (both of which inherit from FileSystemInfo). An optional parameter gives a pattern to match. This method does not recursively search subdirectories.
LastAccessTime	Gets or sets the directory's last access time.
LastAccessTimeUtc	Gets or sets the directory's last access time in UTC.
LastWriteTime	Gets or sets the directory's last write time.
LastWriteTimeUtc	Gets or sets directory's last write time in UTC.
MoveTo	Moves the directory and its contents to a new path.
Name	The directory's name without the path information.
Parent	Returns a DirectoryInfo object, representing the directory's parent. If the directory is its file system's root (for example, C:\), this returns null.
Refresh	Refreshes the DirectoryInfo object's data.
Root	Returns a DirectoryInfo object representing the root of the directory's file system.
ToString	Returns the directory's fully qualified path and name.

FileInfo

A FileInfo object represents a file. You can use its properties and methods to create and delete files. The following table describes the most useful public properties and methods provided by the FileInfo class.

PROPERTY OR METHOD	PURPOSE
AppendText	Returns a StreamWriter that appends text to the file.
Attributes	Gets or sets the file's attributes. This is a combination of FileAttributes flags that can include Archive, Compressed, Device, Directory, Encrypted, IntegrityStream, Hidden, Normal, NoScrubData, NotContextIndexed, Offline, ReadOnly, ReparsePoint, SparseFile, System, and Temporary.
CopyTo	Copies the file and returns a FileInfo object, representing the new file. A parameter lets you indicate whether the copy should overwrite an existing file. If the destination path is relative, it is relative to the application's current directory, not to the FileInfo object's directory.
Create	Creates the file and returns a FileStream object attached to it. (Create a FileInfo object, passing its constructor the name of a file that doesn't exist, and then call the Create method to create the file.)
CreateText	Creates the file and returns a StreamWriter attached to it. (Create a FileInfo object, passing its constructor the name of a file that doesn't exist, and then call the CreateText method to create the file.)
CreationTime	Gets or sets the file's creation time.
CreationTimeUtc	Gets or sets the file's creation time in UTC.
Delete	Deletes the file.
Directory	Returns a DirectoryInfo object representing the file's directory.
DirectoryName	Returns the name of the file's directory.
Exists	Returns true if the file exists.
Extension	Returns the extension part of the file's name. For example, the extension for scores.txt is .txt.
FullName	Returns the file's fully qualified path and name.
IsReadOnly	Returns true if the file is marked read-only.
LastAccessTime	Gets or sets the file's last access time.
LastAccessTimeUtc	Gets or sets the file's last access time in UTC.
LastWriteTime	Gets or sets the file's last write time.
LastWriteTimeUtc	Gets or sets the file's last write time in UTC.
Length	Returns the number of bytes in the file.

continues

(continued)

PROPERTY OR METHOD	PURPOSE
MoveTo	Moves the file to a new location. If the destination uses a relative path, it is relative to the application's current directory, not to the `FileInfo` object's directory. When this method finishes, the `FileInfo` object is updated to refer to the file's new location.
Name	The file's name without the path information.
Open	Opens the file with various mode (`Append`, `Create`, `CreateNew`, `Open`, `OpenOrCreate`, or `Truncate`), access (`Read`, `Write`, or `ReadWrite`), and sharing (`Read`, `Write`, `ReadWrite`, or `None`) settings. This method returns a `FileStream` object attached to the file.
OpenRead	Returns a read-only `FileStream` attached to the file.
OpenText	Returns a `StreamReader` with UTF-8 encoding attached to the file for reading.
OpenWrite	Returns a write-only `FileStream` attached to the file.
Refresh	Refreshes the `FileInfo` object's data.
Replace	Takes three file paths as parameters, representing a source file, a destination file, and a backup file. If the backup file exists, this method permanently deletes it. It then moves the destination file to the backup file, and moves the source file to the destination file.
ToString	Returns the file's fully qualified name.

FileSystemWatcher

The `FileSystemWatcher` class keeps an eye on part of the file system and raises events to let your program know if something changes. For example, a `FileSystemWatcher` can monitor a directory and raise an event when a new file appears so your program can process the file.

The `FileSystemWatcher` class's constructor takes parameters that tell it which directory to watch and that give it a filter for selecting files to watch. For example, the filter `*.txt` makes it watch for changes to text files. The default filter is `*.*`, which catches changes to all files that have extensions.

The following table describes the `FileSystemWatcher` class's most useful properties.

PROPERTY	PURPOSE
EnableRaisingEvents	Determines whether the watcher is enabled. (This property is `false` by default, so the watcher does not raise any events until you set it to `true`.)

PROPERTY	PURPOSE
Filter	Determines the files for which the watcher reports events. (You cannot watch for multiple file types as in *.txt and *.dat. Instead use multiple FileSystemWatchers.)
IncludeSubdirectories	Determines whether the object watches subdirectories below the main directory.
InternalBufferSize	Determines the size of the internal buffer. If the watcher is monitoring a very active directory, a small buffer may overflow.
NotifyFilter	Determines the types of changes that the watcher reports. This is a combination of values defined by the NotifyFilters enumeration and can include the values Attributes, CreationTime, DirectoryName, FileName, LastAccess, LastWrite, Security, and Size.
Path	Determines the path of the directory to watch.

The FileSystemWatcher class provides only two useful methods. The first method, Dispose, releases resources used by the component. As usual, be sure to call Dispose when you are done with the object (or use a using statement).

The second method, WaitForChanged, waits for a change synchronously (with an optional timeout). When a change occurs, the method returns a WaitForChangedResult object, giving information about the change that occurred.

When the FileSystemWatcher detects a change asynchronously, it raises an event to let the program know what has happened. The following table describes the class's events.

NAME	DESCRIPTION
Changed	A file or subdirectory has changed.
Created	A file or subdirectory was created.
Deleted	A file or subdirectory was deleted.
Error	The watcher's internal buffer overflowed.
Renamed	A file or subdirectory was renamed.

DESIGN TIME WATCHERS

The FileSystemWatcher class is a component that appears in the Toolbox when you build a Windows Forms application. That means you can add one to a form and give it event handlers at design time.

Path

The `Path` class provides static properties and methods that you can use to manipulate paths. Its methods return the path's filename, extension, directory name, and so forth.

Other methods provide values that relate to system-generated paths. For example, they can give you the system's temporary directory path or the name of a temporary file.

The following table describes the `Path` class's most useful public properties.

PROPERTY	PURPOSE
AltDirectorySeparatorChar	Returns the alternative character used to separate directory levels in a hierarchical path. Typically, this is /.
DirectorySeparatorChar	Returns the character normally used to separate directory levels in a hierarchical path. Typically, this is \ (as in C:\ Users\Rod\PhoneProjects\MrBones.sln).
InvalidPathChars	Returns a character array that holds characters that are not allowed in a path string. Typically, this array includes characters such as ", <, >, and |, as well as nonprintable characters such as those with ASCII values between 0 and 31.
PathSeparator	Returns the character used to separate path strings in environment variables. Typically, this is a semicolon (;).
VolumeSeparatorChar	Returns the character placed between a volume letter and the rest of the path. Typically, this is a colon (:) as in C:\.

The following table describes the `Path` class's most useful methods.

METHOD	PURPOSE
ChangeExtension	Changes a path's extension.
Combine	Returns two path strings concatenated.
GetDirectoryName	Returns a path's directory.
GetExtension	Returns a path's extension.
GetFileName	Returns a path's filename and extension.
GetFileNameWithoutExtension	Returns a path's filename without the extension.
GetFullPath	Returns a path's fully qualified value.
GetInvalidFileNameChars	Returns an array listing characters that are invalid in filenames.

METHOD	PURPOSE
GetInvalidPathChars	Returns an array listing characters that are invalid in file paths.
GetPathRoot	Returns a path's root directory string.
GetRandomFileName	Returns a random filename.
GetTempFileName	Creates a uniquely named, empty temporary file and returns its fully qualified path. Your program can open that file for scratch space, do whatever it needs to do, close the file, and then delete it. A typical filename might be `C:\Users\Rod\AppData\Local\Temp\tmpD4F0.tmp`.
GetTempPath	Returns the path to the system's temporary folder. This is the path part of the filenames returned by `GetTempFileName`.
HasExtension	Returns `true` if a path includes an extension.
IsPathRooted	Returns `true` if a path is an absolute path. This includes `C:\Tests\Logs.txt` and `\Clients\Litigation`, but not `LostFiles\Peter.txt` or `.\Jokes`.

PATH COMBINATIONS

The `Combine` method just tacks two paths together, adding a separator if necessary. For example, the statement `Path.Combine(@"C:\Projects", @"Test\ListFiles")` produces the result `C:\Projects\Test\ListFiles`.

You can also use this method to combine a path with a relative path such as `..`, which represents the directory above the current directory. The result is simply a path with the relative part attached. For example, the statement `Path.Combine(@"C:\Projects\Tests", @"..")` produces the result `C:\Projects\Tests\...`

This isn't useful until you realize that you can pass it to a `Path` class's `GetFullPath` method to resolve the relative path. For example, this statement

```
Path.GetFullPath(Path.Combine(@"C:\Projects\Tests", @".."))
```

produces the following result:

```
C:\Projects
```

This gives you an easy method for resolving relative paths without parsing the paths yourself.

USING THE RECYCLE BIN

Unfortunately, C# doesn't include methods for working with the recycle bin. However, you can use a combination of three different techniques: using the `FileIO.FileSystem` class, using API functions, and using `Shell32.Shell`.

THE API BENEATH IT ALL

The `FileIO.FileSystem` class and `Shell32.Shell` are layered on top of the API, so you could do all the work in the API. However, the `FileIO.FileSystem` class and `Shell32.Shell` are easier to use, so the following sections use the easiest tool for each task.

The ManageRecycleBin example program, which is available for download on this book's website, demonstrates the techniques described in the following sections. Enter a file or directory name and click the corresponding Delete button to move that item into the recycle bin. Click Refresh to refresh the list of files in the recycle bin. Click Empty to permanently remove all the files from the recycle bin. Finally, right-click a file in the recycle bin to see a context menu giving commands you can apply to that file, as shown in Figure 19-1.

You may want to download the ManageRecycleBin example program so that you can refer to it as you read the following sections.

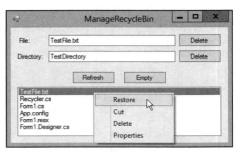

FIGURE 19-1: The ManageRecycleBin example program lets you view and manipulate the files in the recycle bin.

Using the FileIO.FileSystem Class

The `Microsoft.VisualBasic.FileIO` namespace includes a `FileSystem` class that provides `DeleteDirectory` and `DeleteFile` methods. Those methods can take an optional parameter that indicates whether you want to move the directory or file into the recycle bin, or whether you want to delete the directory or file permanently. (They can also take a parameter that lets you decide whether the methods should display progress dialogs.)

Some C# developers prefer not to use classes defined in the `Microsoft.VisualBasic` namespace, feeling they are somehow not C#ish enough. Personally, I think that's just plain silly. If the `Microsoft.VisualBasic` namespace includes tools that you can use to make your life easier, you're only hurting yourself by ignoring them. This class is in the .NET Framework, so it's not like you're sneaking around using some sort of substandard back alley code.

The following code shows the event handlers the ManageRecycleBin program executes when you click one of its Delete buttons.

```
// Delete a file.
private void deleteFileButton_Click(object sender, EventArgs e)
{
    FileSystem.DeleteFile(fileTextBox.Text,
        UIOption.OnlyErrorDialogs, RecycleOption.SendToRecycleBin);
    fileTextBox.Clear();
    ListFiles();
}

// Delete a directory.
private void deleteDirectoryButton_Click(object sender, EventArgs e)
{
    FileSystem.DeleteDirectory(directoryTextBox.Text,
        UIOption.OnlyErrorDialogs, RecycleOption.SendToRecycleBin);
    directoryTextBox.Clear();
    ListFiles();
}
```

The first event handler deletes a file. It calls the `FileSystem` class's `DeleteFile` method, passing it the name of the file to delete, a `UIOption` flag indicating the method should display only error messages (not animations or confirmation dialogs), and a `RecycleOption` value indicating the file should be moved to the recycle bin.

The code then clears the `TextBox` holding the file's name and calls the `ListFiles` method. The `ListFiles` method uses `Shell32.Shell`, which is described shortly in the section "Using `Shell32.Shell`."

REFERENCES REQUIRED

To use the `FileIO` namespace, you must add a reference to `Microsoft.VisualBasic` to your program.

To use `Shell32.Shell`, you need add a reference to "Microsoft Shell Controls And Automation" on the Reference Manager's COM tab.

Using API Functions

The `FileIO.FileSystem` class lets you easily move directories and files into the recycle bin, but it doesn't give you any other tools for working with the recycle bin. It doesn't let you determine the number or sizes of the items in the recycle bin, restore items from the recycle bin, or empty the recycle bin.

Fortunately, you can use the `SHEmptyRecycleBin` API function to empty the recycle bin relatively easily. This API function takes a parameter that is of the `RecycleFlags` enumerated type. (Actually, the function itself takes a uint as a parameter, but the enumeration makes it easier for your code to specify the wanted options.) The following code shows the enumeration's definition.

```
[Flags]
private enum RecycleFlags : uint
{
    SHERB_NOCONFIRMATION = 0x1,
    SHERB_NOPROGRESSUI = 0x2,
    SHERB_NOSOUND = 0x4
}
```

The following code shows the API function's declaration.

```
[DllImport("shell32.dll")]
static extern int SHEmptyRecycleBin(
    IntPtr hWnd, string pszRootPath, uint dwFlags);
```

Here shell32.dll is the library that contains the SHEmptyRecycleBin API function. This is different from the Shell32.Shell techniques described in the next section.

The ManageRecycleBin program uses the following EmptyRecycleBin method, which wraps the call to SHEmptyRecycleBin.

```
public static void EmptyRecycleBin(bool showProgress, bool playSound,
    bool confirm)
{
    RecycleFlags options = 0;
    if (!showProgress) options |= RecycleFlags.SHERB_NOPROGRESSUI;
    if (!playSound) options |= RecycleFlags.SHERB_NOSOUND;
    if (!confirm) options |= RecycleFlags.SHERB_NOCONFIRMATION;

    SHEmptyRecycleBin(IntPtr.Zero, null, (uint)options);
}
```

This method uses its parameters to create an appropriate RecycleFlags value. It then simply invokes the API function.

When you click the Empty button, the program uses the following code to invoke the EmptyRecycleBin method.

```
// Empty the recycle bin.
private void emptyButton_Click(object sender, EventArgs e)
{
    // Empty with sounds and making the user confirm.
    EmptyRecycleBin(false, true, true);

    // Refresh the list.
    ListFiles();
}
```

Using Shell32.Shell

Shell32.Shell is an interface for working with the Windows shell. One of the things you can do with the Shell interface is interact with virtual objects representing such things as remote printers and the recycle bin.

> ## MORE ABOUT SHELL
>
> Shell and other Windows shell items are interfaces representing COM (Component Object Model) objects, which are not the same as .NET objects. (That's why the text refers to them as interfaces.)
>
> For more information about working with the Windows shell, see "Windows Shell" at msdn.microsoft.com/library/windows/desktop/bb773177.aspx.

The files in the recycle bin are represented by FolderItems. To work with the files, the ManageRecycleBin program needs to keep track of those FolderItems. To do so, it stores information about the files in the following RecycleItemInfo class.

```
// A class to hold a FolderItem and return its name.
private class RecycleItemInfo
{
    public FolderItem Item;
    public RecycleItemInfo(FolderItem item)
    {
        Item = item;
    }
    public override string ToString()
    {
        return Item.Name;
    }
}
```

This class simply holds a FolderItem. It provides a constructor for easy initialization and overrides its ToString method to return the name of the file it represents.

The following code shows the ManageRecycleBin program's ListFiles method.

```
// List the files in the recycle bin.
private void ListFiles()
{
    const int RECYCLE_BIN_NAMESPACE = 10;

    Shell shell = new Shell();
    Folder bin = shell.NameSpace(RECYCLE_BIN_NAMESPACE);

    // List the files.
    filesListBox.Items.Clear();
    foreach (FolderItem item in bin.Items())
    {
        filesListBox.Items.Add(new RecycleItemInfo(item));
    }
}
```

The method creates a new Shell interface and uses its NameSpace method to get a Folder interface representing the recycle bin. The parameter, which has value 10, is simply the "magic number" that represents the recycle bin.

Next, the method empties the file `ListBox` and loops through the `FolderItems` returned by the recycle `Folder`'s `Items` method. For each `FolderItem`, the program creates a `RecycleItemInfo` object and adds it to the `ListBox`.

Because the `RecycleItemInfo` class's `ToString` method returns the `FolderItem`'s `Name` property, that is what is displayed by the `ListBox`.

The following code shows how the program responds when you right-click a file's entry in the `ListBox`.

```
// On right-mouse down, display the item's verbs in a menu.
private void filesListBox_MouseDown(object sender, MouseEventArgs e)
{
    // Make sure it's the right button.
    if (e.Button != MouseButtons.Right) return;

    // Find the item under the mouse.
    int index = filesListBox.IndexFromPoint(e.Location);
    if (index < 0) return;

    // Select that item.
    filesListBox.SelectedIndex = index;

    // Get the item's RecycleItemInfo.
    RecycleItemInfo info = filesListBox.SelectedItem as RecycleItemInfo;

    // Get the item's FolderInfo object.
    FolderItem item = info.Item;

    // Make the context menu.
    ContextMenu menu = new ContextMenu();
    foreach (FolderItemVerb verb in item.Verbs())
    {
        MenuItem menuItem = new MenuItem(verb.Name, ContextMenuItem_Click);
        menuItem.Tag = verb;
        menu.MenuItems.Add(menuItem);
    }
    menu.Show(filesListBox, e.Location);
}
```

This code creates a context menu appropriate for the item that the user right-clicked. First, the method exits if the button pressed isn't the right mouse button.

Next, the program uses the `ListBox`'s `IndexFromPoint` method to get the index of the item under the mouse. If there is no item there, the method exits. If there is an item below the mouse, the code selects it.

The code then converts the selected item into the `RecycleItemInfo` object that is stored in the `ListBox` and gets the `FolderItem` stored inside the object.

The method then creates a `ContextMenu` and loops through the list returned by the `FolderItem`'s `Verbs` method. Each of those items is a `FolderItemVerb` interface that represents something the `FolderItem` can do.

The code creates a new MenuItem representing each verb. The MenuItem displays its verb's name and is associated with the ContextMenuItem_Click event handler. The code stores the FolderItemVerb in the MenuItem's Tag property.

After it has created the ContextMenu and the verbs' MenuItems, the program displays the ContextMenu.

The following code shows the ContextMenuItem_Click event handler.

```
// Perform some action on a file.
private void ContextMenuItem_Click(object sender, EventArgs e)
{
    // Get the MenuItem.
    MenuItem menuItem = sender as MenuItem;

    // Get the verb.
    FolderItemVerb verb = menuItem.Tag as FolderItemVerb;

    // Invoke the verb.
    verb.DoIt();

    // Redisplay the files.
    ListFiles();
}
```

First, this code gets the MenuItem that was clicked. It gets the corresponding FolderItemVerb from the MenuItem's Tag property. The code invokes the FolderItemVerb's DoIt method to make it perform whatever action it should take. It finishes by calling ListFiles to refresh the file list in case the verb changed the files in the recycle bin, for example, by restoring a file.

Download the ManageRecycleBin program to see additional details. The program isn't exactly simple, but it does demonstrate techniques you can use to work with the recycle bin.

SUMMARY

The System.IO namespace offers many classes that let you manipulate files and directories. Classes such as Directory, DirectoryInfo, File, and FileInfo make it easy to create, examine, move, rename, and delete directories and files. The File class's ReadAllText and WriteAllText methods make it particularly easy to read or write an entire file.

The FileSystemWatcher class lets an application keep an eye on a file or directory and take action when it is changed. For example, a program can watch a spooling directory and take action when a new file appears in it.

The Path class provides miscellaneous support for working with paths. For example, it provides methods you can use to combine paths and resolve relative paths.

There is considerable overlap among these tools, so you don't need to feel that you have to use them all. Take a good look so that you know what's there, and then pick the tools that you find the most comfortable.

Finally this chapter explained techniques you can use to manage the recycle bin. Some of them are fairly complex, but at least the `FileIO.FileSystem` class makes moving a file or directory into the recycle reasonably simple.

So far the chapters in this book have explained how to do things locally on the user's computer. The next chapter explains how a program can move off of the local computer to download files from the Internet.

EXERCISES

1. Write a program that lets the user select a directory and displays its creation, last access, and last write times.

2. Write a program that lets the user select a file and displays its creation, last access, and last write times. Let the user change the times and then set them for the file.

3. Write a program that lets the user get and set a file's attributes. Use `CheckBoxes` to display and let the user specify attributes.

4. Write a program that uses `File.ReadAllText` and `File.WriteAllText` to save and restore the contents of a text file when it starts and stops. Compare your solution to the solution for Exercise 18-3.

5. Write a program that sorts the lines in a file. (Hint: Use `File.ReadAllLines` to get the lines, sort them, and then use `File.WriteAllLines` to write them back into the file.)

6. Write a program that lists the computer's drives and whatever drive information is available from the `DriveInfo` class.

7. Modify the program you wrote for Exercise 6 so that it displays sizes in KB, MB, GB, or TB as appropriate.

8. Write a program that displays the name of the directory two levels higher than the directory where the program is executing. What happens if you run the program near the top of the directory hierarchy, for example, in `C:\`?

9. Write a program that lets the user enter a directory path and a pattern. When the user clicks the Search button, the program should search the directory and its subdirectories for files matching the pattern.

10. Modify the program you wrote for Exercise 9 so that it shows the selected filenames (without paths) and their sizes.

11. Write a program that uses a `FileSystemWatcher` to watch the directory where the program is executing for changes. When a change occurs, the program should display the date and time, the type of change, and the changing file's name.

12. Write a program that lets the user enter a filename and then uses the `FileIO` class to move the file into the recycle bin. (That's all many programs need to do anyway. You can use the recycle bin on your desktop to manage its contents.)

20

Networking

WHAT'S IN THIS CHAPTER

- ➤ Networking overview
- ➤ Uploading and downloading data
- ➤ Getting remote file information with FTP
- ➤ Sending e-mail and text messages

WROX.COM DOWNLOADS FOR THIS CHAPTER

Please note that all the code examples for this chapter are available as a part of this chapter's code download on the book's website at www.wrox.com/go/csharp5programmersref on the Download Code tab.

Networking is a complicated topic. Understanding all the protocols, addresses, routing, data layers, network hardware, and everything else that goes into building a network is a difficult task and outside the scope of this book.

Fortunately, most programs use only a few main networking techniques such as:

- ➤ Upload a file
- ➤ Download a file
- ➤ Get information about a file
- ➤ Get a directory listing
- ➤ Post information to a form
- ➤ Send e-mail

Rather than trying to cover all there is to know about network programming in detail, this chapter explains how to perform these common chores.

If you want to get into network programming, you should look for a book that focuses on just that. If you search your favorite online bookstore for **C# Networking,** you should find a few good choices. You can also look at the following articles.

➤ "Network Programming in the .NET Framework" `msdn.microsoft.com/library/4as0wz7t.aspx`

➤ "An Introduction to Socket Programming in .NET Using C#" `www.codeproject.com/Articles/10649/An-Introduction-to-Socket-Programming-in-NET-using`

➤ "Network Programming Samples" `msdn.microsoft.com/library/vstudio/ee890485.aspx`

NETWORKING CLASSES

The .NET Framework defines several namespaces containing networking classes. Most of those namespaces, and some of the most useful classes, are contained in the `System.Net` namespace.

At the lower levels, the `System.Net.Sockets` namespace provides classes that manipulate Windows sockets (Winsock). These let you create and manage sockets, which provide relatively low-level access to the network. Sockets let you accept incoming connection requests, connect to remote hosts, and send and receive datagrams.

DATAGRAM

A *datagram* is a basic unit of data sent over a packet-switched network (a network that packages data into datagrams). Datagrams may not arrive in the order in which they were sent.

Typically, a large message might be split into several datagrams that are sent separately. Higher protocol levels reassemble the datagrams to recover the original message.

The `HttpListener` class lets you create a listener that responds to HTTP requests. Using a listener, you can make a program that runs on a server and responds to incoming requests from other programs.

HTTP

HyperText Transfer Protocol (HTTP) is a protocol that defines how messages are formatted and transmitted. It sits at a higher level than sockets and datagram communications.

The `WebRequest` and `WebResponse` classes are abstract classes that define a request/response model for fetching URIs. A program uses a class derived from `WebRequest` to request a URL (for example, a web page). When the file returns from the network, the program receives a `WebResponse` object fulfilling the request (if nothing went wrong). Classes derived from `WebRequest` include `FileWebRequest`, `FtpWebRequest`, and `HttpWebRequest`. Similarly classes derived from `WebResponse` include `FileWebResponse`, `FtpWebResponse`, and `HttpWebResponse`.

URLS, URNS, AND URIS

A *Uniform Resource Location (URL)* is an address that specifies where a resource is and the protocol that is its primary means of access. For example, `http://www.CSharpHelper.com/howto_index.html` is a URL that refers to the web page located at the address `www.CSharpHelper.com/howto_index.html` and obtainable with HTTP. This is the kind of address that is most familiar to Internet users. Other URLs may refer to files in a directory hierarchy, or relative paths to web documents or files on a filesystem.

A *Uniform Resource Name (URN)* is a name that identifies something but doesn't necessarily refer to a "physical" location. For example, `urn:isbn:978-1118847282` is a URN that uses the *International Standard Book Number (ISBN)* to refer to this book. There are many copies of this book, so the URN cannot be the address of a physical copy of the book. A URL corresponding to this URN might give you the street address and shelf location of a copy of the book in a particular bookstore.

A more confusing use of URNs is to create a universally unique name that will never change. For example, a new WPF application starts with the following code.

```
<Window x:Class="WpfApplication1.MainWindow"
    xmlns="http://schemas.microsoft.com/winfx/2006/xaml/presentation"
    xmlns:x="http://schemas.microsoft.com/winfx/2006/xaml"
    Title="MainWindow" Height="350" Width="525">
    <Grid>

    </Grid>
</Window>
```

The two pieces of text highlighted in bold are URNs that identify namespaces used by the program. Even though these look like URLs, if you try to open them in a browser, you'll find that there are no files there. They are URNs but not URLs.

Note that a URL is a URN because it is both a location and a name for something.

Uniform Resource Identifiers (URIs) includes both URLs and URNs.

People often confuse URIs for URLs. In practice, they often mean URLs.

The `WebClient` class provides some of the same features as the request/response classes but at a higher level. It's not quite as flexible, but it's much easier to use.

The `System.Net.Mail` namespace includes classes for sending e-mail messages to a Simple Mail Transfer Protocol (SMTP) server so that they can be forwarded to the recipient(s).

The following sections explain how you can use these classes to download and upload information, get information about remote files and directories, and send e-mail.

DOWNLOADING INFORMATION

The following sections explain how to download data using `WebClient` and `WebRequest` classes. It's easier to use `WebClient`, so I recommend that you try that approach first. The `WebRequest` class gives you more control over cookies, request and response headers, and other details that don't matter for simple file uploads and downloads.

Downloading with WebClient

The `WebClient` class provides four sets of methods for downloading data from a URL into a file, `string`, `byte` array, or stream. Each set has one synchronous and two asynchronous methods. The following sections describe these four sets of methods.

Downloading Files

The `WebClient` class's first set of methods downloads the data at a URL into a local file. Its methods are `DownloadFile`, `DownloadFileAsync`, and `DownloadFileTaskAsync`. The synchronous method, `DownloadFile`, is remarkably easy to use. Simply create a new object and call the method, passing it the URL of the file you want to download and the name of the file where you want to place the result. The following code shows an example.

```
WebClient client = new WebClient();
client.DownloadFile(
    "http://www.csharphelper.com/howto_index.html",
    "howto_index.html");
```

This code downloads the web page `http://www.csharphelper.com/howto_index.html` and stores it in the local file `howto_index.html`. The new file is placed in the program's current directory, which by default is its startup directory.

The `DownloadFileAsync` method starts an asynchronous file download. You can catch the `WebClient`'s `DownloadProgressChanged` event to monitor the download's progress. Catch the `DownloadFileCompleted` event to get the result of the download. While the download is in progress, you can cancel it by calling the `WebClient`'s `CancelAsync` method.

The second asynchronous file download method is `DownloadFileTaskAsync`. Like `DownloadFileAsync`, this method starts an asynchronous download. The difference is that this method uses a separate task to start the download, so you can use the `await` keyword to wait for the method to finish downloading the file. The code runs asynchronously and then execution resumes after the `await` keyword when the asynchronous task has finished. (For more information on `await`, see the section "Using `async` and `await`" in Chapter 6, "Methods.")

Downloading Strings

The WebClient class's second set of downloading methods is similar to the first set, except it down-loads data into a string instead of a file. The string downloading methods are DownloadString, DownloadStringAsync, and DownloadStringTaskAsync.

As is the case when you download a file asynchronously, you can catch the DownloadProgressChanged event to monitor the download's progress, and you can use the CancelAsync method to cancel the download. Catch the DownloadStringCompleted event to get the downloaded string.

The DownloadStringAsync example program, which is available for download on this book's website, uses code similar to the following to download a web page as a string. (The code isn't exactly the same because the program has some extra user interface code that makes the program easier to use, but that isn't part of the download process.)

```
// The WebClient. (Needed for canceling.)
private WebClient Client = null;

// Start downloading.
private void downloadButton_Click(object sender, EventArgs e)
{
    // Make a Uri.
    Uri uri = new Uri(urlTextBox.Text);

    // Start the download.
    Client = new WebClient();
    Client.DownloadProgressChanged += Client_DownloadProgressChanged;
    Client.DownloadStringCompleted += Client_DownloadStringCompleted;
    Client.DownloadStringAsync(uri);
}

// Report on download progress.
private void Client_DownloadProgressChanged(object sender,
    DownloadProgressChangedEventArgs e)
{
    downloadProgressBar.Value = e.ProgressPercentage;
    downloadStatusLabel.Text = e.ProgressPercentage.ToString() + "%";
}

// The download has finished.
void Client_DownloadStringCompleted(object sender,
    DownloadStringCompletedEventArgs e)
{
    // See what the result was.
    if (e.Error != null)
    {
        MessageBox.Show(e.Error.Message);
    }
    else if (e.Cancelled)
    {
        MessageBox.Show("Canceled");
    }
    else
    {
```

```
            // Display the downloaded file.
            MessageBox.Show(e.Result);
        }

        Client.Dispose();
    }

    // Cancel the download.
    private void cancelButton_Click(object sender, EventArgs e)
    {
        // Cancel.
        Client.CancelAsync();
    }
```

The program declares a WebClient at the module level, so it is visible to all the program's methods, in particular the methods that start and cancel the download.

When you click the program's Download button, the downloadButton_Click event handler starts the download. It first creates a Uri object to represent the URL to download. (The Async methods take a Uri object as a parameter. The synchronous and TaskAsync methods can take either a string or a Uri as a parameter.)

This is a bit different from the DownloadFile method, which can take the URL as a string parameter. The DownloadString method requires a Uri object.

The code creates a new WebClient object, associates event handlers with the DownloadProgressChanged and DownloadStringCompleted events, and then calls the DownloadStringAsync method to start the download.

The DownloadProgressChanged event handler updates a ToolStripProgressBar and a ToolStripStatusLabel to keep the user informed of the progress. The e.ProgressPercentage parameter is an int holding the percentage of the download that is complete.

The DownloadStringCompleted event handler checks the result to see if there was an error or if the download was canceled. If the download completed successfully, the result string is stored in the e.Result parameter.

If the user clicks the program's Cancel button before the download completes, the cancelButton_Click event handler calls the WebClient's CancelAsync method.

Figure 20-1 shows the DownloadStringAsync example program displaying a web page from the C# Helper website.

Downloading byte Arrays

The WebClient class's third set of downloading methods is similar to the first two except it downloads data into a byte array. Its methods are DownloadData, DownloadDataAsync, and DownloadDataTaskAsync.

As before, when you download data asynchronously, you can catch the DownloadProgressChanged event to monitor the download's progress, and you can use the CancelAsync method to cancel the download. Catch the DownloadDataCompleted event to get the downloaded bytes.

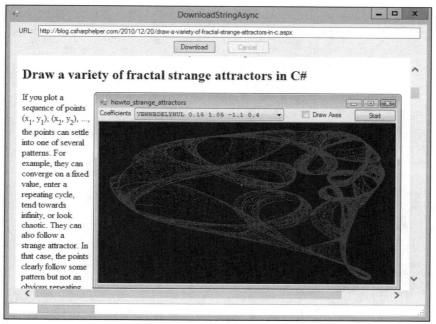

FIGURE 20-1: The DownloadStringAsync example program lets you download and view web pages.

Downloading Streams

The WebClient class's final set of downloading methods is somewhat similar to the others, but the fact that these methods download data in a stream lead to some differences. This group's methods are OpenRead, OpenReadAsync, and OpenReadTaskAsync.

The asynchronous methods do not fire the DownloadProgressChanged event, so you cannot monitor the download's progress, but you can still use the CancelAsync method to cancel the download.

Catch the OpenReadCompleted event to process the stream. If the download was successful, the e.Result parameter contains the stream.

Downloading with WebRequest

To download data with a WebRequest object, use the WebRequest class's Create method to create a new object. This method takes as a parameter either a URL or a Uri object. The method examines its parameter and returns an appropriate object of a class that inherits from WebRequest. For example, if the URL string begins with http://, the Create method returns an HttpWebRequest object. Usually, you can ignore the specific class and just treat the result as a WebRequest.

After you create the request object, set its Method property to indicate the type of operation you want to perform. The WebRequestMethods namespace defines the three classes Http, Ftp, and File that provide strings that define methods that you can use. For example, WebRequestMethods.Http.Get represents a download command that uses the HTTP protocol.

REQUEST TYPES

The `WebRequest` class's `Create` method understands the prefixes `http://`, `https://`, `ftp://`, and `file://`. You can derive other classes from `WebRequest` to support custom request types. Creating request objects to support custom request protocols is outside the scope of this book. For more information, see "Programming Pluggable Protocols" at `msdn.microsoft.com/library/1f6c88af.aspx`.

The following table briefly summarizes the HTTP methods, which are the most confusing.

METHOD	PURPOSE
Connect	Represents an HTTP CONNECT command for use with a proxy.
Get	Represents an HTTP GET command, which downloads a resource.
Head	Represents an HTTP HEAD command. This is similar to a GET command except it returns only headers and not the actual resource.
MkCol	Represents an HTTP MKCOL command, which creates a new collection (for example, a collection of pages).
Post	Represents an HTTP POST command, which basically creates a new resource.
Put	Represents an HTTP PUT command, which can create or update a resource.

The `Ftp` and `File` methods are more self-explanatory. The following list shows the `Ftp` methods.

- ➤ AppendFile
- ➤ DeleteFile
- ➤ DownloadFile
- ➤ GetDateTimeStamp
- ➤ GetFileSize
- ➤ ListDirectory
- ➤ ListDirectoryDetails
- ➤ MakeDirectory
- ➤ PrintWorkingDirectory
- ➤ RemoveDirectory
- ➤ Rename
- ➤ UploadFile
- ➤ UploadFileWithUniqueName

The `WebRequestMethods.File` class defines only two methods, both of which have self-explanatory names: `DownloadFile` and `UploadFile`.

After you create the `WebRequest` object and set its `Method` property, call the request's `GetResponse` method to get a `WebResponse` object.

WEBRESPONSES

The `GetResponse` method returns one of the `WebResponse` subclasses `HttpWebResponse`, `FtpWebResponse`, or `FileWebResponse`. Usually you can ignore the specific type and treat it as a `WebResponse`.

You can examine the response's properties to get information about the response. For example, you can look at the `ContentLength` and `ContentType` properties to learn about the response's contents. The `IsFromCache` property indicates whether the contents were loaded from cache or from the original source.

The response's `GetResponseStream` method returns a stream that contains the requested content (if nothing went wrong). Now you can write code to use this stream to process the content appropriately.

The following list summarizes the steps for using a `WebRequest`.

1. Use `WebRequest.Create` to create the request object.
2. Set the request's `Method` property.
3. Call the request's `GetResponse` method to get a `WebResponse`.
4. Call the response's `GetResponseStream` method to get the response stream.
5. Process the stream.

> **WARNING** *Be sure to close the stream when you finish using it so that it can free its system resources.*

The WebRequestDownloadData example program, which is available for download on this book's website, uses the following code to download an image file from an `http://` URL.

```
try
{
    // Make the WebRequest.
    WebRequest request = WebRequest.Create(urlTextBox.Text);

    // Use the Get method to download the file.
    request.Method = WebRequestMethods.Http.Get;

    // Get the response.
    WebResponse response = request.GetResponse();

    // Get the image from the response stream.
```

```
        // (You must close the stream when finished.)
        using (Stream stream = response.GetResponseStream())
        {
            Bitmap bitmap = new Bitmap(stream);

            // Display the result.
            imagePictureBox.Image = bitmap;
        }
    }
    catch (Exception ex)
    {
        MessageBox.Show(ex.Message);
    }
```

Most of this code follows the basic steps fairly closely. The only new part is the code that processes the stream. In this example, the program passes the stream to the `Bitmap` class's constructor to create a copy of the downloaded image. The code then displays the `Bitmap` in a `PictureBox`.

Figure 20-2 shows the WebRequestDownloadData example program displaying an image downloaded from the Internet.

FIGURE 20-2: The WebRequestDownloadData example program downloads and displays images from the Internet.

WEBCLIENT VERSUS WEBREQUEST

The `WebRequest` class certainly works, but for a simple download such as this one, the `WebClient` class also works and is simpler. When you need to download (or upload) a resource, consider the `WebClient` class first and see if it can get the job done.

UPLOADING INFORMATION

You can use the `WebClient` and `WebRequest` classes to upload data as well as download it. The process is fairly similar to the steps you follow for downloading resources, with a few changes to the methods you use. The following sections explain how you can use the `WebClient` and `WebRequest` classes to upload data.

Uploading with WebClient

Using a `WebClient` to upload a file is similar to using a `WebClient` to download a file. One big difference, however, is security.

Most of the Internet's material is freely available for download, but to upload anything you usually need a username and password for the destination server. In most cases you can supply those by setting the `WebRequest`'s `Credentials` property to a `NetworkCredential` object.

The following code shows how a program could use a `WebClient` to upload a file.

```
WebClient client = new WebClient();
client.Credentials = new NetworkCredential(username, password);
client.UploadFile(url, filename);
```

The `WebClient` class's `UploadFile`, `UploadData`, and `UploadString` methods correspond to their downloading counterparts. They also come in the asynchronous versions `UploadFileAsync`, `UploadDataAsync`, and `UploadStringAsync`.

The `OpenWrite` and `OpenWriteAsync` methods open streams into which the program can write. (These correspond to the `OpenRead` and `OpenReadAsync` methods that open streams for reading downloaded data.)

The `UploadValues` and `UploadValuesAsync` methods send a name/value collection for the server to process in some way.

> ### NEVER INCLUDE PASSWORDS!
>
> You should never include passwords in a program, its resources, or its configuration files. Otherwise, a cyber-villain could read the program's IL code or look at the configuration or resource files and easily recover the passwords.
>
> Always require the user to enter any password your program needs.

Uploading with WebRequest

When you use a `WebRequest` object to download data, you get a stream from a `WebResponse` object and then process the data in the stream. To use a `WebRequest` object to upload data, you get a stream and write data into it.

The following list summarizes the steps for using a `WebRequest` to upload a file.

1. Use the `WebRequest` object's `Create` method to create a `WebRequest` object.

2. Set the `WebRequest`'s `Method` property to indicate the method that you want to perform.

3. Set the `WebRequest`'s `Credentials` property to specify the username and password you want to use on the server.

4. Call the `WebRequest`'s `GetRequestStream` method to get a stream.

5. Write the data into the stream.

The following code shows how a program might use a `WebRequest` object to upload a byte array (highlighted in bold).

```
// Make the WebRequest.
WebRequest request = WebRequest.Create(url);

// Use the UploadFile method.
request.Method = WebRequestMethods.Ftp.UploadFile;

// Set network credentials.
request.Credentials = new NetworkCredential(username, password);

// Write the bytes into the request stream.
using (Stream stream = request.GetRequestStream())
{
    stream.Write(bytes, 0, bytes.Length);
}
```

From here, you can upload a file, `string`, image, or other data by converting it into a `byte` array and then using similar code to upload the array.

GETTING FTP INFORMATION

File Transfer Protocol (FTP) defines protocols for transferring files from one host to another on a *Transmission Control Protocol* (TCP) network such as the Internet.

These transfers are more storage-oriented than a typical Internet user's browser uses. A user typically uses a web browser to request a file and the browser displays it. FTP transfers typically move files, for example, between your computer and a host somewhere on the Internet.

FTP also allows you to ask a server file-related questions. For example, it lets you ask a server for a file's size or for a directory listing.

In addition to letting you upload and download files, the `WebRequest` class also lets you perform FTP queries. The steps are similar to those you use to download files.

1. Use `WebRequest.Create` to create the request object.

2. Set the request's `Method` property, in this case to an FTP method.

3. Set the object's `Credentials` property.

4. Call the request's `GetResponse` method to get a `WebResponse`.

5. Call the response's `GetResponseStream` method to get the response stream.

6. Process the stream.

The FtpGetFileInfo example program, which is available for download on this book's website, uses the following code to get the length of a file.

```
// Use FTP to get a remote file's size.
private long FtpGetFileSize(string url, string username, string password)
{
    // Make a FtpRequest object.
    WebRequest request = WebRequest.Create(url);
    request.Method = WebRequestMethods.Ftp.GetFileSize;

    // Set network credentials.
    request.Credentials = new NetworkCredential(username, password);

    using (WebResponse response = request.GetResponse())
    {
        // Return the size.
        return response.ContentLength;
    }
}
```

This code simply follows the steps outlined earlier.

The program uses the following code to get a file's last modification time.

```
// Use FTP to get a remote file's timestamp.
private DateTime FtpGetFileTimestamp(string uri, string username, string password)
{
    // Get the object used to communicate with the server.
    WebRequest request = WebRequest.Create(uri);
    request.Method = WebRequestMethods.Ftp.GetDateTimestamp;

    // Get network credentials.
    request.Credentials = new NetworkCredential(username, password);

    // Return the last modification time.
    using (FtpWebResponse response = (FtpWebResponse)request.GetResponse())
    {
        return response.LastModified;
    }
}
```

This code also follows the previously described steps but with one twist. The `LastModified` property is defined in the `FtpWebResponse` class, not in the `WebResponse` parent class. That means the code must cast the generic `WebResponse` returned by the `GetReponse` method into its true identity: an `FtpWebResponse` object.

ANONYMOUS ACCESS

There are two ways you will probably access FTP servers. First, you can use a normal username and password.

In contrast, some FTP servers allow anonymous downloads, uploads, or both. In that case, you should still create network credentials, but you should set the username to "anonymous" or "ftp." Some servers accept "Anonymous" but others are case-sensitive and require a lowercase username.

You can set the password to anything. Sometimes people use the password "guest." Many websites request that you use your e-mail address as the password so that they have a log of who's using their sites. Some sites require an e-mail address so that they won't allow "guest" as a password; although, they don't actually verify the e-mail address.

While you are testing FTP programs, you may want to find an anonymous FTP server. The examples provided in this chapter and the solutions to the exercises use the anonymous FTP server directory `ftp://nssdcftp.gsfc.nasa.gov/photo_ gallery/hi-res/astro`, which contains high-resolution NASA astronomy photographs. If you point your browser at this URL, you can see a listing of the directory.

Figure 20-3 shows the FtpGetFileInfo example program displaying information about a file on an anonymous FTP server.

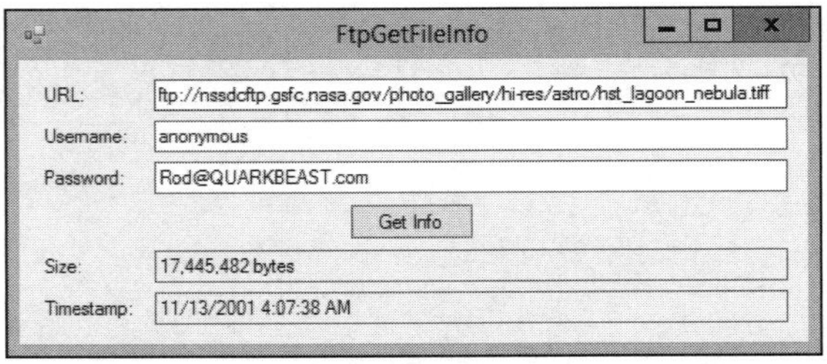

FIGURE 20-3: The FtpGetFileInfo example program displays information about files on FTP servers.

Other FTP commands such as `DeleteFile`, `ListDirectory`, and `ListDirectoryDetails` work more or less the same way; although, they return different results in their response streams.

SENDING E-MAIL

The `System.Net.Mail` namespace includes classes that let you send e-mail. The process is straightforward but somewhat cumbersome because there are a lot of options that can go along with an e-mail message. A message can have

➤   Subject

- ➤ Sender name and e-mail address

- ➤ Multiple primary, CC, and BCC recipient names and e-mail addresses

- ➤ Message body

- ➤ Multiple attachments

- ➤ Different priorities

- ➤ Delivery notification options

- ➤ Reply to addresses

Fortunately, these features are fairly easy to use. You simply create a `MailMessage` object and set its properties to provide all the necessary information.

The SendEmail example program, which is available for download on this book's website, uses the following `SendEmailMessage` method to send a simple e-mail message.

```
// Send an email.
private void SendEmailMessage(string toName, string toEmail,
    string fromName, string fromEmail,
    string host, int port, bool enableSsl, string password,
    string subject, string body)
{
    // Make the mail message.
    MailAddress fromAddress = new MailAddress(fromEmail, fromName);
    MailAddress toAddress = new MailAddress(toEmail, toName);
    MailMessage message = new MailMessage(fromAddress, toAddress);
    message.Subject = subject;
    message.Body = body;

    // Get the SMTP client.
    SmtpClient client = new SmtpClient()
    {
        Host = host,
        Port = port,
        EnableSsl = enableSsl,
        UseDefaultCredentials = false,
        Credentials = new NetworkCredential(fromAddress.Address, password),
    };

    // Send the message.
    client.Send(message);
}
```

The method starts by creating two `MailAddress` objects to represent the sender's name and e-mail address and the recipient's name and e-mail address. It then uses those objects to make a `MailMessage` object representing an e-mail message from the sender to the recipient. The code finishes preparing the `MailMessage` by setting its `Subject` and `Body` properties.

Next, the code creates an `SmtpClient` object to send the message. It sets the object's `Host` and `Port` properties to indicate the mail server that will process the message.

> ### SMTP
>
> *Simple Mail Transfer Protocol (SMTP)* is an Internet protocol for transmitting e-mail messages across an *Internet Protocol (IP)* network.

The code sets the `SmtpClient`'s `EnableSsl` property to enable or disable *Secure Sockets Layer (SSL)* to encrypt the connection with the host. The example program enables SSL.

> ### HOSTS, PORTS, AND SSL
>
> The SMTP host and port you use depends on your mail server. The SendEmail example program sets `Host` to `smtp.gmail.com` and the `Port` to `587`, which works for sending e-mail from Gmail accounts.
>
> For Hotmail accounts, try setting `Host` to `smtp.live.com` and `Port` to `587`.
>
> For other mail servers, search the Internet or your mail server's website for the correct host and port settings.
>
> Note also that many mail servers require that you enable SSL.

To prevent an evildoer from using your e-mail account to send spam about Nigerian oil money to everyone in North America, you must use a `NetworkCredential` object to log in to the mail server. The program creates this object using the sender's e-mail address and the password entered on the example program's form. Enter the password that you use to access your e-mail account.

Finally, when the `SmtpClient` object knows all the details about how it should send the message, the code simply calls its `Send` method, passing it the `MailMessage` that it should send.

SENDING TEXT MESSAGES

When you know how to write a program that sends e-mail, it's not too hard to write one that sends SMS text messages. To send an SMS message, send an e-mail message to an e-mail address with the format `number@gateway` where

➤ `number` is the recipient's telephone number with no special characters such as -, (,), or +.

➤ `gateway` is the SMS e-mail gateway used by the recipient's telephone carrier.

> ### SMS
>
> *Short Message Service (SMS)* uses standardized protocols to send text messages to phones.

For example, the following e-mail address would send a text message to the phone number 1-234-567-8901 assuming that phone number's carrier is Air Fire Mobile.

```
12345678901@sms.airfiremobile.com
```

The following web page contains a long list of telephone carriers and their SMS e-mail gateways.

```
https://github.com/cubiclesoft/email_sms_mms_gateways/blob/master/
sms_mms_gateways.txt
```

Unfortunately, this method still requires you to know the recipient's telephone carrier so that you can look up the SMS gateway address. (I don't know how to learn the carrier automatically from just the phone number. If you figure it out, please e-mail me at RodStephens@CSharpHelper.com. For bonus points, write a program to e-mail me the information.)

As you do for any e-mail message, you need to include a mail host and port, and a sender e-mail address and password. The message body and subject define the message that the recipient receives. On my phone, a typical message might look like the following:

thesender@somemailserver.com / This is the subject / This is the message body.

IMPLEMENTING NOTIFICATION MESSAGES

A program that sends SMS messages can have more uses than simply annoying your friends. Suppose you write a service process that runs on a computer and monitors some long-running process. For example, it might track the number of files in a spool directory and process them somehow. If the directory starts to grow large, that might indicate a problem with the processing application. In that case, the monitor might send you an SMS message telling you about the problem.

Unfortunately, this approach would require the program to know your password on the mail server and, as mentioned earlier in this chapter, you should never include a password in a program.

Similarly, the program would need to know your phone number and telephone carrier, two things that you probably don't want some hacker to stumble across.

You can mitigate the problem somewhat by obfuscating these sensitive values. You can store the values in some sort of encrypted or scrambled format and then make the program decode them. Of course, a determined hacker could easily study the IL code to see how the program decodes this information.

A better approach would be to start the program interactively and provide your e-mail address, password, phone number, and gateway server at that time. Then those values are never stored inside the program's code or configuration information.

You can also create a separate e-mail account just for this purpose. Then if a hacker gets hold of your e-mail address and password, you can stop using that account.

Finally, you should run the program (and store its code) only on a trusted computer. A hacker who can't find your program can't decode your information.

SUMMARY

The `WebClient` class makes uploading and downloading files relatively simple. In situations in which the `WebClient` class doesn't give you enough control, you can use the `WebRequest` and `WebResponse` classes to move data to and from a network with streams.

The `SmtpClient`, `MailMessage`, and `MailAddress` classes let you send e-mails quite easily. By sending a message to the proper e-mail address, you can send SMS text messages to a phone.

Together these classes provide some powerful tools for interacting with networks such as the Internet.

In addition to describing these classes, this chapter also defined a bunch of terms and abbreviations. The following table recaps those definitions.

TERM	MEANING
datagram	A basic unit of data sent over a packet-switched network. Datagrams may arrive out of order.
HTTP (HyperText Transfer Protocol)	A protocol that defines how messages are formatted and transmitted. It sits at a higher level than socket and datagram communications.
URL (Uniform Resource Location)	An address that specifies where some resource is located. Typical web addresses that you open with a browser are URLs.
URN (Uniform Resource Name)	A name that identifies something but doesn't necessarily refer to a "physical" resource location.
ISBN (International Standard Book Number)	A unique value that identifies a book. Because an ISBN does not tell you where to find a particular copy of the book, an ISBN is a URN but not a URL.
URI (Uniform Resource Identifier)	Includes both URLs and URNs.
TCP (Transmission Control Protocol)	One of the protocols used by the Internet that specifies how to move data from one point in the network to another. TCP provides reliable delivery of data in its correct order. TCP and IP are used together so frequently that they are often called TCP/IP.

TERM	MEANING
IP (Internet Protocol)	One of the protocols used by the Internet that specifies how to move data from one point in the network to another. IP ensures delivery of data based on an addressing scheme. TCP and IP are used together so frequently that they are often called TCP/IP.
FTP (File Transfer Protocol)	Defines protocols for transferring files from one host to another on a TCP network such as the Internet.
SMTP (Simple Mail Transfer Protocol)	An Internet protocol for transmitting e-mail messages across an IP (Internet Protocol) network.
SSL (Secure Sockets Layer)	Encrypts communications between Internet locations such as between an e-mail client and an e-mail server.
SMS (Short Message Service)	A service that uses standardized protocols to send text messages to phones.

When your program sends e-mails or text messages, you might like to parse the addressing information to see if it makes sense. For example, you cannot send e-mail to the address this@is@a@test.com and you cannot send an SMS message to the phone number 1-111-111.

Depending on the patterns you need to recognize, parsing values can be difficult. The following chapter describes regular expressions, a powerful tool you can use to make this sort of pattern recognition easier.

EXERCISES

1. Write a program that uses the WebClient's DownloadFile method to download the file http://www.csharphelper.com/howto_index.html and save it as the local file howto_index.html.

2. Write a program that uses the WebClient's DownloadString method to download the file http://blog.csharphelper.com/2010/07/02/draw-a-filled-chrysanthemum-curve-in-c.aspx. For bonus points, display it in a WebBrowser control.

   Hints: To display HTML text in a WebBrowser control, first add the following code to the form's Load event handler to initialize the WebBrowser.

   ```
   webBrowser1.Navigate("about:blank");
   ```

   Then use code similar to the following to display the HTML stored in the string variable html in the control.

   ```
   webBrowser1.Document.Body.InnerHtml = html;
   ```

3. Download the `DownloadStringAsync` example program (or write your own version) and modify it so that it uses the `DownloadStringTaskAsync` method.

Hints: Use the following statement to start the download.

```
string result = await client.DownloadStringTaskAsync(uri);
```

You can still use a `DownloadStringCompleted` event handler if you like, but you don't need to because you can move its code right after the call to `DownloadStringTaskAsync` (with a few error handling modifications).

4. The main benefit of using `await` in Exercise 3 is that it simplifies the code by allowing you to remove the `DownloadStringCompleted` event handler. How large is the benefit in this case? How could you increase the benefit?

5. Write a program that uses the `WebClient`'s `OpenStream` method to download an image file and display it in a `PictureBox`. Test the program by downloading the file `http://www.csharphelper.com/howto_filled_chrysanthemum_curve.png`. (Hint: The `Bitmap` class has a constructor that takes a stream as an argument.)

6. Modify the program you wrote for Exercise 5 so that it uses the `DownloadStreamAsync` method. Allow the user to cancel the download, but remember that this method doesn't fire the `DownloadProgressChanged` event.

7. Write a program that uses the `WebClient`'s `DownloadData` method to download an image file and display it in a `PictureBox`. Test the program by downloading the file `http://www.csharphelper.com/howto_filled_chrysanthemum_curve.png`. (Hint: The `MemoryStream` class has a constructor that takes a `byte[]` as an argument.)

8. Write a program that uses the `WebRequest` class's `Http.Get` method to download and display an image file. Test the program on the file `http://www.csharphelper.com/howto_vortex_fractal_smooth4.png`.

9. Write a program that uses the `WebClient`'s `UploadFile` method to upload a file to a web server. (You need to provide your own server, username, and password.)

10. Write a program that uses the `WebClient`'s `UploadString` method to upload a string into a file on a web server. (You need to provide your own server, username, and password.)

11. Write a program that uses the `WebRequest` class to upload a file to a web server. (You need to provide your own server, username, and password.) (Hint: Write an `UploadBytesIntoFile` method that uploads a `byte` array. Then write an `UploadFile` method that reads a file into a `byte` array and then calls `UploadBytesIntoFile` to do the real work.)

12. Write a program that uses the `WebRequest` class to upload a `string` to a web server. (You need to provide your own server, username, and password.) (Hint: Use the `UploadBytesIntoFile` method you wrote for Exercise 11.)

13. Write a program that uses the `ListDirectory` FTP command to list the files in an FTP directory. (For testing, you can use the anonymous FTP directory `ftp://nssdcftp.gsfc.nasa.gov/photo_gallery/hi-res/astro`.)

14. Modify the program you wrote for Exercise 13 so that it uses the `ListDirectoryDetails` FTP command.

15. Modify the program you wrote for Exercise 14 so that it displays the results ordered by file size. (Hint: This isn't as simple as you might like because different FTP servers may return the information in different formats. For this exercise, don't worry about a general solution. Pick a specific FTP directory such as the NASA server listed in Exercise 13 and parse the data from that directory.)

16. Modify the SendEmail example program so that you can add one CC recipient. (Hint: Add a new `MailAddress` object to the `MailMessage` object's `CC` collection.)

Note that some mail servers are clever enough to combine multiple copies of the same message sent to the same recipient. In this exercise, for example, if you use your own e-mail address as both the recipient and the CC recipient, your mail server may combine the two copies and you'll receive only one of them.

To test your solution, use my e-mail address `RodStephens@CSharpHelper.com` for one of the addresses. I'll send you a reply saying I got it. (Please try to send me only one message when you have the program debugged. Don't spam me with dozens of messages while you're working on early versions of the program.)

17. Modify your solution to Exercise 16 so that you can enter a comma-delimited series of e-mail addresses and the program sends BCC copies of the message to them. (Hint: Use the `MailMessage`'s `Bcc` collection.)

> **NOTE** *BCC stands for Blind Carbon Copy. BCC recipients receive a copy of the mail message, but other recipients don't see the BCC recipients' names or e-mail addresses.*

18. Write a program that sends your phone an SMS text message.

PART V
Advanced Topics

21

Regular Expressions

WHAT'S IN THIS CHAPTER

- ➤ Regular expression syntax
- ➤ Using regular expressions to detect matches, find matches, and make replacements
- ➤ Using regular expressions to parse input

WROX.COM DOWNLOADS FOR THIS CHAPTER

Please note that all the code examples for this chapter are available as a part of this chapter's code download on the book's website at `www.wrox.com/go/csharp5programmersref` on the Download Code tab.

Many applications enable the user to type information but the information should match some sort of pattern. For example, the string 784-36λ9 is not a valid phone number and Rod@Stephens@C#Helper.com is not a valid e-mail address.

One approach for validating this kind of input is to use string methods. You could use the `string` class's `IndexOf`, `LastIndexOf`, `Substring`, and other methods to break the input apart and see if the pieces make sense. For all but the simplest situations, however, that would be a huge amount of work.

Regular expressions provide another method for verifying that the user's input matches a pattern. A *regular expression* is a string that contains characters that define a pattern. For example, the regular expression `^\d{3}-\d{4}$` represents a pattern that matches three digits followed by a hyphen followed by four more digits as in 123-4567. (This isn't a great pattern for matching U.S. phone numbers because it enables many invalid combinations such as 111-1111 and 000-0000.)

The .NET Framework includes classes that can use regular expressions to see if an input string matches the pattern. They also provide methods for locating patterns within input text and for making complex substitutions.

This chapter provides an introduction to regular expressions. It explains how to create regular expressions and how to use them to see if a complete string matches a pattern, find matches within a string, use patterns to make replacements, and parse inputs.

THE REGULAREXPRESSIONS NAMESPACE

The .NET regular expression classes as in the System.Text.RegularExpressions namespace so, while you work with regular expressions, you may want to include that namespace in your program with a using directive.

NOT ALL REGULAR EXPRESSIONS ARE EQUAL

Different programming languages and environments may use different regular expression formats. For example, C++ running on a Linux system uses a different regular expression language than the one used by .NET. The languages use similar symbols so that they are often close enough to be confusing.

When you search the Internet for regular expression patterns to match a particular format such as UK phone numbers or Canadian postal codes, be certain the patterns you find use the .NET syntax and not some other syntax.

The following section explains the regular expression syntax used by .NET. The sections after that one explain how to determine whether a string matches a pattern, find matches within a string, and make replacements.

BUILDING REGULAR EXPRESSIONS

Before you can write code to see if an input string matches a pattern, you need to know how to build a regular expression to represent that pattern.

A regular expression can contain literal characters that the input must match exactly and characters that have special meanings. For example, the sequence [0-9] means the input must match a single digit 0 through 9.

Regular expressions can also contain special character sequences called *escape sequences* that match specific patterns or that control the behavior of a regular expression class. For example, the escape sequence \d makes the pattern match a single digit just as [0-9] does.

If you want to include a special character such as \ or [in a regular expression without it taking on its special meaning, you can "escape it" as in \\ or \[.

The tools you use to build regular expressions can be divided into six categories: character escapes, character classes, anchors, grouping constructs, quantifiers, and alternation constructs. The following sections describe those categories. The section after that describes some example regular expressions that match common input patterns such as telephone numbers.

ESCAPING ESCAPES

Remember that C# programs also use the \ character to begin escape sequences within strings. For example, \n represents a newline character and \t represents a tab character. That makes using \ as an escape in a regular expression awkward.

For example, suppose you want to match \ followed by a digit followed by \. The regular expression is \\\d\\. As if this weren't confusing enough, if you want to include this expression in a string defined inside your code, you need to escape the \ characters, so you get a mess similar to the following code.

```
string pattern = "^\\\\\\d\\\\$";
```

You can make your code easier to read by using the @ symbol to define any pattern strings in your code. The following statement initializes the same string as before, but it uses the @ symbol to make things slightly easier to read.

```
string pattern = @"^\\\d\\$";
```

The backslashes still make this somewhat confusing, but it's a lot easier to read than the first version.

Character Escapes

A *character escape* matches special characters such as [Tab] that you cannot simply type into a string. The following table lists the most useful character escapes.

ESCAPE	MEANING
\t	Matches the tab character
\r	Matches the return character
\n	Matches the newline character
\nnn	Matches a character with ASCII code given by the two or three octal digits nnn
\xnn	Matches a character with ASCII code given by the two hexadecimal digits nn
\unnnn	Matches a character with Unicode representation given by the four hexadecimal digits nnnn

For example, the regular expression \u00A7 matches the section symbol § (because 00A7 is that character's hexadecimal Unicode value).

Character Classes

A *character class* matches one of the items in a set of characters. For example, \d matches a digit 0 through 9. The following table lists the most useful character class constructs.

CONSTRUCT	MEANING
[chars]	Matches one of the characters inside the brackets. For example, [aeiou] matches a single lowercase vowel.
[^chars]	Matches a character that is not inside the brackets. For example, [^aeiouAEIOU] matches a single nonvowel character such as Q, ?, or 3.
[first-last]	Matches a character between the character *first* and the character *last*. For example, [a-z] matches any lowercase letter between a and z. You can combine multiple ranges as in [a-zA-Z], which matches uppercase or lowercase letters.
.	This is a wildcard that matches any single character except \n. (To match a period, use the \. escape sequence.)
\w	Matches a single "word" character. Normally, this is equivalent to [a-zA-Z_0-9], so it matches letters, the underscore character, and digits.
\W	Matches a single nonword character. Normally, this is equivalent to [^a-zA-Z_0-9].
\s	Matches a single whitespace character. Normally, this includes [Space], [Form feed], [Newline], [Return], [Tab], and [Vertical tab].
\S	Matches a single nonwhitespace character. Normally, this matches everything except [Space], [Form feed], [Newline], [Return], [Tab], and [Vertical tab].
\d	Matches a single decimal digit. Normally, this is equivalent to [0-9].
\D	Matches a single character that is not a decimal digit. Normally, this is equivalent to [^0-9].

DASHING DASHES

If you want to include a dash character inside a bracketed group, place it at the beginning or end so that it's not confused with the dash used to make a range of characters. For example, the patterns [-a-z] and [a-z-] both match the dash character – or a lowercase letter a through z.

For example, the regular expression [A-Z]\d[A-Z] \d[A-Z]\d matches a Canadian postal code of the form A1A 1A1 where A represents a letter and 1 represents a digit.

NO JOKE

The Canadian postal service Canada Post gave Santa Claus his own postal code: H0H 0H0.

Anchors

An *anchor* (also called an *atomic zero-width assertion*) represents a state that the input string must be in at a certain point to achieve a match. Anchors have a position in the string but do not use up characters.

For example, the ^ and $ characters represent the beginning and ending of a line or the string, depending on whether you work on multiline or single-line input.

The following table lists the most useful anchors.

ANCHOR	MEANING
^	Matches the beginning of the line or string
$	Matches the end of the string or before the \n at the end of the line or string
\A	Matches the beginning of the string
\Z	Matches the end of the string or before the \n at the end of the string
\z	Matches the end of the string
\G	Matches where the previous match ended
\B	Matches a nonword boundary

REGEX OPTIONS

The Framework's regular expression classes provide options to let you change the way they process input strings. For example, options enable you to specify whether a class should treat a multiline input string as a series of lines that should be matched separately or as a single, long string that happens to contain multiple lines.

You can specify regular expression options in three ways.

First, you can pass a `RegexOptions` parameter to a `Regex` object's constructor or pattern matching methods such as `IsMatch`.

Second, you can use the syntax `(?options)` to include inline options within a regular expression. These options, which are described shortly, can include any of the values i, m, n, s, or x. If the list begins with a – character, then the following options are turned off. The options remain in effect until a new set of inline options reset their values.

Third, you can use the syntax `(?options:subexpression)` within a regular expression. In this case, `options` is as before, and `subexpression` is the part of a regular expression during which the options should apply.

The following table lists the available options.

OPTION	MEANING
i	Ignore case.
m	Multiline. Here ^ and $ match the beginning and ending of lines instead of the beginning and ending of the whole input string.
s	Single-line. Here . matches all characters including \n.
n	Explicit capture. This makes the method not capture unnamed groups. See the following section "Grouping Constructs" for more information on groups.
x	Ignore unescaped whitespace in the pattern and enable comments after the # character.

For more information on these options, see "Regular Expression Options" at `msdn.microsoft.com/library/yd1hzczs.aspx`.

Grouping Constructs

Grouping constructs enables you to define *capture groups* within matching pieces of a string. For example, in a U.S. Social Security number with the format 123-45-6789, you could define groups to hold the pieces 123, 45, and 6789. The program could later refer to those groups either with C# code or later inside the same regular expression.

Parentheses create groups. For example, consider the expression `(\w)\1`. The parentheses create a numbered group that in this example matches a single word character. Later in the expression, the text `\1` refers to group number 1. That means this regular expression matches a word character followed by itself. If the string is "book," then this pattern would match the "oo" in the middle.

GROUP INDEXES

In regular expressions, numbered groups are numbered starting at 1, not 0.

There are several kinds of groups, some of which are fairly specialized and confusing. The two most common are numbered and named groups.

To create a numbered group, simply enclose a subexpression in parentheses as shown in the previous example.

To create a named group, use the syntax `(?<name>subexpression)` where `name` is the name you want to assign to the group and `subexpression` is a subexpression.

To use a named group in a regular expression, use the syntax `\k<name>`.

For example, the expression `(?<twice>\w)\k<twice>` is equivalent to the previous expression `(\w)\1` except the group is named `twice`.

Quantifiers

A *quantifier* makes the regular expression engine match the previous element a certain number of times. For example, the expression `\d{3}` matches any digit exactly 3 times. The following table describes regular expression quantifiers.

QUANTIFIER	MEANING
*	Matches the previous element 0 or more times
+	Matches the previous element 1 or more times
?	Matches the previous element 0 or 1 times
{n}	Matches the previous element exactly n times
{n,}	Matches the previous element n or more times
{n,m}	Matches the previous element between n and m times (inclusive)

If you follow one of these with `?`, the pattern matches the preceding expression as few times as possible. For example, the pattern `BO+` matches B followed by 1 or more Os, so it would match the BOO in BOOK. The pattern `BO+?` also matches a B character followed by 1 or more Os, but it matches as few Os as possible, so it would match only the BO in BOOK.

Alternation Constructs

An *alternation construct* uses the | character to allow a pattern to match either of two subexpressions. For example, the expression ^(true|yes)$ matches either true or yes.

For a more complicated example, the pattern ^(\d{3}-\d{4}|\d{3}-\d{3}-\d{4})$ matches 7-digit U.S. phone numbers of the form 123-4567 and 10-digit U.S. phone numbers of the form 123-456-7890.

Sample Regular Expressions

The following list describes several useful regular expressions.

➤ ^\d{3}-\d{4}$

This is a simple 7-digit phone number format and allows several illegal phone numbers such as 111-1111 and 000-0000.

^—Match the start of the string, so the phone number must start at the beginning of the string.

\d—Match any digit.

{3}—Repeat the previous (match any digit) 3 times. In other words, match 3 digits.

- —Match the - character.

\d—Match any digit.

{4}—Match 4 digits.

➤ ^[2-9][0-9]{2}-\d{4}$

This matches a 7-digit U.S. phone number more rigorously. The exchange code at the beginning must match the pattern NXX where N is a digit 2-9 and X is any digit 0-9.

➤ ^[2-9][0-8]\d-[2-9][0-9]{2}-\d{4}$

This pattern matches a 10-digit U.S. phone number with the format NPA-NXX-XXXX where N is a digit 2-9, P is a digit 0-8, A is any digit 0-9, and X is any digit 0-9.

➤ ^([2-9][0-8]\d-)?[2-9][0-9]{2}-\d{4}$

This pattern matches a U.S. phone number with an optional area code such as 202-234-5678 or 234-5678. The part of the pattern ([2-9][0-8]\d-)? matches the area code. The ? at the end means the preceding group can appear 0 or 1 times, so it's optional. The rest of the pattern is similar to the earlier pattern that matches a 7-digit U.S. phone number.

➤ ^\d{5}(-\d{4})?$

This pattern matches a U.S. ZIP code with optional +4 as in 12345 or 12345-6789.

➤ ^[A-Z]\d[A-Z] \d[A-Z]\d$

This pattern matches a Canadian postal code with the format A1A 1A1 where A is any capital letter and 1 is any digit.

➤ `^[a-zA-Z0-9.-]{3,16}$`

This pattern matches a username with 3 to 16 characters that can be dashes, letters, digits, periods, or underscores. You may need to modify the allowed characters to fit your application.

➤ `^[a-zA-Z][a-zA-Z0-9._-]{2,15}$`

This pattern matches a username that includes a letter followed by 2 to 15 dashes, letters, digits, periods, or underscores. You may need to modify the allowed characters to fit your application.

➤ `^[a-zA-Z0-9._%+-]+@[a-zA-Z0-9._%+-]+\.[a-zA-Z]{2,4}$`

This pattern matches an e-mail address.

The sequence `[a-zA-Z0-9._%+-]` matches letters, digits, underscores, %, +, and –. The plus sign after that group means the string must include one or more of those characters.

Next, the pattern matches the `@` symbol.

The pattern then matches another letter one or more times, followed by a `.`, and then between two and four letters.

For example, this pattern matches `RodStephens@CSharpHelper.com`. This pattern isn't perfect but it matches most valid e-mail addresses.

➤ `^[+-]?[a-fA-F0-9]{3}$`

This pattern matches a 3-digit hexadecimal value with an optional sign + or – as in +A1F.

➤ `^(https?://)?([\w-]+\.)+[\w-]+$`

This pattern matches a top-level HTTP web address such as `http://www.csharphelper.com`.

The pattern `(https?://)?` matches `http`, followed by an `s` zero or one times, followed by `://`. The whole group is followed by `?`, so the whole group must appear zero or one times.

The pattern `([\w-]+\.)+` matches a word character (letter, digit, or underscore) or dash one or more times followed by a period. This whole group is followed by `+` so the whole group must appear one or more times.

The final piece `[\w-]+` matches one or more letters, digits, underscores, or dashes one or more times.

This pattern isn't perfect. In particular it doesn't validate the final part of the domain, so it would match `www.something.whatever`.

➤ `^(https?://)?([\w-]+\.)+[\w-]+(/(([\w-]+)(\.[\w-]+)*)*)*$`

This pattern matches an HTTP web URI such as `http://www.csharphelper.com/howto_index.html`. It starts with the same code used by the preceding pattern. The new part is highlighted in bold.

The entire new piece is surrounded by parentheses and followed by *, so the whole thing can appear zero or more times.

The new piece begins with a /, so the text must start with a / character.

The rest of the new piece is surrounded with parentheses and followed by *, so that part can appear zero or more times. This allows the URL to end with a /.

The rest of the pattern is ([\w-]+)(\.[\w-]+)*). The first part ([\w-]+) requires the string to include one or more letters, digits, underscores, or dashes. The second part (\.[\w-]+)*) requires the string to contain a period followed by one or more letters, digits, underscores, or dashes. This second part is followed by *, so it can appear zero or more times. (Basically this piece means the URL can include characters separated by periods but it cannot end with a period.)

Again, this pattern isn't perfect and doesn't handle some more advanced URLs such as those that include =, ?, and # characters, but it does handle many typical URLs.

Notice that all these patterns begin with the beginning-of-line anchor ^ and end with the end-of-line anchor $, so each pattern matches the entire string not just part of it. For example, the pattern ^\d{5}(-\d{4})?$ matches complete strings that look like ZIP codes such as 12345. Without the ^ and $, the pattern would match strings that *contain* a string that looks like a ZIP code such as x12345x.

TESTING REGULAR EXPRESSIONS

Using the techniques described in the following sections, you can write C# programs to use and test regular expressions. However, tools are available that let you test regular expressions without building programs around them. For example, you can use the following tools.

➤   regexhero.net/tester

➤   derekslager.com/blog/posts/2007/09/a-better-dotnet-regular-expression-tester.ashx

➤   www.myregextester.com/

Remember that some programming languages have slightly different regular expressions syntax. For example, in JavaScript regular expressions don't allow named groups so a tool that uses JavaScript would not be able to use the expression (?<double>.)\k<double> to detect double letters. Be sure the tool you pick uses the syntax used by .NET.

USING REGULAR EXPRESSIONS

The Regex class provides objects that you can use to work with regular expressions. The following table summarizes the Regex class's most useful methods.

METHOD	PURPOSE
IsMatch	Returns `true` if a string satisfies a regular expression.
Match	Searches a string for the first part of it that satisfies a regular expression.
Matches	Returns a collection giving information about all parts of a string that satisfy a regular expression.
Replace	Replaces some or all the parts of the string that match a regular expression with a new value. (This is much more powerful than the `string` class's `Replace` method.)
Split	Splits a string into an array of substrings delimited by pieces of the string that match a regular expression.

Many of the methods described in the table have multiple overloaded versions. In particular, many take a `string` as a parameter and can optionally take another parameter that gives a regular expression. If you don't pass the method a regular expression, then the method uses the expression you passed into the object's constructor.

The `Regex` class also provides static versions of these methods that take both a `string` and a regular expression as parameters. For example, the following code determines whether the text in `inputTextBox` satisfies the regular expression in `patternTextBox`.

```
if (Regex.IsMatch(inputTextBox.Text, patternTextBox.Text))
    resultLabel.Text = "Match";
else
    resultLabel.Text = "No match";
```

The static methods make simple regular expression testing easy.

The following sections explain how to use the `Regex` class to perform common regular expression tasks such as finding matches, making replacements, and parsing input strings.

Matching Patterns

The `Regex` class's static `IsMatch` method gives you an easy way to determine whether a string satisfies a regular expression. The MatchPattern example program, which is available for download and shown in Figure 21-1, uses this method to determine whether a string matches a pattern.

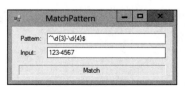

FIGURE 21-1: The MatchPattern example program determines whether a string satisfies a regular expression.

When you modify the regular expression or the string, the program executes the following code.

```
// See if the text matches the pattern.
private void CheckForMatch()
```

```
{
    try
    {
        if (Regex.IsMatch(inputTextBox.Text, patternTextBox.Text))
            resultLabel.Text = "Match";
        else
            resultLabel.Text = "No match";
    }
    catch (Exception ex)
    {
        resultLabel.Text = ex.Message;
    }
}
```

The code passes the `Regex.IsMatch` method the string to validate and the regular expression. The method returns `true` if the string satisfies the expression. The program then displays an appropriate message in `resultLabel`.

This example uses a `try catch` block to protect itself from improperly formed regular expressions. For example, suppose you want to use the expression `(.)\1` to detect repeated characters. At one point while you're typing you will have entered just `(`, which is not a valid regular expression.

Finding Matches

The MatchPattern example program described in the preceding section determines whether a string satisfies a regular expression. For example, it can use the pattern `(.)\1` to verify that the string `bookkeeper` contains a double letter. However, that program won't tell you where the double letter is. In this example, `bookkeeper` contains three double letters: `oo`, `kk`, and `ee`.

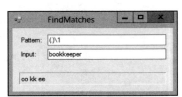

FIGURE 21-2: The FindMatches example program finds the parts of a string that match a pattern.

The `Regex` class's `Matches` method can give you information about places where a string matches a regular expression. The FindMatches example program, which is available for download and shown in Figure 21-2, displays the parts of a string that match a pattern.

The FindMatches program uses the following code to locate matches.

```
// Display matches.
private void FindMatches()
{
    try
    {
        // Make the regex object.
        Regex regex = new Regex(patternTextBox.Text);

        // Find the matches.
        string matches = "";
        foreach (Match match in regex.Matches(inputTextBox.Text))
        {
```

```
                    // Display the matches.
                    matches += match.Value +" ";
                }
                resultLabel.Text = matches;
            }
            catch (Exception ex)
            {
                resultLabel.Text = ex.Message;
            }
        }
```

This code creates a `Regex` object, passing its constructor the regular expression pattern. It then calls the object's `Matches` method, passing it the input string. It loops through the resulting collection of `Match` objects and adds each match's `Value` to a result string. When it is finished, it displays the results in `resultLabel`.

The following table lists the `Match` class's most useful properties.

PROPERTY	PURPOSE
Groups	Returns a collection of objects representing any groups captured by the regular expression. The `Group` class has `Index`, `Length`, and `Value` properties that describe the group.
Index	The index of the match's first character.
Length	The length of the text represented by this match.
Value	The text represented by this match.

Making Replacements

The `Regex` class's static `Replace` method lets you replace the parts of a string that match a pattern with a new string. The MakeReplacements example program, which is available for download and shown in Figure 21-3, replaces parts of a string that match a pattern with a new string.

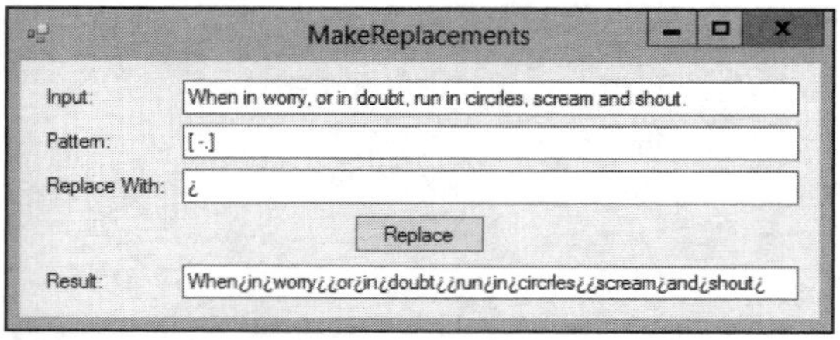

FIGURE 21-3: The MakeReplacements example program replaces matching parts of a string with a new value.

The following code shows how the MakeReplacements program makes replacements.

```
// Make the replacements.
private void replaceButton_Click(object sender, EventArgs e)
{
    resultTextBox.Text = Regex.Replace(
        inputTextBox.Text,
        patternTextBox.Text,
        replaceWithTextBox.Text);
}
```

This code simply calls the `Replace` method, passing it the input string, the pattern to match, and the replacement text.

Parsing Input

In some situations, you can use a `Regex` object to parse an input string by using capture groups. After matching a string, you can loop through a `Regex` object's `Matches` collection to find parts of the string that matched the expression. You can then use each `Match`'s `Groups` collection, indexed by number or name (if the groups are named), to get the pieces of the match in the groups.

The ParsePhoneNumber example program, which is available for download and shown in Figure 21-4, uses a `Regex` object to find the pieces of a 10-digit phone number.

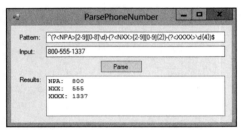

FIGURE 21-4: The ParsePhoneNumber example program parses out the pieces of a phone number.

The ParsePhoneNumber program uses the following code to find the phone number's pieces.

```
// Find matching groups.
private void parseButton_Click(object sender, EventArgs e)
{
    groupsListBox.Items.Clear();

    Regex regex = new Regex(patternTextBox.Text);
    foreach (Match match in regex.Matches(inputTextBox.Text))
    {
        groupsListBox.Items.Add("NPA:  " + match.Groups["NPA"]);
        groupsListBox.Items.Add("NXX:  " + match.Groups["NXX"]);
        groupsListBox.Items.Add("XXXX: " + match.Groups["XXXX"]);
    }
}
```

This code clears its `ListBox` and then creates a `Regex` object, passing its constructor the pattern to match. It then calls the `Matches` method, passing it the input string, and loops through the resulting collection of matches.

If the input string contains a single phone number, there will be only one match in the `Matches` collection. In fact, the pattern shown in Figure 21-4 can contain at most one match.

For each match, the code uses the Groups collection to get the text in the named groups NPA, NXX, and XXXX. It adds the values it finds to the result ListBox.

SUMMARY

The string class provides methods that you can use to examine a string to see if it matches a particular pattern. Unfortunately, using those methods can be a lot of work if the pattern is complicated.

The Regex class provides another approach that is often much easier. Instead of breaking a string apart to see if it matches a pattern, the Regex class lets you define a regular expression and then see whether the string satisfies the expression. The class's methods also let you find parts of a string that match the expression, make replacements, and parse a string to find pieces that match parts of a regular expression.

Chapter 8, "LINQ," described PLINQ, which lets you perform multiple LINQ queries in parallel. PLINQ isn't the only way a program can perform multiple tasks at the same time. The following chapter explains other methods in which you can use parallelism to improve performance on multiple CPU or multicore systems.

EXERCISES

1. Write a program that takes an input string, removes leading and trailing whitespace, and replaces sequences of multiple whitespace characters with single spaces. For example, with the input string " **This   is   a test.   ** " the program should produce the result "This is a test."

2. Write a program that uses Regex.Split to list the words in a string.

3. Modify the FindMatches example program shown in Figure 21-2 so that it displays matches in a ListBox. Then run the program with the regular expression \w* and the input string abc;def;;;ghi;;. Why doesn't the program display only the three strings abc, def, and ghi? How can you make it display only those strings?

4. The ParsePhoneNumber example program shown in Figure 21-4 cannot match a phone number that is missing the area code. It can parse 800-555-1337 but cannot parse 555-1337. What regular expression can you use to parse phone numbers with or without an area code? What does the program do if a phone number is missing the area code?

5. Modify the ParsePhoneNumber example program so that it parses multiple phone numbers in a multiline string. Display each phone number's pieces on a separate line in the ListBox as in NPA: 800, NXX: 555, XXXX: 1337.

   Hints: When you create the Regex object, use the Multiline option. That makes the ^ and $ characters match the start and end of each line instead of the entire string. Also note that the Regex object considers [Newline] to mark the end of a line but a TextBox uses the [Return] [Newline] combination to mark the end of a line. Modify the regular expression so it can remove the [Return] characters as needed.

6.   Write a regular expression that matches integers with digit grouping such as –1,234 and +91. Use the MatchPattern example program shown in Figure 21-1 to check your result.

7.   Write a regular expression that matches floating-point numbers such as –1234.56 and +65.43. If a number has a decimal point, require at least one digit after it.

8.   Write a regular expression that matches floating-point numbers with digit grouping such as –1,234.5678.

9.   Replacement patterns let the Regex.Replace method use groups and other parts of a match in replacement text. For example, within the replacement text, you can use $1 to represent the text in the first match group.

Write a program that lets you type a series of names of the form **Ann Archer**. When you click the Rearrange button, make the program use replacement patterns to rewrite the names in the form Archer, Ann.

Hints: Remember to remove the trailing [Return] character from each line. Use replacement patterns to restore it in the result so each name appears on a separate line.

22

Parallel Programming

One way to improve a program's performance is to run it on a faster computer, but there's a limit to how many instructions per second even a fast CPU can execute.

Another approach is to run different parts of the program on different processors. Some computers have multiple processors and many these days have multiple *cores*, separate *central processing units (CPUs)* on a single chip. Two core systems are the norm these days and processors with four, eight, or even more cores are available.

To execute commands on different CPUs, a .NET application creates multiple threads. A *thread* is the smallest unit of code to which an operating system allocates CPU time. In *multithreading*, a single process has multiple threads of execution. If the system has multiple CPUs, the threads can run in parallel on different CPUs.

MULTITHREADING ADVANTAGES

Multithreading has other advantages in addition to executing code in parallel. For example, many programs perform tasks that take a long time to finish. Perhaps the program needs to check a dozen websites to get pricing information for a particular product. If the program does everything in a single thread, then the main program is blocked until the web search finishes. That means the user interface is stuck and the user can't do anything except watch the screen refuse to refresh. If you run the user interface and the web search on separate threads, the program can remain responsive even while the search is still running.

Multithreading can also sometimes simplify your code. Suppose a program needs to monitor several processes. Perhaps it needs to periodically check a collection of websites for news and stock prices. You could write a program that repeatedly loops through each of the websites to check them one after another. That might be somewhat complicated because the code to deal with each website would be intermingled with the code needed to loop through the sites, handle timeouts, and deal with other potential problems on each site.

Another approach would be to assign a separate thread to each website and let each thread run independently. Now each thread's code can focus on a single website. Also if one thread's website is having problems, it won't affect the performance of the other threads.

The .NET Framework provides several methods for multithreading including the following.

➤ **PLINQ**—You saw this in Chapter 8, "LINQ."

➤ `BackgroundWorker`—This component executes code on a separate thread. It uses events to communicate with the main user interface thread (the UI thread).

➤ **Task Parallel Library (TPL)**—These tools let you easily run multiple methods in different threads or run multiple instances of the same method with different parameters.

➤ **Tasks**—The `Task` class lets you create and run threads. The `Task` class defines some methods to make certain typical operations easier such as creating and starting a task in a single step, waiting for a group of tasks to finish, or waiting until any one of a group of tasks finishes.

➤ **Threads**—The `Thread` class gives you lower level access to threads. These are more complicated that using other methods but they provide greater control.

This chapter explains how you can use `BackgroundWorker`, TPL, threads, and tasks to execute code on multiple threads simultaneously. (See the section "PLINQ" in Chapter 8 for information about PLINQ.)

Multiprocessing is a big topic so this chapter provides only an overview of the most common parallel programming techniques. Threads are particularly complicated, so this chapter doesn't cover them exhaustively. PLINQ, the `BackgroundWorker` component, TPL, and the `Task` class are much simpler than threads and provide much of the same basic functionality.

Before you can learn how to use those tools, however, you need to learn a bit about how threads can interact with the user interface's controls. The following section explains those interactions. The sections after that describe `BackgroundWorker`, TPL, and threads.

THE NEED FOR SPEED

Actually, there are several other ways you can improve a program's performance in addition to multithreading.

If performance is limited by disk speed, you can buy faster disks. Many programs, particularly database applications and data-oriented programs, are limited by how fast the program can move data to and from storage rather than how fast the code executes. In that case, faster disks can greatly improve performance. Fast hard drives, solid state disks, and hybrid drives (which combine hard drives and solid state memory) can greatly improve performance over slower drives. *Redundant arrays of independent disks (RAID)* can also improve performance by distributing data across several physical disks. This is sort of like parallel processing for disk storage.

If the application is limited by available memory, you can buy more memory. If a computer's applications use up all its physical memory, the computer must *page* some applications' memory to disk so that it can use that memory for other programs. When the paged program is ready to run again, its memory must be paged back from disk into memory. Paging is extremely slow compared to normal memory access, so this degrades the performance of the entire system. Buying more memory (and you can buy memory with different access speeds) can eliminate paging and greatly improve performance.

Many applications are limited by critical sections of code. Although parts of the application may be fast enough, other parts may limit overall performance. In that case it may be worth spending some extra time writing an algorithm to optimize the critical sections of code. (For information about some interesting algorithms, see my book *Essential Algorithms: A Practical Approach to Computer Algorithms*, Rod Stephens, Wiley, 2013.)

The history of the drive to improve transistor density and processor speed is also fascinating. See `en.wikipedia.org/wiki/Moore's_law` for information about *Moore's Law*, the trend that the number of transistors on integrated circuits roughly doubles every 2 years. Gordon E. Moore made this observation in 1965 and it has proven amazingly accurate ever since.

INTERACTING WITH THE USER INTERFACE

Windows Forms controls are not thread-safe. That means they can safely be manipulated only by the thread that created them: the UI thread. If a program runs multiple threads, only the UI thread can safely interact with the controls. If a non-UI thread tries to manipulate a control, it might succeed sometimes but often it crashes the program.

Sometimes, a thread might need to interact with the user interface to provide information to the user. For example, a thread that monitors stock prices might need to display a new price or draw a graph showing prices over time.

A non-UI thread cannot directly modify the UI controls, but it can modify them indirectly. To interact with the UI controls, a thread should follow these steps.

1. Check the InvokeRequired property for a control that was created in the UI thread. This property is true if that control was created on a thread other than the thread that is calling InvokeRequired. (Typically a thread checks the form's InvokeRequired property, so the property is true if the thread is not the UI thread.)

2. If InvokeRequired is true, the thread should call the control's Invoke method, passing it a delegate. The Invoke method then executes the delegate on the thread that created the control. (Again the control is typically the form, so Invoke executes the delegate on the UI thread because it created the form.)

3. The delegate executes on the control's thread. Because it is running in the control's thread, the delegate can safely interact with the control. (Typically, the control was created in the UI thread, so the delegate can interact with all the UI controls.)

If this seems a bit confusing, that's because it is. The Invoke example program, which is available for download on this book's website, provides a simple example that uses two techniques to update two different labels. (Unfortunately, even a simple example such as this one can be fairly confusing.)

This example uses a Timer component created at design time to update a label to show the current time. At design time I set the Timer's Enabled property to true so that the Timer starts running automatically. I also set its Interval property to 500 so that it fires its Tick event every 500 milliseconds (every one-half second).

The following code shows the Timer's Tick event handler.

```
// Update the first clock.
private void clock1Timer_Tick(object sender, EventArgs e)
{
    clock1Label.Text = DateTime.Now.ToString("T");
}
```

The Tick event handler runs in the UI thread so that it can access the clock1Label control directly. That makes this nice and simple.

TIMER ISN'T MULTITHREADING

I didn't count the Timer component as an option for multithreading because it doesn't let you use multiple processors. The Tick event runs on the UI thread, so all the work done by the Timer is done in the UI thread, not in a separate thread.

The following code shows how the program creates and launches a thread to update its second clock label.

```
// Start a thread to update the second clock.
private void Form1_Load(object sender, EventArgs e)
{
    // Create the thread.
    Thread thread = new Thread(UpdateClock2);

    // Start the thread.
    thread.Start();
}
```

The form's Load event handler declares and instantiates the thread variable, passing its constructor the method that the thread should execute: UpdateClock2. It then calls the object's Start method to start the thread.

The following code shows the UpdateClock2 method that the thread executes.

```
// The method that the thread executes.
private void UpdateClock2()
{
    // Loop forever.
    for (; ; )
    {
        // This doesn't work.
        //clock2Label.Text = DateTime.Now.ToString("T");

        // This works.
        if (this.InvokeRequired)
            this.Invoke(new Action(DoUpdateClock2));

        // Sleep for 1/2 second.
        Thread.Sleep(500);
    }
}
```

The method enters an infinite loop. Inside the loop, commented code tries to directly set the text displayed by the clock2Label control. Because that control was created by the UI thread, this code fails. If you uncomment this statement, you'll get the following exception message.

An unhandled exception of type 'System.InvalidOperationException' occurred in System.Windows.Forms.dll.

Additional information: Cross-thread operation not valid: Control 'clock2Label' accessed from a thread other than the thread it was created on.

After the commented code, the method checks `InvokeRequired` to see if the code is executing on a non-UI thread. (Actually in this example we know for certain that the code is executing on a non-UI thread, so you could skip this check and just call `Invoke`.) If `InvokeRequired` is `true`, the program calls `Invoke`, passing it the method that should be invoked, in this case `DoUpdateClock2`.

After invoking `DoUpdateClock2`, the loop sleeps for one-half a second before the next update.

> ### SELF-INVOCATION
>
> Some programmers use a single method to perform an action from the UI thread or from some other thread. The method checks `InvokeRequired` to see if it is executing on a non-UI thread. If `InvokeRequired` is `true`, the method invokes itself. If `InvokeRequired` is `false`, the method performs whatever action it needs to take on the UI thread.
>
> This technique lets you use one method instead of two, but it may be confusing. Use whichever technique you find easiest to understand.

The following code shows the `DoUpdateClock2` method that updates the second clock label on the UI thread.

```
// Perform the update for the second clock.
private void DoUpdateClock2()
{
    clock2Label.Text = DateTime.Now.ToString("T");
}
```

This method runs on the UI thread, so it simply sets the `clock2Label` control's `Text` property directly.

There's one more complication to using the thread in this way. When you close the main form, the thread keeps running. The form closes but the application doesn't end.

There are a couple ways you can handle this. First, you can stop the thread in either the form's `Closing` or `Closed` event handler. If you declare the thread variable at the class level, the event handler can call the thread's `Abort` method to make it stop.

You can also make the `Closing` or `Closed` event handler call `Environment.Exit`. This ends the application immediately, stopping all threads.

A better solution is to set the thread's `IsBackground` property to `true`. When all foreground threads end, the application stops any background threads and terminates. Initially the main form's UI thread is the only foreground thread. If you don't create any others, then when you close the main form, its UI thread stops, so the application stops.

The following code shows the full version of the Invoke example program's `Load` event handler. The code that sets the `IsBackground` property is highlighted in bold.

```
// Start a thread to update the second clock.
private void Form1_Load(object sender, EventArgs e)
{
    // Create the thread.
    Thread thread = new Thread(UpdateClock2);
    thread.IsBackground = true;

    // Start the thread.
    thread.Start();
}
```

BACKGROUNDWORKER

Understanding how to use `InvokeRequired` and `Invoke` is one of the harder parts of using threads. Compared to accessing UI controls from other threads, using `BackgroundWorker` is relatively simple.

The `BackgroundWorker` component provides a relatively simple way to run a separate thread of execution. The basic process follows.

1. Create a `BackgroundWorker`. Because this is a component, you can place one on a form at design time if you want.

2. To make the worker start running, call its `RunWorkerAsync` method. This starts a new thread and raises the worker's `DoWork` event handler on that thread.

3. The worker must catch its `DoWork` event. This event handler is where the worker executes its code. This event handler runs on a separate thread, so it and the UI thread may run on different processors.

If you like, the `BackgroundWorker` can provide feedback to the main UI thread. To do that, add these steps to those described in the preceding list.

1. Before starting the `BackgroundWorker`, set its `WorkerReportsProgress` property to `true`.

2. Catch the worker's `ProgressChanged` event. This event handler runs in the UI thread, so it can manipulate the user interface controls without messing with `InvokeRequired` and `Invoke`.

If you want the main program to stop the worker, follow these steps.

1. Before starting the `BackgroundWorker`, set its `WorkerSupportsCancellation` property to `true`.

2. To stop the worker, call its `CancelAsync` method.

3. In the `DoWork` event handler, periodically check the worker's `CancellationPending` property. If that property is `true`, the event handler should exit. If you like, the code can set the `e.Cancel` parameter to indicate that the work was canceled.

If you declare the `BackgroundWorker` in code instead of adding it to a form at design time, you must keep a reference to it at the class level so that the code can call its `CancelAsync` method in step 2.

The worker raises its `RunWorkerCompleted` event if the `DoWork` event handler ends, if the `DoWork` event handler throws an exception, or if the worker is stopped by a call to its `CancelAsync` method.

If the `DoWork` event handler exits, the worker stops. The event handler can set its `e.Result` parameter to return a value to the `RunWorkerComplete` event handler.

TPL

The `BackgroundWorker` component uses events to interact with the UI thread without the hassle of using `InvokeRequired` and `Invoke`. Because it uses event handlers, it breaks the code up into pieces that cannot be easily run in a sequence.

For example, suppose you want to perform several complicated calculations and display the results to the user. You could use a separate `BackgroundWorker` to calculate each of the results. Unfortunately, the main method that created the workers would then need to end. The program would later catch the workers' `RunWorkerCompleted` events. It would then need to figure out when all the workers had finished and display the combined result. If the program needed to use the results to calculate further results, the whole process might start again. The finished code would be filled with event handlers and code to coordinate them.

TPL provides much better methods for performing multiple calculations on separate threads and waiting for them all to complete. Those methods are `Parallel.For`, `Parallel.ForEach`, and `Parallel.Invoke`.

Parallel.For

The `Parallel.For` method takes as parameters a starting value, an ending value, and a delegate. It invokes the delegate for each of the values between the starting value (including that value) and the ending value (not including that value). The method blocks until all the calls to the delegate have completed and then the code continues.

The ParallelFor example program, which is available for download on this book's website, uses the following code to calculate Fibonacci numbers.

```
// Use recursion (the slow way) to calculate Fibonacci(N).
private long Fibonacci(long N)
{
    if (N <= 1) return 1;
    return Fibonacci(N - 1) + Fibonacci(N - 2);
}
```

This code simply implements the following recursive definition of Fibonacci numbers.

$$F_0 = 1$$

$$F_1 = 1$$

$$F_N = F_{N-1} + F_{N-2}$$

This isn't the most efficient way to calculate Fibonacci numbers. This example uses it because it's simple and slow enough to show a benefit from multithreading.

The program uses the following code to calculate four Fibonacci numbers at the same time.

```
// Arrays for holding N and results.
private long[] Numbers = new long[4];
private long[] Results = new long[4];

// Calculate a Fibonacci number and save it in Results[index].
private void FindFibonacci(int index)
{
    Results[index] = Fibonacci(Numbers[index]);
}
```

First, the code declares the `Numbers` array to hold the index of the Fibonacci numbers to calculate. For example, if `Numbers[0]` is 10, the program should calculate F_{10}. (The code that initializes the `Numbers` array isn't shown here.)

Next, the code declares the `Results` array to hold results. If `Numbers[0]` is 10, the program will store the value F_{10} in `Results[0]`.

The `FindFibonacci` method takes as a parameter the index of the value in the `Numbers` and `Results` arrays that it should calculate. It calls the `Fibonacci` method described earlier to perform the calculation and saves the result in the correct position in the `Results` array.

The following code shows how the example program calculates four Fibonacci numbers in parallel.

```
Parallel.For(0, 4, FindFibonacci);
```

The `Parallel.For` method calls the `FindFibonacci` method four times, passing it the parameters 0, 1, 2, and 3. Each call receives 0, 1, 2, or 3 as a parameter and looks in the appropriate `Numbers` array entry to see which value it should calculate. It performs its calculations and save its results in the `Results` array.

After the call to `Parallel.For` finishes, the program resumes execution as it would if it had called `FindFibonacci` four times in sequence.

If the computer has multiple CPUs available, the four calls to `FindFibonacci` may run on separate threads, possibly saving time.

Figure 22-1 shows the ParallelFor program after it has calculated four Fibonacci numbers sequentially and then in parallel. If you look at the figure you'll see that calculating the values sequentially took 12.39 seconds and calculating them in parallel took 7.57 seconds.

My computer has two cores, so performing the calculations on separate threads did save some time. The parallel trial used a bit more than one-half as long as the sequential trial because the system uses some time starting and coordinating the threads. Still the parallel trial took only 61 percent as long as the sequential trial.

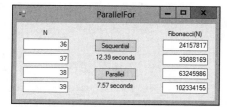

FIGURE 22-1: The ParallelFor example program uses `Parallel.For` to calculate Fibonacci numbers in parallel.

A TPL DRAWBACK

There is one small drawback to using TPL methods such as `Parallel.For`: The program is blocked and cannot provide feedback while the method is running. The sequential code in the ParallelFor example program displays each value as soon as it is calculated. The parallel code must wait until all the calculations are finished and then displays them all at once. The total time spent is smaller, but the user doesn't get to see any partial results.

Parallel.ForEach

The `Parallel.For` method invokes a method passing it the values between starting and ending values. This is analogous to how a `for` loop works, assuming the loop uses a simple integer as a looping variable.

The `Parallel.ForEach` method is analogous to a `foreach` loop. It also invokes a method several times in different threads. Instead of passing the method different integer values in each call, `Parallel.ForEach` passes the method different items from some sort of group of objects.

The ParallelForEach example program, which is available for download on this book's website, uses this technique to calculate Fibonacci numbers in parallel.

Because `Parallel.ForEach` passes the method items from a collection, the example program must create some sort of item to hold information about the Fibonacci calculations. This example uses the following simple class to hold that information.

```
private class FibInfo
{
    public long N, Result;
}
```

The `N` field holds the index of the Fibonacci number to calculate. When the program performs the calculation, it stores the Fibonacci number in the object's `Result` field.

The following code shows this example's version of the `FindFibonacci` method.

```
private void FindFibonacci(FibInfo info)
{
    info.Result = Fibonacci(info.N);
}
```

This method takes a `FibInfo` object as a parameter. It calls the `Fibonacci` method, which is the same as the version used in the ParallelFor example program, passing it the `FibInfo` object's `N` field. It stores the result in the object's `Result` field.

The following code shows the part of the program that uses `Parallel.ForEach`.

```
// Save the numbers N.
FibInfo[] infos = new FibInfo[4];
```

```
for (int i = 0; i < OutputTextBoxes.Length; i++)
{
    infos[i] = new FibInfo() { N = long.Parse(InputTextBoxes[i].Text) };
}

// Calculate.
Parallel.ForEach(infos, FindFibonacci);

// Display the results.
for (int i = 0; i < OutputTextBoxes.Length; i++)
{
    OutputTextBoxes[i].Text = infos[i].Result.ToString();
}
```

The code creates an array of `FibInfo` objects and sets their `N` fields from the values in the `TextBoxes` in the `InputTextBoxes` array. (That array is initialized when the program starts.)

The code then calls `Parallel.ForEach`, passing it the array of `FibInfo` objects and the `FindFibonacci` method that it should call.

The code then displays the results in the `TextBoxes` in the `OutputTextBoxes` array (which is also initialized when the program starts).

Parallel.Invoke

The `Parallel.For` and `Parallel.ForEach` methods invoke the same delegate for different parameters. Sometimes you might want to invoke several different methods. The `Parallel.Invoke` method lets you do that. Simply pass the method one or more action delegates for the method to execute.

The ParallelInvoke example program, which is available for download on this book's website, uses the following code to calculate four Fibonacci values in parallel.

```
Parallel.Invoke(
    FindFibonacci0,
    FindFibonacci1,
    FindFibonacci2,
    FindFibonacci3
);
```

The following code shows the `FindFibonacci0` method.

```
private void FindFibonacci0()
{
    Results[0] = Fibonacci(Numbers[0]);
}
```

The other methods are similar.

> **NOTE** *The performance of* `Parallel.For`, `Parallel.ForEach`, *and* `Parallel.Invoke` *are roughly the same.*

TASKS

The `System.Threading.Tasks.Task` class lets you create threads and run them asynchronously. If the system has multiple CPUs, then `Tasks` may run simultaneously.

The following table summarizes the `Task` class's most useful properties.

PROPERTY	PURPOSE
Exception	Returns an `AggregateException` object containing information about any exceptions that caused the `Task` to end early.
Factory	Provides access to `TaskFactory` class methods that you can use to create `Tasks`. (This is explained in more detail shortly.)
IsCanceled	Returns `true` if the `Task` was canceled.
IsCompleted	Returns `true` if the `Task` has finished processing.
IsFaulted	Returns `true` if the `Task` stopped because of an unhandled exception.
Status	Returns the `Task`'s status. This can be one of `Canceled`, `Created`, `Faulted`, `RanToCompletion`, `Running`, `WaitingForActivation`, `WaitingForChildrenToComplete`, or `WaitingToRun`.

The following table lists the `Task` class's most useful methods.

METHOD	PURPOSE
ConfigureAwait	Configures an "awaiter" object that you can use with the `await` keyword to wait for the `Task` to complete.
ContinueWith	Creates a continuation `Task` that executes when a target `Task` finishes.
Delay	Creates a `Task` that completes after a specified amount of time has passed.
Run	This static method creates a `Task` and queues it to start running. (This is basically a simplified version of `Task.Factory.StartNew`, which is described later in this section.)
RunSynchronously	Runs a `Task` synchronously.
Start	Starts a `Task` that was previously created.
Wait	Waits for the `Task` to complete.
WaitAll	This static method waits until all the `Tasks` in a set complete.

METHOD	PURPOSE
WaitAny	This static method waits until any one of the Tasks in a set completes.
WhenAll	Creates a Task that completes when all the specified Tasks complete.
WhenAny	Creates a Task that completes when any one of the specified Tasks completes.

There are several ways you can create and start a Task. First, you can use a Task class constructor to create a Task and then call its Start method to start it.

Second, you can use a TaskFactory object. The Task class's Factory method returns a TaskFactory object that you can use to create different kinds of Tasks. The Task.Factory.StartNew method creates and starts a Task in a single step. This method has many overridden versions that let you specify various options.

Third, you can call Task.Run. This is basically a simplified version of Task.Factory.StartNew. It has fewer options so it is less flexible, but the reduced number of options also makes it a bit less confusing.

In addition to the StartNew method, the TaskFactory class provides two methods that create continuation Tasks that start running when other Tasks complete. The ContinueWhenAll method creates a Task that starts when all of a set of Tasks completes. The ContinueWhenAny method creates a Task that starts when any one of a set of Tasks completes.

The FiboTasks example program demonstrates the more cumbersome method for using Tasks. The following code shows how the program creates four tasks and then waits for them to complete.

```
// Start four tasks.
Task task0 = new Task(FindFibonacci, 0);
task0.Start();
Task task1 = new Task(FindFibonacci, 1);
task1.Start();
Task task2 = new Task(FindFibonacci, 2);
task2.Start();
Task task3 = new Task(FindFibonacci, 3);
task3.Start();

// Wait for the tasks to complete.
task0.Wait();
task1.Wait();
task2.Wait();
task3.Wait();
```

The code creates each Task and calls its Start method to start it running. After it starts the fourth Task, the program calls each Task's Wait method to wait for the Task to complete.

The rest of the example program is similar to the Fibonacci number examples described in the earlier section "TPL."

THREADS

The `System.Threading.Thread` class gives you more control over threads than you can get from the other techniques described in this chapter. Using threads is more complicated, however, so normally you should try to use one of the other methods first. In most cases a `Task` object is a better choice than a thread.

The following table lists the `Thread` class's most useful properties.

PROPERTY	MEANING
IsAlive	Returns `true` if the thread has been started and has not ended or aborted.
IsBackground	Determines whether the thread is a background thread.
Priority	Determines the thread's priority. This can be `Highest`, `AboveNormal`, `Normal`, `BelowNormal`, or `Lowest`.
ThreadState	Returns the thread's state. This can be a combination of the values `Aborted`, `AbortRequested`, `Background`, `Running`, `Stopped`, `StopRequested`, `Suspended`, `SuspendRequested`, `Unstarted`, and `WaitSleepJoin`.

The following table lists the `Thread` class's most useful methods.

METHOD	PURPOSE
Abort	Raises a `ThreadAbortException` on the thread to make it terminate.
Join	Blocks the thread on which the method is called until the thread terminates. (This is how programs normally wait for a thread to finish.)
ResetAbort	Cancels an `Abort` for the current thread.
Sleep	This static method suspends a thread for a specified amount of time.
Start	Starts the thread.
Yield	Yields execution to another thread if one is ready to run.

Using a simple thread typically involves the following steps.

1. Create the `Thread` object.
2. Call the `Start` method to start the thread.
3. To stop the thread, call its `Abort` method.
4. To wait for the thread, call its `Join` method.

Creating and managing Threads takes some overhead, so you should use only Threads if you have multiple large calculations that you want to run on multiple CPUs.

COORDINATING TASKS

All the examples used so far in this chapter have been rigged for success. Each computation running in parallel worked only with its own data and never tried to look at the data used by any other computation. Each computation used InvokeRequired and Invoke to safely interact with the UI thread.

If you can arrange your computations in this way so that they never interfere with each other, then concurrent programming is relatively simple. Unfortunately in some applications different computations must access the same resources. In that case several conflicts can arise. Two of the most common of these are race conditions and deadlocks.

Race Conditions

A race condition can occur when two concurrent computations try to read and update the same value at roughly the same time. For example, suppose threads A and B each perform a random search trying to find the best possible solution to some difficult problem. When they finish their calculations, they must check variable BestSolution and update it if they find a better solution (one that is a larger integer).

The following code shows how a thread might perform this operation in C#.

```
if (mySolution > BestSolution)
{
    BestSolution = mySolution;
}
```

For this example, suppose BestSolution is initially 10, thread A finds a solution with value 15, and thread B finds a solution with value 20. Now consider the sequence of events shown in the following table.

THREAD A STEPS	THREAD B STEPS
Get BestSolution value (10)	
	Get BestSolution value (10)
	20 > 10 so set BestSolution = 20
15 > 10 so set BestSolution = 15	

Thread A starts execution and gets the value of BestSolution, which is initially 10.

The system then switches execution to thread B. Thread B gets the value of BestSolution, which is still 10. Thread B compares its solution value 20 to BestSolution. Because 20 > 10, thread B's solution is an improvement, so it saves its solution and sets BestSolution to 20.

Next, the system switches execution back to thread A. Thread A compares its solution value 15 to the value it saved for BestSolution, which is 10. Because 15 > 10, thread A thinks its solution is an improvement, so it updates BestSolution to 15.

In this example, thread B has the better solution, but thread A overwrites thread B's solution. Thread A "wins" the race by setting its value second.

RACE FRUSTRATION

The maddening thing about race conditions is that they happen only when exactly the right sequence of events occurs. In this example, there is no problem if thread A reads and updates BestSolution before thread B does, or vice versa. The program may work 99 times in a row. Just when you think everything is debugged and working perfectly, you run the 100th test, the race condition occurs, and you get the wrong solution. (In this example, you might not even know that a better solution was discarded and be unaware that there is a problem!)

You can avoid race conditions by ensuring that the critical sequence of steps is performed atomically. In this example if each thread reads and updates variable BestSolution atomically, the other thread cannot interfere and cause a race condition.

ATOMIC SEQUENCE OF STEPS

An *atomic* sequence of events is one that cannot be subdivided. The steps are marked so they must be run together without being interrupted by another process.

You can use the lock statement to prevent race conditions. The lock statement marks a section as a *critical region* that cannot be interrupted by other concurrent paths of execution.

The lock statement uses an instance of an object to mark the region. When a thread enters the region, it obtains an exclusive lock on the object. Other threads cannot lock that object until it is released so they cannot enter a similar critical region until the first thread has finished and released its lock.

The following code shows how you might revise the preceding code to use the lock statement.

```
// Create and initialize BestSolution.
private int BestSolution = 10;

// Create the lock object.
private object UpdateLock = new object();

...

// Thread A updates BestSolution
lock (UpdateLock)
{
```

```
    if (mySolution > BestSolution)
    {
        BestSolution = mySolution;
    }
}
```

When the program starts, it creates and initializes `BestSolution`. It also creates an object named `UpdateLock` to use for locking critical regions of code. This object is declared at the class level so all code in the class can use it.

Later when thread A needs to update `BestSolution`, it uses a `lock` statement to obtain an exclusive lock on the object `UpdateLock`. Now thread B cannot enter its critical section of code because it cannot lock the object until thread A is done with it.

Deadlocks

A *deadlock* occurs when two or more threads are all stuck waiting for resources that are held by the other threads. For example, suppose thread A and thread B both need to access resources M and N. The resources might be files that the threads need to lock, variables that must be accessed within critical regions to prevent race conditions, or anything else that the threads must access exclusively.

Now suppose thread A has locked resource M and thread B has locked resource N. Thread A cannot continue because it cannot get resource N and thread B cannot continue because it cannot get resource M. The two are deadlocked and neither can continue.

In this simple example there's a simple solution: Both threads can try to lock the resources in the same order. When both try to lock resource M, one succeeds and one is blocked waiting. Whichever succeeds can then lock resource N and continue. When that thread has finished, it releases its locks, the other thread locks both resources, and it can continue.

If you can, you should structure the code so deadlocks are impossible. That's not hard in this example. If you have many threads possibly written by different programmers all trying to update a large set of objects in different orders, it can sometimes be hard to figure out if a deadlock might occur.

One way to break deadlocks is to use a timeout on operations that might cause trouble. For example, the `Monitor` class's `TryEnter` method tries to obtain an exclusive lock on an object much as the `lock` statement does, but the `TryEnter` method also allows you to specify a timeout period. If the method acquires the lock, it returns `true`. If the method times out, it returns `false`.

When a thread is finished with a critical region, it should call the `Monitor` class's `Exit` method to release its lock on the lock object.

The following code shows how a thread could attempt to enter a critical section of code that might cause a deadlock with other threads.

```
// Create the lock object.
private object UpdateLock = new object();
...
// Try to lock the lock object.
if (Monitor.TryEnter(UpdateLock, 500))
```

```
{
    try
    {
        // Critical code goes here ...
    }
    finally
    {
        Monitor.Exit(UpdateLock);
    }
}
else
{
    // Do something if we time out.
}
```

The code creates the lock object `UpdateLock` as before. Later it uses `Monitor.TryEnter` to try to enter the critical region of code. If `TryEnter` succeeds, the thread enters its critical region and does whatever it needs to do with the resources. The `finally` section of the `try finally` block ensures that the code calls `Monitor.Exit` when it is done with the critical region.

If the call to `TryEnter` returns `false`, the thread timed out and failed to obtain the lock. In that case the code should do something to recover, possibly trying again to obtain the lock.

LIMITED DO-OVERS

If your code fails to obtain a lock, you may want to limit the number of times it can try again. If a thread becomes permanently stuck inside the critical region, it will block any other thread that must access that region.

Of course, if the program is in that situation, it may be impossible to get anything done, and you may want close it and start over.

The following table lists the most useful `Monitor` class methods.

METHOD	PURPOSE
Enter	Acquires an exclusive lock on an object.
Exit	Releases an exclusive lock on an object.
IsEntered	Returns `true` if the current thread has a lock on a specific object.
TryEnter	Tries to acquire an exclusive lock on an object.
Wait	Releases the lock on an object and then blocks until it reacquires a lock on that object. This is useful if the thread needs to allow another thread to take some action before it can continue.

OTHER LOCKING CLASSES

The .NET Framework provides a few other primitive classes that you can use to provide locking mechanisms. Usually the `lock` statement and the `Monitor` class are easier to use, so you should use those if possible.

The `Mutex` class lets a process acquire a lock much as the `Monitor` class does. One big difference between `Mutex` and `Monitor` is that a `Mutex` can wait for a *named mutex* that is defined systemwide. That means you can use `Mutex` to coordinate among threads running in different programs.

The `SpinLock` structure is like a high-performance `Monitor` class. Obtaining and managing locks involves some overhead, so creating and using a `Monitor` object can slow a thread down. Instead of creating a `Monitor` object, when a thread uses a `SpinLock` to enter a critical region, it enters a loop and spins until it can acquire the lock. This can improve performance if the thread will acquire the lock quickly. If the thread must spin for a long time (more than a few dozen milliseconds), then its loop will use up more CPU cycles than a `Monitor` object would, so the `SpinLock` will degrade the performance of other threads.

The `ReaderWriterLockSlim` class is useful if a writer object needs exclusive write access to a resource and any number of reader objects need nonexclusive read access to the resource.

The `Semaphore` class is similar to the `Mutex` class. The difference is that the `Mutex` class allows only one thread to access a critical region at one time, whereas a `Semaphore` allows a fixed number of threads to access a critical region at one time. For example, you could use a `Semaphore` to allow up to four threads to access a resource at the same time. Both `Mutex` and `Semaphore` let you lock threads locally within the same program or systemwide.

For more information on these and a few even more exotic synchronization classes, see "Overview of Synchronization Primitives" at `msdn.microsoft.com/library/ms228964.aspx`.

THREAD-SAFE OBJECTS

An object is *thread-safe* if it is safe for it and other objects of that class or other classes to run on different threads at the same time. For example, in the race condition example described earlier, the objects running in threads A and B were not thread-safe because they tried to read and update the same variable in an unsafe manner.

If a class accesses only its own instance variables and no other class accesses those variables, then it is thread-safe.

PRIVATE ISN'T ALWAYS SAFE

Making instance variables `private` does not guarantee that a class is thread-safe. Different instances of a class can access each other's private variables so they could interfere with each other. However, if the instances don't mess with each other's variables, the class is thread-safe.

At some point most threads need to somehow get information from the main program or send the main program results. To be thread-safe, you need to ensure that those operations are performed safely. If each thread interacts with the main program through variables assigned to it alone, then they are probably safe, as long as the main program doesn't interfere with those variables.

If multiple threads (including the main program's thread) need to manipulate the same variables, you should use locking mechanisms to coordinate them.

Writing your own thread-safe classes isn't too hard if you're careful to write the classes so that objects won't interfere with each other when running on other threads. One situation that some programmers overlook is the case in which their class uses another class that is not thread-safe.

For example, the `List<>` class is not thread-safe. That means if two threads try to share information in the same `List<>`, they may cause race conditions.

The `System.Collections.Concurrent` namespace defines several collection classes that are thread-safe. The following table lists these concurrent classes.

COLLECTION	PURPOSE
`BlockingCollection<T>`	A thread-safe collection.
`ConcurrentDictionary<TKey, TValue>`	A thread-safe dictionary class.
`ConcurrentQueue`	A thread-safe queue.
`ConcurrentStack`	A thread-safe stack.
`ConcurrentBag`	A thread-safe bag (unordered collection of objects).

SUMMARY

This chapter explained several classes that you can use to perform different kinds of tasks in parallel. The `BackgroundWorker` component performs a task and uses events to return progress and completion information. If you set its `WorkerSupportsCancellation` property to `true`, the program can interrupt a worker before it finishes.

TPL provides methods that let you easily perform operations in parallel and wait for them to finish. The `Task` class lets you perform multiple tasks simultaneously with greater flexibility than the `BackgroundWorker` or TPL. Finally, the `Thread` class provides even more options and flexibility; although, it's more complicated than the `Task` class.

These classes let you write programs that perform operations separately. Treating each operation individually often makes the code simpler than it would be if you tried to handle every operation in a single piece of code. These classes also let you run pieces of code truly in parallel, if the computer has multiple CPUs.

Parallel programming is a huge topic, and this chapter scratched only the surface. For more information on parallel programming, find a good book on the subject or search the Internet. You can start with the following links.

➤ "Parallel Programming in the .NET Framework" at `msdn.microsoft.com/library/dd460693.aspx`

➤ "Parallel Programming with .NET blog" at `blogs.msdn.com/b/pfxteam`

Parallel programming can sometimes make a program faster if it is CPU-bound. Distributing calculations across multiple CPUs can improve performance. However, that won't work if the program is limited by resources other than CPU power.

For example, if the program spends most of its time reading and writing to disk, multiple threads of execution probably won't improve performance much. Database applications are often disk-bound in this manner. The program spends most of its time waiting for user input or reading and writing data to the database. The next chapter provides an introduction ADO.NET, one of the tools you can use to write database programs in C#.

EXERCISES

1. The `System.Threading.Timer` class provides a timer similar to the `System.Windows.Forms.Timer` component that you can place on a form. Write a program that uses the former to display an updating clock.

Hint: Create the `Timer` as in the following code.

```
System.Threading.Timer timer =
    new System.Threading.Timer(TimerTick, null, 0, 500);
```

Here `TimerTick` is the name of the callback method the `Timer` should invoke periodically; `null` is a parameter that the `Timer` will pass to the callback method; 0 is the delay in milliseconds before the callback method is first invoked; and 500 is the delay in milliseconds between calls to the callback method.

2. Modify the FiboTasks example program so that it uses the `Task.WaitAll` method to wait for all the tasks to complete.

3. The `Task.Factory.StartNew` method creates a new `Task` and starts it. Modify the program you wrote for Exercise 2 so that it uses this method to create and start its tasks instead of performs those actions in two steps.

4. Modify the program you wrote for Exercise 3 so that it uses `Task.WaitAny` instead of `Task.WaitAll`. Run the program several times to find different Fibonacci values until you understand the program's behavior. When one of the tasks finishes, what happens to the other tasks?

5. Modify the ParallelFor example program so that it uses lambda expressions instead of the `FindFibonacci` method.

6. Suppose a program creates four `Tasks` (or threads) and then waits for them all to complete. Does it matter in what order the program waits for the `Tasks`?

7. The `Task` class has a generic version that takes as a parameter the kind of result the task returns. For example, a `Task<long>` represents a thread that executes a method that returns a `long` result. When you use this kind of `Task`, its `Result` property returns the result.

Modify the program you wrote for Exercise 3 so that it uses `Task<long>.Factory.StartNew` to run the Fibonacci function without using the `FindFibonacci` method or the `Results` array.

8. Modify the FiboTasks example program so that it uses `Threads` instead of `Tasks`. Is there a difference in performance?

9. The DeadLock example program, which is available for download on this book's website, uses two `Task` objects to execute the following two methods at the same time.

```
// Task A.
private void TaskA()
{
    Console.WriteLine("TaskA: Locking A");
    lock (LockObjectA)
    {
        Thread.Sleep(500);
        Console.WriteLine("TaskA: Locking B");
        lock (LockObjectB)
        {
            // Update the value.
            BestValue = ValueA;
        }
    }
}

// Task B.
private void TaskB()
{
    Console.WriteLine("TaskB: Locking B");
    lock (LockObjectB)
    {
        Thread.Sleep(500);
        Console.WriteLine("TaskB: Locking A");
        lock (LockObjectA)
        {
            // Update the value.
            BestValue = ValueB;
        }
    }
}
```

The following text shows the program's Console window output.

```
TaskA: Locking A
TaskB: Locking B
TaskA: Locking B
TaskB: Locking A
```

Explain briefly why the `Tasks` are now in deadlock and how they got into that state. Then download and rewrite the program so that it uses the `Monitor` class to avoid the deadlock. Use the `Console.WriteLine` method to indicate when each `Task` attempts to get a lock, fails to get a lock, and updates the variable `BestValue`.

How many times do the `Tasks` fail to obtain a lock? Can you think of a way to reduce the number of failures?

Can you think of better ways to avoid the deadlock?

10. Modify the program you wrote for Exercise 9 so that the two `Tasks` try to lock objects in the same order. What is the result?

11. What happens if a `Task` calls `Monitor.Exit` for an object that it didn't lock?

12. What happens if a `Task` doesn't call `Monitor.Exit` for an object that it locked?

23

ADO.NET

WHAT'S IN THIS CHAPTER

➤ Connecting to databases

➤ Bound controls

➤ `DataGridView`, `DataGrid`, and detail interfaces

➤ `DataSet`s

➤ ADO.NET

WROX.COM DOWNLOADS FOR THIS CHAPTER

Please note that all the code examples for this chapter are available as a part of this chapter's code download on the book's website at www.wrox.com/go/csharp5programmersref on the Download Code tab.

Databases play an important role in many software applications. A large percentage of business applications use databases to store, arrange, and otherwise manipulate data.

Because databases play such an important role in so many programs, companies such as Microsoft have spent a huge amount of time building database tools. As a consequence, there are several methods you can use to work with databases. Some of the most recent methods include the Entity Framework and LINQ to ADO.NET, which includes LINQ to SQL, LINQ to Entities, and LINQ to DataSet. Those techniques were covered briefly in Chapter 8, "LINQ."

This chapter provides a brief introduction to ADO.NET, a set of classes that provide more direct access to the underlying database. It also shows how you can use bound database components and controls to quickly build simple applications that let you create, edit, and delete database records.

RELATIONAL INTRO

Relational databases are particularly common because they are relatively intuitive and because they map naturally to the data used by many businesses.

A relational database stores data in tables. Each table contains a collection of records or rows. Each record contains fields that hold values that belong to a record.

The "relational" part of the name "relational database" refers to the fact that fields within the tables define relationships among the tables. Typically, records in one table correspond to records in another table where the two sets of records share some common value.

For example, this chapter's examples and exercises use the SchoolData.accdb Access database file, which is available for download on this book's website. That database contains two tables: Students and TestScores.

The Students table has three fields: StudentId, FirstName, and LastName. The TestScores table also has three fields: StudentId, TestNumber, and Score.

The StudentId field provides the relational link between the two tables. For example, suppose the student Dean Diamond has the StudentId value 4. Then the Students table contains a single record with StudentId value 4 that contains Dean's first and last names. The TestScores table contains one or more records with StudentId value 4 that contain Dean's test scores.

The SchoolData.accdb database also includes some integrity checks. For example, it won't let you create a TestScores record with a StudentId that doesn't exist in the Students table. (You can't make test scores for a student that doesn't exist.) The database also verifies that Score values are between 0 and 100. (Sorry, no extra credit.)

The examples in Chapter 8 also worked with databases built inside the program's code so they didn't work with databases stored on the computer's hard drive. The examples in this chapter show how you can load and query databases stored on disk. When you know how to load data from a database, you can modify the examples described in Chapter 8 to select data from the database. This chapter won't make you a database expert, but it will at least get you started writing database programs and enable you to use LINQ to query databases.

SELECTING A DATABASE

Because database applications are so important, a lot of companies have created databases and database tools. A small sampling of databases includes Microsoft SQL Server, Microsoft SQL Server Express, Microsoft Access, MySQL, MariaDB, PostgreSQL, SQLite, Oracle, SAP, dBASE, FoxPro, IBM DB2, LibreOffice Base, and FileMaker Pro. Some of these are expensive, whereas others are free. Some are designed for large volumes of data and many concurrent users, whereas others are designed for more limited use by a single user. You can search the Internet for database comparisons and recommendations.

Four databases that I've used in C# programs are SQL Server, SQL Server Express, MySQL Community Edition, and Access. SQL Server and MySQL are designed to handle large amounts of data and concurrent users. Both have free versions with limited features (SQL Server Express and MySQL Community Edition). The full-featured versions are similar to the free editions, so many developers start with the free editions and later upgrade if necessary.

Access is more suited for smaller desktop applications. One advantage it has over SQL Server is that Access databases are stored in simple files, and a C# program can open them without any additional tools (other than database drivers, which are needed for any database). In contrast, to use a SQL Server database, you need to have the database server installed and running on your computer. SQL Server can store data in a separate file, but you can't distribute it to other computers unless they have SQL Server installed.

You can use the Microsoft Access database product to create Access database files and modify their structures. For example, Access lets you build tables, add fields to tables, and create relational constraints between tables. A C# program can use those database files even if you don't have Access installed. You can write programs to manipulate the data and copy the program and its Access files to another computer without needing to install Access on the destination computer.

For those reasons, the examples in this chapter use Access database files. You can download them from this book's website and use them in your programs. You do need database drivers to let your program connect to the database, but they may have already been installed by Visual Studio and are relatively easy to install if they're missing. The feature "Connecting Rejection" in the section "Making a Data Source later in this chapter says more about installing missing drivers.

USING BOUND CONTROLS

One approach to using a database is to use controls bound to the data. As you move through the data, the bound controls update to display pieces of the data. For example, when the program visits an `Employee` record, bound `TextBoxes` might display the employee's first name, last name, employee ID, and other values.

Before you can use bound controls, you need to create a data source that can connect to the database. The following section explains how you can make that data source. The sections after that explain how you can quickly build some simple programs that use bound controls.

Making a Data Source

You can use Visual Studio to make a data source at design time. This has the advantage that you can test the connection right away to make sure the program can connect to the database. It also lets you define a `DataSet` to hold data loaded from the data source. You can then bind data components to the `DataSet`. This lets you quickly build simple database applications with very little code.

FINDING THE DATA

Some of this chapter's example programs use relative paths to find their databases at run time. If you preserve the directory structure of this chapter's files, they should work without modification.

However, some of the examples use database connections that were built interactively at design time. Their database connection strings are tied to locations on my computer that probably won't match the database's location on your computer. If you try to run these programs without modifying them, they will look for their databases, fail to find them, and halt with runtime errors. These examples include the programs:

➤ AddStudent

➤ BoundControls

➤ BoundControlsDataGrid

➤ BoundControlsDataGridView

➤ BoundControlsDetails

➤ LinqTestScores

➤ ListStudentNames

Fortunately you should be able to modify the programs to work without rebuilding them from scratch.

Load one of the programs, open Solution Explorer, and double-click the App.config file. That file should contain a `connectionString` element similar to the following. (I've added some new lines to make the element fit in this book, but in the App.config file it will be on one long line.)

```
connectionString="Provider=Microsoft.ACE.OLEDB.12.0;
Data Source=&quot;C:\Users\Rod\Work\Writing\Books\
C# Prog Ref\Src\847282ch23src\SchoolData.accdb&quot;"
```

Within the Data Source part of the `connectionString`, replace the bold text with the location of the database on your system. Now when you run the program, it will load the database from that location.

The following steps explain how to create a data source, database connection, and `DataSet`.

1. Start a new C# project. (This example assumes you're making a Windows Forms application.)

2. Open the Data Sources window. (If you can't find it, select View ➪ Other Windows ➪ Data Sources.)

3. Click the Add New Data Source button (in the upper-left corner) to open the Data Source Configuration Wizard.

4. The wizard's first page lets you select a data source type from the choices Database, Service, and Object. Select Database and click Next.

5. The wizard's next page lets you pick a database model from the choices Dataset and Entity Data Model. Select Dataset and click Next.

6. The wizard's next page, which is shown in Figure 23-1, lets you pick a database connection. If Visual Studio already knows about database connections, you can select one from the drop-down list.

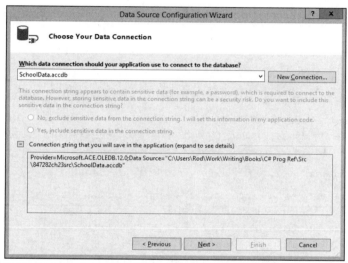

FIGURE 23-1: This page in the Data Source Configuration Wizard lets you select a data connection.

7. If you need to create a new connection, follow these steps.

    a. Click New Connection to display the dialog shown in Figure 23-2. Select the data source type you want to use.

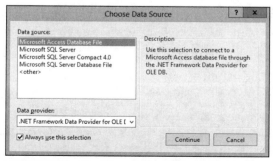

FIGURE 23-2: The Choose Data Source dialog lets you select the kind of database you will use.

b. For this example, select Microsoft Access Database File. (Note that the description says this data source will use an OLE DB data provider.) Click Continue to display the dialog shown in Figure 23-3.

c. Enter or select the database file's name. If the database is password protected, enter a username and password.

d. Click Test Connection to see if Visual Studio can connect to the database.

e. If the connection test works, click OK.

8. After you create the connection, a dialog displays the following self-explanatory message.

The connection you selected uses a local data file that is not in the current project. Would you like to copy the file to your project and modify the connection?

CONNECTION REJECTION

Step 7d, where you test the connection, is the first place things are likely to go seriously wrong. There are several reasons why you might be unable to connect to the database. Here are some things you can try to fix the problem.

If you use SQL Server, make sure SQL Server is installed and running.

If you use a 64-bit computer (which is common these days), you may not have the best database drivers. In some 64-bit systems, only 32-bit Access drivers are installed by default. In that case a program targeted for 64-bit systems won't connect to Access databases. You can try two approaches to solve this problem.

First, you can target the application for x86 (32-bit) computers only. The program can still run on a 64-bit system, but it will use the 32-bit Access database drivers. To do this, follow these steps:

1. Select Build ⇨ Configuration Manager. (If Configuration Manager isn't visible in the Build menu, select Tools ⇨ Options ⇨ Projects and Solutions ⇨ General and check the Show Advanced Build Configurations box.)

2. In the Active Solution Platform drop-down, select <New...>.

3. In the upper platform drop-down, select x86 and click OK.

4. In the Configuration Manager, make sure the new x86 configuration is selected and click Close.

I have used this approach successfully on some systems; although, it didn't work on my newest Windows 8 system. For that system, the second approach worked.

For the second approach, download and install the 2007 Office System Driver: Data Connectivity Components at `www.microsoft.com/download/confirmation .aspx?id=23734`. That package installs 64-bit drivers for Access databases so that the program can target x86 or 64-bit systems.

If you copy the data file to your project, it will be copied to the project's output directory each time you run the application. Press F1 for information on controlling this behavior.

Copying the database file into the project's executable location can be helpful for testing. Your program can modify the data, and when you run it again, it starts with a fresh copy of the database.

FIGURE 23-3: The Add Connection dialog lets you select the kind of database you will use.

9. Next the Data Source Configuration Wizard asks if you want to save the connection string in the application's configuration file. This makes it easier to change the location of the database later. For this example, check the Yes, Save the Connection As box and click Next.

SENSITIVE DATA

If you refer to Figure 23-1, you can see two disabled radio buttons that enable you to decide whether the connection string should include sensitive data. If the database in this example were password protected, those radio buttons would be enabled.

If you click the second radio button and you include the username and password in the Add Connection dialog (refer to Figure 23-3), the connection string will include the username and password. If you then decide to save the connection string in the configuration file, that file will contain the username and password.

In general it's not a good idea to save usernames and passwords in configuration files because anyone can read them. To make the program safer, edit the configuration file and replace the username and password with the tokens **USERNAME** and **PASSWORD**. Then at run time, ask the user for the necessary values and use `string` methods to replace the tokens with the values the user entered.

10. Now the wizard displays the screen shown in Figure 23-4 to let you select the database objects you want to include in the data source. Check the tables and views (if they are defined by the database) that you want to include. Enter the name you want to give the new `DataSet` and click Finish.

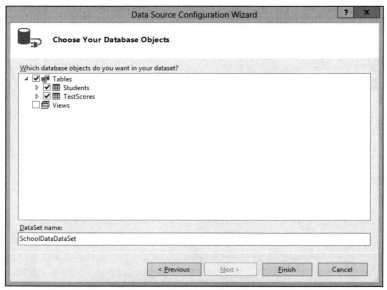

FIGURE 23-4: This screen lets you pick the database objects that will be included in the data source.

Figure 23-5 shows the Data Sources window after I created a data source to work with the SchoolData.accdb database that is included in this chapter's downloads. The `DataSet` shows the tables that it contains, and the tables show the fields they contain.

Now that you've created a data source, you can use it to build simple data-bound user interfaces. The following two sections explain how you can use drag-and-drop to build `DataGridView` and detail style interfaces. The section after that describes a third approach that lets you view multiple tables in a `DataGrid`.

FIGURE 23-5: The Data Sources window shows the new `DataSet` and its selected tables.

Making a DataGridView Interface

To make a `DataGridView` display, open the Data Sources window, right-click the table you want to display, and select DataGridView, as shown in Figure 23-6.

FIGURE 23-6: The Data Sources window can create `DataGridView` or `Details` views for a table.

Now click and drag the table onto the form to make Visual Studio automatically add the following components to the form.

➤ A `DataGridView` to display and edit the data.

➤ A `DataSet` to hold the data.

➤ A `BindingSource` to bind the `DataSet` to the `DataGridView`.

➤ A `TableAdapter` to move data between the `DataSet` and the database.

➤ A `TableAdapterManager` to manage the table adapter.

➤ A `BindingNavigator` to provide a user interface allowing simple navigation through the data.

Many of these components sit in the component tray below the form designer. Only the `DataGridView` control and the `BindingNavigator` are visible on the form itself.

Together these components create the user interface shown in Figure 23-7. (I rearranged the `DataGridView` so it fills the form.) You can use the `DataGridView` to modify the data. You can use either the `DataGridView` or the `BindingNavigator` at the top of the form to navigate through the data and add or delete records. Click the `BindingNavigator`'s Save Data button (which looks like a floppy disk) to save changes.

Visual Studio also automatically adds code behind the scenes to load the data when the program starts and to save any changes when you click the `BindingNavigator`'s Save Data button.

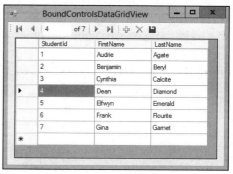

FIGURE 23-7: You can drag-and-drop a table from the Data Sources window onto a form to quickly build a grid-style program to edit a table's data.

If the database defines constraints, it verifies those constraints when you try to save changes. For example, if a field must contain a value between 0 and 100 and you try to set its value to 200, the program throws an exception when you try to save the data.

This program is rather primitive and is missing some features that you would want to include if you were going to give it to a customer. For example, if you close the program without saving changes, the changes are lost. The program also doesn't provide validation to prevent you from entering invalid values, and it doesn't handle the exceptions that occur if you try to save changes that violate the database's constraints

Still this program is easy to build. You might not want to give this program to a customer, but if you just need an easy way to edit the records in a table, this program may suffice.

Making a Details Interface

To make a details view interface, create the data source as before. Open the Data Sources window and right-click the table you want to display. This time select the Details option shown in Figure 23-6.

Now click and drag the table onto the form as before. Visual Studio automatically adds the same components as it did for the `DataGridView` display, but this time it includes a series of `Labels` and `TextBoxes` instead of a `DataGridView` control. Figure 23-8 shows the result.

Use the `BindingNavigator`'s buttons to navigate through the records or to add and remove records. Use the `TextBoxes` to view and edit the records' field values.

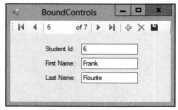

FIGURE 23-8: Use the `BindingNavigator` to navigate through the records in a details view.

This simple program has the same advantages and disadvantages that the grid view does. It's missing some important features (such as warning you if you try to close when there are unsaved changes) and doesn't handle exceptions, but it's also easy to create. You might not want to give it to a customer, but it may be good enough to let you manage a database table.

Making a DataGrid Interface

The two previous techniques have the disadvantage that they let you view data from only one table at a time. There are ways you can make a form work with multiple tables (the section "Using ADO.NET" later in this chapter describes one method), but they're more work.

Another approach that can be useful is to display a `DataSet`'s data in a `DataGrid` control. The `DataGrid` control can display data from multiple tables linked by the relationships defined by the database. To use this method, follow these steps.

1. Create the data source and `DataSet` as before.

2. Add some controls and components that you will need to the Toolbox.

    a. Open the form and the Toolbox window.

b. In the General section at the bottom of the Toolbox, right-click and select Choose Items.

c. On the .NET Framework Components tab, select DataGrid (System.Windows.Forms) and OleDbDataAdapter. Then click OK to add those components to the Toolbox.

3. Create a data adapter for the Students table.

a. Double-click the OleDbDataAdapter tool in the Toolbox to start the Data Adapter Configuration Wizard shown in Figure 23-9. Select the connection you created earlier and click Next.

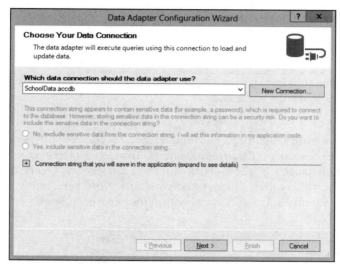

FIGURE 23-9: Select or create the database connection that you want to use.

ABANDONED ADAPTERS

When you double-click the OleDbDataAdapter tool in the Toolbox, Visual Studio adds the adapter to the form. It then launches the Data Adapter Configuration Wizard to let you configure the adapter.

If you cancel the wizard, the adapter is still on the form. In that case, you may want to remove it.

---

b. On the wizard's next page, shown in Figure 23-10, select Use SQL Statements and click Next.

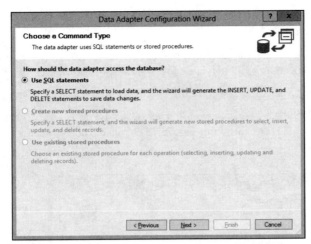

FIGURE 23-10: Select the method you want the adapter to use to access the database.

c. On the wizard's next page, shown in Figure 23-11, enter the SQL query that you want to use to select data from the table. To select all the Student table's data, use the query SELECT * FROM Students. (You can also use Query Builder to create the SQL query if you like. Query Builder isn't described here, but it's fairly easy to use, so you can probably figure it out with some experimentation.)

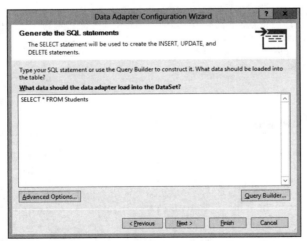

FIGURE 23-11: Enter a SQL select statement or click Query Builder and use the Query Builder to create a select statement.

d. After you enter the SQL select statement, you can click Finish to finish creating the data adapter, or you can click Next to see the summary shown in Figure 23-12. In this case the summary indicates that the wizard configured the adapter to give it the tools it needs to modify the data. After you view the summary, click Finish to create the data adapter and close the wizard.

e. Use the Properties window to change the new data adapter's name to **studentsDataAdapter**.

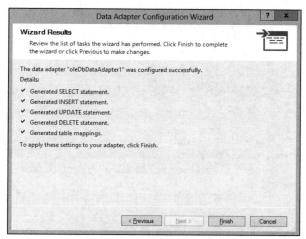

FIGURE 23-12: The Data Adapter Configuration Wizard's summary screen tells you what the wizard will do when it creates a data adapter.

4. Repeat the previous steps to create a data adapter for the `TestScores` table named `testScoresDataAdapter`.

5. Add a `DataSet` to the form.

a. Expand the Toolbox's Data section and double-click the `DataSet` tool.

b. On the Add Dataset dialog shown in Figure 23-13, click the "Typed dataset" option and select the `DataSet` type you created while making the original data source, and click OK.

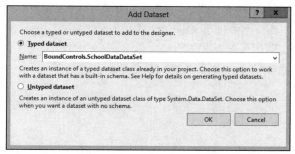

FIGURE 23-13: Use the Add Dataset dialog to create an instance of a `DataSet`.

SQL

Structured Query Language (SQL) is a command language with an English-like syntax that lets you insert, select, update, and delete data in a relational database such as SQL Server or Access. The syntax is somewhat similar to LINQ, or actually LINQ is somewhat similar to SQL because SQL has been around since the early 1970s.

Although SQL is easy to use, it's also a fairly large language, so there isn't room to cover it in detail here. The SELECT statement, which is one of the most commonly used commands, has the following basic syntax:

```
SELECT fields FROM tables WHERE condition ORDER BY order_by_fields
```

Here:

fields—The database fields for which you want to select data. If you use multiple tables that have fields with the same names, use the table name to differentiate them as in TestScores.StudentId. You can set *fields* to * to select all of a table's fields.

tables—The table(s) from which you want to select data. If you use multiple tables, you probably also want to use a WHERE clause to indicate how records from the tables are combined.

condition—A condition that specifies how records in multiple tables are combined or that filters the results. For example, this could be Students.StudentId = TestScores.StudentId or Score < 60.

order_by_fields—The fields that should be used to sort the results.

For example, the following query selects all student and test score data. The WHERE clause matches Students records with the corresponding TestScores records.

```
SELECT Students.StudentId, FirstName, LastName, TestNumber, Score
FROM Students, TestScores
WHERE Students.StudentId = TestScores.StudentId
ORDER BY FirstName, LastName
```

In this example you set the first data adapter's query to SELECT * FROM Students. This statement has no WHERE clause, so it selects all the records in the Students table. It has no ORDER BY clause, so the results are not returned in any particular order.

SQL is case-insensitive; although, many developers write the SQL keywords in ALL CAPS, so they are easy to distinguish from field and table names.

For more information on SQL, search online. For example, see the SQL tutorial at www.w3schools.com/sql/default.asp.

6. Create the `DataGrid` control.

a. In the Toolbox's General section, double-click the `DataGrid` control.

b. Arrange the control as you want it, perhaps docking it to fill the form or setting its `Anchor` property.

c. In the Properties window, select the `DataGrid`'s `DataSource` property and open the drop-down, as shown in Figure 23-14. Expand the drop-down's options until you find the `DataSet` and select it. (This actually sets the `DataSource` to a new binding source for the `DataSet`, not to the `DataSet` itself. This is just another layer between the control and the `DataSet`.)

FIGURE 23-14: Use the Properties window to set the `DataGrid`'s `DataSource` property.

7. Give the form a `Load` event handler and add the following code to it.

```
private void Form1_Load(object sender, EventArgs e)
{
    // Use the connection string stored in App.config.
    oleDbConnection1.ConnectionString =
        Properties.Settings.Default.SchoolDataConnectionString;

    studentsDataAdapter.Fill(schoolDataDataSet1.Students);
    testScoresDataAdapter.Fill(schoolDataDataSet1.TestScores);
}
```

This code starts by setting the OLE DB connection object's connect string to the value saved in the App.config file. You don't need to do this if the database is at the same location it was when you built the program, but it enables you to easily change the database's location.

Next the code makes the data adapters load the data from their respective database tables into the `DataSet`.

8. Give the form a `FormClosing` event handler and add the following code to it.

```
private void Form1_FormClosing(object sender, FormClosingEventArgs e)
{
    studentsDataAdapter.Update(schoolDataDataSet1.Students);
    testScoresDataAdapter.Update(schoolDataDataSet1.TestScores);
}
```

This code makes the data adapters save any changes in the `DataSet` back into the database.

Figure 23-15 shows the finished program. You can click the links to navigate from a `Students` record to the corresponding records in the `TestScores` table.

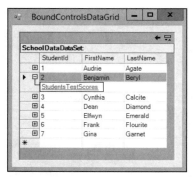

FIGURE 23-15: A `DataGrid` control provides links between records in related tables.

BOUND EXAMPLES

The BoundControls directory in this chapter's downloads contains a program that defines a data source for working with the SchoolData.accdb database. The BoundControlsDataGridView, BoundControlsDetails, and BoundControlsDataGrid directories contain copies of that program that have been modified to demonstrate the three methods described in the preceding sections.

These examples show only a few ways you can bind controls to data in a Windows Forms application. There are so many other ways to use data binding that you would need a whole book to cover them all. For more information about data binding, look through some books on database programming or search the Internet. The following links can help get you started.

➤ "Displaying Data Overview" at `msdn.microsoft.com/library/2b4be09b(v=vs.90).aspx`

➤ "Binding Controls to Data in Visual Studio" at `msdn.microsoft.com/library/ms171923.aspx`

LOADING DATASETS

The previous examples displayed data in bound controls. Sometimes, you might want a program to use data without binding it to controls. For example, you might want to loop through a customer database and print out invoices for customers with outstanding balances. In that case, there's no need to display the data in bound controls. You can write this kind of program by loading the data into a DataSet and then examining it there.

The example described in the preceding section, which displays from multiple tables in a DataGrid control, does almost exactly what you need for this kind of program. When the program starts, it loads data into a DataSet and displays the data in a DataGrid control. The only difference is that the new type of program doesn't need the DataGrid.

To build the new kind of program, follow the same steps described in the previous section but skip step 6, which creates the DataGrid control. If you don't need to save any changes to the database, you can also skip step 8, which uses the form's Closing event handler to save changes when the program is closing.

After the form's Load event handler loads the data, the program can use the DataSet and the tables it contains to examine the data. For example, you can use the LINQ to DataSet techniques described in Chapter 8 to select data from the DataSet and display the results.

The ListStudentNames program, which is available for download on this book's website, uses a DataSet and data adapter to load the Students table in the SchoolData.accdb database. It uses the following code to load and display the students' names.

```
private void Form1_Load(object sender, EventArgs e)
{
    // Load the data.
    studentsDataAdapter.Fill(schoolDataDataSet1);

    // Display the students' names.
    ListStudents();
}

// List the students.
private void ListStudents()
{
    studentsListBox.Items.Clear();

    // Display the students' names.
    foreach (DataRow row in schoolDataDataSet1.Students.Rows)
    {
        string name =
            row.Field<string>("FirstName") + " " +
            row.Field<string>("LastName");
        studentsListBox.Items.Add(name);
    }
}
```

The code starts by calling the data adapter's `Fill` method to load data into the `DataSet`'s `Students` table. It then calls the `ListStudents` method to display the students' names.

The `ListStudents` method loops through the table's rows. The code gets each row's `FirstName` and `LastName` values and concatenates them to form the student's name. It then adds the name to the `studentsListBox` control.

Using similar techniques you can write programs that load and manipulate data. If you need to save changes, simply call the data adapters' `Update` methods.

The AddStudent example program, which is shown in Figure 23-16 and available for download on this book's website, lets you add new students to the `Students` table.

FIGURE 23-16: This example adds new students to the Students table.

When the program starts, its `Form_Load` event handler loads the student data and displays student names just as the ListStudentNames example program did.

If you enter a new first and last name and click Add, the following code executes.

```
// Add the new student.
private void addButton_Click(object sender, EventArgs e)
{
    // Create the new row.
    DataRow row = schoolDataDataSet1.Students.NewRow();
    row.SetField<string>("FirstName", firstNameTextBox.Text);
    row.SetField<string>("LastName", lastNameTextBox.Text);

    // Add the new row to the Students table.
    schoolDataDataSet1.Students.Rows.Add(row);

    // Clear the TextBoxes.
    firstNameTextBox.Clear();
    lastNameTextBox.Clear();

    // Redisplay the data.
    ListStudents();
}
```

This code uses the `Students` table's `NewRow` method to create a new `DataRow` object that has the right fields to make a row in that table. It sets the row's `FirstName` and `LastName` values and adds the new row to the table's `Rows` collection.

The code finishes by clearing the `TextBoxes` and redisplaying the list of students.

If you click Save, the following code saves any new rows into the database.

```
// Save the data.
private void saveButton_Click(object sender, EventArgs e)
{
```

```
        studentsDataAdapter.Update(schoolDataDataSet1);
    }
```

This code simply uses the data adapter's `Update` method to save the changes.

USING ADO.NET

This chapter's examples so far used wizards to create and configure data adapters and `DataSets` to load, manipulate, and save data. Behind the scenes, the wizards created ADO.NET code to handle all the details. (ADO.NET is the .NET version of ADO, which stands for ActiveX Data Objects.) Instead of using the wizards and the objects they create, you can use ADO.NET directly.

The program first makes a database connection that it can use to interact with the database. It then creates a command object associated with the connection. The command's methods let the program execute SQL commands that manipulate the database.

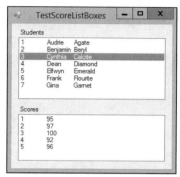

FIGURE 23-17: The TestScoreListBoxes example program uses ADO.NET to display student and test score data.

The TestScoreListBoxes example program, which is shown in Figure 23-17 and available in this chapter's downloads, uses ADO.NET to display student and test score data.

The program uses classes in the System.IO and System.Data.OleDb namespaces, so it includes `using` directives for them.

When the program starts, it uses the following code to display the students' names.

```
    // The database connection.
    private OleDbConnection Connection = null;

    // Load the data.
    private void Form1_Load(object sender, EventArgs e)
    {
        // Use a relative path to the database.
        string dbPath = Path.GetFullPath(Path.Combine(
            Application.ExecutablePath,
            @"..\..\..\.."));
        string connectString =
            @"Provider=Microsoft.ACE.OLEDB.12.0;" +
            @"Data Source='" + dbPath + @"\SchoolData.accdb';" +
            @"Persist Security Info=True;";

        // Create the database connection.
        Connection = new OleDbConnection(connectString);

        // Create a command object to select student names.
        string query =
            "SELECT StudentId, FirstName, LastName " +
```

```
                    "FROM Students " +
                    "ORDER BY FirstName, LastName";

            // Open the connection.
            Connection.Open();

            // Execute the command.
            using (OleDbCommand command = new OleDbCommand(query, Connection))
            {
                // Execute the command.
                using (OleDbDataReader reader = command.ExecuteReader())
                {
                    while (reader.Read())
                    {
                        int studentId = reader.GetInt32(0);
                        string firstName = reader.GetString(1);
                        string lastName = reader.GetString(2);
                        studentsListBox.Items.Add(studentId.ToString() + "\t" +
                            firstName + "\t" + lastName);
                    }
                }

                // Close the connection.
                Connection.Close();
            }
        }
```

The code first declares an `OldDbConnection` object. It declares this object outside of any method so all the form's code can use it.

The form's `Load` event handler defines a connection string that it can use to connect to the database. Figuring out exactly what needs to be in this string can be tricky because the requirements vary depending on the type of database you are using. One method for building this string is to make a data source at design time and use the connection string created by the Data Source Configuration Wizard. If you refer to Figure 23-1, you can see a connecting string that works with this example's database. I modified the code slightly to make the database's location relative to the example program's executable directory.

After defining the connection string, the program uses it to initialize the connection object. That gives the new connection the information it needs to connect to the database, but it doesn't yet open the connection.

The program then defines the SQL query it will execute. In this example the query selects the `StudentId`, `FirstName`, and `LastName` fields from the `Students` table and orders the result by `FirstName` and `LastName`.

Next, the code opens the database connection. It then makes a new `OleDbCommand` object, passing its constructor the query string and the connection.

This query selects multiple rows of data, so the program uses the command's `ExecuteReader` method to execute the query and retrieve an object that can read the returned results.

EXECUTING COMMANDS

This example uses a query that returns multiple rows of data, so it uses the command's ExecuteReader method. Other types of SQL commands can select a single value (in which case you would use the command's ExecuteScalar method) or perform actions without selecting data (in which case you would use the ExecuteNonQuery method).

The program now uses the reader to loop the returned results. The reader's Read method advances the reader to the next row of results and returns true if such a row exists. (In other words, it returns true if the reader has not reached the end of the results.)

For each returned row, the program gets the row's StudentId, FirstName, and LastName values. It concatenates them and adds the result to the studentsListBox.

When it finishes processing the returned results, the program closes the database connection.

When you select a student from the upper ListBox, the following event handler displays that student's test scores in the lower ListBox.

```
// Display the selected student's scores.
private void studentsListBox_SelectedIndexChanged(object sender, EventArgs e)
{
    // Clear the ListBox.
    scoresListBox.Items.Clear();

    // Get the selected student's ID.
    string studentId = studentsListBox.SelectedItem.ToString().Split('\t')[0];

    // Create a command object to select student names.
    string query =
        "SELECT TestNumber, Score " +
        "FROM TestScores " +
        "WHERE StudentId=" + studentId.ToString() + " " +
        "ORDER BY TestNumber";

    // Open the connection.
    Connection.Open();

    // Execute the command.
    using (OleDbCommand command = new OleDbCommand(query, Connection))
    {
        // Execute the command.
        using (OleDbDataReader reader = command.ExecuteReader())
        {
            while (reader.Read())
            {
                int testNumber = reader.GetInt32(0);
                int score = reader.GetInt32(1);

                scoresListBox.Items.Add(testNumber.ToString() + "\t" +
```

```
                              score.ToString());
                    }
              }
        }

        // Close the connection.
        Connection.Close();
}
```

This code is similar to the code the program uses to display the students' names. The biggest difference is that it uses a different query to select a specific student's test scores. For example, if you select the student with StudentId equal to 1, the program uses the following query.

```
SELECT TestNumber, Score FROM TestScores WHERE StudentId=1 ORDER BY TestNumber
```

The code follows these steps:

1. Open the database connection.
2. Create a command to use the query on the connection.
3. Execute the query and get a reader to fetch the returned records.
4. For each record, display the record's data in a ListBox.
5. Close the database connection.

This technique of using ADO.NET directly is more work than using drag-and-drop to build simple interfaces. It's also more work to debug and maintain over time, but it gives you a lot more control and flexibility.

SUMMARY

Because database programming is such an important topic for so many businesses, there are a huge number of tools, databases, and books available. No book, not even one solely dedicated to database programming, can cover everything there is to know about databases and database programming. This chapter barely scratches the surface. It doesn't include enough material to make you an expert, but it explains some techniques you can use to build a quick interface to let you manage a database. It also explains how you can use ADO.NET to build more complicated database programs. You can use the Internet and database programming books to learn more.

The databases used in this chapter are relational databases that store data in tables containing rows, but there are other kinds of databases. For example, hierarchical databases store data that is arranged in tree-like structures (such as an organizational chart).

XML files can also store hierarchical data. Related technologies such as XPath and XSL provide additional database-like features such as searching and the capability to transform XML data into other forms such as HTML, text documents, or rearranged XML. The next chapter provides an introduction to XML and explains how you can use it to store and manipulate XML data in your C# programs.

EXERCISES

1. Write a program similar to the one shown in Figure 23-18 that uses a `DataSet` and LINQ to display test score data. Hint: Follow the steps described in the section "Making a `DataGridView` interface" to make a `DataSet` and data adapters. When the program starts, use data adapters to load a `DataSet`. Then use LINQ code similar to the code used by the LinqToDataSetScores example program in Chapter 8 to select and display the required data.

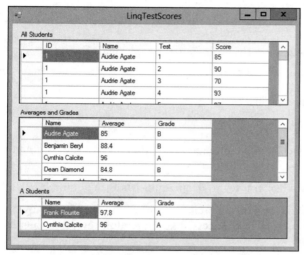

FIGURE 23-18: This program uses LINQ to select and display test score data.

2. In the AddStudent example program described in the section "Loading `DataSet`s," what happens if you add a student and then close the program without clicking Save?

3. Programs that use data adapters to load and save data in `DataSet`s load all the data when the program starts and save changes before the program ends (or when the user clicks a Save button). The ADO.NET examples described in this chapter load data as it is needed. Does one approach seem better than the other? Does the size or location of the database matter? What about the number of users?

4. An ADO.NET program can execute many more SQL statements than just SELECT. For example, it can create tables, insert new records, modify or delete existing records, and drop tables.

    Write a program that connects to the SchoolData.accdb database and performs the following tasks by using the indicated SQL statements.

    ➤   Create an `Instructors` table.

    ```
    CREATE TABLE Instructors (InstructorId int, FirstName varchar(255),
        LastName varchar(255), Department varchar(255))
    ```

➤ Insert a new record into the Instructors table.

```
INSERT INTO Instructors (InstructorId, FirstName, LastName, Department)
     VALUES (1001, 'Fred', 'Flourite', 'Mathematics')
```

➤ Fetch and display the data in the Instructors table.

```
SELECT InstructorId, FirstName, LastName, Department FROM Instructors
```

➤ Update the record in the Instructors table.

```
UPDATE Instructors SET FirstName='Fran' WHERE InstructorId=1001
```

➤ Fetch and display the data in the Instructors table again.

```
SELECT InstructorId, FirstName, LastName, Department FROM Instructors
```

➤ Drop the Instructors table.

```
DROP TABLE Instructors
```

Hints: Use the command object's ExecuteNonQuery method to execute commands that don't fetch data.

Does the database warn you when you try to drop a table that isn't empty?

5. What happens if a program tries to open a database connection that is already open? How does this affect programs that create a connection at the module level and then use the connection in multiple methods?

6. Modify the program you wrote for Exercise 4 so that it inserts three records into the Instructors table. What happens if you omit the UPDATE statement's WHERE clause? Hint: You can simplify the program by creating an InsertInstructorsRecord method.

7. Write a program that lets the user enter an SQL SELECT statement and execute it to see results in a ListBox. Test the program by executing the following queries:

```
SELECT * FROM Students, TestScores
    WHERE Students.StudentId = TestScores.StudentId

SELECT FirstName, LastName, AVG(Score)
    FROM Students, TestScores
    WHERE Students.StudentId = TestScores.StudentId
    GROUP BY FirstName, LastName
```

Hints: Use error handling in case the SQL statement is incorrectly formed. Use the OleDbDataReader's GetValues method to fetch all the values for a row. Use those values' ToString methods to convert the values into text.

Note that you generally shouldn't execute SQL statements entered by the user because the user could enter malicious code that damages the database. For example, the user could enter a DROP TABLE statement. This sort of tool should be available only to trusted users who understand SQL.

24

XML

WROX.COM DOWNLOADS FOR THIS CHAPTER

Please note that all the code examples for this chapter are available as a part of this chapter's code download on the book's website at `www.wrox.com/go/csharp5programmersref` on the Download Code tab.

Relational database engines such as SQL Server, Access, and MySQL let you store data that includes records grouped into tables. They use indexes to let you select records based on criteria, join records from multiple tables, and order the results.

Sometimes you might not need the features a relational database provides. If you just want to store some data and you don't need to search, join, or sort it, then a relational database is overkill.

eXtensible Markup Language (XML) is a data storage language that uses a hierarchical collection of *element*s to represent data. You can write data into an XML file. Later you can read the file to recover the data. Because this is an industry-standard language, other programs possibly running on different operating systems can read, write, and share XML files.

Like all the topics in this part of the book, XML is a big topic. In fact, entire books have been written about it. (I even coauthored one: *Visual Basic .NET and XML: Harness the Power of XML in VB.NET* by Rod Stephens and Brian Hochgurtel, Wrox, 2002.)

There isn't room in this chapter to cover every detail of XML, so I won't try. This chapter explains the basics of XML, so you can use it in your programs to save and restore data and to read data stored by other programs. For additional details, find a good book about these languages or search the Internet.

SERIALIZATION DEFERRED

Serialization is the process of converting an object such as a `Book` or `Employee` into a stream representation, usually in the form of text. *Deserialization* is the process of converting a serialization back into the object it represents.

You can use XML to serialize and deserialize objects. Serialization and deserialization are somewhat specialized, but they are quite useful in many applications. Rather than trying to squeeze them into this chapter, they are explained in the next chapter.

The following section explains XML syntax. The sections after that explain how you can use XML in your C# programs.

BASIC XML SYNTAX

Each element is represented by an opening *tag* and a corresponding closing tag. Opening tags are enclosed in brackets < and >. Closing tags look like opening tags except they begin with </ instead of just <.

For example, the following XML code stores information about two students.

```
<Students>
    <Student>
        <FirstName>Larry</FirstName>
        <LastName>Liverpool</LastName>
    </Student>
    <Student>
        <FirstName>Miranda</FirstName>
        <LastName>McQuaid</LastName>
    </Student>
</Students>
```

RIGHTSPACE

Methods that process XML ignore whitespace including newlines, tabs, and spaces. You can insert any whitespace you like to make an XML file easier to read. For example, you can use indentation to show which elements are contained inside other elements.

Elements are sometimes called *nodes*, particularly when you want to emphasize the hierarchical tree-like nature of the data.

Elements must be properly nested. For example, the following is not valid XML because the `FirstName` and `LastName` elements overlap.

```
<Student>
    <FirstName>
        Larry
    <LastName>
        Liverpool
    </FirstName>
    </LastName>
<Student>
```

Note that the names of the elements are completely up to you. You can define them on the fly as you build the file if you like. There's nothing special about the elements `Students`, `Student`, `FirstName`, and `LastName` used in the previous examples. They can use Pascal case as in this example, be all lowercase, or use whatever casing scheme you like.

An element's value is whatever is contained inside its opening and closing tags. In addition to a value, an element can have attributes. An *attribute* gives additional information about an element. To make an attribute, insert its name, an equal sign, and the value it should have within quotes all inside the opening tag.

For example, consider the following XML.

```
<Students>
    <Student StudentId="128977">
        <FirstName>Larry</FirstName>
        <LastName>Liverpool</LastName>
        <StudentId>3981</StudentId>
    </Student>
    <Student StudentId="348722">
        <FirstName>Miranda</FirstName>
        <LastName>McQuaid</LastName>
        <StudentId>2711</StudentId>
    </Student>
</Students>
```

In this code, the `Student` elements have nested `FirstName` and `LastName` elements. The `StudentId` attribute gives each `Student`'s ID number.

You can mix and match nested elements and attributes in any way you like to make the XML code easier to read and process.

If an element contains no nested elements, you can omit the closing tag if you end it with `/>` instead of the usual `>`. For example, the following code shows a `Contact` element with no nested subelements.

```
<Contact Phone="800-555-1234" />
```

CONCISE XML

If you store values in attributes instead of nested elements, you can omit closing tags and make the XML code more concise. For example, the following code holds the same data as the previous student code, but it uses only attributes.

```
<Students>
    <Student FirstName="Larry" LastName="Liverpool"
        StudentId="128977" />
    <Student FirstName="Miranda" LastName="McQuaid"
        StudentId="348722" />
</Students>
```

This code is certainly more concise. You may also find it easier to read.

Which version you use is largely a matter of preference. The only real restriction is that any code that writes the data must use the same arrangement as any code that must later read the data.

You can include a comment in XML code by starting it with `<!--` and ending it with `-->` as in the following code.

```
<!-- This is an XML comment -->
```

Because XML is a hierarchical language, all the data in an XML file must be contained within a single top-level node that has no parent node called the *root node*. However, there is one important exception to this rule. Many XML files begin with a single XML declaration that gives information about the file itself. That declaration begins with `<?` and ends with `?>`. For example, the following code shows the `App.config` file for a C# program.

```
<?xml version="1.0" encoding="utf-8" ?>
<configuration>
    <startup>
        <supportedRuntime version="v4.0" sku=".NETFramework,Version=v4.5" />
    </startup>
</configuration>
```

The directive at the top of the code indicates that this file uses XML version 1.0 and contains characters from the UTF-8 character encoding.

Just as you sometimes want to include special characters such as \ in a C# string as in \n, you might want to include special characters in XML code. XML defines the five special characters listed in the following table.

CHARACTER	CODE
<	&lt;
>	&gt;
&	&amp;

CHARACTER	CODE
'	'
"	"

For example, the following code represents the equation 17 < 21.

```
<equation>17 &lt; 21</equation>
```

There's one other way you can include special characters inside XML code: a CDATA section. A CDATA section begins with `<![CDATA[` and includes all the following text until it reaches the closing sequence `]]>`. The CDATA can include carriage returns, ampersands, quotes, and other special characters.

That's all there is to basic XML. There are plenty of other details, some of which will be explained later in this chapter, but this is enough to let you save and restore data in XML files.

The following text shows an XML file that demonstrates the features described so far.

```
<?xml version="1.0" encoding="utf-8" ?>
<Students>
  <Description>
    <![CDATA[This is some text that describes the XML file.
It's a multi-line description.
< > ' " &
This is its last line.]]>
  </Description>
  <!-- This Student's data is stored in sub-elements. -->
  <Student>
    <FirstName>Arthur</FirstName>
    <LastName>Andrews</LastName>
    <StudentId>83746</StudentId>
  </Student>
  <!-- This Student's data is stored in attributes. -->
  <Student FirstName="Bethany" LastName="Bechtold" StudentId="12653" />
</Students>
```

> **NOTE** *Several of the examples described later in this chapter create or read this XML data.*

The code is relatively straightforward so I won't describe it line by line.

One thing worth mentioning is that the CDATA element contains special characters and multiple lines. The content starts right after the `<![CDATA[`. If the content began on the following line, it would contain the initial new line after the `<![CDATA[`.

Similarly, the CDATA content ends immediately before the `]]>`. If the `]]>` were on the following line, the content would include a final new line.

The following sections explain several ways you can write XML data into a file. The sections after that explain how you can read XML data from files or strings.

WRITING XML DATA

The .NET Framework provides two main ways to write XML data: the `XmlWriter` class and the XML Document Object Model. The following two sections describe these approaches.

USING NAMESPACES

The classes that read and write XML files are in the `System.Xml` and `System.Xml.Linq` namespaces. When you write code that manipulates XML data, you may want to include one or both of the following `using` directives.

```
using Systen.Xml;
using Systen.Xml.Linq;
```

XmlWriter

The `XmlWriter` class provides methods for writing the pieces of an XML file. To use an `XmlWriter` to write XML data into a file, call the class's `Create` method to create the file. Then use the other methods to write the pieces of the XML document into the file. For example, the `WriteComment` method adds a comment to the file and the `WriteStartElement` method writes an element's starting tag into the file.

The following table lists the most useful `XmlWriter` methods.

METHOD	PURPOSE
`Close`	Closes the writer's underlying stream.
`Create`	Creates an `XmlWriter` associated with a file, stream, `StringBuilder`, or other object.
`Dispose`	Frees the writer's resources. (You can use the `using` statement to ensure that the writer is disposed.)
`Flush`	Flushes output to the underlying stream.
`WriteAttributeString`	Writes an attribute with a specified name and value.
`WriteCData`	Writes CDATA.
`WriteComment`	Writes a comment.
`WriteElementString`	Writes an element with a specified name and text value.
`WriteEndAttribute`	Ends an attribute started with `WriteStartAttribute`.
`WriteEndDocument`	Ends the document.
`WriteName`	Writes a name.
`WriteStartAttribute`	Starts an attribute.

METHOD	PURPOSE
`WriteStartDocument`	Starts the document.
`WriteStartElement`	Starts an element.
`WriteString`	Writes a string, escaping special characters such as < and > if necessary.
`WriteValue`	Writes a value such as a `bool`, `int`, or `double`.

The UseXmlWriter example program, which is available for download on this book's website, uses the following code to create an XML file holding the student data shown earlier.

```
    // Create the writer.
    using (XmlWriter writer = XmlWriter.Create(fileTextBox.Text))
    {
        // Write the start element.
        writer.WriteStartDocument();

        writer.WriteStartElement("Students");        // <Students>
        writer.WriteStartElement("Description");      // <Description>

        // Write the Description's content.
        string cdata = @"This is some text that describes the XML file.
It's a multi-line description.
< > ' "" &
This is its last line.";
        writer.WriteCData(cdata);

        writer.WriteComment("This Student's data is stored in sub-elements.");
        writer.WriteStartElement("Student");          // <Student>
        writer.WriteElementString("FirstName", "Arthur");
        writer.WriteElementString("LastName", "Andrews");
        writer.WriteElementString("StudentId", "83746");
        writer.WriteEndElement();                      // </Student>

        writer.WriteComment("This Student's data is stored in attributes.");
        writer.WriteStartElement("Student");          // <Student>
        writer.WriteAttributeString("FirstName", "Bethany");
        writer.WriteAttributeString("LastName", "Bechtold");
        writer.WriteAttributeString("StudentId", "12653");
        writer.WriteEndElement();                      // </Student>

        writer.WriteEndElement();                      // </Description>
        writer.WriteEndElement();                      // </Students>
    }
```

This code is fairly straightforward. The only thing worth special mention is the way the program uses a multiline `string` to create CDATA. Recall that a C# string literal begins with @" and includes all characters including new lines up to the closing " character. Because this example needs to include a " character within the CDATA, the code doubles the character in the string literal to place a single instance of the character in the string.

Figure 24-1 shows the UseXmlWriter program displaying the resulting XML file in a `TextBox`. Notice that the file's text is all run together with no whitespace except the whitespace included within strings such as the `Description` element's CDATA content. Other programs can read the file with no problems but this is hard for a human to read.

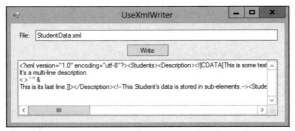

FIGURE 24-1: The UseXmlWriter example program builds and displays an XML file.

The `XmlTextWriter` class, which inherits from `XmlWriter`, works much as `XmlWriter` does, but it can produce nicely indented output.

The FormatXml example program, which is available for download on this book's website, is shown in Figure 24-2.

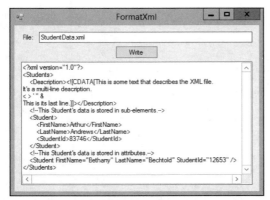

FIGURE 24-2: The FormatXml example program uses an `XmlTextWriter` object to produce nicely indented XML code.

To produce indented XML code, the FormatXml example program creates an `XmlTextWriter` instead of an `XmlWriter`. It sets the `XmlTextWriter`'s `Formatting` property to `Indented` and then creates the XML file exactly as before.

The following code shows the statements that create the XmlTextWriter and set its Formatting property.

```
// Create the writer.
using (XmlTextWriter writer = new XmlTextWriter(fileTextBox.Text, null))
{
    // Make it pretty.
    writer.Formatting = Formatting.Indented;

    // Generate the XML code as before...
}
```

The XmlWriter class is a fast tool for writing XML output. It works "forward only" so after it has written something, you can't go back and change it.

It's also noncached so it doesn't remember what it wrote in the past. The writer keeps track of the path it took to get to its current position but that's all. For example, it might know that it took the following path to get to a LastName element.

```
<Students>
    <Student>
        <LastName>
```

The writer doesn't remember any other elements that it might have written along the way such as other Student elements or other elements within this Student element.

Document Object Model

The XmlWriter and XmlTextWriter classes let you build XML data but they're rather cumbersome. For example, they require you to end each element that you start and to do so in the proper sequence. Ending an element in the wrong place can mean the difference between this:

```
<Student>
    <FirstName>
        Bethany
    </FirstName>
    <LastName>
        Bechtold
    </LastName>
</Student>
```

And this:

```
<Student>
    <FirstName>
        Bethany
        <LastName>
            Bechtold
        </LastName>
    </FirstName>
</Student>
```

> **TIP** *If you forget to end an open element, the writer automatically ends it at the end of the file.*

Another way to build an XML document is to use the *XML Document Object Model (DOM)*. The DOM uses objects to create an in-memory model of an XML document. After you build such a model, you can use its methods to manipulate the model and save the result into an XML file or string.

The WriteDom example program, which is available for download on this book's website, uses the following code to create an XML file holding the student data shown earlier.

```
// Write a text file.
private void writeButton_Click(object sender, EventArgs e)
{
    // Create the document.
    XDocument document = new XDocument();

    // Create the root element
    XElement students = new XElement("Students");          // <Students>
    document.Add(students);

    XElement description = new XElement("Description");     // <Description>
    students.Add(description);

    // Write the Description's content.
    string cdata = @"This is some text that describes the XML file.
It's a multi-line description.
< > ' "" &
This is its last line.";
    description.Add(new XCData(cdata));

    students.Add(new XComment(                              // Comment.
        "This Student's data is stored in sub-elements."));

    XElement student = new XElement("Student");             // <Student>
    students.Add(student);

    student.SetElementValue("FirstName", "Arthur");        // <FirstName>
    student.SetElementValue("LastName", "Andrews");        // <LastName>
    student.SetElementValue("StudentId", "83746");         // <StudentId>

    students.Add(new XComment(                              // Comment.
        "This Student's data is stored in attributes."));

    student = new XElement("Student");                      // <Student>
    students.Add(student);

    student.SetAttributeValue("FirstName", "Bethany");     // FirstName
    student.SetAttributeValue("LastName", "Bechtold");     // LastName
    student.SetAttributeValue("StudentId", "12653");       // StudentId
```

```
    // Save the document in a file.
    using (XmlTextWriter writer = new XmlTextWriter(fileTextBox.Text, null))
    {
        // Make it pretty.
        writer.Formatting = Formatting.Indented;

        document.WriteTo(writer);
    }

    // Display the file.
    resultTextBox.Text = File.ReadAllText(fileTextBox.Text);
}
```

The code first creates an XDocument object to represent the XML code.

Next, it creates an XElement object to represent the file's Students element and uses the document's Add method to add it to the document's child collection.

The code creates another XElement to represent the Description element and adds it to the Students element. It then adds a new XCData object to hold the Description's data.

The rest of the code follows a similar pattern, creating new objects and adding them to the child collections of the objects that should contain them.

After it finishes building the document, the program creates an XmlTextWriter much as the FormatXml example program did. It sets the writer's Formatting property and then uses the document object's WriteTo method to make the document write its XML code into a file.

The program finishes by displaying the resulting XML file.

ANOTHER DOM

The WriteDom example program uses System.Xml.Linq classes to build an XML document object model. The System.Xml namespace contains other versions of similar classes. For example, it includes XmlDocument, XmlElement, XmlComment, and other classes. Building an XML document object model with those classes is similar to building one with the System.Xml.Linq classes, with some minor differences. Building objects models is easier with the newer System.Xml.Linq classes, however, so you should probably use them.

Two of the most important classes for manipulating the DOM are XDocument and XElement.

The XDocument class's most useful properties are Declaration, which gets or sets the document's XML declaration, and Root, which returns the document's root element. The following table lists the XDocument class's most useful methods.

METHOD	PURPOSE
Add	Adds an item to the document's child collection. (Note that you can add only one child, the root element, to the document.)
DescendantNodes	Returns a collection of XNode objects that are descendants of the document.
Descendants	Returns a collection of XElement objects that are descendants of the document. If you specify a name, the method returns only elements with that name.
Load	Loads the document from a filename, stream, or XmlReader.
Parse	Creates a new XDocument from an XML string.
Save	Saves the document into a file, stream, or writer.
ToString	Returns the document's indented XML code.
WriteTo	Writes the document into an XmlWriter.

The following table lists the XElement class's most useful properties.

PROPERTY	PURPOSE
Document	Returns the XDocument that contains the element.
FirstAttribute	Gets the element's first attribute.
FirstNode	Gets the element's first child node.
HasAttributes	Returns true if the element has attributes.
HasElements	Returns true if the element has child elements.
IsEmpty	Returns true if the element contains no content. (It still might have attributes.)
LastAttribute	Gets the element's last attribute.
LastNode	Gets the element's last child node.
Name	Gets or sets the element's name.
NextNode	Returns the next node in the element's parent's child list.
NodeType	Gets the node's type.
Parent	Gets the element's parent element.
PreviousNode	Returns the previous node in the element's parent's child list.
Value	Gets or sets the node's text contents.

The following table lists the XElement class's most useful methods.

METHOD	PURPOSE
Add	Adds an item at the end of the element's child collection.
AddAfterSelf	Adds an item to the parent's child collection after this element.
AddBeforeSelf	Adds an item to the parent's child collection before this element.
AddFirst	Adds an item at the beginning of the element's child collection.
Ancestors	Returns a collection of XElement objects that are ancestors of the element. If you specify a name, the method returns only elements with that name.
Attribute	Returns an attribute with a specific name.
Attributes	Returns a collection containing this element's attributes. If you specify a name, the collection includes only attributes with that name.
DescendantNodes	Returns a collection of XNode objects that are descendants of the element.
Descendants	Returns a collection of XElement objects that are descendants of the element. If you specify a name, the method returns only elements with that name.
DescendantsAndSelf	Returns a collection of XElement objects that includes this element and its descendants. If you specify a name, the method returns only elements with that name.
Element	Returns the first child element with a specified name.
Elements	Returns a collection holding the element's children. If you specify a name, the method returns only elements with that name.
ElementsAfterSelf	Returns a collection holding the element's siblings that come after this element. If you specify a name, the method returns only elements with that name.
ElementsBeforeSelf	Returns a collection holding the element's siblings that come before this element. If you specify a name, the method returns only elements with that name.
IsAfter	Returns true if this node comes after another specified node in document.
IsBefore	Returns true if this node comes before another specified node in document.
Load	Loads the element from a filename, stream, or reader.

continues

(continued)

METHOD	PURPOSE
Nodes	Returns a collection holding this element's child nodes.
NodesAfterSelf	Returns a collection holding the node's siblings that come after this node.
NodesBeforeSelf	Returns a collection holding the node's siblings that come before this node.
Parse	Creates an XElement from an XML string.
Remove	Removes this element from its parent.
RemoveAll	Removes all nodes and attributes from this element.
RemoveAttributes	Removes this element's attributes.
RemoveNodes	Removes this element's child nodes.
ReplaceAll	Replaces the element's child nodes and attributes with specified new ones.
ReplaceAttributes	Replaces the element's attributes with specified new ones.
ReplaceNodes	Replaces the element's child nodes with specified new ones.
ReplaceWith	Replaces this node with new specified content.
Save	Saves the element into a file, stream, or writer.
SetAttributeValue	Sets, adds, or removes an attribute.
SetElementValue	Sets, adds, or removes a child element.
SetValue	Sets the element's value.
ToString	Returns the element's indented XML code.
WriteTo	Writes the element into an XmlWriter.

An object model is handy if you need to roam through its structure to examine data and make changes, but the XmlWriter class still has its uses. A document model must contain all the elements that make up the XML data. If you're building an enormous model, the DOM structure will take up a lot of memory.

In contrast an XmlWriter doesn't remember what it wrote in the past so it can write even huge XML documents without using up a lot of memory. However, many programmers find XmlWriter more cumbersome than the DOM so they prefer the DOM.

XML Literals

The `XmlWriter` class and the DOM both let a program build an XML document, but both require a fairly large amount of code. They're a lot easier to use if you can loop through an array, list, or other data structure containing objects and generate XML data for the objects.

However, sometimes you might simply want to create an XML object hierarchy within a program. Visual Basic allows you to use string literals as in the following code.

```
Dim arthur As XElement =
    <Student>
        <FirstName>Arthur</FirstName>
        <LastName>Andrews</LastName>
        <StudentID>83746</StudentID>
    </Student>
```

C# doesn't support XML literals. (Although I wouldn't be surprised if it did some day.) Fortunately, C# does support multiline string literals and that works almost as well. Simply use the `XElement.Parse` method to parse a multiline string holding the XML code. The following code shows an example.

```
XElement student = XElement.Parse(
    @"<Student>
        <FirstName>Arthur</FirstName>
        <LastName>Andrews</LastName>
        <StudentID>83746</StudentID>
    </Student>");
```

The XML string can include any amount of nested XML code, so you can use this technique to build an XML document of arbitrary complexity.

READING XML DATA

The previous sections explained how you can use `XmlTextWriter` and DOM classes to create XML documents. The .NET Framework provides corresponding techniques to read XML documents. The following two sections explain how you can use the `XmlTextReader` class and the document object model to read XML code.

XmlTextReader

The `XmlWriter` class and subclasses such as `XmlTextWriter` provide fast, forward-only, noncached methods for writing XML data. Similarly, the `XmlTextReader` class provides fast, forward-only, noncached methods for reading XML data. It provides methods to move through an XML file one node at a time and to examine the data provided by each node.

To use an `XmlTextReader`, use the class's constructor or the `XmlReader` class's static `Create` method to create an object associated with the file or input stream that you want to read. Use the object's `Read` method to read the next node from the XML data. After you read a node, you can use the reader's properties and methods to determine the node's name, type, attributes, content, and other properties.

The following table lists the most useful `XmlReader` properties.

PROPERTY	MEANING
AttributeCount	Returns the number of attributes the node has.
Depth	Returns the depth of the current node in the XML hierarchy.
EOF	Returns `true` when the reader is at the end of the XML data.
HasAttributes	Returns `true` if the node has attributes.
HasValue	Returns `true` if the node can have a value.
IsEmptyElement	Returns `true` if the node is an empty element as in `<Overdue />`.
Item	Gets a node attribute by index or name. (This is the class's indexer, so you use it as in `reader[0]` instead of invoking the `Item` property explicitly.)
Name	Returns the node's name.
Value	Returns the text value of the current node.

The following table lists the `XmlReader` class's most useful methods.

METHOD	PURPOSE
Create	Creates a new reader associated with a string, stream, file, or other data source.
Dispose	Frees the object's resources. You can include a `using` statement to automatically call `Dispose`.
GetAttribute	Gets an attribute for the current node by index or name. (Similar to the `Item` property.)
IsName	Returns `true` if its parameter is a valid XML name.
MoveToAttribute	Moves the reader to an attribute specified by index or name.
MoveToContent	Moves the reader to the current node's content.
MoveToElement	Moves the reader to the element containing the reader's current position. For example, if you move the reader to examine an element's attributes, the method moves the reader back to the element's node.
MoveToFirstAttribute	Moves the reader to the current node's first attribute node.
MoveToNextAttribute	Moves the reader to the current node's next attribute node.

METHOD	PURPOSE
Read	Reads the next node from the XML data.
ReadInnerXml	Returns the current node's descendants as an XML string.
ReadOuterXml	Returns the current node's subtree (including the current node) as an XML string.
ReadToDescendant	Moves the reader to a subelement with a specified name.
ReadToNextSibling	Moves the reader past the rest of the current node to its next sibling.
Skip	Skips the current node's children.

The ReadXml example program, which is available for download on this book's website, uses the following code to read an XML file.

```
// Read the XML data.
private void readButton_Click(object sender, EventArgs e)
{
    string result = "";

    // Open a reader for the XML file.
    using (XmlReader reader = XmlReader.Create(fileTextBox.Text))
    {
        // Read tags from the file.
        while (reader.Read())
        {
            switch (reader.NodeType)
            {
                case XmlNodeType.Element:
                    result += "Element: " + reader.Name + "\r\n";
                    if (reader.HasAttributes)
                    {
                        for (int i = 0; i < reader.AttributeCount; i++)
                            result += "    Attribute: " + reader[i] + "\r\n";
                    }
                    break;
                case XmlNodeType.EndElement:
                    result += "EndElement: " + reader.Name + "\r\n";
                    break;
                case XmlNodeType.Text:
                    result += "Text: " + reader.Value + "\r\n";
                    break;
                case XmlNodeType.CDATA:
                    result += "CDATA: [" +
                        reader.Value.Replace("\n","\r\n") + "]\r\n";
                    break;
                case XmlNodeType.Comment:
                    result += "Comment: " + reader.Value + "\r\n";
                    break;
```

```
            }
         }
      }
      resultTextBox.Text = result;
}
```

The code uses `XmlReader.Create` to create an `XmlReader` associated with an XML file. It then enters a loop that continues as long as the `Read` method returns `true` to indicate that there is more data to read.

Within the loop, the code checks the reader's `NodeType` property to see what kind of node it is reading. If the node is an element (such as `<Student>`), the code displays its name and its attributes if it has any.

If the node is the end of an element (such as `</Student>`), the code displays its name.

If the node is a text node, the code displays the text it contains. For example, in the XML code `<FirstName>Arthur</FirstName>`, the `FirstName` element contains a text element that holds the text `Arthur`.

If the node is a CDATA node, the code displays its data. Within the data, the code replaces the `\n` character with the string `\r\n` so newlines will be displayed correctly in the result `TextBox`.

Finally, if the node is a comment, the code displays its value.

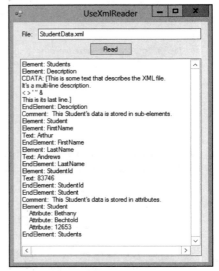

FIGURE 24-3: The UseXmlReader example program reads an XML file and displays information about the nodes it contains.

After it has processed all the file's nodes, the program displays the results in a `TextBox`.

Figure 24-3 shows the UseXmlReader program after it has read the students XML data shown earlier in this chapter. If you look closely, you can see the pieces of the data in the result.

Document Object Model

The `XmlReader` and `XmlTextReader` classes are fast but somewhat awkward because they let you move only forward through the data. They can be efficient if you know the structure of the data or if you are looking for specific nodes, but they don't let you explore the structure of an XML file.

Just as you can use the DOM to build an XML file, you can also use the DOM to study an existing XML file. Then your program can move over its nodes to examine its structure, find values, copy subtrees, and use the document's full structure to otherwise study and manipulate the data.

To load an object model from XML data, simply call the `XDocument` class's static `Load` method passing it a filename, stream, or `XmlReader`.

The ReadDom example program, which is available for download on this book's website, uses the following code to read and display an XML file holding the student data shown earlier.

```
// Load the XML file into a DOM.
XDocument document = XDocument.Load(fileTextBox.Text);

// Display the document's XML text.
resultTextBox.Text = document.ToString();
```

It doesn't get much simpler than that! Of course, in a real program you would need to use the XDocument object's properties and methods to find the data you want and do something with it.

RELATED TECHNOLOGIES

By itself, an XML file simply holds data. It doesn't select, sort, rearrange, or otherwise manipulate the data. Those operations are often useful, however, so lots of related technologies have sprung up to work with XML data. Some of those technologies include the following.

- ➤ **XSL (Extensible Style Sheet Language)**—This refers to a family of languages and tools for reformatting XML data. It includes the following.

  - ➤ **XSLT (XSL Transform)**—A language for transforming XML data into other formats such as plain text, HTML, rearranged XML documents, or XSL FO.

  - ➤ **XSL FO (XSL Formatting Objects)**—A language for formatting XML data for output for screen, PDFs, printers, and so forth.

  - ➤ **XPath**—This is a query language used by XSL and other XML tools to find and identify items within XML data.

- ➤ **XQuery**—A somewhat SQL-like language for querying XML data.

- ➤ **DTD (Document Type Definition)**—An XML data file validation language. You use DTD to define the required structure of an XML file. Then you can validate a particular XML file to see if it satisfies those requirements.

- ➤ **XSD (XML Schema Definition)**—Another XML data file validation language. See DTD.

- ➤ **XLink**—A language for defining hyperlinks in XML data.

- ➤ **SOAP (Simple Object Access Protocol)**—A protocol that lets applications (often running on different computers) exchange data.

- ➤ **WSDL (Web Services Definition Language)**—A language for describing web services.

- ➤ **RSS (Really Simple Syndication)**—A format for XML news feeds and sites that post news-like items.

There isn't room to cover all these technologies here, but I would like to provide at least a brief introduction to two of these: XPath and XSLT.

XPath

XPath is a language for identifying items in XML data. For example, you can use XPath to select nodes with a particular name, nodes that have certain attributes, and nodes that have certain relationships with other nodes.

To use XPath in C#, you first define an XPath query to identify the elements that you want to select. You then call an XDocument or XElement object's XPathSelectElement or XPathSelectElements method to find the wanted elements.

> ### WHERE ARE XPATHSELECTELEMENT AND XPATHSELECTELEMENTS?
>
> The XPathSelectElement and XPathSelectElements methods are extension methods defined in the System.Xml.XPath namespace. To make using them easier, you may want to add the following using directive to programs that use XPath.
>
> ```
> using System.Xml.XPath;
> ```

The XPath query looks vaguely like a file's pathname in a directory hierarchy. The query can also include operators that work as wildcards, filter the results, and specify relationships among nodes. For example, the following statement selects XElement objects representing Student elements that have a GradePointAverage attribute with value less than 2.5.

```
IEnumerable<XElement> students =
    document.XPathSelectElements("//Student[@GradePointAverage < 2.5]");
```

The following table lists the most useful operators that you can use in an XPath query.

OPERATOR	MEANING
/	Selects an immediate child.
//	Selects descendants.
.	The current node.
..	The current node's parent.
*	Matches anything.
@	Attribute prefix for matching an attribute. For example, @Cost matches an attribute named Cost.
@*	Selects all attributes.
( )	Groups operations.
[ ]	Applies a filter. For example, //Planet[@Name="Earth"] matches Planet elements that have a Name attribute with value Earth.

OPERATOR	MEANING
[ ]	Subscript operator for accessing items in a collection.
+	Addition.
-	Subtraction.
div	Floating-point division.
*	Multiplication.
mod	Modulus.

When a query filters results, it can include the boolean and comparison operators listed in the following table.

OPERATOR	MEANING
and	Logical AND
or	Logical OR
not()	Logical NOT
=	Equals
!=	Not equals
<	Less than
<=	Less than or equal
>	Greater than
>=	Greater than or equal

The UseXPath example program, which is available for download on this book's website, uses XPath to display information about planets. The program gets its data from the file `Planets.xml`, which has the following structure.

```
<SolarSystem>
  <Planets>
    <Planet>
      <Name>Mercury</Name>
      <Distance>57.91</Distance>
      <Radius>2340</Radius>
      <LengthOfYear>0.24085</LengthOfYear>
      <Day>88</Day>
      <Mass>0.054</Mass>
    </Planet>
```

```
    ... Other planets omitted ...

  </Planets>
</SolarSystem>
```

When the program starts, it uses the following code to load the XML file and to fill a ComboBox with the names of the planets defined in the file.

```
// The DOM.
XDocument Document = XDocument.Load("Planets.xml");

// Load the XML data.
private void Form1_Load(object sender, EventArgs e)
{
    // Load the XML file.
    Document = XDocument.Load("Planets.xml");

    // List planets.
    foreach (XElement element in Document.XPathSelectElements("//Planet/Name"))
    {
        planetComboBox.Items.Add(element.Value);
    }

    // Select the first planet.
    planetComboBox.SelectedIndex = 0;
}
```

The Load event handler first loads the XML document. It then calls the document's XPathSelectElements method, passing it the XQuery //Planet/Name. The // operator allows the query to descend to any depth in the document. The Planet/Name piece makes the query select Name elements that are direct children of Planet elements.

The code loops through the returned XElement objects and adds each object's Value property to the ComboBox.

When the user selects a planet from the ComboBox, the program executes the following code.

```
// Display the selected planet's data.
private void planetComboBox_SelectedIndexChanged(object sender, EventArgs e)
{
    string name = planetComboBox.Text;
    string query = "//Planet[Name=\"" + name + "\"]";
    XElement planet = Document.XPathSelectElement(query);
    string info = "";
    foreach (XElement child in planet.Elements())
    {
        info += child.Name.ToString() + ": " + child.Value + "\r\n";
    }
    infoTextBox.Text = info;
}
```

This code gets the selected planet's name and uses it to build an XPath query with the following format.

```
//Planet[Name="Mercury"]
```

This query selects `Planet` elements at any depth in the document where the `Planet`'s `Name` child has value `Mercury`.

The program then calls the `XDocument` object's `XPathSelectElement` method to get the first (and in this case the only) element that satisfies the query. The code then loops through the `Planet` element's children and adds their names and values to a result string. When it is finished, the program displays the result.

Figure 24-4 shows the UseXPath example program displaying information for Mercury.

FIGURE 24-4: The UseXPath example program uses XPath queries to display information about planets.

For more information on XPath, see the following links.

➤ "XPath Reference" at `msdn.microsoft.com/library/ms256115.aspx`

➤ "XPath Examples" at `msdn.microsoft.com/library/ms256086.aspx`

XSLT

XSLT is a language that you can use to transform XML data into a new format. It's a fairly complicated language, so there isn't room to cover it in any depth here. To really learn the language, see the following links.

➤ "XSLT Tutorial" at `www.w3schools.com/xsl/default.asp`

➤ "XSLT Elements Reference" at `www.w3schools.com/xsl/xsl_w3celementref.asp`

➤ "XSL Transformations (XSLT) Version 1.0" at `www.w3.org/TR/xslt`

Rather than explaining the whole XSLT language, the rest of this section explains an example. The TransformPlanets example program uses XSLT to transform the `Planets.xml` file described in the preceding section into an HTML file.

Recall that the `Planets.xml` file has the following structure.

```
<SolarSystem>
  <Planets>
    <Planet>
      <Name>Mercury</Name>
      <Distance>57.91</Distance>
      <Radius>2340</Radius>
      <LengthOfYear>0.24085</LengthOfYear>
      <Day>88</Day>
      <Mass>0.054</Mass>
    </Planet>

    ... Other planets omitted ...

  </Planets>
</SolarSystem>
```

The following code shows the XSLT file `PlanetsToHtml.xslt`.

```xml
<?xml version="1.0" encoding="utf-8"?>
<xsl:stylesheet version="1.0"
    xmlns:xsl="http://www.w3.org/1999/XSL/Transform"
    xmlns:msxsl="urn:schemas-microsoft-com:xslt"
    exclude-result-prefixes="msxsl"
>
    <xsl:output method="html" indent="yes"/>

    <xsl:template match="Planets">
      <HTML>
        <BODY>
          <TABLE BORDER="2">
            <TR>
              <TH>Planet</TH>
              <TH>Distance to Sun</TH>
              <TH>Length of Year</TH>
              <TH>Length of Day</TH>
            </TR>
            <xsl:apply-templates select="Planet"/>
          </TABLE>
        </BODY>
      </HTML>
    </xsl:template>
    <xsl:template match="Planet">
      <TR>
        <TD>
          <xsl:value-of select="Name"/>
        </TD>
        <TD>
          <xsl:value-of select="Distance"/>
        </TD>
        <TD>
          <xsl:value-of select="LengthOfYear"/>
        </TD>
        <TD>
          <xsl:value-of select="Day"/>
        </TD>
      </TR>
    </xsl:template>
</xsl:stylesheet>
```

The `xsl:output` element indicates that the resulting output file should be in HTML format and that it should include indenting.

This file contains two templates. The first matches `Planets` nodes. When the XSLT processor works through the XML input file and encounters a `Planets` element, this template executes. (In this example, the `Planets.xml` file has only one `Planets` element so this template executes only once.)

The body of the template makes the processor emit the following text.

```
<HTML>
  <BODY>
    <TABLE BORDER="2">
      <TR>
        <TH>Planet</TH>
        <TH>Distance to Sun</TH>
        <TH>Length of Year</TH>
        <TH>Length of Day</TH>
      </TR>
      <xsl:apply-templates select="Planet"/>
    </TABLE>
  </BODY>
</HTML>
```

This is ordinary HTML code except for the line highlighted in bold. That line uses the xsl:apply-templates element to tell the processor to apply the templates for Planet child nodes.

In this example, the first template finds the Planets element and applies the template that matches Planet elements to that element's children.

The second template matches Planet elements and emits the following text for them.

```
<TR>
  <TD>
    <xsl:value-of select="Name"/>
  </TD>
  <TD>
    <xsl:value-of select="Distance"/>
  </TD>
  <TD>
    <xsl:value-of select="LengthOfYear"/>
  </TD>
  <TD>
    <xsl:value-of select="Day"/>
  </TD>
</TR>
```

Again this is plain HTML text except for the bold statements. Those statements use the xsl:value-of element to select values from the Planet element's children.

The following HTML code shows the result.

```
<HTML>
<BODY>
  <TABLE BORDER="2">
    <TR>
      <TH>Planet</TH>
      <TH>Distance to Sun</TH>
      <TH>Length of Year</TH>
      <TH>Length of Day</TH>
```

```
          </TR>
          <TR>
            <TD>Mercury</TD>
            <TD>57.91</TD>
            <TD>0.24085</TD>
            <TD>88</TD>
          </TR>
          <TR>
            <TD>Venus</TD>
            <TD>108.21</TD>
            <TD>0.61521</TD>
            <TD>230</TD>
          </TR>

          ... Other planets omitted ...

          <TR>
            <TD>Pluto</TD>
            <TD>5910</TD>
            <TD>247.687</TD>
            <TD>6.39</TD>
          </TR>
        </TABLE>
      </BODY>
  </HTML>
```

The following code shows how the TransformPlanets program uses the XSLT file to transform the XML file.

```
// Transform Planets.xml.
private void Form1_Load(object sender, EventArgs e)
{
    // Load the style sheet.
    XslCompiledTransform xslt = new XslCompiledTransform();
    xslt.Load("PlanetsToHtml.xslt");

    // Transform the file.
    xslt.Transform("Planets.xml", "Planets.html");

    // Display the result.
    string filename = Path.GetFullPath(
        Path.Combine(Application.StartupPath, "Planets.html"));
    planetsWebBrowser.Navigate(filename);
}
```

The program creates and initializes an `XslCompiledTransform` object. It then uses its `Load` method to load the XSLT file. Next, the program calls the object's `Transform` method to transform the input XML file and save the result in the new HTML file.

That's all that's needed to perform the transformation. The program finishes by displaying the HTML file in a `WebBrowser` control.

Figure 24-5 shows the TransformPlanets example program displaying its HTML output file.

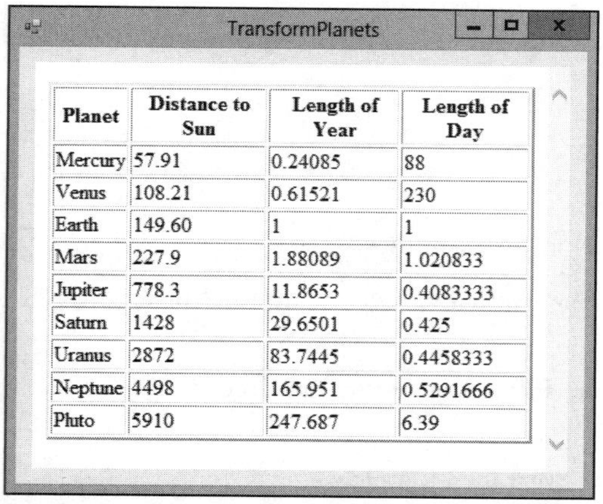

FIGURE 24-5: The TransformPlanets example program uses XSLT to transform an XML file into an HTML file and then displays the result in a `WebBrowser` control.

SUMMARY

XML is a hierarchical data storage language. Using the tools provided by the .NET Framework, you write C# programs that read and write XML data. Because XML is standardized, your program can exchange XML data with other programs, possibly running on different computers or even operating systems.

By itself, an XML file just holds data. Other related technologies such as XPath and XSLT let you search and transform XML data. This chapter didn't have room to cover those technologies in detail but it did provide some examples that you can use to start with XPath and XSLT.

Often XML files are used to hold data such as information about employees, customer orders, plants, or planets. XML files can also be used to hold representations of objects. In a process called serialization, a program can write information describing an object into an XML file. Later, it or another program can read that data to re-create (or deserialize) the object. The next chapter explains how a C# program can serialize and deserialize objects.

EXERCISES

1. Use an `XmlTextWriter` to create an XML file containing random plant data. The file should have the following structure.

```xml
<?xml version="1.0" encoding="utf-8"?>
<Plants>
  <Plant>
    <Name>ut nibh morbi</Name>
    <Zone>3</Zone>
```

```
    <Light>Shade</Light>
  </Plant>

  ... Other Plant elements omitted ...

</Plants>
```

Follow these steps to prepare to generate random plant names.

a. Place a `TextBox` on the form so that the user can enter the number of `Plant` elements to create.

b. Place a multiline `TextBox` on the form. Fill it with a few hundred words from `www.lipsum.com/feed/html`.

c. Get the text from the `TextBox` and convert it to lowercase.

d. Use regular expressions to remove periods and commas from the text.

e. Use `string.Split` to split the text into words using spaces, \r, and \n as word separators, removing empty entries.

The following code shows two methods you can use to create random plant names and light values.

```
// Return a random name.
private Random Rand = new Random();
private string RandomName(string[] words)
{
    return
        words[Rand.Next(0, words.Length)] + " " +
        words[Rand.Next(0, words.Length)] + " " +
        words[Rand.Next(0, words.Length)];
}

// Return a random light value.
private string RandomLight()
{
    string[] values =
    {
        "Shade", "Partial Shade", "Partial Sun", "Full Sun"
    };
    return values[Rand.Next(0, values.Length)];
}
```

The program should pass the array of words it built during preparation into the `RandomName` method.

2. Modify the program you wrote for Exercise 1 so that it uses the DOM instead of an `XmlTextWriter`. Which version of the program do you prefer? Are there situations in which one would be better than the other?

3. Write a program similar to the one shown in Figure 24-6 to display the plant data generated by the program you wrote for Exercise 1 or 2.

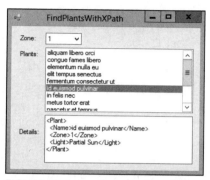

FIGURE 24-6: For Exercise 3, write a program that displays the plant data you generated in Exercises 1 and 2.

When it starts, the program should load the plant XML file into a DOM. It should use the XDocument object's Descendants method to find Zone elements and use LINQ and to display a sorted list of the distinct Zone values in the form's ComboBox.

When the user selects a zone, the program should display the names of the plants in that zone in the Plants ListBox. (Hints: Use the Descendants method to find Zone elements. Use LINQ to select the elements with the selected zone. Loop through the selected elements. Use each element's Parent property to get to its Plant element. Then use the parent's Element method to get the Name subelement.)

When the user clicks a plant in the Plants ListBox, display the information about that plant. (Hints: Use Descendants again to find Name elements and use LINQ to select the one with the selected name. Get the first selected element's parent and call the parent's ToString method.)

4. Write a program that reads the plant data generated by the program you wrote for Exercise 1 or 2 and displays a list of the plant records' names. (Hints: Scan the file to find Name elements. With those elements, use the reader's ReadElementContentAsString or ReadInnerXml method to get the element's content.)

Compare this program with the one you wrote for Exercise 3. Under what circumstances is one better than the other?

5. Modify the program you wrote for Exercise 3 so that it uses XPath instead of LINQ to find the elements it needs.

6. Modify the TransformPlanets example program so that it transforms the Plants.xml file created by the program you wrote for Exercise 1 or Exercise 2 and displays it in an HTML page.

7. Write a program that uses XSLT to transform the `Planets.xml` file into the `Planets2.xml` file that has the following format.

```
<?xml version="1.0" encoding="utf-8"?>
  <Planets>
    <Planet Name="Mercury" Distance="57.91"
        LengthOfYear="0.24085" LengthOfDay="88" />
    <Planet Name="Venus" Distance="108.21"
        LengthOfYear="0.61521" LengthOfDay="230" />

    ... Other planets omitted ...

    <Planet Name="Pluto" Distance="5910"
        LengthOfYear="247.687" LengthOfDay="6.39" />
</Planets>
```

Hints: In the XSLT file, use the child nodes' names in braces to set an attribute's value as in `Name="{Name}"`. Also note that the new format uses the name `LengthOfDay` value instead of `Day`. Finally, don't worry about indenting.

25

Serialization

WHAT'S IN THIS CHAPTER

- ➤ Serialization and deserialization
- ➤ XML, JSON, and binary serialization
- ➤ Using attributes to control serialization

WROX.COM DOWNLOADS FOR THIS CHAPTER

Please note that all the code examples for this chapter are available as a part of this chapter's code download on the book's website at www.wrox.com/go/csharp5programmersref on the Download Code tab.

Serialization is the process of converting one or more objects into a serial, stream-like format, often text. *Deserialization* is the reverse: restoring an object from its serialization.

Like the XML files described in the preceding chapter, serialization gives you a portable way to store data. You can serialize an object and send the serialization to another program, and then that program can deserialize the object.

You can also use serialization to allow a program to save and restore its state. For example, a drawing program might build a complicated data structure containing the objects the user drew. To save the drawing, the program could write the data structure's serialization into a file. Later it could reload the serialization and display the objects.

The objects serialized can be relatively simple, such as a `Customer` or `Person` object, or they can be complex data structures including objects that have references to other objects. For example, you could serialize a `CustomerOrder` object that includes an array of `Order` objects each containing a list of `OrderItem` objects.

For something that can be so complicated, serialization is surprisingly easy in .NET.

This chapter explains serialization. It explains how to serialize and deserialize objects. It also explains attributes that you can use to control how objects of a particular class are serialized.

The .NET Framework gives you three choices for how data is stored in a serialization: XML data, JSON data, or binary data. The following sections explain how you can use each of these three choices.

SERIALIZATION NAMESPACES

The `System.Xml.Serialization` namespace includes XML serialization classes. To make that kind of serialization easier, you may want to include the following `using` directive in your code.

```
using System.Xml.Serialization;
```

The `System.Runtime.Serialization.Json` namespace includes JSON serialization classes. To make that kind of serialization easier, you may want to include the following `using` directive in your code.

```
using System.Runtime.Serialization.Json;
```

The JSON classes are included in the `System.ServiceModel.Web` library. If you will be using those classes, use Project ⇨ Add Reference to add a reference to that library to your project.

XML SERIALIZATION

To serialize and deserialize objects in XML format, you use the `XmlSerializer` class's `Serialize` and `Deserialize` methods. The methods work only for classes that have a parameterless constructor, either the default constructor or one that you created. They also work only for public properties and fields. All other properties and fields are ignored.

WHY A PARAMETERLESS CONSTRUCTOR?

If you think about it, you'll realize why serialization has these restrictions. To serialize an object, the serializer must get an object's property and field values. If a property or field is not public, the serializer cannot see it.

When you deserialize an object, the serializer must create a new object and then set its values. If the class doesn't have a parameterless constructor, it would need some way to figure out which constructor to use and what values to pass into it. You might cook up some scheme for telling it which constructor to use and how, but it would make deserialization more complicated. It's just easier to require a parameterless constructor.

The Serialize and Deserialize methods are fairly easy to use; although, you do need to pass them some slightly exotic parameters. For example, you might expect the Serialize method to simply return a serialization string. Actually, it requires a stream, XmlWriter, or TextWriter parameter where it can write the serialization.

The following section explains the basic process of serializing and deserializing objects. The section after that describes some attributes you can use to change the way values are serialized.

Performing Serialization

The SerializeCustomer example program, which is available for download on this book's website, demonstrates XML serialization and deserialization. Before you look at the code, here's an overview of what the program does.

The example uses three classes: Customer, Order, and OrderItem. When it starts, the program creates a Customer object, which contains Order objects, which contain OrderItem objects. It then displays the Customer object's data. It serializes the Customer object and displays the serialization. Finally, the program deserializes the XML data to create a new object and displays that object's data.

Figure 25-1 shows the program displaying the Customer objects' data and the serialization. If you look closely, you can see that the data in the left and right TextBoxes is the same, so the program did successfully serialize and deserialize the Customer object.

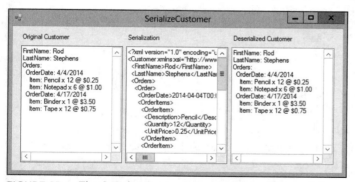

FIGURE 25-1: The SerializeCustomer example program serializes and deserializes a Customer object.

The following code shows the OrderItem class.

```
public class OrderItem
{
    public string Description;
    public int Quantity;
    public decimal UnitPrice;

    public OrderItem() { }
    public OrderItem(string description, int quantity, decimal unitPrice)
    {
```

```
            Description = description;
            Quantity = quantity;
            UnitPrice = unitPrice;
        }
    }
```

This class has `Description`, `Quantity`, and `UnitPrice` fields; a parameterless constructor; and an initializing constructor.

The following code shows the `Order` class.

```
public class Order
{
    public DateTime OrderDate;
    public OrderItem[] OrderItems;

    public Order() { }
    public Order(DateTime orderDate, params OrderItem[] orderItems)
    {
        OrderDate = orderDate;
        OrderItems = orderItems;
    }
}
```

This class includes an `OrderDate` field and an array of `OrderItem` objects. It also has a parameterless constructor and an initializing constructor.

The following code shows the `Person` class.

```
// Customer and related classes.
public class Customer
{
    public string FirstName, LastName;
    public List<Order> Orders = new List<Order>();

    public Customer() { }
    public Customer(string firstName, string lastName, params Order[] orders)
    {
        FirstName = firstName;
        LastName = lastName;
        foreach (Order order in orders) Orders.Add(order);
    }
}
```

This class has `FirstName` and `LastName` fields. It holds information about orders in a `List<Order>`.

When the program starts, it uses the following code to create a `Customer` object and display its data.

```
// Create some OrderItems.
OrderItem item1 = new OrderItem("Pencil", 12, 0.25m);
OrderItem item2 = new OrderItem("Notepad", 6, 1.00m);
OrderItem item3 = new OrderItem("Binder", 1, 3.50m);
OrderItem item4 = new OrderItem("Tape", 12, 0.75m);
```

```
// Create some Orders.
Order order1 = new Order(new DateTime(2014, 4, 4), item1, item2);
Order order2 = new Order(new DateTime(2014, 4, 17), item3, item4);

// Create a Customer.
Customer customer = new Customer("Rod", "Stephens", order1, order2);

// Display the Customer.
DisplayCustomer(originalTextBox, customer);
```

This code just creates some objects and sets their fields' values. It then calls the DisplayCustomer method to display the Customer object's values in a TextBox. It isn't very interesting so it isn't shown here. Download the example to see how it works.

Next, the program uses the following code to serialize the Customer object and display the serialization.

```
// Create a serializer that works with the Customer class.
XmlSerializer serializer = new XmlSerializer(typeof(Customer));

// Create a TextWriter to hold the serialization.
string serialization;
using (TextWriter writer = new StringWriter())
{
    // Serialize the Customer.
    serializer.Serialize(writer, customer);
    serialization = writer.ToString();
}

// Display the serialization.
serializationTextBox.Text = serialization;
```

The code first creates an XmlSerializer object to perform the serialization (and later the deserialization). It passes the XmlSerializer constructor the type of the class that it will serialize. In this example, the serializer object knows only how to serialize and deserialize Customer objects.

The serializer can serialize only into streams, XmlWriters, and TextWriters, so this example creates a TextWriter to hold the serialization. It calls the serializer's Serialize method, passing it the Customer object to serialize. The program saves the serialization in a string and displays the string in a TextBox.

The following code shows how the program deserializes the serialization.

```
// Create a stream from which to read the serialization.
using (TextReader reader = new StringReader(serialization))
{
    // Deserialize.
    Customer newCustomer = (Customer)serializer.Deserialize(reader);

    // Display the deserialization.
    DisplayCustomer(deserializedTextBox, newCustomer);
}
```

The serializer can deserialize only from streams, XmlReaders, and TextReaders, so the program creates a reader to read from the serialization string.

The program then calls the Deserialize method, passing it the reader. The Deserialize method returns a nonspecific object so the program casts it into a Customer object.

The program finishes by displaying the deserialized object.

The following code shows the object's serialization.

```xml
<?xml version="1.0" encoding="utf-16"?>
<Customer xmlns:xsi="http://www.w3.org/2001/XMLSchema-instance"
          xmlns:xsd="http://www.w3.org/2001/XMLSchema">
  <FirstName>Rod</FirstName>
  <LastName>Stephens</LastName>
  <Orders>
    <Order>
      <OrderDate>2014-04-04T00:00:00</OrderDate>
      <OrderItems>
        <OrderItem>
          <Description>Pencil</Description>
          <Quantity>12</Quantity>
          <UnitPrice>0.25</UnitPrice>
        </OrderItem>
        <OrderItem>
          <Description>Notepad</Description>
          <Quantity>6</Quantity>
          <UnitPrice>1.00</UnitPrice>
        </OrderItem>
      </OrderItems>
    </Order>
    <Order>
      <OrderDate>2014-04-17T00:00:00</OrderDate>
      <OrderItems>
        <OrderItem>
          <Description>Binder</Description>
          <Quantity>1</Quantity>
          <UnitPrice>3.50</UnitPrice>
        </OrderItem>
        <OrderItem>
          <Description>Tape</Description>
          <Quantity>12</Quantity>
          <UnitPrice>0.75</UnitPrice>
        </OrderItem>
      </OrderItems>
    </Order>
  </Orders>
</Customer>
```

If you look through the serialization, it makes reasonably intuitive sense. A Customer element represents a Customer object. It contains FirstName and LastName elements to hold its simple data values. The Orders element holds a sequence of Order elements to represent the Customer object's List<Order>.

Each `Order` element holds other elements that contain information about the program's `Order` object. The `OrderItems` element holds a sequence of `OrderItem` objects to represent an `OrderItem` object's `OrderItems` array.

> **OBVIOUS XML**
>
> The XML serialization's structure is so intuitive that you could easily serialize and deserialize objects yourself by hand if necessary. The only remarkable thing about it is that it all happens automatically. You don't need to tell the serializer what properties and fields the `Customer`, `Order`, and `OrderItem` classes have; what their data types are; or whether they are simple values (such as `int` and `string`) or complex values (such as `OrderItem` and `List<Order>`). The serializer figures that out all by itself.
>
> The serializer uses reflection to analyze the classes and determine what values it must save and what their names are. You'll learn how your programs can use reflection in the next chapter.

Controlling Serialization

The serialization shown in the preceding section is straightforward and reasonably intuitive, but there are times when you might want to change the way an object is serialized.

For example, the previous serialization is easy to understand but it's quite verbose. Perhaps you would rather store this data:

```
<OrderItem>
  <Description>Tape</Description>
  <Quantity>12</Quantity>
  <UnitPrice>0.75</UnitPrice>
</OrderItem>
```

Like this:

```
<OrderItem Description="Tape" Quantity="12" UnitPrice="0.75" />
```

The result is more concise and possibly easier to read.

For another example, suppose your program saves a customer's order data and you want to use that data in another program. Unfortunately, the other program stores a `Customer` object's order information in an `Order[]` named `CustomerOrders` instead of a `List<Order>` named `Orders`.

At this point you might realize that you could use XSLT to transform your serialization into a format that the other program could deserialize. That would certainly work (and would let you make other transformations that you can't with the techniques that follow) but it would be extra work and require another processing step.

Fortunately, the `System.Xml.Serialization` namespace defines attributes that you can use to gain some control over the serialization process. You add these attributes to classes or the properties and fields of classes that you want to serialize. They can indicate that a value should be stored in the serialization as an attribute instead of an element. They can also change the name of a value in the serialization or indicate that a value should be completely ignored.

For example, consider the following versions of the Customer, Order, and OrderItem classes. Here I've removed the constructors (which are the same as the previous versions) to save space. The attributes are highlighted in bold.

```
public class Customer
{
    [XmlAttribute]
    public string FirstName, LastName;

    [XmlArray("CustomerOrders")]
    public List<Order> Orders = new List<Order>();
}

public class Order
{
    [XmlIgnore]
    public DateTime OrderDate;

    [XmlArray("Items")]
    public OrderItem[] OrderItems;
}

public class OrderItem
{
    [XmlAttribute]
    public string Description;

    [XmlAttribute]
    public int Quantity;

    [XmlAttribute("PriceEach")]
    public decimal UnitPrice;
}
```

In the Customer class, the XmlAttribute attribute indicates that the FirstName and LastName fields should be serialized as XML attributes instead of elements. The XmlArray attribute indicates that the Customer class's Orders list should be called CustomerOrders in the serialization. (Lists and arrays are both serialized in the same way so that the XmlArray attribute doesn't change the way this is serialized. It just changes the name.)

ATTRIBUTE ATTRIBUTES

Yes, it sounds strange to say XmlAttribute attribute. Actually, the class that provides this attribute is XmlAttributeAttribute and you can even use that name instead of the shorter XmlAttribute. Similarly, the class that provides the XmlArray attribute is called XmlArrayAttribute.

In the Order class, the XmlIgnore attribute indicates that the OrderDate field should not be serialized at all. The XmlArray attribute makes the OrderItems array serialize with the name Items.

IGNORE ME

Why would you want to ignore a field or property in a serialization? There are a few good reasons.

First, suppose a class provides more than one property that accesses the same data. For example, it might have DegreesFahrenheit and DegreesCelsius properties. Both store their data in the same backing variable (possibly one of those two properties) and return it in different formats. In this case, there's no point to saving and restoring the same temperature value in two different formats.

Second, the XmlSerializer class cannot store some kinds of data. For example, it cannot store images. If the Student class includes a Picture field that holds a picture of the student, you can use the XmlIgnore attribute to let the serializer skip it instead of getting confused and crashing.

Finally, you might just want to omit some data. For example, suppose a drawing application uses the Picture class to represent a drawing, and suppose that class has a History property that contains undo and redo information. You can use a serialization to save a drawing into a file, but you probably don't want to save the undo and redo information. In that case, you can simply mark the History property with the XmlIgnore attribute.

In the OrderItem class, the three XmlAttribute attributes indicate that all three fields should be stored as XML attributes and that the UnitPrice field should be stored as PriceEach in the serialization.

The SerializeCustomerWithAttributes example program is identical to the SerializeCustomer program except it uses the new definitions of the Customer, Order, and OrderItem classes. The following code shows the XML serialization it produces.

```
<?xml version="1.0" encoding="utf-16"?>
<Customer xmlns:xsi="http://www.w3.org/2001/XMLSchema-instance"
          xmlns:xsd="http://www.w3.org/2001/XMLSchema"
          FirstName="Rod" LastName="Stephens">
  <CustomerOrders>
    <Order>
      <Items>
        <OrderItem Description="Pencil" Quantity="12" PriceEach="0.25" />
        <OrderItem Description="Notepad" Quantity="6" PriceEach="1.00" />
      </Items>
    </Order>
    <Order>
      <Items>
        <OrderItem Description="Binder" Quantity="1" PriceEach="3.50" />
        <OrderItem Description="Tape" Quantity="12" PriceEach="0.75" />
```

```
        </Items>
      </Order>
    </CustomerOrders>
  </Customer>
```

This is still reasonably intuitive and more concise than the previous version.

The following table lists the most useful attributes that you can use to control serialization. (The names of the classes that implement these attributes all end with `Attribute`. For example, the `XmlArray` attribute is implemented by the `XmlArrayAttribute` class. If you want to look up any of these online, use their full class names.)

ATTRIBUTE	PURPOSE
XmlArray	Changes the name by which the array or list is serialized.
XmlArrayItem	Indicates a type that can be in an array. For example, suppose the `People` array contains `Person` objects, some of which might be from the `Author` subclass. Then you would use `XmlArrayItem` twice to indicate that the array might contain `Person` and `Author` objects.
XmlAttribute	Serializes a field as an attribute instead of an element. Optionally sets the name of the attribute.
XmlElement	Specifically indicates the field will be serialized as an XML element. This attribute allows you to change the XML element's name.
XmlEnum	Enables you to specify the names by which enumeration values are serialized. For example, suppose the enumeration `MealSize` defines values `Small`, `Medium`, and `Large`. You could use this attribute to make the serialization call those values `Tall`, `Grande`, and `Brobdignagian`.
XmlIgnore	Makes the serializer omit a field from the serialization.
XmlRoot	Controls the name and namespace for the element generated for a serialization's root element. For example, the attribute `[XmlRoot("Client")]` in front of the `Customer` class would make the serializer name the root element `Client`. This would not affect `Customer` objects that are not the root element. (See `XmlType`.)
XmlText	Makes the serializer store a value as XML text. An object can have only one text value. (The serializer cannot put more than one text value between the object's start and end tags.)
XmlType	Controls the name and namespace for the element generated for a class. For example, if you place the attribute `[XmlType("Item")]` in front of the `OrderItem` class, then all `OrderItem` objects are serialized as `Item` elements.

The `DataContractSerializer` class can also use XML to serialize and deserialize objects. The process is similar to using the `DataContractJsonSerializer` class, which is described in the next section.

JSON SERIALIZATION

Like XML, *JSON* (*JavaScript Object Notation*) is a data storage language. JSON is somewhat simpler and often more concise than XML so it is preferred by some developers.

JSON data mostly consists of `name:value` pairs where names are text and values can have one of the following data types:

➤ Number

➤ String

➤ Boolean

➤ Array (a sequence of values separated by commas and enclosed in brackets `[ ]`)

➤ Object (a collection of `key:value` pairs with pairs separated by commas and the whole collection surrounded by braces `{ }`)

➤ `null`

The following code shows a JSON representation of a `Customer` object that contains two `Order` objects; each `Order` object holds two `OrderItem` objects.

```
{
  "FirstName":"Rod",
  "LastName":"Stephens",
  "Orders":
  [
    {
      "OrderDate":"\/Date(1396591200000-0600)\/",
      "OrderItems":
        [
          {"Description":"Pencil","Quantity":12,"UnitPrice":0.25},
          {"Description":"Notepad","Quantity":6,"UnitPrice":1.00}
        ]
    },
    {
      "OrderDate":"\/Date(1397714400000-0600)\/",
      "OrderItems":
      [
        {"Description":"Binder","Quantity":1,"UnitPrice":3.50},
        {"Description":"Tape","Quantity":12,"UnitPrice":0.75}
      ]
    }
  ]
}
```

As is the case with XML serialization, you can use attributes to control how classes are serialized by the `DataContractJsonSerializer` class. The following section explains the basic JSON serialization and deserialization processes. The section after that describes attributes you can use to control the serialization.

Performing Serialization

The `DataContractJsonSerializer` class serializes and deserializes objects using the JSON format. The class's `WriteObject` method serializes an object. Its `ReadObject` method deserializes an object.

The SerializeCustomerJson example program, which is available for download on this book's website, uses the following code to serialize and deserialize a `Customer` object in the JSON format.

```
// Create a serializer that works with the Customer class.
DataContractJsonSerializer serializer =
    new DataContractJsonSerializer(typeof(Customer));

// Create a stream to hold the serialization.
using (MemoryStream stream = new MemoryStream())
{
    // Serialize the Customer.
    serializer.WriteObject(stream, customer);

    // Convert the stream into a string.
    stream.Seek(0, SeekOrigin.Begin);
    string serialization;
    using (StreamReader reader = new StreamReader(stream))
    {
        serialization = reader.ReadToEnd();

        // Display the serialization.
        serializationTextBox.Text = serialization;

        // Deserialize from the stream.
        stream.Position = 0;
        Customer newCustomer = (Customer)serializer.ReadObject(stream);

        // Display the deserialization.
        DisplayCustomer(deserializedTextBox, newCustomer);
    }
}
```

The code first creates a `DataContractJsonSerializer` object.

That object can write serializations into a stream, `XmlDictionaryWriter`, or `XmlWriter`. This example creates a `MemoryStream` to hold the serialization. The code then calls the serializer's `WriteObject` method to write the `Customer` object's serialization into the stream.

To get the serialization as a `string`, the program rewinds the stream and creates a `StreamReader` associated with the stream. It uses that object's `ReadToEnd` method to get the text from the stream and displays the serialization in a `TextBox`.

To deserialize the `Customer` object, the program uses the same `MemoryStream` (because it already contains the serialization). The code rewinds the stream and uses the serializer's `ReadObject` method to read the `Customer` object from the serialization.

The code finishes by calling the `DisplayCustomer` method (not shown here) to display the object's data.

Controlling Serialization

You can use attributes to control a JSON serialization much as you can use attributes to control an XML serialization. JSON is a simpler format, however, so there are fewer attributes available. For example, JSON doesn't let you store values as element attributes (as in `<Customer FirstName="Zaphod">`) so there's no attribute for that.

If you don't give a class any attributes, the serializer tries to serialize all of its public properties and methods.

You can use the `XmlSerializable` attribute to explicitly mark a class as serializable. If you do, the serializer still tries to serialize all its public properties and methods.

In both of these cases, when you don't give a class any attributes or you give it the `XmlSerializable` attribute, you can give a field the `IgnoreDataMember` attribute to indicate that the field should not be serialized.

In addition to using the `XmlSerializable` attribute, you can mark a class as serializable by giving it the `DataContract` attribute. This attribute's properties also let you change the name used to represent the class in the serialization.

If you give a class the `DataContract` attribute, then the serializer's default behavior changes. Instead of serializing all public fields and properties that are not marked with `IgnoreDataMember`, the serializer serializes only public fields and properties that are marked with the `DataMember` attribute. The `DataMember` attribute also lets you change a member's name or set the order in which it is included in the object's serialization.

The following code shows an `OrderItem` class with some serialization control attributes.

```
[DataContract(Name = "Item")]
public class OrderItem
{
    [DataMember]
    public string Description;

    [DataMember]
    public int Quantity;

    [DataMember(Name = "PriceEach")]
    public decimal UnitPrice;
}
```

The `DataContract` attribute indicates that the class is serializable and that any fields or properties without the `DataMember` attribute will be ignored. It also makes the serializer use the name `Item` when it writes an `OrderItem` into a serialization.

The first two `DataMember` attributes indicate that the `Description` and `Quantity` fields should be included in serializations.

The last `DataMember` attribute indicates that the `PriceEach` field should be included in serializations and that it should be called `PriceEach` in serializations.

BINARY SERIALIZATION

The XML and JSON serializers are fairly easy to use and produce reasonably intuitive results. However, they have a couple of drawbacks. For example, there are some data types such as images that they cannot serialize. (Exercise 4 explains one way around the problem.) They also cannot serialize data structures that contain cycles.

For example, suppose you build an organizational model with `Department` objects representing your company's departments and `Employee` objects representing employees. The `Department` class has an `Employees` property that is a `List<Employee>` that contains references to the employees in that department. The `Employee` class has a `Department` property that is a reference to the department where that employee works.

The XML and JSON serializers cannot serialize this structure because the `Department` object contains references to `Employee` objects, and the `Employee` objects have references to the `Department` object. These references form a cycle and the serializers don't know how to handle cycles.

The `BinaryFormatter` class serializes and deserializes data and can handle both images and cycles.

The SerializeDepartment example program, which is available for download on this book's website, demonstrates the `BinaryFormatter`. It uses the following `Department` and `Employee` classes (constructors omitted).

```
[Serializable]
public class Department
{
    public Image Logo;
    public string Name;
    public List<Employee> Employees = new List<Employee>();
}

[Serializable]
public class Employee
{
    public string Name;
    public Department Department;
}
```

The `BinaryFormatter` can work only with classes that are decorated with the `Serializable` attribute.

IGNORE IGNORED

The BinaryFormatter doesn't care about attributes other than Serializable. There's no point trying to use an attribute to change an element's name in the serialization because the serialization is in binary so you can't read it anyway. Furthermore the BinaryFormatter ignores the XmlIgnore attribute so all properties and fields are serialized.

In fact, the BinaryFormatter even ignores privacy. It barges into an object and grabs all its fields and properties even if they're marked private.

The example program uses the following code to serialize and deserialize a Department object.

```
// Create a BinaryFormatter.
IFormatter formatter = new BinaryFormatter();

// Create a stream to hold the serialization.
using (MemoryStream stream = new MemoryStream())
{
    // Serialize.
    formatter.Serialize(stream, department);

    // Display a textual representation of the serialization.
    byte[] bytes = stream.ToArray();
    string serialization = BitConverter.ToString(bytes).Replace("-", " ");

    // Display the serialization.
    serializationTextBox.Text = serialization;

    // Deserialize.
    stream.Seek(0, SeekOrigin.Begin);
    Department newDepartment = (Department)formatter.Deserialize(stream);

    // Display the new Department's data.
    deserializedPictureBox.Image = newDepartment.Logo;
    deserializedTextBox.Text = DisplayDepartment(newDepartment);
}
```

The code starts by creating a BinaryFormatter object. A BinaryFormatter uses only streams for serialization, so the program creates a MemoryStream. It then uses the formatter's Serialize method to serialize the Department object into the stream.

Next, the code converts the serialization stream into a byte array. It converts that array into a string showing the serialization's hexadecimal contents and displays the result in a TextBox.

To deserialize the serialization, the code rewinds the MemoryStream, and then calls the formatter's Deserialize method. The code finishes by displaying the reconstituted Department object's logo and employee data. (The DisplayDepartment method is straightforward and unrelated to serialization, so it isn't shown here. Download the example to see how it works.)

SUMMARY

This chapter explained techniques you can use to serialize and deserialize data. It explained how you can use the XmlSerializer class to use XML serializations, the DataContractJsonSerializer class to use JSON serializations, and the BinaryFormatter class to make binary serializations.

Binary serializations have the disadvantage that you can't easily read them to see what they contain. They have the advantage that they can contain data types such as images that the other serializations cannot. They can also serialize data that contains cyclical references.

You can use attributes to influence the way objects are stored in XML and JSON serializations, but most of the process is automatic. The serializers use reflection to determine what data is included in a class. The next chapter explains how you can use reflection in your programs to get information about the properties, methods, and events contained in a class.

EXERCISES

1. Write a program similar to the SerializeCustomer example program but that works with an array of Student objects. Give the Student class FirstName and LastName properties (not fields). The program should

   ➤ Create an array of Students.

   ➤ Display the original Students.

   ➤ Serialize the array storing FirstName and LastName as attributes.

   ➤ Display the serialization.

   ➤ Deserialize the array.

   ➤ Display the deserialized Students.

   Hint: Override the Student class's ToString method. Then set a ListBox's DataSource property equal to an array to display the Students it contains.

2. Make a classroom editor similar to the one shown in Figure 25-2. Make the program store Student objects in a List<Student>. Display the list by setting a ListBox's DataSource property equal to it. When the program ends, save the list's serialization into a file. When the program restarts, reload the serialization.

   Hints: Note that you don't need to use strings to serialize and deserialize. Just serialize and deserialize directly in and out of a file. Before you change the list to add, remove, or edit a Student, set the ListBox's DataSource property to null. After the change, set the DataSource property back to the list.

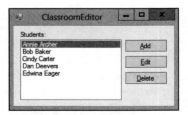

FIGURE 25-2: For Exercise 2, make a classroom editor that saves and restores a list of Student objects when the program stops and starts.

3. Make a static XmlTools class. Give it generic Serialize and Deserialize methods that serialize and deserialize objects to and from strings. Modify the program you wrote for Exercise 1 to test the methods.

4. The XmlSerializer class cannot serialize images, but you can help it along by creating a public property that gets and sets an image in a format that it understands.

Write a program similar to the SerializeCustomer example program but that works with a single Student object. Give the Student class FirstName, LastName, and Picture properties.

Hint: Also give the class the following property that gets and sets the picture as an array of bytes.

```
// Return the Picture as a byte stream.
public byte[] PictureBytes
{
    get     // Serialize
    {
        if (Picture == null) return null;
        using (MemoryStream stream = new MemoryStream())
        {
            Picture.Save(stream, ImageFormat.Png);
            return stream.ToArray();
        }
    }
    set     // Deserialize.
    {
        if (value == null) Picture=  null;
        else
        {
            using (MemoryStream stream = new MemoryStream(value))
            {
                Picture = new Bitmap(stream);
            }
        }
    }
}
```

5. Make a friendship tracking program similar to the one shown in Figure 25-3. When the user clicks a name in the ListBox on the left, the program checks that person's friends in CheckedListBox on the right.

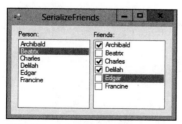

FIGURE 25-3: For Exercise 5, make a friendship editor that saves and restores a list of Person objects when the program stops and starts.

Use the following `Person` class to store information about the people.

```
public class Person
{
    public string Name;
    public List<Person> Friends = new List<Person>();
    public override string ToString()
    {
        return Name;
    }
}
```

Hints: Store the person information in a `List<Person>`. Serialize and deserialize the data into a file when the program stops and starts. If the data file doesn't exist when the program starts, just create some `Person` objects. (A real application would let the user add, edit, and delete `Person` objects, perhaps as in the program you wrote for Exercise 2.)

26

Reflection

WHAT'S IN THIS CHAPTER

- ➤ Learning about assemblies
- ➤ Enumerating fields, properties, methods, and events
- ➤ Getting and setting property values
- ➤ Creating add-ins
- ➤ Compiling and executing scripts at run time

WROX.COM DOWNLOADS FOR THIS CHAPTER

Please note that all the code examples for this chapter are available as a part of this chapter's code download on the book's website at www.wrox.com/go/csharp5programmersref on the Download Code tab.

Reflection is a process by which a program can examine and manipulate program objects at run time. For example, serialization (described in the preceding chapter) uses reflection to figure out what values an object has and what their data types are so that it can save and restore them. IntelliSense also uses reflection to describe the parameters that a method takes while you are entering those parameters.

Reflection is a fairly advanced technique that isn't necessary for most programs. Usually, when you write a program, you know what you want it to do and what methods you need to call to do it. It's unusual, for example, to be working with an `Invoice` class and not know what properties, methods, and events that class defines. Even if you don't know what's in a class and you use reflection to find out, it would be quite hard to make the program use those discovered items effectively.

Still there are a few situations in which reflections can be useful. Some of the more common uses of reflection include

➤ Load assemblies at run time.

➤ Learn what assembly defines a particular item such as a class or enumeration.

➤ List a class's fields and properties.

➤ List a class's constructors and other methods.

➤ List a class's events.

➤ Get information about a property such as its type and whether it is read-only.

➤ Get and set a property's value.

➤ Get information about the parameters passed to a method.

➤ Get information about an item's attributes.

Some reflection classes even let you create new types and execute code at run time.

This chapter describes some of the more useful things you can do with reflection. It explains how to learn about classes, get and set property values, invoke methods, and compile and execute scripts.

LEARNING ABOUT CLASSES

A class's type provides properties and methods that provide a wealth of information about the class. You can get a class's type by using `typeof(TheClass)` or by calling the `GetType` method on an instance of the class.

The `System.Type` class provides many properties and methods that give information about a type. Most of these are reasonably self-explanatory. One detail that may not be obvious is that some of these properties and methods return objects that describe the information you want rather than the information itself. The reason they do that is many of these items are more complicated than you might at first realize.

For example, suppose the `MusicalInstrument` class is defined in some DLL. You can use reflection to determine the module that defines the class. You might think of the module as simply the name of the DLL containing the class, but the `Type` class's `Module` property returns a `Module` object that includes lots of information about the module including its name, assembly (which is also an object containing a lot of information), custom attributes, fully qualified name, global fields, and types (which includes classes, enumerations, delegate types, and any other types defined in the module).

Some of the more useful informational classes include the obviously named `FieldInfo`, `PropertyInfo`, `ConstructorInfo`, `MethodInfo`, and `EventInfo` classes. Two other classes that are returned by some reflection methods are `MethodBase` (the parent class of `MemberInfo` and `ConstructorInfo`) and `MemberInfo` (the parent class of `FieldInfo`, `PropertyInfo`, `MethodBase`, and `EventInfo`).

The CustomerClassInformation example program, which is available for download on this book's website, demonstrates many useful reflection properties and methods to display information about a

Customer class. This class is derived from the Person class and contains a list of Order objects. The following code shows the Person, Customer, and Order classes.

```
public class Person
{
    public string FirstName, LastName;
}

public sealed class Customer : Person
{
    public struct Address
    {
        public string Street, City, State, Zip;
    }

    public string EmailAddress { get; set; }
    public Address MailingAddress { get; set; }
    public List<Order> Orders = new List<Order>();

    public Customer() { }
    public Customer(string firstName, string lastName, params Order[] orders)
    {
        FirstName = firstName;
        LastName = lastName;
        foreach (Order order in orders) Orders.Add(order);
    }

    public delegate void PaymentReceivedDelegate(decimal amount);
    public event PaymentReceivedDelegate PaymentReceived;

    public void SendEmail(string message) { }
}

public class Order
{
}
```

The Person class is almost empty. It's just there to be the Customer class's parent class.

The Customer class contains a nested Address structure, properties (EmailAddress and MailingAddress), fields (Orders and the inherited FirstName and LastName fields), two constructors, a delegate type, an event, and the SendEmail method.

The Order class is empty. It's just there so that the Customer class can contain a List<Order>.

The program uses the following code to display information about the Customer class.

```
// Display information about the Customer class.
private void Form1_Load(object sender, EventArgs e)
{
    Type type = typeof(Customer);
    AddItem("Name: ", type.Name);
    AddItem("Assembly: ", type.Assembly.FullName);
    AddItem("Attributes: ", type.Attributes.ToString());
    AddItem("BaseType: ", type.BaseType.Name);
    AddItem("FullName: ", type.FullName);
```

```
        AddItem("IsAbstract: ", type.IsAbstract.ToString());
        AddItem("IsAutoLayout: ", type.IsAutoLayout.ToString());
        AddItem("IsClass: ", type.IsClass.ToString());
        AddItem("IsNested: ", type.IsNested.ToString());
        AddItem("IsNotPublic: ", type.IsNotPublic.ToString());
        AddItem("IsPrimitive: ", type.IsPrimitive.ToString());
        AddItem("IsPublic: ", type.IsPublic.ToString());
        AddItem("IsSealed: ", type.IsSealed.ToString());
        AddItem("IsSerializable: ", type.IsSerializable.ToString());
        AddItem("IsSubclassOf(Person): ",
            type.IsSubclassOf(typeof(Person)).ToString());
        AddItem("IsValueType: ", type.IsValueType.ToString());
        AddItem("IsVisible: ", type.IsVisible.ToString());
        AddItem("Module: ", type.Module.Name);
        AddItem("Namespace: ", type.Namespace);

        AddItem("NestedTypes:", "");
        foreach (Type nestedType in type.GetNestedTypes())
        {
            AddItem("    ", nestedType.ToString());
        }

        AddItem("Fields:", "");
        foreach (FieldInfo info in type.GetFields())
        {
            AddItem("    ", info.ToString());
        }
        AddItem("Properties:", "");
        foreach (PropertyInfo info in type.GetProperties())
        {
            AddItem("    ", info.ToString());
        }

        AddItem("Constructors:", "");
        foreach (ConstructorInfo info in type.GetConstructors())
        {
            AddItem("    ", info.ToString());
        }
        AddItem("Methods:", "");
        foreach (MethodInfo method in type.GetMethods())
        {
            AddItem("    ", method.Name);
        }

        AddItem("Events:", "");
        foreach (EventInfo info in type.GetEvents())
        {
            AddItem("    ", info.ToString());
        }

        // Size the ListView's columns.
        infoListView.Columns[0].Width = -1;
        infoListView.Columns[1].Width = -1;
    }
```

The program first gets an object representing the Customer class's type. It then invokes a series of that object's properties to display various pieces of information about the Customer class. The code uses the AddItem method (described shortly) to display the values in the program's ListView control.

Next, the program calls several Type methods to get information about features of the Customer class. Those methods include GetNestedTypes, GetFields, GetProperties, GetConstructors, GetMethods, and GetEvents. All these methods return objects (such as MethodInfo or EventInfo objects) providing detailed information about particular Customer class features. This example simply lists the features' names.

The following code shows the AddItem method.

```
// Add an item and value to the ListView.
private void AddItem(string item, string value)
{
    ListViewItem newItem = infoListView.Items.Add(item);
    newItem.SubItems.Add(value);
}
```

This method simply adds a new item and subitem to the program's ListView control.

Figure 26-1 shows the CustomerClassInformation example program scrolled down to display information about the Customer class's properties, constructors, and methods.

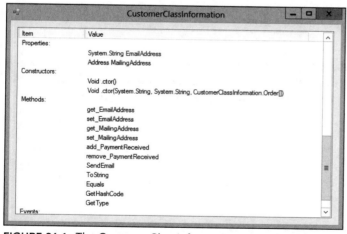

FIGURE 26-1: The CustomerClassInformation example program uses reflection to display information about a Customer class.

GETTING AND SETTING PROPERTIES

The CustomerClassInformation example program just lists the names of the fields, properties, methods, and other complex items that it finds. However, a program can do much more with those items. For example, it can use a PropertyInfo object to get or set the value of its property, or it can use a MethodInfo object to invoke its method.

The GetSetPersonProperties example program, which is shown in Figure 26-2 and available for download on this book's website, uses reflection to get and set a `Person` class's fields and properties.

FIGURE 26-2: The GetSetPersonProperties example program uses reflection to get and set property and field values.

The program uses the following simple `Person` class.

```
public class Person
{
    public string FirstName { get; set; }
    public string LastName { get; set; }
    public string Street, City, State, Zip;
}
```

Most of the program's code creates the `Labels` and `TextBoxes` that it uses to display property and field values. The following code shows how the program gets values. To save space, I removed the code that creates the `Labels` and `TextBoxes`. Download the example to see all the details.

```
// The Person object.
private Person ThePerson = new Person()
{
    FirstName = "Rufus",
    LastName = "Firefly",
    Street = "1933 Duck Soup Pl",
    City = "Hollywood",
    State = "CA",
    Zip = "90027"
};

// The Labels and TextBoxes we create.
private List<Label> Labels;
private List<TextBox> TextBoxes;

// Display the object's fields and properties.
private void getValuesButton_Click(object sender, EventArgs e)
{
    // List fields and properties.
    foreach (MemberInfo info in ThePerson.GetType().FindMembers(
        MemberTypes.Field | MemberTypes.Property,
```

```
            BindingFlags.Public | BindingFlags.Instance,
            new MemberFilter((x, y) => true),
            null))
    {
        // Create a Label and TextBox.
        ...
        Labels.Add(label);
        ...
        textBox.Tag = info;
        TextBoxes.Add(textBox);
        ...

        // Get the value.
        if (info is FieldInfo)
        {
            FieldInfo fieldInfo = info as FieldInfo;
            textBox.Text = fieldInfo.GetValue(ThePerson).ToString();
            label.BackColor = Color.LightGray;
        }
        else if (info is PropertyInfo)
        {
            PropertyInfo propertyInfo = info as PropertyInfo;
            textBox.Text = propertyInfo.GetValue(ThePerson).ToString();
            label.BackColor = Color.White;
        }
    }

    setValuesButton.Enabled = true;
}
```

The code starts by creating a `Person` object and declaring lists to hold `Labels` and `TextBoxes`.

When you click the Get Values button, the program uses `ThePerson.GetType().FindMembers` to get information about the `Person` class's fields and properties. That method takes four parameters, which in this example have the following values:

➤ `MemberTypes.Field | MemberTypes.Property`—This tells the method to select information about fields and properties.

➤ `BindingFlags.Public | BindingFlags.Instance`—This makes the method return information about members that are `public` instance members (as opposed to `private` or `static` members).

➤ `new MemberFilter((x, y) => true)`—This parameter is a `MemberFilter` delegate that examines objects discovered by `FindMembers` and returns `true` to select the ones you want to select. It takes as parameters a `MemberInfo` object and an object that you can set to give the method some extra information. This example uses a lambda expression that returns `true` for any input so it selects every field and property.

➤ `null`—This is the extra value passed into the method provided in the third parameter. In this example, this value means the lambda expression receives `null` as its second parameter.

BINDING FLAGS REQUIRED

The `BindingFlags` parameter must include either `Static` or `Instance`, and either `Public` or `NonPublic` or else the `FindMembers` method won't return any results.

The program loops over the `MemberInfo` objects returned by the call to `FindMembers`. For each item, it creates a `Label` and `TextBox`. It stores the new controls in the `Labels` and `TextBoxes` lists. It also stores the `MemberInfo` object in the `TextBox`'s `Tag` property for later use.

Next, the code displays the member's value in the `TextBox`. It also changes the `Label`'s background color to indicate whether the member is a field (darker) or property (lighter).

After the program displays the values, you can modify them by typing in the `TextBoxes`. If you then click the Set Values button, the following code executes.

```
// Set the values.
private void setValuesButton_Click(object sender, EventArgs e)
{
    // Delete the Labels.
    foreach (Label label in Labels) label.Parent = null;

    // Save the TextBox values.
    foreach (TextBox textBox in TextBoxes)
    {
        // See if this TextBox represents a field or property.
        MemberInfo info = textBox.Tag as MemberInfo;
        if (info is FieldInfo)
        {
            // Save the field's value.
            FieldInfo fieldInfo = info as FieldInfo;
            fieldInfo.SetValue(ThePerson, textBox.Text);
        }
        else
        {
            // Save the property's value.
            PropertyInfo propertyInfo = info as PropertyInfo;
            propertyInfo.SetValue(ThePerson, textBox.Text);
        }

        // Remove the TextBox.
        textBox.Parent = null;
    }

    setValuesButton.Enabled = false;
}
```

This code starts by looping through the `Labels` it created and removing them from the form. It then loops through the `TextBoxes` and gets each `TextBox`'s `MemberInfo` object. It converts the object into the appropriate subclass, `FieldInfo` or `PropertyInfo`, and uses that object's `SetValue` method to update the member's value. The code then removes the `TextBox` from the form.

GETTING ASSEMBLY INFORMATION

An assembly is the fundamental unit of deployment and version control in Visual Studio. An assembly can contain an executable application, a *dynamic-link library (DLL)*, or a control library. Usually, a project is contained in a single assembly.

The Assembly Information dialog box shown in Figure 26-3 lets you define information that should be associated with the assembly, including the assembly's company name, description, copyright, trademark, name, product name, title, and version (which includes major, minor, revision, and build values).

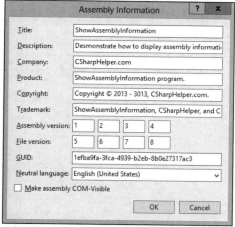

FIGURE 26-3: The Assembly Information dialog lets you set a project's assembly information.

Most of the items in this dialog box, such as the application's title and description, are self-explanatory. They are simply strings that the assembly carries around for identification. The assembly and file versions are used by the Visual Studio run time to verify compatibility between an application's components. The *GUID* (which stands for *globally unique identifier* and is pronounced to rhyme with "squid") uniquely identifies the assembly and is generated by Visual Studio. The Make Assembly COM-Visible check box lets you determine whether the assembly should make types defined in the assembly visible to COM applications. For more information on this dialog box, see `msdn.microsoft.com/1h52t681.aspx`.

Unfortunately, learning these values at run time isn't easy. To get most of these values, you need to follow these steps:

1. Use `Assembly.GetExecutingAssembly` to get an `Assembly` object representing the currently running assembly.

2. Call the `Assembly` object's `GetCustomAttributes` method, passing it as a parameter an assembly attribute type such as `AssemblyTitleAttribute`. The `GetCustomAttributes` method returns an array of attribute objects of the requested type.

3. Use the appropriate property for the returned attribute. For example, use an `AssemblyTitleAttribute` object's `Title` property.

Unfortunately, some of the attribute objects may not always be defined, so your code must watch out for `null` object references.

A C# program uses a different method to obtain the assembly version information. To get that information, the program calls the `Assembly` object's `GetName` method and then uses the returned object's `Version` property.

The ShowAssemblyInformation example program uses the following `GetAssemblyAttribute` method to make fetching assembly attributes a little easier.

```
// Return a particular assembly attribute value.
public static T GetAssemblyAttribute<T>(Assembly assembly) where T : Attribute
{
    // Get attributes of this type.
    object[] attributes = assembly.GetCustomAttributes(typeof(T), true);

    // If we didn't get anything, return null.
    if ((attributes == null) || (attributes.Length == 0)) return null;

    // Convert the first attribute value into the desired type and return it.
    return (T)attributes[0];
}
```

The method takes a type as a generic parameter. That should be the type of attribute that you want to retrieve. The method also takes as a parameter the assembly that you want to use.

The code calls the `Assembly` object's `GetCustomAttributes` method to fetch an array containing the assembly's attribute objects that have the right type. If the result is `null` or an empty array, the method returns `null`.

If the code gets a nonempty array, it converts the first element in it into the desired attribute type and returns it.

The following code shows how the ShowAssemblyInformation program uses the `GetAssemblyAttribute` method to display attribute information.

```
private void Form1_Load(object sender, EventArgs e)
{
    // Get the running assembly.
    Assembly assembly = Assembly.GetExecutingAssembly();

    // Get values from the assembly.
    AssemblyTitleAttribute titleAttr =
        GetAssemblyAttribute<AssemblyTitleAttribute>(assembly);
    if (titleAttr != null) titleTextBox.Text = titleAttr.Title;

    AssemblyDescriptionAttribute descrAttr =
        GetAssemblyAttribute<AssemblyDescriptionAttribute>(assembly);
    if (descrAttr != null) descriptionTextBox.Text = descrAttr.Description;

    ... Code omitted ...

    assemblyVersionTextBox.Text = assembly.GetName().Version.ToString();

    ... Code omitted ...
}
```

The code uses `Assembly.GetExecutingAssembly` to get an object representing the executing assembly. It then uses the `GetAssemblyAttribute` method to get attribute objects representing the assembly's attributes. After checking that each result isn't `null`, the code displays the attribute values.

The one exception is the assembly version information. To get that value, the code simply calls `assembly.GetName().Version.ToString()`.

INVOKING METHODS

Reflection provides objects that let you load and examine assemblies. After you load an assembly, you can dig through the types it defines and use the properties, methods, and other features defined by those types.

This section describes the InvokeEchoer example program, which is available for download on this book's website. That example demonstrates several important techniques for working with an assembly loaded at run time.

The tasks performed by the InvokeEchoer program include

- ➤ Load an assembly at run time.
- ➤ Get information about the `Echoer` class defined by the assembly.
- ➤ Create an instance of the `Echoer` class.
- ➤ Set a field value for the instance.
- ➤ Invoke the object's `ShowMessage` method.

The `EchoDll` example, which is also available for download on this book's website, creates a control library (DLL) that the InvokeEchoer program can load. (The `EchoDll` example must be compiled for the InvokeEchoer example to work properly.) It uses the following code to define the `Echoer` class.

```
public class Echoer
{
    // The objexct's message.
    public string Message = "Message not set";

    // Display the message in a MessageBox.
    public void ShowMessage(string caption)
    {
        MessageBox.Show(Message, caption);
    }
}
```

This class has a public `string` field named `Message` and a public method named `ShowMessage`.

The following code shows how the InvokeEchoer program loads and uses the EchoDll library.

```
// Load the DLL, create an Echoer, and invoke the ShowMessage method.
private void invokeButton_Click(object sender, EventArgs e)
{
    // Load the DLL assembly.
    Assembly dll = Assembly.LoadFile(dllTextBox.Text);

    // Find the Echoer class's Type.
    Type echoer = dll.GetType("EchoDll.Echoer");

    // Create an Echoer object.
    object myEchoer = Activator.CreateInstance(echoer);

    // Set the Message field.
    FieldInfo fieldInfo = echoer.GetField("Message");
    fieldInfo.SetValue(myEchoer, messageTextBox.Text);

    // Get a MethodInfo for the ShowMessage method.
    MethodInfo methodInfo = echoer.GetMethod("ShowMessage");

    // Invoke the method on the object.
    object[] args = { captionTextBox.Text };
    methodInfo.Invoke(myEchoer, args);
}
```

The program first uses the `Assembly.LoadFile` method to load the EchoDll assembly.

It then uses the `Assembly`'s `GetType` method to get a `Type` object that represents the `Echoer` class's type.

Next, the code uses the `System.Activator` class to create an instance of the `Echoer` type. If you pass the `Activator` class's `CreateInstance` method additional parameters, it invokes the class's constructor that best fits the parameters. In this example, the `Echoer` class has no constructors, so the code doesn't pass any extra parameters to the `CreateInstance` method.

The program then sets the value of the Echoer object's Message field. It uses the Echoer type's GetField method to get a FieldInfo object representing the field. It then uses the FieldInfo object's SetValue method to set the field's value for the Echoer instance.

The last task the program must perform is invoking the Echoer object's ShowMessage method. To do that, it calls the Echoer type's GetMethod method to get a MethodInfo object representing the ShowMessage method. It creates an array of objects to hold the parameters that should be passed to the ShowMessage. Finally, it calls the MethodInfo object's Invoke method, passing it the Echoer instance for which it should invoke the method and the argument array.

This is an awful lot of work to simply display a message box, but the techniques used by the InvokeEchoer program show how to load and explore an assembly at run time. With a little more work and experimentation, you could modify the program to perform other tasks such as

➤ Discover the classes defined by an assembly.

➤ Create instances of a class.

➤ Learn what fields, properties, and methods are defined by each class.

➤ Get and set field and property values.

➤ Invoke static methods and instance methods.

DANGEROUS DLLS

Load an assembly at run time only if you are sure it is safe. If a hacker inserts a bogus DLL in a directory where your code is looking for assemblies, you might be tricked into executing dangerous code.

RUNNING SCRIPTS

Reflection lets a program learn about existing code. The classes in the System.CodeDom.Compiler namespace enable a program to compile completely new code at run time. You can then use refection to execute the methods defined by the newly compiled code.

TIME SAVER

Compiling code at run time is fairly slow, so it's not a good way to provide features that you know about at design time. If you know at design time that the program needs to do something, just compile that code right into the executable program. You only need to compile code at run time to run scripts and execute code that you can't predict ahead of time.

To compile code, the program creates a code provider. It sets any parameters needed by the provider and adds references to any assemblies the script uses. It then calls the provider's `CompileAssemblyFromSource` method to compile the script. If the compilation succeeds, the program can use reflection to find and use the classes, methods, and other items defined by the script.

The TurtleScript example program, which is shown in Figure 26-4 and available for download on this book's website, lets the user write scripts that control a drawing turtle similar to the one described in Chapter 3, "Program and Code File Structure."

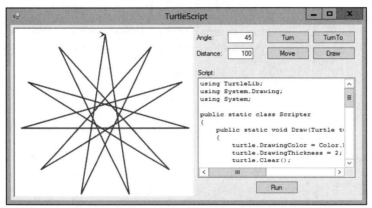

FIGURE 26-4: The TurtleScript example program compiles and executes code entered at run time.

The script you enter can include `using` directives just as any other C# program can. It should define a static `Scripter` class. That class should provide a static `Draw` method that takes a `Turtle` object as a parameter and uses it to draw something. The code can include loops, `if-then` tests, other classes, methods, and most anything else you can put in a C# program. The following code shows a script's basic structure.

```
using TurtleLib;
using System.Drawing;
using System;

public static class Scripter
{
    public static void Draw(Turtle turtle)
    {
        // Draw stuff here...
    }
}
```

The following code shows how the TurtleScript program compiles and executes the script.

```
// Run the script.
private void RunScript()
{
    // Make a C# code provider.
    CodeDomProvider codeProvider = CodeDomProvider.CreateProvider("C#");
```

```csharp
    // Generate a non-executable assembly in memory.
    CompilerParameters parameters = new CompilerParameters();
    parameters.GenerateInMemory = true;
    parameters.GenerateExecutable = false;

    // Add references to the assemblies used by the program.
    var query =
        from Assembly assembly in AppDomain.CurrentDomain.GetAssemblies()
        where !assembly.IsDynamic
        select assembly.Location;
    parameters.ReferencedAssemblies.AddRange(query.ToArray());

    // Compile the code.
    CompilerResults results =
        codeProvider.CompileAssemblyFromSource(parameters, scriptTextBox.Text);

    // See if there are errors.
    if (results.Errors.Count > 0)
    {
        string errors = "";
        foreach (CompilerError error in results.Errors)
        {
            errors +=
                "Error:\r\n" +
                "    Line: " + error.Line + "\r\n" +
                "    Error Number: " + error.ErrorNumber + "\r\n" +
                "    Text: " + error.ErrorText + "\r\n";
        }
        throw new ApplicationException(errors);
    }

    // Get the Scripter class.
    Type scripterType = results.CompiledAssembly.GetType("Scripter");
    if (scripterType == null)
        throw new MissingMethodException("Cannot find class Scripter");

    // Get a MethodInfo object describing the Draw method.
    MethodInfo methodInfo = scripterType.GetMethod("Draw");
    if (methodInfo == null)
        throw new MissingMethodException(
            "Cannot find method Draw(Turtle turtle)");

    // Make sure the method takes a single Turtle as a parameter.
    ParameterInfo[] paramInfos = methodInfo.GetParameters();
    if ((paramInfos.Length != 1) ||
        (paramInfos[0].ParameterType.Name != "Turtle"))
            throw new ArgumentException(
                "The Draw method must take a single Turtle parameter.");

    // Make the parameter list.
    object[] methodParams = new object[] { TheTurtle };

    // Execute the method.
    methodInfo.Invoke(null, methodParams);
}
```

The code starts by creating a `CodeDomProvider` for C#. (The .NET Framework also includes JScript and Visual Basic compilers.) It then creates a `CompilerParameters` object and sets its properties to indicate that the compiler should compile the script into memory (as opposed to into a DLL file) and that it should not create an executable program.

Next, the program must add references to any assemblies that the script needs. You could write code to add specific references one at a time. This example takes a somewhat heavier-handed approach and simply adds references to every assembly that the main program references. To do that, it uses a LINQ query that selects from the assemblies returned by `AppDomain.CurrentDomain.GetAssemblies`. It picks nondynamic assemblies (those not loaded at run time) and selects their locations.

The program then adds the selected assemblies to the `CompilerParameters` object's `ReferencedAssemblies` collection.

The program then calls the code provider's `CompileAssemblyFromSource` method to compile the script with the selected compiler parameters. If the compilation has errors, the program composes an error message and displays it to the user.

SCRIPTING SUPPORT

Compilation error messages are useful but they're far from perfect. They provide basic information and the line number where the error occurred, but the compiler isn't integrated into your program as closely as it is in Visual Studio. For example, the user cannot double-click an error to jump to the line containing the problem. You could add that feature to your code, but it would mean extra work.

The `TextBox` you use to let the user enter a script is even less integrated. Unlike Visual Studio's code editor, it doesn't provide IntelliSense, refactoring tools, or debugging features such as watches and breakpoints.

If your users are advanced enough to benefit from those tools, you may want to have them use Visual Studio to create an add-in DLL and then use reflection to load it at run time as described in the preceding section.

Next, the program uses reflection to find the script's `Scripter` class and that class's `Draw` method, which must take a `Turtle` object as a parameter. If it successfully finds this method, the program invokes it, passing it the class-level `TheTurtle` variable as a parameter.

SUSPICIOUS SCRIPTS

As is the case with DLLs loaded at run time, you must be sure any scripts you execute come from trusted sources. A hacker who uses your program to execute scripts might make your program do all sorts of dangerous things such as deleting files. In general you should not allow nontrusted users to run programs that allow scripting.

SUMMARY

Most programs can do without reflection. Usually, you know what a program needs to do, so you can write the necessary code at design time. However, reflection is occasionally useful for exploring assemblies. It lets you find properties, fields, and methods at run time. It lets you discover what's hidden in undocumented libraries. It even lets you implement add-ins by allowing you to search for add-in classes and methods inside DLLs. Together add-ins and the ability to compile and execute scripts at run time let you make applications that are extensible even after they have been compiled.

One problem with add-ins and scripts is that a hacker could use them to make your program execute code that isn't safe. In general, you shouldn't allow nontrusted users to install DLLs or write and execute scripts.

Even without add-ins and scripting, many applications have problems with hackers. One of the biggest of those problems occurs when a hacker gets hold of crucial data. Every year millions (if not hundreds of millions) of customer records are stolen, often including sensitive information such as usernames, passwords, or credit card numbers.

One way you can protect this kind of data is to encrypt it. If a data thief steals your password file, your data is still safe if the file is properly encrypted.

The .NET Framework includes tools that you can use to encrypt and decrypt files, calculate hash values for files, digitally sign documents, and perform other cryptographic tasks. The next chapter describes some of the most useful of those tools and explains how you can use them to protect your data.

EXERCISES

1. The `PropertyGrid` control uses reflection to let a user view and edit the properties of an object much as the Properties window lets you view and edit properties at design time. Write a program that uses the `PropertyGrid` to let the user view and edit a `Person` object's properties.

    Create a `Person` class with the properties `FirstName`, `LastName`, `Street`, `City`, `State`, `PostalCode`, and `EmailAddress`. Give each property a `Description` attribute explaining its purpose and a `Category` attribute to group it with other related properties. For example, the following code shows how you might declare the `PostalCode` property.

    ```
    [Category("Address")]
    [Description("The address's postal code.")]
    public string PostalCode { get; set; }
    ```

    Hint: The `Description` and `Category` attribute classes are defined in the `System.ComponentModel` namespace.

    When the program starts, create and initialize a `Person` object. Then set a `PropertyGrid` control's `SelectedObject` property to that `Person` object.

    When you run the program, what do the `Description` and `Category` attributes do? What happens when you click the `PropertyGrid`'s Alphabetical button?

MORE ABOUT PROPERTYGRIDS

The `PropertyGrid` control can do a lot more than what's demonstrated by this exercise. For example, it provides support for custom visualizers and editors that you can build to let the user view and set property values. (For example, the Properties window uses a special editor to let you set the `Anchor` property graphically.)

For more information on the `PropertyGrid` control, see "Getting the Most Out of the .NET Framework PropertyGrid Control" at `msdn.microsoft.com/en-us/library/aa302326.aspx`.

---

2. Modify the program you wrote for Exercise 1 by adding a `ContactTypes` enumeration to the `Person` class. Give it the values `Personal`, `Billing`, `Shipping`, and `Admin`. Then give the class a new `ContactType` property that has this type. How does the `PropertyGrid` display the new property?

3. Write a program similar to the one shown in Figure 26-5. (If you don't want to write a graphics program, create different tools that do something like display messages so that you know which tool has been invoked.)

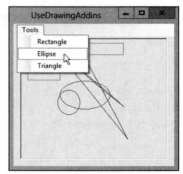

FIGURE 26-5: The DrawingAddIns example program loads add-in methods at run time.

At run time, this program should do the following:

➤ Search its current directory for DLLs.

➤ Search each DLL for classes that have a static `Draw` method that takes a `Graphics` object as a parameter.

➤ For each such class, the program should add an item to the Tools menu. The name of that item should be specified by the class's `DisplayName` attribute. (If the class doesn't have that attribute, use the class's name.)

➤ Each `Draw` method should draw something on the `Graphics` object it is passed.

Hint: To get a class's `DisplayName` attribute value, get the class's type and use the type's `GetCustomAttribute` method. Cast the returned `Attribute` into a `DisplayNameAttribute` and use its `DisplayName` property.

The following code shows an example add-in method.

```
[DisplayName("Rectangle")]
public static class RectangleDrawer
{
    public static void Draw(Graphics gr)
    {
        // Draw something...
    }
}
```

Hint: When you find an appropriate `Draw` method, store its `MethodInfo` object in the `Tag` property of its menu item. That way when the user clicks that item, you can find the corresponding `MethodInfo` to invoke the method.

4. The program you built for Exercise 3 looks for DLLs that hold classes that define a single `Draw` method. Alternatively, you could allow the classes to hold any number of add-in methods. Modify the program you wrote for Exercise 3 so it does that. It should use any method that takes a `Graphics` object as a parameter and that has a `DisplayName` attribute.

5. The program you built for Exercise 4 assumes that any method that takes a `Graphics` object as a parameter and that has a `DisplayName` attribute is a drawing add-in. That works but is somewhat restrictive because it prevents you from having any other similar methods that are not add-ins. Another approach is to define your own custom attribute class and apply it to methods that are add-ins.

Modify the program and DLL(s) you wrote for Exercise 4 to use this approach. In the DLL(s), create a `DrawingAddInAttribute` attribute class. Place it inside the `DrawingAddIn` namespace. (The rest of the DLL doesn't need to be in that namespace.) The following code shows how you can create this attribute.

```
namespace DrawingAddIn
{
    // An attribute that flags a method as a drawing add-in tool.
    [AttributeUsage(AttributeTargets.Method)]
    public class DrawingAddInAttribute : Attribute
    {
    }
}
```

The important things here are the `AttributeUsage` attribute (which indicates that the new attribute applies only to methods) and the fact that the class is inside the `DrawingAddIn` namespace.

Next, modify the program that uses the DLL(s). When it processes a DLL, make it use the following code to get the new attribute's type from the DLL.

```
Type addInType = dll.GetType("DrawingAddIn.DrawingAddInAttribute");
```

(This is why you need the `DrawingAddInAttribute` class to be in the `DrawingAddIn` namespace, so this statement can find the class's type.)

When the code considers a method, have it use code similar to the following to see if the method has this attribute.

```
// Make sure the method has DrawingAddIn attribute.
Attribute drawingAttribute = methodInfo.GetCustomAttribute(addInType);
if (drawingAttribute == null) continue;
```

6. The description of Exercise 5 says the `DrawingAddInAttribute` class should be defined in the `DrawingAddIn` namespace so you can find it later. Can you avoid that restriction?

27

Cryptography

WHAT'S IN THIS CHAPTER

- ➤ Symmetric key encryption and decryption
- ➤ Asymmetric key encryption and decryption
- ➤ Creating, saving, and retrieving public and private keys
- ➤ Cryptographic random numbers
- ➤ Generating keys, initialization vectors, and salts

WROX.COM DOWNLOADS FOR THIS CHAPTER

Please note that all the code examples for this chapter are available as a part of this chapter's code download on the book's website at www.wrox.com/go/csharp5programmersref on the Download Code tab.

Cryptography is the study of methods for protecting communications between two people in the presence of an adversary who wants to intercept the communications. Early forms of cryptography, which were used thousands of years ago, use techniques such as rearranging letters or replacing letters with other letters. For example, in a Caesar substitution cipher (named after Julius Caesar who used it more than 2,000 years ago), you shift letters by some fixed amount. For a shift of 3, A becomes D, B becomes E, C becomes F, and so forth.

These encryption schemes are interesting and fun to experiment with, but they're relatively easy to break with modern techniques. My book *Essential Algorithms: A Practical Approach to Computer Algorithms* (John Wiley and Sons, 2013) includes a chapter that describes some of these historical methods and how to break them (mostly for entertainment value).

Other books such as *Applied Cryptography: Protocols, Algorithms, and Source Code in C* (by Bruce Schneier, John Wiley and Sons, 1996) explain modern cryptographic techniques that cannot be easily broken even by today's computers.

This chapter describes only a few of the most useful cryptographic methods provided by the .NET Framework. Those include generating cryptographically secure random numbers, symmetric encryption, and asymmetric encryption.

This chapter explains only how to use .NET Framework tools to perform those tasks, but it should be enough to get you started with cryptography. Unfortunately, there isn't room here to explain all the methods for performing even those limited tasks or to explain how those methods work. See a book about cryptography (such as Bruce Schneier's book) for details about how some of these algorithms work.

LEISURE READING

The history of cryptography contains truly remarkable stories involving spies and counterspies, ingenious contraptions, breaking unbreakable codes, and using clever artifice to convince the enemy that its code is secure even after it's broken. If you have the time, it makes fascinating reading.

Cryptography was originally used to send messages from one person to another securely. Modern cryptography has expanded to include other sorts of secure communication. The following section describes some of the operations that modern cryptographic programs perform. The sections after that explain some of the cryptographic tools you can use in your C# programs.

CRYPTOGRAPHY NAMESPACES

The `System.Security.Cryptography` namespace includes cryptographic classes. To make using these classes easier, you may want to include the following `using` directive in your code.

```
using System.Security.Cryptography;
```

CRYPTOGRAPHIC OPERATIONS

The following list describes some of the most common cryptographic operations.

➤ *Symmetric key encryption (private key encryption)*—This technique uses a secret key to encrypt and decrypt messages. You use the key to encrypt a message. You then send the result to someone else who knows the key. That person uses the key to decrypt the message.

➤ *Asymmetric key encryption (public key encryption)*—This technique uses two keys, a public key and a secret key, to encrypt and decrypt messages. Everyone knows the public key that is used to encrypt messages. Only those who know the secret key (typically a single person) can decrypt the messages. (This is sort of like a mail slot in a door. Anyone can slip a message through the slot, but only the person with the key to the door can open the door and read the messages.)

➤ *Hashing*—This technique uses the contents of a file to produce a *hash code* that represents the file, sort of like a fingerprint. Hash codes have the property that two files are extremely unlikely to have the same hash code. If you know a file's hash code, then you can rehash the file to see if it has the same hash code. If it does not, then the file has been modified since the original code was calculated.

➤ *Authentication*—This is the process of verifying a person's identity. For example, if someone sends you a message, authentication lets you determine that the message was sent by the person you think it is and not some imposter.

➤ *Message signing*—Digital message signing plays a role similar to signing a document in the physical world: It lets you verify that the signer created the message. For example, if Microsoft sends you a software update, its digital signature guarantees that the update actually came from Microsoft and not some imposter.

➤ *Random number generation*—This is the process of generating cryptographically strong random numbers.

RANDOM THOUGHTS

Actually the "random" numbers produced by any deterministic method are not truly random. If you knew the algorithm used to produce the numbers and the internal state of the algorithm (the values of its variables), you could predict the numbers it would generate.

To get truly random numbers, you need some source of nondeterministic randomness such as a device that measures particles coming from a radioactive sample or that measures fluctuations in radio background noise.

To keep things simple, this chapter uses the word "random" but "pseudorandom" is usually more technically correct.

The last item, random number generation, deserves a little more explanation.

RANDOMNESS

Cryptographic techniques do not all use random number generators but randomness is closely tied with cryptography. If you have a good source of random numbers, you can use it to encrypt messages. Conversely, if you have a good encryption scheme, you can use it to generate random numbers. Because you can use random numbers to encrypt and vice versa, the two are in some sense equivalent.

The following two sections explain this equivalency. The section after that explains cryptographically secure randomness.

Using Random Numbers for Encryption

Suppose you have a good random number generator. (I'll say more about what "good" means shortly.) To use random numbers to encrypt a message, generate a new random byte R for each byte P in the message. The byte's encrypted value is $C = P \oplus R$.

PS AND CS

Usually when discussing cryptography, the unencrypted message is called the *plaintext*, so the letter P represents the unencrypted message byte. Similarly, the encrypted message is usually called the *ciphertext*, so the letter C represents the encrypted message byte.

Here $\oplus$ is the bitwise exclusive-or (XOR) operation. (In C# the XOR operator is ^.) A bit in the result is 1 if exactly one of the corresponding bits in the two input bytes is 1. For example, $1 \oplus 0 = 1$ because exactly one of the input bits is 1. In contrast, $1 \oplus 1 = 0$ because both input bits are 1.

To decrypt the message, simply repeat the previous steps, because $(P \oplus R) \oplus R = P$, which restores the original plaintext bytes.

Note that the message's receiver must use the same sequence of bytes that the sender used to encrypt the message. The information needed to produce the same sequence of bytes forms the system's private key that is shared by the sender and receiver. For example, the key might be a password or sequence of numbers that both the sender and receiver can use to initialize their random number generators.

Using Encryption for Random Numbers

Suppose you have a good encryption algorithm that converts plaintext bytes into unpredictable ciphertext. Then to produce random numbers, simply encrypt the values 1, 1, 1, and so forth for as many bytes as you need. If the encryption algorithm is good, this should produce a stream of apparently random bytes.

If the resulting stream of bytes does not appear random, then the algorithm is not a good secure encryption algorithm.

Cryptographically Secure Randomness

In cryptography, a "good" stream of random numbers roughly means one that is unpredictable. If I give you a sequence of numbers produced by a random number generator, you should not be able to predict with any certainty what the next number will be.

A "good" cryptographic algorithm also produces uncertainty. The bytes of a ciphertext message should look random to an attacker.

The .NET Framework includes a Random class that you can use to generate random numbers, but the algorithm it uses is not cryptographically secure. To see why, you need to know that you can initialize a Random object by passing its constructor a 32-bit integer as a *seed value*. If you use a Random object to encrypt messages, the seed value is basically the key.

A 32-bit integer can hold 2^{32} (4.3 billion) different values, so there are approximately 4.3 billion ways you can initialize a `Random` object. To think of it another way, there are roughly 4.3 billion possible keys. That may seem like a lot of keys, but to a computer it's actually not many. It wouldn't be hard to write a program that tries every possible seed value.

For each seed value, the program would try to decrypt the message. If the result looks like English (or whatever language you use), the seed is probably correct. For example, in English some letters such as E appear more often than others. If the seed is correct, some letters should appear more often than others. If the seed is incorrect, all the letters should appear with roughly the same frequency.

Generating Random Numbers

Generating cryptographically strong random numbers is actually fairly easy in C#. Simply create a cryptographic random number generator object and use its methods to generate the numbers. The .NET Framework's `RNGCryptoServiceProvider` class provides this kind of random number generator. (The "RNG" at the beginning of the class's name stands for "random number generator.")

The RandomNumbers example program, which is available for download on the book's website, uses the following code to generate a list of random numbers.

```
// Generate random numbers.
private void generateButton_Click(object sender, EventArgs e)
{
    numbersListBox.Items.Clear();
    int numNumbers = int.Parse(numNumbersTextBox.Text);

    // Make the RNG.
    RNGCryptoServiceProvider rand = new RNGCryptoServiceProvider();

    // Make a buffer to hold 4 random bytes.
    byte[] bytes = new byte[4];

    // Make the random numbers.
    for (int i = 0; i < numNumbers; i++)
    {
        // Get 4 random bytes.
        rand.GetBytes(bytes);

        // Convert the bytes into an integer.
        int number = BitConverter.ToInt32(bytes, 0);

        // Display the number.
        numbersListBox.Items.Add(number);
    }
}
```

The program starts by clearing its output `ListBox` and parsing the number of random numbers it should generate.

The code then creates an `RNGCryptoServiceProvider` object. That object generates random bytes but this program needs to display random numbers. To convert bytes into numbers, the program creates a `byte` array large enough to hold the number of bytes it needs. This program generates `int` values, which are 4-byte integers, so it makes an array holding 4 bytes.

DATA TRANSLATIONS

In the past, cryptography encrypted and decrypted only text messages. Modern cryptography must encrypt any kind of data including text, databases, images, audio, video, and anything else you can imagine. That means an encrypted message may not be a simple string of letters. In fact, most modern techniques produce seemingly random sequences of bytes.

That makes the cryptographic algorithms strong and flexible, but it makes visualizing the encrypted data difficult. There are a few tools you can use to make visualizing and working with encrypted data easier.

The `UnicodeEncoding` class provides `GetBytes` and `GetString` methods that let you convert between `string`s and `byte` arrays. You can use `GetBytes` to turn a `string` into a `byte` array so that you can encrypt the `bytes`. After you decrypt some encrypted data, the result is another `byte` array. You can then use the `GetString` method to turn the result back into a `string`.

The `BitConverter.ToString` method converts many data types (including `byte` arrays) into a `string` that includes the `bytes`' values. The `string` consists of a sequence of two-digit hexadecimal numbers representing the array's `byte` values, separated by hyphens as in F9-9A-98-6F-BC-9F. This method lets you display `byte` arrays textually.

Unfortunately, the `BitConverter` class doesn't provide a reverse method for translating a `string` of the form F9-9A-98-6F-BC-9F back into a `byte` array. Fortunately, it's not hard to write one.

```
// Convert a string created by BitConverter.ToString into a byte[].
private byte[] StringToBytes(string input)
{
    string[] byteStrings = input.Split('-');
    byte[] result = new byte[byteStrings.Length];
    for (int i = 0; i < result.Length; i++)
        result[i] = Convert.ToByte(byteStrings[i], 16);
    return result;
}
```

This method uses the `string` class's `Split` method to split the input `string` into an array of two-character `string`s holding the `bytes`' hexadecimal values. Next, it creates a `byte` array long enough to hold the `bytes`. It then loops through the `bytes`' hexadecimal values and uses `Convert.ToByte` to convert them into their `byte` values.

As you write cryptographic programs, you can use these tools to

➤ Convert plaintext `string`s into `byte` arrays so that you can encrypt them.

➤ Display textual representations of `byte` arrays.

➤ Convert textual representations of `byte` arrays back into arrays.

➤ Convert a `byte` array containing a `string` into the `string`.

The program then enters a loop to generate the values. For each value, it uses the `RNGCryptoServiceProvider` object's `GetBytes` method to fill the `byte` array with random bytes. It then uses the `BitConverter` class's `ToInt32` method to convert the bytes into an integer value. Finally, it adds the result to the `ListBox`.

This example uses four random bytes to generate an integer value, so it can produce any possible value. If you want to generate values between lower and upper bounds, you need to do some more work.

The first step is to generate a random floating-point value. The following code snippet shows one way you can generate a value in the range 0 (inclusive) and 1 (exclusive).

```
RNGCryptoServiceProvider rand = new RNGCryptoServiceProvider();
byte[] bytes = new byte[8];
rand.GetBytes(bytes);
UInt32 randomInt = BitConverter.ToUInt32(bytes, 0);
float randomFloat = randomInt / (1.0 + UInt32.MaxValue);
```

RANGES

You can represent a range of values by specifying the lower and upper bounds inside parentheses or brackets. A parenthesis means the adjacent bound is not part of the range, and a bracket means the bound is part of the range. For example, [0, 1) indicates the values between 0 inclusive and 1 exclusive.

The code creates an `RNGCryptoServiceProvider` and uses it to fill a 4-byte array with random bytes. It then converts the result into a `UInt32`.

Next, the code divides the random `UInt32` by 1 more than the largest possible `UInt32`. Because the random `UInt32` is between 0 and the largest possible value, the result of the division is between 0 and a tiny bit less than 1.

IMPERFECT RANDOMNESS

This method for generating random floating-point values is pretty good but not completely perfect. For a discussion of some of the issues involved, see the article "Tales from the CryptoRandom" at msdn.microsoft.com/en-us/magazine/cc163367.aspx.

Now that you can generate random floating-point values, you can use those values to generate integers within a range. The following code shows how you can generate an integer in the range [min, max).

```
int randomInRange = (int)(min + (randomFloat * (max - min)));
```

ADVANTAGES OF RANDOM

The `RNGCryptoServiceProvider` class provides values that are "more random" than those produced by the `Random` class, but there are still reasons why you might want to use `Random` under some circumstances.

First, using `Random` is easier. The `Random` class doesn't make you fill arrays of bytes and then translate those bytes into integers. The `Random` class has a `NextDouble` method that returns a value in the range [0, 1), and overloaded versions of a `Next` method that returns integers or an integer within a range.

Second, generating cryptographically random numbers is a lot of work, so `Random` is faster than `RNGCryptoServiceProvider`.

Finally, `Random` can produce a repeatable sequence of numbers. If you initialize a `Random` object with the same seed value, you'll get the same sequence of "random" numbers. That can be useful for testing or creating the same "random" data multiple times.

If you just need values that look random but won't be attacked by hackers, the values produced by `Random` are probably good enough.

SYMMETRIC KEY ENCRYPTION

One of the most obvious uses for encryption is to encrypt and decrypt strings or files. The .NET Framework's encryption services work with streams, so you can use them to encrypt and decrypt anything that you can treat as a stream. That includes strings, files, arrays of bytes, serializations, or just about any other piece of data.

The basic idea is reasonably straightforward: Create a *cryptographic service provider* object and use its methods to write data into an output stream. As data passes through the provider, it is encrypted or decrypted. Unfortunately, the details are rather confusing, so they are described in the following sections.

Simple Encryption and Decryption

The DefaultKeyAndIV example program, which is shown in Figure 27-1 and available for download on the book's website, is one of the simplest programs you can write to encrypt and decrypt a string.

When you enter a string and click Encrypt, the program encrypts and then decrypts the string. The following code shows how the program encrypts the string.

```
private void encryptButton_Click(object sender, EventArgs e)
{
    // Get the plaintext.
    string plaintext = plaintextTextBox.Text;
```

```csharp
// Create an AesManaged provider.
using (AesManaged provider = new AesManaged())
{
    // Make a byte array to hold the encrypted result.
    byte[] cipherbytes;

    // Encrypt. Create an encryptor.
    using (ICryptoTransform encryptor =
        provider.CreateEncryptor(provider.Key, provider.IV))
    {
        // Create a memory stream to hold the result.
        using (MemoryStream ms = new MemoryStream())
        {
            // Create an associated CryptoStream.
            using (CryptoStream cs =
                new CryptoStream(ms, encryptor, CryptoStreamMode.Write))
            {
                // Make a StreamWriter associated with the CryptoStream
                // so we can write into it.
                using (StreamWriter writer = new StreamWriter(cs))
                {
                    // Write the message into the writer.
                    writer.Write(plaintext);
                }

                // Save the resulting ciphertext bytes.
                cipherbytes = ms.ToArray();

                // Display the key, IV, and encrypted bytes.
                keyTextBox.Text = BitConverter.ToString(provider.Key);
                ivTextBox.Text = BitConverter.ToString(provider.IV);
                cipherbytesTextBox.Text = BitConverter.ToString(cipherbytes);
            }
        }
    }
}
```

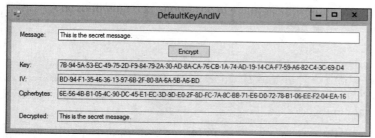

FIGURE 27-1: The DefaultKeyAndIV example program encrypts and decrypts a string.

The code gets the message text and then creates an AesManaged object. This is a managed object that lets C# programs easily interact with an Advanced Encryption Standard (AES) service provider.

Next, the code creates the variable `cipherbytes` to hold the encrypted data later. It then creates an *encryptor* object that it can use to encrypt the string.

To use the encryptor, the program must create one stream from which to read data and a second stream into which to write results. The program creates a `MemoryStream` to hold the results.

The program then creates a `CryptoStream` object to transform any data written into the input stream. It passes the memory stream and the encryptor into the `CryptoStream`'s constructor, so it knows where to write results and what encryptor to use to transform the data. It also passes the constructor the value `CryptoStreamMode.Write` so the `CryptoStream` knows it will be writing into the memory stream.

Next, the code creates a `StreamWriter` into which it can write the plaintext data. It associates the writer with the `CryptoStream`.

Finally, the code calls the `StreamWriter`'s `Write` method to write the string.

Figure 27-2 shows the process schematically. The plaintext is written into the `StreamWriter`. The `StreamWriter` writes the data into the `CryptoStream`. The `CryptoStream` uses the associated encryptor to transform the data and writes the result into the `MemoryStream`.

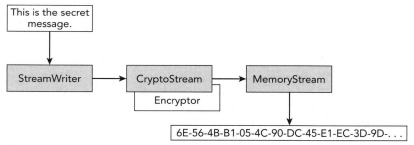

FIGURE 27-2: To encrypt a message, a `StreamWriter` writes data into a `CryptoStream`, which transforms the data and writes the result into a `MemoryStream`.

After the program writes the data, it saves the `MemoryStream`'s contents in a `byte` array.

Next, the program displays the `AesManaged` object's `Key` and `IV` values, and the encrypted bytes. (The following section says more about the `Key` and `IV` values.) It uses the `BitConverter.ToString` method to convert each of those values, all of which are `byte` arrays, into strings displaying the bytes as sequences of hexadecimal numbers.

After it encrypts the message string, the program uses the following code to decrypt the encrypted bytes.

```
// Decrypt. Create a decryptor.
using (ICryptoTransform decryptor =
    provider.CreateDecryptor(provider.Key, provider.IV))
{
    // Create a memory stream from which to read the encrypted bytes.
    using (MemoryStream ms = new MemoryStream(cipherbytes))
```

```
    {
        // Create an associated CryptoStream.
        using (CryptoStream cs =
            new CryptoStream(ms, decryptor, CryptoStreamMode.Read))
        {
            // Make a StreamReader associated with the CryptoStream
            // so we can read from it.
            using (StreamReader reader = new StreamReader(cs))
            {
                // Read the message from the reader.
                string decrypted = reader.ReadToEnd();

                // Display the result.
                decryptedTextBox.Text = decrypted;
            }
        }
    }
        }
    }
}
```

The general pattern of this code is similar to the code that encrypts the string. The biggest difference is that this code uses a decryptor instead of an encryptor.

The code starts by creating the decryptor, passing its constructor the Key and IV values that were used to encrypt the message. It then creates a MemoryStream associated with the encrypted bytes so it can read from it.

The program then creates a CryptoStream associated with the MemoryStream and decryptor, this time passing the constructor the CryptoStreamMode.Read parameter, so the CryptoStream knows it will be reading data from the MemoryStream.

The code makes a StreamReader to read from the CryptoStream and uses its ReadToEnd method to read the data from the stream. Finally, the program displays the decrypted result.

Figure 27-3 shows the decryption process schematically. The StreamReader's ReadToEnd method pulls data from the CryptoStream. The CryptoStream pulls data from the MemoryStream and uses its associated decryptor to decrypt the data.

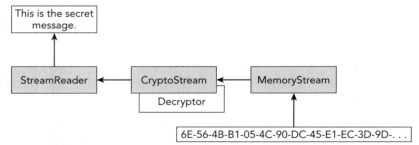

FIGURE 27-3: To decrypt a message, a StreamReader pulls data from a CryptoStream, which pulls data from the MemoryStream and uses its associated decryptor to decrypt it.

Keys and Initialization Vectors

Recall from the earlier discussion of randomness that there are only approximately 4.3 billion seeds you can use to initialize a System.Random object. That means this class can't give you a very secure encryption scheme because an attacker can simply try all possible seed values until finding the right one.

To avoid this problem, cryptographic service providers allow far more initialization values than those available to the Random class. Those values are grouped into two pieces: a *key* and an *initialization vector* (*IV*). Both the key and IV are arrays of bytes, so they don't map to easily remembered passwords.

If you don't care what values the key and IV have, you can simply create an AesManaged object as is done by the example in the preceding section and it will randomly generate those values for you.

That works for this simple example, but only because the same program performs the encryption and decryption. When it decrypts the message, it knows the AesManaged object's Key and IV values.

What if you want to encrypt a message and send it to someone else? They need to use the same Key and IV values if they want to decrypt the message. Somehow you must get them those values or the message is meaningless.

One solution is to have the encryption program write the Key and IV values onto a flash drive or piece of paper. (You could even write the values on a microdot and hide them in the secret compartment of a ring, so you can feel like you're in a Tom Clancy novel.) Then you can transfer those values to the receiver through secure means. For example, you might have a courier carrier the flash drive or paper (or ring) to the recipient.

> ## SPLIT PERSONALITIES
>
> The sender and receiver could be the same person. For example, you might encrypt some important document so that you can read it at a later date. In that case you could write the Key and IV values onto a flash drive or piece of paper and lock it away in a safe or safe deposit box. Later when you need to read the document, you can retrieve the Key and IV.

In this example, that may seem like more work than it's worth. If you look closely at Figure 27-1, you'll see that the Key contains 32 bytes and the IV contains 16 bytes, whereas the entire encrypted message contains only 32 bytes. You could just as easily have had the courier carry the original plaintext message to the receiver and skip the encryption.

However, the same Key and IV values could be used to encrypt a message of any size. As long as the courier gets those values to the receiver safely, you could encrypt and transmit an entire encyclopedia securely.

Another approach would be to generate a collection of Key and IV values and send them securely to the receiver in advance. Then when you need to send an encrypted message, the receiver can use the next Key and IV values in the collection to decrypt the message.

HOW SECURE IS IT?

The `System.Random` class isn't secure enough to use for encryption in large part because it has only 2^{32} possible initialization values. If the bytes in the `Key` and `IV` are truly scrambled, so an attacker cannot guess them, then in this example there are $2^{(32+16)*8} = 2^{384}$ possible combinations of values for the `Key` and `IV` bytes.

How good is that? Suppose the attacker has a computer that can examine 2^{32} possible initialization values per second (which seems fantastically optimistic by modern standards). Then it would take $2^{384} / 2^{32} = 2^{384-32} = 2^{352}$ seconds or roughly 2.9×10^{98} years to try every possible value. Even if the attacker uses a million computers and gets lucky and guesses the correct values 0.01 percent of the way through the search, your secrets will still be safe for 2.9×10^{90} years or so.

Generating Key and IV Values

These methods work reasonably well (assuming you can safely carry the `Key` and `IV` values to the receiver), but unless you have an amazing memory, you're unlikely to remember the `Key` and `IV` values.

Often large pseudorandom arrays of bytes make good keys and IVs. If you truly want to use a password, however, you can use one to generate a key and IV.

The `Rfc2898DeriveBytes` class provides a `GetBytes` method that returns an array containing a specified number of bytes.

The following code shows a method that uses this class to initialize key and IV arrays.

```
// Use a password to generate key and IV bytes.
private static void MakeKeyAndIV(string password, byte[] salt,
    int iterations, int numKeyBytes, int numIVbytes, out byte[] key, out byte[] iv)
{
    Rfc2898DeriveBytes deriver =
        new Rfc2898DeriveBytes(password, salt, iterations);

    key = deriver.GetBytes(numKeyBytes);
    iv = deriver.GetBytes(numIVbytes);
}
```

The method starts by creating a new `Rfc2898DeriveBytes` object, passing its constructor the password, a salt, and a number of iterations.

The *salt* is an array of bytes that you specify to make it harder for an attacker to build a dictionary containing key and IV values for all possible passwords. Basically, this serves as an initialization vector for the `Rfc2898DeriveBytes` object.

The number of iterations tells the object how many times to apply the object's internal algorithm. This number is intended to slow the operation down. If you know the correct password, repeating the algorithm 1,000 or so times will slow you down only a few milliseconds. However, if you're an attacker trying to guess all possible passwords, performing all those iterations for every possible password will add up and slow down your attack. (Microsoft recommends that you use at least 1,000 iterations.)

After it has initialized the `Rfc2898DeriveBytes` object, the code simply calls its `GetBytes` method to generate however many bytes it needs for the key and IV values.

ASYMMETRIC KEY ENCRYPTION

Asymmetric key encryption uses a public key known to everyone (or at least everyone you want to be a message sender) and a private key known only to the message receiver. Anyone can encrypt messages but only the receiver can decrypt them.

The most widely known asymmetric algorithm is *RSA*, which was named for the three people who first publicized it: Ron Rivest, Adi Shamir, and Leonard Adleman. RSA is interesting but it's also fairly complicated, so there's no room to explain how it works here. The rest of this section provides an overview of how to use RSA in a C# program. The sections that follow show code that performs the steps.

> **FURTHER READING**
>
> Many books, including my book *Essential Algorithms: A Practical Approach to Computer Algorithms* and Bruce Schneier's book (both mentioned earlier in this chapter), explain how RSA works.
>
> Microsoft's description of the `RSAParameters` structure at `msdn.microsoft.com/library/system.security.cryptography.rsaparameters.aspx` provides a brief description of how Microsoft's implementation of RSA works.
>
> Finally you can look at more general descriptions of RSA such as Wikipedia's article "RSA (Cryptosystem)" at `en.wikipedia.org/wiki/RSA_(algorithm)`.

For now what you need to know is that RSA uses a collection of numbers to encrypt and decrypt data. Two of the numbers, called `Exponent` and `Modulus`, make up the public key. The others, which are called `D`, `DP`, `DQ`, `InverseQ`, `P`, and `Q`, make up the private key.

The .NET Framework's `RSACryptoServiceProvider` class uses RSA to encrypt and decrypt data. It uses the `RSAParameters` structure to store the public and private key data.

To retrieve key data from an `RSACryptoServiceProvider` object, you call the object's `ExportParameters` method, passing it the parameter `false` if you want only the object's public parameters and `true` if you also want the object's private parameters.

To load key values into an `RSACryptoServiceProvider` object, you call the object's `ImportParameters` method, passing it an `RSAParameters` structure holding the necessary parameters.

Unlike the key and IV data used by the AES algorithm, the bytes used in RSA's keys are not random. They are carefully selected large integers that satisfy specific mathematical relationships. These numbers are also enormous (64 bytes or longer) so finding numbers that work isn't as simple as generating random bytes.

You can create a new set of key parameters by making an instance of the RSACryptoServiceProvider class. You can then publish the public parameters and save the private parameters so that you can later decrypt messages.

Microsoft correctly points out that you should never store key values in plaintext on a computer, so cyber-crooks can't find them. You could write down the D, DP, DQ, InverseQ, P, and Q parameters on a piece of paper, but that's a lot of data.

To help solve this problem, Microsoft suggests that you store key information in a *key container*, an object that stores key information encrypted, so it's not easy to steal.

If this all seems complicated, you're right, it is.

The following list summarizes the steps for creating RSA keys in a C# program.

1. Create a new RSACryptoServiceProvider object. (It is created with a usable set of key values.)
2. Use the object's ExportParameters method to extract the key values.
3. Save the key values in a key container for later use.
4. Publish the public key values Exponent and Modulus.

The following list summarizes the steps for using RSA to encrypt data in a C# program.

1. Create a new RSAParameters structure.
2. Initialize the structure's Exponent and Modulus parameters with the public values.
3. Create an RSACryptoServiceProvider object.
4. Call the object's ImportParameters method to set its public key parameters.
5. Call the object's Encrypt method, passing it the bytes to encrypt.

The following list summarizes the steps for using RSA to decrypt data in a C# program.

1. Create an RSACryptoServiceProvider object, initializing its parameters with the values saved in the key container. (Alternatively, you can create the object and then use ImportParameters to load the key parameters from an RSAParameters structure.)
2. Call the provider's Decrypt method, passing it the encrypted bytes.

The following sections show code that performs these steps.

Creating, Saving, and Retrieving Keys

The following code shows how a program might create new RSA key data and save it into a key container.

```
// Create the parameters object and set the container name.
CspParameters parameters = new CspParameters();
```

```
    parameters.KeyContainerName = "TestKey";

    // Create an RSACryptoServiceProvider that uses the parameters.
    return new RSACryptoServiceProvider(parameters);
```

The code first creates a `CspParameters` object and sets its `KeyContainerName` property to the name of the key's container. It then creates a new `RSACryptoServiceProvider` object, passing its constructor the `CspParameters` object.

If the key container already exists, the new `RSACryptoServiceProvider` object is loaded with the saved key information.

If the container does not already exist, the `RSACryptoServiceProvider` object is loaded with a new set of valid RSA keys and they are saved in a new key container.

Encrypting Data

The following `RSAEncrypt` method uses RSA to encrypt data.

```
    private byte[] RSAEncrypt(byte[] plainbytes, RSAParameters publicParams)
    {
        // Create a RSACryptoServiceProvider.
        using (RSACryptoServiceProvider provider = new RSACryptoServiceProvider())
        {
            // Import the public key information.
            provider.ImportParameters(publicParams);

            // Encrypt the data and return the result. (Don't use OAEP padding.)
            return provider.Encrypt(plainbytes, false);
        }
    }
```

This method first creates an `RSACryptoServiceProvider` object. It then calls the object's `ImportSettings` method to import the public key information in the `RSAParameters` structure passed into the routine as a parameter.

The method finishes by calling the provider's `Encrypt` method. It passes the method the data to encrypt and returns the resulting encrypted data.

Decrypting Data

The following `RSADecrypt` method uses RSA to decrypt data.

```
    private byte[] RSADecrypt(byte[] cipherbytes, RSAParameters privateParams)
    {
        // Create a RSACryptoServiceProvider.
        using (RSACryptoServiceProvider provider = new RSACryptoServiceProvider())
        {
            // Import the private key information.
            provider.ImportParameters(privateParams);

            // Decrypt the data and return the result. (Don't use OAEP padding.)
            return provider.Decrypt(cipherbytes, false);
        }
    }
```

This method is similar to the `RSAEncrypt` method. The only differences are that its `privateParams` parameter contains the private RSA key parameters rather than the public parameters, and that the method calls the provider's `Decrypt` method instead of its `Encrypt` method.

Example Encryption

The RSAEncryptDecrypt example program, which is shown in Figure 27-4 and available for download on the book's website, demonstrates RSA encryption and decryption. You can see from the figure that all the key values except `Exponent` are quite large. In this example running on my computer, `Exponent` is a 3-byte integer, `D` and `Modulus` are 128-byte integers, and the other values are 64-byte integers.

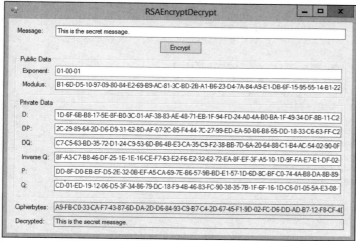

FIGURE 27-4: The RSAEncryptDecrypt example program uses RSA to encrypt and decrypt a string.

The following code shows how the example encrypts and decrypts data when you click the Encrypt button.

```
private void encryptButton_Click(object sender, EventArgs e)
{
    // Get the plaintext.
    string plaintext = plaintextTextBox.Text;

    // Create a UnicodeEncoding object to convert between byte array and string.
    UnicodeEncoding converter = new UnicodeEncoding();

    // Make byte arrays to hold the original, encrypted, and decrypted data.
    byte[] plainbytes = converter.GetBytes(plaintextTextBox.Text);
    byte[] cipherbytes;
    byte[] decryptedbytes;

    // Create an RSA provider.
    using (RSACryptoServiceProvider provider = new RSACryptoServiceProvider())
    {
```

```
                // Get the provider's public key properties.
                RSAParameters publicParams = provider.ExportParameters(false);

                // Use the public parameters to encrypt the data.
                cipherbytes = RSAEncrypt(plainbytes, publicParams);

                // Display the encrypted bytes.
                cipherbytesTextBox.Text = BitConverter.ToString(cipherbytes);

                // Display public properties.
                exponentTextBox.Text = BitConverter.ToString(publicParams.Exponent);
                modulusTextBox.Text = BitConverter.ToString(publicParams.Modulus);

                // Decrypt.
                // Get the provider's private key properties.
                RSAParameters privateParams = provider.ExportParameters(true);

                // Use the private parameters to decrypt the data.
                decryptedbytes = RSADecrypt(cipherbytes, privateParams);

                // Display private properties.
                DTextBox.Text = BitConverter.ToString(privateParams.D);
                DPTextBox.Text = BitConverter.ToString(privateParams.DP);
                DQTextBox.Text = BitConverter.ToString(privateParams.DQ);
                inverseQTextBox.Text = BitConverter.ToString(privateParams.InverseQ);
                PTextBox.Text = BitConverter.ToString(privateParams.P);
                QTextBox.Text = BitConverter.ToString(privateParams.Q);

                // Display the result.
                decryptedTextBox.Text = converter.GetString(decryptedbytes);
            }
        }
```

The code starts by getting the plaintext to encrypt. It then creates a `UnicideEncoding` object to translate between `strings` and `byte` arrays. It converts the plaintext into `bytes` and makes two other `byte` arrays to hold the encrypted and decrypted data.

The program then creates an `RSACryptoServiceProvider` object. That object is initialized with new RSA key information.

The program calls the provider's `ExportParameters` method to get its public key values. It passes those parameters and the data to encrypt into the `RSAEncrypt` method described earlier to encrypt the data.

The program then displays the encrypted data and the public key parameters.

Next, the program calls the provider's `ExportParameters` method again, this time to get its private key values. It passes those and the encrypted data to the `RSADecrypt` method described earlier to decrypt the data.

The program finishes by displaying the private key parameters and the decrypted message.

LENGTH LIMITATIONS

RSA is relatively slow compared to symmetric key algorithms, so the .NET Framework limits the size of the messages it encrypts with RSA. If you exceed the allowed length, the provider throws a `CryptographicException` with the rather unhelpful message "Bad Length."

Symmetric algorithms break messages into blocks and then encrypt them separately, so they can handle messages of any length.

Together the two kinds of algorithms are effective. For example, you could use the following steps to send a long message to a receiver even if you have not exchanged private keys for symmetric encryption.

1. Generate a private key for symmetric encryption.

2. Use asymmetric encryption to send the private key to the receiver.

3. Send the symmetrically encrypted message to the receiver.

SUMMARY

Cryptography is a fascinating topic. Modern cryptographic tools use sophisticated mathematics to let you perform such operations as encrypting and decrypting files and strings, hashing files to see if they have been modified, digitally signing files to provide assurance that you actually wrote the file, and generating cryptographically secure random numbers.

There isn't room to cover all these topics here, so this chapter focused on three of the most useful tasks: generating cryptographically secure random numbers, symmetric encryption, and asymmetric encryption. This should provide enough introduction for you to continue your study of the .NET Framework's cryptographic methods on your own.

For more information about cryptographic tools in the .NET Framework, see "Cryptographic Services" at msdn.microsoft.com/library/92f9ye3s.aspx.

EXERCISES

1. Write a program that uses the `Random` class to encrypt and decrypt messages.

   Unfortunately, if you use the XOR operator `^` to combine a letter with a random byte, the result may not be a letter, so it's hard to visualize the result. To make it easier to visualize the results, assume the message contains only uppercase letters A through Z. (For bonus points, use string methods and LINQ to convert the plaintext.) To encrypt a letter, shift it by a random number of letters between 0 and 25. For example, A + 1 = B, A + 2 = C, and so forth.

Use the program to encrypt a message and then decrypt the result to make sure it works properly. (For testing purposes, the message "This is a test" with key 123456 should be ZJIBDEFDSNV.)

2. Write a program similar to the one shown in Figure 27-5 that breaks the encryption you used for Exercise 1.

FIGURE 27-5: The BreakRandomCipher example program uses character frequencies to break the encryption scheme used in Exercise 1.

Make the program loop through possible key values. (To reduce the search slightly, use only non-negative keys.) For each possible key, decipher the ciphertext and use LINQ to calculate the frequencies of the letters in the resulting plaintext. Compare the maximum frequency in the plaintext to the test value entered by the user. If the maximum frequency is greater than the test value, display the plaintext so that the user can see if it looks like a message. (If you look closely at Figure 27-5, you can see that the plaintext doesn't make sense. In that case, you should increase the test frequency and try again.)

To test your program, decrypt the text in the file DecipherMe.txt available in this chapter's downloads. What is the name of the author of the encrypted quote?

3. Will the approach you used for Exercise 2 work for short messages? Why?

4. The instructions for Exercise 2 tell you to look at the maximum frequency of the letters in the decrypted plaintext. Why don't you need to look at all the letters' frequencies? What are the advantages and disadvantages of this approach? Can you think of a simple way to make the search more reliable?

5. What changes would you need to make for the solution you wrote for Exercise 2 to work with other languages such as French or German?

6. The RandomNumbers example program described in the section "Generating Random Numbers" works but is long and cumbersome. Write a static `MyRandom` class that has a `GetInt` method that returns a cryptographically secure random integer. Then rewrite the example program to use the new method.

7. Rewrite the program you wrote for Exercise 6 so that it generates random `doubles` in the range [0, 1). (Hint: Add a `NextDouble` method to the `MyRandom` class to generate the random value, and make the main program use that method.)

8. Rewrite the program you wrote for Exercise 6 so that it generates integers between minimum and maximum values entered by the user. (Hint: Use the `NextDouble` method you added for Exercise 7 to add an overloaded version of `GetInt` that takes lower and upper bounds as parameters.)

9. The DefaultKeyAndIV example program encrypts and decrypts a string within its button `Click` event handler. That's not a reusable approach. Rewrite the program to move the encryption and decryption steps into separate methods. (Hints: Make the methods take the key and IV values as parameters. Make the main program create an `AesManaged` object and use its default key and IV values.)

10. Modify the program you wrote for Exercise 9 to move the encryption and decryption methods into extension methods.

11. Write a program similar to the one shown in Figure 27-6 to encrypt and decrypt strings. What happens if you try to decrypt a message with the wrong password? What if the password is wrong only by a single character?

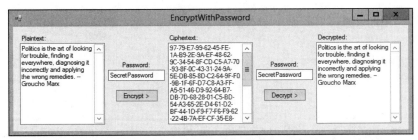

FIGURE 27-6: For Exercise 11, write a program that uses a password to encrypt and decrypt messages.

12. Write programs to act as a sender and receiver for RSA communication. The receiver program should have these features:

a. When it starts, the program should create an `RSACryptoServiceProvider` object associated with a key stored in a key container. (If the key already exists, it will load into the provider. If the key doesn't yet exist, the provider will create a key and store it in the container.)

b. After it has created the provider, the program should display the public key values `Exponent` and `Modulus` in TextBoxes. (You can also make it display the private data if you like.)

c. The user should enter encrypted data in the format used by the `BitConverter.ToString` method (as in F9-9A-98-6F-BC-9F).

d. When the user clicks the Decrypt button, the program should convert the entered data into a `byte` array and use the private key data to decrypt it.

The sender program should have these features:

a. The user should copy and paste the public key data from the receiver program into `TextBoxes` in the sender. (The sender should not know the public key data.)

b. When the user enters a message and clicks Encrypt, the program should use the private key data to encrypt the message and display the result. (Remember to use a short message because the RSA provider won't encrypt long ones.)

To test the programs:

a. Run both programs.

b. Copy and paste the public key data from the receiver into the sender.

c. Enter a message in the sender and encrypt it.

d. Copy and paste the encrypted data from the sender to the receiver.

e. Use the receiver to decrypt the message and verify that it is correct.

PART VI
Appendices

Continues

Solutions to Exercises

All the programmatic exercise solutions are available for download in the downloads for their chapters. For example, the ConsoleShowArgs example program that solves Exercise 1 in Chapter 2, "Writing a First Program," is contained in the downloads for Chapter 2.

This appendix shows the most interesting parts of many of the programs, but to save space some of the less interesting details are omitted. Download the examples from www.wrox.com/go/csharp5programmersref to see all the code.

CHAPTER 1

1. Figure A-1 shows the major steps that Visual Studio performs when you write a C# program and press F5 to run it.

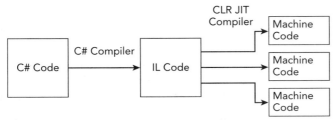

FIGURE A-1: The C# compiler converts C# code into IL code. Then the CLR's JIT compiler converts the IL code into machine code. The JIT compiler compiles only methods as they are needed.

2. In the first application, there will be a small delay because each method is compiled the first time the user selects the corresponding tool. The delay is small, so the user probably won't notice anything.

In the second application, all the compilation delays occur when the program starts. It is possible that those delays could add up to enough time for the user to notice. However, the time spent by the methods' code will probably be far larger, so the user would notice a delay in any case.

If you precompile the programs and install them in the GAC, they would run slightly faster because their methods wouldn't need to compile to machine code on first use. The difference will probably be small, however. This is probably not worth doing for the first application because the user will see any compilation delay as part of the time needed to click a button. It's questionable whether it's worth the effort for the second program, either.

3. Using NGen and the GAC will be most useful for the code library and the control library. Their code would be precompiled and ready to run for any application that uses those libraries.

4. Calling all the methods when the program starts would force the CLR to compile them, so they would be ready to run if they were called again later. However, this technique would make the code more confusing, and it's not clear that it would save enough time to be noticeable to the user, so it may be best to not do this.

CHAPTER 2

1. The ConsoleShowArgs example program does this.

The first time you run the program, a console window appears and displays the text `Press Enter to continue`. When you press Enter, it closes.

When you run the program after entering the command-line arguments, the window displays the following text.

```
Red
Green
Blue
Press Enter to continue.
```

2. When you run the program from Windows Explorer, a console window appears and displays the text `Press Enter to continue`. The command-line arguments you entered for Exercise 1 are passed to the program only when you run it from inside Visual Studio.

3. When you run the program from the shortcut, a console window appears displaying the following text.

```
Apple
Banana
Cherry
Press Enter to continue.
```

This technique enables you to easily start a program with command-line arguments.

4. The first time you run the program, the console window displays `Press Enter to continue`. When you press Enter, the window displays a command prompt and doesn't disappear.

When you run the program again with the program's name followed by command-line arguments, the window displays the following text.

```
Ant
Bear
Cat
Press Enter to continue
```

5. The WindowsFormsShowArgs example program does this.

   If you worked through the previous exercises, you may think the program will show nothing because you haven't specified any command-line arguments for it. Actually, the `Environment.GetCommandLineArgs` method treats the program's name as an argument, so the program lists that. In this example, the name should include the path to the executable and then end in WindowsFormsShowArgs.vshost.exe. This is the program that Visual Studio is actually executing.

   After you set the command-line arguments Red, Green, and Blue, the program displays the executable program's name and those three values.

6. On the basis of the results of Exercises 2 and 5, you probably think the program will display only the executable program's name. This time you're right.

7. On the basis of the results of Exercises 3 and 5, you probably think the program will display the executable program's name followed by the command-line arguments Apple, Banana, and Cherry. You're right again.

8. As in Exercise 5, the program initially displays the executable program's name (the vshost.exe version). After you define the command-line arguments, the program displays the executable program's name and the arguments.

9. As in Exercises 2 and 6, the program displays only the executable program's name.

10. As in Exercises 3 and 7, the program displays the executable program's name followed by the command-line arguments Apple, Banana, and Cherry.

CHAPTER 3

For Exercises 1 through 5, see the program Ex03-01.

1. Initially the button is centered.

   a. When you resize the form, the button remains centered on the form.

   b. If Anchor is Top, Left, the button remains the same distance from the form's upper and left sides.

   c. If Anchor is Bottom, Right, the button remains the same distance from the form's lower and right sides.

   d. If Anchor is Top, Bottom, Left, Right, the button remains the same distance from all the form's sides. That makes it grow to use any available new size.

2. When you resize the form, the button resizes, too.

    a. If you make the form very small, the button shrinks until it disappears.

    b. Yes, if the button has focus, then you can still "click" it by pressing Enter or Space.

    c. If the button's `MinimumSize` property is `50, 15` and you make the form small, the button will not shrink below the minimum size.

3. When you click the button, the picture displays on the form's background.

    a. Initially the form tiles with copies of the picture.

    b. If `BackgroundImageLayout` is `None`, a single copy of the picture displays in the form's upper-left corner.

    c. If `BackgroundImageLayout` is `Center`, a single copy of the picture displays centered on the form. If the image doesn't fit, it is placed in the upper-left corner.

    d. If `BackgroundImageLayout` is `Stretch`, a copy of the picture stretches to fill the form. This can distort the image if the picture's and form's aspect ratios are different.

    e. If `BackgroundImageLayout` is `Zoom`, a copy of the picture stretches as large as possible without distorting it.

4. The button's background becomes yellow and its text becomes red.

5. When you click the button, its text becomes blue. This code sets the form's `ForeColor` and `BackColor` properties to red and blue, respectively. Some controls inherit certain properties from the control that contains them. The `Button` control inherits `ForeColor` but not `BackColor` because it has its own ideas about what a button's background should look like.

    The form doesn't display a red background because it is already displaying a background image. If you comment out the code that sets the image, the form's background becomes red.

6. A `/*` begins a comment that extends to the next `*/`. In this case, that means the bold lines in the following code are commented out.

    ```
    /*
    Comment.

    /*
    Inner comment.
    */

    */
    ```

    The remaining `*/` is not commented out, so Visual Studio complains.

7. Visual Studio ignores any text on the line after the `#region` and `#endregion` directives, so the region names don't actually matter to Visual Studio. It simply matches each `#endregion` with the most recent `#region`. That means the code is equivalent to the following.

    ```
    #region Region1
    // Code Block 1 ...
    #region Region2
    ```

```
// Code Block 2 ...
#endregion Region2
// Code Block 3 ...
#endregion Region1
```

    a. If you collapse Region1, all this code is hidden.

    b. If you collapse Region2, only Code Block 3 is hidden.

CHAPTER 4

1. The equivalent statement is

```
if (person is Student)
    student = (Student)person;
else
    student = null;
```

2. The following statement creates and initializes the `fibonacci` array.

```
int[] fibonacci = { 1, 1, 2, 3, 5, 8, 13, 21, 33, 54, 87 };
```

3. The following statement creates an 8×8 array of `Person` objects.

```
Person[,] board = new Person[8, 8];
```

4. The following statement creates an array of eight arrays each holding eight `Person` objects.

```
Person[][] board =
{
    new Person[8],
    new Person[8],
    new Person[8],
    new Person[8],
    new Person[8],
    new Person[8],
    new Person[8],
    new Person[8],
};
```

5. The smallest number type that can hold large five-digit ZIP codes is `int`, so the `Zip` field must be an `int`. The following code defines the `Person` class.

```
public class Person
{
    public string FirstName, LastName, Street, City, State;
    public int Zip;
}
```

6. The following code creates the necessary array.

```
Person[,] people =
{
```

```
    {
        new Person() { FirstName="Ann", LastName="Archer"},
        new Person() { FirstName="Ben", LastName="Baker"},
    },
    {
        new Person() { FirstName="Cindy", LastName="Cant"},
        new Person() { FirstName="Dan", LastName="Deevers"},
    },
};
```

7. The following code declares and initializes the required three-dimensional array.

```
string[, ,] values =
{
    {
        { "000", "001", "002" },
        { "010", "011", "012" },
    },
    {
        { "100", "101", "102" },
        { "110", "111", "112" },
    },
};
```

8. Visual Studio flags the method call with an error similar to "Use of unassigned local variable 'value'."

9. The code works whether the calling method initializes the value or not. The method doesn't assume the value is initialized but doesn't mind if it is.

10. Visual Studio flags the statement that tries to double the parameter with as error similar to "Use of unassigned out parameter 'number'."

11. Visual Studio flags the method with an error similar to "The out parameter 'number' must be assigned to before control leaves the current method."

12. If you try to pass an expression into a method for a ref parameter, Visual Studio flags the method call with the error "A ref or out argument must be an assignable variable."

13. The following Oven class shows one possible solution.

```
public class Oven
{
    // Backing field for temperature in degrees Celsius.
    private float DegreesCelsius = 0;

    // Get and set the temperature in degrees Fahrenheit.
    public float TempFahrenheit
    {
        get
        {
            return DegreesCelsius * 5f / 9f + 32f;
        }
        set
        {
            DegreesCelsius = (value - 32f) * 5f / 9f;
```

```
        }
    }

    // Get and set the temperature in degrees Celsius.
    public float TempCelsius
    {
        get
        {
            return DegreesCelsius;
        }
        set
        {
            DegreesCelsius = value;
        }
    }
}
```

14. The following code shows the two methods.

```
private string Combine1(int row, int column)
{
    return "(" + row + ", " + column + ")";
}

private string Combine2(int row, int column)
{
    return "R" + row + "C" + column;
}
```

The following code declares a delegate variable to refer to the methods and tests them.

```
Func<int, int, string> combiner;

combiner = Combine1;
Console.WriteLine(combiner(1, 2));
combiner = Combine2;
Console.WriteLine(combiner(1, 2));
```

Alternatively, the program could use the following code to define a delegate type.

```
public delegate string CombinerType(int row, int column);
```

It would then declare the delegate variable as in the following code.

```
CombinerType combiner;
```

CHAPTER 5

1. You cannot use both the pre- and post-increment operators on the same variable as in ++x++. Because the post-increment operator has higher precedence than the pre-increment operator, this is equivalent to ++(x++). The post-increment operator returns x's original value. The pre-increment operator would then try to increment the result. But the result isn't x; it's basically a copy of x's value. The pre-increment operator can work only on items such as variables that it can increment, so it fails.

If you enter ++x++ in the code, Visual Studio flags it with this error:

The operand of an increment or decrement operator must be a variable, property or indexer

2. The following code uses if statements instead of ?: and ??.

```
if (amount < 0) amountLabel.ForeColor = Color.Red;
else amountLabel.ForeColor = Color.Blue;

Customer orderedBy;
if (customer != null) orderedBy = customer;
else orderedBy = new Customer();
```

The following code shows a slightly more concise way to set orderedBy.

```
Customer orderedBy = customer;
if (customer == null) orderedBy = new Customer();
```

3. The code starts by using System.Object.ReferenceEquals to see if the operands refer to the same object. If they are both null, then they refer to the same null object, so the method returns true.

4. The following code shows a subtraction operator for the Complex class.

```
public static Complex operator -(Complex operand1, Complex operand2)
{
    return new Complex()
    {
        Re = operand1.Re - operand2.Re,
        Im = operand1.Im - operand2.Im
    };
}
```

Alternatively, because the class already defines addition and unary negation, you could use the following simpler subtraction operator.

```
public static Complex operator -(Complex operand1, Complex operand2)
{
    return operand1 + (-operand2);
}
```

5. The following code shows a simple Fraction class with * and / operators.

```
public class Fraction
{
    public double Numerator = 0;
    public double Denominator = 0;

    public static Fraction operator *(Fraction operand1, Fraction operand2)
    {
        return new Fraction()
        {
            Numerator = operand1.Numerator * operand2.Numerator,
            Denominator = operand1.Denominator * operand2.Denominator
```

```
            };
        }

        public static Fraction operator /(Fraction operand1, Fraction operand2)
        {
            return new Fraction()
            {
                Numerator = operand1.Numerator * operand2.Denominator,
                Denominator = operand1.Denominator * operand2.Numerator
            };
        }
    }
```

6. Any fraction can be represented as a `double`, possibly with the loss of some precision, so this is a widening conversion. That means this should be an implicit conversion. The following code shows the conversion operator.

```
public static implicit operator double(Fraction fraction)
{
    return fraction.Numerator / fraction.Denominator;
}
```

7. If you provide the > operator, then you must also provide the < operator. The following code uses the `double` conversion operator defined in Exercise 6 to implement those operators for the `Fraction` class.

```
public static bool operator <(Fraction operand1, Fraction operand2)
{
    return (double)operand1 < (double)operand2;
}

public static bool operator >(Fraction operand1, Fraction operand2)
{
    return (double)operand1 > (double)operand2;
}
```

8. If you provide the == operator, then you must also provide the != operator and you must override the `Equals` and `GetHashCode` methods. The following code uses the `double` conversion operator defined in Exercise 6 to do this for the `Fraction` class.

```
public override bool Equals(object obj)
{
    if (obj == null) return false;
    if (!(obj is Fraction)) return false;

    Fraction fraction = obj as Fraction;
    return (double)this == (double)fraction;
}

public override int GetHashCode()
{
    double value = (double)this;
    return value.GetHashCode();
}
```

```
public static bool operator ==(Fraction operand1, Fraction operand2)
{
    // If both refer to the same object (reference equality), return true.
    if ((object)operand1 == (object)operand2) return true;

    // If one is null but not the other, return false.
    if (((object)operand1 == null) || ((object)operand2 == null)) return false;

    // Compare the values.
    return (double)operand1 == (double)operand2;
}

public static bool operator !=(Fraction operand1, Fraction operand2)
{
    return !(operand1 == operand2);
}
```

9. The results of the statements are

a. `1 + 2 * 3 - 4 / 5 = 7`

b. `9 * 5 / 10 = 4`

c. `2 * 5 / 10 = 1`

d. `2 / 10 * 5 = 1`

e. `12 / 6 * 4 / 8 = 1`

10. The following parenthesized statements are true.

a. `4 * 4 - 4 / 4 + 4 = 19`

b. `4 * 4 - 4 / (4 + 4) = 16`

c. `4 * 4 - (4 / 4 + 4) = 11`

d. `4 * (4 - 4) / 4 + 4 = 4`

e. `4 * (4 - 4) / (4 + 4) = 0`

11. The following table shows the values of x and y after each statement.

STATEMENT	x	y
`int y = x / 4;`	11	2
`int y = x++ / 4;`	12	2
`int y = ++x / 4;`	12	3
`float y = x / 4;`	11	2.0
`double y = x / 4f;`	11	2.75

12. The following statements make y equal 3.5.

    a. `float y = x / 2f;`

    b. `float y = (float)x / 2;`

    c. `float y = x / (float)2;`

13. In the statement `float y = x / 2.0`, the value `2.0` is a `double`, so `x / 2.0` is also a `double`. Storing a `double` value in the `float` variable `y` is a narrowing conversion, so it cannot be done implicitly. This statement tries to perform the conversion implicitly, so it raises an error.

One way to fix the statement is to explicitly cast the result to a `float` as in `float y = (float)(x / 2.0)`.

14. If `||=` existed, it would be a conditional Or operator. Suppose A and B are `bool`s. Then A `||=` B would examine A. If A is `true`, then it would be left alone. If A is `false`, the program would set A = A `|` B.

If `&&=` existed, it would be a conditional And operator. Suppose A and B are `bool`s. Then A `&&=` B would examine A. If A is `false`, then it would be left alone. If A is `true`, the program would set A = A `&` B.

These would provide some benefit because they wouldn't evaluate B unless necessary. If B is a slow method call instead of a variable, that could save some time.

CHAPTER 6

1. The following code shows the `IContactable` interface.

```
interface IContactable
{
    bool Contact(string message);
}
```

2. The following code shows an `Emailable` class that implicitly implements the `IContactable` interface.

```
class Emailable : IContactable
{
    public bool Contact(string message)
    {
        return true;
    }
}
```

3. The following code shows an `Emailable` class that explicitly implements the `IContactable` interface.

```
class Textable : IContactable
{
    bool IContactable.Contact(string message)
    {
```

```
        return true;
    }
}
```

4. To define a method without providing any implementation, the method's declaration must include the abstract keyword. If the class contains an abstract method, its declaration must also include the abstract keyword. The following code shows the Contactable class.

```
abstract class Contactable
{
    abstract public bool Contact(string message);
}
```

5. The following code shows a Mailable class that inherits from Contactable and implements the Contact method.

```
class Mailable : Contactable
{
    public override bool Contact(string message)
    {
        return true;
    }
}
```

6. The following code shows an implementation of the Root extension method.

```
static class DoubleExtensions
{
    public static double Root(this double number)
    {
        return (Math.Sqrt(number));
    }
}
```

7. The following code shows an overloaded version of the Root extension method. (In the same DoubleExtensions class used in Exercise 6.)

```
public static double Root(this double number, int rootBase)
{
    return (Math.Pow(number, 1.0 / rootBase));
}
```

8. If the program is going to use Piece variables to represent Pieces and Kings, the CanMoveTo method must be virtual and the King class must override the method. Then if the program uses a Piece variable to invoke CanMoveTo for a King object, it executes the King's version of the method.

The following code shows the Piece class.

```
class Piece
{
    public virtual bool CanMoveTo(int row, int column)
    {
        return false;
    }
}
```

The following code shows the `King` class.

```
class King : Piece
{
    public override bool CanMoveTo(int row, int column)
    {
        return true;
    }
}
```

9. The following statement defines the `ManagersFromEmployeesDelegate` type.

```
delegate Manager[] ManagersFromEmployeesDelegate(Employee[] employees);
```

The following code shows the `Promote` method that matches the delegate type.

```
private Manager[] Promote(Employee[] employees)
{
    return null;
}
```

The following statement creates a variable that holds a reference to the `Promote` method.

```
ManagersFromEmployeesDelegate del = Promote;
```

10. Covariance lets a method return a more derived type than the delegate. In this example, the delegate returns `Manager[]`, so the new method should return the more derived type `Executive[]`.

Contravariance lets a method take parameters that are a less derived type than those taken by the delegate. In this example, the delegate takes an `Employee[]` as a parameter, so the new method should take the less derived parameter type `Person[]`.

The following code shows the new version of the `Promote` method.

```
private Executive[] Promote2(Person[] people)
{
    return null;
}
```

The following statement creates a variable that holds a reference to the new version of the `Promote` method.

```
ManagersFromEmployeesDelegate del2 = Promote2;
```

11. The ColorizeImage program, which is available for download on this book's website, does this. Download the program to see how it works. In one test on my dual-core computer, processing an image took roughly 1.78 seconds synchronously and 0.92 seconds asynchronously.

Because the computer has two cores, you might expect the asynchronous version to take one-half the time used by the synchronous version, but there is some overhead in setting up and coordinating the threads. The result is still an impressive reduction in time, however, and would be even greater on a computer with more cores.

12. There would not be a big advantage to using callbacks or `async` and `await`. Those techniques would allow the program's user interface to respond to the user while the program was processing images. The only things the user could do at that time, however, would be to load a new image, close the program, or start more threads processing the images. Letting the user do those things while the program is processing images doesn't seem like it would be useful.

CHAPTER 7

1. The first block of code uses `else` statements, so the program skips all the tests after it finds a match. For example, if `person.Type` is `Customer`, then it skips the tests that compare `person.Type` to `Employee` and `Manager`.

The second block of code performs all three comparisons even if `person.Type` matches one of the early ones. That makes the second block of code slightly less efficient than the first. In this example, where the conditions are simple comparisons, the difference will be small. If the tests called complicated methods, then the difference in speed could be significant.

2. The following code uses a `switch` statement instead of `if` statements.

```
switch (person.Type)
{
    case PersonType.Customer:
        //...
        break;
    case PersonType.Employee:
        //...
        break;
    case PersonType.Manager:
        //...
        break;
}
```

3. A series of `if-else` statements would call the `GetBirthMonth` method 12 times. A `switch` statement would call the method only once. Because `GetBirthMonth` accesses a database, it would be inefficient to call it 12 times instead of once, so the `switch` statement is better.

4. The following code uses a `switch` statement to determine the person's birthstone.

```
string birthstone="";

switch (person.GetBirthMonth())
{
    case 1:
        birthstone = "Garnet";
        break;
    case 2:
        birthstone = "Amethyst";
        break;
    case 3:
        birthstone = "Aquamarine";
        break;
```

```
    case 4:
        birthstone = "Diamond";
        break;
    case 5:
        birthstone = "Emerald";
        break;
    case 6:
        birthstone = "Alexandrite";
        break;
    case 7:
        birthstone = "Ruby";
        break;
    case 8:
        birthstone = "Peridot";
        break;
    case 9:
        birthstone = "Sapphire";
        break;
    case 10:
        birthstone = "Tourmaline";
        break;
    case 11:
        birthstone = "Topaz";
        break;
    case 12:
        birthstone = "Zircon";
        break;
}
```

The problem with the series of if-else statements is that the most obvious version calls the GetBirthMonth method 12 times, once for each if statement. You can avoid those calls if you call the method once and save the result to use in the if statements. The following code shows this version.

```
string birthstone="";
int month = person.GetBirthMonth();

if (month == 1) birthstone = "Garnet";
else if (month == 2) birthstone = "Amethyst";
else if (month == 3) birthstone = "Aquamarine";
else if (month == 4) birthstone = "Diamond";
else if (month == 5) birthstone = "Emerald";
else if (month == 6) birthstone = "Alexandrite";
else if (month == 7) birthstone = "Ruby";
else if (month == 8) birthstone = "Peridot";
else if (month == 9) birthstone = "Sapphire";
else if (month == 10) birthstone = "Tourmaline";
else if (month == 11) birthstone = "Topaz";
else if (month == 12) birthstone = "Zircon";
```

This version is more concise and easier to read than the switch statement. (Actually you can place the case keyword, the line of code, and the break keyword all on one line to make the switch version more concise. It looks a bit crowded but which version you prefer is mostly a matter of personal preference.)

5. To do this in a `switch` statement, you would need 100 separate `case` statements, one for each possible test score. You could reduce that number to 40 `case` statements if you let the default case handle all the values less than 60 (which give the grade F).

In contrast, an `if` statement can evaluate boolean expressions so that each `if` statement can handle a range of test scores. That makes it much more concise.

The following code uses a series of `if` statements to assign grades.

```
int score = 89;
string grade = "";

if (score >= 90) grade = "A";
else if (score >= 80) grade = "B";
else if (score >= 70) grade = "C";
else if (score >= 60) grade = "D";
else grade = "F";
```

6. The following code shows the rewritten loop.

```
int a = 0;
int b = 1;
int c = 1;

for (; a < 1000; )
{
    Console.WriteLine("a: " + a);

    a = b;
    b = c;
    c = a + b;
}
```

7. The following `for` loop adds up the numbers in the array values.

```
int total = 0;
for (int i = 0; i < values.Length; i++)
    total += values[i];
```

8. The following `while` loop adds up the numbers in the array values.

```
int total = 0;
int i = 0;
while (i < values.Length)
{
    total += values[i];
    i++;
}
```

9. The following `do` loop adds up the numbers in the array values.

```
int total = 0;
int i = 0;
do
{
```

```
        total += values[i];
        i++;
    } while (i < values.Length);
```

10. The following `for` loop displays the letters A through Z.

```
for (char ch = 'A'; ch <= 'Z'; ch++)
    Console.WriteLine(ch);
```

11. The following code sets the `Bill` object's `Penalty` property without using the `?:` operator.

```
if (bill.Status == BillStatus.Overdue)
{
    if (bill.Balance < 50m) bill.Penalty = 5m;
    else bill.Penalty = bill.Balance * 0.1m;
}
else
{
    bill.Penalty = 0m;
}
```

12. The following code initializes the `student` variable without using the `??` operator.

```
Student student = GetStudent("Steward Dent");
if (student == null) student = new Student("Steward Dent");
```

13. The following code displays the multiples of 3 between 0 and 100 in largest-to-smallest order.

```
for (int i = 99; i >= 0; i -= 3) Console.WriteLine(i);
```

14. Each time the loop executes, the increment statement doubles the looping variable `i`, so the loop displays the powers of 2 between 1 and 100: 1, 2, 4, 8, 16, 32, and 64.

15. The following code displays Friday the 13ths a year at a time until the user stops it.

```
// Start at the beginning of this year.
int year = DateTime.Now.Year;

// Loop until stopped.
do
{
    for (int month = 1; month <= 12; month++)
    {
        DateTime date = new DateTime(year, month, 13);
        if (date.DayOfWeek == DayOfWeek.Friday)
            Console.WriteLine(date.ToShortDateString());
    }
    year++;
} while (MessageBox.Show("Continue for " + year.ToString() + "?",
    "Continue?", MessageBoxButtons.YesNo) == DialogResult.Yes);
```

16. The following code shows the `foreach` loop without a `continue` statement.

```
foreach (Employee employee in employees)
{
    if (!employee.IsExempt)
    {
```

```
        // Process the employee.
        ...
    }
}
```

This code uses an `if` statement to avoid using a `continue` statement. That causes an extra level of indentation, which makes the code a bit harder to read than the version with the `continue` statement.

If the code contained several tests that allowed it to skip processing an employee, then it would need several `if` tests. That could increase the level of indentation quite a bit. (Alternatively, you could use a single `if` statement with a complicated test.) The `continue` statement avoids that.

The `continue` statement is also useful if there are several places inside the loop where you may discover that you don't need to continue that iteration of the loop.

CHAPTER 8

Note that there may be many solutions to these exercises depending on what kind of information is selected in the LINQ queries and what kind of information is generated in `foreach` loops.

1. Example program FunctionalVolleyballData does this. The code is fairly long, so it isn't shown here. Download the example to see the solution.

2. Simply add the following two lines at the beginning of the example program's `Main` method.

```
XElement root = XElement.Parse(XmlString());
Console.WriteLine(root.ToString());
```

3. There are a couple of ways you can do this. The following code shows one method.

```
// Select the teams.
var teams =
    from team in root.Element("Teams").Descendants("Team")
    select team;

// Loop through the teams displaying them and their players.
foreach (var team in teams)
{
    // Display the team's name.
    Console.WriteLine(team.Attribute("Name").Value);

    // Display the team's players.
    foreach (var player in team.Descendants("Player"))
        Console.WriteLine("     " +
            player.Attribute("FirstName").Value + " " +
            player.Attribute("LastName").Value);
}
```

This code uses LINQ to start at the `root` element, finds that element's `Teams` children (in this case there's only one), and then looks for `Team` descendants of that element. Moving into `Element("Teams")` makes the query only consider elements in the `Teams` subtree. That prevents the query from selecting the `Team` elements that are inside the `Matches` subtree.

After selecting the `Team` elements inside the `Teams` subtree, the code loops through those elements. For each `Team`, the code displays the `Team`'s name and then loops through the `Team`'s `Player` elements, displaying their names.

Another approach uses the following code to select objects with an anonymous type holding the `Teams` and their `Players`.

```
// Select the teams.
var teams =
    from team in root.Element("Teams").Descendants("Team")
    select new
    {
        Team = team,
        Players = team.Descendants("Player")
    };

// Loop through the teams displaying them and their players.
foreach (var team in teams)
{
    // Display the team's name.
    Console.WriteLine(team.Team.Attribute("Name").Value);

    // Display the team's players.
    foreach (var player in team.Players)
        Console.WriteLine("      " +
            player.Attribute("FirstName").Value + " " +
            player.Attribute("LastName").Value);
}
```

Like the preceding solution, this query searches for `Team` elements that are in the `Teams` subtree. It then selects those `Teams` plus their `Player` descendants. The code loops through the selected objects displaying each `Team`'s name and its `Players`.

Example program VolleyballTeamsAndPlayers demonstrates both of these approaches. (These two solutions use similar loops to display their results. The second version feels more LINQ-like, but the first seems more intuitive so I prefer the first solution.)

4. Example program VolleyballTeamsAndScores does this. It uses the following code to match the appropriate team and match score records.

```
// Join teams and match results.
var teamResults =
    from team in root.Element("Teams").Descendants("Team")
    join result in root.Element("Matches").Descendants("Team")
        on team.Attribute("Name").ToString()
            equals result.Attribute("Name").ToString()
    select new
    {
        Team = team.Attribute("Name").Value,
        Score = int.Parse(result.Attribute("Score").Value)
    };

string format = "{0,-20}{1,10}";
Console.WriteLine(string.Format(format, "Team", "Points"));
Console.WriteLine(string.Format(format, "====", "======"));
foreach (var obj in teamResults)
```

```
{
    Console.WriteLine(string.Format(format, obj.Team, obj.Score));
}
```

The query matches `Team` elements inside the `Teams` subtree with `Team` elements inside the `Matches` subtree. For each selected pair, the query selects the team's `Name` attribute and the match result's `Score` attribute.

Notice that the code compares the team and match `Name` attributes after converting them into strings. The attributes themselves are `XAttribute` objects. They hold the same value but the `XAttribute` objects are different, so if you compare those objects you'll never find any matches.

After selecting the corresponding records, the program loops through the query's results and displays the team names and scores.

5.   Example program VolleyballTeamsAndTotals does this. It uses the following code to calculate and display the teams' total wins and points.

```
// Select the teams and their results.
// Total each team's wins and points.
var teamResults =
    from team in root.Element("Teams").Descendants("Team")
    join result in root.Element("Matches").Descendants("Team")
        on team.Attribute("Name").Value
            equals result.Attribute("Name").Value
    group result by team into teamMatches
    orderby teamMatches.Count(r => r.Attribute("Score").Value == "25") descending,
            teamMatches.Sum(r => (int)r.Attribute("Score")) descending
    select new
    {
        Team = teamMatches.Key.Attribute("Name").Value,
        Wins = teamMatches.Count(r => r.Attribute("Score").Value == "25"),
        Points = teamMatches.Sum(r => (int)r.Attribute("Score"))
    };

string format = "{0,-20}{1,10}{2,10}";
Console.WriteLine(string.Format(format, "Name", "Wins", "Points"));
Console.WriteLine(string.Format(format, "====", "====", "======"));
foreach (var results in teamResults)
{
    Console.WriteLine(string.Format(format,
        results.Team, results.Wins, results.Points));
}
```

Like the solution to Exercise 4, this program joins teams with match results. It groups the results by team and calls the groups `teamMatches`.

To determine the number of matches a team won, the query counts the matches where the `Score` attribute has value 25.

To determine a team's total number of points, the query takes the sum of the match values' `Score` attribute values converted into integers.

The query orders its results by both the number of wins and the total number of points. Finally, it selects the team's name together with the number of wins and total number of points.

Next, the program loops through the query and displays the results. Because the query selects simple string and integer values, displaying the results is easy.

6. Example program CreateVolleyballDataSet does this. The code is fairly long, so it isn't shown here. Download the example to see the solution.

7. Example program VolleyballTeamsAndPlayersDataSet does this.

The program demonstrates two approaches. The following code shows the first approach.

```
// Loop through the teams displaying them and their players.
foreach (DataRow team in teamsTable.AsEnumerable())
{
    // Display the team's name.
    Console.WriteLine(team.Field<string>("TeamName"));

    // Select the team's players.
    string teamName = team.Field<string>("TeamName");
    var players =
        from player in playersTable.AsEnumerable()
        where player.Field<string>("TeamName") == teamName
        select player;

    // Display the players.
    foreach (var player in players)
        Console.WriteLine("     " +
            player.Field<string>("FirstName") + " " +
            player.Field<string>("LastName"));
}
```

This code loops through the records from the Teams table. (Note that the items returned by the table's AsEnumerable method are DataRow objects. Note also that you could loop over the table's Rows collection instead of using AsEnumerable.)

For each team, the program displays the team's name, selects the corresponding records in the Players table, and displays the selected players.

The program's second approach uses the following code.

```
// Select the teams joined with the players.
var teams =
    from team in teamsTable.AsEnumerable()
    join player in playersTable.AsEnumerable()
        on team.Field<string>("TeamName") equals player.Field<string>("TeamName")
    group player by team into teamPlayers
    select teamPlayers;

// Loop through the teams displaying them and their players.
foreach (var team in teams)
{
    // Display the team's name.
    Console.WriteLine(team.Key.Field<string>("TeamName"));
```

```
    // Display the team's players.
    foreach (var player in team)
    {
        Console.WriteLine("     " +
            player.Field<string>("FirstName") + " " +
            player.Field<string>("LastName"));
    }
}
```

This code selects records from the `Teams` and `Players` tables, joined on their `TeamName` fields. It groups the players by team.

The program loops through the selected team groups. For each group, it displays the group's team name and then loops through the team's players displaying their names.

8. Example program VolleyBallTeamsAndScoresDataSet uses the following query to select its data.

```
// Join teams and match results.
var teamResults =
    from team in teamsTable.AsEnumerable()
    join result in matchesTable.AsEnumerable()
        on team.Field<string>("TeamName") equals result.Field<string>("TeamName")
    select new
    {
        Team = team.Field<string>("TeamName"),
        Score = result.Field<int>("Score")
    };
```

This query selects data from the `Teams` and `Matches` tables and joins them by `TeamName`. It selects the team names and scores so the program can later display those values.

9. Example program VolleyballTeamsAndTotalsDataSet uses the following query to select its data.

```
// Select the teams and their results.
// Total each team's wins and points.
var teamResults =
    from team in teamsTable.AsEnumerable()
    join result in matchesTable.AsEnumerable()
        on team.Field<string>("TeamName") equals
            result.Field<string>("TeamName")
    group result by team into teamMatches
    orderby teamMatches.Count(r => r.Field<int>("Score") == 25) descending,
        teamMatches.Sum(r => r.Field<int>("Score")) descending
    select new
    {
        Team = teamMatches.Key.Field<string>("TeamName"),
        Wins = teamMatches.Count(r => r.Field<int>("Score") == 25),
        Points = teamMatches.Sum(r => r.Field<int>("Score"))
    };
```

This is similar to the code used in Exercise 5 except it selects its data from tables instead of XElement objects.

10. Example program VolleyballTeamsRankings does this. It uses a query named `pointsFor` that is similar to the one used by the solution to Exercise 9 to select team name, number of wins, and points "for."

Next, the program uses a second query named `pointsAgainst` to select team name, number of losses, and points "against." This query is similar to the first except it matches the `Teams` table's `TeamName` field to the `Matches` table's `VersusTeamName` field.

The program then uses the following query to join the results of the `pointsFor` and `pointsAgainst` queries.

```
// Join the win and loss data.
var combined =
    from dataFor in pointsFor
    join dataAgainst in pointsAgainst
        on dataFor.Team equals dataAgainst.Team
    orderby
        100 * (dataFor.Wins / (float)dataAgainst.Losses) descending,
        dataFor.PointsFor - dataAgainst.PointsAgainst descending
    select new
    {
        Team = dataFor.Team,
        Wins = dataFor.Wins,
        Losses = dataAgainst.Losses,
        WinPercent = 100 *
            (dataFor.Wins / (float)(dataFor.Wins + dataAgainst.Losses)),
        PointsFor = dataFor.PointsFor,
        PointsAgainst = dataAgainst.PointsAgainst,
        PointDifferential = dataFor.PointsFor - dataAgainst.PointsAgainst
    };
```

Finally, the program loops through the selected data and displays the results.

11. Example program AddStandingsToXml does this in two different ways.

The first method uses the same queries as the solution to Exercise 10. After it builds the `combined` query, the program uses the following code to build the new XML elements.

```
// Add the results to a new Standings XML element.
XElement standings = new XElement("Standings");
root.Add(standings);
foreach (var results in combined)
{
    standings.Add(
        new XElement("Team",
            new XAttribute("Name", results.Team),
            new XAttribute("Wins", results.Wins),
            new XAttribute("Losses", results.Losses),
            new XAttribute("WinPercent", results.WinPercent),
            new XAttribute("PointsFor", results.PointsFor),
            new XAttribute("PointsAgainst", results.PointsAgainst),
            new XAttribute("PointDifferential", results.PointDifferential)
        )
    );
}
```

This code starts by creating a new `Standings` `XElement` and adding it to the `root` element. It then loops through the `combined` query. For each item in the query's results, the program uses the item's properties to create a new `Team` element and adds that element to the `Standings` element.

The program's second approach uses the following code.

```
// Join the win and loss data.
var combined =
    from dataFor in pointsFor
    join dataAgainst in pointsAgainst
        on dataFor.Team equals dataAgainst.Team
    orderby
        100 * (dataFor.Wins / (float)dataAgainst.Losses) descending,
        dataFor.PointsFor - dataAgainst.PointsAgainst descending
    select new XElement("Team",
        new XAttribute("Name", dataFor.Team),
        new XAttribute("Wins", dataFor.Wins),
        new XAttribute("Losses", dataAgainst.Losses),
        new XAttribute("WinPercent",
            100 * (dataFor.Wins / (float)(dataFor.Wins + dataAgainst.Losses))),
        new XAttribute("PointsFor", dataFor.PointsFor),
        new XAttribute("PointsAgainst", dataAgainst.PointsAgainst),
        new XAttribute("PointDifferential",
            dataFor.PointsFor - dataAgainst.PointsAgainst)
    );

// Add the results to a new Standings XML element.
root.Add(new XElement("Standings", combined));
```

This version makes the LINQ query create `XElement` objects to represent the standings data. It then creates the `Standings` element and passes that element's constructor the query. Because the query returns an `IEnumerable` containing `XElements`, the constructor makes those elements children of the `Standings` element.

The first approach uses a query that selects the data the program needs and then loops through the query's result to create the `XElements`. The second approach makes the LINQ query create the `XElements`. In general you should use whichever approach you find more intuitive.

CHAPTER 9

1. To allow the program to detect changes to the classes' values, all the values must be converted into properties. The properties' `set` accessors can then validate new values for the properties. The following code shows the revised class.

```
public class Student
{
    private string _Name;
    public string Name
    {
```

```
        get { return _Name; }
        set
        {
            Debug.Assert(value != null, "Name must not be null");
            Debug.Assert(value.Length > 0, "Name must have non-zero length");
            _Name = value;
        }
    }

    private List<Course> _Courses = new List<Course>();
    public List<Course> Courses
    {
        get { return _Courses; }
        set
        {
            Debug.Assert(value != null, "Courses list must not be null");
            _Courses = value;
        }
    }

    // Constructor.
    public Student(string name)
    {
        Name = name;
    }
}
```

Note that the constructor doesn't need to do any validation because it uses the Name property to set the new object's name, and that property performs validation.

(You can find this code in the StudentTest example program in this chapter's downloads.)

2. The following code shows the revised class.

```
public class Student
{
    private string _Name;
    public string Name
    {
        get { return _Name; }
        set
        {
            Contract.Requires(value != null, "Name must not be null");
            Contract.Requires(value.Length > 0, "Name must have non-zero length");
            Contract.Ensures(_Name != null, "Name must not be null");
            Contract.Ensures(_Name.Length > 0, "Name must have non-zero length");
            _Name = value;
        }
    }

    private List<Course> _Courses = new List<Course>();
    public List<Course> Courses
    {
        get { return _Courses; }
        set
```

```
        {
            Contract.Requires(value != null, "Courses list must not be null");
            Contract.Ensures(_Courses != null, "Courses list must not be null");
            _Courses = value;
        }
    }
}

    // Constructor.
    public Student(string name)
    {
        Name = name;
    }
}
```

Could you remove the postconditions? Of course, you could. The preconditions guarantee that the postconditions are satisfied.

That's exactly the sort of thinking that makes developers assume their code is correct when it actually isn't. This is also why it's good to write contracts before writing the code inside the method. Knowing what these property set accessors do, you can convince yourself that the postconditions are unnecessary. In a nontrivial method, the same pressures may lead you to omit the postconditions.

Note that the postconditions are not exactly the same as the preconditions. The preconditions test the inputs to the accessors (if the accessors made other assumptions, the preconditions would verify them, too) and the postconditions check the wanted results.

(You can find this code in the StudentTest example program in this chapter's downloads.)

3. The following code shows the revised class.

```
public class Student
{
    public string Name { get; set; }
    public List<Course> Courses { get; set; }

    // Constructor.
    public Student(string name)
    {
        Name = name;
        Courses = new List<Course>();
    }

    [ContractInvariantMethod]
    private void CheckValuesNotNull()
    {
        Contract.Invariant(this.Name != null);
        Contract.Invariant(this.Name.Length > 0);
        Contract.Invariant(this.Courses != null);
    }
}
```

In this version, the Name and Courses values are auto-implemented properties. Because their set accessors are public methods, they invoke the class's invariant method after they set their values.

Because an auto-implemented property cannot be initialized in its declaration, this version's constructor initializes the object's Courses property so that property is not null when the constructor finishes.

(You can find this code in the StudentTest example program in this chapter's downloads.)

4. The following code shows the revised class.

```
public class Student
{
    private string _Name;
    public string Name
    {
        get { return _Name; }
        set
        {
            if (value == null) throw new ArgumentNullException("Name",
                "Name must not be null");
            if (value.Length <= 0) throw new ArgumentOutOfRangeException("Name",
                "Name must have non-zero length");
            _Name = value;
        }
    }

    private List<Course> _Courses = new List<Course>();
    public List<Course> Courses
    {
        get { return _Courses; }
        set
        {
            if (value == null) throw new ArgumentNullException("Courses",
                "Courses list must not be null");
            _Courses = value;
        }
    }

    // Constructor.
    public Student(string name)
    {
        Name = name;
    }
}
```

(You can find this code in the StudentTest example program in this chapter's downloads).

5. The program will throw an exception if you enter a non-numeric value such as "ten" or "weasel" in the console window. Also if you enter numeric values other than 1, 2, or 3, the program ignores them.

6. The ConsoleUnexpectedInputs example program in this chapter's downloads uses the following code to handle unexpected inputs. The new lines are highlighted in bold.

```
static void Main(string[] args)
{
    // Install the event handler.
    AppDomain.CurrentDomain.UnhandledException += UnhandledException;

    // Loop forever.
    for (; ; )
    {
        Console.WriteLine("1 - Continue, 2 - Throw exception, 3 - Exit");
        Console.Write("> ");
        string text = Console.ReadLine();

        // If the input cannot be parsed, set choice to 0.
        int choice;
        if (!int.TryParse(text, out choice)) choice = 0;

        switch (choice)
        {
            case 1:
                // Continue.
                Console.WriteLine("Continuing...\n");
                break;

            case 2:
                // Throw an exception.
                Console.WriteLine("Throwing exception...\n");
                throw new ArgumentException();

            case 3:
                // Exit.
                return;

            default:
                // Handle other inputs.
                Console.WriteLine("Unexpected input: " + text + "\n");
                break;
        }
    }
}
```

7. The ConsoleTryCatch example program in this chapter's downloads uses the following code to avoid using the UnhandledException event handler.

```
static void Main(string[] args)
{
    // Loop forever.
    for (; ; )
    {
        // Catch all exceptions.
        try
        {
```

```
Console.WriteLine("1 - Continue, 2 - Throw exception, 3 - Exit");
Console.Write("> ");
string text = Console.ReadLine();
int choice = int.Parse(text);

switch (choice)
{
    case 1:
        // Continue.
        Console.WriteLine("Continuing...\n");
        break;

    case 2:
        // Throw an exception.
        Console.WriteLine("Throwing exception...\n");
        throw new ArgumentException();

    case 3:
        // Exit.
        return;
}
}
catch (Exception ex)
{
    Console.WriteLine("Caught exception:");
    Console.WriteLine(ex.Message);
    Console.WriteLine("\n\n");
}
}
}
```

One advantage of this method is that it can prevent the program from closing. An `UnhandledException` event handler cannot.

One disadvantage of this method is that the program could get stuck in an infinite loop. This example doesn't have this problem (at least if you wrote it correctly), but a program could throw an exception, display an error message, and then throw the same exception again when it resumes its main loop. An `UnhandledException` event handler cannot stop the program from ending, so it doesn't have this problem. (Although that's a bit like saying you don't have trouble parking because your car got repossessed. You don't have the problem because you have a worse problem.)

8. The main program calls the `Factorial` method with values entered by the user. The `Debug.Assert` statement and code contracts help flush out bugs during testing, but the user may still enter invalid values in the release build. You could use those methods to look for bugs, but the program needs to handle invalid inputs and run correctly in any case, so it would be more useful to handle problems in `try-catch` blocks.

There are two places the original code can fail: in the `calculateButton_Click` event handler and in the `Factorial` method. The event handler can fail to parse the user's input. The `Factorial` method can fail if its input is negative or too big. Each of those pieces of code should protect itself.

The Factorial example program in this chapter's downloads uses the following code to protect itself from invalid inputs.

```
// Calculate the entered number's factorial.
private void calculateButton_Click(object sender, EventArgs e)
{
    try
    {
        // Clear the result label in case we fail.
        resultLabel.Text = "";

        // Try to parse the number entered by the user.
        long number;
        if (!long.TryParse(numberTextBox.Text, out number))
        {
            MessageBox.Show("Please enter a number.");
            numberTextBox.Select(0, numberTextBox.Text.Length);
            numberTextBox.Focus();
            return;
        }

        // Display the factorial.
        resultLabel.Text = Factorial(number).ToString();
    }
    catch (OverflowException)
    {
        MessageBox.Show("Please enter a number between 0 and 20.");
    }
    catch (ArgumentOutOfRangeException)
    {
        MessageBox.Show("Please enter a number between 0 and 20.");
    }
    catch (Exception ex)
    {
        Console.WriteLine("Exception: " + ex.GetType().Name);
        MessageBox.Show(ex.Message);
    }
}

// Return number!
private long Factorial(long number)
{
    // Make sure the number is non-negative.
    if (number < 0)
        throw new ArgumentOutOfRangeException("number",
            "Argument number must be non-negative.");

    // Check for overflow.
    checked
    {
        long result = 1;
        for (long i = 2; i <= number; i++) result *= i;
        return result;
    }
}
```

The button's event handler does all its work inside a `try-catch` block. The first two `catch` sections display messages that the user can understand. The third `catch` section handles unexpected exceptions. Because it doesn't know what kinds of exceptions to expect, it can't display a user-friendly message. Instead it just writes the exception's name into the Console window (so you can add a `catch` section for it) and displays the exception's message to the user.

The `Factorial` function throws an `ArgumentOutOfRangeException` if its parameter is negative. It then uses a `checked` block to watch for arithmetic errors and calculates the factorial. (See the section "Casting Numbers" in Chapter 4, "Data Types, Variables, and Constants," for a review of `checked` blocks.)

CHAPTER 10

1. The TraceFactorial example program, which is available in this book's downloads, includes code for Exercises 1, 2, and 4. It uses the following code to solve Exercise 1. (Notice how the code needs to separate the recursive call from the `return` statement so that it can display the method's result before returning.)

```
private long Factorial(long number)
{
    Debug.WriteLine("Factorial(" + number.ToString() + ")");
    Debug.Indent();

    long result;
    if (number <= 1) result = 1;
    else result = number * Factorial(number - 1);

    Debug.Unindent();
    Debug.WriteLine("Result: " + result.ToString());
    return result;
}
```

2. The TraceFactorial example program uses the following code to solve Exercise 2.

```
private long Factorial(long number)
{
    long result;
    if (number <= 1) result = 1;
    else result = number * Factorial(number - 1);

    Debug.WriteLine("Factorial(" + number.ToString() +
        ") = " + result.ToString());
    return result;
}
```

3. You can't do this efficiently with `Debug` statements alone because each call to the `Factorial` method would need to know its result so that it can display it before it calls itself recursively. But it needs to call itself recursively to find out its result.

4. One solution is to build a string holding the entire trace and then display it at the end. The TraceFactorial example program uses the following version of the `Factorial` method to solve Exercise 4.

```
private long Factorial(long number, ref string trace)
{
    long result;
    if (number <= 1) result = 1;
    else result = number * Factorial(number - 1, ref trace);

    // Add our information at the beginning of the trace.
    trace = "Factorial(" + number.ToString() +
        ") = " + result.ToString() + '\n' + trace;

    return result;
}
```

The method takes a second `ref` parameter that holds a string containing the method `trace`. When the method is called, it calculates its value by calling itself recursively. The recursive call sets `trace` equal to the trace for the recursive call (and any further recursive calls it makes).

When the recursive call returns, the current method call adds its information to the beginning of the `trace` string.

The program uses the following code to call the `Factorial` method.

```
string trace = "";
resultLabel.Text = Factorial(number, ref trace).ToString();

// Display the trace.
Debug.WriteLine(trace);
```

This code initializes a blank `trace` string, calls the `Factorial` method and then displays `trace`.

5. The DebugLevels example program, which is available in this book's downloads, uses the following code to write appropriate messages.

```
        // Display the message if the debug level is low enough.
        private void PrintMessage(int level, string message)
        {
#if DEBUG1
            if (level <= 1) Console.WriteLine(message);
#elif DEBUG2
            if (level <= 2) Console.WriteLine(message);
#elif DEBUG3
            if (level <= 3) Console.WriteLine(message);
#elif DEBUG4
            if (level <= 4) Console.WriteLine(message);
#elif DEBUG5
            if (level <= 5) Console.WriteLine(message);
#endif
        }
```

An obvious advantage of this method is that it gives as many debugging levels as you like instead of just the two provided by the Debug and Trace classes.

One disadvantage is that it requires you to write a separate line of code for each possible debug level. It also doesn't support trace listeners, so you can't use multiple listeners to send the message to multiple locations the way the Debug and Trace classes can.

You can solve the first problem if you use a variable instead of preprocessor symbols to determine the program's current debugging level. That also lets you load the value in different ways that may be more convenient that recompiling. For example, the program can load the value at run time from a text file, configuration file, or registry setting. Then you could change the debug level and rerun the program without needing to recompile it.

If you make the method use the Trace class to display its results, you can also take advantage of trace listeners.

The following code shows an improved version of the method.

```
// The debug level. Load it from a text file, config file, registry setting, etc.
private int DebugLevel = 2;

// Display the message if the debug level is low enough.
private void PrintMessage(int level, string message)
{
    if (level <= DebugLevel) Trace.WriteLine(message);
}
```

6. The MessageLog example program, which is available in this book's downloads, uses the following code to write messages into the message file.

```
static void Main(string[] args)
{
    // Remove the default Debug listener and
    // add a new TextWriterTraceListener.
    Debug.Listeners.RemoveAt(0);
    Stream stream = File.Open("Messages.txt",
        FileMode.Append, FileAccess.Write, FileShare.Read);
    Debug.Listeners.Add(new TextWriterTraceListener(stream));

    // Make Debug and Trace autoflush.
    Debug.AutoFlush = true;
    Trace.AutoFlush = true;

    // Write some messages.
    Debug.WriteLine(DateTime.Now.ToString() + ": Debug message 1");
    Trace.WriteLine(DateTime.Now.ToString() + ": Trace message 1");
    Console.WriteLine(DateTime.Now.ToString() + ": Console message 1");

    Debug.WriteLine(DateTime.Now.ToString() + ": Debug message 2");
    Trace.WriteLine(DateTime.Now.ToString() + ": Trace message 2");
    Console.WriteLine(DateTime.Now.ToString() + ": Console message 2");

    // Make the user press Enter before exiting.
    Console.WriteLine("Press Enter to exit.");
```

```
        Console.ReadLine();

        // Close the logs.
        Debug.Close();
        Trace.Close();
    }
```

7. The DebugAndTraceLogs example program, which is available in this book's downloads, uses the following code to write messages into the message files.

```
static void Main(string[] args)
{
    // Write some messages.
    LogMessage("DebugLog.txt", "Debug message 1");
    LogMessage("TraceLog.txt", "Trace message 1");
    Console.WriteLine(DateTime.Now.ToString() + ": Console message 1");

    LogMessage("DebugLog.txt", "Debug message 2");
    LogMessage("TraceLog.txt", "Trace message 2");
    Console.WriteLine(DateTime.Now.ToString() + ": Console message 2");

    // Make the user press Enter before exiting.
    Console.WriteLine("Press Enter to exit.");
    Console.ReadLine();

    // Close the logs.
    Debug.Close();
    Trace.Close();
}

// Append a message to a text file.
private static void LogMessage(string filename, string message)
{
    System.IO.File.AppendAllText(filename,
        DateTime.Now.ToString() + ": " +
        message + '\n');
}
```

CHAPTER 11

1. You could add a new `PartTimeProgrammer` but it would duplicate features of the `Secretary` class. The solution is to abstract those two classes to give them a common `HourlyEmployee` parent class. Figure A-2 shows the new hierarchy.

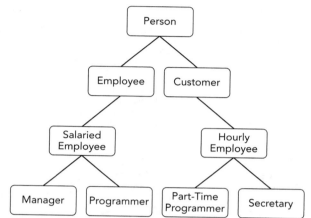

FIGURE A-2: The `HourlyEmployee` class is an abstraction of the `PartTimeProgrammer` and `Secretary` classes.

2. The following code avoids using the `is` statement.

```
foreach (Person person in AllPeople)
{
    Employee employee = person as Employee;
    if (employee != null)
    {
        // Do something Employee-specific with the person...
        ...
    }
}
```

Which version is better is a matter of personal preference and style. There isn't much difference.

3. Figure A-3 shows the inheritance hierarchy.

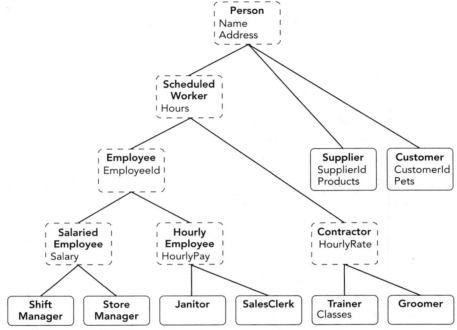

FIGURE A-3: This inheritance hierarchy represents classes used to represent people for a pet store application. Classes with dashed outlines show abstract classes.

The classes with dashed outlines can be abstract because they don't represent concrete real-world objects. For example, the program will never need to create an `Employee` object. Instead it can create an instance of the appropriate kind of `Employee`: `ShiftManager`, `StoreManager`, `Janitor`, or `SalesClerk`. The program can still treat the objects as if they were `Employee` objects if that is convenient.

In fact, the program should make those classes abstract so that no one tries to instantiate them. Trying to create an `Employee` object is probably an indication of a bug. (You can always make a class concrete later if you decide you need to instantiate it.)

You would make the classes abstract by including the `abstract` keyword, but they don't need to contain any abstract members.

4. The PetStoreHierarchy example program shows one way to define the classes shown in Figure A-3. In this solution, each property is defined in only one class and is inherited by other classes.

5. The "is-a" and "has-a" relationships lead to a good solution. A player "is-a" `Human`, `Elf`, or `Dwarf`, and a player "has-a" weapon. That means the `Player` class should be part of an inheritance hierarchy that includes the races. It should have a property that is an instance of a weapon.

Figure A-4 shows the program's inheritance hierarchies.

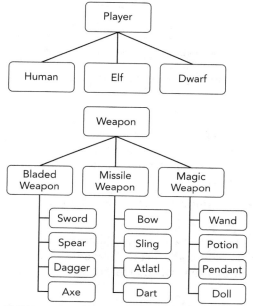

FIGURE A-4: The role-playing game needs two inheritance hierarchies, one for race and one for weapon.

6. This situation is a bit tricky because a player "is-a" race and also "is-a" profession. For example, a specific player "is-a" `Dwarf` and "is-a" `Chemist`. This might suggest that you should use multiple inheritance (implemented with interface inheritance).

The problem with that approach is it would lead to lots of classes to cover all the possible combinations: `Human/Fighter`, `Human/MagicUser`, `Dwarf/Illusionist`, `Elf/Witch`, and so forth. If you have N races and M professions and specialties, you would need to make N × M classes to cover every possible combination. For the example so far, there would be 3 × 8 = 24 such combinations.

A better approach is to think a player "has-a" profession. Then you can give the `Player` class a property to hold the player's profession.

Figure A-5 shows the `Profession` inheritance hierarchies.

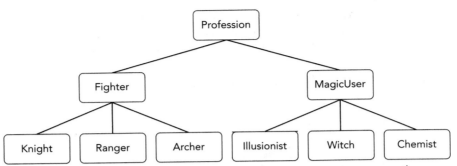

FIGURE A-5: Players can have the generic class `Fighter` or `MagicUser`, so those classes are not abstract.

7. This situation is actually fairly simple as long as you don't try to use inheritance. A developer "is-not-a" department, so there's no inheritance relationship between the developer and the department. Similarly, developer "is-not-a" project, so there's no inheritance relationship between the developer and the project.

In this case, you can simply make the department and any assigned projects be properties of the `Developer` class.

8. The tricky part of this problem is that there are two key inheritance paths: one for students and one for employees. The problem arises from the fact that `TeachingAssistants` and `ResearchAssistants` are both students and employees. (The `StudentId` and `EmployeeId` properties are the clues.)

Figure A-6 shows the inheritance hierarchy. Dashed lines represent multiple inheritance. Alternatively, you could make the lines from `ResearchAssistant` and `TeachingAssistant` to `Student` solid and make the lines from those classes to `Employee` dashed.

This hierarchy changes the names of the `Instructor` properties `CurrentClasses` and `PastClasses` to `CurrentClassesTaught` and `PastClassesTaught` to make them the same as the corresponding properties in the `TeachingAssistant` class. That clarifies the differences between a class that is being taken and a class that is being taught.

Because C# doesn't allow multiple inheritance, you should implement the hierarchy with interface inheritance. The program should define an `IStudent` interface for the `Student`, `ResearchAssistant`, and `TeachingAssistant` classes to implement.

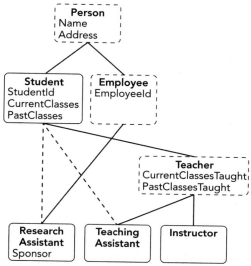

FIGURE A-6: The ResearchAssistant and TeachingAssistant classes use multiple inheritance.

9. The StudentHierarchy example program defines the hierarchy. The most interesting classes are those that implement the IStudent interface. The following code shows the IStudent interface and TeachingAssistant class, which implements it.

```
// A student interface.
public interface IStudent
{
    int StudentId { get; set; }
    string CurrentClasses{ get; set; }
    string PastClasses{ get; set; }
}

public class TeachingAssistant : Person, IStudent
{
    public int StudentId { get; set; }
    public string CurrentClasses { get; set; }
    public string PastClasses { get; set; }
}
```

10. The StudentHierarchy2 example program defines the revised hierarchy. It includes a StudentImplementer class that implements IStudent. The following code shows the updated StudentImplementer and TeachingAssistant classes.

```
// A class that implements IStudent.
public class StudentImplementer : IStudent
{
    public int StudentId { get; set; }
    public string CurrentClasses { get; set; }
```

```
        public string PastClasses { get; set; }
    }

public class TeachingAssistant : Teacher, IStudent
{
    // Delegate IStudent to a private Student object.
    private Student MyStudent = new Student();
    public int StudentId
    {
        get { return MyStudent.StudentId; }
        set { MyStudent.StudentId = value; }
    }
    public string CurrentClasses
    {
        get { return MyStudent.CurrentClasses; }
        set { MyStudent.CurrentClasses = value; }
    }
    public string PastClasses
    {
        get { return MyStudent.PastClasses; }
        set { MyStudent.PastClasses = value; }
    }
}
```

This version has the disadvantage that it is much longer than the previous one. It has the advantage that all the classes that implement IStudent share the same code in the StudentImplementer class because they delegate their properties to an object of that class. That means if you need to debug or modify that code, you can do it in one place.

11. You could do that but the Student class inherits from Person. The TeachingAssistant and ResearchAssistant classes also inherit from Person via a different path through the tree. If you make those classes delegate to Student, they essentially have the Person class in their ancestry twice. In this example, the Person class defines Name and Address properties, so TeachingAssistant and ResearchAssistant have two different ways to define those values. You could simply ignore one, but it would introduce a possible source of confusion and error.

(Languages that allow multiple inheritance have methods for determining which inherited version of a multiply defined property to use.)

12. The new LabAssistant class wouldn't need to worry about the IStudent interface. The ResearchAssistant class already implements that interface, so LabAssistant would inherit its implementation.

CHAPTER 12

The example programs that solve these exercises are fairly long, so their code isn't shown here. Download them to see how they work.

1. Figure A-7 shows this memory arrangement.

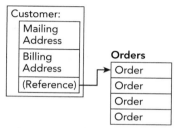

FIGURE A-7: The Customer class contains two embedded Address structures and an array of Order structures.

2. Figure A-8 shows this memory arrangement.

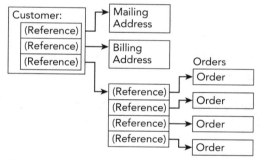

FIGURE A-8: The Customer class contains two references to Address objects and an array of references to Order objects.

3. Because Customer is a class, there is little difference when passing either version of the class. When passing by value, the program sends the method a copy of the Customer object's reference. When passing by reference, the program sends the method a reference to the original reference to the Customer object. In either case, the method receives only a reference, so the program doesn't need to send much data to the method.

If Customer were a structure passed by reference, the program would still need to pass only a reference into the method, so there would be little difference between the two structures.

If Customer were a structure passed by value, the program would need to copy the Customer instance and send the copy to the method. The version of Customer used in Exercise 1 would require the program to copy two Address structures and a reference to the Orders array. The version of `Customer` used in Exercise 2 would require the program to copy only references to the two `Address` objects and a reference to the `Orders` array. If the `Address` structure or class is large, the version used by Exercise 2 would be more efficient because it would pass only references to `Address` objects instead of copying `Address` structures entirely. (However, unless the `Address` structure or class is *really* large, the practical difference will be small. In that case, you should pick the design that makes the most logical sense instead of worrying about a tiny performance difference.)

4. If you "invoke" an event handler and no object is registered to receive it, the program throws a `System.NullReferenceException`.

5. The BankAccount example program does this.

6. The OverdraftAccount example program does this.

7. The OnOverdrawn example program does this.

8. The OverdraftAccount2 example program does this. When you run the modified program and try to reduce the account balance to a value less than –$100.00, the program does not display a message box, but it doesn't update the balance either.

The program behaves this way because this version of the `OverdraftAccount` class hides the `Overdrawn` event but overrides the `Balance` property.

The main program uses this code to create its account object.

```
private BankAccount Account = new OverdraftAccount();
```

This code creates an `OverdraftAccount` object but saves it in a `BankAccount` variable.

Later, the program uses the following code to register to receive the `Overdrawn` event.

```
Account.Overdrawn += Account_Overdrawn;
```

Because the variable `Account` has type `BankAccount`, this registers the event handler to catch the `BankAccount` version of the `Overdrawn` event. (If the `OverdraftAccount` class overrode the event instead of hid it, this statement would register the event handler to catch the `OverdraftAccount` version of the event.)

Finally, the `OverdraftAccount` class overrides the `Balance` property. When the program tries to set the account's balance to a value below –$100.00, the `set` accessor raises the `Overdrawn` event and refuses to update the balance. But it raises the `OverdraftAccount` version of the event and the main program registered to receive the `BankAccount` version. Because no code registered to receive the `OverdraftAccount` version of the event, the event handler doesn't execute.

(This example shows the difference between hiding and overriding an event.)

9. The DelegatedCustomEvent example program does this.

10. The CustomEvent example program does this.

11. The StudentFactory example program does this.

CHAPTER 13

1. First, you can use the following directive to define an alias for the `System.Security`
`.Cryptography` namespace.

```
using Crypto = System.Security.Cryptography;
```

Then, you can refer to the class as `Crypto.SHA512Managed`.

Second, you can use the following directive.

```
using System.Security.Cryptography;
```

Then, you can refer to the class as `SHA512Managed`.

The second solution is more concise but the first is more self-documenting because it tells you
where the class is defined. That can be useful when the class has such a non-intuitive name.

2. First, you could use the fully qualified namespaces for each of the classes. This would be
explicit but verbose.

Second, you could include a `using` directive such as the following to allow easy use of one
of the namespaces.

```
using System.Windows.Controls;
```

Now you can use the `System.Windows.Controls` version of the class without any namespace
prefix. You would need to fully qualify the `System.Globalization` version of the class. This
approach is more concise than the previous version but using the `System.Windows.Controls`
version of the class with no namespace might be confusing because you would need to remember which namespace had a `using` directive.

Third, you could use the following code to define aliases for both namespaces.

```
using Global = System.Globalization;
using Control = System.Windows.Controls;
```

Now you can use the abbreviations to refer to both classes. This is more concise than fully
qualified namespaces but still reminds you of each class's namespace.

The OrderTracker example program demonstrates the solutions to Exercises 3 through 8. Note that
there may be more than one valid solution to each exercise.

3. Code in the `Algorithms` namespace could use the following code.

```
public OrderClasses.Order order1;
public CustomerTools.Fulfillment.Order order2;
```

4. Code in the `OrderTools` namespace could use the following code.

```
public CustomerTools.Fulfillment.Order order1;
public OrderClasses.Order order2;
```

5. You could include the following `using` directives to define the aliases. (You could use different names for the aliases.)

```
using Ord = OrderTracker.OrderTools.OrderClasses;
using Ful = OrderTracker.CustomerTools.Fulfillment;
```

Code in the `Algorithms` namespace could then use the following code to define objects with those aliases.

```
public Ord.Order order1;
public Ful.Order order2;
```

6. You could define an alias for the `OrderTracker.CustomerTools.Fulfillment` class as in Exercise 5. The code could use the other `Order` class without any namespace or alias. The following code shows how the `Customer` class could define both kinds of objects.

```
public Order order1;
public Ful.Order order2;
```

7. The `Billing` namespace doesn't define any classes with names that are used elsewhere in the hierarchy, so you can add the following `using` directive.

```
using OrderTracker.CustomerTools.Billing;
```

Now all code can use the `Invoice` class without including any namespace information.

8. The most obvious improvement would be to rename the classes so that there are no duplicate names. Perhaps you could change the name of the `Fulfillment` namespace's `Order` class to `Shipment` or `PackingList` (depending on the purpose of that class).

A second improvement would be to flatten the namespace hierarchy. The hierarchy doesn't actually help developers keep the code separate. You can do that just as easily by placing different pieces of code in separate modules.

Often namespace hierarchies arise because pieces of an application are implemented in different libraries. The libraries have different namespaces to protect them from name collisions with the other libraries. In this example, however, it's unlikely that each namespace represents a separate library. For example, it's unlikely that the `Fulfillment` and `Billing` code can work without the `Customer` class, so they probably weren't developed as separate libraries.

A final simplification might be to merge the two `Order` classes into a single class. Whether that would be better than leaving them as two separate classes depends on how much they overlap. If they are practically the same class, then merging them would simplify the application. If they serve different purposes, then it may be better to keep them as separate classes.

CHAPTER 14

1. The PalindromeChecker example program uses the following code to do this. The key code is highlighted in bold.

```
private void palindromeTextBox_TextChanged(object sender, EventArgs e)
{
```

```
        string text = palindromeTextBox.Text.ToLower().Replace(" ", "");
        string reverse = new string(text.Reverse().ToArray());
        if (text == reverse)
        {
            isAPalindromeLabel.Text = "is a palindrome";
            isAPalindromeLabel.ForeColor = Color.Green;
        }
        else
        {
            isAPalindromeLabel.Text = "is not a palindrome";
            isAPalindromeLabel.ForeColor = Color.Red;
        }
    }
```

The highlighted code uses the Reverse method to reverse the string's characters and get an IEnumerable<char> holding the string's characters reversed. Next, it uses ToArray to convert the IEnumerable<char> into a char[]. It then passes the char[] to the string class's constructor to get a string holding the reverse of the original string.

Finally, the program compares the original and reversed strings and updates its display to indicate whether they are the same.

2. The BookLists example program uses the following code to create and initialize its dictionary of lists.

```
// The book data.
private Dictionary<string, List<string>> Books =
    new Dictionary<string, List<string>>()
    {
        {"Stephen King",
            new List<string>()
            {"Carrie", "The Shining", "The Stand"}
        },
        {"Tom Clancy",
            new List<string>()
            {"The Hunt for Red October", "Red Storm Rising", "Patriot Games"}
        },
        {"Agatha Christie",
            new List<string>()
            {"The Mysterious Affair at Styles", "The Thirteen Problems"}
        },
    };
```

The dictionary's initialization code contains three key/value pairs. The keys are author names. The values are List<string> objects initialized to hold book titles.

When it loads, the program uses the following code to display the author names.

```
// Display the authors.
private void Form1_Load(object sender, EventArgs e)
{
    var authors =
        from entry in Books
        orderby entry.Key
        select entry.Key;
```

```
        authorListBox.DataSource = authors.ToArray();
}
```

This code uses LINQ to select the keys (author names). It converts the result into an array and displays the names by setting the author `ListBox`'s `DataSource` property.

When the user clicks on an author, the following code displays that author's book titles.

```
// Display the books by the selected author.
private void authorListBox_SelectedIndexChanged(object sender, EventArgs e)
{
    string author = authorListBox.SelectedItem.ToString();
    List<string> books = Books[author];
    booksListBox.DataSource = books;
}
```

This code gets the selected author's name and then uses it to get the value for that author. The value is a `List<string>` containing the author's book titles. The program converts that into an array and displays the result in the book `ListBox`.

3. The BookNameValueCollection example program uses the following code to create and initialize its `NameValueCollection`.

```
// The book data.
private NameValueCollection Books =
    new NameValueCollection
    {
        {"Stephen King",
            "Carrie,The Shining,The Stand"},
        {"Tom Clancy",
            "The Hunt for Red October,Red Storm Rising,Patriot Games"},
        {"Agatha Christie",
            "The Mysterious Affair at Styles,The Thirteen Problems"},
    };
```

The collection's initialization code contains three name/value pairs. The keys are author names. Each of the values is a string holding an author's book titles separated by commas.

When it loads, the program uses the following code to display the author names.

```
// Display the authors.
private void Form1_Load(object sender, EventArgs e)
{
    var authors =
        from name in Books.AllKeys
        orderby name
        select name;
    authorListBox.DataSource = authors.ToArray();
}
```

This code uses LINQ to select the `NameValueCollection`'s keys (author names). It converts the result into an array and displays the names by setting the author `ListBox`'s `DataSource` property.

When the user clicks on an author, the following code displays that author's book titles.

```
// Display the books by the selected author.
private void authorListBox_SelectedIndexChanged(object sender, EventArgs e)
{
    string author = authorListBox.SelectedItem.ToString();
    string value = Books[author];
    string[] books = value.Split(',');
    booksListBox.DataSource = books;
}
```

This code gets the selected author's name and then uses it to get the value for that author. It uses the `Split` method to split the value string into an array of book titles and sets the books `ListBox`'s `DataSource` property to the resulting array.

4. The CarList example program does this. Download the example to see how it works.

5. The ReverseList example program uses the following code to create and reverse its list of characters.

```
private void Form1_Load(object sender, EventArgs e)
{
    // Make the original list.
    List<char> original = new List<char>() { 'A', 'B', 'C', 'D', 'E' };
    originalListTextBox.Text = new string(original.ToArray());

    // LINQ.
    var linq =
        from char letter in original
        orderby letter descending
        select letter;
    linqTextBox.Text = new string(linq.ToArray());

    // Reverse.
    List<char> reversed = new List<char>(original);
    reversed.Reverse();
    reverseTextBox.Text = new string(reversed.ToArray());

    // Stack.
    Stack<char> stack = new Stack<char>();

    // Add the characters to the stack.
    foreach (char ch in original) stack.Push(ch);

    // Remove the characters from the stack.
    List<char> result = new List<char>();
    while (stack.Count > 0) result.Add(stack.Pop());

    // Display the result.
    stackTextBox.Text = new string(result.ToArray());
}
```

6. A method that returns a collection is similar to an iterator, and you can use a `foreach` loop to enumerate the items returned by either.

One difference is that a method returning a collection would need to generate all the items at once and add them to the collection before the `foreach` loop started. In contrast, the iterator generates items only as they are needed by the `foreach` loop. That can save some work if the program doesn't know how many items it must examine before it can stop.

For example, suppose the program must loop through `Employee` objects until it finds one that hasn't used 40 hours of work yet this week. A method that returned a collection would have to build a collection containing every `Employee`. An iterator would only yield `Employee` objects until the program found one that worked. The program could then exit its `foreach` loop. (Exercise 8 gives you a chance to try this.)

7. The ListPrimes example program does this. It uses the following `Primes` iterator.

```
// Enumerate prime numbers between startNumber and stopNumber.
public IEnumerable Primes(int startNumber, int stopNumber)
{
    // Define a lambda method that tests
    // primality of odd numbers at least 3.
    Func<int, bool> isPrime = x =>
    {
        for (int i = 3; i * i <= x; i += 2)
            if (x % i == 0) return false;
        return true;
    };

    // Return 2 if it is between startNumber and stopNumber.
    if ((2 >= startNumber) && (2 <= stopNumber)) yield return 2;

    // Make sure startNumber is positive and odd.
    if (startNumber < 3) startNumber = 3;
    if (startNumber % 2 == 0) startNumber++;

    // Loop through odd numbers in the range.
    for (int i = startNumber; i <= stopNumber; i += 2)
    {
        // If this number is prime, enumerate it.
        if (isPrime(i)) yield return i;
    }
}
```

The program uses the following code to display the primes.

```
// List primes between the two numbers.
private void listPrimesButton_Click(object sender, EventArgs e)
{
    int startNumber = int.Parse(startNumberTextBox.Text);
    int stopNumber = int.Parse(stopNumberTextBox.Text);

    primesListBox.Items.Clear();
    foreach (int i in Primes(startNumber, stopNumber))
        primesListBox.Items.Add(i);
}
```

8. The ListAllPrimes example program does this. It uses the following `AllPrimes` iterator.

```
// Enumerate prime numbers indefinitely.
public IEnumerable AllPrimes()
{
    // Define a lambda method that tests
    // primality of odd numbers at least 3.
    Func<int, bool> isPrime = x =>
    {
        for (int i = 3; i * i <= x; i += 2)
            if (x % i == 0) return false;
        return true;
    };

    // Return 2.
    yield return 2;

    // Loop through odd numbers.
    for (int i = 3; ; i += 2)
    {
        // If this number is prime, enumerate it.
        if (isPrime(i)) yield return i;
    }
}
```

The main program uses the following code to list primes.

```
// List primes between the two numbers.
private void listPrimesButton_Click(object sender, EventArgs e)
{
    int stopNumber = int.Parse(stopNumberTextBox.Text);

    primesListBox.Items.Clear();
    foreach (int i in AllPrimes())
    {
        if (i > stopNumber) break;
        primesListBox.Items.Add(i);
    }
}
```

CHAPTER 15

1. The PriorityQueue example program does this. The most interesting part of the program is the following `PriorityQueue` class.

```
public class PriorityQueue<TKey, TValue>
    where TKey : IComparable<TKey>
{
    // The list to hold the keys and values.
    List<KeyValuePair<TKey, TValue>> List =
        new List<KeyValuePair<TKey, TValue>>();

    // Add an item to the queue.
```

```csharp
        public void Enqueue(TKey key, TValue value)
        {
            List.Add(new KeyValuePair<TKey, TValue>(key, value));
        }

        // Remove an item from the queue.
        public void Dequeue(out TKey key, out TValue value)
        {
            if (List.Count == 0)
                throw new InvalidOperationException("The PriorityQueue is empty");

            // Find the item with the lowest valued key.
            int bestIndex = 0;
            TKey bestKey = List[0].Key;
            for (int index = 1; index < List.Count; index++)
            {
                // See if this key is less than the previous best key.
                TKey testKey = List[index].Key;
                if (testKey.CompareTo(bestKey) < 0)
                {
                    // Save this key.
                    bestIndex = index;
                    bestKey = testKey;
                }
            }

            // Return the best pair.
            key = bestKey;
            value = List[bestIndex].Value;

            // Remove the pair we are returning.
            List.RemoveAt(bestIndex);
        }

        // Return the number of items in the list.
        public int Count
        {
            get { return List.Count; }
        }
    }
}
```

The class's declaration includes generic type parameters for the keys and values that the program will store. To find the key with the lowest value, the class must compare keys so the TKey type must implement IComparable<TKey>.

The class uses a List<KeyValuePair<TKey, TValue>> to hold the keys and values. The Enqueue method simply adds a new KeyValuePair object to the list.

The Dequeue method loops through the list to find the pair with the lowest key. It sets its return values and then removes that pair from the list.

The PriorityQueue class's Count property returns the number of items in the list. The example program uses that property to determine when the list is empty, so the Dequeue button should be disabled.

Download the example to see other details.

2. The IncreasingQueue example program does this. The following code shows the IncreasingQueue class.

```
public class IncreasingQueue<T>
    where T : IComparable<T>
{
    // The queue that holds the items.
    private Queue<T> Items = new Queue<T>();

    // The previously added item.
    private T LastValue;

    // Constructor.
    public IncreasingQueue(T lowerBound)
    {
        LastValue = lowerBound;
    }

    // Enqueue.
    public void Enqueue(T value)
    {
        // If this isn't the first item, make sure
        // it's bigger than the previous value.
        if (value.CompareTo(LastValue) <= 0)
            throw new ArgumentOutOfRangeException("value",
                "New value was not larger than the previous value");

        // Add the item.
        Items.Enqueue(value);

        // Save this value.
        LastValue = value;
    }

    // Dequeue.
    public T Dequeue()
    {
        return Items.Dequeue();
    }

    // Return the number of items.
    public int Count
    {
        get { return Items.Count; }
    }
}
```

This class takes a single generic type parameter. Like the previous example, this program needs to compare items, so the type T must implement IComparable<T>.

The class starts by declaring a Queue<T> to hold the queue's items. It then declares variable LastValue to keep track of the last value added to the queue.

The class's constructor sets LastValue to the lower bound it receives as a parameter.

The Enqueue method does the most interesting work. It compares the new value to the last value added to the queue and throws an exception if the new value is not larger. If the new value is okay, the method adds it to the queue and updates LastValue.

The rest of the class simply delegates the Dequeue method and the Count property to its internal queue.

Download the example to see other details.

3. The following code shows one possible BoundValues method.

```
public static class NumberMethods
{
    // Make sure all values are between lowerBound and upperBound.
    public static void BoundValues<T>(T[] values, T lowerBound, T upperBound)
        where T : IComparable<T>
    {
        for (int i = 0; i < values.Length; i++)
        {
            if (values[i].CompareTo(lowerBound) < 0)
                values[i] = lowerBound;
            if (values[i].CompareTo(upperBound) > 0)
                values[i] = upperBound;
        }
    }
}
```

Notice that the NumberMethods class isn't generic but the BoundValues method is. The method simply loops through the array setting any values that are out of bounds to the upper or lower bound.

4. The following code shows one possible BoundValues method.

```
public static class NumberMethods
{
    // Make sure all values are between lowerBound and upperBound.
    public static List<T> BoundValues<T>(IEnumerable<T> values,
        T lowerBound, T upperBound)
        where T : IComparable<T>
    {
        List<T> result = new List<T>();
        foreach (T value in values)
        {
            if (value.CompareTo(lowerBound) < 0)
                result.Add(lowerBound);
            else if (value.CompareTo(upperBound) > 0)
                result.Add(upperBound);
            else
                result.Add(value);
        }
        return result;
    }
}
```

This code creates a List<T>. Then for each item in the IEnumerable<T>, it adds one of the item, the lower bound, or the upper bound to the result list. After it finishes its loop, the method returns the list.

5. The following code shows one possible MiddleValue method.

```
public static class NumberMethods
{
    public static T MiddleValue<T>(T value1, T value2, T value3)
        where T : IComparable<T>
    {
        T[] values = new T[] { value1, value2, value3 };
        Array.Sort(values);
        return values[1];
    }
}
```

This method saves the three values into an array, sorts the array, and returns the middle value.

6. The following code shows one possible CircularQueue class.

```
public class CircularQueue<T>
{
    // A list to hold items.
    private List<T> List = new List<T>();

    // The index of the current item.
    private int CurrentItem = -1;

    // Add an item to the queue.
    public void Enqueue(T value)
    {
        List.Add(value);
    }

    // Return the next item in the queue.
    public T NextItem()
    {
        if (List.Count == 0)
            throw new InvalidOperationException("The CircularQueue is empty");

        // Move to the next item, wrapping around to 0 if necessary.
        CurrentItem = (CurrentItem + 1) % List.Count;

        // Return the item.
        return List[CurrentItem];
    }
}
```

7. The following code shows one possible Bundle class.

```
public class Bundle<T>
{
    List<T> List = new List<T>();

    public void Add(T value)
```

```
    {
        List.Add(value);
    }

    public override string ToString()
    {
        string result = "";
        foreach (T value in List)
            result += ";" + value.ToString();
        if (result.Length > 0) result = result.Substring(1);
        return result;
    }
}
```

8. The following code shows one possible revised Bundle class.

```
public class Bundle<T> : List<T>
{
    public override string ToString()
    {
        string result = "";
        foreach (T value in this)
            result += ";" + value.ToString();
        if (result.Length > 0) result = result.Substring(1);
        return result;
    }
}
```

CHAPTER 16

1. The PrintStars example program does this. The following code shows the program's BeginPrint event handler.

```
// The number of pages printed.
private int NumPagesPrinted = 0;

// Start at the first page.
private void starsPrintDocument_BeginPrint(object sender, PrintEventArgs e)
{
    NumPagesPrinted = 0;
}
```

This code declares the NumPagesPrinted variable to keep track of the number of pages that have been printed. The BeginPrint event handler simply sets that value to 0 before starting a new print job.

The following code shows the program's PrintPage event handler.

```
// Draw stars on three pages.
private void starsPrintDocument_PrintPage(object sender, PrintPageEventArgs e)
{
    switch (++NumPagesPrinted)
```

```
    {
        case 1:
            DrawStar(5, e);
            break;
        case 2:
            DrawStar(7, e);
            break;
        case 3:
            DrawStar(9, e);
            break;
    }
    e.HasMorePages = (NumPagesPrinted < 3);
}
```

This code simply increments the page number and calls the following `DrawStar` method, passing the number of points the star should have and the `PrintPageEventArgs` object.

```
// Draw a star with a given number of points.
private void DrawStar(int numPoints, PrintPageEventArgs e)
{
    // Find the center of the page.
    double cx = (e.MarginBounds.Left + e.MarginBounds.Right) / 2;
    double cy = (e.MarginBounds.Top + e.MarginBounds.Bottom) / 2;

    // Calculate the radius.
    double radius = e.MarginBounds.Width / 2;

    // Get the points.
    List<PointF> points = StarPoints(cx, cy, radius, numPoints);

    // Draw the star.
    e.Graphics.SmoothingMode = SmoothingMode.AntiAlias;
    using (Pen pen = new Pen(Color.Blue, 20))
    {
        e.Graphics.DrawPolygon(pen, points.ToArray());
    }
}
```

The `DrawStar` method does all the interesting work. First, it calculates the center of the printed page and the radius it will use to find the points on the star. It uses one-half of the page's width for that radius.

Next, the code calls the `StarPoints` method shown in the exercise's statement to get the points that make up the star. It finishes by drawing a polygon that connects the points.

2. The PrintName example program does this. The following code shows the program's `PrintPage` event handler.

```
// Draw the name.
private void namePrintDocument_PrintPage(object sender, PrintPageEventArgs e)
{
    // Insert your name here.
    const string name = "Rod Stephens";
```

```
    // Loop through bigger and bigger fonts until the name won't fit.
    int bestSize = 10;
    for (int fontSize = 10; ; fontSize++)
    {
        // Make a font if this size.
        using (Font font = new Font("Times New Roman", fontSize))
        {
            // See if the name will fit.
            SizeF size = e.Graphics.MeasureString(name, font);
            if (size.Width > e.MarginBounds.Width)
            {
                // Use this size.
                bestSize = fontSize - 1;
                break;
            }
        }
    }

    // Print the name with the best font size.
    using (Font font = new Font("Times New Roman", bestSize))
    {
        // Measure the text at this font size.
        SizeF size = e.Graphics.MeasureString(name, font);

        // Center the text.
        float x = e.MarginBounds.Left + (e.MarginBounds.Width - size.Width) / 2;
        float y = e.MarginBounds.Top + (e.MarginBounds.Height - size.Height) / 2;

        // Draw the name.
        e.Graphics.DrawString(name, font, Brushes.Green, x, y);
    }

    // We're done.
    e.HasMorePages = false;
}
```

This code starts with a font size of 10 points and loops through bigger and bigger font sizes. For each size, it uses `e.Graphics.MeasureString` to see how big the string will be when printed at that size. When it reaches a size that's too big, the code saves the previous size (that last one that let the name fit) and breaks out of its loop.

The code then makes a font with the best size and draws the name centered.

3. The PrintPrimes example program does this. The following code shows the program's `PrintPage` event handler.

```
// Print primes.
private void primesPrintDocument_PrintPage(object sender, PrintPageEventArgs e)
{
    // Draw the margin bounds.
    e.Graphics.DrawRectangle(Pens.Red, e.MarginBounds);

    // Keep track of the next available X coordinate.
    float x = e.MarginBounds.Left;
    float y = e.MarginBounds.Top;
```

```
    // Make the font.
    using (Font font = new Font("Times New Roman", 12))
    {
        // Measure a line's height.
        SizeF size = e.Graphics.MeasureString("M", font);

        // Print primes.
        foreach (int prime in AllPrimes())
        {
            // Draw this prime.
            e.Graphics.DrawString(prime.ToString(),
                font, Brushes.Black, x, y);

            // Move to the next line.
            y += size.Height * 1.2f;

            // See if we're out of room.
            if (y + size.Height > e.MarginBounds.Bottom) break;
        }
    }

    // We're done.
    e.HasMorePages = false;
}
```

The event handler starts by drawing the margin bounds. It then sets the x and y variables to the coordinates of the margin bounds' upper-left corner.

The code makes a 12-point font. It measures the M character in the font to calculate line height.

The event handler then loops indefinitely through the values generated by the AllPrimes iterator. See the solution to Chapter 14, "Collection Classes," Exercise 8 for information about that iterator.

For each prime, the program draws the prime and increases y by the height of a line. It then checks to see if there is enough room to draw the next line of text. If the program has run out of room, it exits its foreach loop and is done.

4. The WpfStars example program does this. Download the example to see the details.

5. The WpfFixedStars example program does this. The following code shows the most interesting parts of the program.

```
// Create the FixedDocument's pages.
private void window_Loaded(object sender, RoutedEventArgs e)
{
    // Add the pages.
    starsFixedDocument.Pages.Add(MakePage(5));
    starsFixedDocument.Pages.Add(MakePage(7));
    starsFixedDocument.Pages.Add(MakePage(9));
}

// Make a PageContent object with a star on it.
private PageContent MakePage(int numPoints)
```

```
{
    // Build this hierarchy:
    //  PageContent
    //      FixedPage
    //          Grid
    //              Polygon
    PageContent pageContent = new PageContent();
    pageContent.Width = 850;
    pageContent.Height = 1100;

    FixedPage fixedPage = new FixedPage();
    fixedPage.Width = 850;
    fixedPage.Height = 1100;
    pageContent.Child = fixedPage;

    Grid grid = new Grid();
    fixedPage.Children.Add(grid);

    Polygon star = new Polygon();
    star.Stroke = Brushes.Blue;
    star.StrokeThickness = 20.0;
    star.Points = StarPoints(425, 550, 300, numPoints);
    grid.Children.Add(star);

    // Return the PageContent object.
    return pageContent;
}
```

At design time, I gave the XAML code a FixedDocument element named starsFixedDocument. When the program's window loads, the window_Loaded event handler executes. It calls the MakePage method three times to generate three pages of content and adds those pages to the starsFixedDocument element's Pages collection.

The MakePage method creates a PageContent element that contains a FixedPage element. It sets the sizes of those elements to 850 by 1100 (8.5" by 11").

Next, the method adds a Grid. It then adds a Polygon to the Grid. It uses the StarPoints method to generate the polygon's points. This method is based on the code given as a hint for Exercise 1.

Finally, the method returns the PageContent object that contains all the content. (Download the solution for additional details.)

CHAPTER 17

1. Example program SystemEnvironment does this. The program uses the following code to display the values in a dictionary returned by a call to GetEnvironmentVariables.

```
// Display the values in this dictionary.
private void ShowValues(ListBox lst, IDictionary values)
{
    foreach (string key in values.Keys)
```

```
        lst.Items.Add(key + " = " + values[key].ToString());
}
```

The program uses this method as in the following code, which adds the machine-level environment variables to the `valuesListBox`.

```
ShowValues(valuesListBox,
    System.Environment.GetEnvironmentVariables(
        EnvironmentVariableTarget.Machine));
```

2. Example program VisualStudioVersion uses the following code to do this.

```
versionLabel.Text = "Visual Studio version " +
    System.Environment.GetEnvironmentVariable(
        "VisualStudioVersion");
```

This is a process-level variable defined by Visual Studio when it starts. It is inherited by the executing program because Visual Studio starts that program. If you run the program outside of Visual Studio, the variable hasn't been defined, so the program cannot display the version.

3. Example program ShowPaths uses the following code to do this.

```
// Display the paths in the Path variable.
private void Form1_Load(object sender, EventArgs e)
{
    string paths = System.Environment.GetEnvironmentVariable("PATH");
    pathsListBox.DataSource = paths.Split(new char[] { ';' });
}
```

4. Example program SaveControlValues does this. It uses the `RegistryTools` class and `SetValue` and `GetValue` methods similar to those described in the chapter. The following code shows how the program saves and restores `TextBox` and `ComboBox` values.

```
// Load TextBox and ComboBox values.
private void Form1_Load(object sender, EventArgs e)
{
    foreach (Control ctl in Controls)
    {
        if (ctl is TextBox) ctl.Text = GetValue(ctl.Name, ctl.Text);
        else if (ctl is ComboBox) ctl.Text = GetValue(ctl.Name, ctl.Text);
    }
}

// Save TextBox and ComboBox values.
private void Form1_FormClosing(object sender, FormClosingEventArgs e)
{
    foreach (Control ctl in Controls)
    {
        if (ctl is TextBox) SetValue(ctl.Name, ctl.Text);
        else if (ctl is ComboBox) SetValue(ctl.Name, ctl.Text);
    }
}
```

5. Example program ConfigLabel uses the following code to make its label use the font specified in the config file.

```
private void Form1_Load(object sender, EventArgs e)
{
    greetingsLabel.Font = Properties.Settings.Default.GreetingFont;
}
```

(Alternatively, you could bind the label's font to the dynamic setting. Then you wouldn't need to use code to set it at run time.)

If you modify the config file and run the compiled executable, you see the new font. In fact, if you run the program from Visual Studio, you still see the new font because the modified config file is in the same directory as the executable being run by Visual Studio.

If you delete the config file and run the compiled executable, you get the original font back. Next, if you run the program from Visual Studio, you get the original font and Visual Studio replaces the original config file.

6. Example program LocalizedStrings uses the following code to do this.

```
public Form1()
{
    // Set the culture and UI culture to French.
    Thread.CurrentThread.CurrentCulture = new CultureInfo("fr-FR");
    Thread.CurrentThread.CurrentUICulture = new CultureInfo("fr-FR");

    InitializeComponent();
}

// Display a greeting.
private void Form1_Load(object sender, EventArgs e)
{
    MessageBox.Show(MyStrings.Greeting);
}
```

When the program loads the fr-FR locale, it displays the message Salut. Visual Studio creates a subdirectory named fr and puts the localized resource file LocalizedStrings.resources.dll in it.

7. Example program ShowCurrency uses the following code to do this.

```
private void Form1_Load(object sender, EventArgs e)
{
    DateTime date = DateTime.Now;
    decimal amount = 12345.67m;
    string[] cultures =
        { "fr-FR", "de-DE", "de-CH", "es-MX", "es-ES", "en-US", "en-GB" };

    foreach (string culture in cultures)
    {
        Thread.CurrentThread.CurrentCulture = new CultureInfo(culture);
        resultsListBox.Items.Add(culture + "\t" +
            date.ToShortDateString() + "\t" +
            amount.ToString("C"));
    }
}
```

The following text shows sample results.

```
fr-FR    21/04/2014    12 345,67 €
de-DE    21.04.2014    12.345,67 €
de-CH    21.04.2014    Fr. 12'345.67
es-MX    21/04/2014    $12,345.67
es-ES    21/04/2014    12.345,67 €
en-US    4/21/2014     $12,345.67
en-GB    21/04/2014    £12,345.67
```

CHAPTER 18

1. The WriteIntoMemoryStream example program contains the following commented out code to do this.

```
// Create the stream.
using (MemoryStream stream = new MemoryStream())
{
    // Write into the stream.
    using (BinaryWriter writer = new BinaryWriter(stream))
    {
        writer.Write(textTextBox.Text);

        // Read from the stream.
        stream.Seek(0, SeekOrigin.Begin);
        using (BinaryReader reader = new BinaryReader(stream))
        {
            MessageBox.Show(reader.ReadString());
        }
    }
}
```

Which version seems easier to read is a matter of personal preference. The way the parentheses nest the `BinaryReader` inside the `BinaryWriter`'s using statement seems odd to me, but you should use whichever technique seems most natural to you.

2. If you don't free a stream attached to a file, the file may remain locked until the program ends. While it is locked, you may be unable to read, edit, or delete the file.

In contrast, if you don't free a memory stream, the stream's memory remains allocated until the program ends.

A locked file can affect other programs and can be annoying if you try to read or delete the file with Windows Explorer. Locked memory doesn't actually affect other programs, so in some sense failing to free a file stream is worse than failing to free a memory stream. (Both are sloppy programming, however.)

3. The LoadAndSaveFile example program uses the following code to do this.

```
// Load the file, if it exists.
private void Form1_Load(object sender, EventArgs e)
{
    // See if the file exists.
```

```
        if (File.Exists("Notes.txt"))
        {
            // Read the file.
            using (StreamReader reader = new StreamReader("Notes.txt"))
            {
                notesTextBox.Text = reader.ReadToEnd();
            }
        }
    }

    // Save the file.
    private void Form1_FormClosing(object sender, FormClosingEventArgs e)
    {
        using (StreamWriter writer = File.CreateText("Notes.txt"))
        {
            writer.Write(notesTextBox.Text);
        }
    }
```

4. The `WriteLine` method adds a new line after the text it is writing into the file. When the program starts, it reads that new line as part of the text it displays in the `TextBox`. If the program uses `WriteLine` to save the text, it will write the original new line plus another one into the file. The result is the program adds another new line every time it starts and stops. (Try it and see.)

You can avoid that by using the `Write` method instead of `WriteLine`.

5. The LoadAndSaveFileWithPrompt example program uses the following Form_Closing event handler to prompt the user if the text file exists.

```
    // Save the file.
    private void Form1_FormClosing(object sender, FormClosingEventArgs e)
    {
        // See if the file exists.
        if (File.Exists("Notes.txt"))
        {
            // Prompt the user.
            DialogResult result =
                MessageBox.Show("The file exists. Do you want to overwrite it?",
                    "Overwrite?",
                    MessageBoxButtons.YesNoCancel,
                    MessageBoxIcon.Question);

            // If the user clicked No, exit without saving.
            if (result == DialogResult.No) return;

            // If the user clicked Cancel, cancel.
            if (result == DialogResult.Cancel)
            {
                e.Cancel = true;
                return;
            }

            // If the user clicked Yes, continue to overwrite the file.
        }
```

```
    // Save the text.
    using (StreamWriter writer = File.CreateText("Notes.txt"))
    {
        writer.Write(notesTextBox.Text);
    }
}
```

6. The IsFileSorted example program uses the following `FileIsSorted` method to determine whether a file's contents are sorted.

```
// Return true if the file's lines are sorted.
// This method throws an exception if the file doesn't exist.
private bool FileIsSorted(string filename)
{
    // Open the file.
    using (StreamReader reader = new StreamReader(filename))
    {
        // Start with a line <= any string.
        string previousLine = "";

        // Read the lines.
        while (!reader.EndOfStream)
        {
            string nextLine = reader.ReadLine();
            if (nextLine.CompareTo(previousLine) < 0) return false;
            previousLine = nextLine;
        }
    }

    // If we get here, the file is sorted.
    return true;
}
```

7. The StreamPrimes example program uses the following code to display primes and write them in the text file. The modified code is highlighted in bold.

```
// List primes between the two numbers.
private void listPrimesButton_Click(object sender, EventArgs e)
{
    int stopNumber = int.Parse(stopNumberTextBox.Text);

    primesListBox.Items.Clear();

    using (StreamWriter writer = new StreamWriter("Primes.txt"))
    {
        foreach (int i in AllPrimes())
        {
            if (i > stopNumber) break;
            primesListBox.Items.Add(i);
            writer.Write(i.ToString() + " ");
        }
    }
}
```

The code that defines the `AllPrimes` iterator is the same as in the earlier program, so it isn't shown here. See the solution to Exercise 14-8 for that code.

8. The StreamPrimesBinary example program uses the following code to display primes and write them in the data file.

```
// List primes between the two numbers.
private void listPrimesButton_Click(object sender, EventArgs e)
{
    int stopNumber = int.Parse(stopNumberTextBox.Text);

    primesListBox.Items.Clear();

    // Generate and list the primes.
    foreach (int i in AllPrimes())
    {
        if (i > stopNumber) break;
        primesListBox.Items.Add(i);
    }

    // Create a file stream.
    using (FileStream stream = new FileStream("Primes.dat", FileMode.Create))
    {
        // Create an associated BinaryWriter.
        using (BinaryWriter writer = new BinaryWriter(stream))
        {
            // Save the number of primes.
            writer.Write(primesListBox.Items.Count);

            // Save the primes.
            for (int i = 0; i < primesListBox.Items.Count; i++)
            {
                writer.Write((int)primesListBox.Items[i]);
            }
        }
    }
}
```

This version is different in two main ways. First, it uses a `BinaryWriter` instead of a `StreamWriter`. Because it uses a `BinaryWriter`, it needs to create a file stream first for the `BinaryWriter` to manipulate.

The second main difference is that it enumerates the primes before it starts writing the file. Because it needs to save the number of primes at the beginning of the file, it needs to have generated the primes before it writes the file so it knows how many there are.

The following code shows how the program loads the saved primes when the program starts.

```
// Load the saved primes.
private void Form1_Load(object sender, EventArgs e)
{
    if (File.Exists("Primes.dat"))
    {
        // Create a file stream.
        using (FileStream stream = new FileStream("Primes.dat", FileMode.Open))
```

```
        {
            // Create an associated BinaryReader.
            using (BinaryReader reader = new BinaryReader(stream))
            {
                // Get the number of primes.
                int numPrimes = reader.ReadInt32();

                // Read the primes.
                for (int i = 0; i < numPrimes; i++)
                {
                    primesListBox.Items.Add(reader.ReadInt32());
                }
            }
        }
    }
}
```

If the file exists, the program creates a `FileStream` and an associated `BinaryReader`. The reader first reads the number of primes the file holds and then reads that many primes.

CHAPTER 19

1. The GetDirectoryTimes example program uses the following code to display a directory's times.

```
private void getTimesButton_Click(object sender, EventArgs e)
{
    string dirname = directoryTextBox.Text;
    creationTimeTextBox.Text =
        Directory.GetCreationTime(dirname).ToString();
    accessTimeTextBox.Text =
        Directory.GetLastAccessTime(dirname).ToString();
    writeTimeTextBox.Text =
        Directory.GetLastWriteTime(dirname).ToString();
}
```

2. The GetSetFileTimes example program does this. The code that gets the file's times is similar to the code shown for the solution to Exercise 19-1 except it works with a file instead of a directory. The following code shows how the program sets the file's times.

```
private void setTimesButton_Click(object sender, EventArgs e)
{
    string filename = fileTextBox.Text;
    Directory.SetCreationTime(filename,
        DateTime.Parse(creationTimeTextBox.Text));
    Directory.SetLastAccessTime(filename,
        DateTime.Parse(accessTimeTextBox.Text));
    Directory.SetLastWriteTime(filename,
        DateTime.Parse(writeTimeTextBox.Text));
    MessageBox.Show("Done");
}
```

3. The GetSetFileAttributes example program does this. The following code shows how the program gets a file's attributes. The program gets all of the attributes in the same way, so only
a few are shown here.

```
private void getAttributesButton_Click(object sender, EventArgs e)
{
    string filename = fileTextBox.Text;
    FileAttributes attributes = File.GetAttributes(filename);

    archiveCheckBox.Checked =
        (int)(attributes & FileAttributes.Archive) != 0;
    compressedCheckBox.Checked =
        (int)(attributes & FileAttributes.Compressed) != 0;
    deviceCheckBox.Checked =
        (int)(attributes & FileAttributes.Device) != 0;
    ...
}
```

The following code shows how the program sets a file's attributes. The program sets all of the attributes in the same way, so only a few are shown here.

```
private void setAttributesButton_Click(object sender, EventArgs e)
{
    string filename = fileTextBox.Text;
    FileAttributes attributes = 0;

    if (archiveCheckBox.Checked) attributes |= FileAttributes.Archive;
    if (compressedCheckBox.Checked) attributes |= FileAttributes.Compressed;
    if (deviceCheckBox.Checked) attributes |= FileAttributes.Device;
    ...

    File.SetAttributes(filename, attributes);
    MessageBox.Show("Done");
}
```

Note that the filesystem won't allow certain combinations of attributes. For example, the Normal attribute means the file has no other associated attributes. If the program tries to set conflicting attributes, the SetAttributes method silently fixes them.

Also the program cannot set some attributes. For example, setting the Compressed attribute does not magically compress a file and setting the Directory attribute cannot turn a file into a directory. If the program tries to set one of these attributes, the SetAttributes method silently ignores them.

4. The LoadAndSaveFile2 example program uses the following code to do this.

```
// Load the saved file.
private void Form1_Load(object sender, EventArgs e)
{
    if (File.Exists("Notes.txt"))
        notesTextBox.Text = File.ReadAllText("Notes.txt");
}

// Save the text.
```

```
private void Form1_FormClosing(object sender, FormClosingEventArgs e)
{
    File.WriteAllText("Notes.txt", notesTextBox.Text);
}
```

This is much simpler than the solution to Exercise 18-3, which uses file streams to read and write the notes file. (Unless you noticed the `File` class's `ReadAllText` and `WriteAllText` methods while you were working on Exercise 18-3. In that case, well done! But you might want to repeat the exercise using streams just to see what they're like.)

5. The SortFileLines example program uses the following code to do this.

```
private void sortFileButton_Click(object sender, EventArgs e)
{
    string filename = fileTextBox.Text;
    string[] lines = File.ReadAllLines(filename);
    Array.Sort(lines);
    File.WriteAllLines(filename, lines);

    // Display the result.
    resultTextBox.Text = File.ReadAllText(filename);
}
```

6. The ListDriveProperties example program uses the following code to do this.

```
private void Form1_Load(object sender, EventArgs e)
{
    string results = "";
    foreach (DriveInfo info in DriveInfo.GetDrives())
    {
        results += info.Name +
            "\r\n    DriveType: " + info.DriveType.ToString() +
            "\r\n    IsReady: " + info.IsReady.ToString() +
            "\r\n    RootDirectory: " + info.RootDirectory.ToString() +
            "\r\n";
        if (info.IsReady)
        {
            results +=
                "    AvailableFreeSpace: " + info.AvailableFreeSpace.ToString() +
                "\r\n    DriveFormat: " + info.DriveFormat.ToString() +
                "\r\n    TotalFreeSpace: " + info.TotalFreeSpace.ToString() +
                "\r\n    TotalSize: " + info.TotalSize.ToString() +
                "\r\n    VolumeLabel: " + info.VolumeLabel +
                "\r\n";
        }
        resultsTextBox.Text = results;
    }
}
```

7. The ListDrivePropertiesWithSizes example program does this. This version of the program uses the following `ToFileSize` method to format a file size.

```
public static string ToFileSize(long value)
{
```

```
    string[] suffixes = { "bytes", "KB", "MB", "GB", "TB",
        "PB", "EB", "ZB", "YB" };
    for (int i = 0; i < suffixes.Length; i++)
    {
        if (value <= (Math.Pow(1024, i + 1)))
        {
            return ThreeNonZeroDigits(value / Math.Pow(1024, i)) + " " +
                suffixes[i];
        }
    }

    return ThreeNonZeroDigits(value / Math.Pow(1024, suffixes.Length - 1)) +
        " " + suffixes[suffixes.Length - 1];
}
```

This code finds the first power i where value $\leq 1024^{i+1}$. It then divides the value by 1024^i and returns the value's first three digits with the appropriate suffix: KB, GB, and so forth.

For example, suppose the value is 10,000,000. Then $1024^3 = 1,073,741,824$ is greater than 10,000,000, so the code divides 10,000,000 by $1024^2 = 1,048,576$ and gets 9.54. The method returns 9.54 MB.

The following code shows the ThreeNonZeroDigits method, which returns a value's first three digits.

```
private static string ThreeNonZeroDigits(double value)
{
    if (value >= 100)
    {
        // No digits after the decimal.
        return value.ToString("0,0");
    }
    else if (value >= 10)
    {
        // One digit after the decimal.
        return value.ToString("0.0");
    }
    else
    {
        // Two digits after the decimal.
        return value.ToString("0.00");
    }
}
```

If the value is at least 100, then it has three digits before the decimal point. In that case the method simply returns the value with any digits after the decimal point removed.

If the value is less than 100 but at least 10, the method returns the value formatted with one digit after the decimal point.

If the value is less than 10, the method returns the value formatted with two digits after the decimal point.

8. The ShowGrandparent example program uses the following code to do this.

```
private void Form1_Load(object sender, EventArgs e)
{
    grandparentTextBox.Text = Path.GetFullPath(
        Path.Combine(Application.StartupPath, "..\\.."));
}
```

If you run the program near the top of the directory hierarchy, the result is simply the top of the hierarchy. For example, if you run the program in the directory C:\, the program displays C:\.

9. The FindFiles example program uses the following code to do this.

```
private void searchButton_Click(object sender, EventArgs e)
{
    filesListBox.Items.Clear();
    foreach (string filename in Directory.GetFiles(
        directoryTextBox.Text, patternTextBox.Text,
        SearchOption.AllDirectories))
    {
        filesListBox.Items.Add(filename);
    }
}
```

10. The FindFilesAndSizes example program uses the following code to do this.

```
private void searchButton_Click(object sender, EventArgs e)
{
    string results = "";
    foreach (string filename in Directory.GetFiles(
        directoryTextBox.Text, patternTextBox.Text,
        SearchOption.AllDirectories))
    {
        FileInfo info = new FileInfo(filename);
        results += info.Name + "\r\n";
        results += "    " + ToFileSize(info.Length) + "\r\n";
    }
    filesTextBox.Text = results;
}
```

11. The WatchForChanges example program uses the following event handlers to display information about directory changes in the resultsTextBox.

```
private void myFileSystemWatcher_Changed(object sender, FileSystemEventArgs e)
{
    resultsTextBox.AppendText(
        DateTime.Now.ToShortDateString() + ": Changed " +
        e.Name + "\r\n");
}

private void myFileSystemWatcher_Created(object sender, FileSystemEventArgs e)
{
    resultsTextBox.AppendText(
        DateTime.Now.ToShortDateString() + ": Created " +
```

```
            e.Name + "\r\n");
    }

    private void myFileSystemWatcher_Deleted(object sender, FileSystemEventArgs e)
    {
        resultsTextBox.AppendText(
            DateTime.Now.ToShortDateString() + ": Deleted " +
            e.Name + "\r\n");
    }

    private void myFileSystemWatcher_Renamed(object sender, RenamedEventArgs e)
    {
        resultsTextBox.AppendText(
            DateTime.Now.ToShortDateString() + ": Renamed " +
            e.Name + "\r\n");
    }
```

12. The MoveToRecycleBin example program uses the following code to move a file into the recycle bin.

```
// Move the file into the recycle bin.
private void recycleButton_Click(object sender, EventArgs e)
{
    FileSystem.DeleteFile(fileTextBox.Text,
        UIOption.OnlyErrorDialogs,
        RecycleOption.SendToRecycleBin);
    MessageBox.Show("Done");
}
```

CHAPTER 20

1. The DownloadFile example program uses the following code to do this.

```
try
{
    using (WebClient client = new WebClient())
    {
        client.DownloadFile(urlTextBox.Text, fileTextBox.Text);
    }
    MessageBox.Show("Done");
}
catch (Exception ex)
{
    MessageBox.Show(ex.Message);
}
```

2. The DownloadString example program uses the following code to do this.

```
try
{
    using (WebClient client = new WebClient())
    {
        webBrowser1.Document.Body.InnerHtml =
```

```
            client.DownloadString(urlTextBox.Text);
        }
    }
    catch (Exception ex)
    {
        MessageBox.Show(ex.Message);
    }
```

3. The DownloadStringTaskAsync example program does this. The main change is to the Download button's `Click` event handler shown in the following code. Notice the `async` and `await` keywords highlighted in bold.

```csharp
// Start downloading.
async private void downloadButton_Click(object sender, EventArgs e)
{
    // Get ready to give feedback.
    webBrowser1.Navigate("about:blank");
    downloadProgressBar.Value = 0;
    downloadStatusLabel.Text = "0%";
    downloadButton.Enabled = false;
    cancelButton.Enabled = true;
    Cursor = Cursors.WaitCursor;

    // Make a Uri.
    Uri uri = new Uri(urlTextBox.Text);

    // Start the download.
    Client = new WebClient();
    Client.DownloadProgressChanged += Client_DownloadProgressChanged;

    try
    {
        // Start the download.
        string result = await Client.DownloadStringTaskAsync(uri);

        // Display the result in the WebBrowser.
        webBrowser1.Document.Body.InnerHtml = result;
    }
    catch (WebException ex)
    {
        if (ex.Status == WebExceptionStatus.RequestCanceled)
            MessageBox.Show("Canceled");
        else
            MessageBox.Show(ex.Message);
    }
    catch (Exception ex)
    {
        MessageBox.Show(ex.Message);
    }
    Client.Dispose();

    // Remove the feedback.
    downloadProgressBar.Value = 0;
    downloadStatusLabel.Text = "";
    downloadButton.Enabled = true;
```

```
        cancelButton.Enabled = false;
        Cursor = Cursors.Default;
}
```

The code is the same as the previous version up to the point where the program calls DownloadStringTaskAsync. In the DownloadStringAsync program, the DownloadStringCompleted event handler performs error handling. This program doesn't have a DownloadStringCompleted event handler so error handling must occur here. (Even if you do use a DownloadStringCompleted event handler, the code that calls DownloadStringTaskAsync must perform error handling.)

If the call to DownloadStringTaskAsync throws a WebException, the code determines whether the request was canceled and displays an appropriate message if it was. If any other exception occurred, the code displays its message text.

After the try-catch block, the code performs the tasks that were in the previous program's DownloadStringCompleted event handler.

4. Removing the DownloadStringCompleted event handler is nice but the program still needs to declare its WebClient object at the module level so that the Cancel button's Click event handler can use it. The code also has a separate DownloadProgressChanged event handler. That means the code managing the download is still split into several pieces and the program cannot dispose of the WebClient with a using statement.

If you don't provide download progress and you don't allow the user to cancel the download, then only the Download button's Click event handler needs to use the WebClient. That means you can declare and create the WebClient in that event handler inside a using statement. You also don't need any event handlers. The code is much simpler but it is also less powerful because it doesn't provide progress reports or allow canceling.

5. The DownloadStream example program uses the following code to do this.

```
using (WebClient client = new WebClient())
{
    using (Stream stream = client.OpenRead(urlTextBox.Text))
    {
        // Use the stream to create a Bitmap.
        Bitmap bitmap = new Bitmap(stream);

        // Display the result.
        imagePictureBox.Image = bitmap;
    }
}
```

6. The DownloadStreamAsync example program uses the following code to do this.

```
// The WebClient.
private WebClient Client;

// Download the image file.
private void downloadButton_Click(object sender, EventArgs e)
{
    imagePictureBox.Image = null;
```

```
        // Request the data stream.
        Uri uri = new Uri(urlTextBox.Text);
        Client = new WebClient();
        Client.OpenReadCompleted += Client_OpenReadCompleted;
        Client.OpenReadAsync(uri);
    }

    // Cancel the request.
    private void cancelButton_Click(object sender, EventArgs e)
    {
        Client.CancelAsync();
    }

    // Process the stream.
    private void Client_OpenReadCompleted(object sender, OpenReadCompletedEventArgs e)
    {
        // See what the result was.
        if (e.Error != null)
        {
            MessageBox.Show(e.Error.Message);
        }
        else if (e.Cancelled)
        {
            MessageBox.Show("Canceled");
        }
        else
        {
            // Get the data from the stream.
            // (You must close the stream when finished.)
            using (Stream stream = e.Result)
            {
                // Use the stream to create a Bitmap.
                Bitmap bitmap = new Bitmap(stream);

                // Display the result.
                imagePictureBox.Image = bitmap;
            }
        }

        // Make the form big enough.
        Size size = new Size(
            Math.Max(imagePictureBox.Right + 12, ClientSize.Width),
            Math.Max(imagePictureBox.Bottom + 12, ClientSize.Height));
        ClientSize = size;
    }
```

7. The DownloadData example program uses the following code to do this.

```
using (WebClient client = new WebClient())
{
    byte[] bytes = client.DownloadData(urlTextBox.Text);

    // Make a stream associated with the bytes.
    using (MemoryStream stream = new MemoryStream(bytes))
```

```
    {
        // Make a bitmap from the stream.
        Bitmap bitmap = new Bitmap(stream);

        // Display the result.
        imagePictureBox.Image = bitmap;
    }
}
```

8. The WebRequestDownloadData example program uses the following code to do this.

```
try
{
    // Make the WebRequest.
    WebRequest request = WebRequest.Create(urlTextBox.Text);

    // Use the Get method to download the file.
    request.Method = WebRequestMethods.Http.Get;

    // Get the response.
    WebResponse response = request.GetResponse();

    // Get the image from the response stream.
    // (You must close the stream when finished.)
    using (Stream stream = response.GetResponseStream())
    {
        Bitmap bitmap = new Bitmap(stream);

        // Display the result.
        imagePictureBox.Image = bitmap;
    }
}
catch (Exception ex)
{
    MessageBox.Show(ex.Message);
}
```

9. The UploadFile example program uses the following code to do this.

```
try
{
    WebClient client = new WebClient();
    client.Credentials = new NetworkCredential(
        usernameTextBox.Text, passwordTextBox.Text);
    client.UploadFile(urlTextBox.Text, fileTextBox.Text);
    MessageBox.Show("Done");
}
catch (Exception ex)
{
    MessageBox.Show(ex.Message);
}
```

10. The UploadString example program uses the following code to do this.

```
try
{
    WebClient client = new WebClient();
    client.Credentials = new NetworkCredential(
        usernameTextBox.Text, passwordTextBox.Text);
    client.UploadString(urlTextBox.Text, stringTextBox.Text);
    MessageBox.Show("Done");
}
catch (Exception ex)
{
    MessageBox.Show(ex.Message);
}
```

11. The WebRequestUploadFile example program uses the following code to upload a `byte` array.

```
// Upload an array of bytes into a file.
private void UploadBytesIntoFile(byte[] bytes, string url,
    string username, string password)
{
    // Make the WebRequest.
    WebRequest request = WebRequest.Create(url);

    // Use the UploadFile method.
    request.Method = WebRequestMethods.Ftp.UploadFile;

    // Set network credentials.
    request.Credentials = new NetworkCredential(username, password);

    // Write the bytes into the request stream.
    using (Stream stream = request.GetRequestStream())
    {
        stream.Write(bytes, 0, bytes.Length);
    }
}
```

The program then uses the following method to upload files.

```
// Upload a file.
private void UploadFile(string filename, string url, string username,
    string password)
{
    // Read the file's contents into a byte array.
    byte[] bytes = File.ReadAllBytes(filename);

    // Upload the bytes into a file.
    UploadBytesIntoFile(bytes, url, username, password);
}
```

This method uses `File.ReadAllBytes` to read the file's contents into a `byte` array. It then calls `UploadBytesIntoFile` to upload the array.

12. The WebRequestUploadString example program uses the same `UploadBytesIntoFile` method used by the solution to Exercise 11. The following `UploadString` method uses `UploadBytesIntoFile` to upload a string.

```
// Upload a string into a file.
private void UploadString(string text, string url,
    string username, string password)
{
    // Convert the text into a byte array.
    byte[] bytes = Encoding.UTF8.GetBytes(text);

    // Write the bytes into the file.
    UploadBytesIntoFile(bytes, url, username, password);
}
```

This code uses `Encoding.UTF8.GetBytes` to convert the string into a `byte` array. It then calls `UploadBytesIntoFile` to upload the array.

13. The FtpListDirectory example program uses the following `FtpGetShortDirectoryListing` method to get a directory listing.

```
// Use FTP to get a directory's file list.
private List<string> FtpGetShortDirectoryList(string url,
    string username, string password)
{
    // Make the FtpWebRequest.
    WebRequest request = WebRequest.Create(url);
    request.Method = WebRequestMethods.Ftp.ListDirectory;

    // Set network credentials.
    request.Credentials = new NetworkCredential(username, password);

    using (WebResponse response = request.GetResponse())
    {
        using (StreamReader streamReader =
            new StreamReader(response.GetResponseStream()))
        {
            // Read the response's lines.
            List<string> files = new List<string>();
            while (!streamReader.EndOfStream)
            {
                files.Add(streamReader.ReadLine());
            }
            return files;
        }
    }
}
```

This method creates the `WebRequest`, sets its `Method` and `Credentials` properties, calls `GetResponse`, and calls `GetResponseStream` as usual. Each line of text in the response stream gives information about one file.

The main program calls `FtpGetShortDirectoryList` and displays the files' information in a `ListBox`.

14. The FtpListDirectoryDetail example program does this. The only difference between this version and the solution to Exercise 13 is the following statement that sets the `WebRequest` object's `Method` property.

```
request.Method = WebRequestMethods.Ftp.ListDirectoryDetails;
```

15. The FtpListDirectoryBySize example program lists files ordered by file size. It assumes the directory listing has a format similar to the one returned for the directory `ftp://nssdcftp .gsfc.nasa.gov/photo_gallery/hi-res/astro`.

The program stores information about the files in instances of the following `FileData` class.

```
// A class to hold file size information.
private class FileData
    : IComparable<FileData>
{
    public string Info;
    public long Length;
    public FileData(string info)
    {
        Info = info;
        string lengthString =
            info.Split(new char[] { ' ' },
                StringSplitOptions.RemoveEmptyEntries)[4];
        Length = long.Parse(lengthString);
    }
    public override string ToString()
    {
        return Info;
    }

    // Compare to another FileData.
    public int CompareTo(FileData other)
    {
        return Length.CompareTo(other.Length);
    }
}
```

The class provides an initializing constructor to make creating new instance easier. The program displays `FileData` objects in a `ListBox`, so it overrides the class's `ToString` method so the `ListBox` can display the files' data.

The class implements the `IComparable<FileData>` interface so the program can sort `FileData` objects.

To get the directory listing, this program uses a method similar to the one used by the solution to Exercise 14. The difference is the new version returns a list of `FileData` objects representing the files instead of a list of `strings`.

The following code shows how the program invokes that method, sorts the result, and displays the sorted `FileData` objects in its `ListBox`.

```
try
{
    // Get the directory's file data.
```

```
        FileData[] files =
            FtpGetDetailedDirectoryList(
                urlTextBox.Text, usernameTextBox.Text,
                passwordTextBox.Text).ToArray();

        // Sort the data.
        Array.Sort(files);

        // Display the result.
        filesListBox.DataSource = files;
    }
    catch (Exception ex)
    {
        MessageBox.Show(ex.Message);
    }
```

16. The SendEmailWithCc example program does this. The main difference between this program and the SendEmail example program is that this program uses the following code to add the CC e-mail name address to the `MailMessage`.

```
// Add the CC address.
if ((ccEmail.Length > 0) && (ccName.Length > 0))
    message.CC.Add(new MailAddress(ccEmail, ccName));
```

17. The SendEmailWithBcc example program does this. The main difference between this program and the solution to Exercise 16 is that this program uses the following code to add the BCC e-mail addresses to the `MailMessage`.

```
// Add the BCC addresses.
if (bccEmails.Length > 0) message.Bcc.Add(bccEmails);
```

Here the string `bccEmails` is a comma-delimited list of e-mail addresses.

18. The SendSms example program does this. The code to send the SMS e-mail is included in the SendEmail example program, so it isn't repeated here. Download the SendSms program to see the details.

CHAPTER 21

1. The CompressSpaces example program uses the following code to do this.

```
// Replace multiple whitespace with single spaces.
private void FixString()
{
    string text = inputTextBox.Text;

    // Remove initial and trailing whitespace.
    text = Regex.Replace(text, @"^\s*", "");
    text = Regex.Replace(text, @"\s*$", "");

    // Replace multiple whitespace with single spaces.
    text = Regex.Replace(text, @"\s+", " ");
```

```
    // Display the result.
    resultTextBox.Text = "[" + text + "]";
}
```

The code uses the `Regex` class's `Replace` method three times. First, it matches any number of whitespace characters at the beginning of the string and replaces them with an empty string. It then does the same for whitespace characters at the end of the string.

Next, the code searches for one or more occurrences of whitespace anywhere in the string and replaces those with a single space. It then displays the result.

2. The ListWords example program uses the following code to do this.

```
// List the words.
private void listWordsButton_Click(object sender, EventArgs e)
{
    string text = inputTextBox.Text;

    // Remove apostrophes. (They don't separate words.)
    text = text.Replace("'", "");

    // Split using groups of non-word characters as delimiters.
    string[] words = Regex.Split(text, @"\W+");

    // Display the words.
    wordsListBox.DataSource = words;
}
```

The code first removes apostrophes because they don't represent the beginning of a new word. It uses `Regex.Split` to split the string into pieces delimited by strings of one or more nonword characters and displays the result in its `ListBox`.

3. The ListMatches example program uses the following code to do this.

```
// Display matches in the ListBox.
private void FindMatches()
{
    matchesListBox.Items.Clear();
    try
    {
        // Make the regex object.
        Regex regex = new Regex(patternTextBox.Text);

        // Find the matches.
        foreach (Match match in regex.Matches(inputTextBox.Text))
        {
            // Display the matches.
            matchesListBox.Items.Add(match.Value);
        }
    }
    catch (Exception ex)
    {
        matchesListBox.Items.Add(ex.Message);
    }
}
```

This code calls the `Regex` object's `Matches` method and loops through the result, adding each match to the `ListBox`.

The reason it produces more than just three strings is the regular expression `\w*` matches zero or more occurrences of word characters. For example, the spot between two semicolons matches the expression because it contains zero or more word characters.

You can fix this by changing the regular expression to `\w+` so that it matches one or more word characters.

4. The following text shows a regular expression that allows the program to parse phone numbers with or without area codes. The bold characters show the changes that make the area code optional.

    `^((?<NPA>[2-9][0-8]\d)-)?(?<NXX>[2-9][0-9]{2})-(?<XXXX>\d{4})$`

    If a phone number is missing an area code, the program simply leaves the NPA value blank.

5. The ParsePhoneNumbers example program uses the following code to do this. The code that gives the `Regex` object the `Multiline` option is highlighted in bold.

```
// Find matching groups.
private void parseButton_Click(object sender, EventArgs e)
{
    groupsListBox.Items.Clear();

    Regex regex = new Regex(patternTextBox.Text, RegexOptions.Multiline);
    foreach (Match match in regex.Matches(inputTextBox.Text))
    {
        groupsListBox.Items.Add(
            "NPA: " + match.Groups["NPA"] +
            ", NXX: " + match.Groups["NXX"] +
            ", XXXX: " + match.Groups["XXXX"]);
    }
}
```

The following text shows a regular expression that works for this example. The code that removes the trailing [Return] character on each line is highlighted in bold.

    `^(?<NPA>[2-9][0-8]\d)-(?<NXX>[2-9][0-9]{2})-(?<XXXX>\d{4})\s*$`

6. The following text shows a regular expression that matches this kind of integer.

    `^[-+]?\d{1,3}(,\d{3})*$`

    The `[-+]?` matches a - or + sign zero or one times.

    The `\d{1,3}` matches between one and three digits.

    The next group contains `,\d{3}`, which matches a comma followed by exactly three digits. The group is followed by `*` so it can appear zero or more times.

7. The following text shows a regular expression that matches this kind of floating-point number.

```
^[-+]?\d+(\.\d+)?$
```

The `[-+]?` matches a - or + sign zero or one times.

The `\d+` matches one or more digits.

The `\.\d+` matches a decimal point followed by one or more digits. That group is followed by `?` so it can appear zero or one times, so the expression won't match strings with multiple decimal points.

8. The following text shows a regular expression that matches this kind of floating-point number.

```
^[-+]?\d{1,3}(,\d{3})*(\.\d+)?$
```

The `[-+]?` matches a - or + sign zero or one times.

The `\d{1,3}` matches between one and three digits.

The next group contains `,\d{3}`, which matches a comma followed by exactly three digits. The group is followed by `*` so it can appear zero or more times.

The `\.\d+` matches a decimal point followed by one or more digits. That group is followed by `?` so it can appear zero or one times.

9. The RearrangeNames example program uses the following code to do this.

```
// Rearrange the names.
private void rearrangeButton_Click(object sender, EventArgs e)
{
    resultTextBox.Text = Regex.Replace(
        namesTextBox.Text,
        @"^(\w*)\s*(\w*)(\s*)$",
        @"$2, $1$3",
        RegexOptions.Multiline);
}
```

The following text shows the matching expression.

```
^(\w*)\s*(\w*)(\s*)
```

This expression contains three groups. The first uses `\w*` to match zero or more word characters. (This is the person's first name.)

After the first group the expression uses `\s*` to match zero or more whitespace characters. This is not in a group so anything matched here is lost.

The second group uses `\w*` again to match zero or more word characters. (This is the person's last name.)

The final group uses `\s*` to match zero or more whitespace characters at the end of the line. (This is the [Return] character.)

The following text shows the replacement expression.

```
$2, $1$3
```

This replaces the entire match with the second group, followed by a comma and space, followed by the first group, followed by the third group. The result is last name, comma and space, first name, trailing [Return].

CHAPTER 22

1. The ThreadTimer example program uses the following code to do this.

```
// Create a timer to update the clock.
private void Form1_Load(object sender, EventArgs e)
{
    System.Threading.Timer timer =
        new System.Threading.Timer(TimerTick, null, 0, 500);
}

// Update the clock.
private void TimerTick(object state)
{
    // Invoke to the UI thread.
    this.Invoke((Action)UpdateClockLabel);
}

// Update the clock's label on the UI thread.
private void UpdateClockLabel()
{
    clockLabel.Text = DateTime.Now.ToString("T");
}
```

The only trick here is that the callback method `TimerTick` must use `Invoke` to update the clock label because it is not running in the UI thread.

2. The FiboTasksWaitAll example program does this. The program uses the following code to create its `Tasks` and store them in an array.

```
Task[] tasks =
{
    new Task(FindFibonacci, 0),
    new Task(FindFibonacci, 1),
    new Task(FindFibonacci, 2),
    new Task(FindFibonacci, 3)
};
```

The program then uses the following code to start the `Tasks`.

```
foreach (Task task in tasks) task.Start();
```

Finally, the program uses the following code to wait for all the `Tasks` to finish.

```
Task.WaitAll(tasks);
```

3. The FiboTasksStartAndWaitAll example program uses the following code to create and start its Tasks.

```
Task[] tasks =
{
    Task.Factory.StartNew(FindFibonacci, 0),
    Task.Factory.StartNew(FindFibonacci, 1),
    Task.Factory.StartNew(FindFibonacci, 2),
    Task.Factory.StartNew(FindFibonacci, 3),
};
```

This makes the program's code slightly simpler.

4. The FiboTasksWaitAny example program does this. The following code shows the call to Task.WaitAny.

```
Task.WaitAny(tasks);
```

When one of the Tasks finishes, the others remain running. When the program displays its results, some of the Tasks may not have finished.

The program uses the following code to display results only for any tasks that have finished.

```
for (int i = 0; i < OutputTextBoxes.Length; i++)
{
    if (tasks[i].IsCompleted)
        OutputTextBoxes[i].Text = Results[i].ToString();
}
```

The other Tasks continue running and their results are ignored. (You can also cancel a Task. See "Task Cancellation" at msdn.microsoft.com/library/dd997396.aspx for more information.)

5. The FiboLambdaTPL example program uses the following code to start four threads calculating Fibonacci numbers.

```
Parallel.For(0, 4,
    index => Results[index] = Fibonacci(Numbers[index])
);
```

This simplifies the code somewhat by removing the need for the FindFibonacci method.

6. Not really. If you need to wait for all the Tasks to complete, it doesn't matter in what order you wait.

7. The FiboTaskWithResults example program does this. The program uses the following code to start its Tasks.

```
Task<long>[] tasks =
{
    Task<long>.Factory.StartNew(Fibonacci, Numbers[0]),
    Task<long>.Factory.StartNew(Fibonacci, Numbers[1]),
    Task<long>.Factory.StartNew(Fibonacci, Numbers[2]),
    Task<long>.Factory.StartNew(Fibonacci, Numbers[3]),
};
```

This code creates four Task<long> objects that execute the Fibonacci method (which returns a long result). The Fibonacci method receives as an argument the values Numbers[0], Numbers[1], Numbers[2], and Numbers[4]. (You could even make the Numbers array local to the event handler that creates the Tasks. Its only purpose in this program is to pass the values into the StartNew method.)

Because the StartNew method passes the delegate an object as an argument, the Fibonacci method must be revised to take an object as a parameter. The following code shows the new method.

```
private long Fibonacci(object data)
{
    long N = (long)data;

    if (N <= 1) return 1;
    return Fibonacci(N - 1) + Fibonacci(N - 2);
}
```

This version of the program is somewhat simpler because it doesn't need the FindFibonacci method or a Results array, and the Numbers array can be stored locally in the method that creates the Tasks.

8. The FiboThreads example program does this. The following code shows the key code that creates, starts, and waits for the threads.

```
// Launch four threads.
Thread thread0 = new Thread((ParameterizedThreadStart)FindFibonacci);
thread0.Start(0);
Thread thread1 = new Thread((ParameterizedThreadStart)FindFibonacci);
thread1.Start(1);
Thread thread2 = new Thread((ParameterizedThreadStart)FindFibonacci);
thread2.Start(2);
Thread thread3 = new Thread((ParameterizedThreadStart)FindFibonacci);
thread3.Start(3);

// Wait for the threads to complete.
thread0.Join();
thread1.Join();
thread2.Join();
thread3.Join();
```

This code creates and starts four Threads. It then calls each Thread's Join method to wait for the Thread to complete.

In my tests, there was no significant difference in performance between programs FiboTasks and FiboThreads.

9. The Tasks are in deadlock because each is waiting for a lock on an object that is already locked by the other Task. They got there because Task A locks LockObjectA and then sleeps so Task B has a chance to run. It locks LockObjectB so Task A is blocked. Task A already locked LockObjectA so Task B is also blocked.

The DeadUnlock example program uses the following code for Task A.

```
// Task A.
private void TaskA()
{
    for (int attempts = 0; attempts < 10; attempts++)
    {
        Console.WriteLine("TaskA: Locking A");
        if (Monitor.TryEnter(LockObjectA))
        {
            try
            {
                Thread.Sleep(1);
                Console.WriteLine("TaskA: Locking B");
                if (Monitor.TryEnter(LockObjectB))
                {
                    try
                    {
                        // Update the value.
                        BestValue = ValueA;

                        // We're done. Break out of the retry loop.
                        Console.WriteLine("Task A: Done");
                        return;
                    }
                    finally
                    {
                        Console.WriteLine("Task A: Releasing lock B");
                        Monitor.Exit(LockObjectB);
                    }
                }
                else
                {
                    Console.WriteLine("Task A: Lock B failed");
                }
            }
            finally
            {
                Console.WriteLine("Task A: Releasing lock A");
                Monitor.Exit(LockObjectA);
            }
        }
        else
        {
            Console.WriteLine("Task A: Lock A failed");
        }
    }
}
```

The code used by Task B is similar so it isn't shown here. The only difference is that Task B tries to lock LockObjectB first and LockObjectA second.

When you run this program, the Tasks still have trouble obtaining the locks they need. The two Tasks march along almost synchronized, so they often run through the following sequence of events:

1. Task A locks LockObjectA.

2. Task B locks LockObjectB.

3. Task A fails to lock LockObjectB.

4. Task A releases its lock on LockObjectA.

5. Task A relocks LockObjectA.

6. Task B fails to lock LockObjectA.

7. Task B releases its lock on LockObjectB.

8. Task B relocks LockObjectB.

At this point the objects each have one resource locked so the whole thing repeats from step 3.

This situation in which tasks perform actions that are synchronized enough so that they are not in a deadlock but they still cannot get anywhere is called a *livelock*.

Eventually, the Tasks get a bit out of sync, so one can grab its second resource between the other Task's releasing and relocking it. Then the livelock is broken.

One way to prevent a livelock is to ensure that the Tasks cannot march along almost in synch. In this example, if you make the two Tasks sleep for different amounts of time, the livelock goes away fairly quickly.

In this example, an even more effective solution is to make the Tasks sleep a different amount of time before trying to acquire the first lock. Then the Task that sleeps for less time can grab both locks quickly before the other Task even starts.

An even better solution is to make both Tasks attempt to lock their objects in the same order as explained in Exercise 11.

10. Example program NoDeadlock does this. In this case, whichever Task locks LockObjectA first can then lock object LockObjectB and finish its calculation. The other Task blocks until the first Task finishes. It can then proceed without interference.

(You could also create a single lock object to represent locking both resources A and B. Then each Task needs to acquire only one lock, so they cannot deadlock.)

11. In this case the program throws the following exception.

An exception of type 'System.Threading.SynchronizationLockException' occurred in NoDeadlock.exe but was not handled in user code.

Additional information: Object synchronization method was called from an unsynchronized block of code.

If there is a handler for this exception, the program may be safely continued.

12. In that case the object remains locked. If another Task needs to lock that object, it will never obtain the lock.

CHAPTER 23

1. The LinqTestScores example program does this. The code is similar to the code used by the LinqToDataSetScores example program in Chapter 8 so it isn't shown here. Download the example to see how it works.

2. If you don't click Save, the program doesn't call the data adapter's Update method so no new student records are saved to the database. If you restart the program you won't find the new records.

3. Round trips to the database are relatively expensive, particularly if the database is located on the other side of a network, so it's often better to fetch or save as much data as you will need all at once. That means using data adapters to load and save changes to DataSets can be reasonably efficient in terms of communications costs.

    However, that approach can lead to problems if the database has multiple simultaneous users. For example, suppose two users start the program and edit the same record. Whichever user clicks Save second overwrites the changes made by the first user and the first user's changes are lost.

    You could try to avoid that problem by locking the record so both users cannot edit it at the same time. That works well if you use ADO.NET to fetch one record at a time, but it doesn't work well if you use a data adapter to load an entire table all at once. If one user loads and locks the entire table, the other user can't do anything.

    Another problem with the data adapter approach arises if the database is very large. If the Students table contains thousands of records, the program may be loading far more data than it will ever need.

    In general, using data adapters to load entire tables works well if the tables aren't too big and there is a single user or users who won't try to edit the same records. For really large tables or users who may conflict frequently, it's often better to fetch data in more limited chunks.

4. The CreateAndDropTable example program does this. The code is relatively straightforward but it's long so it isn't shown in its entirety here. The following code shows how the program executes the DROP TABLE command, which doesn't fetch data.

    ```
    string drop = "DROP TABLE Instructors";
    using (OleDbCommand command = new OleDbCommand(drop, connection))
    {
        // Execute the command.
        command.ExecuteNonQuery();
    }
    ```

    No the database doesn't warn you when you try to drop a table that isn't empty. It simply drops the table and any data it contains is lost.

5. If a program tries to open a connection that is already open, it throws a System.InvalidOperationException with the message:

    Additional information: The connection was not closed. The connection's current state is open.

If a program creates a connection at the module level and uses the connection in multiple methods, each method must be certain that it closes the connection before it exits. You can use the `finally` section of a `try-catch-finally` block to ensure that the connection is closed.

Alternatively you could use the following code to open the connection.

```
if (connection.State == ConnectionState.Closed) connection.Open();
```

6. The InsertThreeRecords example program does this. The following code shows its `InsertInstructorsRecord` method.

```
// Insert an Instructors record.
private void InsertInstructorsRecord(OleDbConnection connection, int
instructorId, string firstName, string lastName, string department)
{
    string insert =
      "INSERT INTO Instructors (InstructorId, FirstName, LastName, Department)"
      + "VALUES (" + instructorId.ToString() + ", '"
      firstName + "', '" + lastName + "', '" + department + "')";
    using (OleDbCommand command = new OleDbCommand(insert, connection))
    {
        // Execute the command.
        command.ExecuteNonQuery();
    }
}
```

Download the example to see the other details.

If you omit the UPDATE statement's WHERE clause, it updates all of the records in the table. In this example, that means every instructor's first name is changed to Fran.

7. The AdHocQuery example program does this. The following code shows how the program displays a row's values.

```
// Get the values.
object[] values = new object[reader.FieldCount];
reader.GetValues(values);

// Add the values to a string.
string result = "";
for (int i = 0; i < reader.FieldCount; i++)
{
    result += values[i].ToString() + " ";
}

// Display the result.
resultsListBox.Items.Add(result);
```

Download the example for other details.

CHAPTER 24

1. The RandomPlantsWithWriter example program uses the following code to generate a random XML plant data file.

```
private void createButton_Click(object sender, EventArgs e)
{
    // Get the words to use in building names.
    string text = namesTextBox.Text.ToLower();

    // Remove periods and commas.
    text = Regex.Replace(text, @"[\.,]", "");

    // Split into words.
    char[] chars = { ' ', '\r', '\n' };
    string[] words = text.Split(
        chars, StringSplitOptions.RemoveEmptyEntries);

    // Create the writer.
    using (XmlTextWriter writer = new XmlTextWriter("Plants.xml", null))
    {
        // Make it pretty.
        writer.Formatting = Formatting.Indented;

        // Write the start element.
        writer.WriteStartDocument();

        writer.WriteStartElement("Plants");        // <Plants>

        // Make the plants.
        int numPlants = int.Parse(numPlantsTextBox.Text);
        for (int i = 0; i < numPlants; i++)
        {
            writer.WriteStartElement("Plant");      // <Plant>
            writer.WriteElementString("Name", RandomName(words));
            writer.WriteElementString("Zone", Rand.Next(1, 10).ToString());
            writer.WriteElementString("Light", RandomLight());
            writer.WriteEndElement();               // </Plant>
        }
        writer.WriteEndElement();                   // </Plants>
    }
    MessageBox.Show("Done");
}
```

2. The RandomPlantsWithDom example program uses the following code to generate random XML plant data file.

```
private void createButton_Click(object sender, EventArgs e)
{
    // Get the words to use in building names.
    string text = namesTextBox.Text.ToLower();

    // Remove periods and commas.
    text = Regex.Replace(text, @"[\.,]", "");
```

```
    // Split into words.
    char[] chars = { ' ', '\r', '\n' };
    string[] words = text.Split(
        chars, StringSplitOptions.RemoveEmptyEntries);

    // Make the document.
    XDocument document = new XDocument();

    // Make the root node.
    XElement plants = new XElement("Plants");
    document.Add(plants);

    // Make the plants.
    int numPlants = int.Parse(numPlantsTextBox.Text);
    for (int i = 0; i < numPlants; i++)
    {
        XElement plant = new XElement("Plant");
        plant.SetElementValue("Name", RandomName(words));
        plant.SetElementValue("Zone", Rand.Next(1, 10));
        plant.SetElementValue("Light", RandomLight());
        plants.Add(plant);
    }

    // Save the file.
    document.Save("Plants.xml");

    MessageBox.Show("Done");
}
```

Which version of the program is better is mostly a matter of personal preference.

If you were generating a huge file, perhaps hundreds of thousands or millions of plant records, then the version that uses XmlTextWriter would probably be better because, unlike the version that uses the DOM, it would not need to store the entire XML document in memory all at the same time.

3. The FindPlantsWithDom example program uses the following code to do this.

```
// The DOM.
private XDocument Document;

// Load the XML data.
private void Form1_Load(object sender, EventArgs e)
{
    // Load the XML file.
    Document = XDocument.Load("Plants.xml");

    // Get the zones.
    var zones =
        from XElement zone in Document.Descendants("Zone")
        orderby zone.Value
        select zone.Value;
    zoneComboBox.DataSource = zones.Distinct().ToArray();
}
```

```
// Display plants from the selected zone.
private void zoneComboBox_SelectedIndexChanged(object sender, EventArgs e)
{
    string selectedZone = zoneComboBox.SelectedItem.ToString();

    // Find the selected ZONE elements.
    var zones =
        from XElement zone in Document.Descendants("Zone")
        where zone.Value == selectedZone
        select zone;

    // Loop through the selected ZONE elements.
    plantsListBox.Items.Clear();
    foreach (XElement element in zones)
    {
        // Find the corresponding PLANT element's COMMON element.
        plantsListBox.Items.Add(element.Parent.Element("Name").Value);
    }
}

// Display this plant's details.
private void plantsListBox_SelectedIndexChanged(object sender, EventArgs e)
{
    // Get the selected name.
    string plantName = plantsListBox.SelectedItem.ToString();

    // Find the Name element with this value.
    var plants =
        from XElement name in Document.Descendants("Name")
        where name.Value == plantName
        select name;

    // Get the first plant's element.
    XElement plant = plants.First().Parent;

    // Display the Plant element's data.
    detailsTextBox.Text = plant.ToString();
}
```

4. The FindPlantNamesWithReader example program uses the following code to do this.

```
// Display plant names.
private void Form1_Load(object sender, EventArgs e)
{
    // Open the file.
    using (XmlReader reader = XmlReader.Create("Plants.xml"))
    {
        // Scan the XML file's elements.
        while (reader.Read())
        {
            // See if this is a Name element.
            if (reader.Name == "Name")
            {
                // Display the name.
                //plantsListBox.Items.Add(reader.ReadElementContentAsString());
```

```
                        plantsListBox.Items.Add(reader.ReadInnerXml());
                }
            }
        }
    }
```

This program and FindPlantsWithDom have different purposes, so you can't compare them exactly. FindPlantsWithDom is interactive and displays information when the user selects zones or plant names. Because it might need to display data about any plant, it needs to keep the data around. It can store it in the DOM, or it could reread the XML file every time it needed a value. If the file were big, that would be slow. If the file were extremely big (millions of records), rereading the file would be extremely slow, but that might be necessary to avoid loading the entire file into memory all at once.

The FindPlantNamesWithReader program is not interactive. It needs to scan the data only once to get the information it needs. It doesn't need to keep the zone or light information, so it doesn't need to load all of the data at once.

In summary, FindPlantsWithDom needs to use the DOM because it's interactive and will need to use the data later. FindPlantNamesWithReader is not interactive and can get what it needs by running through the file once.

5. The FindPlantsWithXPath example program does this. The following code shows how it loads its XML data and populates its ComboBox.

```
// The DOM.
private XDocument Document;

// Load the XML data.
private void Form1_Load(object sender, EventArgs e)
{
    // Load the XML file.
    Document = XDocument.Load("Plants.xml");

    // Get the distinct zones.
    List<string> zones = new List<string>();
    foreach (XElement zone in Document.XPathSelectElements("//Zone"))
    {
        if (!zones.Contains(zone.Value)) zones.Add(zone.Value);
    }

    // Sort the zones.
    zones.Sort();

    // Display the zones.
    zoneComboBox.DataSource = zones;
}
```

The code loads the XML document as before. It then uses the XPath query //Zone to find all Zone elements. Because the program wants distinct zones, it checks its zones list and adds only the values that are not already in the list. (You could also use a LINQ query to select the distinct zones, but I'm trying to avoid LINQ in this example.)

The code then sorts the zones and displays them in the ComboBox.

When the user selects a zone from the ComboBox, the program uses the following code to display the plants in that zone.

```
// Display plants from the selected zone.
private void zoneComboBox_SelectedIndexChanged(object sender, EventArgs e)
{
    string selectedZone = zoneComboBox.SelectedItem.ToString();

    // Find Plant elements with the selected Zone children.
    plantsListBox.Items.Clear();

    // Find Plants that have the selected Zone as a child.
    string query = "//Plant[Zone=\"" + selectedZone + "\"]";
    foreach (XElement plant in Document.XPathSelectElements(query))
    {
        // Add the Plant's name to the list.
        plantsListBox.Items.Add(plant.Element("Name").Value);
    }
}
```

This code composes an XPath query similar to the following.

```
//Plant[Zone="1"]
```

This query selects Plant elements that have a Zone child with the value matching the value selected by the user.

The code uses XPathSelectElements to find elements that satisfy the query and loops through them. For each Plant element, the code adds the value of the element's Name child to the plants ListBox.

The following code shows an even more effective query.

```
// Find Names with parents that have the selected Zone as a child.
string query = "//Plant/Name[../Zone=\"" + selectedZone + "\"]";
foreach (XElement name in Document.XPathSelectElements(query))
{
    // Add the Plant's name to the list.
    plantsListBox.Items.Add(name.Value);
}
```

This query has the following format.

```
//Plant/Name[../Zone="1"]
```

The //Plant/Name part of the query selects Name elements that have Plant parents at any depth in the document.

The brackets place a filter on the selected elements. The .. part of the filter moves to the element's parent, in this case the Name's Plant element. The /Zone="1" part of the filter means the parent element must have a child named Zone with value 1.

Taken all together this query means:

Find Name *elements that have parents that are* Plant *elements, and the* Plant *has a* Zone *child with the value 1.*

With this new query, the program needs to loop through the selected Name elements and display their values. The previous query required the program to start at Plant elements and find their Name elements. (Both versions of the query are in the example program, so you can experiment with them.)

When the user selects a plant from the ListBox, the program uses the following code to display information about the plant.

```
// Display this plant's details.
private void plantsListBox_SelectedIndexChanged(object sender, EventArgs e)
{
    // Get the selected name.
    string plantName = plantsListBox.SelectedItem.ToString();

    // Find the Plant with a Name child that has this value.
    string query = "//Plant[Name=\"" + plantName + "\"]";
    XElement plant = Document.XPathSelectElement(query);

    // Display the Plant element's data.
    detailsTextBox.Text = plant.ToString();
}
```

This code composes a query similar to the following.

```
//Plant[Name="id euismod pulvinar"]
```

It then calls XPathSelectElement to select the first Plant element with the selected name. The code then displays that element's data.

6. The TransformPlants example program does this. The following code shows the XSLT file.

```
<?xml version="1.0" encoding="utf-8"?>
<xsl:stylesheet version="1.0"
    xmlns:xsl="http://www.w3.org/1999/XSL/Transform"
    xmlns:msxsl="urn:schemas-microsoft-com:xslt"
    exclude-result-prefixes="msxsl"
>
  <xsl:output method="html" indent="yes"/>

  <xsl:template match="Plants">
    <HTML>
      <BODY>
        <TABLE BORDER="2">
          <TR>
            <TH>Name</TH>
            <TH>Zone</TH>
            <TH>Light</TH>
          </TR>
          <xsl:apply-templates select="Plant"/>
        </TABLE>
      </BODY>
    </HTML>
```

```
    </xsl:template>
    <xsl:template match="Plant">
      <TR>
        <TD>
          <xsl:value-of select="Name"/>
        </TD>
        <TD>
          <xsl:value-of select="Zone"/>
        </TD>
        <TD>
          <xsl:value-of select="Light"/>
        </TD>
      </TR>
    </xsl:template>
</xsl:stylesheet>
```

The following code shows how the program performs the transformation.

```
// Transform Plants.xml.
private void Form1_Load(object sender, EventArgs e)
{
    // Load the style sheet.
    XslCompiledTransform xslt = new XslCompiledTransform();
    xslt.Load("PlantsToHtml.xslt");

    // Transform the file.
    xslt.Transform("Plants.xml", "Plants.html");

    // Display the result.
    string filename = Path.GetFullPath(
        Path.Combine(Application.StartupPath, "Plants.html"));
    planetsWebBrowser.Navigate(filename);
}
```

7. The TransformPlanetsIntoAttributes example program does this. The following code shows the XSLT file.

```
<?xml version="1.0" encoding="utf-8"?>
<xsl:stylesheet version="1.0" xmlns:xsl="http://www.w3.org/1999/XSL/Transform"
    xmlns:msxsl="urn:schemas-microsoft-com:xslt" exclude-result-prefixes="msxsl"
>
  <xsl:output method="xml" indent="yes"/>

  <xsl:template match="Planets">
    <Planets>
      <xsl:apply-templates select="Planet"/>
    </Planets>
  </xsl:template>
  <xsl:template match="Planet">
    <Planet Name="{Name}"
            Distance="{Distance}"
            LengthOfYear="{LengthOfYear}"
            LengthOfDay="{Day}" />
  </xsl:template>
</xsl:stylesheet>
```

The program uses the following code to transform the XML file.

```
// Transform Planets.xml.
private void Form1_Load(object sender, EventArgs e)
{
    // Process without indenting.
    // Load the style sheet.
    XslCompiledTransform xslt = new XslCompiledTransform();
    xslt.Load("PlanetsToAttributes.xslt");

    // Transform the file.
    xslt.Transform("Planets.xml", "Planets2.xml");

    // Display the result.
    resultTextBox.Text = File.ReadAllText("Planets2.xml");
    resultTextBox.Select(0, 0);
}
```

The program also contains code to produce a nicely indented result. Download the example to see how it works.

CHAPTER 25

1. The SerializeStudentArray example program does this. The following code shows the heart of the program.

```
// Display the students.
originalListBox.DataSource = students;

// Create a serializer that works with Student[].
XmlSerializer serializer = new XmlSerializer(typeof(Student[]));

// Create a TextWriter to hold the serialization.
string serialization;
using (TextWriter writer = new StringWriter())
{
    // Serialize the students array.
    serializer.Serialize(writer, students);
    serialization = writer.ToString();
}

// Display the serialization.
serializationTextBox.Text = serialization;

// Create a stream from which to read the serialization.
using (TextReader reader = new StringReader(serialization))
{
    // Deserialize.
    Student[] newStudents = (Student[])serializer.Deserialize(reader);

    // Display the deserialization.
    deserializedListBox.DataSource = newStudents;
}
```

This code is reasonably straightforward. Its most interesting feature is that it works with the Student[] type instead of a class as the SerializeCustomer example does.

2. The ClassroomEditor example program uses the following code to save and load serializations of its Student list.

```
// The Students.
private List<Student> Students;

// Load saved Students.
private void Form1_Load(object sender, EventArgs e)
{
    // See if the serialization file exists.
    if (File.Exists("Students.xml"))
    {
        // Deserialize the file.
        // Create a serializer that works with Student[].
        XmlSerializer serializer = new XmlSerializer(typeof(List<Student>));

        // Create a stream from which to read the serialization.
        using (FileStream reader = File.OpenRead("Students.xml"))
        {
            // Deserialize.
            Students = (List<Student>)serializer.Deserialize(reader);
        }
    }
    else
    {
        // Create an empty student list.
        Students = new List<Student>();
    }

    // Display the Students.
    studentsListBox.DataSource = Students;
}

// Save Students.
private void Form1_FormClosed(object sender, FormClosedEventArgs e)
{
    // Create a serializer that works with Student[].
    XmlSerializer serializer = new XmlSerializer(typeof(List<Student>));

    // Create a StreamWriter to hold the serialization.
    using (StreamWriter writer = File.CreateText("Students.xml"))
    {
        // Serialize the student list.
        serializer.Serialize(writer, Students);
    }
}
```

This code is reasonably straightforward. The code that lets the user create, edit, and delete Student objects is also straightforward (and it's unrelated to the discussion of serialization) so it isn't shown here. Download the example to see how it works.

3. The XmlSerializeToString example program uses the following code to serialize and deserialize objects as XML strings.

```
public static class XmlTools
{
    // Return obj's serialization as a string.
    public static string Serialize<T>(T obj)
    {
        // Create a serializer that works with the T class.
        XmlSerializer serializer = new XmlSerializer(typeof(T));

        // Create a TextWriter to hold the serialization.
        string serialization;
        using (TextWriter writer = new StringWriter())
        {
            // Serialize the object.
            serializer.Serialize(writer, obj);
            serialization = writer.ToString();
        }

        // Return the serialization.
        return serialization;
    }

    // Deserialize a serialization string.
    public static T Deserialize<T>(string serialization)
    {
        // Create a serializer that works with the T class.
        XmlSerializer serializer = new XmlSerializer(typeof(T));

        // Create a reader from which to read the serialization.
        using (TextReader reader = new StringReader(serialization))
        {
            // Deserialize.
            T obj = (T)serializer.Deserialize(reader);

            // Return the object.
            return obj;
        }
    }
}
```

This code should work with any object that the `XmlSerializer` class can understand. (For example, it won't work with images.)

4. The SerializeStudentWithPicture example program does this. The only trick (aside from the `PictureBytes` property that was given as a hint) is that the `Student` class uses the `XmlIgnore` attribute to prevent the serializer from trying to serialize the `Picture` property.

The following code shows the `Student` class (with some code omitted).

```
public class Student
{
    public string FirstName, LastName;
```

```
    [XmlIgnore]
    public Image Picture;

    // Return the Picture as a byte stream.
    public byte[] PictureBytes
    {
        ... Code omitted ...
    }

    ... Constructors omitted ...
}
```

The following text shows a small part of the serialization for a `Student` with a 143×170 pixel picture.

```
<?xml version="1.0" encoding="utf-16"?>
<Student xmlns:xsi="http://www.w3.org/2001/XMLSchema-instance" xmlns:xsd="http://
www.w3.org/2001/XMLSchema">
  <FirstName>Rod</FirstName>
  <LastName>Stephens</LastName>
  <PictureBytes>iVBORw0KGgoAAAANSUhEUgAAAI8AAACqCAYAAACUAhwWAAAABG
    ...96,130 characters omitted ...
  </PictureBytes>
</Student>
```

5. The SerializeFriends example program does this. A `Person` object contains references to other `Person` objects, which may contain references to the first `Person`, so the data may contain cycles. That means you need to use a binary serialization.

The program uses the following code to load the serialization and prepare itself when it starts.

```
// The people.
private List<Person> People = null;

// The currently selected person.
private Person SelectedPerson = null;

// Reload saved data.
private void Form1_Load(object sender, EventArgs e)
{
    if (File.Exists("Friends.dat"))
    {
        // Deserialize the data.
        BinaryFormatter formatter = new BinaryFormatter();
        using (FileStream stream = new FileStream("Friends.dat", FileMode.Open))
        {
            People = (List<Person>)formatter.Deserialize(stream);
        }
    }
    else
    {
        // Create some initial people.
        People = new List<Person>();
        People.Add(new Person() { Name = "Archibald" });
```

```
            People.Add(new Person() { Name = "Beatrix" });
            People.Add(new Person() { Name = "Charles" });
            People.Add(new Person() { Name = "Delilah" });
            People.Add(new Person() { Name = "Edgar" });
            People.Add(new Person() { Name = "Francine" });
        }

        // Add all people to the friends list.
        foreach (Person person in People)
            friendsCheckedListBox.Items.Add(person);

        // Display the people.
        personListBox.DataSource = People;
    }
```

The only non-obvious thing here is that the program uses the variable `SelectedPerson` to keep track of the `Person` who is currently selected in the `ListBox` on the left.

When the user selects a person from the `ListBox` on the left, the following code executes.

```
// Select this person's friends.
private void personListBox_SelectedIndexChanged(object sender, EventArgs e)
{
    // Update the currently selected person's friends.
    UpdateFriends();

    // Update the selected person.
    SelectedPerson = (Person)personListBox.SelectedItem;

    // Check the newly selected person's friends.
    for (int i=0; i<friendsCheckedListBox.Items.Count; i++)
    {
        bool isFriend =
            SelectedPerson.Friends.Contains(friendsCheckedListBox.Items[i]);
        friendsCheckedListBox.SetItemChecked(i, isFriend);
    }
}
```

The code first calls `UpdateFriends` (described shortly) to save any changes to the previously selected person's `Friends` list.

Next, the code saves a reference to the newly selected person in the `SelectedPerson` variable. It then loops through the items in the friends `CheckedListBox` on the right. The program checks or unchecks the people in the `CheckedListBox` depending on whether they are in the newly selected person's `Friends` list.

The following code shows the `UpdateFriends` method.

```
// Update the currently selected person's friends.
private void UpdateFriends()
{
    if (SelectedPerson != null)
    {
        SelectedPerson.Friends = new List<Person>();
```

```
            foreach (object friend in friendsCheckedListBox.CheckedItems)
                SelectedPerson.Friends.Add((Person)friend);
        }
    }
```

If the selected person is not `null`, the code sets that person's `Friends` list to a new `List<Person>`. It then adds the checked items in the `CheckedListBox` on the right to the person's new `Friends` list.

The following code shows how the program saves the friend data when it closes.

```
// Save the friend data.
private void Form1_FormClosed(object sender, FormClosedEventArgs e)
{
    // Update the currently selected person's friends.
    UpdateFriends();

    // Save the data.
    BinaryFormatter formatter = new BinaryFormatter();
    using (FileStream stream = new FileStream("Friends.dat", FileMode.Create))
    {
        formatter.Serialize(stream, People);
    }
}
```

The code calls `UpdateFriends` to save any changes to the currently selected person. It then creates a `BinaryFormatter` and uses it to save the `People` list.

CHAPTER 26

1. The EditPerson example program does this. Download the example to see the details.

When you select a property in the `PropertyGrid`, it displays the `Description` attribute's value to give the user information about the property.

By default, the `PropertyGrid` groups properties by their `Category` attributes. If you click the Alphabetical button, the grid displays the properties alphabetically instead of by category.

2. The EditPerson example program does this. Download the example and search for the following directive to see the new code.

```
#if Exercise2
```

3. The UseDrawingAddIns example program does this. The following code shows how the program searches for DLLs and classes within any DLLs it finds.

```
// Load available tools.
private void Form1_Load(object sender, EventArgs e)
{
    // Create a Bitmap.
    Picture = new Bitmap(
```

```
            imagePictureBox.ClientSize.Width,
            imagePictureBox.ClientSize.Height);
    imagePictureBox.Image = Picture;

    // Look for assemblies.
    foreach (string filename in
        Directory.GetFiles(Application.StartupPath, "*.dll"))
    {
        // Load this assembly.
        Assembly dll = Assembly.LoadFile(filename);

        // Look for classes that have Draw methods.
        foreach (Type type in dll.GetTypes())
        {
            // Make sure this is a class.
            if (!type.IsClass) continue;

            // Find the Draw method.
            MethodInfo methodInfo = type.GetMethod("Draw");
            if (methodInfo == null) continue;

            // Make sure it's a static method.
            if (!methodInfo.IsStatic) continue;

            // Make sure it takes a Graphics object as a parameter.
            ParameterInfo[] parameters = methodInfo.GetParameters();
            if (parameters.Length != 1) continue;
            if (parameters[0].ParameterType != typeof(Graphics)) continue;

            // We can use this method!

            // Get the class's DisplayName atttribute.
            Attribute attribute =
                type.GetCustomAttribute(typeof(DisplayNameAttribute));
            string toolName;
            if (attribute == null) toolName = type.Name;
            else
            {
                DisplayNameAttribute attr = attribute as DisplayNameAttribute;
                toolName = attr.DisplayName;
            }

            // Create a menu item for this method.
            ToolStripItem item = toolsMenu.DropDownItems.Add(toolName);
            item.Tag = methodInfo;

            // Set a Click event handler for the menu item.
            item.Click += item_Click;
        }
    }
}
```

The following code shows how the program invokes a tool.

```
// The bitmap we are displaying.
private Bitmap Picture;

// Invoke a menu item's method.
private void item_Click(object sender, EventArgs e)
{
    using (Graphics gr = Graphics.FromImage(Picture))
    {
        // Get the menu item's MethodInfo.
        ToolStripMenuItem item = sender as ToolStripMenuItem;
        MethodInfo methodInfo = item.Tag as MethodInfo;

        // Invoke the method.
        object[] args = { gr };
        methodInfo.Invoke(null, args);
    }

    imagePictureBox.Refresh();
}
```

The UseDrawingAddIns program uses DLLs built by the DrawingAddIns and MoreDrawingAddIns example projects.

4. The UseDrawingAddIns2 example program does this. The MultipleDrawingAddIns project creates a DLL that this program can load. Download the examples to see how they work.

5. The UseDrawingAddIns3 example program uses this approach. The MultipleDrawingAddIns2 project creates a DLL that this program can load. Download the examples to see how they work.

6. There are a couple ways you can avoid the restriction of putting the DrawingAddInAttribute class in the DrawingAddIn namespace.

If you allow the class to be defined in any namespace, you can search the DLL to find the class. That takes more effort but should work. It has problems, however, if the DLL defines a DrawingAddInAttribute class in more than one namespace. In that case, an add-in method could use any of the defined classes and you wouldn't know which of the attribute types to use.

Another approach would be to use GetCustomAttributes to iterate through the method's attributes. You could then use each attribute's ToString method to see if its name were DrawingAddInAttribute.

CHAPTER 27

1. The EncryptWithRandom example program does this. The following code shows how the program gets the user's inputs.

```
// Encrypt.
private void encryptButton_Click(object sender, EventArgs e)
{
    // Get the plaintext converted to uppercase.
    string plaintext = plaintextTextBox.Text.ToUpper();

    // Remove non-alphabetic characters.
    plaintext = Regex.Replace(plaintext, "[^A-Z]", "");

    // Get the key.
    int key = int.Parse(keyTextBox.Text);

    // Encrypt.
    ciphertextTextBox.Text = Encrypt(key, plaintext);
}
```

The program gets the plaintext and uses the ToUpper string method to convert it into uppercase. It then uses the Regex regular expression class to remove all non-alphabetic characters.

The code gets the user's key and calls the following Encrypt method to encrypt the message.

```
private string Encrypt(int key, string plaintext, bool encrypting = true)
{
    // Make the Random object.
    Random rand = new Random(key);

    // Encrypt.
    string ciphertext = "";
    foreach (char ch in plaintext)
    {
        int chNum = ch - 'A';

        // Add or remove a random number between 0 and 26.
        if (encrypting) chNum += rand.Next(0, 26);
        else chNum -= rand.Next(0, 26) - 26;

        chNum = chNum % 26;

        ciphertext += (char)('A' + chNum);
    }

    return ciphertext;
}
```

This method uses the key to initialize a Random object. It then loops through the message characters.

It converts each character into a number between 0 and 25 where A = 0, B = 1, and so forth. If it is encrypting, the method adds a random value between 0 and 25 to each character. If it is decrypting, the method subtracts a random value between 0 and 25 from each character. It takes the new value modulo 26 and converts the result back into a letter.

The oddest trick here is that the code adds 26 to the character's number if it is decoding. For example, if the ciphertext letter is B = 1 and the random value subtracted is 10, then 1 − 10 = −9. In C# the modulus operator `%` doesn't care if its result is negative, so it leaves this value −9, which does not convert back into a letter. The code adds 26, so the program calculates `(-9 + 26) % 26 = 17 % 26 = 17`, which converts to the letter R.

2. The BreakRandomCipher example program does this. It's mostly straightforward, so download the example to see how it works. The following code shows the trickiest part, which uses LINQ to find the largest letter frequency.

```
// Get the letter frequencies.
var query =
    from char ch in plaintext
    group ch by ch into g
    select g.Count();

// See how big the largest frequency is.
if (query.Max() / (float)plaintext.Length > maxFrequency)
{
    // Hopefully this is it.
    ...
}
```

This code uses LINQ to get the letter counts in the plaintext. It then divides the largest count by the number of letters in the message and compares that to the test frequency.

3. This approach doesn't work well for short messages because the letter frequencies in short messages may not match normal language usage. For example, in English the letter E appears most often, but it doesn't appear at all in the message "All good plans will bring victory!"

4. You could look at a measure of the distribution of the letters in the plaintext to see if it matches what you expect for a correct decryption. For example, you could see if the top three letters have frequencies around 12 percent, 9 percent, and 8 percent, the frequencies of the letters E, T, and A in English, respectively. Or you could see if the standard deviations of the letters are large. Unfortunately, both of those techniques are relatively time-consuming. The method described in the exercise is less reliable, so it won't work well with short messages, but it is much faster.

You might make the test a bit more reliable if you look at the largest and smallest frequencies.

5. This program looks only at relative letter frequencies, so it should work with any language where messages have uneven frequency distributions. The biggest change would be to allow the program to work with characters that don't lie between A and Z such as ö and ß.

6. The RandomIntegers example program uses the following code to provide the `GetInt` method.

```
public static class MyRandom
{
    // The RNG.
    private static RNGCryptoServiceProvider Rand = new RNGCryptoServiceProvider();
```

```
// Return a random int.
public static int GetInt()
{
    // A buffer to hold random bytes.
    byte[] bytes = new byte[4];

    // Get 4 random bytes.
    Rand.GetBytes(bytes);

    // Convert the bytes into an integer.
    return BitConverter.ToInt32(bytes, 0);
}
}
```

7. The RandomFloats example program uses the following code to return random `double` values between 0 and 1.

```
public static double NextDouble()
{
    byte[] bytes = new byte[8];
    Rand.GetBytes(bytes);
    UInt64 randomInt = BitConverter.ToUInt64(bytes, 0);
    return randomInt / (1.0 + UInt64.MaxValue);
}
```

8. The RandomInRange example program uses the following code to provide the `NextDouble` method and the new version of the `GetInt` method.

```
// Return a random integer within a range.
// Includes min and excludes max.
public static int GetInt(int min, int max)
{
    return (int)(min + (NextDouble() * (max - min)));
}

// Return a double between 0 (inclusive) and 1 (exclusive).
public static double NextDouble()
{
    byte[] bytes = new byte[8];
    Rand.GetBytes(bytes);
    UInt32 randomInt = BitConverter.ToUInt32(bytes, 0);
    return randomInt / (1.0 + UInt32.MaxValue);
}
```

9. The DefaultKeyAndIVMethods example program does this. The code in the encryption and decryption methods is similar to the code used by the original DefaultKeyAndIV program, so it isn't shown here.

10. The DefaultKeyAndIVExtensions example program does this. The encryption and decryption code is similar to the code used by the original DefaultKeyAndIV program, so it isn't shown here.

11. The EncryptWithPassword example program does this. Download it to see how it works.

If you try to decrypt a message with the wrong password, even a password that is wrong by a single character, the decryption operation throws an exception.

A BAD PAD

In my tests, the decryption operation throws a `ListDictionaryInternalException` with the message, "Padding is invalid and cannot be removed." The `AesManaged` class uses a block cipher, which means it breaks the message up into blocks and encrypts them separately. It uses a padding scheme to make the blocks the length it requires. This exception basically means the object tried to decrypt the encrypted bytes but the result didn't have the required padding.

To make a long story short, the decryption failed.

If you set the `AesManaged` object's `Padding` property to `PaddingMode.None` during decryption, the decryption will not worry about padding and will return a decrypted result. However, if the password is even a little wrong, the result is complete gibberish.

---

12. The RSAReceiver and RSASender example programs do this. They're relatively straight-forward, so download them to see how they work.

B

Data Types

The following table summarizes the C# data types.

TYPE	SIZE	VALUE
bool	2 bytes	Must be true or false.
byte	1 byte	0 to 255 (unsigned byte).
sbyte	1 byte	−128 to 127 (signed byte).
char	2 bytes	0 to 65,535 (unsigned character).
short	2 bytes	−32,768 to 32,767.
ushort	2 bytes	0 through 65,535 (unsigned short).
int	4 bytes	−2,147,483,648 to 2,147,483,647.
uint	4 bytes	0 through 4,294,967,295 (unsigned integer).
long	8 bytes	−9,223,372,036,854,775,808 to 9,223,372,036,854,775,807.
ulong	8 bytes	0 through 18,446,744,073,709,551,615 (unsigned long).
decimal	16 bytes	0 to +/−79,228,162,514,264,337,593,543,950,335 with no decimal point. 0 to +/−7.9228162514264337593543950335 with 28 significant diits.
float	4 bytes	−3.4028235E+38 to −1.401298E-45 (negative values). 1.401298E−45 to 3.4028235E+38 (positive values).
double	8 bytes	−1.79769313486231570E+308 to −4.94065645841246544E−324 (negative values). 4.94065645841246544E−324 through 1.79769313486231570E+308 (positive values).

continues

(continued)

TYPE	SIZE	VALUE
string	varies	Depending on the platform, approximately 0 to 2 billion Unicode characters.
DateTime	8 bytes	January 1, 0001 0:0:00 to December 31, 9999 11:59:59 p.m.
object	4 bytes	Points to any type of data.
(class)	varies	Class members have their own ranges.
(structure)	varies	Structure members have their own ranges.

CASTING AND CONVERTING VALUES

You can use a cast to convert a value into a compatible data type. For example, the following code declares and initializes a long variable. It then uses a cast to convert the long into an int and save the result in a new int variable. The cast operator is highlighted in bold.

```
long longValue = 10;
int intValue = (int)longValue;
```

The Convert class also provides methods for converting from one data type to another. The following table lists the most useful Convert class functions.

FUNCTION	
ToBoolean	ToInt64
ToByte	ToSByte
ToChar	ToSingle
ToDateTime	ToString
ToDecimal	ToUInt16
ToDouble	ToUInt32
ToInt16	ToUInt64
ToInt32	

All the Convert class methods provide many overloaded versions to convert different kinds of values. For example, ToInt32 has different versions that take parameters that are bool, byte, string, and other data types.

The integer functions ToInt16, ToInt32, ToInt64, ToUInt16, ToUInt32, and ToUInt64 also provide overloaded versions that take as parameters a string value and a base, which can be 2, 8, 10, or 16 to indicate whether the string is in binary, octal, decimal, or hexadecimal, respectively. For example, the following statement converts the binary value 00100100 into the integer value 36.

```
int value = Convert.ToInt32("00100100", 2)
```

The BitConverter class provides methods for converting variables to and from arrays of bytes.

Widening and Narrowing Conversions

In a widening conversion, the destination data type can hold any value held by the source data type. For example, a long can hold any value that fits in an int, so the following code is a widening conversion.

```
int intValue = 100;
long longValue = intValue;
```

Because this conversion must succeed, no casting or other operation is required.

In a narrowing conversion, the destination data type may not hold any value held by the source data type. For example, an int cannot necessarily hold any value that fits in a long, so the following code is a narrowing conversion.

```
long longValue = 100;
int intValue = (long)longValue;
```

Because this is a narrowing conversion, the casting operator is required, and the operation may throw an exception if the value cannot fit in the destination data type.

Converting Objects

Converting an object into a less derived ancestor class is a widening conversion, so it doesn't require casting. Conversely converting an object into a more derived descendant class is a narrowing conversion, so it requires casting.

For example, suppose the Employee class is derived from the Person class. Then the following code shows a widening conversion followed by a narrowing conversion.

```
Employee employee = new Employee();
Person person = new Person();
Employee employee2 = (Employee)person;
```

The as Operator

The as operator provides a shorthand for converting objects from one type to another. The following code converts the value in variable person into a Student and saves it in variable student.

```
student = person as Student;
```

If the value cannot be converted into a Student (for example, if person is a Janitor), then the as operator returns null.

Casting Arrays

You can cast variables of array types. For example, an array of Student objects is also an array of Person objects because a Student is a type of Person. The following code demonstrates implicit and explicit array conversions.

```
// Make an array of Students.
Student[] students = new Student[10];

// Implicit cast to an array of Persons.
// (A Student is a type of Person.)
Person[] persons = students;

// Explicit cast back to an array of Students.
students = (Student[])persons;
```

PARSING VALUES

Data types have parsing methods that convert string values into values of the data type. For example, the following code parses the text in the TextBox named numValuesTextBox and saves the result in the integer variable numValues.

```
int numValues = int.Parse(numValuesTextBox.Text);
```

The data types also provide TryParse methods that attempt to parse a string and return a boolean value indicating whether they succeeded.

Variable Declarations

The following code shows the syntax for declaring a variable inside a method.

```
«const» type«[]» name «= value»;
```

The following list describes the pieces of this declaration.

- ➤ const—If you include this, the variable is a constant and its value cannot be changed later. Use the *value* to assign the constant a value.

- ➤ *type*—The data type you want the variable to have.

- ➤ []—Include empty square brackets [] to make an array.

- ➤ *name*—The name you want the variable to have.

- ➤ = *value*—The value you want the variable to initially have.

C# enables you to declare and initialize more than one variable in a single declaration statement, but this can make the code more difficult to read.

The following code shows the syntax for declaring a variable outside of any method (at the class level).

```
«attributes» «accessibility»
    «const | readonly | static | volatile | static volatile»
    type«[]» name «= value»
```

The following list describes the pieces of this declaration.

- ➤ *attributes*—Attributes that specify extra properties for the variable.

- ➤ *accessibility*—One of public, internal, protected, internal protected, or private. The default is private.

- ➤ const—If you include this, the variable is a constant and its value cannot be changed later. Use the *value* to assign the constant a value.

- ➤ readonly—If you include this, the variable is similar to a constant except its value can be set either with a *value* clause or in the class's constructor.

➤   static—This keyword indicates the variable is shared by all instances of the class.

➤   volatile—This keyword indicates the variable might be modified by code running in multiple threads running at the same time.

➤   type—The data type you want the variable to have.

➤   []—Include empty square brackets [] to make an array.

➤   name—The name you want the variable to have.

➤   = value—The value you want the variable to initially have.

INITIALIZATION EXPRESSIONS

Initialization expressions assign a value to a new variable. Simple expressions assign a literal value to a simple data type. The following example sets the value of a new string variable.

```
string txt = "Test";
```

The assignment expression can also initialize a variable to the result of a method or constructor, as in the following example.

```
Person person = new Person("Rod", "Stephens");   // Constructor.
int numTools = CountTools();                      // Method.
```

An initialization expression for an object can specify values for the object's public properties as in the following example, which sets the object's FirstName and LastName properties.

```
Person rod = new Person() { FirstName = "Rod", LastName = "Stephens" };
```

To create an array of a certain size, set it equal to a new array of the required type with the number of items in its dimensions inside brackets. For example, the following code creates an array that holds 10 entries with indices 0 through 9.

```
decimal[] salaries = new decimal[10];
```

To initialize a one-dimensional array, put the array's values inside braces separated by commas, as in the following code.

```
int[] fibonacci = { 1, 1, 2, 3, 5, 8, 13, 21, 34, 55, 89 };
```

To initialize higher-dimensional arrays, place lower-dimensional array values inside braces and separate them with commas, as in the following example, which initializes a two-dimensional array.

```
int[,] values =
{
    {1, 2, 3},
    {4, 5, 6}
};
```

To initialize a collection class that provides an `Add` method, create a new instance of the class followed by initial values enclosed in braces, as in the following code.

```
List<string> pies = new List<string>()
{
    "Apple", "Banana", "Cherry", "Coconut Cream"
};
```

If the collection's `Add` method takes more than one parameter, group parameters in brackets, as in the following example.

```
Dictionary<string, string> directory = new Dictionary<string, string>()
{
    {"Alice Artz", "940-283-1298"},
    {"Bill Bland", "940-237-3827"},
    {"Carla Careful", "940-237-1983"}
};
```

USING

To make it easy to call an object's `Dispose` method, you can declare the object inside a `using` statement. When the code reaches the end of the `using` block, the program automatically calls the object's `Dispose` method.

For example, the following code creates a `Graphics` variable named `gr` that is automatically disposed when the `using` block ends.

```
using (Graphics gr = Graphics.FromImage(bm))
{
    ...
}
```

ENUMERATED TYPE DECLARATIONS

The syntax for declaring an enumerated type is as follows.

```
«attributes0» «accessibility» enum name
    «: type»
{
    «attributes1» name1 «= value1»,
    «attributes2» name2 «= value2»,
    ...
}
```

The pieces of this declaration are as follows.

➤ *attributes0*—Attributes that specify extra properties for the enumeration.

➤ *accessibility*—This determines which code can access the variable.

➤ *name*—The name you want to give the enumeration.

➤   : *type*—All enumerations are stored internally as integer values. By default, an enumeration's type is `int`. You can use this part of the declaration to change the underlying type to `byte`, `sbyte`, `short`, `ushort`, `int`, `uint`, `long`, or `ulong` (any integer type except `char`).

➤   *attributes1*, *attributes2*—Attributes that specify extra properties for the enumerators.

➤   *name1*, *name2*—The names of the enumerators.

➤   *value1*, *value2*—The integer value that should be used to store this enumerator. By default, the first enumerator is represented by 0, and the values of subsequent enumerators are increased by 1.

Constant Declarations

Constant declarations are similar to the variable declarations described in Appendix C, "Variable Declarations." The main differences are you must include an initialization statement to give the constant a value and you cannot change the value after the constant is initialized.

You may also need to use a literal type character to explicitly give a value's type. For example, the following code attempts to create a `float` constant and set its value to 5.8. Unfortunately, C# interprets the literal string 5.8 as a `double` and not a `float`, so Visual Studio flags this as an error.

```
const float taxRate = 5.8;
```

To avoid this problem, or to make your code more explicit, you can follow a literal value with a literal type character to indicate the value's data type, as in the following code.

```
const float taxRate = 5.8F;
```

The following table lists C#'s literal type characters.

CHARACTER	DATA TYPE
U	uint
L	long
UL, LU	ulong
F	float
D	double
M	decimal

You can use either uppercase or lowercase for literal type characters.

You can also precede an integer literal with 0x or 0X to indicate that it is a hexadecimal value.

Operators

The C# operators fall into four main categories: arithmetic, comparison, logical, and bitwise. The following sections explain these categories and the operators they contain. The end of this appendix describes operator precedence and special operators, as well as operator overloading.

ARITHMETIC OPERATORS

The following table lists the arithmetic operators provided by C#.

OPERATOR	PURPOSE	EXAMPLE	RESULT
++	Increment	x++ or ++x	Sets x = x + 1
--	Decrement	x-- or --x	Sets x = x - 1
-	Negation	-x	Sets x = -x
+	Unary plus	+x	Sets x = +x (leaves x unchanged)
*	Multiplication	2 * 3	6
/	Division	3.0 / 2	1.5
%	Modulus	17 % 5	2
+	Addition	2 + 3	5
+	Concatenation	"Bob " + "Baker"	"Bob Baker"
-	Subtraction	3 - 2	1
<<	Bit left shift	10110111 << 1	01101110
>>	Bit right shift	10110111 >> 1	01011011

COMPARISON OPERATORS

The following table lists the comparison operators provided by C#.

OPERATOR	PURPOSE	EXAMPLE	RESULT
==	Equals	A == B	true if A equals B.
!=	Not equals	A != B	true if A does not equal B.
<	Less than	A < B	true if A is less than B.
<=	Less than or equal to	A <= B	true if A is less than or equal to B.
>	Greater than	A > B	true if A is greater than B.
>=	Greater than or equal to	A >= B	true if A is greater than or equal to B.
is	Object is or inherits from a certain type	obj is Manager	true if obj is an object that inherits from Manager.

LOGICAL OPERATORS

The following table summarizes the C# logical operators.

OPERATOR	PURPOSE	EXAMPLE	RESULT
!	Negation	!A	true if A is false.
&	And	A & B	true if A and B are both true.
|	Or	A | B	true if A or B or both are true.
^	Xor (Exclusive Or)	A ^ B	true if A is true or B is true but both are not true.
&&	And with short-circuit evaluation	A && B	true if A and B are both true.
||	Or with short-circuit evaluation	A || B	true if A or B or both are true.

BITWISE OPERATORS

Bitwise operators work much as logical operators do, except that they compare values 1 bit at a time. C# provides bitwise versions of the &, |, and ^ operators. It also provides ~, the bitwise negation operator.

ASSIGNMENT OPERATORS

Many operators have assignment versions. For example, the following code adds 10 to the value x and saves the result in variable x.

```
x += 10;
```

The complete list of assignment operators is: =, +=, -=, *=, /=, %=, &=, |=, ^=, <<=, and >>=.

CONDITIONAL AND NULL-COALESCING OPERATORS

The conditional operator ?: (sometimes called the ternary operator) takes three operands. If the first operand is `true`, it returns the second operand. Otherwise it returns the third operand.

The null-coalescing operator ?? takes two operands. It returns its left operand if its value is not `null`. If the left operand is `null`, it returns its right operand.

OPERATOR PRECEDENCE

The following table lists the operators in order of precedence. When evaluating an expression, the program evaluates an operator before it evaluates those in a lower section of the list.

OPERATOR	DESCRIPTION
( )	Grouping (parentheses)
x++	Post-increment
x--	Post-decrement
+	Unary plus
-	Numeric negation
!	Logical negation
~	Bitwise negation
++x	Pre-increment
--x	Pre-decrement
(T)	Casting

continues

(continued)

OPERATOR	DESCRIPTION
*	Multiplication
/	Division
%	Modulus
+	Concatenation
+	Addition
-	Subtraction
<<	Left shift
>>	Right shift
<	Less than
>	Greater than
<=	Less than or equal to
>=	Greater than or equal to
is	Inherits from
==	Equals
!=	Does not equal
&	Logical And
^	Logical Xor
|	Logical Or
&&	Conditional And
||	Conditional Or
??	Null-coalescing
? :	Conditional
=	Assignment operators
+=	
-=	
...	

When operators are in the same section in the table, or if an expression contains more than one instance of the same operator, the program evaluates them in left-to-right order.

Use parentheses to change the order of evaluation and to make expressions easier to read.

DATETIME AND TIMESPAN OPERATORS

The `DateTime` and `TimeSpan` data types are related through their operators. The following list shows the relationships between these two data types.

➤ `DateTime - DateTime = TimeSpan`

➤ `DateTime + TimeSpan = DateTime`

➤ `TimeSpan + TimeSpan = TimeSpan`

➤ `TimeSpan - TimeSpan = TimeSpan`

The following table lists examples demonstrating convenient methods provided by the `DateTime` data type.

SYNTAX	MEANING
`newDate = date1.Add(timespan1)`	Returns `date1` plus `timespan1`
`newDate = date1.AddYears(numYears)`	Returns `date1` plus the indicated number of years
`newDate = date1.AddMonths(numMonths)`	Returns `date1` plus the indicated number of months
`newDate = date1.AddDays(numDays)`	Returns `date1` plus the indicated number of days
`newDate = date1.AddHours(numHours)`	Returns `date1` plus the indicated number of hours
`newDate = date1.AddMinutes(numMinutes)`	Returns `date1` plus the indicated number of minutes
`newDate = date1.AddSeconds(numSeconds)`	Returns `date1` plus the indicated number of seconds
`newDate = date1.AddMilliseconds(numMilliseconds)`	Returns `date1` plus the indicated number of milliseconds
`newDate = date1.AddTicks(numTicks)`	Returns `date1` plus the indicated number of ticks (100 nanosecond units)
`newTimespan = date1.Subtract(date2)`	Returns the time span between `date2` and `date1`
`resultInt = date1.CompareTo(date2)`	Returns a value indicating whether `date1` is greater than, less than, or equal to `date2`
`resultBool = date1.Equals(date2)`	Returns `true` if `date1` equals `date2`

OPERATOR OVERLOADING

To overload an operator, create a `static` method that returns the appropriate data type. Instead of giving the method a name, use the keyword `operator` followed by the operator symbol you want to overload. Next, define the parameters that the operator takes. Finally, write the code that the operator should execute.

For example, the following code defines a + operator for a simple `Complex` class.

```
public static Complex operator +(Complex operand1, Complex operand2)
{
    return new Complex()
    {
        Re = operand1.Re + operand2.Re,
        Im = operand1.Im + operand2.Im
    };
}
```

Unary operators that you can overload include: +, -, !, ~, ++, --, `true`, and `false`.

Binary operators that you can overload include: +, -, *, /, %, &, |, ^, <<, and >>. If you overload `true`, `false` 7, and |, the && and || operators are automatically overloaded for you.

Note that the second operand for the shift operators << and >> must be an `int`.

The assignment operators are automatically overloaded if you overload the corresponding operator. For example, if you overload *, then C# overloads *= for you.

See Chapter 5, "Operators," for more information about overloading comparison, logical, and type conversion operators.

Method Declarations

This appendix provides information about method declarations. A property procedure includes a pair of methods, which are also described here.

METHODS

In C# all methods must be inside a class. The syntax for creating a method is as follows.

```
«attributes» «accessibility» «modifiers» return_type name(«parameters»)
{
    code...
}
```

The following list describes the pieces of this declaration.

➤ *attributes*—Attributes that specify extra properties for the method.

➤ *accessibility*—One of public, internal, protected, internal protected, or private.

➤ *modifiers*—One of new (hides a parent class's version of the method), static (shared by all instances of the class), virtual (the method can be overridden in a descendant class), override (the method is overriding a version in an ancestor class), sealed (indicates an overriding method cannot be further overridden), abstract (defines only the method's signature), or extern (the method is defined outside of the assembly).

➤ *return_type*—The type of the data that the method returns. If the method doesn't return a value, this should be void.

➤ *name*—The name you want the method to have.

➤ *parameters*—The method's parameters.

➤ *code*—The code that the method should execute.

Use a return statement to exit the method and return a value (if the method returns a value).

PROPERTY PROCEDURES

Properties have `get` and `set` accessors. The syntax for creating a read/write property is as follows.

```
public data_type name
{
    get
    {
        ...
        return value;
    }
    set
    {
        ...
    }
}
```

To create a read-only or write-only property, simply omit the accessor that you don't need.

To create an auto-implemented property, simply omit the body of the accessors, as in the following example.

```
public string Name { get; set; }
```

LAMBDA FUNCTIONS AND EXPRESSIONS

A *lambda expression* is a method defined within the flow of the program's code instead of as a separate method.

An *expression lambda* consists of a list of zero or more parameters, the `=>` operator, and a single expression that evaluates to some result. For example, the following code creates an delegate named root and sets it equal to an expression lambda. It then displays the value of root(13).

```
Func<float, double> root = (value) => Math.Sqrt(value);
Console.WriteLine(root(13));
```

A *statement lambda* is similar to an expression lambda except it can execute multiple statements inside braces and uses the `return` statement to return its result. The following code demonstrates a statement lambda.

```
Func<int, int, int, int> middle = (v1, v2, v3) =>
    {
        // Sort the items.
        int[] values = { v1, v2, v3 };
        Array.Sort(values);

        // Return the middle item.
        return values[1];
    };
Console.WriteLine(middle(2, 3, 1));
```

An *async lambda* is a lambda expression with the async keyword added, so the program can execute it asynchronously. For example, the following code adds an asynchronous statement lambda to the countButton control's Click event.

```
private void Form1_Load(object sender, EventArgs e)
{
    countButton.Click += async (button, args) =>
    {
        for (int i = 0; i < 5; i++)
        {
            Console.WriteLine(i);
            await System.Threading.Tasks.Task.Delay(1000);
        }
    };
}
```

EXTENSION METHODS

To make an extension method, place a static method in a static class. Add the keyword this before the method's first parameter and give that parameter the type that you want to extend. For example, the following code defines a RemoveNonLetters string extension method.

```
public static class StringExtensions
{
    public static string RemoveNonLetters(this string text)
    {
        string result = "";
        foreach (char ch in text)
            if (((ch >= 'a') && (ch <= 'z')) ||
                ((ch >= 'A') && (ch <= 'Z')))
                result += ch;
            else
                result += "?";

        return result;
    }
}
```

Useful Attributes

The .NET Framework defines more than 500 attribute classes, so only a handful of the most commonly used are described here.

The names of attribute classes end with `Attribute`. If you want to search for an attribute's class, add `Attribute` to the end of the name. For example, the `ReadOnly` attribute class's name is `ReadOnlyAttribute`.

To create a custom attribute, simply create a new class derived from the `Attribute` class. By convention, the custom attribute class's name should end with `Attribute`.

For more information about attributes, see `msdn.microsoft.com/library/system .attribute.aspx`. If you scroll to the bottom, you can see a list of classes that inherit from the `Attribute` class.

USEFUL XML SERIALIZATION ATTRIBUTES

The following table lists attributes that are useful when performing XML serializations.

ATTRIBUTE	PURPOSE
`XmlArray`	Indicates the name that should be given to an array in an XML serialization.
`XmlArrayItem`	Indicates a type that can be in an array in an XML serialization.
`XmlAttribute`	Indicates that a property should be serialized as an attribute rather than an element in an XML serialization. Optionally indicates the attribute's name in the serialization.
`XmlElement`	Specifically indicates the field will be serialized as an XML element. This attribute allows you to change the XML element's name.

continues

(continued)

ATTRIBUTE	PURPOSE
XmlEnum	Enables you to specify the names by which enumeration values are serialized.
XmlIgnore	Indicates that an XML serialization should not serialize a property.
XmlRoot	Controls the name and namespace for the element generated for an XML serialization's root element.
XmlText	Indicates that a value should be serialized as a text value in an XML serialization.
XmlType	Controls the name and namespace for the element generated for a class in an XML serialization.

USEFUL JSON SERIALIZATION ATTRIBUTES

The following table lists attributes that are useful when performing JSON serializations.

ATTRIBUTE	PURPOSE
CollectionDataContract	Allows you to control serialization of collections.
DataContract	Indicates that a type is serializable by a serializer such as a `DataContractSerializer`.
DataMember	Indicates that a property should be serialized.
EnumMember	Indicates that a property is an enumeration and should be serialized.
IgnoreDataMember	Indicates that a property should not be included in the serialization.
OptionalField	Indicates that a property is optional in a serialization.

BINARY SERIALIZATION ATTRIBUTES

The `BinaryFormatter` class understands only one attribute, `Serializable`, which you should use to mark a class as serializable. The serialization includes all properties and fields, even those with restricted access such as those marked `private`.

OTHER USEFUL ATTRIBUTES

The following table summarizes particularly useful attributes available to C# programs.

ATTRIBUTE	PURPOSE
AssemblyCompany	Stores an assembly's company name.
AssemblyCopyright	Stores an assembly's copyright information.
AssemblyCulture	Stores the culture that an assembly supports.
AssemblyDescription	Stores an assembly's description.
AssemblyProduct	Stores an assembly's product name.
AssemblyTitle	Stores an assembly's title.
AssemblyTrademark	Stores an assembly's trademark information.
AssemblyVersion	Stores an assembly's version information.
AttributeUsage	Indicates the kinds of items (class, method, property, and so on) to which a custom attribute may be applied.
Browsable	Indicates whether a property should be visible to editors such as the Properties window or the PropertyGrid control.
Category	Indicates the category that should include a property in an editor such as the Properties window.
Conditional	Hides a method's body if a compile-time symbol is undefined. The method is still callable; it just doesn't do anything.
DebuggerHidden	Indicates a method should be hidden from the debugger. The debugger will not stop inside or step through the method.
DebuggerStepThrough	Makes the debugger skip over the method if you try to step over or into it. The debugger will still stop inside the method if you set a breakpoint there.
DefaultEvent	Indicates a class's default event.
DefaultProperty	Indicates a class's default property.
DefaultValue	Sets a property's default value for use by editors such as the Properties window. (If you right-click a property in the Properties window and select Reset, the property is given this value.)
Description	Specifies the description that an editor such as the Properties window should display for an object's property. (Use XML comments to specify a description for use by IntelliSense.)

continues

(continued)

ATTRIBUTE	PURPOSE
DisplayName	Indicates the name that editors such as the Properties window should display for a property.
Flags	Indicates that an enumeration should be considered a bit mask, so a variable can include one or more of the enumeration's values simultaneously.
Localizable	Indicates that a property is localizable, and its value should be stored in the appropriate resource files.
Mergable	Indicates an editor such as the Properties window should allow the user to get and set the property for multiple objects at the same time. (For example, if you select two TextBoxes, you can set both of their Text properties at the same time. In contrast, you cannot set their Name properties at the same time.)
Obsolete	Marks a method as obsolete. The program can still use the method, but Visual Studio flags calls to it with warnings.
ParenthesizePropertyName	Tells property editors such as the Properties window to display a property's name surrounded by parentheses. When displayed alphabetically, the property comes at the top of the list.
ReadOnly	Indicates that a property is read-only to editors such as the PropertyGrid control.

Control Statements

Control statements tell an application which other statements to execute under a particular set of circumstances.

The two main categories of control statements are decision statements and looping statements. The following sections describe the decision and looping statements provided by C#.

DECISION STATEMENTS

A decision statement represents a branch in the program. It marks a place where the program can execute one set of statements or another or possibly no statements at all.

if-else Statements

The if-else statement has the following syntax.

```
if (condition1) block1;
else if (condition2) block2;
else if (condition3) block3;
...
else blockElse;
```

The program evaluates each condition and executes the first block for which the condition is true.

If none of the conditions is true, then the final blockElse block is executed. If the final else statement and the blockElse are not provided, no code is executed.

Each block could be a single statement or a sequence of statements included in braces.

switch

A switch statement lets a program execute one of several pieces of code based on a test value. The switch statement is roughly equivalent to a sequence of if-else statements.

The basic syntax is as follows.

```
switch (value)
{
    case expression1:
        statements1;
        break;
    case expression2:
        statements2;
        break;
    ...
    «default:
        statementsDefault
        break;»
}
```

The program compares *value* to the expressions until it finds one that matches or it runs out of expressions to test. The expressions must be constant statements and cannot duplicate each other.

If the program finds a match, it executes the corresponding code. If the program runs out of expressions, it executes the statements in the default section (if it is present).

You can place multiple case statements in a group to make them all execute the same code. However, you cannot allow the code from one case section to fall through to the next. If a section contains lines of code, then it must end with a break statement before the next case begins.

Conditional and Null-coalescing Operators

The conditional and null-coalescing operators are actually operators, but they behave like decision statements so their descriptions are included here.

The conditional operator ?: (sometimes called the ternary operator) takes three operands. If the first operand is true, it returns the second operand. Otherwise, it returns the third operand.

The null-coalescing operator ?? takes two operands. It returns its left operand if its value is not null. If the left operand is null, it returns its right operand.

LOOPING STATEMENTS

Looping statements make the program execute a series of statements repeatedly. C# provides four kinds of loops: for loops, while loops, do loops, and foreach loops.

for Loops

A for loop has the following syntax.

```
for («initialization»; «test»; «increment») block;
```

Here:

- ➤ *initialization*—This piece of code initializes the loop.

- ➤ *test*—Each time the program is about to execute the code inside the loop, it evaluates this as a boolean expression. If the result is `true`, the loop continues. If the result is `false`, the loop ends.

- ➤ *increment*—After the program has executed the code inside the loop but before it checks *test* again, it executes this code.

- ➤ *block*—This is the piece of code, which could be a single statement or a sequence of statements surrounded by braces, that is executed repeatedly as long as *test* is `true`.

while Loops

A `while` loop has the following syntax.

```
while (test)
    block;
```

As long as the *test* evaluates to `true`, the loop executes the block, which can be a single statement or a sequence of statements enclosed in braces. Note that this means the loop might not execute even once if the test is `false` when the loop starts.

You cannot omit the *test* but you can set it to `true` to make the `while` loop repeat indefinitely.

do Loops

A `do` loop has the following syntax.

```
do
    block;
while (test);
```

A `do` loop is similar to a `while` loop except it performs its test after the loop has executed instead of before it executes. That means a `do` loop always executes at least once.

foreach Loops

A `foreach` loop iterates over the items in a collection, array, or other container class that supports `foreach` loops. A `foreach` loop has the following syntax.

```
foreach (variable in group)
    statement;
```

Here, *group* is a collection, array, or other object that supports `foreach`.

Enumerators

An *enumerator* is an object that lets you move through the objects contained by some sort of container class.

You can use an enumerator to view the objects in a collection but not to modify the collection itself. You can use the enumerator to alter the objects in the collection (for example, to change their properties), but you can generally not use it to add, remove, or rearrange the objects in the collection.

Initially, an enumerator is positioned before the first item in the collection. The following table summarizes methods that an enumerator provides to let you move through its collection.

METHOD	PURPOSE
MoveNext	Moves to the next item in the collection. This method returns true if it successfully moves to a new item.
Reset	Restores the enumerator to its original position before the first object.
Current	Returns the object that the enumerator is currently reading.

Iterators

An *iterator* is similar in concept to an enumerator. Iterators also provide methods for moving through a collection of items.

Iterators are more specialized than enumerators. How you use them depends on what you need to do and on the kind of iterator, so they are not described in detail here.

break and continue Statements

Inside a loop, the break statement makes a program immediately break out of the closest enclosing loop without executing any statements inside the loop that follow the break statement.

The continue statement makes a program jump to the beginning of the closest containing loop without executing any statements inside the loop that follow the continue statement.

Error Handling

A program can use `try-catch-finally` blocks to protect itself from exceptions. The syntax is as follows.

```
try
{
    tryStatements...
}
catch (exceptionType1 variable1)
{
    exceptionStatements1...
}
catch (exceptionType2 variable2)
{
    exceptionStatements2...
}
...
catch
{
    finalExceptionStatements...
}
finally
{
    finallyStatements...
}
```

When an error occurs, the program examines the `catch` statements in order until it finds one that matches the current exception and executes the corresponding code. If the exception doesn't match any of the `catch` statements, the program executes the code in the final `catch` statement, which doesn't specify an exception type.

After executing the code in the `try` section and possibly a `catch` section, the program executes the code in the `finally` section.

The `catch` and `finally` sections are optional; although, the `try-catch-finally` block must include at least one `catch` section or the `finally` section.

THROWING EXCEPTIONS

Use the `throw` statement to throw an exception, as in the following code.

```
throw new ArgumentException("Width must be greater than zero");
```

Exception classes provide several overloaded constructors, so you can indicate such things as the basic error message, the name of the variable that caused the exception, and an inner exception.

For information on useful exception classes and custom exception classes, see Appendix O, "Useful Exception Classes."

LINQ

This appendix provides syntax summaries for the most useful LINQ methods. For more detailed information, see Chapter 8, "LINQ."

BASIC LINQ QUERY SYNTAX

The following text shows the typical syntax for a LINQ query.

```
from ... where ... orderby ... select ...
```

The following sections describe these four standard clauses. The sections after those describe some of the other most useful LINQ clauses.

from

The `from` clause tells where the data comes from and defines the name by which it is known within the LINQ query.

```
from queryVariable in dataSource
```

Examples:

```
var customerQuery =
    from person in customers
    select person;
var scoresQuery =
    from student in students
    from score in testScores
    where student.StudentId == score.StudentId
    select new {student, score};
```

Usually, if you select data from multiple sources, you will want to use a `where` clause to join the results from the sources.

where

The where clause applies filters to the records selected by the from clause. The syntax follows.

```
where conditions
```

Use comparison operators (>, <, and ==), logical operators (!, |, and &&), object methods (ToString and Length), and functions to build complex conditions.

For example, the following query selects student and test score data, matching students to their test scores.

```
var scoresQuery =
    from student in students
    from score in testScores
    where student.StudentId == score.StudentId
    select new {student, score};
```

The following example selects students with last names starting with S.

```
var scoresQuery =
    from student in students
    from score in testScores
    where student.StudentId == score.StudentId
        && student.LastName.StartsWith("S")
    select new {student, score};
```

orderby

The orderby clause makes a query sort the selected objects. For example, the following query selects students and their scores ordered by student last name followed by first name.

```
var scoresQuery =
    from student in students
    from score in testScores
    where student.StudentId == score.StudentId
    orderby student.LastName, student.FirstName
    select new {student, score};
```

Add the descending keyword to sort a field in descending order.

select

The select clause lists the fields that the query should select into its result. Optionally, you can add an alias to the result.

The following query selects the customers' FirstName and LastName values concatenated and gives the result the alias Name.

```
var customerQuery = from person in customers
    select Name = person.FirstName + " " + person.LastName;
```

You can pass values from the data sources into functions or constructors. For example, suppose the `Person` class has a constructor that takes first and last names as parameters. Then the following query returns a group of `Person` objects created from the selected customer data.

```
var customerQuery = from person in customers
    select new Person(person.FirstName, person.LastName);
```

join

The `join` keyword selects data from multiple data sources matching up corresponding fields. The following pseudo-code shows the `join` command's syntax.

```
from variable1 in dataSource1
join variable2 in dataSource2
  on variable1.field1 equals variable2.field2
```

For example, the following query selects `Customer` objects from the `customers` array. For each `Customer` object, it selects `Order` objects from the `orders` array where the two records have the same `CustomerId` value.

```
var query =
    from customer in customers
    join order in orders
    on customer.CustomerId equals order.CustomerId
    select new { customer, order };
```

Note that you can get a similar result by using a `where` clause. The following query selects a similar set of objects without using the `join` keyword.

```
var query =
    from customer in customers
    from order in orders
    where customer.CustomerId == order.CustomerId
    select new { customer, order };
```

group by

The `group by` clause lets a program select data from a flat, relational style format and build a hierarchical arrangement of objects. The following code shows a simple example.

```
var query =
    from order in orders
    group order by order.CustomerId;
```

This query selects `Order` objects from the `orders` array and groups the selected objects by their `CustomerId` values.

The result is a list of objects representing the groups. Each of those objects has a `Key` property that gives the value that was used to build that group. In this example, the `Key` is the value of the objects' `CustomerId` values.

Each of the group objects is also enumerable, so the program can loop through the objects that are in its group.

Aggregate Values

When you group data, you can use aggregate methods to select combined values from the groups.

The following query selects orders grouped by `CustomerId`. The `Sum` aggregate method highlighted in bold selects the sum of the prices of the orders in each group.

```
var query =
    from order in orders
    group order by order.CustomerId into Orders
    select new
    {
        ID = Orders.Key,
        Orders,
        TotalPrice = Orders.Sum(order => order.Price)
    };
```

Limiting Results

The following list summarizes methods that LINQ provides for limiting the results returned by a query.

➤ `First`—Returns the first result and discards the rest. If the result includes no values, this throws an exception.

➤ `FirstOrDefault`—Returns the first result and discards the rest. If the query contains no results, it returns a default value.

➤ `Last`—Returns the last result and discards the rest. If the result includes no values, this throws an exception.

➤ `LastOrDefault`—Returns the last result and discards the rest. If the query contains no results, it returns a default value.

➤ `Single`—Returns the single item selected by the query. If the query does not contain exactly one result, this throws an exception.

➤ `SingleOrDefault`—Returns the single item selected by the query. If the query contains no results, this returns a default value. If the query contains more than one item, this throws an exception.

➤ `Skip`—Discards a specified number of results and keeps the rest.

➤ `SkipWhile`—Discards results as long as some condition is `true` and then keeps the rest. (The condition is given by a method, often a lambda expression.)

➤ `Take`—Keeps a specified number of results and discards the rest.

➤ `TakeWhile`—Keeps results as long as some condition is `true` and then discards the rest.

LINQ FUNCTIONS

The following table summarizes LINQ useful extension methods that are not available from C# LINQ query syntax.

FUNCTION	PURPOSE
Aggregate	Uses a function specified by the code to calculate a custom aggregate
Concat	Concatenates two sequences into a new sequence
Contains	Returns `true` if the result contains a specific value
DefaultIfEmpty	Returns the query's result or a default value if the query returns an empty result
ElementAt	Returns an element at a specific position in the query's result
ElementAtOrDefault	Returns an element at a specific position in the query's result or a default value if there is no such position
Empty	Creates an empty `IEnumerable`
Except	Returns the items in one `IEnumerable` that are not in a second `IEnumerable`
Intersection	Returns the intersection of two `IEnumerable` objects
Range	Creates an `IEnumerable` containing a range of integer values
Repeat	Creates an `IEnumerable` containing a value repeated a specific number of times
SequenceEqual	Returns `true` if two sequences are identical
Union	Returns the union of two `IEnumerable` objects

The following table summarizes LINQ data type conversion methods.

FUNCTION	PURPOSE
AsEnumerable	Converts the result to `IEnumerable<T>`
AsQueryable	Converts an `IEnumerable` to `IQueryable`
OfType	Removes items that cannot be cast into a specific type
ToArray	Places the results in an array

continues

(continued)

FUNCTION	PURPOSE
ToDictionary	Places the results in a `Dictionary`
ToList	Converts the result to `List<T>`
ToLookup	Places the results in a `Lookup` (one-to-many dictionary)

LINQ TO XML

The following sections describe LINQ methods to move data in and out of XML.

XML Literals

C# does not support XML literals, but you can pass a string containing XML data into an XML object's `Parse` method, as shown in the following code.

```
XElement xelement = XElement.Parse(
@"<Employees>
    <Employee FirstName=""Ann"" LastName=""Archer""/>
    <Employee FirstName='Ben' LastName='Baker'/>
    <Employee>
      <FirstName>Cindy</FirstName>
      <LastName>Cant</LastName>
    </Employee>
  </Employees>
");
```

LINQ into XML

LINQ's XML classes provide constructors that enable you to build XML documents relatively easily. Each constructor's parameter list ends with a parameter array, so you can pass any number of items into it. The following code uses functional construction to build an XML structure.

```
XElement employees = new XElement("Employees",
    new XElement("Employee",
        new XAttribute("FirstName", "Ann"),
        new XAttribute("LastName", "Archer")
    ),
    new XElement("Employee",
        new XAttribute("FirstName", "Ben"),
        new XAttribute("LastName", "Baker")
    ),
    new XElement("Employee",
        new XElement("FirstName", "Cindy"),
        new XElement("LastName", "Cant")
    )
);
```

LINQ out of XML

XML classes such as XElement provide LINQ functions that enable you to use LINQ queries on them just as you can select data from IEnumerable objects.

The following code searches the XElement named document for descendants named "Employee" and selects their FirstName and LastName attributes.

```
var selectEmployee =
    from employee in document.Descendants("Employee")
    select new
    {
        FirstName = employee.Attribute("FirstName").Value,
        LastName = employee.Attribute("LastName").Value
    };
```

The following table describes other methods supported by XElement that a program can use to navigate through an XML hierarchy. Most of the functions return IEnumerable objects that you can use in LINQ queries.

FUNCTION	RETURNS
Ancestors	IEnumerable containing all ancestors of the element.
AncestorsAndSelf	IEnumerable containing this element followed by all its ancestors.
Attribute	The element's attribute with a specific name.
Attributes	IEnumerable containing the element's attributes.
Descendants	IEnumerable containing all descendants of the element.
DescendantsAndSelf	IEnumerable containing this element followed by all its descendants.
DescendantNodes	IEnumerable containing all descendant nodes of the element. These include all nodes such as XElement and XText.
DescendantNodesAndSelf	IEnumerable containing this element followed by all its descendant nodes.
Element	The first child element with a specific name.
Elements	IEnumerable containing the immediate children of the element.
ElementsAfterSelf	IEnumerable containing the siblings of the element that come after this element.
ElementsBeforeSelf	IEnumerable containing the siblings of the element that come before this element.

continues

(continued)

FUNCTION	RETURNS
Nodes	IEnumerable containing the nodes that are immediate children of the element. These include all nodes such as XElement and XText.
NodesAfterSelf	IEnumerable containing the sibling nodes of the element that come after this element.
NodesBeforeSelf	IEnumerable containing the sibling nodes of the element that come before this element.

LINQ TO ADO.NET

LINQ to ADO.NET provides tools that enable you to apply LINQ-style queries to objects used by ADO.NET to store and interact with relational data. LINQ to ADO.NET includes three components: LINQ to SQL, LINQ to Entities, and LINQ to DataSet.

Building and managing SQL Server databases and the Entity Framework are topics too large to cover in this book, so LINQ to SQL and LINQ to Entities are not described in more detail here. For more information, consult the online help or Microsoft's website.

LINQ to DataSet lets a program use LINQ-style queries to select data from DataSet objects.

For example, suppose the testScoresDataSet object contains tables named Students and TestScores. Then the following code gets references to the DataTable objects that represent the tables.

```
DataTable studentsTable = testScoresDataSet.Tables["Students"];
DataTable scoresTable = testScoresDataSet.Tables["TestScores"];
```

You can then use LINQ to query the DataTable table objects. For example, the following code selects the names of students with LastName before "F" alphabetically.

```
var namesBeforeFQuery =
    from student in studentsTable.AsEnumerable()
    where (student.Field<string>("LastName").CompareTo("F") < 0)
    orderby student.Field<string>("LastName")
    select new
    {
        FirstName = student.Field<string>("FirstName"),
        LastName = student.Field<string>("LastName")
    };
namesBeforeDDataGrid.DataSource = namesBeforeFQuery.ToList();
```

The following list summarizes the key differences between a LINQ to DataSet query and a normal LINQ to Objects query.

➤ The LINQ to DataSet query must use the `DataTable` object's `AsEnumerable` method to make the object queryable.

➤ The code can access the fields in a `DataRow`, as in `student.Field<string>("LastName")`.

➤ If you want to display the results in a bound control such as a `DataGrid` or `ListBox`, use the query's `ToList` method.

PLINQ

Adding parallelism to LINQ is remarkably simple. First, add a reference to the System.Threading library to your program. Then add a call to `AsParallel` to the enumerable object that you're searching. For example, the following code uses `AsParallel` to select the even numbers from the array `numbers`.

```
var evens =
    from int number in numbers.AsParallel()
    where number % 2 == 0
    select number;
    join order in orders on customer.CustomerId equals order.CustomerId
```

Classes and Structures

This appendix provides information about class and structure declarations.

CLASSES

The syntax for declaring a class follows.

```
«attributes» «accessibility» «abstract|sealed|static» «partial»
    class name «inheritance»
{
    statements
}
```

The following list describes the declaration's pieces.

➤ *attributes*—This can include any number of attribute specifiers.

➤ *accessibility*—This can be one of public, internal, private, protected, or protected internal.

➤ abstract—This keyword means you cannot create instances of the class. Instead you can make instances of derived classes.

➤ sealed—This keyword means you cannot derive other classes from the class.

➤ static—This keyword means you cannot derive other classes from the class or create instances of it. You invoke the members of a static class by using the class's name instead of an instance. All members of a static class must also be declared static.

➤ partial—This keyword indicates that this is only part of the class declaration and that the program may include other partial declarations for this class.

➤ *name*—This is the name you want to give the class.

➤ *inheritance*—This clause can include a parent class, one or more interfaces, or both a parent class and interfaces. If the declaration includes a parent class and interfaces, the parent class must come first.

STRUCTURES

The syntax for writing a structure follows.

```
«attributes» «accessibility» «partial» struct name «interfaces»
{
    statements
}
```

The structure's *attributes*, *accessibility*, and partial clauses are the same as those for classes. See the previous section for details.

Structures cannot inherit, so they cannot have *inheritance* clauses. Instead they have *interfaces* clauses that specify any interfaces the structure implements.

Following are the major differences between a structure and a class.

➤   Structures cannot inherit.

➤   Structures cannot use the abstract, sealed, or static keywords because you cannot inherit from a structure.

➤   Structures are *value types*, whereas classes are *reference types*. See the section "Value Versus Reference Types" in Chapter 12, "Classes and Structures," for information on the consequences of this difference.

CONSTRUCTORS

A *constructor* is a special method that has no name and that returns the type of the class or structure that contains it. Alternatively, you can think of a constructor as having the same name as its class and returning no type, not even void.

Class constructors can take any number of parameters. If you provide no constructors, C# creates a default parameterless constructor that takes no parameters. If you provide *any* constructor, C# does not provide a default parameterless constructor. If you want to allow the program to use a parameterless constructor in that case, you must either provide one or provide a constructor with all optional parameters.

Structure constructors are similar to class constructors with two major exceptions. First, you cannot make a structure constructor that takes no parameters. Second, C# always provides a default parameterless constructor, even if you give the structure other constructors.

DESTRUCTORS

A *destructor* is a method that executes when an object is destroyed. Before it permanently destroys an object, the garbage collector calls that object's destructor so that the destructor can clean up unmanaged resources. Keep in mind that finalization is nondeterministic, so you generally don't know when the destructor will be called.

To create a destructor, create a method named after the class with a ~ character in front of it. For example, the following code shows a destructor for the `Person` class.

```
~Person()
{
    // Free unmanaged resources here.
    ...
}
```

To allow a program to free resources before an object is destroyed, you can give the class a `Dispose` method and implement the `IDisposable` interface.

The following list summarizes the key destruction issues.

➤ The destructor is called automatically when an object is destroyed.

➤ The destructor cannot refer to managed objects because they may have already been destroyed. In particular, the destructor cannot free managed resources because they may have already been destroyed.

➤ The destructor must free unmanaged resources. This is the last chance the object has for freeing those resources.

➤ Instead of making the program wait an unknowable amount of time for the destructor to execute, you can provide a `Dispose` method that disposes of all resources when the object is done with them.

➤ If you implement the `IDisposable` interface, the `using` statement calls `Dispose` automatically.

➤ Either it must be safe for the `Dispose` method and the destructor to both run, or you can ensure that they both can't run by making the `Dispose` method call `GC.SuppressFinalize`.

EVENTS

An *event* lets an object notify the application that something potentially interesting has occurred.

Following is the syntax for declaring an event.

```
«attributes» «accessibility» «new|virtual|override|abstract|sealed» «static»
    event delegate name;
```

The following list describes the declaration's pieces.

➤ `attributes`—Attributes provide extra information about the event for use by the compiler, the runtime system, and other tools.

➤ `accessibility`—This can be `public`, `private`, `protected`, `internal`, or `protected internal` and is similar to the accessibility for other items such as classes, properties, and methods.

➤ `new|virtual|override|abstract|sealed`—These are similar to the keywords used by methods described in Chapter 6, "Methods." They have the following meanings:

➤ `new`—Hides an event with the same name defined in an ancestor class.

➤ `virtual`—If you mark an event as virtual, you can later replace it in a derived class by overriding it.

➤ `override`—If an ancestor class defines a virtual event, you can use the `override` keyword to override it.

➤ `abstract`—This keyword indicates the event is abstract, so derived classes must override the event to give it an implementation. As is the case with `abstract` methods, a class that contains an `abstract` event must be `abstract` and cannot be instantiated.

➤ `sealed`—This keyword indicates the event is no longer `virtual`, so it cannot be overridden in derived classes.

➤ `static`—This indicates the class itself raises the event rather than instances of the class.

➤ `delegate`—This is a delegate type that defines the parameters that will be passed to event handlers for the event.

➤ `name`—This is the name you want to give the event.

To raise an event, first determine whether any other pieces of code have registered to receive the event by comparing the event to `null`. If code has registered to receive the event, invoke the event by name, passing it any necessary parameters.

For example, suppose the `Student` class has a `GradeChanged` event. Then the following snippet inside the `Student` class raises the event, passing it the current `Student` object as a parameter.

```
if (GradeChanged != null) GradeChanged(this);
```

To subscribe to an event, use the `+=` operator to "add" the event handler to the event. The following code shows how a program could register the `MyPerson_NameChanged` event handler to handle the `MyPerson` object's `NameChanged` event.

```
MyPerson.NameChanged += MyPerson_NameChanged;
```

If you subscribe an event handler to an event multiple times, it executes multiple times when the event occurs.

To unsubscribe from an event, use the `-=` operator, as in the following code.

```
MyPerson.NameChanged -= MyPerson_NameChanged;
```

Unsubscribing from an event more times than the event handler was originally registered does not throw an exception.

Collection Classes

This appendix provides information about collection classes.

ARRAYS

Arrays are relatively simple collection classes that enable you to store and retrieve items by using their indexes in the array. C# provides two kinds of arrays: simple arrays and array objects that are instances of the `Array` class.

Simple Arrays

The syntax for declaring and allocating a one-dimensional array follows.

```
type[] name = new type[length];
```

Here *type* is the data type that the array should hold, *name* is the name you want to give the array, and *length* is the number of items the array should hold. The array's indexes range from 0 to *length* - 1.

The syntax for declaring and allocating a two-dimensional array follows.

```
type[,] name = new type[length1, length2];
```

The only difference between this declaration and the preceding one is that you need to specify the number of items the array should hold in each dimension. For example, the following statement creates an array of integers with 10 rows and 20 columns.

```
int[,] values = new int[10, 20];
```

To make higher-dimensional arrays, use a similar syntax with more commas in the declaration and more lengths in the allocation part.

To initialize an array when it is declared, include the values it should hold inside braces, as in the following code.

```
int[] primes = { 2, 3, 5, 7, 11 };
```

To initialize multidimensional arrays, include each dimension's values inside their own braces. The following code declares and initializes a 2 × 4 array of integers.

```
int[,] values =
{
    {11, 12, 13, 14},
    {21, 22, 23, 24},
};
```

Array Objects

The `Array` class provides another method for creating arrays. Simple arrays give much faster performance than `Array` objects, so use them whenever possible.

One reason you may want to use an `Array` object is so that you can give the array nonzero lower bounds. The following code creates a two-dimensional `Array` object with row indexes ranging from 2001 to 2010 and column indexes ranging from 1 to 4. It then uses the `SetValue` method to set the value `sales[2005, 3]`.

```
int[] lengths = {10, 4};
int[] lowerBounds = {2001, 1};
Array sales = Array.CreateInstance(typeof(decimal), lengths, lowerBounds);
sales.SetValue(10000m, 2005, 3);
```

The following table summarizes some of the most useful `Array` class methods.

PROPERTY/METHOD	PURPOSE
BinarySearch	Returns the index of an item in the previously sorted array. The items must implement the `IComparable` interface, or you must provide an `IComparer` object.
Clear	Removes all the items from the array.
ConvertAll	Converts an array of one type into an array of another type.
Copy	Copies some or all the items from a position in one array to a position in another.
Exists	Determines whether the array contains a particular item.
IndexOf	Returns the index of the first item with a given value.
LastIndexOf	Returns the index of the last item with a given value.
Resize	Resizes the array.
Reverse	Reverses the order of the items in the array.
Sort	Sorts the items in the array. The items must implement the `IComparable` interface, or you must provide an `IComparer` object.

You can use these `Array` methods to manipulate simple arrays as well as `Array` objects.

COLLECTIONS

Collection classes store items in different data structures so that they can provide special features. For example, dictionaries enable you to use keys to locate objects. The following sections describe collection classes and how to initialize them.

Specialized Collections

The following list describes classes available in the `System.Collections` and `System.Collections.Specialized` namespaces.

➤ `ArrayList`—A simple resizable array implemented internally as a list.

➤ `StringCollection`—Similar to an `ArrayList` except it can hold only `strings`.

➤ `NameValueCollection`—A collection that can hold one or more `string` values for a particular key.

➤ Dictionaries—Collections that keys and values. The `System.Collections.Specialized` namespace defines the following dictionary classes.

>   ➤ `ListDictionary`—A dictionary that internally stores its items as a linked list. This is good for short lists but not long ones.

>   ➤ `Hashtable`—A dictionary that internally stores its items in a hash table. This provides fast access but imposes some memory overhead, so it is good for long lists but not short ones.

>   ➤ `HybridDictionary`—A dictionary that uses a linked list when the number of items is small and a hash table when the number of items is large.

>   ➤ `StringDictionary`—A dictionary that uses a hash table to store string values with string keys.

>   ➤ `SortedList`—A combination of `Hashtable` and `Array`.

➤ `Stack`—A list that stores and retrieves items in last-in-last-out (LIFO) order.

➤ `Queue`—A list that stores and retrieves items in first-in-first-out (FIFO) order.

Generic Collections

The collection classes in the `System.Collections.Generic` namespace use generic parameters to provide strong type checking. You should use them instead of the specialized collections described in the preceding section whenever possible. The following list describes these collections and related classes.

➤ `Dictionary`—A strongly typed dictionary

➤ `LinkedList`—A strongly typed linked list

➤ `LinkedListNode`—A strongly typed node in a linked list

➤ `List`—A strongly typed list

➤ `Queue`—A strongly typed queue

➤ SortedDictionary—A strongly typed sorted dictionary

➤ SortedList—A strongly typed sorted list

➤ Stack—A strongly typed stack

Collection Initializers

If a collection class has an Add method, you can initialize a new instance of the collection by including values inside braces after the new statement. The following code initializes a new List<Author>.

```
List<Author> authors = new List<Author>()
{
    new Author("Terry", "Pratchett"),
    new Author("Jasper", "Fforde"),
    new Author("Tom", "Holt"),
};
```

If a class's Add method takes multiple parameters, include them in their own braces. The following code initializes a Dictionary<string, string>.

```
Dictionary<string, string> phoneNumbers = new Dictionary<string, string>()
{
    {"Arthur", "808-567-1543"},
    {"Betty", "808-291-9838"},
    {"Charles", "808-521-0129"},
    {"Debbie", "808-317-3918"},
};
```

ITERATORS

The foreach statement enables you to iterate over the objects in a collection. C# also enables you to write your own iterators to yield a sequence of results.

To make an iterator, create a method that returns IEnumerable or a generic type such as IEnumerable<String>. Make the method generate its values and use a yield return statement to return them to the code that is looping over the iteration.

The following iterator yields a list of prime numbers between startNumber and stopNumber.

```
// Enumerate prime numbers between startNumber and stopNumber.
public IEnumerable Primes(int startNumber, int stopNumber)
{
    // Define a lambda expression that tests primality.
    Func<int, bool> isPrime = x =>
    {
        if (x == 1) return false;      // 1 is not prime.
        if (x == 2) return true;       // 2 is prime.
        if (x % 2 == 0) return false;  // Even numbers are not prime.
        for (int i = 3; i * i <= x; i += 2)
            if (x % i == 0) return false;
        return true;
```

```
    };

    for (int i = startNumber; i <= stopNumber; i++)
    {
        // If this number is prime, enumerate it.
        if (isPrime(i)) yield return i;
    }
}
```

This code first makes a lambda expression that returns true if a number is prime. It then loops through the values between startNumber and stopNumber and uses a yield return statement for those that are prime.

The following code loops through the values yielded by the Primes iterator and displays them in a ListBox.

```
foreach (int i in Primes(1, 100)) primesListBox.Items.Add(i);
```

Generic Declarations

This appendix summarizes generic classes and methods. The final section in this appendix describes items that you cannot make generic.

GENERIC CLASSES

To define a generic class, make a class declaration as usual. After the class name, add one or more type names for data types surrounded by brackets. The following code defines a generic BinaryNode class with the generic type highlighted in bold.

```
public class BinaryNode<T>
{
    public T Value;
    public BinaryNode<T> LeftChild, RightChild;
}
```

The class's declaration includes one type parameter T. The class's code declares a Value field of type T. It also uses the type to declare the LeftChild and RightChild fields of type BinaryNode<T>.

You can add constraints on the generic types, as in the following code.

```
public class SortedBinaryNode<T> where T : IComparable<T>
{
    ...
}
```

The code where T : IComparable<T> indicates that the generic type T must implement the interface IComparable<T>.

A generic type's where clause can include one or more of the elements shown in the following table.

ELEMENT	MEANING
struct	The type must be a value type.
class	The type must be a reference type.
new()	The type must have a parameterless constructor.
«*baseclass*»	The type must inherit from *baseclass*.
«*interface*»	The type must implement *interface*.
«*typeparameter*»	The type must inherit from *typeparameter*.

The following code defines the StrangeGeneric class where type T1 must implement IComparable<T1> and must provide a parameterless constructor, type T3 must inherit from the Control class, and type T2 must inherit from type T3.

```
public class StrangeGeneric<T1, T2, T3>
    where T1 : IComparable<T1>, new()
    where T3 : Control
    where T2 : T3
{

}
```

GENERIC METHODS

You can also give a class (generic or otherwise) a generic method. Just as a generic class is not tied to a particular data type, the parameters of a generic method are not tied to a specific data type.

To make a generic method, include type parameters similar to those you would use for a generic class. The following code defines a generic Switch method inside the static Switcher class.

```
public static class Switcher
{
    // Switch two values.
    public static void Switch<T>(ref T value1, ref T value2)
    {
        T temp = value1;
        value1 = value2;
        value2 = temp;
    }
}
```

Printing and Graphics

This appendix provides information about printing and the graphics classes used by Windows Forms applications. Printing is different in Windows Forms and WPF applications. The next sections explain how to print in a Windows Forms application. The sections after that explain how to print in a WPF application.

WINDOWS FORMS PRINTING

The following section explains the basic printing process in a Windows Forms application. The section after that summarizes graphics classes and methods used to print in that kind of application.

Printing Steps

The following steps summarize how to print in a Windows Forms application.

1. Create a PrintDocument object either at design time or at run time.

2. Start the printing process by doing one of the following:

    a. To send a printout to a printer, call the PrintDocument object's Print method.

    b. To display a print preview in a PrintPreviewDialog:

        i. Create a PrintPreviewDialog object either at design time or at run time.

        ii. Set the object's Document property equal to the PrintDocument object you created in Step 1.

        iii. Call the dialog's ShowDialog method to display it.

    c. To display a print preview in a PrintPreviewControl:

        i. Create a PrintPreviewControl object either at design time or at run time.

        ii. Set the object's Document property equal to the PrintDocument object you created in Step 1.

3. Catch the `PrintDocument` object's events to generate the printout.

The following list summarizes the events raised by the `PrintDocument` object.

➤ `BeginPrint`—This event indicates that printing is about to begin. The program can use this event to prepare for printing.

➤ `QueryPageSettings`—This event occurs when the `PrintDocument` object is about to generate a new page. The program can use this event to make changes that are specific to the page it is about to print.

➤ `PrintPage`—This event is raised to generate a page of output. The program catches this event and uses the `e.Graphics` parameter to generate output. After it finishes printing the page, the program sets the value `e.HasMorePages` to indicate whether there are more pages to print.

➤ `EndPrint`—This event is raised when printing is finished. The program can use it to clean up any data structures or resources it used while printing.

The `PrintPage` event receives a parameter `e` that includes several properties that are useful when printing. The following list summarizes those properties.

➤ `Cancel`—Set this to `true` to cancel the printout.

➤ `Graphics`—This is a `Graphics` object that the program can use to produce graphics.

➤ `HasMorePages`—Set this to `true` or `false` to indicate whether there are more pages to print after the current one.

➤ `MarginBounds`—This indicates the page boundaries inside the page's margins. Normally you should draw inside these bounds.

➤ `PageBounds`—This indicates the page's printable boundaries.

➤ `PageSettings`—This gives the page settings such as the paper size, a value indicating whether the page is printing in landscape mode, and the printer's resolution.

Graphics Namespaces

The following list summarizes the most important graphics namespaces and their most useful classes, structures, and enumerated values.

➤ `System.Drawing`—This namespace defines the most important graphics objects including `Bitmap`, `Brush`, `Color`, `Font`, `FontFamily`, `Graphics`, `Icon`, `Image`, `Metafile`, `Pen`, `Pens`, `Point`, `PointF`, `Rectangle`, `RectangleF`, `Region`, `Size`, `SizeF`, and `SolidBrush`.

➤ `System.Drawing.Drawing2D`—This namespace contains classes for more advanced two-dimensional drawing and classes that refine more basic drawing classes. Classes and enumerations defined in this namespace include `Blend`, `ColorBlend`, `DashCap`, `DashStyle`, `GraphicsPath`, `HatchBrush`, `HatchStyle`, `LinearGradientBrush`, `LineCap`, `LineJoin`, `Matrix`, and `PathGradientBrush`.

➤ `System.Drawing.Imaging`—This namespace contains classes that deal with more advanced bitmap graphics including `ColorMap`, `ColorPalette`, `ImageFormat`, `Metafile`, `MetafileHeader`, `MetaHeader`, and `WmfPlaceableFileHeader`.

➤ `System.Drawing.Printing`—This namespace contains objects used for printing and managing the printer's characteristics including `Margins`, `PageSettings`, `PaperSize`, `PaperSource`, `PrinterResolution`, and `PrinterSettings`.

➤ `System.Drawing.Text`—This namespace contains classes for working with installed fonts including `FontCollection`, `InstalledFontCollection`, and `PrivateFontCollection`.

Drawing Graphics

The basic steps for drawing in C# are to obtain a `Graphics` object and use its methods to draw shapes. `Brush` classes determine how shapes are filled, and `Pen` classes determine how lines are drawn.

The following sections describe the most useful properties and methods provided by key drawing classes.

Graphics

The `Graphics` object represents a drawing surface. The following table lists the `Graphics` object's drawing methods.

DRAWING METHOD	PURPOSE
DrawArc	Draws an arc of an ellipse
DrawBezier	Draws a Bézier curve
DrawBeziers	Draws a series of connected Bézier curves
DrawClosedCurve	Draws a smooth closed curve that connects a series of points, joining the final point to the first point
DrawCurve	Draws a smooth curve that connects a series of points
DrawEllipse	Draws an ellipse
DrawIcon	Draws an `Icon` onto the `Graphics` object's drawing surface
DrawIconUnstretched	Draws an `Icon` object onto the `Graphics` object's drawing surface without scaling
DrawImage	Draws an `Image` object onto the `Graphics` object's drawing surface
DrawImageUnscaled	Draws an `Image` object onto the drawing surface without scaling
DrawLine	Draws a line

continues

(continued)

DRAWING METHOD	PURPOSE
DrawLines	Draws a series of connected lines
DrawPath	Draws a `GraphicsPath` object
DrawPie	Draws a pie slice taken from an ellipse
DrawPolygon	Draws a polygon
DrawRectangle	Draws a rectangle
DrawRectangles	Draws a series of rectangles
DrawString	Draws text

The following table lists the `Graphics` object's area filling methods.

FILLING METHOD	PURPOSE
FillClosedCurve	Fills a smooth curve that connects a series of points
FillEllipse	Fills an ellipse
FillPath	Fills a `GraphicsPath` object
FillPie	Fills a pie slice taken from an ellipse
FillPolygon	Fills a polygon
FillRectangle	Fills a rectangle
FillRectangles	Fills a series of rectangles
FillRegion	Fills a `Region` object

The following table lists other useful `Graphics` object properties and methods.

PROPERTIES AND METHODS	PURPOSE
AddMetafileComment	Adds a comment to a metafile
Clear	Clears the `Graphics` object and fills it with a specific color
Clip	Determines the `Region` object used to clip any drawing the program does on the `Graphics` surface
Dispose	Releases the resources held by the `Graphics` object

PROPERTIES AND METHODS	PURPOSE
DpiX	Returns the horizontal number of dots per inch (DPI) for this object's surface
DpiY	Returns the vertical number of dots per inch (DPI) for this object's surface
EnumerateMetafile	Invokes a callback method for each record defined in a metafile
ExcludeClip	Updates the Graphics object's clipping region to exclude the area defined by a Region or Rectangle
FromHdc	Creates a new Graphics object from a device context handle (hDC)
FromHwnd	Creates a new Graphics object from a window handle (hWnd)
FromImage	Creates a new Graphics object to draw on an Image object
InterpolationMode	Controls anti-aliasing when drawing scaled images to determine how smooth the result is
IntersectClip	Updates the Graphics object's clipping region to be the intersection of the current clipping region and the area defined by a Region or Rectangle
IsVisible	Returns true if a specified point is within the Graphics object's visible clipping region
MeasureCharacterRanges	Returns an array of Region objects that show where each character in a string will be drawn
MeasureString	Returns a SizeF structure that gives the size of a string drawn on the Graphics object with a particular font
MultiplyTransform	Multiplies the Graphics object's current transformation matrix by another transformation matrix
PageScale	Determines the amount by which drawing commands are scaled
PageUnit	Determines the units of measurement: Display (depends on the device, typically pixel for monitors and 1/100 inch for printers), Document (1/300 inch), Inch, Millimeter, Pixel, or Point (1/72 inch)
RenderingOrigin	Determines the point used as a reference when hatching
ResetClip	Resets the object's clipping region so that the drawing is not clipped
ResetTransformation	Resets the object's transformation matrix to the identity matrix

continues

(continued)

PROPERTIES AND METHODS	PURPOSE
Restore	Restores the `Graphics` object to a state saved by the `Save` method
RotateTransform	Adds a rotation to the object's current transformation
Save	Saves the object's current state
ScaleTransform	Adds a scaling transformation to the `Graphics` object's current transformation
SetClip	Sets or merges the `Graphics` object's clipping area to another `Graphics` object, a `GraphicsPath` object, or a `Rectangle`
SmoothingMode	Controls anti-aliasing when drawing lines, curves, or filled areas
TextRenderingHint	Controls anti-aliasing and hinting when drawing text
Transform	Gets or sets the `Graphics` object's transformation matrix
TransformPoints	Applies the object's current transformation to an array of points
TranslateTransform	Adds a translation transformation to the `Graphics` object's current transformation

Pen

The `Pen` object determines the appearance of drawn lines. The following table lists the `Pen` object's most useful properties and methods.

PROPERTIES AND METHODS	PURPOSE
Alignment	Determines whether the line is drawn inside or centered on the theoretical perfectly thin line specified by the drawing routine
Brush	Determines the `Brush` used to fill the line
Color	Determines the line's color
CompoundArray	Lets you draw a line that is striped lengthwise
CustomEndCap	Determines the line's end cap
CustomStartCap	Determines the line's start cap
DashCap	Determines the cap drawn at the ends of dashes
DashOffset	Determines the distance from the start of the line to the start of the first dash

PROPERTIES AND METHODS	PURPOSE
DashPattern	An array of `floats` that specifies a custom dash pattern
DashStyle	Determines the line's dash style
EndCap	Determines the cap used at the end of the line
LineJoin	Determines how lines are joined by a method that draws connected lines such as `DrawPolygon`
MultiplyTransform	Multiplies the `Pen` object's current transformation by another transformation matrix
ResetTransform	Resets the `Pen` object's transformation to the identity transformation
RotateTransform	Adds a rotation transformation to the `Pen` object's current transformation
ScaleTransform	Adds a scaling transformation to the `Pen` object's current transformation
SetLineCap	This method takes parameters that let you specify the `Pen` object's `StartCap`, `EndCap`, and `LineJoin` properties at the same time
StartCap	Determines the cap used at the start of the line
Transform	Determines the transformation applied to the initially circular "pen tip" used to draw lines
Width	The width of the pen

Brushes

The `Brush` class is an abstract class, so you cannot make instances of it. Instead, you must make instances of one of its derived classes. The following table briefly describes these derived classes.

CLASS	PURPOSE
SolidBrush	Fills areas with a single solid color
TextureBrush	Fills areas with a repeating image
HatchBrush	Fills areas with a repeating hatch pattern
LinearGradientBrush	Fills areas with a linear gradient of two or more colors
PathGradientBrush	Fills areas with a color gradient that follows a path

GraphicsPath

The GraphicsPath object represents a path defined by lines, curves, text, and other drawing commands. The following table lists the GraphicsPath object's most useful properties and methods.

PROPERTIES AND METHODS	PURPOSE
CloseAllFigures	Closes all open figures by connecting their last points with their first points and then starts a new figure.
CloseFigure	Closes the current figure by connecting its last point with its first point and then starts a new figure.
FillMode	Determines how the path handles overlaps when you fill it. This property can take the values Alternate and Winding.
Flatten	Converts any curves in the path into sequences of lines.
GetBounds	Returns a RectangleF structure representing the path's bounding box.
GetLastPoint	Returns the last PointF structure in the PathPoints array.
IsOutlineVisible	Returns true if the indicated point lies beneath the path's outline.
IsVisible	Returns true if the indicated point lies in the path's interior.
PathData	Returns a PathData object that encapsulates the path's graphical data.
PathPoints	Returns an array of PointF structures giving the points in the path.
PathTypes	Returns an array of bytes representing the types of the points in the path.
PointCount	Returns the number of points in the path.
Reset	Clears the path data and resets FillMode to Alternate.
Reverse	Reverses the order of the path's data.
StartFigure	Starts a new figure, so future data is added to the new figure.
Transform	Applies a transformation matrix to the path.
Warp	Applies a warping transformation defined by mapping a parallelogram onto a rectangle to the path.
Widen	Enlarges the curves in the path to enclose a line drawn by a specific pen.

StringFormat

The `StringFormat` object determines how text is formatted. The following table lists the `StringFormat` object's most useful properties and methods.

PROPERTIES AND METHODS	PURPOSE
Alignment	Determines the text's horizontal alignment. This can be Near (left), Center (middle), or Far (right).
FormatFlags	Gets or sets flags that modify the StringFormat object's behavior.
GetTabStops	Returns an array of floats giving the positions of tab stops.
HotkeyPrefix	Determines how the hotkey prefix character is displayed. This can be Show, Hide, or None.
LineAlignment	Determines the text's vertical alignment. This can be Near (top), Center (middle), or Far (bottom).
SetMeasureableCharacterRanges	Sets an array of CharacterRange structures representing ranges of characters that will later be measured by the Graphics object's MeasureCharacterRanges method.
SetTabStops	Sets an array of floats giving the positions of tab stops.
Trimming	Determines how the text is trimmed if it cannot fit within a layout rectangle.

Image

The `Image` class represents the underlying physical drawing surface hidden below the logical layer created by the `Graphics` class. The `Image` is abstract, so you cannot directly instantiate it. Instead, you must instantiate its child classes `Bitmap` and `Metafile`. The following table describes the `Image` class's most useful properties and methods, which are inherited by the `Bitmap` and `Metafile` classes.

PROPERTIES AND METHODS	PURPOSE
Dispose	Frees the resources associated with this image
Flags	Returns attribute flags for the image
FromFile	Loads an image from a file
FromHbitmap	Loads a Bitmap image from a Windows bitmap handle
FromStream	Loads an image from a data stream

continues

(continued)

PROPERTIES AND METHODS	PURPOSE
GetBounds	Returns a `RectangleF` structure representing the rectangle's bounds
GetPixelFormatSize	Returns the color resolution (bits per pixel) for a specified `PixelFormat`
GetThumbnailImage	Returns a thumbnail representation of the image
Height	Returns the image's height
HorizontalResolution	Returns the horizontal resolution of the image in pixels per inch
IsAlphaPixelFormat	Returns `true` if the specified `PixelFormat` contains alpha (opaqueness) information
Palette	Determines the `ColorPalette` object used by the image
PhysicalDimension	Returns a `SizeF` structure giving the image's dimensions in pixels for `Bitmaps` and 0.01 millimeters for `Metafiles`
PixelFormat	Returns the image's pixel format
RawFormat	Returns an `ImageFormat` object representing the image's raw format
RotateFlip	Rotates, flips, or rotates and flips the image
Save	Saves the image in a file or stream with a given data format
Size	Returns a `Size` structure containing the image's width and height in pixels
VerticalResolution	Returns the vertical resolution of the image in pixels per inch
Width	Returns the image's width

Bitmap

The `Bitmap` class represents an image defined by pixel data. The following table describes the class's most useful methods that are not inherited from the `Image` class.

METHOD	PURPOSE
FromHicon	Loads a `Bitmap` image from a Windows icon handle
FromResource	Loads a `Bitmap` image from a Windows resource
GetPixel	Returns a `Color` representing a specified pixel

METHOD	PURPOSE
LockBits	Locks the `Bitmap` image's data in memory, so it cannot move until the program calls `UnlockBits`
MakeTransparent	Makes all pixels with a specified color transparent by setting the alpha component of those pixels to 0
SetPixel	Sets a specified pixel's `Color` value
SetResolution	Sets the `Bitmap` image's horizontal and vertical resolution in dots per inch (DPI)
UnlockBits	Unlocks the `Bitmap` image's data in memory so that the system can relocate it, if necessary

Metafile

The `Metafile` class represents an image defined by metafile records. The following table describes the class's most useful methods that are not inherited from the `Image` class.

METHOD	PURPOSE
GetMetafileHeader	Returns the `MetafileHeader` object associated with this `Metafile`.
PlayRecord	Plays a metafile record. Use the `Graphics` class's `EnumerateMetafile` method to get the data needed to play metafile records.

WPF PRINTING

To create a printout, a WPF application creates objects that represent lines, shapes, text, and whatever else needs to be printed. The program can scale those objects as necessary to fit the printout and the result takes advantage of the printer's capabilities.

There are several ways a WPF application can produce printouts. The following sections describe two of the more useful: using a paginator and creating documents.

Using a Paginator

A *paginator* is an object that generates a printout's pages. To create a printout by using a paginator, derive a new class from the `DocumentPaginator` class. Override the `GetPage` method to create the document's pages. Also override the following properties.

➤ `IsPageCountValid`—Returns `true` if all pages have been created. Returns `false` if some pages have not yet been generated

➤ `PageCount`—Returns the number of pages that have been formatted

➤ `PageSize`—Gets or sets the suggested size of the printed page

➤ `Source`—Returns the element being paginated

Creating Documents

The `FlowDocument` and `FixedDocument` classes allow you to arrange objects on a printout. The classes automatically arrange the objects appropriately. For example, they let you make text flow around other objects. The following sections describe these two document classes.

FlowDocuments

A `FlowDocument` object holds other objects that represent graphical output such as text, images, and shapes. It arranges its objects to take best advantage of whatever space is available, much as a web browser rearranges its contents when it is resized.

The following code shows a short `FlowDocument`.

```
<Window x:Class="WpfFlowDocument.MainWindow"
        xmlns="http://schemas.microsoft.com/winfx/2006/xaml/presentation"
        xmlns:x="http://schemas.microsoft.com/winfx/2006/xaml"
        Title="WpfFlowDocument" Height="350" Width="525">
    <Grid>
        <Grid.RowDefinitions>
            <RowDefinition Height="30"/>
            <RowDefinition Height="*"/>
        </Grid.RowDefinitions>
        <Button Grid.Row="0"
            Content="Print" Click="printButton_Click"
            Width="100" Height="30" VerticalAlignment="Top"/>
        <FlowDocumentReader Grid.Row="1" VerticalAlignment="Top">
            <FlowDocument Name="sampleFlowDocument">
                <Paragraph FontSize="20" FontWeight="Bold">
                    Chapter 1. Lorem Ipsum
                </Paragraph>

                <Paragraph FontSize="16" FontWeight="Bold">
                    Dolor Sit Amet
                </Paragraph>

                <Paragraph>
                    <Floater HorizontalAlignment="Right">
                        <Paragraph>
                            <Grid Width="100" Height="100">
                                <Border BorderBrush="Black" BorderThickness="1"/>
                                <Polygon
                                    Points="50,5 95,50 50,95 5,50"
                                    Stroke="Black" StrokeThickness="5" />
                            </Grid>
                        </Paragraph>
                    </Floater>
                    Consectetur adipiscing elit ...
                </Paragraph>
```

```
                <Paragraph>
                    Nullam dapibus dapibus ...
                </Paragraph>

                <Paragraph>
                    Etiam lacus eros ...
                </Paragraph>

            </FlowDocument>
        </FlowDocumentReader>
    </Grid>
</Window>
```

See the WPF documentation for information about the classes that you can use to produce output.

FixedDocuments

Like a `FlowDocument`, a `FixedDocument` holds graphical objects. Instead of rearranging its objects as space permits, a `FixedDocument` always places its objects in the same positions. This is similar to the way a PostScript document displays items at fixed positions.

The following code shows XAML that defines a `FixedDocument` inside a `DocumentViewer`.

```
<DocumentViewer Grid.Row="1">
    <FixedDocument Name="sampleFixedDocument">
        <PageContent Width="850" Height="1100">
            <FixedPage Width="850" Height="1100" Margin="100">
                ... Page 1 content elements ...
            </FixedPage>
        </PageContent>
        <PageContent Width="850" Height="1100">
            <FixedPage Width="850" Height="1100" Margin="100">
                ... Page 1 content elements ...
            </FixedPage>
        </PageContent>
    </FixedDocument>
</DocumentViewer>
```

FIXEDDOCUMENTS NEED FIXING

There is a well-known bug in Visual Studio's XAML designer that prevents it from correctly displaying XAML code that contains a `FixedDocument`. If you load XAML code into the designer, Visual Studio reports errors such as the following:

Property 'Pages' does not support values of type 'PageContent'.

The property 'Pages' is set more than once.

The specified value cannot be assigned. The following type was expected: "PageContentCollection".

If the XAML code is properly formed, however, the program will compile and run without problems.

Useful Exception Classes

When your program throws an exception, you can use a `try-catch-finally` block to catch the exception and examine it to determine its class. When you want to throw your own exception, however, you must know what exception classes are available so that you can pick the best one to throw. The following sections describe some of the most useful classes for throwing exceptions.

STANDARD EXCEPTION CLASSES

The following table lists some of the most useful exception classes in C#. If possible you should use one of these standard classes when you need to throw an exception.

CLASS	PURPOSE
AmbiguousMatchException	The program could not figure out which overloaded object method to use.
ArgumentException	An argument is invalid.
ArgumentNullException	An argument that cannot be `null` has the value `null`.
ArgumentOutOfRangeException	An argument is out of its allowed range.
ArithmeticException	An arithmetic, casting, or conversion operation has occurred.
ArrayTypeMismatchException	The program tried to store the wrong type of item in an array.
ConfigurationException	A configuration setting is invalid.
ConstraintException	A data operation violates a database constraint.
DataException	The ancestor class for ADO.NET exception classes.

continues

(continued)

CLASS	PURPOSE
DirectoryNotFoundException	A needed directory is missing.
DivideByZeroException	The program tried to divide by zero.
DuplicateNameException	An ADO.NET operation encountered a duplicate name. For example, it tried to create two tables with the same name.
EvaluateException	Occurs when a DataColumn's Expression property cannot be evaluated.
FieldAccessException	The program tried to access a class property improperly.
FormatException	An argument doesn't match its required format.
IndexOutOfRangeException	The program tried to access an item outside of the bounds of an array or other container.
InvalidCastException	The program tried to make an invalid conversion. For example, int.Parse("ten").
InvalidOperationException	The operation is not currently allowed.
IOException	The ancestor class for input/output (I/O) exception classes. A generic I/O error occurred.
EndOfStreamException	A stream reached its end.
FileLoadException	Error loading a file.
FileNotFoundException	Error finding a file.
InternalBufferOverflowException	An internal buffer overflowed.
MemberAccessException	The program tried to access a class member improperly.
MethodAccessException	The program tried to access a class method improperly.
MissingFieldException	The program tried to access a class field that doesn't exist.
MissingMemberException	The program tried to access a class member that doesn't exist.
MissingMethodException	The program tried to access a class method that doesn't exist.

CLASS	PURPOSE
NotFiniteNumberException	A floating-point number is `PositiveInfinity`, `NegativeInfinity`, or `NaN` (Not a Number). You can get these values from the floating-point classes (as in `float.NaN` or `double.PositiveInfinity`).
NotImplementedException	The requested operation is not implemented.
NotSupportedException	The requested operation is not supported. For example, the program might be asking a routine to modify data that was opened as read-only.
NullReferenceException	The program tried to use an object reference that is `null`.
OutOfMemoryException	There isn't enough memory. Note that sometimes a program cannot recover from an `OutOfMemoryException` because it doesn't have enough memory to do anything useful.
OverflowException	An arithmetic, casting, or conversion operation created an overflow. For example, the program tried to assign a large `int` value to a `byte` variable.
PolicyException	Policy prevents the code from running.
RankException	A routine is trying to use an array with the wrong number of dimensions.
ReadOnlyException	The program tried to modify read-only data.
SecurityException	A security violation occurred.
SyntaxErrorException	A `DataColumn`'s `Expression` property contains invalid syntax.
UnauthorizedAccessException	The system is denying access because of an I/O or security error.

Use the `throw` statement to throw an exception. The following code throws a `DivideByZeroException`.

```
throw new DivideByZeroException("No employees are defined.");
```

This code passes the exception class's constructor a message describing the exception. In this case, the divide by zero exception occurred because the application did not have any employees defined. Notice that the message explains the reason for the exception, not just the fact that a division by zero occurred.

CUSTOM EXCEPTION CLASSES

To define a custom exception class, make a class that inherits from the `Exception` class. To give developers who use the class the most flexibility, provide four constructors that delegate their work to the parent class's corresponding constructors.

The following code shows the `InvalidWorkAssignmentException` class. The parameterless constructor passes the `Exception` class's constructor a default error message. The other constructors simply pass their arguments to the `Exception` class's other constructors.

```
public class InvalidWorkAssignmentException : Exception
{
    public InvalidWorkAssignmentException()
        : base("This work assignment is invalid")
    {
    }
    public InvalidWorkAssignmentException(string message)
        : base(message)
    {
    }
    public InvalidWorkAssignmentException(string message, Exception innerException)
        : base(message, innerException)
    {
    }
    public InvalidWorkAssignmentException(SerializationInfo info,
    StreamingContext context)
        : base(info, context)
    {
    }
}
```

For more information on custom exception classes, see the section "Custom Exceptions" in Chapter 9, "Error Handing." Also see the online documentation for topics such as "Designing Custom Exceptions" (msdn.microsoft.com/library/vstudio/ms229064(v=vs.100).aspx) and "Design Guidelines for Exceptions" (msdn.microsoft.com/ms229014.aspx).

Date and Time Format Specifiers

A program uses date and time format specifiers to determine how dates and times are represented as strings. C# provides two kinds of specifiers that you can use to determine a date and time value's format: standard format specifiers and custom format specifiers.

Standard format specifiers are locale-aware, so the result depends on the computer's regional settings. For that reason, you should always use the standard specifiers whenever possible.

The following sections describe the available standard and custom date and time format specifiers.

STANDARD FORMAT SPECIFIERS

A standard format specifier is a single character that you use alone to indicate a standardized format. For example, the format string d indicates a short date format (as in 8/20/2012).

The following table lists standard format specifiers that you can use to format date and time strings. The examples shown in this table are for a typical computer in the United States.

SPECIFIER	MEANING	EXAMPLE
d	Short date.	8/20/2015
D	Long date.	Thursday, August 20, 2015
t	Short time.	2:37 PM
T	Long time.	2:37:18 PM
f	Full date/time with short time.	Thursday, August 20, 2015 2:37 PM
F	Full date/time with long time.	Thursday, August 20, 2015 2:37:18 PM
g	General date/time with short time.	8/20/2015 2:37 PM

continues

(continued)

SPECIFIER	MEANING	EXAMPLE
G	General date/time with long time.	8/20/2015 2:37:18 PM
m or M	Month and date.	August 20
r or R	RFC1123 pattern. Formatting does not convert the time to Greenwich Mean Time (GMT), so you should convert local times to GMT before formatting.	Thu, 20 Aug 2015 14:37:18 GMT
S	Sortable ISO 8601 date/time.	2015-08-20T14:37:18
u	Universal sortable date/time. Formatting does not convert the time to universal time, so you should convert local times to universal time before formatting.	2015-08-20 14:37:18Z
U	Universal full date/time. This is the full universal time, not the local time.	Thursday, August 20, 2015 9:37:18 PM
y or Y	Year and month.	August 2015

CUSTOM FORMAT SPECIFIERS

Custom format specifiers describe pieces of a date or time that you can use to build your own customized formats. For example, the specifier ddd indicates the abbreviated day of the week, as in Wed.

In general, you should use custom date and time formats only to build values used inside the code. The user should never see them.

The following table lists characters that you can use to build custom formats for date and time strings.

SPECIFIER	MEANING	EXAMPLE
d	Date of the month (1–31).	3
dd	Date of the month with two digits (01–31).	03
ddd	Abbreviated day of the week.	Wed
dddd	Full day of the week.	Wednesday
f	Fractions of seconds, one digit. Add additional fs for up to seven digits (fffffff).	8
F	Similar to f except nothing is displayed if the fraction is 0.	8

SPECIFIER	MEANING	EXAMPLE
g or gg	Era.	A.D.
h	Hour, 12-hour clock with one digit (1–12).	1
hh	Hour, 12-hour clock with two digits (01–12).	01
H	Hour, 24-hour clock with one digit (1–24).	13
HH	Hour, 24-hour clock with two digits (01–24).	07
K	Time zone information.	–07:00
m	Minutes with one digit (0–59).	9
mm	Minutes with two digits (00–59).	09
M	Month number with one digit (1–12).	2
MM	Month number with two digits (01–12).	02
MMM	Month abbreviation.	Feb
MMMM	Full month name.	February
s	Seconds with one digit (0–59).	3
ss	Seconds with two digits (00–59).	03
t	AM/PM designator with one character.	A
tt	AM/PM designator with two characters.	AM
y	Year with up to two digits (0–99).	7
yy	Year with two digits (00–99).	07
yyyy	Year with four digits.	2015
yyyyy	Year with five digits.	02015
z	Time zone offset (hours from GMT in the range –12 to +13).	–7
zz	Time zone offset with two digits.	–07
zzz	Time zone offset with two digits of hours and minutes.	–07:00
:	Time separator.	
/	Date separator.	
" . . . "	Quoted string. Displays the enclosed characters without trying to interpret them.	

continues

(continued)

SPECIFIER	MEANING	EXAMPLE
'...'	Quoted string. Displays the enclosed characters without trying to interpret them.	
%	Displays the following character as a custom specifier. (See the following discussion.)	
\	Displays the next character without trying to interpret it.	

Some of the custom specifier characters in this table are the same as characters used by standard specifiers. For example, if you use the character d alone, C# interprets it as the standard specifier for a short date. If you use the character d in a custom specifier, C# interprets it as the date of the month.

If you want to use a custom specifier alone, precede it with the % character. The following shows two queries and their results executed in the Immediate window.

```
DateTime.Now.ToString("d")
"4/1/2015"
DateTime.Now.ToString("%d")
"1"
```

Custom specifiers are somewhat sensitive to the computer's regional settings. For example, they at least know the local names and abbreviations of the months and days of the week.

The standard specifiers have even more information about the local culture, however. For example, the date specifiers know whether the local culture places months before or after days. The d specifier gives the result 8/20/2015 for the en-US culture (English, United States), and it returns 20/08/2015 for the culture en-NZ (English, New Zealand).

To avoid cultural problems on different computers, you should use the standard specifiers whenever possible rather than build your own custom format specifiers. For example, use d instead of M/d/yyyy.

Other Format Specifiers

A program uses format specifiers to determine how objects are represented as strings. C# provides two kinds of specifiers: standard format specifiers and custom format specifiers. Standard format specifiers are locale-aware, so the result depends on the computer's regional settings. If a program uses standard format specifiers and you run the program in a new locale, it automatically produces the formats appropriate for that locale. For that reason, you should always use the standard specifiers whenever possible.

The following sections describe the standard and custom format specifiers.

STANDARD NUMERIC FORMAT SPECIFIERS

Standard numeric format specifiers enable you to easily display commonly used numeric formats. The following table lists the standard numeric specifiers.

SPECIFIER	MEANING
C or c	Currency. If a precision specifier follows the C, it indicates the number of digits that should follow the decimal point. On a standard system in the United States, the value –1234.5678 with the specifier C3 produces ($1,234.568).
D or d	Decimal. This specifier works only with integer types. It simply displays the number's digits. If a precision specifier follows the D, it indicates the number of digits the result should have, padding on the left with zeros, if necessary. If the value is negative, the result has a minus sign on the left. The value –1234 with the specifier D6 produces –001234.

continues

(continued)

SPECIFIER	MEANING
E or e	Scientific notation. The result always has exactly one digit to the left of the decimal point, followed by more digits, an E or e, a plus or minus sign, and at least three digits of exponent (padded on the left with zeros, if necessary). If a precision specifier follows the E, it indicates the number of digits the result should have after the decimal point. The value –1234.5678 with the specifier e2 produces –1.23e+003.
F or f	Fixed point. The result contains a minus sign if the value is negative, digits, a decimal point, and then more digits. If a precision specifier follows the F, it indicates the number of digits the result should have after the decimal point. The value –1234.5678 with the specifier f3 produces –1234.568.
G or g	General. Either scientific or fixed-point notation depending on which is more compact.
N or n	Number. The result has a minus sign if the value is negative, digits with thousands separators, a decimal point, and more digits. If a precision specifier follows the N, it indicates the number of digits the result should have after the decimal point. The value –1234.5678 with the specifier N3 produces –1,234.568.
P or p	Percentage. The value is multiplied by 100 and then formatted according to the computer's settings. If a precision specifier follows the P, it indicates the number of digits that should follow the decimal point. The value 1.2345678 with the specifier P produces 123.46%.
R or r	Round trip. The value is formatted in such a way that the result can be converted back into its original value. Depending on the data type and value, this may require 17 digits of precision. The value 1/7 with the specifier R produces 0.14285714285714285.
X or x	Hexadecimal. This works for integer types only. The value is converted into hexadecimal. The case of the X or x determines whether hexadecimal digits above 9 are written in uppercase or lowercase. If a precision specifier follows the X, it indicates the number of digits the result should have, padding on the left with zeros, if necessary. The value 183 with the specifier x4 produces 00b7.

CUSTOM NUMERIC FORMAT SPECIFIERS

The following table lists characters that you can use to build custom numeric formats.

SPECIFIER	MEANING
0	A digit or zero. If the number doesn't have a digit in this position, the specifier adds a 0. The value 12 with the specifier `000.00` produces 012.00.
#	A digit. If the number doesn't have a digit in this position, nothing is printed.
,	If used between two digits (either 0 or #), this adds thousands separators to the result. Note that it will add as many separators if necessary. The value 1234567 with the specifier `#,#` produces 1,234,567.
,	If used immediately to the left of the decimal point, the number is divided by 1000 for each comma. The value 1234567 with the specifier `#,#,.` produces 1,235.
%	Multiplies the number by 100 and inserts the % symbol where it appears in the specifier. The value `0.123` with the specifier `.00%` produces 12.30%.
E0 or e0	Displays the number in scientific notation inserting an E or e between the number and its exponent. Use # and 0 to format the number before the exponent. The number of 0s after the E determines the number of digits in the exponent. If you place a + sign between the E and 0, the result's exponent includes a + or − sign. If you omit the + sign, the exponent includes a sign only if it is negative. The value 1234.5678 with the specifier `00.000E+000` produces 12.346E+002.
\	Displays the following character literally without interpreting it. Use \\ to display the \ character. The value 12 with the specifier `#\%` produces 12%. The same value with the specifier `#%` produces 1200%.
'ABC' or "ABC"	Displays the characters in the quotes literally. The value 12 with the specifier `#'%'` produces 12%.

NUMERIC FORMATTING SECTIONS

A numeric format specifier may contain one, two, or three sections separated by semicolons. If the specifier contains one section, the specifier is used for all numeric values.

If the specifier contains two sections, the first is used to format values that are positive or zero, and the second is used to format negative values.

If the specifier contains three sections, the first is used to format positive values, the second is used to format negative values, and the third is used to format values that are zero.

The following text shows output from the Immediate window for three values using the format specifier #,#.00;<#,#.00>;ZERO.

```
(1234.5678).ToString("#,#.00; <#,#.00>;ZERO")
"1,234.57"
(-1234.5678).ToString("#,#.00; <#,#.00>;ZERO")
" <1,234.57>"
(0).ToString("#,#.00; <#,#.00>;ZERO")
"ZERO"
```

COMPOSITE FORMATTING

The String.Format, Console.WriteLine, and TextWriter.WriteLine methods provide a different method for formatting strings. These routines can take a composite formatting string parameter that contains literal characters plus placeholders for values. Other parameters to the methods give the values.

The value placeholders have the following format.

```
{index«,alignment»«:format_specifier»}
```

The *index* value gives the index of the parameter (numbered from 0) that should be inserted in this placeholder's position.

The optional *alignment* value tells the minimum number of characters the item should use and the result is padded with spaces, if necessary. If this value is negative, the result is left-justified. If the value is positive, the result is right-justified.

The *format_specifier* indicates how the item should be formatted.

For example, consider the following code.

```
string name = "Crazy Bob";
decimal sales = -12345.67m;
MessageBox.Show(String.Format("{0} {1:earned;lost} {1:c} this year", name, sales));
```

The first placeholder refers to parameter number 0. The first parameter after the format specifier is the name variable, which has value Crazy Bob.

The second placeholder refers to parameter number 1 and includes a two-part format specifier that displays earned if the value is positive or zero, and lost if the value is negative. The third placeholder refers to parameter number 1 again, this time displaying its value formatted as currency.

The following shows the result.

```
Crazy Bob lost ($12,345.67) this year
```

ENUMERATED TYPE FORMATTING

Enumerated values are formatted as string representations rather than as the integer values that represent them. For example, consider the following code.

```
public enum Dessert
{
    Cake = 1,
    Pie = 2,
    Cookie = 3,
    IceCream = 4,
}
...
Dessert selection = Dessert.Cake;
MessageBox.Show(selection.ToString());
```

This code displays the string Cake.

For variables of an enumerated type such as selection, the ToString method can take a specifier that determines how the value is formatted.

The specifier G or g formats the value as a string if possible. If the value is not a valid entry in the enumeration's definition, the result is the variable's numeric value. For example, the previous code does not define a value for the integer 7 so, if you set selection to 7, selection.ToString("G") returns the value 7.

If you define an enumerated type with the Flags attribute, variables of that type can be a combination of the enumeration's values, as shown in the following code.

```
[Flags()]
public enum Dessert
{
    Cake = 1,
    Pie = 2,
    Cookie = 3,
    IceCream = 4,
}
...
Dessert selection = Dessert.IceCream | Dessert.Pie;
Console.WriteLine(selection.ToString("G"));
```

In this case, the G format specifier returns a string that contains all the flag values separated by commas. In this example, the result is Pie, IceCream. Note that the values are returned in the order in which they are defined by the enumeration, not the order in which they are assigned to the variable.

If you do not use the Flags attribute when defining an enumerated type, the G format specifier always returns the variable's numeric value if it is a combination of values rather than a single value from the list. In contrast the F specifier returns a list of comma-separated values if it makes sense. For example, if you omit the Flags attribute from the previous code, selection.ToString("G") returns 6 (because Pie + IceCream = 2 + 4 = 6), but selection.ToString("F") returns Pie, IceCream.

The D or d specifier always formats the variable as a number.

The specifier X or x formats the value as a hexadecimal number.

The following table summarizes the enumeration format specifiers.

SPECIFIER	MEANING
G or g	(The default.) Returns the string value if possible.
	If the value includes multiple enumeration values and the enumeration is marked with the Flags attribute, this returns the values separated by commas.
	If the value is not defined by the enumeration, or if it includes multiple enumeration values but the enumeration does not have the Flags attribute, this returns a numeric value.
F or f	Returns the string value if possible.
	If the value includes multiple enumeration values, this returns the values separated by commas.
	If the value is not defined by the enumeration, this returns a numeric value.
D or d	Always returns a numeric result.
X or x	Always returns a hexadecimal numeric result.

Streams

The .NET Framework provides several classes that treat data as a stream—an ordered series of bytes. These classes are not difficult to use, but they are similar enough to be confusing. This appendix summarizes the stream classes and describes their properties and their methods. See Chapter 18, "Streams," for more information on streams.

STREAM CLASS SUMMARY

The following table lists the .NET Framework stream classes.

CLASS	PURPOSE
BinaryReader, BinaryWriter	Read and write data from an underlying stream using routines that manage specific data types (such as ReadDouble and ReadUInt16).
BufferedStream	Adds buffering to another stream type. This sometimes improves performance on relatively slow underlying devices.
CryptoStream	Applies a cryptographic transformation to its data.
FileStream	Represents a file as a stream. Usually, you can use a helper class such as BinaryReader or TextWriter to make working with a FileStream easier.
MemoryStream	Lets you read and write stream data in memory. This is useful when you need a stream but don't want to read or write a file.
NetworkStream	Sends and receives data across a network connection.
Stream	A generic stream class. This is an abstract class, so you cannot create one directly. Instead, you must instantiate one of its subclasses.

continues

(continued)

CLASS	PURPOSE
StreamReader, StreamWriter	These classes inherit from TextReader and TextWriter. They provide methods for reading and writing text into an underlying stream, usually a FileStream.
StringReader, StringWriter	These classes inherit from TextReader and TextWriter. They provide methods for reading and writing text into an underlying string.
TextReader, TextWriter	These abstract classes define methods that make working with text on an underlying stream easier.

The following sections describe stream classes in greater detail.

STREAM

The following table describes the Stream class's most useful properties.

PROPERTY	PURPOSE
CanRead	Returns true if the stream supports reading.
CanSeek	Returns true if the stream supports seeking to a particular position in the stream.
CanTimeout	Returns true if the stream supports timeouts.
CanWrite	Returns true if the stream supports writing.
Length	Returns the number of bytes in the stream.
Position	Returns the stream's current position in its bytes. For a stream that supports seeking, the program can set this value to move to a particular position.
ReadTimeout	Determines the stream's read timeout in milliseconds.
WriteTimeout	Determines the stream's write timeout in milliseconds.

The following table describes the Stream class's most useful methods.

METHOD	PURPOSE
BeginRead	Begins an asynchronous read.
BeginWrite	Begins an asynchronous write.

METHOD	PURPOSE
Close	Closes the stream and releases any resources it uses (such as file handles).
EndRead	Waits for an asynchronous read to finish.
EndWrite	Ends an asynchronous write.
Flush	Flushes data from the stream's buffers into the underlying storage medium (device, file, and so on).
Read	Reads bytes from the stream and advances its position by that number of bytes.
ReadByte	Reads a byte from the stream and advances its position by 1 byte.
Seek	If the stream supports seeking, sets the stream's position.
SetLength	Sets the stream's length. If the stream is currently longer than the new length, it is truncated. If the stream is shorter than the new length, it is enlarged. The stream must support both writing and seeking for this method to work.
Write	Writes bytes into the stream and advances the current position by this number of bytes.
WriteByte	Writes 1 byte into the stream and advances the current position by 1 byte.

The `FileStream` and `MemoryStream` classes add only a few methods to those defined by the `Stream` class. The most important of those are new constructors specific to the type of stream. For example, the `FileStream` class provides constructors for opening files in various modes (append, new, and so forth).

BINARYREADER AND BINARYWRITER

These are stream helper classes that make it easier to read and write data in specific formats onto an underlying stream. The following table describes the `BinaryReader` class's most useful methods.

METHOD	PURPOSE
Close	Closes the `BinaryReader` and its underlying stream.
PeekChar	Reads the reader's next character but does not advance the reader's position, so other methods can still read the character later.

continues

(continued)

METHOD	PURPOSE
Read	Reads characters from the stream and advances the reader's position.
ReadBoolean	Reads a `bool` from the stream and advances the reader's position by 1 byte.
ReadByte	Reads a `byte` from the stream and advances the reader's position by 1 byte.
ReadBytes	Reads a number of `bytes` from the stream into a `byte` array and advances the reader's position by that number of `bytes`.
ReadChar	Reads a character from the stream and advances the reader's position according to the stream's encoding and the character.
ReadChars	Reads a number of characters from the stream, returns the results in a `char` array, and advances the reader's position according to the stream's encoding and the number of characters.
ReadDecimal	Reads a `decimal` value from the stream and advances the reader's position by 16 bytes.
ReadDouble	Reads a 64-bit double-precision floating-point value (`double`) from the stream and advances the reader's position by 8 bytes.
ReadInt16	Reads a 16-bit signed integer (`short`) from the stream and advances the reader's position by 2 bytes.
ReadInt32	Reads a 32-bit signed integer (`int`) from the stream and advances the reader's position by 4 bytes.
ReadInt64	Reads a 64-bit signed integer (`long`) from the stream and advances the reader's position by 8 bytes.
ReadSByte	Reads a signed `byte` (`sbyte`) from the stream and advances the reader's position by 1 byte.
ReadSingle	Reads a 32-bit single-precision floating-point value (`float`) from the stream and advances the reader's position by 4 bytes.
ReadString	Reads a `string` from the stream and advances the reader's position past it. The string begins with its length.
ReadUInt16	Reads a 16-bit unsigned integer (`ushort`) from the stream and advances the reader's position by 2 bytes.

METHOD	PURPOSE
ReadUInt32	Reads a 32-bit unsigned integer (uint) from the stream and advances the reader's position by 4 bytes.
ReadUInt64	Reads a 64-bit unsigned integer (ulong) from the stream and advances the reader's position by 8 bytes.

The following table describes the BinaryWriter class's most useful methods.

METHOD	DESCRIPTION
Close	Closes the BinaryWriter and its underlying stream.
Flush	Writes any buffered data into the underlying stream.
Seek	Sets the position within the stream.
Write	Writes a value into the stream. This method has many over-loaded versions that write characters, arrays of characters, integers, strings, unsigned 64-bit integers, and so on.

TEXTREADER AND TEXTWRITER

These are stream helper classes that make it easier to read and write text data onto an underlying stream. The following table describes the TextReader class's most useful methods.

METHOD	PURPOSE
Close	Closes the reader and releases any resources that it is using.
Peek	Reads the next character from the text without changing the reader's state so that other methods can read the character later.
Read	Reads data from the input. Overloaded versions of this method read a single character, or an array of characters up to a specified length.
ReadBlock	Reads data from the input into an array of characters.
ReadLine	Reads a line of characters from the input and returns the data in a string.
ReadToEnd	Reads any remaining characters in the input and returns them in a string.

The following table describes the TextWriter class's most useful properties.

PROPERTY	PURPOSE
Encoding	Specifies the data's encoding (ASCII, UTF-8, Unicode, and so forth).
FormatProvider	Returns an object that controls formatting.
NewLine	Gets or sets the stream's new-line sequence.

The following table describes the TextWriter class's most useful methods.

METHOD	PURPOSE
Close	Closes the writer and releases any resources it is using.
Flush	Writes any buffered data into the underlying output.
Write	Writes a value into the output. This method has many overloaded versions that write characters, arrays of characters, integers, strings, unsigned 64-bit integers, and so forth.
WriteLine	Writes data into the output followed by the new-line sequence.

STRINGREADER AND STRINGWRITER

The StringReader and StringWriter classes let a program read and write text in a string. They implement the features defined by their parent classes TextReader and TextWriter. See the section "TextReader and TextWriter" earlier in this appendix for a list of those features.

STREAMREADER AND STREAMWRITER

The StreamReader and StreamWriter classes let a program read and write data in an underlying stream, often a FileStream. They implement the features defined by their parent classes TextReader and TextWriter. See the section "TextReader and TextWriter" earlier in this appendix for a list of the features.

TEXT FILE STREAM METHODS

The System.IO.File class provides several handy methods for working with text files. The following table summarizes these methods.

METHOD	PURPOSE
`AppendText`	Creates a text file or opens it for appending if it already exists. Returns a `StreamWriter` for writing into the file.
`CreateText`	Creates a text file, overwriting it if it already exists. Returns a `StreamWriter` for writing into the file.
`Exists`	Returns `true` if a file exists. It is good practice (and much faster) to only try to open the file if `Exists` returns `true`, rather than just try to open the file and catch errors with a `try-catch-finally` block.
`OpenText`	Opens an existing text file and returns a `StreamReader` to read from it. This method throws a `FileNotFoundException` if the file doesn't exist.

Filesystem Classes

This appendix describes the .NET Framework's filesystem classes. It also summarizes methods you can use to manage the recycle bin.

FRAMEWORK CLASSES

The System.IO namespace provides several classes for working with the filesystem. The following sections describe the properties, methods, and events provided by these classes.

Directory

The Directory class provides static methods for working with directories. The following table summarizes those static methods.

METHOD	PURPOSE
CreateDirectory	Creates a directory and any missing directories along its path.
Delete	Deletes a directory and its contents. It can recursively delete all subdirectories.
Exists	Returns true if the path points to an existing directory.
GetCreationTime	Returns a directory's creation date and time.
GetCreationTimeUtc	Returns a directory's creation date and time in Coordinated Universal Time (UTC).
GetCurrentDirectory	Returns the application's current working directory.
GetDirectories	Returns an array of strings holding the fully qualified names of a directory's subdirectories.

continues

(continued)

METHOD	PURPOSE
GetDirectoryRoot	Returns the directory root for a path, which need not exist (for example, C:\).
GetFiles	Returns an array of strings holding the fully qualified names of a directory's files.
GetFileSystemEntries	Returns an array of strings holding the fully qualified names of a directory's files and subdirectories.
GetLastAccessTime	Returns a directory's last access date and time.
GetLastAccessTimeUtc	Returns a directory's last access date and time in UTC.
GetLastWriteTime	Returns the date and time when a directory was last modified.
GetLastWriteTimeUtc	Returns the date and time when a directory was last modified in UTC.
GetLogicalDrives	Returns an array of strings listing the system's logical drives as in A:\. The list includes drives that are attached. For example, it lists an empty floppy drive and a connected flash drive but doesn't list a flash drive after you disconnect it.
GetParent	Returns a DirectoryInfo object representing a directory's parent directory.
Move	Moves a directory and its contents to a new location on the same disk volume.
SetCreationTime	Sets a directory's creation date and time.
SetCreationTimeUtc	Sets a directory's creation date and time in UTC.
SetCurrentDirectory	Sets the application's current working directory.
SetLastAccessTime	Sets a directory's last access date and time.
SetLastAccessTimeUtc	Sets a directory's last access date and time in UTC.
SetLastWriteTime	Sets a directory's last write date and time.
SetLastWriteTimeUtc	Sets a directory's last write date and time in UTC.

File

The `File` class provides static methods for working with files. The following table summarizes its most useful static methods.

METHOD	PURPOSE
AppendAllText	Adds text to the end of a file, creating the file if it doesn't exist, and then closes the file.
AppendText	Opens a file for appending UTF-8 encoded text and returns a `StreamWriter` attached to it.
Copy	Copies a file.
Create	Creates a new file and returns a `FileStream` attached to it.
CreateText	Creates or opens a file for writing UTF-8 encoded text and returns a `StreamWriter` attached to it.
Delete	Permanently deletes a file.
Exists	Returns `true` if the specified file exists.
GetAttributes	Gets a file's attributes. This is a combination of flags defined by the `FileAttributes` enumeration, which defines the values `Archive`, `Compressed`, `Device`, `Directory`, `Encrypted`, `Hidden`, `Normal`, `NotContextIndexed`, `Offline`, `ReadOnly`, `ReparsePoint`, `SparseFile`, `System`, and `Temporary`.
GetCreationTime	Returns a file's creation date and time.
GetCreationTimeUtc	Returns a file's creation date and time in UTC.
GetLastAccessTime	Returns a file's last access date and time.
GetLastAccessTimeUtc	Returns a file's last access date and time in UTC.
GetLastWriteTime	Returns a file's last write date and time.
GetLastWriteTimeUtc	Returns a file's last write date and time in UTC.
Move	Moves a file to a new location.
Open	Opens a file and returns a `FileStream` attached to it. Parameters let you specify the mode (`Append`, `Create`, `CreateNew`, `Open`, `OpenOrCreate`, or `Truncate`), access (`Read`, `Write`, or `ReadWrite`), and sharing (`Read`, `Write`, `ReadWrite`, or `None`) settings.
OpenRead	Opens a file for reading and returns a `FileStream` attached to it.

continues

(continued)

METHOD	PURPOSE
OpenText	Opens a UTF-8 encoded text file for reading and returns a `StreamReader` attached to it.
OpenWrite	Opens a file for writing and returns a `FileStream` attached to it.
ReadAllBytes	Returns a file's contents in an array of `bytes`.
ReadAllLines	Returns a file's lines in an array of `strings`.
ReadAllText	Returns a file's contents in a `string`.
Replace	This method takes three file paths as parameters representing a source file, a destination file, and a backup file. If the backup file exists, the method permanently deletes it. It then moves the destination file to the backup file and moves the source file to the destination file. This method throws an exception if either the source file or the destination file doesn't exist.
SetAttributes	Sets a file's attributes. This is a combination of flags defined by the `FileAttributes` enumeration, which defines the values `Archive`, `Compressed`, `Device`, `Directory`, `Encrypted`, `Hidden`, `Normal`, `NotContextIndexed`, `Offline`, `ReadOnly`, `ReparsePoint`, `SparseFile`, `System`, and `Temporary`.
SetCreationTime	Sets a file's creation date and time.
SetCreationTimeUtc	Sets a file's creation date and time in UTC.
SetLastAccessTime	Sets a file's last access date and time.
SetLastAccessTimeUtc	Sets a file's last access date and time in UTC.
SetLastWriteTime	Sets a file's last write date and time.
SetLastWriteTimeUtc	Sets a file's last write date and time in UTC.
WriteAllBytes	Creates or overwrites a file, writes an array of `bytes` into it, and closes the file.
WriteAllLines	Creates or overwrites a file, writes an array of `strings` into it, and closes the file.
WriteAllText	Creates or overwrites a file, writes a `string` into it, and closes the file.

DriveInfo

A `DriveInfo` object represents one of the computer's drives. The following table describes the properties provided by this class. The final column in the table indicates whether a drive must be ready for the property to work without throwing an exception. Use the `IsReady` property to see whether the drive is ready before using those properties.

PROPERTY	PURPOSE	MUST BE READY?
AvailableFreeSpace	Returns the amount of free space available on the drive in bytes. This value takes quotas into account, so it may not match `TotalFreeSpace`.	True
DriveFormat	Returns the name of the filesystem type such as NTFS or FAT32. (For more information on NTFS and FAT filesystems, search the web. For example, the page www.ntfs.com/ntfs_vs_fat.htm compares the FAT, FAT32, and NTFS filesystems.)	True
DriveType	Returns a `DriveType` enumeration value indicating the drive type. This value can be `CDRom`, `Fixed`, `Network`, `NoRootDirectory`, `Ram`, `Removable`, or `Unknown`.	False
IsReady	Returns `true` if the drive is ready. Many `DriveInfo` properties are unavailable and throw exceptions if you try to access them while the drive is not ready.	False
Name	Returns the drive's name. This is the drive's root name as in `A:\` or `C:\`.	False
RootDirectory	Returns a `DirectoryInfo` object representing the drive's root directory. See the following section, "DirectoryInfo," for more information.	False
TotalFreeSpace	Returns the total amount of free space on the drive in bytes.	True
TotalSize	Returns the total amount of space on the drive in bytes.	True
VolumeLabel	Gets or sets the drive's volume label.	True

DirectoryInfo

A `DirectoryInfo` object represents a directory. The following table summarizes its most useful properties and methods.

PROPERTY OR METHOD	PURPOSE
Attributes	Gets or sets flags from the `FileAttributes` enumeration for the directory. These flags can include `Archive`, `Compressed`, `Device`, `Directory`, `Encrypted`, `Hidden`, `Normal`, `NotContentIndexed`, `Offline`, `ReadOnly`, `ReparsePoint`, `SparseFile`, `System`, and `Temporary`.
Create	Creates the directory. You can create a `DirectoryInfo` object, passing its constructor the fully qualified name of a directory that doesn't exist. You can then call the object's `Create` method to create the directory.
CreateSubdirectory	Creates a subdirectory within the directory and returns a `DirectoryInfo` object representing it. The subdirectory's path must be relative to the `DirectoryInfo` object's directory but can contain intermediate subdirectories. For example, the statement `dir_info.CreateSubdirectory("Tools\Bin")` creates the `Tools` subdirectory and the `Bin` directory inside that.
CreationTime	Gets or sets the directory's creation time.
CreationTimeUtc	Gets or sets the directory's creation time in UTC.
Delete	Deletes the directory if it is empty. A parameter lets you tell the object to delete its contents, too, if it isn't empty.
Exists	Returns `true` if the directory exists.
Extension	Returns the extension part of the directory's name. Normally, this is an empty string for directories.
FullName	Returns the directory's fully qualified path.
GetDirectories	Returns an array of `DirectoryInfo` objects representing the directory's subdirectories. An optional parameter gives a pattern to match. This method does not recursively search the subdirectories.
GetFiles	Returns an array of `FileInfo` objects representing files inside the directory. An optional parameter gives a pattern to match. This method does not recursively search subdirectories.

PROPERTY OR METHOD	PURPOSE
GetFileSystemInfos	Returns a strongly typed array of `FileSystemInfo` objects representing subdirectories and files inside the directory. The items in the array are `DirectoryInfo` and `FileInfo` objects, both of which inherit from `FileSystemInfo`. An optional parameter gives a pattern to match. This method does not recursively search subdirectories.
LastAccessTime	Gets or sets the directory's last access time.
LastAccessTimeUtc	Gets or sets the directory's last access time in UTC.
LastWriteTime	Gets or sets the directory's last write time.
LastWriteTimeUtc	Gets or sets the directory's last write time in UTC.
MoveTo	Moves the directory and its contents to a new path.
Name	Returns the directory's name without the path information.
Parent	Returns a `DirectoryInfo` object representing the directory's parent. If the directory is its filesystem's root (for example, `C:\`), this returns `null`.
Refresh	Refreshes the `DirectoryInfo` object's data. For example, if the directory has been accessed since the object was created, you must call `Refresh` to load the new `LastAccessTime` value.
Root	Returns a `DirectoryInfo` object representing the root of the directory's filesystem.
ToString	Returns the directory's fully qualified path and name.

FileInfo

A `FileInfo` object represents a file. The following table summarizes its most useful properties and methods.

PROPERTY OR METHOD	PURPOSE
AppendText	Returns a `StreamWriter` that appends text to the file.
Attributes	Gets or sets flags from the `FileAttributes` enumeration for the file. These flags can include `Archive`, `Compressed`, `Device`, `Directory`, `Encrypted`, `Hidden`, `Normal`, `NotContentIndexed`, `Offline`, `ReadOnly`, `ReparsePoint`, `SparseFile`, `System`, and `Temporary`.

continues

(continued)

PROPERTY OR METHOD	PURPOSE
CopyTo	Copies the file and returns a FileInfo object representing the new file. A parameter lets you indicate whether the copy should overwrite the destination file if it already exists. If the destination path is relative, it is relative to the application's current directory, not to the FileInfo object's directory.
Create	Creates the file and returns a FileStream object attached to it. For example, you can create a FileInfo object passing its constructor the name of a file that doesn't exist. Then you can call the Create method to create the file.
CreateText	Creates the file and returns a StreamWriter attached to it. For example, you can create a FileInfo object passing its constructor the name of a file that doesn't exist. Then you can call the CreateText method to create the file.
CreationTime	Gets or sets the file's creation time.
CreationTimeUtc	Gets or sets the file's creation time in UTC.
Delete	Deletes the file.
Directory	Returns a DirectoryInfo object representing the file's directory.
DirectoryName	Returns the name of the file's directory.
Exists	Returns true if the file exists.
Extension	Returns the extension part of the file's name including the period. For example, the extension for game.txt is .txt.
FullName	Returns the file's fully qualified path and name.
IsReadOnly	Returns true if the file is marked read-only.
LastAccessTime	Gets or sets the file's last access time.
LastAccessTimeUtc	Gets or sets the file's last access time in UTC.
LastWriteTime	Gets or sets the file's last write time.
LastWriteTimeUtc	Gets or sets the file's last write time in UTC.
Length	Returns the number of bytes in the file.
MoveTo	Moves the file to a new location. If the destination uses a relative path, it is relative to the application's current directory, not to the FileInfo object's directory. When this method finishes, the FileInfo object is updated to refer to the file's new location.

PROPERTY OR METHOD	PURPOSE
Name	The file's name without the path information.
Open	Opens the file with specified mode (`Append`, `Create`, `CreateNew`, `Open`, `OpenOrCreate`, or `Truncate`), access (`Read`, `Write`, or `ReadWrite`), and sharing (`Read`, `Write`, `ReadWrite`, or `None`) settings. This method returns a `FileStream` object attached to the file.
OpenRead	Returns a read-only `FileStream` attached to the file.
OpenText	Returns a `StreamReader` with UTF-8 encoding attached to the file for reading.
OpenWrite	Returns a write-only `FileStream` attached to the file.
Refresh	Refreshes the `FileInfo` object's data. For example, if the file has been accessed since the object was created, you must call `Refresh` to load the new `LastAccessTime` value.
Replace	Replaces a target file with this one, renaming the old target as a backup copy. If the backup file already exists, it is deleted and replaced with the target.
ToString	Returns the file's fully qualified name.

FileSystemWatcher

The `FileSystemWatcher` class lets an application watch for changes to a file or directory. The following table summarizes its most useful properties.

PROPERTY	PURPOSE
EnableRaisingEvents	Determines whether the component is enabled. Note that this property is `false` by default, so the watcher will not raise any events until you set it to `true`.
Filter	Determines the files for which the watcher reports events. You cannot watch for multiple file types as in `*.txt` and `*.dat`. Instead, use multiple `FileSystemWatchers`. If you like, you can use `AddHandler` to make all the `FileSystemWatchers` use the same event handlers.
IncludeSubdirectories	Determines whether the object watches subdirectories within the main path.
InternalBufferSize	Determines the size of the internal buffer. If the watcher is monitoring an active directory, a small buffer may overflow.

continues

(continued)

PROPERTY	PURPOSE
NotifyFilter	Determines the types of changes that the watcher reports. This is a combination of values defined by the NotifyFilters enumeration and can include the values Attributes, CreationTime, DirectoryName, FileName, LastAccess, LastWrite, Security, and Size.
Path	Determines the path to watch.

The following table summarizes the FileSystemWatcher class's two most useful methods.

METHOD	PURPOSE
Dispose	Releases resources used by the object.
WaitForChanged	Synchronously waits for a change to the target file or directory.

The following table summarizes the class's events.

NAME	DESCRIPTION
Changed	A file or subdirectory has changed.
Created	A file or subdirectory was created.
Deleted	A file or subdirectory was deleted.
Error	The watcher's internal buffer overflowed.
Renamed	A file or subdirectory was renamed.

Path

The Path class provides static properties and methods that you can use to manipulate paths. The following table summarizes its most useful public properties.

PROPERTY	PURPOSE
AltDirectorySeparatorChar	Returns the alternate character used to separate directory levels in a hierarchical path (typically /).
DirectorySeparatorChar	Returns the character used to separate directory levels in a hierarchical path (typically \, as in C:\Tests\Billing\2010q2.dat).

PROPERTY	PURPOSE
InvalidPathChars	Returns a character array that holds characters that are not allowed in a path string. Typically, this array includes characters such as ", <, >, and |, as well as nonprintable characters such as those with ASCII values between 0 and 31.
PathSeparator	Returns the character used to separate path strings in environment variables (typically ;).
VolumeSeparatorChar	Returns the character placed between a volume letter and the rest of the path (typically :, as in C:\Tests\Billing\2010q2.dat).

The following table summarizes the Path class's most useful methods.

METHOD	PURPOSE
ChangeExtension	Changes a path's extension.
Combine	Returns two path strings concatenated. This does not simplify the result like the GetFullPath method does.
GetDirectoryName	Returns a path's directory.
GetExtension	Returns a path's extension.
GetFileName	Returns a path's filename and extension.
GetFileNameWithoutExtension	Returns a path's filename without the extension.
GetFullPath	Returns a path's fully qualified value. This can be particularly useful for converting a partially relative path into an absolute path. For example, the statement Path.GetFullPath("C:\Tests\OldTests\Software\..\..\New\Code") returns C:\Tests\New\Code.
GetInvalidFileNameChars	Returns a character array that holds characters that are not allowed in filenames.
GetPathRoot	Returns a path's root directory string. For example, the statement Path.GetPathRoot("C:\Invoices\Unpaid\Deadbeats") returns C:\.
GetRandomFileName	Returns a random filename.

continues

(continued)

METHOD	PURPOSE
GetTempFileName	Creates a uniquely named, empty temporary file and returns its fully qualified path. Your program can open that file for scratch space, do whatever it needs to do, close the file, and then delete it. A typical filename might be C:\Users\Rod\AppData\Local\Temp\tmpFCC6.tmp.
GetTempPath	Returns the path to the system's temporary folder. This is the path part of the filename returned by GetTempFileName.
HasExtension	Returns true if a path includes an extension.
IsPathRooted	Returns true if a path is an absolute path. This includes \Temp\Wherever and C:\Clients\Litigation, but not Temp\Wherever or ..\Uncle.

SPECIAL FOLDERS

The System.Environment.SpecialFolder enumeration defines SpecialFolder objects representing folders such as MyDocuments, History, and CommonProgramFiles. Use a SpecialFolder object's ToString method to get the folder's name. Use Environment.GetFolderPath to get the directory's path.

The following code lists special folders.

```
foreach (Environment.SpecialFolder folderType
    in Enum.GetValues(typeof(Environment.SpecialFolder)))
{
    Console.WriteLine(
        String.Format("{0,-25}{1}",
            folderType.ToString(),
            Environment.GetFolderPath(folderType)
        )
    );
}
```

RECYCLE BIN

C# doesn't provide tools for working with the recycle bin, but you can manage the recycle bin by using a combination of three techniques: using the FileIO.FileSystem class, using API functions, and using Shell32.Shell.

FileIO.FileSystem

The `Microsoft.VisualBasic.FileIO` namespace includes a `FileSystem` class that provides `DeleteDirectory` and `DeleteFile` methods. Those methods can take an optional parameter that indicates whether you want to move the directory or file into the recycle bin, or whether you want to delete the directory or file permanently. (They can also take a parameter that lets you decide whether the methods should display progress dialogs.)

To use the `FileSystem` class to move files and directories into the recycle bin, add a reference to the `Microsoft.VisualBasic` library. Then use the class's static `DeleteFile` and `DeleteDirectory` methods.

API Functions

The `SHEmptyRecycleBin` API function lets you empty the recycle bin. To use this function, add the following code to a class outside any methods.

```
[Flags]
private enum RecycleFlags : uint
{
    SHERB_NOCONFIRMATION = 0x1,
    SHERB_NOPROGRESSUI = 0x2,
    SHERB_NOSOUND = 0x4
}
[DllImport("shell32.dll")]
static extern int SHEmptyRecycleBin(
    IntPtr hWnd, string pszRootPath, uint dwFlags);
```

This code defines the `RecycleFlags` enumeration and the `SHEmptyRecycleBin` API function.

Now you can call the function, passing it appropriate parameters. The following `EmptyRecycleBin` method wraps the call to the API function to make it a bit easier to use.

```
public static void EmptyRecycleBin(bool showProgress, bool playSound,
    bool confirm)
{
    RecycleFlags options = 0;
    if (!showProgress) options |= RecycleFlags.SHERB_NOPROGRESSUI;
    if (!playSound) options |= RecycleFlags.SHERB_NOSOUND;
    if (!confirm) options |= RecycleFlags.SHERB_NOCONFIRMATION;

    SHEmptyRecycleBin(IntPtr.Zero, null, (uint)options);
}
```

This method uses its parameter values to compose an appropriate `RecycleFlags` value and then calls the API function.

Shell32.Shell

Shell32.Shell is an interface for working with the Windows shell. It enables you to interact with virtual objects representing such things as the recycle bin.

To use Shell32.Shell, first add a reference to "Microsoft Shell Controls And Automation" on the Reference Manager's COM tab. To make using the Shell class easier, add the following using directive to the program.

```
using Shell32;
```

Now you can use code similar to the following to enumerate the files in the recycle bin.

```
const int RECYCLE_BIN_NAMESPACE = 10;

Shell shell = new Shell();
Folder bin = shell.NameSpace(RECYCLE_BIN_NAMESPACE);

// List the files.
foreach (FolderItem item in bin.Items())
{
    Console.WriteLine(item.Name + "\n    " + item.Path);
}
```

This code creates a new Shell object and uses that object's NameSpace method to get a Folder object representing the recycle bin. It then loops through the items returned by the Folder's Items method, displaying each item's name and path.

Regular Expressions

This appendix summarizes methods of creating and using regular expressions.

CREATING REGULAR EXPRESSIONS

This section describes the characters you can use to define regular expressions.

Character Escapes

Character escapes are character sequences that match special characters. The following table summarizes useful character escapes.

ESCAPE	MEANING
\t	Matches the tab character
\r	Matches the return character
\n	Matches the new-line character
\nnn	Matches a character with ASCII code given by the two or three octal digits nnn
\xnn	Matches a character with ASCII code given by the two hexadecimal digits nn
\unnnn	Matches a character with Unicode representation given by the four hexadecimal digits nnnn

Character Classes

A character class matches one of a set of characters. The following table summarizes useful character class constructs.

CONSTRUCT	MEANING
[*chars*]	Matches one of the characters inside the brackets. For example, [aeiou] matches a single lowercase vowel.
[^*chars*]	Matches a character that is not inside the brackets. For example, [^aeiouAEIOU] matches a single nonvowel character such as Q, ?, or 3.
[*first-last*]	Matches a character between the character *first* and the character *last*. For example, [a-z] matches any lowercase letter between a and z. You can combine multiple ranges as in [a-zA-Z], which matches uppercase or lowercase letters.
.	This is a wildcard that matches any single character except \n. (To match a period, use the \. escape sequence.)
\w	Matches a single "word" character. Normally, this is equivalent to [a-zA-Z_0-9], so it matches letters, the underscore character, and digits.
\W	Matches a single nonword character. Normally, this is equivalent to [^a-zA-Z_0-9].
\s	Matches a single whitespace character. Normally, this includes space, form feed, new line, return, tab, and vertical tab.
\S	Matches a single nonwhitespace character. Normally, this matches everything except space, form feed, new line, return, tab, and vertical tab.
\d	Matches a single decimal digit. Normally, this is equivalent to [0-9].
\D	Matches a single character that is not a decimal digit. Normally, this is equivalent to [^0-9].

Anchors

An anchor matches a part of the input without reading any characters from it. The following table summarizes useful anchors.

ANCHOR	MEANING
^	Matches the beginning of the line or string
$	Matches the end of the string or before the \n at the end of the line or string
\A	Matches the beginning of the string
\Z	Matches the end of the string or before the \n at the end of the string
\z	Matches the end of the string
\G	Matches where the previous match ended
\B	Matches a nonword boundary

REGULAR EXPRESSION OPTIONS

You can specify regular expression options in three ways:

➤ Pass a `RegexOptions` parameter to a `Regex` object's constructor or to a pattern matching methods such as `IsMatch`.

➤ Use the syntax (`?options`) to include inline options within a regular expression. Options can include i, m, n, s, and x. If the list begins with a - character, the following options are turned off.

➤ Use the syntax (`?options:subexpression`) within a regular expression. In this case, `options` is as before and `subexpression` is the part of a regular expression during which the options should apply.

The following table lists the available options.

OPTION	MEANING
i	Ignore case.
m	Multiline. Here ^ and $ match the beginning and ending of lines instead of the beginning and ending of the whole input string.
s	Single-line. Here . matches all characters including \n.
n	Explicit capture. This makes the method not capture unnamed groups. See the following section "Grouping Constructs" for more information on groups.
x	Ignore unescaped whitespace in the pattern and enable comments after the # character.

Grouping Constructs

Grouping constructs let you define *capture groups* within matching pieces of a string. Parentheses create groups. There are several kinds of groups, some of which are fairly specialized and confusing. The two most common are numbered and named groups.

To create a numbered group, simply enclose a subexpression in parentheses as in `(\w)\1`. The `\w` in this expression matches a single word character. The parentheses mean this character is in the first numbered group. The `\1` that follows matches whatever is in group 1, in this case a single word character. That means this expression matches a single word character that appears twice.

To create a named group, use the syntax `(?<name>subexpression)` where *name* is the name you want to assign to the group and *subexpression* is a subexpression. Use the syntax `\k<name>` to refer to a named group.

For example, the expression `(?<twice>\w)\k<twice>` is equivalent to the previous expression `(\w)\1` except the group is named `twice`.

Quantifiers

A *quantifier* makes the regular expression engine match the previous element a certain number of times. The following table describes regular expression quantifiers.

QUANTIFIER	MEANING
`*`	Matches the previous element 0 or more times
`+`	Matches the previous element 1 or more times
`?`	Matches the previous element 0 or 1 times
`{n}`	Matches the previous element exactly n times
`{n,}`	Matches the previous element n or more times
`{n,m}`	Matches the previous element between n and m times (inclusive)

If you follow one of these with `?`, the pattern matches the preceding expression as few times as possible. For example, the pattern `BO+` matches `B` followed by 1 or more `O`s, so it would match the `BOO` in `BOOK`. The pattern `BO+?` also matches `B` followed by 1 or more `O`s, but it matches as few `O`s as possible, so it would match only the `BO` in `BOOK`.

Alternation Constructs

An *alternation construct* uses the `|` character to allow a pattern to match either of two subexpressions. For example, the expression `^(true|yes)$` matches either `true` or `yes`.

Sample Regular Expressions

The following list shows several useful regular expressions.

➤ `^\d{3}-\d{4}$`—Matches a simple 7-digit phone number.

➤ `^[2-9][0-9]{2}-\d{4}$`—Matches a 7-digit phone number more precisely.

➤ `^[2-9][0-8]\d-[2-9][0-9]{2}-\d{4}$`—Matches a 10-digit U.S. phone number with the format NPA-NXX-XXXX where N is a digit 2-9, P is a digit 0-8, A is any digit 0-9, and X is any digit 0-9.

➤ `^([2-9][0-8]\d-)?[2-9][0-9]{2}-\d{4}$`—Matches a U.S. phone number with an optional area code such as 202-234-5678 or 234-5678.

➤ `^\d{5}(-\d{4})?$`—Matches a U.S. ZIP code with optional +4 as in 12345 or 12345-6789.

➤ `^[A-Z]\d[A-Z] \d[A-Z]\d$`—Matches a Canadian postal code with the format A1A 1A1 where A is any capital letter and 1 is any digit.

➤ `^[a-zA-Z0-9._-]{3,16}$`—Matches a username with 3 to 16 characters that can be dashes, letters, digits, periods, or underscores.

➤ `^[a-zA-Z][a-zA-Z0-9._-]{2,15}$`—Matches a username that includes a letter followed by 2 to 15 dashes, letters, digits, periods, or underscores.

➤ `^[a-zA-Z0-9._%+-]+@[a-zA-Z0-9._%+-]+\.[a-zA-Z]{2,4}$`—Matches an e-mail address. (This pattern isn't perfect but it matches most valid e-mail addresses.)

➤ `^[+-]?[a-fA-Z0-9]{3}$`—Matches a 3-digit hexadecimal value with an optional sign + or − as in +A1F.

➤ `^(https?://)?([\w-]+\.)+[\w-]+$`—Matches a top-level HTTP web address such as `http://www.csharphelper.com`. (This pattern isn't perfect. In particular it doesn't validate the final part of the domain, so it would match `www.something.whatever`.)

➤ `^(https?://)?([\w-]+\.)+[\w-]+(/(([\w-]+)(\.[\w-]+)*)*)*$`—Matches an HTTP web URI such as `http://www.csharphelper.com/howto_index.html`. (Again this pattern isn't perfect and doesn't handle some more advanced URLs such as those that include =, ?, and # characters, but it does handle many typical URLs.)

USING REGULAR EXPRESSIONS

The Regex class provides objects that you can use to work with regular expressions. The following table summarizes the Regex class's most useful methods.

METHOD	PURPOSE
IsMatch	Returns true if a string satisfies a regular expression.
Match	Searches a string for the first part of it that satisfies a regular expression.

continues

(continued)

METHOD	PURPOSE
`Matches`	Returns a collection giving information about all parts of a string that satisfy a regular expression.
`Replace`	Replaces some or all the parts of the string that match a regular expression with a new value. (This is much more powerful than the `string` class's `Replace` method.)
`Split`	Splits a string into an array of substrings delimited by pieces of the string that match a regular expression.

The `Regex` class also provides static versions of these methods that take both a `string` to examine and a regular expression as parameters.

The following sections summarize how to use the `Regex` class to perform common regular expression tasks.

Matching Patterns

The `Regex` class's static `IsMatch` method gives you an easy way to determine whether a string satisfies a regular expression. The following code tests whether the text in variable `text` matches the pattern in variable `pattern`.

```
if (Regex.IsMatch(text, pattern))
    result = "Match";
else
    result = "No match";
```

Finding Matches

The `Regex` class's `Matches` method can give you information about places where a string matches a regular expression. The following code locates pieces of the string in variable `text` that match the pattern in variable `pattern`.

```
// Make the regex object.
Regex regex = new Regex(pattern);

// Find the matches.
foreach (Match match in regex.Matches(text))
{
    // Display the match.
    Console.WriteLine(match.Value);
}
```

The following table lists the `Match` class's most useful properties.

PROPERTY	PURPOSE
Groups	Returns a collection of objects representing any groups captured by the regular expression. The `Group` class has `Index`, `Length`, and `Value` properties that describe the group.
Index	The index of the match's first character.
Length	The length of the text represented by this match.
Value	The text represented by this match.

Making Replacements

The `Regex` class's static `Replace` method enables you to replace the parts of a string that match a pattern with a new string. The following code examines the string in variable `text`, locates pieces that match the pattern in variable `pattern`, and replaces them with the text in variable `replaceWith`.

```
string result = Regex.Replace(
    text,
    pattern,
    replaceWith);
```

For example, the following code replaces vowels in a string with question marks.

```
string result =
    Regex.Replace("The quick brown fox jumps over the lazy dog", "[aeiou]", "?")
```

The following text shows the result.

```
Th? q??ck br?wn f?x j?mps ?v?r th? l?zy d?g
```

Parallel Programming

This appendix summarizes C# parallel programming techniques.

INTERACTING WITH THE USER INTERFACE

Code can directly interact with user interface elements if the code is running inside the thread that created those elements. For example, code executing in a separate thread cannot safely change the text displayed in a TextBox or Label.

To interact with the UI controls, a thread should follow these steps.

1. Check the InvokeRequired property for a control that was created in the UI thread.

2. If InvokeRequired is true, the thread should call the control's Invoke method, passing it a delegate.

3. The delegate executes on the control's thread. Because it is running in the control's thread, the delegate can safely interact with the control.

PLINQ

Parallel LINQ (PLINQ pronounced "plink") allows a program to execute LINQ queries across multiple processors or cores in a multi-core system. Simply add a call to the AsParallel extension method to the enumerable object from which the query selects data.

The following code uses a PLINQ query to select the even numbers in the array numbers. The call to AsParallel is highlighted in bold.

```
var evens =
    from int number in numbers.AsParallel()
    where number % 2 == 0
    select number;

foreach (int number in evens) Console.WriteLine(number);
```

This code composes the query and includes the call to `AsParallel`. It then loops through the query's results and displays them.

BACKGROUNDWORKER

The `BackgroundWorker` component provides a relatively simple way to run a separate thread of execution. It provides events to provide feedback to the main UI thread so that you can display results without needing to use `InvokeRequired` and the `Invoke` method.

Following is the basic process.

1. Create a `BackgroundWorker` at design time or run time.

2. Call its `RunWorkerAsync` method. This starts a new thread and raises the worker's `DoWork` event handler on that thread.

3. Catch the `DoWork` event, and make its event handler execute the code you want to run on the new thread.

To provide feedback, add these steps to those described in the preceding list.

1. Before starting the `BackgroundWorker`, set its `WorkerReportsProgress` property to `true`.

2. Catch the worker's `ProgressChanged` event. This event handler runs in the UI thread, so it can manipulate the user interface controls without messing with `InvokeRequired` and `Invoke`.

If you want the main program to stop the worker, follow these steps.

1. Before starting the `BackgroundWorker`, set its `WorkerSupportsCancellation` property to `true`.

2. To stop the worker, call its `CancelAsync` method.

3. In the `DoWork` event handler, periodically check the worker's `CancellationPending` property. If that property is `true`, the event handler should exit. If you like, the code can set the `e.Cancel` parameter to indicate that the work was canceled.

TPL

Task Parallel Library (TPL) provides methods for executing multiple calculations on separate threads and waiting for them all to complete. Those methods are `Parallel.For`, `Parallel.ForEach`, and `Parallel.Invoke`.

Because all three of these methods call delegates that might execute on separate threads, the calls may not finish in any particular order.

Parallel.For

The `Parallel.For` method takes as parameters a starting value, an ending value, and a delegate. It invokes the delegate for each of the values between the starting value (including that value) and the ending value (not including that value). The method blocks until all the calls to the delegate have completed and then the code continues.

The following code shows how a program might invoke the `FindFibonacci` method with the parameters 0, 1, 2, and 3.

```
Parallel.For(0, 4, FindFibonacci);
```

Parallel.ForEach

The `Parallel.ForEach` method takes as parameters an enumerable collection of values and a delegate. The `ForEach` method invokes the delegate, passing it each of the parameter values. The method blocks until all the calls to the delegate have completed.

The following code shows how a program might call the `FindFibonacci` method, passing it the input parameters 0, 2, 4, 6, and 8.

```
int[] numbers = {0, 2, 4, 6, 8};
Parallel.ForEach(numbers, FindFibonacci);
```

Parallel.Invoke

The `Parallel.Invoke` method lets you invoke one or more possibly different delegates. It executes the delegates, possibly on different threads, and blocks until they all complete.

The following code shows how a program might use `Parallel.Invoke` to execute the `ResetParameters`, `LoadGame`, and `BuildWorld` methods in parallel.

```
Parallel.Invoke(ResetParameters, LoadGame, BuildWorld);
```

TASKS

The `System.Threading.Tasks.Task` class enables you to create threads and run them asynchronously. The following table summarizes the `Task` class's most useful properties.

PROPERTY	PURPOSE
Exception	Returns an `AggregateException` object containing information about any exceptions that caused the `Task` to end early.
Factory	Provides access to `TaskFactory` class methods that you can use to create `Tasks`. (This is explained in more detail shortly.)
IsCanceled	Returns `true` if the `Task` was canceled.

continues

(continued)

PROPERTY	PURPOSE
IsCompleted	Returns `true` if the `Task` has finished processing.
IsFaulted	Returns `true` if the `Task` stopped because of an unhandled exception.
Status	Returns the `Task`'s status. This can be one of `Canceled`, `Created`, `Faulted`, `RanToCompletion`, `Running`, `WaitingForAactivation`, `WaitingForChildrenToComplete`, or `WaitingToRun`.

The following table lists the `Task` class's most useful methods.

METHOD	PURPOSE
ConfigureAwait	Configures an "awaiter" object that you can use with the `await` keyword to wait for the `Task` to complete.
ContinueWith	Creates a continuation `Task` that executes when a target `Task` finishes.
Delay	Creates a `Task` that completes after a specified amount of time has passed.
Run	This static method creates a `Task` and queues it to start running. (This is basically a simplified version of `Task.Factory.StartNew`, which is described later in this section.)
RunSynchronously	Runs a `Task` synchronously.
Start	Starts a `Task` that was previously created.
Wait	Waits for the `Task` to complete.
WaitAll	This static method waits until all the `Tasks` in a set complete.
WaitAny	This static method waits until any one of the `Tasks` in a set completes.
WhenAll	Creates a `Task` that completes when all the specified `Tasks` complete.
WhenAny	Creates a `Task` that completes when any one of the specified `Tasks` completes.

The following list describes different methods you can use to create and start a `Task`.

➤ Use a `Task` class constructor to create a `Task` and then call its `Start` method to start it.

➤ Use a `TaskFactory` object. The `Task` class's `Factory` method returns a `TaskFactory` object that you can use to create different kinds of `Tasks`. The `Task.Factory.StartNew` method creates and starts a `Task` in a single step.

➤ Call `Task.Run`. This is basically a simplified version of `Task.Factory.StartNew`.

➤ Call the `TaskFactory` class's `ContinueWhenAll` or `ContinueWhenAny` methods to create `Tasks` that start after some or all of a set of previous `Tasks` completes.

The following code shows one of the simplest cases in which a program starts four `Tasks` and then waits for them all to complete.

```
// Start four tasks.
Task task0 = new Task(FindFibonacci, 0);
task0.Start();
Task task1 = new Task(FindFibonacci, 1);
task1.Start();
Task task2 = new Task(FindFibonacci, 2);
task2.Start();
Task task3 = new Task(FindFibonacci, 3);
task3.Start();

// Wait for the tasks to complete.
task0.Wait();
task1.Wait();
task2.Wait();
task3.Wait();
```

THREADS

The `System.Threading.Thread` class gives you more control over threads than you can get from the other techniques described in this appendix, but using it is more complicated. The following table lists the `Thread` class's most useful properties.

PROPERTY	MEANING
`IsAlive`	Returns `true` if the thread has been started and has not ended or aborted.
`IsBackground`	Determines whether the thread is a background thread.
`Priority`	Determines the thread's priority. This can be `Highest`, `AboveNormal`, `Normal`, `BelowNormal`, or `Lowest`.
`ThreadState`	Returns the thread's state. This can be a combination of the values `Aborted`, `AbortRequested`, `Background`, `Running`, `Stopped`, `StopRequested`, `Suspended`, `SuspendRequested`, `Unstarted`, and `WaitSleepJoin`.

The following table lists the `Thread` class's most useful methods.

METHOD	PURPOSE
Abort	Raises a `ThreadAbortException` on the thread to make it terminate.
Join	Blocks the thread on which the method is called until the thread terminates. (This is how programs normally wait for a thread to finish.)
ResetAbort	Cancels an `Abort` for the current thread.
Sleep	This static method suspends a thread for a specified amount of time.
Start	Starts the thread.
Yield	Yields execution to another thread if one is ready to run.

Using a simple thread typically involves the following steps.

1. Create the `Thread` object.
2. Call the `Start` method to start the thread.
3. To stop the thread, call its `Abort` method.
4. To wait for the thread, call its `Join` method.

XML

This appendix summarizes useful XML topics and techniques.

SPECIAL CHARACTERS

The following table lists five special characters defined for use in XML files.

CHARACTER	CODE
<	&lt;
>	&gt;
&	&amp;
'	&apos;
"	&quot;

You can also include special characters inside CDATA sections. A CDATA section begins with `<![CDATA[` and includes all the following text until it reaches the closing sequence `]]>`. The CDATA can include carriage returns, ampersands, quotes, and other special characters.

WRITING XML DATA

The .NET Framework provides two main ways to write XML data: the XmlWriter class and the XML Document Object Model. The following two sections describe these approaches.

XmlWriter

The XmlWriter class provides methods for writing the pieces of an XML file. To use an XmlWriter to write XML data into a file, call the class's Create method to create the file. Then use the other methods to write the pieces of the XML document into the file.

The following table lists the most useful XmlWriter methods.

METHOD	PURPOSE
Close	Closes the writer's underlying stream.
Create	Creates an XmlWriter associated with a file, stream, StringBuilder, or other object.
Dispose	Frees the writer's resources. (You can use the using statement to ensure that the writer is disposed.)
Flush	Flushes output to the underlying stream.
WriteAttributeString	Writes an attribute with a specified name and value.
WriteCData	Writes CDATA.
WriteComment	Writes a comment.
WriteElementString	Writes an element with a specified name and text value.
WriteEndAttribute	Ends an attribute started with WriteStartAttribute.
WriteEndDocument	Ends the document.
WriteName	Writes a name.
WriteStartAttribute	Starts an attribute.
WriteStartDocument	Starts the document.
WriteStartElement	Starts an element.
WriteString	Writes a string, escaping special characters such as < and > if necessary.
WriteValue	Writes a value such as a bool, int, or double.

The XmlTextWriter class, which inherits from XmlWriter, works much as XmlWriter does but it can produce nicely indented output. Simply create an XmlTextWriter instead of an XmlWriter, set its Formatting property to Indented, and create the XML file using the methods described in the preceding table.

Document Object Model

The *XML Document Object Model* (*DOM*) provides a more structured way to build XML documents. It uses objects to create an in-memory model of an XML document. You can then manipulate the model and save the result into an XML file or string.

Two of the most important classes for manipulating the DOM are XDocument and XElement.

The XDocument class represents an XML document. Its most useful properties are Declaration, which gets or sets the document's XML declaration, and Root, which returns the document's root element.

The following table lists the XDocument class's most useful methods.

METHOD	PURPOSE
Add	Adds an item to the document's child collection. (Note that you can add only one child, the root element, to the document.)
DescendantNodes	Returns a collection of XNode objects that are descendants of the document.
Descendants	Returns a collection of XElement objects that are descendants of the document. If you specify a name, the method returns only elements with that name.
Load	Loads the document from a filename, stream, or XmlReader.
Parse	Creates a new XDocument from an XML string.
Save	Saves the document into a file, stream, or writer.
ToString	Returns the document's indented XML code.
WriteTo	Writes the document into an XmlWriter.

The XElement class represents an element in an XML document. The following table lists the XElement class's most useful properties.

PROPERTY	PURPOSE
Document	Returns the XDocument that contains the element.
FirstAttribute	Gets the element's first attribute.
FirstNode	Gets the element's first child node.
HasAttributes	Returns true if the element has attributes.
HasElements	Returns true if the element has child elements.

continues

(continued)

PROPERTY	PURPOSE
IsEmpty	Returns true if the element contains no content. (It still might have attributes.)
LastAttribute	Gets the element's last attribute.
LastNode	Gets the element's last child node.
Name	Gets or sets the element's name.
NextNode	Returns the next node in the element's parent's child list.
NodeType	Gets the node's type.
Parent	Gets the element's parent element.
PreviousNode	Returns the previous node in the element's parent's child list.
Value	Gets or sets the node's text contents.

The following table lists the XElement class's most useful methods.

METHOD	PURPOSE
Add	Adds an item at the end of the element's child collection.
AddAfterSelf	Adds an item to the parent's child collection after this element.
AddBeforeSelf	Adds an item to the parent's child collection before this element.
AddFirst	Adds an item at the beginning of the element's child collection.
Ancestors	Returns a collection of XElement objects that are ancestors of the element. If you specify a name, the method returns only elements with that name.
Attribute	Returns an attribute with a specific name.
Attributes	Returns a collection containing this element's attributes. If you specify a name, the collection includes only attributes with that name.
DescendantNodes	Returns a collection of XNode objects that are descendants of the element.
Descendants	Returns a collection of XElement objects that are descendants of the element. If you specify a name, the method returns only elements with that name.

METHOD	PURPOSE
DescendantsAndSelf	Returns a collection of XElement objects that includes this element and its descendants. If you specify a name, the method returns only elements with that name.
Element	Returns the first child element with a specified name.
Elements	Returns a collection holding the element's children. If you specify a name, the method returns only elements with that name.
ElementsAfterSelf	Returns a collection holding the element's siblings that come after this element. If you specify a name, the method returns only elements with that name.
ElementsBeforeSelf	Returns a collection holding the element's siblings that come before this element. If you specify a name, the method returns only elements with that name.
IsAfter	Returns true if this node comes after another specified node in a document.
IsBefore	Returns true if this node comes before another specified node in a document.
Load	Loads the element from a filename, stream, or reader.
Nodes	Returns a collection holding this element's child nodes.
NodesAfterSelf	Returns a collection holding the node's siblings that come after this node.
NodesBeforeSelf	Returns a collection holding the node's siblings that come before this node.
Parse	Creates an XElement from an XML string.
Remove	Removes this element from its parent.
RemoveAll	Removes all nodes and attributes from this element.
RemoveAttributes	Removes this element's attributes.
RemoveNodes	Removes this element's child nodes.
ReplaceAll	Replaces the element's child nodes and attributes with specified new ones.
ReplaceAttributes	Replaces the element's attributes with specified new ones.
ReplaceNodes	Replaces the element's child nodes with specified new ones.
ReplaceWith	Replaces this node with new specified content.

continues

(continued)

METHOD	PURPOSE
Save	Saves the element into a file, stream, or writer.
SetAttributeValue	Sets, adds, or removes an attribute.
SetElementValue	Sets, adds, or removes a child element.
SetValue	Sets the element's value.
ToString	Returns the element's indented XML code.
WriteTo	Writes the element into an XmlWriter.

XML Literals

C# doesn't support XML literals but it does support multiline string literals and they work almost as well. Simply use the XElement.Parse method to parse a multiline string holding the XML code, as in the following example.

```
XElement student = XElement.Parse(
    @"<Student>
        <FirstName>Arthur</FirstName>
        <LastName>Andrews</LastName>
        <StudentID>83746</StudentID>
    </Student>");
```

READING XML DATA

The following two sections explain how you can use the XmlTextReader class and the Document Object Model to read XML code.

XmlTextReader

The XmlTextReader class provides fast, forward-only, noncached methods for reading XML data. It provides methods to move through an XML file one node at a time and to examine the data provided by each node.

To use an XmlTextReader, use the class's constructor or the XmlReader class's static Create method to create an object associated with the file or input stream that you want to read. Use the object's Read method to read the next node from the XML data. After you read a node, you can use the reader's properties and methods to determine the node's name, type, attributes, content, and other properties.

The following table lists the most useful XmlReader properties.

PROPERTY	MEANING
AttributeCount	Returns the number of attributes the node has.
Depth	Returns the depth of the current node in the XML hierarchy.
EOF	Returns true when the reader is at the end of the XML data.
HasAttributes	Returns true if the node has attributes.
HasValue	Returns true if the node can have a value.
IsEmptyElement	Returns true if the node is an empty element as in <Overdue />.
Item	Gets a node attribute by index or name. (This is the class's indexer, so you use it as in reader[0] instead of invoking the Item property explicitly.)
Name	Returns the node's name.
Value	Returns the text value of the current node.

The following table lists the XmlReader class's most useful methods.

METHOD	PURPOSE
Create	Creates a new reader associated with a string, stream, file, or other data source.
Dispose	Frees the object's resources. You can include a using statement to automatically call Dispose.
GetAttribute	Gets an attribute for the current node by index or name. (Similar to the Item property.)
IsName	Returns true if its parameter is a valid XML name.
MoveToAttribute	Moves the reader to an attribute specified by index or name.
MoveToContent	Moves the reader to the current node's content.
MoveToElement	Moves the reader to the element containing the reader's current position. For example, if you move the reader to examine an element's attributes, the method moves the reader back to the element's node.
MoveToFirstAttribute	Moves the reader to the current node's first attribute node.
MoveToNextAttribute	Moves the reader to the current node's next attribute node.
Read	Reads the next node from the XML data.

continues

(continued)

METHOD	PURPOSE
ReadInnerXml	Returns the current node's descendants as an XML string.
ReadOuterXml	Returns the current node's subtree (including the current node) as an XML string.
ReadToDescendant	Moves the reader to a subelement with a specified name.
ReadToNextSibling	Moves the reader past the rest of the current node to its next sibling.
Skip	Skips the current node's children.

Document Object Model

You can use the DOM to load and study an existing XML file.

To load an object model from XML data, simply call the XDocument class's static Load method, passing it a filename, stream, or XmlReader.

RELATED TECHNOLOGIES

The following list summarizes some XML-related technologies.

➤ XSL (Extensible Stylesheet Language)—This refers to a family of languages and tools for reformatting XML data. It includes

  ➤ XSLT (XSL Transform)—A language for transforming XML data into other formats such as plain text, HTML, rearranged XML documents, or XSL FO.

  ➤ XSL FO (XSL Formatting Objects)—A language for formatting XML data for output for screen, PDFs, printers, and so forth.

  ➤ XPath—This is a query language used by XSL and other XML tools to find and identify items within XML data.

➤ XQuery—A somewhat SQL-like language for querying XML data.

➤ DTD (Document Type Definition)—An XML data file validation language. You use DTD to define the required structure of an XML file. Then you can validate a particular XML file to see if it satisfies those requirements.

➤ XSD (XML Schema Definition)—Another XML data file validation language. See DTD.

➤ XLink—A language for defining hyperlinks in XML data.

➤ SOAP (Simple Object Access Protocol)—A protocol that lets applications (often running on different computers) exchange data.

➤ WSDL (Web Services Definition Language)—A language for describing web services.

➤ RSS (Really Simple Syndication)—A format for XML news feeds and sites that post news-like items.

The following sections provide more information about XPath and XSLT.

XPath

XPath is a language for identifying items in XML data. An XPath query looks vaguely like a file's pathname in a directory hierarchy. The query can also include operators that work as wildcards, filter the results, and specify relationships among nodes.

The following table lists the most useful operators that you can use in an XPath query.

OPERATOR	MEANING
/	Selects an immediate child.
//	Selects descendants.
.	The current node.
..	The current node's parent.
*	Matches anything.
@	Attribute prefix for matching an attribute. For example, @Cost matches an attribute named Cost.
@*	Selects all attributes.
()	Groups operations.
[ ]	Applies a filter. For example, //Planet[@Name="Earth"] matches Planet elements that have a Name attribute with value Earth.
[ ]	Subscript operator for accessing items in a collection.
+	Addition.
-	Subtraction.
Div	Floating-point division.
*	Multiplication.
Mod	Modulus.

When a query filters results, it can include the boolean and comparison operators listed in the following table.

OPERATOR	MEANING
And	Logical AND
Or	Logical OR
not()	Logical NOT
=	Equals
!=	Not equals
&lt;	Less than
<=	Less than or equal
&gt;	Greater than
>=	Greater than or equal

For more information on XPath, see the following links.

➤ "XPath Reference" at msdn.microsoft.com/library/ms256115.aspx

➤ "XPath Examples" at msdn.microsoft.com/library/ms256086.aspx

XSLT

XSLT is a language that you can use to transform XML data into a new format. It's a fairly complicated language, so there isn't room to cover it in any depth here. To learn the language, see the following links.

➤ "XSLT Tutorial" at www.w3schools.com/xsl/default.asp

➤ "XSLT Elements Reference" at www.w3schools.com/xsl/xsl_w3celementref.asp

➤ "XSL Transformations (XSLT) Version 1.0" at www.w3.org/TR/xslt

For an example, see the section "XSLT" in Chapter 24, "XML."

Serialization

This appendix summarizes useful serialization topics and techniques.

XML SERIALIZATION

To serialize and deserialize objects in XML format, you use the XmlSerializer class's Serialize and Deserialize methods. The methods work only for classes that have a parameterless constructor, either the default constructor or one that you created. They also work only for public properties and fields. All other properties and fields are ignored.

To serialize an object, follow these steps.

1. Create an XmlSerializer, passing its constructor the object's type.

2. Create a TextWriter to hold the serialization.

3. Call the serializer's Serialize method, passing it the TextWriter and the object to serialize.

The following code shows how a program might serialize a Customer object.

```
// Create a serializer that works with the Customer class.
XmlSerializer serializer = new XmlSerializer(typeof(Customer));

// Create a TextWriter to hold the serialization.
string serialization;
using (TextWriter writer = new StringWriter())
{
    // Serialize the Customer.
    serializer.Serialize(writer, customer);
    serialization = writer.ToString();
}

// Display the serialization.
serializationTextBox.Text = serialization;
```

To deserialize a serialization, follow these steps.

1. Create an `XmlSerializer`, passing its constructor the object's type.

2. Create a `TextReader` from which to read the serialization.

3. Call the serializer's `Deserialize` method, passing it the `TextReader`. Cast the result into the object's type.

The following code shows how a program might deserialize a `Customer` object's serialization.

```
// Create a serializer that works with the Customer class.
XmlSerializer serializer = new XmlSerializer(typeof(Customer));

// Create a stream from which to read the serialization.
using (TextReader reader = new StringReader(serialization))
{
    // Deserialize.
    Customer newCustomer = (Customer)serializer.Deserialize(reader);

    // Display the deserialization.
    DisplayCustomer(deserializedTextBox, newCustomer);
}
```

Controlling Serialization

The following table lists the most useful attributes that you can use to control serialization. (The names of the classes that implement these attributes all end with `Attribute`. For example, the first `XmlArray` attribute is implemented by the `XmlArrayAttribute` class. If you want to look up any of these online, use their full class names.)

ATTRIBUTE	PURPOSE
XmlArray	Changes the name by which the array or list is serialized.
XmlArrayItem	Indicates a type that can be in an array. For example, suppose the `People` array contains `Person` objects, some of which might be from the `Author` subclass. Then you would use `XmlArrayItem` twice to indicate that the array might contain `Person` and `Author` objects.
XmlAttribute	Serializes a field as an attribute instead of an element. Optionally sets the name of the attribute.
XmlElement	Specifically indicates the field will be serialized as an XML element. This attribute allows you to change the XML element's name.
XmlEnum	Enables you to specify the names by which enumeration values are serialized. For example, suppose the enumeration `MealSize` defines values `Small`, `Medium`, and `Large`. You could use this attribute to make the serialization call those values `Tall`, `Grande`, and `Brobdignagian`.

ATTRIBUTE	PURPOSE
XmlIgnore	Makes the serializer omit a field from the serialization.
XmlRoot	Controls the name and namespace for the element generated for a serialization's root element. For example, the attribute [XmlRoot("Client")] in front of the Customer class would make the serializer name the root element Client. This would not affect Customer objects that are not the root element. (See XmlType.)
XmlText	Makes the serializer store a value as XML text. An object can have only one text value. (The serializer cannot put more than one text value between the object's start and end tags.)
XmlType	Controls the name and namespace for the element generated for a class. For example, if you place the attribute [XmlType("Item")] in front of the OrderItem class, then all OrderItem objects are serialized as Item elements.

The DataContractSerializer class can also use XML to serialize and deserialize objects. The process is similar to using the DataContractJsonSerializer class, which is summarized in the next section.

JSON SERIALIZATION

JavaScript Object Notation (JSON) is a data storage language that mostly consists of name:value pairs where names are text and values can have one of the following data types.

> Number

> String

> Boolean

> Array (a sequence of values separated by commas and enclosed in brackets [ ])

> Object (a collection of key:value pairs with pairs separated by commas and the whole collection surrounded by braces { })

> Null

The following section summarizes the basic JSON serialization and deserialization processes. The section after that describes attributes you can use to control the serialization.

Performing Serialization

The DataContractJsonSerializer class serializes and deserializes objects using the JSON format. The class's WriteObject method serializes an object. Its ReadObject method deserializes an object.

The following code serializes and deserializes a `Customer` object in the JSON format.

```
// Create a serializer that works with the Customer class.
DataContractJsonSerializer serializer =
    new DataContractJsonSerializer(typeof(Customer));

// Create a stream to hold the serialization.
using (MemoryStream stream = new MemoryStream())
{
    // Serialize the Customer.
    serializer.WriteObject(stream, customer);

    // Convert the stream into a string.
    stream.Seek(0, SeekOrigin.Begin);
    string serialization;
    using (StreamReader reader = new StreamReader(stream))
    {
        serialization = reader.ReadToEnd();

        // Display the serialization.
        serializationTextBox.Text = serialization;

        // Deserialize from the stream.
        stream.Position = 0;
        Customer newCustomer = (Customer)serializer.ReadObject(stream);

        // Display the deserialization.
        DisplayCustomer(deserializedTextBox, newCustomer);
    }
}
```

Controlling Serialization

The following table lists attributes that are useful when performing JSON serializations.

ATTRIBUTE	PURPOSE
CollectionDataContract	Allows you to control serialization of collections
DataContract	Indicates that a type is serializable by a serializer such as a `DataContractSerializer`
DataMember	Indicates that a property should be serialized
EnumMember	Indicates that a property is an enumeration and should be serialized
IgnoreDataMember	Indicates that a property should not be included in the serialization
OptionalField	Indicates that a property is optional in a serialization

BINARY SERIALIZATION

The XML and JSON serializers cannot serialize some data types and cannot serialize a data structure that contains reference loops. However, the `BinaryFormatter` class can handle both of these issues.

The `BinaryFormatter` can work only with classes that are decorated with the `Serializable` attribute.

The following code shows how a program might use a `BinaryFormatter` to serialize and deserialize a `Department` object.

```
// Create a BinaryFormatter.
IFormatter formatter = new BinaryFormatter();

// Create a stream to hold the serialization.
using (MemoryStream stream = new MemoryStream())
{
    // Serialize.
    formatter.Serialize(stream, department);

    // Display a textual representation of the serialization.
    byte[] bytes = stream.ToArray();
    string serialization = BitConverter.ToString(bytes).Replace("-", " ");

    // Display the serialization.
    serializationTextBox.Text = serialization;

    // Deserialize.
    stream.Seek(0, SeekOrigin.Begin);
    Department newDepartment = (Department)formatter.Deserialize(stream);

    // Display the new Department's data.
    deserializedPictureBox.Image = newDepartment.Logo;
    deserializedTextBox.Text = DisplayDepartment(newDepartment);
}
```

Reflection

A class's type provides properties and methods that provide a wealth of information about the class. You can get a `Type` object representing a class by using `typeof(TheClass)` or by calling the `GetType` method on an instance of the class.

The following section summarizes the `Type` class's most useful properties and methods. The sections after that summarize other useful reflection classes.

TYPE

The following table lists the `Type` class's most useful properties.

PROPERTY	DESCRIPTION
Assembly	Gets the assembly where the type is declared.
Attributes	Gets the type's attributes.
BaseType	Gets the type's parent class.
ContainsGenericParameters	Indicates whether the type has generic type parameters.
CustomAttributes	Gets the type's custom attributes.
FullName	Gets the type's fully qualified name, which includes the type's namespace but not its assembly.
IsAbstract	Returns `true` if the type is abstract.
IsArray	Returns `true` if the type is an array.
IsAutoLayout	Returns `true` if the type's fields are laid out automatically by the CLR.

continues

(continued)

PROPERTY	DESCRIPTION
IsByRef	Returns true if the type is passed by reference.
IsClass	Returns true if the type is a class.
IsCOMObject	Returns true if the type is a COM object.
IsEnum	Returns true if the type is an enumeration.
IsExplicitLayout	Returns true if the type's fields are laid out explicitly.
IsGenericType	Gets a value indicating whether the current type is a generic type.
IsImport	Returns true if the type was imported from a COM library.
IsInterface	Returns true if the type is an interface.
IsLayoutSequential	Returns true if the type's fields are laid out sequentially.
IsMarshalByRef	Returns true if the type is marshaled by reference.
IsNested	Returns true if the type's definition is contained inside another type's definition.
IsNestedAssembly	Returns true if the type is nested and visible only within its assembly.
IsNestedFamANDAssem	Returns true if the type is nested and visible only to classes in its family in its class and derived classes) and its assembly.
IsNestedFamily	Returns true if the type is nested and visible only to classes in its family.
IsNestedFamORAssem	Returns true if the type is nested and visible only to classes either in its family or in its assembly.
IsNestedPrivate	Returns true if the type is nested and private.
IsNestedPublic	Returns true if the type is nested and public.
IsNotPublic	Returns true if the type is not public.
IsPointer	Returns true if the type is a pointer.
IsPrimitive	Returns true if the type is a primitive type.
IsPublic	Returns true if the type is public.
IsSealed	Returns true if the type is sealed.
IsSerializable	Returns true if the type is serializable.

PROPERTY	DESCRIPTION
IsValueType	Returns true if the type is a value type.
IsVisible	Returns true if the type is visible to code outside the assembly.
Module	Returns the module where the type is defined.
Name	Returns the type's name.
Namespace	Returns the type's namespace.
StructLayoutAttribute	Returns a StructLayoutAttribute describing the type's layout.
TypeInitializer	Gets the type's initializer.

The following table lists the Type class's most useful methods.

METHOD	DESCRIPTION
FindInterfaces	Returns a filtered list of interfaces that the type implements.
FindMembers	Returns a filtered array of MemberInfo objects of the specified member type. Member type can be All, Constructor, Custom, Event, Field, Method, NestedType, Property, or TypeInfo.
GetArrayRank	Returns the number of an array's dimensions.
GetConstructor	Returns information about a constructor matching specific parameter types.
GetConstructors	Returns all the type's public constructors.
GetCustomAttributes	Returns an array of the type's custom attributes.
GetDefaultMembers	Returns the type's default members.
GetElementType	For an array, pointer, or reference type, returns the type of items contained by the type.
GetEnumName	For an enumeration type, returns the name corresponding to a specific value. (For example, if the Desserts enumeration represents the value Cookie with the integer value 3, then GetEnumName(3) returns Cookie.)

continues

(continued)

METHOD	DESCRIPTION
GetEnumNames	For an enumeration type, returns the names of the enumeration's values.
GetEnumUnderlyingType	For an enumeration type, returns the integer data type used to store the enumeration's values.
GetEnumValues	For an enumeration type, returns an array of the integer values used to store the enumeration's values.
GetEvent	Returns an EventInfo object representing a specified public event.
GetEvents	Returns EventInfo objects representing all the type's public events.
GetField	Returns a FieldInfo object representing a specified public field.
GetFields	Returns FieldInfo objects representing all the type's public fields.
GetGenericArguments	Returns an array of type objects representing the type's generic type arguments.
GetGenericParameterConstraints	Returns an array of type objects representing constraints on a generic type parameter.
GetInterface	Returns a type representing an interface implemented by the type.
GetInterfaces	Returns an array of types representing interfaces implemented by the type.
GetMember	Returns an array of MemberInfo objects containing information about the type's public members that match search criteria.
GetMembers	Returns an array of MemberInfo objects containing information about all the type's public members.
GetMethod	Returns a MethodInfo object representing a public method that matches search criteria.
GetMethods	Returns an array of MethodInfo objects representing the type's public methods.

METHOD	DESCRIPTION
GetNestedType	Returns type information representing a nested type that matches search criteria.
GetNestedTypes	Returns an array of type information representing all the type's nested types.
GetProperties	Returns an array of `PropertyInfo` objects representing properties that match search criteria.
GetProperty	Returns a `PropertyInfo` object representing a property that matches search criteria.
GetType	This static method returns a `Type` object representing a type that matches search criteria.
GetTypeArray	Returns an array of `Type` objects for objects in an array.
GetTypeFromCLSID	Returns the type with a given class identifier (CLSID) specified as a GUID.
InvokeMember	Invokes a member.
IsAssignableFrom	Returns `true` if an instance of the type can be assigned from an instance of another specified type.
IsEnumDefined	For an enumeration type, returns `true` if the enumeration defines a specific value.
IsInstanceOfType	Returns `true` if a specific object is an instance of the type.
IsSubclassOf	Returns `true` if the type is a subclass of another type.
MakeArrayType	Returns a new `Type` object representing an array of the current type.
MakeByRefType	Returns a new `Type` object representing the current type when passed by reference.
MakeGenericType	Returns a new `Type` object representing the current generic type with specific types substituted in for the generic type parameters.
MakePointerType	Returns a new `Type` object representing a pointer to the current type.

MEMBERINFO

The MemberInfo class is the parent class of EventInfo, MethodInfo, FieldInfo, and PropertyInfo. The following table lists useful MemberInfo properties.

PROPERTY	DESCRIPTION
CustomAttributes	Returns a collection containing information about the member's custom attributes
DeclaringType	Returns the class that includes this member
MemberType	Returns the member's type
Module	Returns the module that contains the type that defines this member
Name	Returns the member's name
ReflectedType	Returns the object that was used to get this MemberInfo object

The following sections describe the most useful properties and methods provided by the EventInfo, MethodInfo, FieldInfo, and PropertyInfo classes.

EVENTINFO

An EventInfo object contains information about an event. The following table lists the most useful EventInfo properties that are not inherited from the MemberInfo class.

PROPERTY	DESCRIPTION
AddMethod	Returns the method used to add a delegate to the event
Attributes	Returns the event's attributes
EventHandlerType	Returns a Type representing the event's event handler delegate
RaiseMethod	Returns the method that is called when the event is raised
RemoveMethod	Returns the method that removes a delegate from the event handler

The following table lists the most useful EventInfo methods that are not inherited from the MemberInfo class.

METHOD	DESCRIPTION
AddEventHandler	Adds an event handler to the event
GetAddMethod	Returns the method used to add a delegate to the event
GetRaiseMethod	Returns the method that is called when the event is raised
GetRemoveMethod	Returns the method that removes a delegate from the event handler
RemoveEventHandler	Removes an event handler from the event

METHODINFO

A MethodInfo object contains information about a method. This class is derived from MethodBase, which is derived from MemberInfo.

The following table lists the most useful MethodInfo properties that are not inherited from the MemberInfo class. (Some of these properties are inherited from MethodBase, but that class is abstract, so this appendix doesn't describe it separately.)

PROPERTY	DESCRIPTION
ContainsGenericParameters	Returns true if the method has generic parameters.
IsAbstract	Returns true if the method is abstract.
IsAssembly	Returns true if the method is visible only to code within the same assembly.
IsConstructor	Returns true if the method is a constructor.
IsFamily	Returns true if the method is visible only within this class and derived classes.
IsFamilyAndAssembly	Returns true if the method is visible only to its family (its class and derived classes) and only within the same assembly.
IsFamilyOrAssembly	Returns true if the method is visible to its family (its class and derived classes) and to code within the same assembly.
IsFinal	Returns true if the method is final.

continues

(continued)

PROPERTY	DESCRIPTION
IsGenericMethod	Returns `true` if the method is an instance of a generic method.
IsGenericMethodDefinition	Returns `true` if the method is a generic method definition.
IsPrivate	Returns `true` if the method is private.
IsPublic	Returns `true` if the method is public.
IsStatic	Returns `true` if the method is static.
IsVirtual	Returns `true` if the method is virtual.
ReturnParameter	Returns a `ParameterInfo` object representing the method's return type.
ReturnType	Returns the method's return type.

The following table lists the most useful `MethodInfo` methods that are not inherited from the `MemberInfo` class.

METHOD	DESCRIPTION
CreateDelegate	Returns a delegate for the method.
GetGenericArguments	Returns an array of `Type` objects representing the method's generic arguments.
GetGenericMethodDefinition	For an instance of a generic method, returns a `MethodInfo` object representing the method's generic definition.
GetParameters	Returns information about the method's parameters.
Invoke	Invokes the method, passing it specified parameters.
MakeGenericMethod	For a generic method definition, returns a `MethodInfo` representing the method with specific types inserted in place of the generic type parameters.

FIELDINFO

A `FieldInfo` object contains information about a field. The following table lists the most useful `FieldInfo` properties that are not inherited from the `MemberInfo` class.

PROPERTY	DESCRIPTION
Attributes	Returns the field's attributes
FieldType	Returns the field's type
IsAssembly	Returns `true` if the field is visible only to code within the assembly
IsFamily	Returns `true` if the field is visible only to code in its family (its class and derived classes)
IsFamilyAndAssembly	Returns `true` if the field is visible only to code in its family that is in the same assembly
IsFamilyOrAssembly	Returns `true` if the field is visible to code in its family and to code in the same assembly
IsInitOnly	Returns `true` if the field's value can be set only in the class's constructor
IsLiteral	Returns `true` if the field is initialized at compile time and cannot be changed later
IsNotSerialized	Returns `true` if the field is marked with the `NotSerialized` attribute
IsPrivate	Returns `true` if the field is private
IsPublic	Returns `true` if the field is public
IsStatic	Returns `true` if the field is static

The following table lists the `FieldInfo` class's most useful methods.

METHOD	DESCRIPTION
GetValue	Returns the field's value
GetValueDirect	Returns the value of a field supported by a given object
SetValue	Sets the field's value

PROPERTYINFO

A `PropertyInfo` object contains information about a property. The following table lists the most useful `PropertyInfo` properties that are not inherited from the `MemberInfo` class.

PROPERTY	DESCRIPTION
Attributes	Returns the property's attributes
CanRead	Returns `true` if the property can be read
CanWrite	Returns `true` if the property can be written
GetMethod	Returns the property's `get` accessor
PropertyType	Returns the property's type
SetMethod	Returns the property's `set` accessor

The following table lists the `PropertyInfo` class's most useful methods.

METHOD	DESCRIPTION
GetAccessors	Returns an array of `MethodInfo` objects representing the property's accessors
GetGetMethod	Returns a `MethodInfo` object representing the property's `get` accessor
GetIndexParameters	For indexed properties, returns an array of `ParameterInfo` objects giving information about the property's indexes
GetSetMethod	Returns a `MethodInfo` object representing the property's `set` accessor
GetValue	Returns the property's value
SetValue	Sets the property's value

PARAMETERINFO

A `ParameterInfo` object contains information about a parameter. The following table lists the most useful `ParameterInfo` properties.

PROPERTY	DESCRIPTION
Attributes	Returns the parameter's attributes
CustomAttributes	Returns the parameter's custom attributes

PROPERTY	DESCRIPTION
DefaultValue	Returns the parameter's default value, if it has one
HasDefaultValue	Returns true if the parameter has a default value
IsIn	Returns true if the parameter is an input parameter
IsOptional	Returns true if the parameter is optional
IsOut	Returns true if the parameter is an output parameter
Member	Returns the member that uses the parameter
Name	Returns the parameter's name
ParameterType	Returns the parameter's type
Position	Returns the parameter's position (numbered from 0) in a parameter list

The ParameterInfo class's most useful method is GetCustomAttributes, which returns information about the parameter's custom attributes.

INDEX

N

S